BLOODY SHOVEL

Volume 2
Spandrell

West Martian Limited Company
2nd Edition, October 2023

Content from Bloody Shovel is property of Spandrell, and is used with permission by West Martian Limited Company.

First printing 2023

Second printing 2023

The publisher can be contacted at westmartian.com

ISBN-13: 979-8-218-23441-6 Paperback

Table of Contents

Conspiracies

2015-12-04 // europe, negroes, bluegov, power

I've been writing for so time now the idea that bad things happen not necessarily because bad people are out there conspiring to do them, but because humans are, well, just a species of highly social monkeys, cooperation is difficult, large scale societies are weird, and sometimes bad things happen even when nobody really wants it that way.

In 1966 probably nobody wanted to end up worshiping mangoes as Mao's holy fruit[1]. And Mao himself didn't want that to happen. But it did, because of bad incentives feeding into human's SP cognitive process. And there are plenty of examples of the same thing happening all over our thousands of years of history. This includes of course the collapse of Western Civilization occurring just as I write this.

But you know the saying. The fact that you're paranoid doesn't mean that they're not really out there to get you. Take a look at this:

https://www.youtube.com/watch?v=ZqIdghXyOP8

Insane, right? Apparently Merkel has not had enough with the Afghan teenagers ravaging the German countryside. A million Muslims is not enough, she wants more. And she wants to not just open the doors; she wants to go out there to tell them to come! To Africa! To be fair the word "propaganda" means just advertising, it's not necessarily associated with Goebbels alone in German, but still. Look at the faces of her audience. They're not happy. They're not buying this stuff at all.

But then again look at her face. At her voice. At her body language. Does she look like a woman who is convinced she is right, and has an important message to tell? Does she look like Hillary Clinton in a debate? Hell no. She sounds scared to me. Really positively terrified. She doesn't look to be enjoying this at all. In fact she seems to have been fed some lines, and just repeating them from memory. That stuff about "90 types of jobs with shortages". Somebody sold her that and she's has to sell it even though she doesn't really buy it herself. That's what her tone of voice tells me.

An SP interpretation of the Refugee Crisis tends to be that, you know, Merkel is a braindead progressive and she wants to do the progressive thing. Certainly not lose to those perfid Swedes! She'll bring all the Muslims and go to the history books as the glorious woman who brought multiculturalism to Germany. But that doesn't fit with

---

[1]   https://spandrell.com/2015/02/19/explaining-the-cultural-revolution-signalling-arms-races-as-bad-fiat-currency/

her biography at all. A recent biopic on her[2]) who did the rounds this year explicitly shows her as a machiavelian politician who has absolutely no principles whatsoever; and relies on her laser-sharp instinct to tell what is popular to go ahead and win elections. And indeed she seems very good at that. Hell, she's been president for 10 years, and nobody really likes her that much.

So her latest enthusiasm for bringing Muslims to Germany can't possibly be a matter of principle. She has none. Then why is she doing this? Why is she destroying her country? Look at the video again.

Now there's two possible explanations to her uneasy demeanor. Maybe somebody told her that this refugee thing is going to cost her the presidency, that she's gonna get demoted from the presidency, publicly disowned by her party, fired and banished to solitary retirement, where her barrenness will torment her as not even her husband bothers visiting. However she has no escape now, she must double down whatever the costs, as she has committed herself to the open borders policy, and any backtrack would be just as disastrous anyway. If she were to admit her error, some Bavarian who was critic of her from the start would come out as the winner, and become the obvious replacement for this old GDR cat woman who almost destroyed the nation because of some stupid error of judgment. Merkel is now between a rock and a hard place, and she can't find the way of getting out of this, leading to her complete lack of confidence in the video.

Or maybe it's not her who is putting her in this dilemma. Maybe it is something else who is forcing her into it. Someone she can't overpower. Maybe there is a conspiracy of bad people who are behind the bad things that affect us all.

Steve Sailer has a subtly concealed them at his blog, and if I'm reading between the lines correctly, I think he means to say that, you know, maybe there is a conspiracy out there. You never know, right? Look at Turkey, it's a mess and nobody really knows what's going on and who is pulling the strings or how he got there. Why should it be any simpler over here?

Of course a conspiracy doesn't really imply that there are cartoon-like evil men who do evil things just for the fun of it. Powerful people also form groups, they come up with stupid ideas to signal loyalty, they make new ideas to try to fight for status, and all that stuff produces the same social dynamics where everybody is unhappy even though nobody really wants to. The difference is that in smaller groups, the influence of individual personality is somewhat greater. An important manifestation of this principle is Jim's Law of Committees: when decision is taken collectively, the evil and insane always win, because they never compromise, and the good and sane people have

---

[2]   https://www.vanityfair.com/news/2015/01/angela-merkel-profile

been brought up to compromise, which they do. So in this sort of dynamic, if there's some evil, insane and stubborn old fuck who is convinced that making the all whites are potential Nazis or Gaia-killers or whatever, he might get the idea across and it can snowball on forever.

And even if he's not around anymore, remember that all human groups organize around stupid, no, preposterous ideas[3] as the optimal way to create cohesion and assess loyalty. And once the idea is out there in explicit or implicit form, and everybody has committed itself to it in order to signal their loyalty and get access, well the racket can snowball and go on forever.

And most people don't even need to know. Imagine this old evil insane man made his master plan in the 1940s. He didn't say it openly, he just said that diversity is strength, multiculturalism is good, and the economy needs new blood to do the jobs that the lazy natives won't do. He used his evil and insane stubborness to get the idea across, and eventually is stuck. Everybody accepted the plan and went on to implement it. Two generations later, the new ruling class might still be going on with the idea without really knowing why. They just know they've committed themselves publicly to it, and thus it must be done, or else. And they will conspire to get it done and whatever the cost, or else their own place in the conspiracy is in danger, as is the place of any defector in any human group.

Who is doing this to you, Merkel? The American State Department? The German corporate mafia? The EU? Or just your pitiful little pride? Whichever it is, you're still dead. Everybody hates you and they will hate you whatever you do right now. However if you backtrack now you will get your name into history as doing the right thing.

I envy the Indians. They could curse her saying she'd be reincarnated into a filthy dog eating shit in a dump. But no, all Christian can say is she'll go to hell. But that's where all her friends are anyway.

---

[3] https://spandrell.com/2015/03/09/religion/

Что Делать

2015-12-16 // wat do, france, demographics, blackpill

Many of you may know that France doesn't take statistics by race, because being French is about having French values. Or in other words, being French is what the French government says it is, so shut up already.

The French are the kings of bullshit. There's been an academic paper doing the rounds these days, called On the Reception of Pseudoprofound Bullshit.[4] Well, you know Pseudoprofound Bullshit? The French are kings of that. Fortunately there is also a (smaller) group of French which are serious scientists. Some of them are in the healthcare business, and they publish stats of screening for sickle-cell anaemia. Sickle-cell anaemia is a genetic aftereffect of malaria resistance in Africans, so France only screens Africans (both blacks and Maghrebians). Here's the most recent map.

---

[4]   https://www.valuewalk.com/2015/11/on-the-reception-and-detection-of-pseudo-profound-bullshit/2/

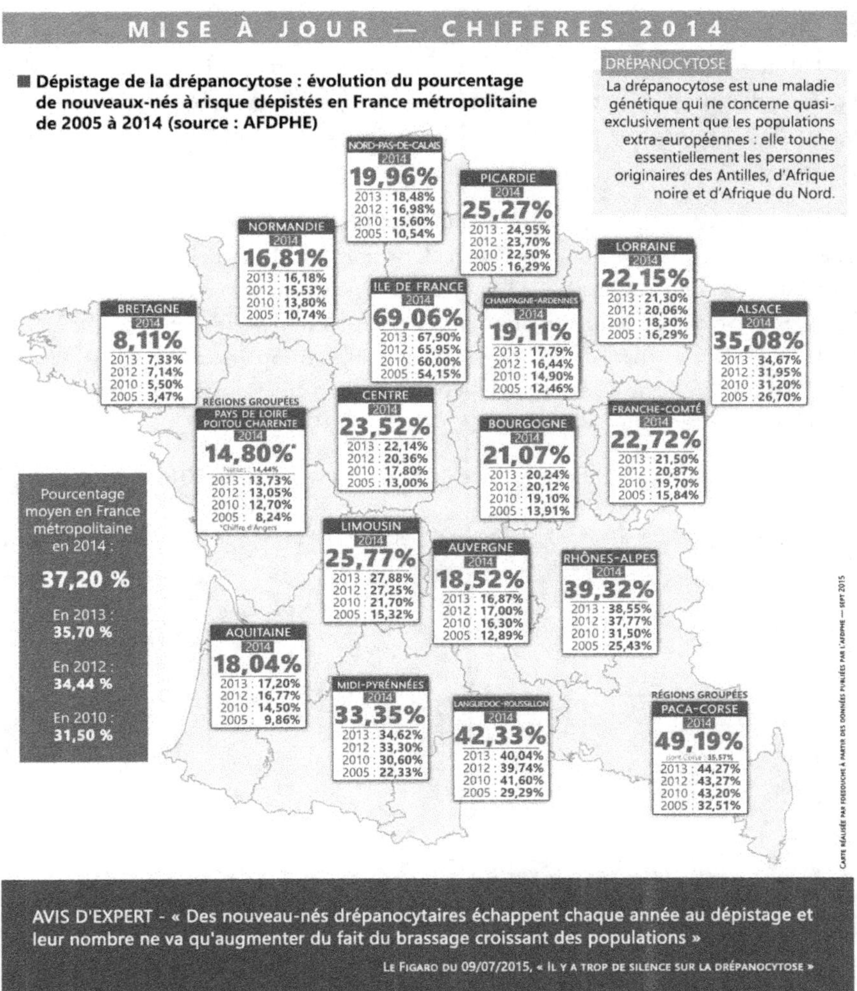

37.20% of newborns in France are of African descent. It is increasing at a rate of around 1.5% per year. That means in 10 years half of all French newborns will be of African descent. In 30 years, half of all French 20 year olds will be of African descent. I often talk about Brazilification. But even Brazil is whiter than that.

Now, France may deserve this because of their invention of pseudoprofound bullshit. I do feel a certain amount of schadenfraude. When French rightists start to pay attention to this stats, the French newspaper started running articles about how sickle-cell is a "European disease too", and how we are stigmatizign "the disease of the OTHER (caps in original)", and how differential screening is a "inequality of France". Leftists of all kinds started calling for every single baby in France to be screened. It is impossible for white kids to have sickle-cell. The purpose of screening white kids is obviously to fudge the data so that people can't make maps about it. This will probably happen in a few years, so this map may be the last one which gives you an accurate picture of how France died.

Which again, given the contribution of France to intellectual history of the world, may not be a bad thing. But it's not only France. One third of all babies in Britain have one foreign-born parent.[5] Those are 2011 figures. And plenty of foreigners are not foreign-born by now. So a good approximation may be 40% of non-white babies in Britain by now. It will take less than in France to achieve 50%. In Spain, a relative backwater which most migrants only pass through in order to get further north, 25% of babies are born to foreign parents.

US readers might know that the 50% threshold was crossed around 2011:

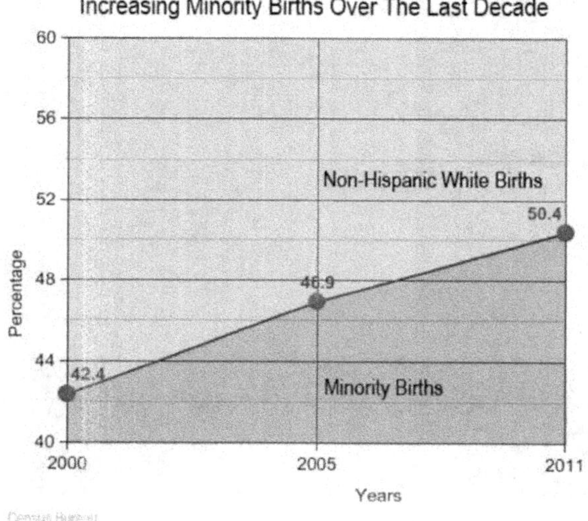

However US census count Middle-Easterners as white, so the line may have been crossed somewhat earlier. Still, the situation isn't much different in Europe.

What is to be done? The trends are clear, we are heading to Brazilification, or something worse. Perufication? Worst case scenario is South Africa. You may think that whites will always be the elite, and living in a fancy guarded compound isn't that bad. You get to use cheap labor! Cheap nannies and lawnmowers and all that. Yes but do not forget. Rich elites always have lower fertility. South African whites are legally second-class

---

[5]   https://www.telegraph.co.uk/news/uknews/10029547/Third-of-children-born-in-England-has-foreign-born-parent.html

citizens already. Many are falling in poverty. They still have less babies than blacks. Brazil's white population, as loosely defined as it is, is losing ground too.

https://www.youtube.com/watch?v=oWWzAdb2wbU

So these are the odds. Do you still want to talk about the tax rate?

Facts are useless

2015-12-17 // theory, psychology, status, leftism

My post on the Chinese Cultural Revolution and Mao's mangoes still gets a lot of traffic, which is nice. I do feel like the title wasn't very elegant, but I wanted to make the point about ideology as "currency". Unfortunately it didn't get through. Let's see if I can explain myself better.

An inspiration for that metaphor was a post by Nick Szabo (who apparently isn't the inventor of Bitcoin. I hope at least he did become an early adopter and is now filthy rich), about the origins of currency[6]. He talks about how humans have been collecting and making completely useless stuff such as shells or beads since way before agriculture. Money often was not only useless, it was completely harmful, like the Chinese toy swords and plows[7]. Metal is useful. You make weapons and farming tools with them. You don't fucking waste precious copper in making toy knives. But they did. Of course they did.

Szabo's point is that the point of money is to be a cognitive aid for remembering favors. I did something for you, if I am not to be a sucker I'll want to get something back from you eventually. So grab me that shiny shell you use as a wristband, so I can remember. David Graeber made a similar point on his famous book about Debt[8], which is pretty good if you get the fact that Graeber is a lame communist and adjust your skimming accordingly.

The problem is that this tech we use to remember favors leads us to spent huge amount of valuable labor in manufacturing shell accessories, beads, mining metal and wasting it in making coins. Whole empires were built, entire nations killed and enslaved in the process of looking for mines where perfectly good metal could be extracted to waste in making little coins with the face of a king to distribute so people can remember who made a favor to whom. That's how it works though.

I am endlessly fascinated by this kind of evolutionary process where everybody runs around doing completely pointless stuff which nobody benefits from. Ideology is the

---

[6] https://szabo.best.vwh.net/shell.html

[7] https://en.wikipedia.org/wiki/Ancient_Chinese_coinage

[8] https://en.wikipedia.org/wiki/Debt:_The_First_5000_Years

same. See Mao's mangoes. And see the last Republican debate. As a commenter said at Sailer's[9]:

Every single word thus far in the undercard debate has been about ISIS. Our obsession with this region of lunatics on the other side of the world is bizarre.

Indeed it is stupid. It beggars belief. But ISIS is not the point. The point is that you have a bunch of men in that room, and you're supposed to make a judgment about them. You need to compare. And comparisons require a yardstick. What do we compare about them?

How tall and handsome they are? Well that works in some places. How well they dance or sing? That happens in many places too. How strong and brave they are in single combat? Lots of cultures did that too. But we don't. We resent tall and handsome men are privileged enough in the sexual marketplace, so fuck that. Fuck dancers too, those get women also. And fuck single combat, the average voter isn't a good fighter. We don't want to give high status to tall, strong men with good dancing feet. That would make us feel inadequate. And with good reason, in Africa they give high status to all those men and it sucks.

Our culture gives high status to men with ideas. Everybody can claim to have good ideas. It doesn't take good genes, nor dancing or fighting skills. Everybody can learn to parrot bullshit after a little practice. Bullshit is the most egalitarian arena, so all status contests are done in the realm of bullshit. Now bullshit requires a topic too. Remember in middle school, when a bunch of friends got together and stared asking: "What would you do if you were invisible?" Or "Batman or Spiderman?" What's the point of those questions? Nobody's gonna become invisible. But by asking stupid questions you get people to talk, and through their answers you get to know their character. The question doesn't matter. The more outlandish the better. You can't get to know people by asking them a factual question. It *has to* be bullshit.

And adults do the same thing. In the Cultural Revolution people liked to discuss materialist dialectics. The Republican party likes to talk National Security. Why? Did peasants in Jingzhou give a shit about Hegel? Of course not. Does anybody in the USA really care about Raqqa? No. So why won't people shut up about it?

"You gotta talk about something!". That's what my mother tells me when I ask her why does she like discussing the news about stuff she absolutely has no clue about. And... that's all there is to it. There's a bunch of old dudes on TV, and you gotta choose one. Experience says they're all lying their asses anyway. But you gotta choose one. And how do you choose one? You throw some bullshit topic at them and look at how they

---

9 https://www.unz.com/isteve/gop-debate-open-thread-2/#comment-1262162

respond. Then you have something to make judgment about. How they talk. Tone of voice, body language. Logic. This guy sounds smart. Oh this guy's a doofus. Hey this guys sounds like fun to have a beer with.

You then choose a guy who you like, or more accurately, you choose the guy because saying that you like that guy makes you look good with your friends. And you made that decision after seeing him speak about ISIS. What's ISIS? I don't know. Who gives a shit. I just kinda like the guy who said we should bomb them. So yeah, let's bomb them. What, we just spent 2 trillion bombing some other guy? Who gives a shit, it's not like I know the difference. They're not gonna lower my taxes if I choose not to bomb someone, right? So anyway, yeah I like that bomb-ISIS guy. And that Palestinian-rights guy too. Where's Palestine? I don't know. Who gives a shit? But my girlfriends talks about it a lot, and I wanna look good to her.

I imagine some little nephew of Emperor Claudius asking him:

-Uncle Claudius, why in hell are we invading Britain?

=Oh, they have metal there.

-And what do we want the metal for?

=We gotta make little discs and give them to our soldiers.

-We are going to send a hundred thousand young men to their deaths in some god forsaken barbarian island because we need to make metal discs and give it to them?

=Yep.

-Mmm ok.

Fast forward 2000 years:

-Uncle, why are we invading Syria?

=Oh, I promised in my electoral campaign.

-Why did you promise?

=People asked me my opinion on ISIS.

-But you don't really care about ISIS. I know, you always change the TV channel when they come up on TV.

=Yeah, but people asked my opinion, and I needed to sound tough, so I said I'd invade Syria.

-So we are going to send a hundred thousand young men to get shot at in some god forsaken barbarian desert because you needed to sound tough on TV?

=Yep.

-At least you're getting some money out of this.

=Not really, but I know my advisors are.

-Mmm... ok.

Truth

2015-12-28 // hbd, signaling, WNANR

Good old Mencken said:

(pause your adblock or Ghostery or similar extensions to see embedded Tweets)

https://twitter.com/HLMenckenBot/status/680636693829951488

Well, as I always say, there are no mysteries in life. Reality isn't strange, you just have a bad model. Not that I'm innocent of that mistake. I'm known of chanting how the truth will always prevail[10], even when most people obviously prefer bullshit, and have always done so. I, like Mencken, like Orwell, also used to pick my brains out about why people just didn't see what is in front of their noses. I had a habit of pointing at the truth, and it never made me any friends.

Now I know why; you just can't make friends with the truth. It's like trying to buy stuff without money. To catch people's attention you need conversational currency[11], i.e. you need bullshit. Controversy, nonsense, whatever gets people to talk and do things. Then you can watch them talk, and do things, judge their characters according to what they say and do, and choose your friends accordingly. Compared to that, the truth is of much more limited application. If there's a wolf, knowing there is a wolf, and that wolves are dangerous is very useful. But if there are no wolves, who the hell cares if they're dangerous? In the absence of wolves, talking of wolves is just signaling. Say you like wolves, and you come out as an animal lover. Say you hate wolves, and you come out as a creepy animal hater. Why would you hate wolves if you've never been close to one? You read they are bad for farmers? Oh who cares. Cree-py.

Let's talk HBD. HBD is even closer than wolves. We have people of all races living together in the West now. The differences are beyond obvious. We have heaps of data. Most human traits are normally distributed in a bell curve, and averages differ between any population group which has been inbreeding for long enough. That applies to races, but also to a lesser extent to social classes too.

And yet nobody cares about the data. There are two positions on HBD: nananananacan't-hear-you denialism. It's all in the head, all you need is better education.

---

[10] https://spandrell.com/2013/04/30/optimizing-for-truth/

[11] https://spandrell.com/2015/12/17/facts-are-useless/

And then there's the Nazis: whites are supreme, the whiter the better, everyone else is scum, Asians have a smaller standard deviation, everyone else sucks, even southern whites suck too frankly speaking.

And that's all there is. Well there's a tiny minority of people who try to actually look at the data. But Nazis outnumber us 1 million to one. And denialists are of course the state religion, and have been so forever. Even Confucianism and Islam are denialist.

For good reason of course, genetic determinism is just not a useful idea. The elite wants to sell its product, which is that access to the elite depends on culture, and by the way we happen to sell that culture, and it's not cheap. Saying that access to the elite depends on innate talent uncovers the fact that the culture the elite sells is just an arbitrary barrier to entry into a privileged social club, and that elite status is not earned through effort, and just a genetic fluke.

And nobody benefits from knowing about HBD. The poor don't like to hear they are fucked up because they are born that way and their children will most likely be equally fucked up. And the talented don't like to hear that their children will likely regress to the mean and not be as talented as they are.

Nobody wins from HBD. The Nazis win from a wrong interpretation. Sure, people differ and it's genetic. We're the master race and we should rule the world. Or even just good old nationalism we're not superior, we're just special, and yes in our eyes maybe just a tiny bit better than others, so let us have our countries for ourselves at least. That doesn't quite follow from the data. You can't derive modern nations from their genepool. But the countries are out there, so nationalism gets people excited. It gets people to feel superior, which makes them happy, gets them to organize, get together, maybe burn a refugee camp, or threaten some cuck politician.

The truth doesn't get anybody moving. All it goes is get people pissed and depressed. That's why we got Nazis out there outnumbering us in 2015. Nobody likes the truth, for completely unmysterious reasons. The truth sucks. We need a lie. A good one, that gets people moving in the right direction, and with enough appeal to beat denialism. Which is not easy: denialism is not a modern progressive heresy, it's the default opinion of all human civilizations. A stable alternative is not gonna be easy. What have we got?

Men doing their own thing

2015-12-30 // men, china, history, signaling, psychology

Basically means doing steroids and denying that those have any bad effect.

You'll remember a post I did a while ago[12] on the Chinese classical novel, the Water Margin. That's a 14th century novel, thought to be based on the peasant rebellions that overthrew the Mongol Yuan Dynasty in China in the 1350s. So that's 665 years ago. The novel is a historical novel of a previous rebellion in the 1110s. Rebellions are of course stories of men, and the Water Margin is an epic story of 108 men who are forced to leave society by evil men, and thus go up the mountain to do their own thing. To this day, when a man says "fuck it" and leaves polite society to do his own thing, in Chinese you say he is "forced to climb to mount Liang", which is the hideout of the rebels in the Water Margin.

So what did these great bros do up at Liangshan? Bully each other into a signaling spiral of binge drinking, binge eating, pointless fighting and destruction of normal family life. And completely disregard for women. The only women in the novel are bros too, women fighers who can beat 100 men while handling huge spears on horseback. Those are cool. Other women are hoes, and hoes are not cool. The sheer nonsense and sometimes pure evil that the novel describes as being the honorable and manly thing to do is just amazing. One of the stories that amazed me the most was how 秦明 Qin Ming joined the gang.

Oh sorry, I forgot that Chinese names just don't register as human to foreign ears. So let's call him Archibald Cooper. Well Cooper was a general of the dynasty, working as chief of the garrison of Qingzhou (you'll allow me to use the original placenames), and as such he was ordered to crack down on the hero-rebels which were hiding on the mountains. Crack down he did, and he fought them valiantly. He had a reputation for being extremely brave and reckless in battle, never losing the will to fight. But of course he was fighting the hero-rebels, and so he lost. He was captured after the battle, and taken to the rebel HQ, where he expected to be tortured and killed. But no, the hero-rebels told him they admired his reputation for honor and bravery, and wanted him to join the rebel army. Obviously he was a bro, and all bros of the world should join the rebel army.

It's a funny argument, kinda Islamic. All moral people should be Muslim, as it's the right thing to do. So all good people are supposed to convert eventually. Apostasy is

---

[12] https://spandrell.com/2015/09/30/male-culture/

unthinkable. Once a bro always a bro! Thus thought the medieval Chinese too. All good men are bros.

However our friend Cooper couldn't just join the rebels after a defeat. He has sworn an oath of loyalty to the dynasty, and a bro is supposed to uphold his oaths. The rebels understood that, them being also hero-bros. So he was left to go back to his post at the garrison, just like that.

However the rebels had no intention of just letting such a good bro leave. They sent a bunch of bros, impersonating Cooper, and went on a killing rampage close to Qingzhou. The whole town around the castle was massacred and burnt, hundreds of men, women and children killed in the process. Then they shouted to the walls: I'm Archibald Cooper, and I joined the rebels! Mwahaha!

Some hours later the real Cooper arrives, and sees the carnage, not knowing what was all that about. He calls to the gates to request passage into the city, but he is of course refused. The local governor comes out and shouts to him that he is a despicable traitor, and that his whole family inside the city has been tortured and killed. The severed head of his father, wife and children are posted on pikes and shown above the city walls, for him to see.

Imagine that. You come back home exhausted after a war, and the severed head of your father, wife and children are posted on pikes. Thanks for that. Being chased out of the city, and not really knowing what had happened, he goes back to the rebel HQ to ask for help in killing the local governor, that he blames for the assault. Once he gets there, though, the rebel-bros tell them that actually... all that was their fault. They respected him so much, you know, bro, you're so awesome, we wanted you to join us so badly, so we made this little plan, to impersonate you and make it impossible for you to go back to the garrison. We planned to get your family and take them here with us after the thing, but the gates were closed, and we just couldn't manage. Sorry 'bout that, bro. Our intentions were good!

Imagine that. Surely Cooper took out his sword and killed everything on the spot. Right? Right? No. He fell on his knees and cried, but he understood that what is done is done, his father, wife and children are all dead and their heads are on spikes. But the real bad man is the city governor, who killed his family without checking with him. The bros who impersonated him and killed hundreds of civilians were good bros with good intentions. So after being offered the sister of one bro in marriage as compensation, he resolved to join the bro-army, and he became one of their best fighters.

Bros before hoes! And before fathers. And children. Yes, always bros.

Now of course in the 21st century we don't have rebel armies in Liangshan, hiding from the evil dishonorable men that don't give them the status they deserve as hero-bros. But now we have men-doing-their-own-thing. Or going their own way, whatever. Now, don't get me wrong. I totally get the motivation. Feminism has made life completely pointless for many men. It just doesn't pay to marry or even cohabitate. With the average woman you need to be a dark-triad psychopath in order to have her respect you. So it's no wonder that many men just say fuck it and go climb a metaphorical Mount Liang and do their own thing. Sure, porn, movies and videogames have also made the average men have a rather excessive expectation of what a woman should be. Most men would find their young grandmothers to be short, ugly, boring and uptight, completely unworthy of courtship, yet grandpa had no qualms in marrying them. But still, modern women are unpleasant. Very unpleasant. And so men withdraw.

But what do men after withdrawal. What do men do when in the company of other men, without unpleasant and rapacious women to bother them. This is what they do.[13] They seek manliness. They become bros, the ultimate bros. They go to the gym, they work out, they build muscle. Muscle is good, muscle is manly. So they work out some more. They compete to see who has more muscles, who is the better bro, who is more manly. They take steroids. They work out some more. The steroids get into their brains, clouding their judgment. Their testicles atrophy. They crash their cars. They become a complete nuissance to everyone. They go online and leave comments about how steroids are cool and completely harmless. How can they be bad? They make you more manly. That's good, because being manly is good. Surely being more manly can only be better! They are bros, and that's all that matters.

You'll have noticed this is not at all different to how women bully themselves into being increasingly more annoying, ugly and unreasonable, because being feminist is good, surely being more feminist can only be better! Being Maoist is good, surely worshipping Mao's mangoes[14] is only reasonable. You get the picture.

If Sailer is onto something, and long term steroid use messes with your hormones so much you develop an uncontrollable desire to become a tranny after your 50s, all those Men Going their Own Way are gonna be a funny sight in 20 years time. At least now they can marry each other!

---

[13] https://www.unz.com/isteve/cops-on-steroids/

[14] https://spandrell.com/2015/02/19/explaining-the-cultural-revolution-signalling-arms-races-as-bad-fiat-currency/

What to do about Censorship

2016-01-03 // wat do, power

I sometimes get asked if learning foreign languages is worth it, especially if you don't make money from them, or actually have a need for them. It's a though question. Learning Chinese was hard. I don't live there now, I did for a while, but most likely will never do again. Chinese upper-middle class people are leaving the country in droves, especially people with children. It certainly isn't a very comfortable place to live with a family.

Was it a waste then? I personally don't think so. There's always books and movies to make it worthwhile. And China in particular is a very interesting place, which is very worth knowing about. First of all it was the first modern state in many ways. Centralized government, meritocratic bureaucracy, universal education, state-run economy. All of that was invented in China, they run it for thousands of years, and it's not that different from what modern liberal democracies have become. I strongly think that understanding the political dynamics of ancient China is very useful to understand how Western states work today, even more so than understanding the history of the West itself. Our bureaucracies in many ways have more in common with the mandarinate in the Song Dynasty that they have to a 17th century European kingdom.

And this convergence is actually increasing. Look at this:

Facebook, Twitter, Google Collude With German Government To Censor Discussion On Immigration[15]

As Western states give up with the pretence of democracy, representative government and free speech; as radical ideology dominates all the media and academic world, what is the West going to resemble? China, of course. Before everybody started talking about censoring "hate speech" in the Internet, the Chinese were running the Great Firewall. Before SJWs started "doxxing" people on Twitter and Tumblr, the Chinese internet was doing "human searches" and getting people shamed in public. Before Twitter became the most important place for political speech in the Internet, Weibo had 500 million users, and all sorts of political agitation was going on there.

As you'll imagine the Communist Party wasn't very happy with party members being shown on Weibo every other day naked with their mistresses, or drinking too much, or

---

[15] https://www.breitbart.com/tech/2015/12/15/facebook-twitter-google-collude-with-german-government-to-censor-discussion-on-immigration/

with solid gold watches. They also weren't happy with extreme Maoists saying we need a new Cultural Revolution, or which Cathedral-spies talking about human rights and about how backward China is in comparison to Great America. So what the government did was a huge crackdown on political speech on the Internet. Massive censorship, banned accounts, and finally a real-name registration system. To get on Weibo or any big forum (imagine Reddit), you need to use your real name and ID number.

Given that Twitter and Facebook will soon start to censor everything white males say as racist and evil, you may be worried about what to do. Well what did the Chinese do? Leave Weibo in droves. And where did they go? To WeChat.

WeChat is a chat app, not that different from WhatsApp or many others. You may have heard of it; it's available out of China too, they're promoting all around the world, and it's translated to any language. How can a chat service supplant Weibo? Well, first of all WeChat has a "moments" tab where you can post stuff like you would on Facebook. You can also run open-accounts, where people follow celebrities who post regularly.

The point is that Chinese now keep to themselves. There is no public speech. If you wanna shit on the government, you can. Everybody does it, all the time. Hell, they won't shut up about it. But not in public. You do it with your friends, or people you can trust. WeChat gets censored too, if you start planning about how much you love the Dalai Lama, your "moment" will get deleted and police will knock to your door. But as long as you're discrete and shit on Oobama instead of Obama, or on Seerian refugees instead of Syrians, you are safe.

So now you know: learn from the Chinese, and leave the public sphere. The government is going to kick you out anyway. All you can do is retreat to the private sphere and do what you have to do, share what you have to share. It's OK, in many ways it's actually better. A good video will get shared anyway. Interesting news will get passed down too. All you need is put more skin in the game.

The case for voting for Clinton

2016-01-29 // demographics, bluegov

Yes, Trump is lots of fun. Having Mexico build a wall makes me giggle too. Shitting on Saudi princes on Twitter is priceless. But, but, Trump may not be all that cracked up when he gets the presidency. He's doing lots of stupid stuff too. Bombing ISIS? Come on. Pandering to conservakin voters has its backside too.

Take this:[16]

WATCH: Planned Parenthood Capitalizes on Zika Tragedy to Promote Abortion in Latin America

Fuck yeah. That's exactly that they should be doing. That's perhaps the best, the most important single policy that any country on earth can be pursuing. Go promote abortion in the third world. Go limit their fertility. Don't liberals like to talk about root causes? Well folks, the root causes of third world immigration into Europe and America is overpopulation in the third world. Wanna fix that? Then send Obama's minions and go tell them about grrl rights and abortion. Great stuff. Please, fund Planned Parenthood. Fund it lavishly. Give it tons of money. And staff. Lots of staff. Diverse stuff. Whatever. Just send them away to preach their mission.

Having planned parenthood go to poor countries is even more important than stopping the rapefugee crisis in Europe. I'll sign a treaty allowing 2 million refugees a year in exchange for Planned Parenthood having full authority in any refugee-sending country. In 20 years you get their TFR to 0.9. Then after they have a demographic crisis, you can send the rapefugees from Europe back home. Win-win.

So hey, vote Clinton. Shit is fubar already, Trump probably ain't gonna help much. Crushing anti-abortion activism though could actually save the day.

---

[16] https://www.breitbart.com/big-government/2016/01/29/planned-parenthood-capitalizes-on-zika-tragedy-to-promote-abortion-in-latin-america/

Blood is thicker than water

2016-01-31 // nationalism, europe

Donald Trump has swept the American political establishment by promising to kick out 10 million immigrants and forbidding Muslims from entering the US. The refugee crisis in Europe has turned awry so fast and so dramatically (assaulting young women in New Years has to be the worst PR ever in leftist history), that nativists all over the West are ecstatic and full of energy. The time has come, it almost appears. Everybody is running to Twitter and making small scale demonstrations all over the West, to take advantage of the momentum.

Some of this outburst of energy has reach this blog. Now I've been critical of white nationalism for quite some time. I just don't see it working out, and I have good reasons for it. I know my history, I know what nationalism is, how it was born, how it died, and what would it take to bring it back to life. And I just don't see it working out. Some people accuse me of being a bourgeois snob looking down at working class whites. Others have called me a rootless cosmopolitan who just doesn't have skin in the game.

Well, guilty as charged. But that's putting the cart before the horses. I took my skin out of the game because I didn't see how we're going to win this game. So I bailed. It happened that I had a good way out. And yes, I think working class whites are retarded. But I think that of high class whites too. I'm not into sports, which makes it hard to build rapport with working class people. But I'm not into charity, or homos, or any other bourgeois signaling crap either, so I find it even harder to build rapport with most upper-middle class people. I don't get along with anyone; it's nothing personal. That's why I have a fucking blog.

All that said, it's not that I don't understand white nationalism, or that I don't think it's a good idea. Stuff like this does get me excited:

https://www.youtube.com/watch?v=fA6XcyXsxXU

https://www.youtube.com/watch?v=BvoGPd6Yjo8

It probably shouldn't though. In the remote case that the nativist opposition won, then a nativist signaling spiral would get started in order to get to the top of the new power vacuum, and I'd probably be branded an evil rootless cosmopolitan, a rice-niger fifth columnist, a bourgeois dilettante who has belittled our glorious religion and racial theories. I've little to gain short term by a victory of nativism, and lots to lose.

But I can't help rooting for a group of white thugs attacking a bunch of smelly dumb Muslims. Those guys look like me. And decades after victory, perhaps after I'm dead, when the nativist signaling spiral settles down, Europe would be free of barbarians insulting our men and assaulting our women. Imagine that.

In all honestly, I don't see it happening. But I wish them the best of luck. Don't listen to me fellas. Keep on fighting.

The Easy Way Out

2016-02-04 // islam, wat do, europe, religion

A modest proposal. Don't take it too seriously.

Western elites are hell-bent in allowing unrestricted immigration into Europe and America. Even if they're all ISIS operatives. Muslims are not deemed to be a threat to the progressive establishment the same way that white-nationalism is, and they're mostly right about that.

Given present demographic trends, at this rate large swathes of the West will be Muslim in 20 years time; and again the progressive establishment will do nothing about that; because doing something about that would strengthen the hand of white-nationalists, and that directly threatens the power of the progressive establishment. So odds are for a Brazil - Mexico style situation, where a white-ish progressive elite rules over a mixed demographic of various shades of brown. Living standards plummet on average, but the elites still do great, and a white middle class which keeps the lights on still manages to make a tolerable living. But note that progressivism is still the state religion, and that means a large proportion of white people will still buy the whole package, i.e. hedonism, low fertility, feminism, the whole thing. That means dysgenic fertility goes on forever; the end of that road is South Africa.

The only way out is for whites to stop being progressive. And that means whites to stop being white. This means whites must stop being distinctly white, i.e. they must join non-whites at something so that the state can't just point at some group (besides progressivism), find it's white, and crack down on it because non-progressive whites are traitors and thus evil. The easy way out, as Houellebecq recently found out, is for whites to convert to Islam.

You don't have to be good Muslims. Just tolerably good ones. Islam sucks in many ways, but on the whole it's preferable to progressivism. Muslims get married and can control their wives. Muslims breed, and the influence of polygamy is way overhyped. Polygamy just formalizes what happens everywhere; some married men get poon on the side. Big deal. I'd rather they take a second wife than bang someone else's. Still very few do so. Being a second wife is way less glamorous than being a sexy mistress who has some hope of getting the first wife dumped and replace her. Being a second wife is a sign of poverty and shame. Chinese literature is full of women lamenting having to become second wives because their parents couldn't afford to sustain them.

Any obviously white group is going to be targeted by progressivism as being the obvious threat that it is. And, like it or not, the progressive state has the capability of crushing any attempt at subversion, and is going to have it for the foreseeable future. The only way to avoid detection is to join a non-white group, a group that the progressive state just can't attack. Islam is much less vulnerable to progressive attack. There's a reason it's been around for so long. While it sucks to join a group formed by smelly Arabs and inbred South Asians, eventually the cream rises to the top. And Islam needn't suck as badly as it does. Wahabbism is a modern fad. Muslims historically also used to drink and be merry. Once whites get some weight in Islam, naturally it'd evolve into White Islam. And the examples we have of White Islam in the Balkans are a joke. Who the hell is going to bother learning Arabic? Oh yeah praise Allah. Friday's off. Big deal. At least we could cover up our women and tell them to stop being such sluts.

A characteristic of Islam is that it requires of the faithful to take power once it has the numbers to achieve it. A 50% Muslim country, let alone an 80% one, wouldn't remain progressive for long. Eventually the Muslims will take over. The question is who is going to be part of that. You could remain defiant, and become a jizya-paying white minority, to be squeezed and bullied forever. Or you can convert early and join the fun before the Arabs get too uppity. Ever seen the pictures of the Ottoman sultans? They're whiter than me. Ever seen the Istanbul elite? They're whiter than you.

So think about it. I'd certainly do so if I were 18.

Choices

2016-02-04 // china, history

I hadn't thought about it, but my last post on Whites converting to Islam has a somewhat similar theme to a very famous episode in Chinese history. It's been a while since I write another Chinese history tale, and this is one of my favorites. So let's talk about Wu Sangui 吳三桂.

The year is 1644. The Ming Dynasty is in ruins. It is actually in ruins; a peasant rebellion led by a man called Li Zicheng 李自成 has been ravishing the country for a decade, conquering and utterly destroying much of the central and western areas of the country. The rebel leader had already conquered the largest city in the west, Xi'an 西安, and had proclaimed himself as the king of the Shun 順 Dynasty. The Shun army raced from Xi'An up through the province of Shanxi 山西, where most of the cities openly surrendered to him without bloodshed. In no time he crossed the western passes close to Beijing, and on May 26, the capital fell. The emperor of the Ming Dynasty stabbed his wives and daughters with his own hand, and then hanged himself on a nearby hill.

A resistance had formed in the south, where several imperial princes were proclaimed as emperors in different provinces. The north though was completely in control of the rebels of the Shun Dynasty. They felt safe, and spent 10 days sacking Beijing, raping the wives and daughters of the mandarins and merchants, and torturing them to extort untold quantities of gold and silver. Then one advisor to the rebel army came with news: we haven't completely conquered the north. There is still Wu Sangui.

Most maps you can see of the Ming Dynasty are complete bullshit, because they throw in every place where the Ming ever had a garrison during its 270 years of life. And this guys had lots of garrisons around at first, but they soon abandoned most of them. For all purposes, the effective northern borders of the Ming Dynasty were the Great Wall, which they built. Here's an accurate map of the north.

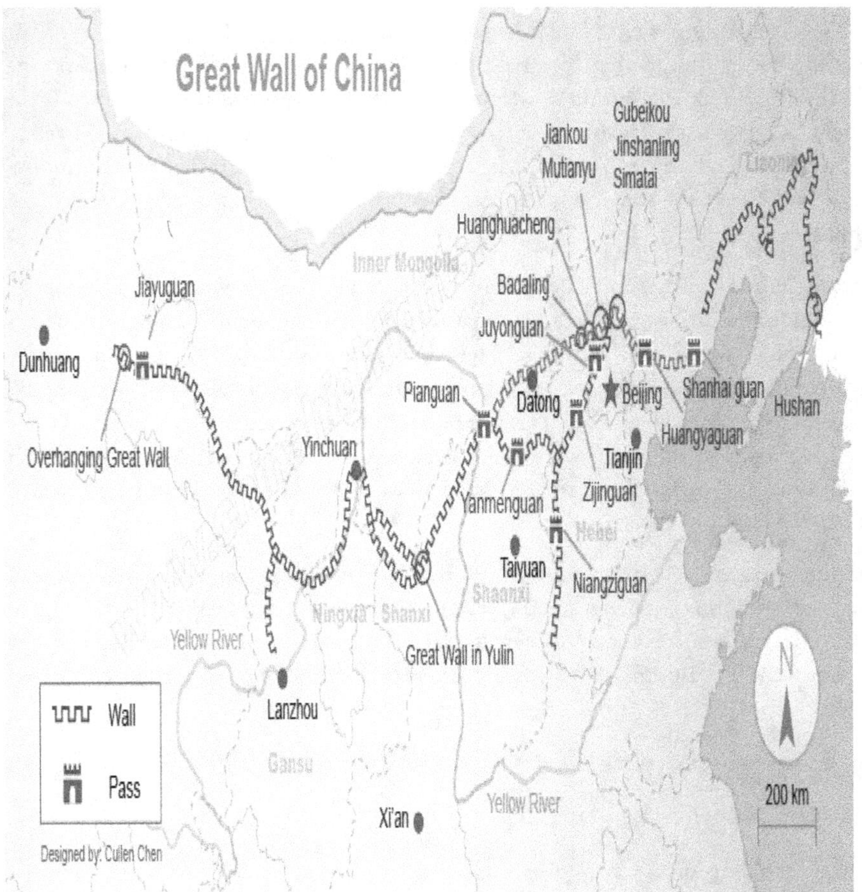

By this time, May 1644, mostly everything south of the wall and north of Yang-tze river has fallen to the Shun rebels, and most Ming generals in the area had surrendered and joined the fun. All except the most important. You'll see in this map that there's a weird discontinuous piece of wall up in the Northeast. That's Liaodong 遼東. That used to be firm Ming territory, settled with Han farmers, but since the 1600s a nearby tribal people, the Manchus (Jurchens back then) had built a very strong state, and conquered most of the Ming settlements in the area. The Manchus were extremely good fighters, they had managed to beat the Mongols and put them in their army, and had been raiding inside China for decades, doing massive damage. By 1644 there was only one fortress left in Liaodong, the castle of Ningyuan 寧遠. And Wu Sangui was its commander.

Weeks before Beijing fell to the rebels, the Ming emperor had sent an edict to Wu Sangui, ordering him to abandon the fortress and come with his troops to defend the capital. He was actually on his way, not far from Beijing, when the city fell and the emperor killed himself. Unsure what to do, Wu Sangui got his army and moved back to the Northeast, and set camp at Shanhaiguan 山海關, the last fortress of the continuous Great Wall, where the wall meets the sea. The fortress was very strong, and he decided to hold up there.

Soon the rebels having fun at Beijing decided that all Ming generals had surrendered, surely this one would surrender too. What is he going to do, fight us? The conquerors of the capital? Good luck with that. The rebels soon found that Wu Sangui's family was all in Beijing, 38 persons in all, led by his father, who had been chief of the capital's garrison at the time. They... persuaded the man to write a letter to his son, saying how virtuous and sagely the rebels were, that the game was over, and his duty as a filial son was to obey and surrender to the rebels. He'll be given a title of nobility and treated with all the honor he deserves.

The letter gets to the fortress, alongside shitloads of gold and silver for his soldiers. Wu Sangui sees that this is a pretty good deal, gets his army and marches towards Beijing in order to formally surrender to his new lord. On his second journey to Beijing in a few days, he suddenly bumps into two servants of his household. "What are you doing here?"

-Oh you have no idea, young lord.

What happened? How is my father?

They got him, my lord.

Who got him? What happened to him?

One rebel general came to father, and asked him for your concubine, Chen Yuan. Your father refused, said she wasn't there, that she was with you, but they refused to believe, and they tortured him. They tortured all of us, it was awful, only we two were able to escape. Father Lord was tortured so badly that he's likely to be dead by now. You should prepare yourself, young master.

Not good. Not good at all. These rebel bastards were scamming him. They didn't want him to surrender and join their army as a general. No, they wanted to lure him to the capital to kill him and get rid of a problem. That they didn't wait to steal my women and torture my father is proof that nothing good expected him at Beijing. Oh, this won't do. Wu Sangui again got his army and led them back to the Great Wall fortress.

What could he do, though. His army was perhaps the best in the empire. Tough, hardly men from the Northeast frontier, seasoned by constant war with the fierce Manchus.

He had a sizable army, but could he beat the rebels? All of them? Soon he heard that Li Zicheng, the rebel emperor himself was personally leading a 100k strong army to kill him. And behind his back, on the other side of the Great Wall, Dorgon, the effective king of the Manchus had departed from their capital with two thirds of the fierce Manchu army. He obviously knew that his Chinese enemies had collapsed and he wanted part of the fun.

So there he is, our famed general, holding the strongest fortress on the Chinese empire, facing a 100,000 rebel army on his front, and another 100,000 army of Manchu riders on his back. What can he do now? The Manchus are on his back. His uncle are with them; he was captured years ago, and had surrendered to the Manchus. He was now a very high status nobleman in the Manchu state, and he sent letters to his nephew to surrender. These are good people too, manly, virtuous, just men, not like the corrupt and decadent mandarins who used to rule over us. You cannot trust them, nephew. They maybe Chinese like you and us, share our culture and language. But they are evil, false men, and you know that. Join the Manchu army, they know of you, admire your martial skills, they'll make you into a prince and give you untold riches and honor.

The rebel leader though has brought Wu Sangui's father with him. He tells him it has all been a misunderstanding. One of the top rebel generals got a bit carried away. But the Shun emperor guarantees his safety, and he seems to mean it. He calls him to fulfill his duty towards his father and his country. The Mandate of Heaven has changed, the Shun now has it. His duty as a general is to follow him, and start a new glorious dynasty. Once the old corrupt mandarins of the Ming Dynasty are dealt with, the new, vigorous armies of the Chinese nation will come back north, where he can take part on the glorious retaking of the Northeast from the evil barbarians. Do the right thing, general. Your family and your nation need you.

Guess what he did?[17] 2 days later his father alongside the 38 members of his family were killed. 2 days later he was made a prince. The Manchus ruled China until 1911.

---

[17] https://www.amazon.com/Great-Enterprise-Reconstruction-Imperial-Seventeenth-Century/dp/0520235185/ref=sr_1_1?ie=UTF8&qid=1454611553&sr=8-1&keywords=wakeman+enterprise

Means, goals and signaling

2016-02-06 // wat do, signaling, blackpill, rightwingers

As I said in a recent post, the euphoria caused by the Donald Trump candidacy and the recent breakdown of public order in Western Europe has given renewed energy to white nationalism in both sides of the Atlantic. Now it seems like the time is ripe for revolution. Surely when Ivy League universities are openly staging rallies saying white people are evil by definition, and when white women are being openly assaulted by Middle Eastern migrants in the streets of Sweden and Germany, now white people in all sides can unite and fight back!

... Have they? Haven't seen that. All I see is the left using the overwhelming power of the state to push back with ruthless efficiency. I see German mayors not even bothering to pretend that they care that 9 year old german girls are being harassed on his streets

https://www.youtube.com/watch?v=XdSsJQ-fvOU

I see the Christian Church in Sweden building mosques adjacent to empty churches

And we recently saw like the neomasculine King Roosh was cowed into submission by the overwhelming force of leftist media.

Anonymous doxxed my family's address. Whatever I've done in life, they don't deserve to be harassed or harmed.

And not only was Roosh was beaten so badly that he's fearing for his own life. The progressive establishment is now using him and his followers as scapegoats for the epidemic of sexual assault by Muslim immigrants.[18]

---

[18] https://www.mirror.co.uk/news/uk-news/home-office-minister-implies-pro-7308510

Ms Champion added: "Rape of women has increased by 41 per cent in the last year. I'm appalled that the Government are sitting idly by whilst a group who believe women are pieces of meat without any rights are allowed to spread their poisonous ideology in the UK."How can the Government allow disgusting "meet-ups" led by a man and a group that have promoted rape to take place in the UK at a time when sex crimes against women are going through the roof?

People, you can't win. If you had half a brain, and knew how popular movements are run, you'd know you're doing it wrong. You can't openly call for rebellion and expect for it to work. Rebellions are crushed. That's what states are for. The State isn't a social contract for the protection of property rights. The State is a bunch of thugs assembled for the extermination of opposition to their power.

But of course men being men, when you get a bunch of dumb guys getting together, the first thing they do is signal their masculinity, and the signaling spiral devolves into everybody bragging about who is more macho, brave and reckless, and they go on Twitter rambling about how White Men should behead all the traitors. I posted a humble thought experiment[19] about how perhaps we should do a collective Flight from White to troll the progressives into allowing us to survive, and I get nazi hotheads calling for my murder in my own fucking blog. And I'm supposed to publish that. Right.

Not a few people lament that Hitler had it right all along, and if Germany had won WW2 we wouldn't have to face the likely death of white nations across the world. And there's a point to that. But you know, there are no ifs in history. Hitler was a white supremacist, running the most populous and advanced white nation in Europe. And he lost. He lost the war, Germany lost half its territory, millions dead, 12 million Germans exiled from across all Europe. It not only didn't work, it was a complete disaster. Hitler wanted the German race to be supreme. His temerity caused the likely death of the German nation 100 years later. Some great leader.

Look, this is a blog. A small, inconsequential blog. I'm not running a political party, an army, a band of brothers, or any kind of organization. I'm not running an advocacy program. I just write, using my brains to come out with ideas that none of you have thought of. I'm not personally converting to Islam. I'm not saying you should. But given the situation for most white people, I do think odds are the white race as a race has a better chance of surviving if whites converted to Islam, than if whites kept on being progressive, let alone if whites went nazi and openly rebelled against the state.

What do you care about? The survival of your people? Or signaling how edgy and manly you are on the internet? If Roosh had actually walked the walk and converted to his father's religion, he wouldn't be a semi-depressed lonely expat drifting around the

---

[19] https://spandrell.com/2016/02/04/the-easy-way-out/

second world looking for a woman that accepts his authority. Alas, he chose not to, he chose to get his dopamine kicks by signaling how manly and edgy he is on Twitter by openly confronting the progressive state. And all he achieved with that is putting his family in danger, and becoming a convenient scapegoat for the actual crime wave of brown and black people assaulting white people in Europe. Thanks dude. Now every time I say anything marginally red-pill, people will associate me with a hairy rape-apologist.

Now I may be wrong about Flight from White being a good strategy, and I may be wrong about Islam being the best place to flee to. But one thing I know, chances of survival are way higher than by going Nazi. White converts get to be shown as heroes in TV shows[20]. While nationalists are still shown as the epitome of all evil. Muslims breed, nazis go to their soccer matches, drink a lot, have their fun, and then fail to have children.

Now of course I'd prefer that whites collectively converted to Mormonism, started pumping white babies, and put all Africans and Middle Easterners in a fleet of boats bound to Liberia, to be taken care by General Butt Naked. But then again I have my doubts about the resilience of Mormons as a people. Defection rates of Mormons into progressivism are way higher than those for Muslims.

So again, I'm not converting. I don't give a shit if you do. But I think it's a fun idea to contemplate. Houellebecq seems pretty sold to the idea, and he's a sharp guy. The best for this idea would be for some small group of whites to convert en masse. Like the

---

[20] https://en.wikipedia.org/wiki/Nicholas_Brody

Subbotnik Jews.[21] See what happens. Maybe some Parisian banlieu. Or some enterprising American prophet in Michigan. If there's some smart Muslim out there, stop putting lame bombs, and go proselitizing. It could be fun.

I do understand this post suffers of severely bad timing. Trump still looks like he could win the election, and a complete moratory on Muslim immigration would be a massive victory for the alt-right. This post would be more suited for early 2018, when people start to notice that Trump was full of shit, that Muslim immigration hasn't stopped, and that half of the 20 year old cohort in Germany is already Muslim. If that happens, I'll repost this article to say I told you so. If it doesn't, and I dearly hope so, it will remain as historical proof of how bad things were back in 2016.

---

[21] https://en.wikipedia.org/wiki/Subbotnik_Jews

Power

2016-02-07 // wat do, power, rightwingers

In 1927, the young Chinese Communist Party was having a meeting, and all those young Chinese Communists were doing their thing, discussing stuff using arcane Marxist jargon. Mao Zedong cut the discussion short, telling them: "People, cut the crap. We gotta focus on the military stuff. Governments are born out of the barrel of a gun."

History proved him right, and his comrades know it. They know it so well that even after the Cultural Revolution killed and maimed most of his old comrades, his successors never disowned Mao or tarnished his legacy, the way Kruschov publicly said Stalin was an evil bastard. During the Cultural Revolution Deng was purged three times, his whole family imprisoned, sent away. His brother was forced to commit suicide. His son was thrown out of the window of his college dorm and became a paraplegic for life. Even then, after Mao was dead, Deng Xiaoping refused to criticize him. Why? "The only reason all of us are here is because Mao won the war". Damn straight.

Now of course Mao's quote isn't completely correct. He didn't grab a gun and win the war by being the best shot in the country. No, he won the war by having the best army. That means having a lot of guns, and having people willing the guns under your orders. So more precisely, power isn't born out of the barrel of a gun. Power is born out of the ability to have people with guns do what you tell them.

Let's apply this dictum to the present situation in Western countries. PEGIDA just run a series of protests against the Islamization of Europe. I've been writing about that these days. Well, what happened during those protests? A commenter was nice enough to post a link from the Daily Mail:

Plainclothes police officers wrestle a man to the ground during the PEGIDA demonstration held in Amsterdam, Holland, today

A man sticks his tongue out at the camera as he is led away from the demonstration by plainclothes police officers

Police officers in Calais, northern France, detain a man taking party in the demonstrations near the town's railway station

https://www.youtube.com/watch?v=TZou9CahPlU

This guy up here is a General of the French army. Leader of men. Alpha of Alphas. Kissing the ground.

If you want to get anything done, if you want to win, you gotta read about people who have won in the past. Like Mao. You need to own the guys with the guns. The police. The army. As long as those guys are against you, as long as those guys are willing to grab an awarded General and make him kiss the ground, all you're doing is LARPing. Which has its place, of course it's important to show that people are angry, and provoking the state gives us iconic images such as poor old General Piquemal. But let's not kid ourselves. LARPing isn't going to solve anything. Leftists don't win because they are masters at protesting and PR. Leftists win because the guys with guns obey them. When General Piquemal goes to protest, he gets arrested and humiliated on national TV. When Antifas trash a whole commercial street, the police make a wall to protect them. When Blacks burnt Ferguson, the police went out to arrest the shopowners who wanted to defend themselves. When Somalis rape Swedish children, the police doesn't answer the phone.

This state of affairs is often called Anarcho-tyranny, a coining of Sam Francis. It's funny because there's no word for that in most languages. Fish don't know what is water; the Chinese don't know what anarcho-tyranny is. Anarcho-tyranny is the natural state of affairs. The word only makes sense if you assume that the state is a social contract made for the defense of the rights of the citizens. But that's a myth. A state is what comes out of the barrel of a gun. In simple evolutionary terms, the state will protect those that the state needs to protect to survive in its present form. You and I don't want the state to survive in its present form, we very much want it to change forms. Well, they won't protect you then.

You wanna get something done? You want to have influence? Then you gotta join those who get things done. Pull a Gramsci and join the police. They're going to be expanding a lot in the next decades.

Influence

2016-02-13 // wat do, islam, europe

(Stop your Ghostery or other extensions to see Twitter links)

https://twitter.com/BreitbartNews/status/698244314858713089

One of the weirdest things in history was Byzantine iconoclasm in the 8th and 9th centuries. The Byzantine imperial house decreed that all pictures and portraits in Orthodox churches were to be destroyed. Not that I'm a fan of the art style of Eastern icons (I find it kinda gloomy and too flat), but that was a waste of perfectly fine artwork. The usual explanation is that the Emperor thought that Islam was strong due to its ascetic religion, and that Byzantines were losing the war because the wasted too much time and effort into drawing lame portraits. Whatever the reason, the Byzantines had adopted an important trait of Islamic culture without surrendering. "Aerial influence", as linguists call it, made the trick.

Another example is the Taoist and Shinto religions. People talk of Taoism in China and Shinto in Japan as if they were ancient religions, with temples, and priests, and the whole package. But that's bunk. When Buddhism came into East Asia, it brought temples, monks, books, influence peddling with rich and powerful, a very strong institutional package. Taoists and Shintoists just copied the whole thing, including the architecture of the temples, and much of its vocabulary. It's like if some neopagans built Gothic Churches, and run weekly rituals where people were fed bread by a professional priest, after giving a homily on the state of the world.

Anyway, I was saying that maybe we should accept Islam, in order to bring some much needed social conservatism into European mores. But we don't need mass conversion, Submission style. The sheer physical danger of having hostile barbarians around, and the refusal of the state to stop them, might bring women back home, make them require and seek the protection of their men, and make them have children so they can have someone to physically protect them after old age.

https://twitter.com/anomalyuk/status/697392363971465216

Just have some strategically placed White Muslims pushing a Salafist agenda so that the curse of affluence disappears. Imagine if Muslims in Europe were able to push the government into pushing women out of the workforce, or at the very least out of male workplaces. Just like that you solved the Two-Income Trap.[22] All we need is to be a bit more tolerant. To stop protesting in the streets, to stop fighting the fight we cannot win, and focus in what's really important: in going on with our lives, protecting our families and our friends.

---

22   https://www.amazon.com/The-Two-Income-Trap-Middle-Class-Parents/dp/0465090907

Picking Sides

2016-02-16 // rationalists, leftism

A while ago I wrote about a funny story[23] in the Chinese classical novel, the Water Margin, where the "heroes" want to poach a strong general, Qin Ming from their enemy. What they did is force the guy to defect, by telling his boss he already had. His boss being an evil asshole didn't bother confirming the news, and vowed to kill him (and beheaded his whole family beforehand). Thus poor Qin Ming had no choice but to fall in the trap and defect. The same tactic was used with another hero-general, Lu Junyi[24].

In fact the tactic is even older. As far as I can recall, it was already used by Liu Bang, the founder of the Han Dynasty during the civil war before he founded the empire, 200 BC. The enemy, Xiang Yu, was an asshole, but he had a very capable general under his command, Ying Bu[25]. Liu Bang sent an envoy to his camp and said to everybody who could hear it "Ying Bu has surrendered to us!". Old boss, being an asshole, vowed to kill him, so the poor guy had to defect now even if he didn't want to. Never fails.

All this was an introduction to paste a recent piece of writing by Scott Alexander. Now, the case isn't exactly equivalent. For starters, there's no need to frame him with a false accusation. He has accused himself. He said this:

People naturally divide into ingroups and outgroups. Although the traditional way of doing this is by race or religion (leading to racism, anti-Semitism, Islamophobia, etc), in modern America this is gradually being replaced by a more complicated division based on social class[26] and political affiliation. Rural working-class people have become a very different tribe ("Red Tribe") than college-educated urban people in gated professions ("Blue Tribe"), with different food preferences, sport preferences, entertainment preferences, dialects, religions, mores, and politics. These two groups are vehemently opposed[27].

---

[23] https://spandrell.com/2015/12/30/men-doing-their-own-thing/

[24] https://en.wikipedia.org/wiki/Lu_Junyi

[25] https://en.wikipedia.org/wiki/Ying_Bu#Defection_to_Liu_Bang

[26] https://slatestarcodex.com/2016/01/30/staying-classy/

[27] https://slatestarcodex.com/2014/09/30/i-can-tolerate-anything-except-the-outgroup/

(if you only read one link in this piece, read that vehemently opposed one. The rest are just citations; that one contains an important piece of the story that's hard to summarize).

While politics is about equally split between them, the media and academia are almost entirely Blue Tribe.

To make the point about the media: a 2008 study[28] found that 88% of contributions by people in the media went to Democrats; a 2004 study with slightly different methodology that limited itself to journalists found an even larger bias[29]. Here's a survey[30] that finds that if journalists were their own congressional district, they would be the most liberal district in the country, much further left even than Berkeley, California.

To make the point about academia: a recent analysis found that 91% of Harvard professors who donated to a presidential campaign donated to Hillary (with the remainder divided between Sanders and all eight GOP candidates). Jon Haidt's does a lot of work on this atheterodoxacademy[31] and finds that[32] there's a 14:1 ration of liberals to conservatives in the non-economics social sciences. Meta-analyses in psychology[33], psychiatry, and economics[34] all find that the personal views of experimenters affect what results they get; the psychology study, which quantifies the results, finds a very large effect size – larger than most effect sizes actually discovered in social science, meaning we have no idea how much of what we know is real effect and how much is experimenter political bias. On a related note, only 30% to 50% of experiments in psychology persist after replication attempts[35] (other academic disciplines are as bad or worse). On a related note, meta-analyses observe clear evidence

---

[28] https://www.washingtonexaminer.com/article/130902

[29] https://www.nytimes.com/2004/09/11/opinion/ruling-class-war.html?_r=0

[30] https://www.washingtontimes.com/news/2004/jun/22/20040622-085207-8465r/?page=all

[31] https://heterodoxacademy.org/

[32] https://heterodoxacademy.org/2015/09/14/bbs-paper-on-lack-of-political-diversity/

[33] https://www.lscp.net/persons/dupoux/teaching/JOURNEE_AUTOMN E_CogMaster_2011-12/readings_deontology/ Rosenthal_1994_interpersonal_expectancy_effects_a_review.pdf

[34] https://fivethirtyeight.com/features/economists-arent-as-nonpartisan-as-we-think/

of publication bias in politically charged domains – for example, this meta-analysis[36] finds that papers are more likely to be published as opposed to file-drawered if they support the liberal position rather than the conservative one. Also, lots and lots of people in academia, even the very liberal people, will admit this is true[37] if you ask them directly. Haidt, Tetlock, et al (see previously cited paper) have found lots of horrifying things like journal editors saying explicitly and proudly they'd refuse to publish articles that support conservative ideas, or professors saying that other academics whose research implies conservative ideas shouldn't be hired or given tenture.

So given the fact that our knowledge of the world is coming from a 90-percent-plus liberal group that's working hard to enforce orthodoxy, and then being filtered and broadcast to us by another 90-percent-plus liberal group that's working hard to enforce orthodoxy, our knowledge of the world is ... about as skewed as you would expect from this process. To give just one example, every number and line of evidence we have suggests that the police do not disproportionately target or kill black people compared to the encounter rate (see Part D here[38] and this study[39]) but the conventional wisdom is absolutely 100% certain they do and anybody who questions it is likely to sound like some kind of lunatic.

Once again, I think of these political differences as secondary to (and proxy for) more complicated tribal/class differences, and these tribes/classes really really hate each other and are trying to destroy each other (remember, multiple experiements – 1[40], 2[41], 3[42] – find that people's party/class/tribe prejudices are stronger than their racial/religious

---

[35]   https://www.psychologytoday.com/blog/the-nature-nurture-nietzsche-blog/201509/quick-guide-the-replication-crisis-in-psychology

[36] https://www.people.vcu.edu/~mamcdani/Publications/Cumulative%20meta-analysis%20as%20a%20publication%20bias%20method%20Final%20SIOP%202009.pdf

[37] https://twitter.com/kph3k/status/698236898100256768

[38]   https://slatestarcodex.com/2014/11/25/race-and-justice-much-more-than-you-wanted-to-know/

[39]   https://www.policeone.com/use-of-force/articles/7653755-Cops-hesitate-more-err-less-when-shooting-black-suspects-study-finds/

[40] https://pcl.stanford.edu/research/2014/iyengar-ajps-group-polarization.pdf

[41] https://psycnet.apa.org/journals/psp/5/2/127.pdf

[42]   https://www.people-press.org/2014/06/12/section-3-political-polarization-and-personal-life/

prejudices). So imagine an institution that's 90% Klansmen, with all its findings interpreted by and transmitted through a second institution that's 90% Klansmen, and consider how useful (or not) the information about black people that eventually reaches you through the conjunction of those two institutions will be.

Because the Blue Tribe's base is in education and the opinion-setting parts of the media, their class interest is to increase the power of these areas. I don't want to sound too conspiratorial by making it sound like this is organized (it's not), but classes tend to[43] evolve distributed ways to pursue their class interests without organization. In this case, that means to enforce credentialism (ie a system where the officialness of your education matters more than your ability) and orthodoxy (whether you hold the right opinions is more important than ability). We see the credentialism in for example the metastatic spread of degree requirements[44]. You need a college degree to have the same opportunities as you'd have gotten from a high school degree in 1960. This isn't because jobs require more knowledge today; there are thousands of jobs that will take you if you've got an Art History degree, not because Art History is relevant to the job, but because they insist on candidates having some, any, college degree. The Blue Tribe protects its own and wants to impoverish anyone who doesn't kowtow to their institutions. For the same reason, we get bizarre occupational licensing restrictions[45] like needing two years of training to braid people's hair, which have been proven time and time again not to work or improve quality, but which effectively lock poor people (and people who just don't do well with structure) out of getting liveable jobs.

The opposite of credentialism is meritocracy – the belief that the best person should get the job whether or not they've given $200,000 to Yale. In my crazy conspiracy theory, social justice is the attack arm of the educated/urban/sophisticated/academic Blue Tribe, which works by constantly insisting all competing tribes are[46] racist and sexist and therefore need to be dismantled/taken over/put under Blue Tribe supervision for their own good. So we get told that meritocracy is racist and sexist. Colleges have pronounced talking about meritocracy to be a microaggression[47], and the media has

---

[43]   https://slatestarcodex.com/2014/09/14/does-class-warfare-have-a-free-rider-problem/

[44]   https://slatestarcodex.com/2015/06/06/against-tulip-subsidies/

[45]   https://reason.com/blog/2015/07/31/white-house-occupational-licenses-report

[46]   https://slatestarcodex.com/2015/02/11/black-people-less-likely/

[47]   https://hotair.com/archives/2015/06/17/newest-campus-microaggression-i-believe-the-most-qualified-person-should-get-the-job/

declared that supporting meritocracy is inherently racist[48]. Likewise, we are all told that standardized tests and especially IQ are racist and hurt minorities, even though in reality this testing helps advance minorities better than the current system[49]. For the same reason, colleges are moving away from the SATs (an actual measure of student intelligence), to how well students do in interviews, how well they write essays, and other things which are obvious proxies for social class and tribal affiliation.

STEM culture and nerd culture is (was?) this weird alternative domain that had Blue Tribe advantages like education and wealth, but also wasn't drinking their Kool-Aid – they took pride in being meritocratic, they didn't care what college you went to as long as you were smart, and they were okay enjoying their own weird culture instead of following sophisticated trend-setters. The Blue Tribe was spooked, so they called in their attack arm, and soon enough we started hearing these constant calls in Blue-affiliated media and circles to destroy nerd culture[50] (2[51], 3[52], etc, etc) because it is inherently misogynistic, racist, etc. It's why we're told that Silicon Valley is full of "brogrammers" and "techbros" (compare "Berniebro", which everyone now agrees[53] was a Hillarysphere attempt to smear Sanders supporters). It's why we're told that tech is "incredibly white and male"[54] and "needs to get less white"[55] and just generally has this huge and unique diversity problem – even though in reality it's possibly the most racially diverse industry in the country, at a full 60% non-white[56]. It's why we're told that there is terrible bias against women in science academia, when in fact anyone can read the studies showing that controlling for

---

[48] https://www.theatlantic.com/business/archive/2015/12/meritocracy/418074/

[49] https://www.theatlantic.com/education/archive/2015/09/inequality-gifted-programs-schools-testing/405013/

[50] https://www.newser.com/story/197232/its-time-to-destroy-nerd-culture.html

[51] https://www.thetakeaway.org/story/misogyny-entitlement-nerd-culture/

[52] https://www.charlestoncitypaper.com/HaireoftheDog/archives/2014/05/28/nerd-culture-is-rape-culture-elliot-rodger-and-the-misogynist-world-of-the-geek

[53] https://fredrikdeboer.com/2016/02/08/if-youre-not-careful-whos-in-and-whos-out-becomes-the-only-question/

[54] https://www.businessinsider.com/silicon-valley-is-incredibly-white-and-male-2015-4

[55] https://thinkprogress.org/economy/2014/06/03/3443112/how-google-and-silicon-valley-can-remedy-its-diversity-problem/

[56] https://www.contracostatimes.com/salaries/ci_22094421

all other factors, women are twice as likely to be hired for tenure-track STEM positions as men bad link *and academic science is [not sexist at all]*[57]. *It's why we're told women fear for their lives in Silicon Valley because of endemic sexual harassment, even though nobody's ever formally investigated if it's worse than anywhere else, and the only informal survey I've ever seen shows harrassment in STEM to be well-below the average harrassment rate*[58].

What's happening at GitHub itself right now[59] is actually a pretty good example. The old CEO was fired because of various accusations (later investigated and found to be false; the firing was not revoked). The new CEO has banned the term "meritocracy", replaced workers managing their own affairs with a system of no-doubt-well-credentialled middle managers, and given lots of power to a "diversity team" that declares all remnants of the old company culture racist and sexist. According to Business Insider[60], there's now a "culture of fear" and a lot of the most talented employees are leaving. People are saying GitHub made some kind of mistake, but I suspect all is going according to plan, the talented employees will be replaced with better-credentialled ones, the media will call everybody who left "techbros" who were suffering from "aggrieved entitlement", GitHub will join the general Silicon Valley 2.0 landscape of open-plan offices and Pointy Haired Bosses, lather, rinse, repeat, and ten years from now bright-but-lower-class unsophisticated people without college degrees won't be able to find a job in Silicon Valley any more than they can on Wall Street or anywhere else.

I am pretty darned Blue Tribe myself – I'm pro-choice, pro-fighting-climate-change, pro-gay, pro-transgender, non-religious, pro-higher-taxes-on-rich, pro-single-payer, anti-gun, ready-for-Hillary, etc – and after having watched the Republican debate tonight I can honestly say I'm terrified at anyone other than the Blue Tribe having power. But just as I can be proud of my Jewish heritage but also upset about the occupation of Palestine, so I can be proud of the Blue Tribe and not too happy about their project of crushing everybody else with an iron fist regardless of the collateral damage. Doing anything about this is a dauntingly large project, but my own comparative advantage is in picking apart some of the sillier studies they use to put a fig-leaf over what they're doing.

---

[57] https://www.nytimes.com/2014/11/02/opinion/sunday/academic-science-isnt-sexist.html?_r=1

[58] https://www.huffingtonpost.com/2015/02/19/1-in-3-women-sexually-harassed-work-cosmopolitan_n_6713814.html

[59] https://www.businessinsider.com/github-the-full-inside-story-2016-2

[60] https://www.businessinsider.com/github-the-full-inside-story-2016-2

I don't know who is boss is, but his metaphorical superior in the Blue Tribe, in the Cathedral, the Polygon, the Left or whatever you want to call it, well by definition the Left is an evil asshole too. So be very aware, this guy is not one of yours. I am not one of yours, and I can't find anything to disagree with this piece of writing. Except the last paragraph, of course, which is retarded.

Not that I want him in my side. The dude has way too much baggage. But there's always something to gain by denying the enemy from a good general. And the guy is smart, and he is the object of admiration of many. Look at his damn blog, he gets hundreds of comments of starry-eyed fans who go there just to share a micro-slice of his fame. I got a link from him a while ago and my referrer stats got flooded with accesses from MIT addresses. Which is very impressive. Surely beats the bunch of nazis I've been getting lately.

But still, if there is some SJW command out there, note that you are more than justified for (metaphorically) killing off this guy's (metaphorical) family, and proscribe him away from your side, into the arms of your enemy. He's not one of yours. He's against everything you stand for. He has openly called for the removal of the racket that sustains your livelihood. He wants to deprive you of your bread! How can you tolerate this guy?

And hey, I do think we could use a psychiatrist. A bitter and resentful genius psychiatrist studying the intricacies of the Leftist Mind, ignoring all established procedure in order to find out what is inside the brains of his enemies, of the people who have tortured him since childhood. Now that sounds interesting.

A biological case against democracy

2016-02-17 // hbd, democracy, theory

This one's not about IQ. Listen up.

All human traits are normally distributed, with few people on each extreme. I don't know to what degree character is inherited, but it sure as hell is innate.

A human trait, like any other, is the thirst for power. Call it sociopathy to get a better image. It's probably not the same thing, but think of the evil striver who lies, fools, scams and does any manner of evil in order to climb the ladder of power and get to lord over others and enjoy riches gained through the exploitation of the people.

Think of Clinton, say. Any of them will do. These guys have an edge. They're driven. They really really want power. And money. Lots of money. Apparently the Clinton's are worth $100 million. Why do they want so much money? Isn't $10 million enough? 20? No, they want more. That's what they do, they seek power, money, and everything that is nice, they seek it in infinite amounts. Why does Hillary want to be president? What for? The satisfaction of power. That's who she is.

But she isn't the only one. There's lots of people like her, in any country, in any institution. Jerry Pournelle had the Iron Law of Bureaucracy: every organization will always end up being led by people devoted to the benefit of the organization, not to doing whatever purpose the organization originally had. Which is another way of saying that any organization will eventually be led by people who only think of benefitting the people who lead the organization, i.e. themselves. The greedy power-hungry. Let's call them Clintons, for lack of a better word. Every organization will eventually always end up being led by Clinton's. Simply because they take care that they end up ruling. They seek power will all their heart, and they get it. That's how you get Conquest's Law too. All organizations not explicitly rightist will always end up turning leftist. Why? Because the left is simply what the Clinton's do. The Left is whatever works at achieving power and keeping it.[61]

In any Open Society™, well all positions are open. There is no privilege of birth, no traditional standards. There is to be open competition. Even the upper reaches of power are to be open to everyone, by free elections. Democracy. Who wins in a democracy? The Clintons. Why? Because they seek power, and have no qualms at doing whatever is necessary. Fraud, lies, treason. Murder. Whatever it takes, they will

---

[61]   https://spandrell.com/2015/03/01/leftism-is-just-an-easy-excuse/

have power. That is what they do. Remember the Selfish Gene? The Hawks and the Doves? Hawks are evil, they hurt everyone. But you can't get rid of them. They're never too many, else they start killing each other. But at small numbers they always win. Michel Houellebecq first became famous with his novel, *The Extension of the Realm of Struggle* (Whatever). He points out how opening the sexual marketplace to competition advantages the ruthless and evil, to the detriment of everyone else. That works in politics too. The right edge of the Bell Curve always wins.

In a traditional aristocratic system, positions of power are given by family prestige. There is some level of striving and merit involved, but mostly it's old families sharing positions of power according to traditional standards, which nobody really understands why are there. Mostly reflecting old Schelling points left by ancient conflicts. But they are there, and they are never touched. You don't get to a position of power if you aren't of the right blood. A Clinton can't get to president. He can join the staff of some aristocrat, and schmoozing him to achieve influence by proxy. But you can only get so far that way; and positions in the staff are also subject to traditional limitations. There's a firewall there.

Traditional power arrangements can be stupid and ineffective. They are by definition nepotistic, and often nothing gets done. But they have the important function of impeding the access of evil sociopaths to the highest reaches of power. You really don't want those people up there; all they do is suck the coffers dry, and hurt everyone they fancy in order to satisfy their greed. Democracy, by opening the levers of power to free competition, all but guarantees that evil sociopaths will end up ruling everything. People who have no issue with giving sick men access to girl's toilets, or bringing hostile barbarians to rape the women of their country.[62] Monarchies can have a bad king. But Democracies always have a bad king.

---

[62] https://www.telegraph.co.uk/news/worldnews/europe/germany/12130843/EU-leaders-No-link-between-Cologne-sex-attacks-and-migrant-crisis.html

It's all Business

2016-02-20 // jews, capitalism

Take a look at this:

Israel calls on world nations to regulate social media anti-Semitism

The Foreign Ministry on Monday called on governments around the world to regulate social media in order to combat anti-Semitism and violent incitement, reiterating the government's support last year for Internet censorship during an anti-racism conference. (...)

"What is YouTube? What is Facebook? What is Twitter? And what is Google?" he asked. "Are they a free speech corner like [London's] Hyde Park or are they more similar to a radio station in the public domain?" Referring to cartoons of Palestinians killing Jews and other such material circulating online, Tor asked why platforms such as Google search, You- Tube, Facebook and Twitter are "tolerating" violent incitement and "saying they are protected in a holy way by free speech."

"How is it possible that the government of France and the European Union all feel that incitement in Arabic on social media in Europe calling for physical attacks on Jews is permitted and that there is no requirement from industry to do something about it," he continued, adding that Israel is working with European partners to push the technology sector to adopt a definition of anti-Semitism so its constituent companies can "take responsibility for what they host."

I got mildly triggered. Man, these Jews. It seems like they're doing it on purpose to piss people off. Then I noticed the ad on the page:

Maybe they are doing it on purpose. To get clicks. An article a while ago put it well, that modern media are "rage profiteers[63]". Maybe Jewish agitation is just a business to get ad clicks. Jews have been at the forefront of the media industry since 18th century newspapers and they pretty much created the modern ad industry.

Europeans discovered continents and conquered most of the world as an afterthought of their quest for cinnamon to put in their mothers' cakes. Britain unleashed the Opium War which resulted in the collapse of the Chinese Empire because they had no other way of buying tea. Ah, the free market.

---

[63] https://www.rooshvforum.com/thread-38925.html

Baby socialism

2016-03-13 // china, women, demographics, redpill

WAR IS PEACE

SLAVERY IS FREEDOM

IGNORANCE IS KNOWLEDGE

DIVERSITY IS...

Inquisition, for the most part. The corporate PR racket sells that diversity is a strength because having different people in your organization gets you different points of view, and that results in better input for discussions and thus better decision-taking. Which is exactly how it doesn't work in practice. Racial diversity is welcome so long as everyone is strictly progressive, and USG has been busy promoting ideological uniformity across its whole empire. In recent years who basically can't get a job if you are caught dissenting with the most trivial progressive dogma. As Trotsky had it, in capitalism those who don't work shan't eat; under communism those who don't obey shan't eat.

The argument itself is true, though. Actual diversity does bring different points of view, which can often be interesting. But that requires actual ideological independence. The ideological landscape in the West is completely owned by USG, and one can hardly found any original ideas that differ even slightly from the progressive platform. But far away in East Asia, people can afford to think for themselves. And they do, for the most part, producing actually interesting ideas. If there's an argument for learning exotic languages, this is it. This blog is proof of that.

The talk of the street these weeks in Japan is a proposal for reforming pre-primary school, and making not only kindergarten (3 to 6 year olds) but even nurseries (0 to 3 year olds) part of mandatory schooling. This might sound similar to the recent "universal pre-K" idea in the US, but the argument here is not about the cognitive benefits of early schooling. The point is purely monetary: if woman are to join the workforce, as Japan's Abe government has publicly proclaimed they must, well somebody should take care of the babies then. Nurseries as of today are regulated by the Ministry of Welfare, which has a bunch of agencies skimming the budget, so that nurseries are underbuilt and baby nurses has laughably low salaries. Corruption is rampant, and the law isn't working, as there's a severe shortage of available nurseries. The idea is to change the law to make nurseries depend on the Ministry of Education, and be run as normal schools. There's no shortage of schools.

Interestingly enough, a similar debate has been going on in China for a while. While the countries are close by geographically, of course China is very different Japan in many ways. China is a communist one-party state, and it has no big issues with their workforce. What China and Japan do have in common is a dire demographic problem. Low fertility.

A while ago there was a post by some man called Ma Qianzu 馬前卒[64], writing about demographic policy. As many of you will know, China has had a One Child Policy for decades, which this year has been finally modified to allow 2 children per couple. The revision of the law of course caused a very big reaction in China, and people have been debating the issue for years. This Ma Qianzu guy is apparently an official intellectual, party member, who basically provides the smart version of government propaganda. He's a smart commie. And there aren't many of those, so people listen to this guy, even if they don't agree with them (public opinion in China, at least among the young, is rabidly anti-government).

While Japan can often produce interesting policy ideas, in the end Japan is still a USG vassal, with tens of thousands of American troops watching over the country. China on contrast is an actually independent country, so they have much more freedom to think about policy in their own way. This article by Ma Qianzu was a good proof of that. It's very first paragraph was such a good example of clear, frank thinking that one could never see in any Western publication. I couldn't believe my own eyes. It made so much sense I got tears in my eyes. It said:

只要阶级跌落的恐惧还在，放开的意义就不大。我周围的育龄人口反应冷淡，原因不是真养不起孩子，而是二胎可能会影响家庭生活水平，让他们所期望的中产阶级生活更渺茫。

As long as the fear of downward mobility remains, opening up the One Child Policy won't change anything. My peers reacted to the new law with derision, not because they can't afford more children, but because a second child would impact their living standards, make the middle-class lifestyle they desire become unachievable.

The original wording is somewhat more dramatic. Downward mobility is stated as "falling from their class". And 'class' is a very charged word in Communist China. Class struggle is still a mainstream concept over there. The guy is an official intellectual of the Communist Party: class struggle is what he writes about. Demographic policy in China is a function of Class Struggle. In this case, the white-collar middle class is refusing to breed because they fear the cost will make them drop out into the proletariat. And they aren't having that.

The writer goes on describing why exactly having a second child would make people think that they would have to abandon middle-class living standards. He aptly says that

---

[64] https://www.letscorp.net/archives/99373

the whole idea of "not being able to afford more children" makes no sense. Our parents, he says, were much poorer than we are (back in the Mao days), yet they all had plenty of children. Of course, children cost less back then; they played out in the street, went to free state schools, healthcare was unavailable so children would die every now and then, which if sad, was still accepted as something that happened. It was no big deal.

Today, though, people have much higher incomes. But that surplus income, and then some, has been taken over by skyrocketing school fees. "Malicious capitalists", as he aptly puts it, are taking advantage of the status anxiety of people, and charging exorbitant fees for children books, cram-schools, and other assorted services for middle-class children. Competition to get into top colleges in China is fierce, so people spend every single dime they have to make sure their children have a chance. And then they complain they can't afford more children.

Part of the issue, Mr. Ma says, is that schools close down too soon. Parents work late, until 8 PM on average, and children leave school at 5 PM. Kids have 3 hours without supervision, so the parents take them to cram schools if only to have them go to some place until they can leave work. Once you get them into cram school, though, the signaling spiral starts. Nobody wants to be that parent who takes his kid to the bad cram school. You want the good one, and the good one is worth money. So cram schools end up charging exorbitant tuition for lousy cram schools, and parents have their small precious discretionary income gone down the drain into education fees.

Well, the author rightly points out, as a Communist Country, we must not allow evil capitalists from taking advantage of the insecurity of our people and make rich from a signaling spiral. China should forbid private ownership of education facilities, cram schools included. Actually, cram schools should be forbidden, period. If children have to spend more time in school, then so be it. Have schools open until late, at least until their parents finish work. If kids are to study, let it be at good Communist schools, and not perfidious capitalist cram schools.

A problem with keeping kids at school until 10 PM is that... the schools don't want the kids around. Parents today are increasingly litigious, and when a kid gets hurt at school parents waste no time suing schools for damages. Under firm Communist principles, that doesn't do. Parents should be stripped of the right to sue schools for what happens to their children inside them. Children spent most of their waking time in schools, not at home. Schools have as much a right to custody over children than their parents do. Sure, people will complain that this goes against natural rights, the sacred property rights of parents over their children. But that, you'll notice, is bad feudal Confucianism. And we are now a Communist country. So no more of that absolute parental rights nonsense. Kids aren't their parents'. You didn't build that.

At this point I started to get uneasy. Hey, hey. There's a reason kids are regarded as being the property of their parents. Parents (generally) have an interest in their children's welfare. Schools don't. A school teacher can be an evil asshole and beat your kid for fun. Or ignore it while other kids bully him into suicide. Overly litigious parents are certainly a drag on the system, but to fix that you don't need to change the whole legal idea of custody.

I got even more uneasy, outright anxious, when the author mentioned how in recent years we see more out-of-wedlock births, with women having children without husbands, and that is a good thing because it shows how old feudal family values are disappearing and moral progress is obviously good. The path to Communism! I didn't see that coming. Don't be fooled by the guy's progressive nonsense; single-motherhood in China is, while certainly increasing, still extremely rare. And for good reason; there is no welfare. Chinese women don't want to have children with their husbands as it costs too much; why would they be willing to have children on their own? That some skank gets knocked up once in a while is obviously just a proof of lack of foresight, not the vanguard of future Communist birth ethics.

Now the whole idea of socializing children in China, or mandatory universal pre-K for 1 year olds in Japan has the common idea that child-rearing is a cost, in both labor and money, and that if the state took care of that cost, people would have more children. And yes, sure, up to a point, child rearing costs money, and it can be a hassle. Some people enjoy taking care of babies, but some people sure don't. I know of plenty of women in Japan who went to work because they found their cubicle jobs easier than their annoying babies. For these people, subsidized daycare would be a godsend.

But there's another side to that equation. If you reduce the costs, you make it easier to consume. But what's the incentive for having kids anyway? If your children are going to be closed up in some government facility for 12 hours a day since age 1 until they leave to college and never come back; what's the point of having children at all if you don't get to see them?

Let's face it, the demand for children in developed countries today is effectively indistinguishable from the demand of pets. People have children because they are adorable, small and cuddly, and many people enjoy having some small cutesy thing to care of.

In the old days, people didn't have pets. They had livestock, they had animals to use them. You had a dog to hunt, or watch the house, you kept a cat so he would eat mice and other vermin. You had cows to milk, pigs to eat, chicken to give you eggs. You didn't take care of animals, take pictures of them, find them cute, watch them or buy them clothes. You had them outside, treated them like shit, and efficiently exploit them as an economic resource. You had as much livestock as you could afford, as they were supposed to be a profitable resource.

Not today though. People don't have animals, because it's cheaper to buy animal products in the supermarket. People who have animals today have them as pets; as small cutesy things to make them company. You pet them, cuddle them, take pictures, watch their every reaction with amusement.

In the same way, in the old days people had children as a resource. Kids weren't found to be cute (the word itself didn't exist until the 19th century); they were annoying brats to be trained into farm hands or money earners for the family. People sent their children away as soon as 8 years old, and had no emotional hangups about it whatsoever. People had a lot of children because they were profitable, or at least there was a gambling chance of getting an awesome kid who raised the whole family out of poverty.

Today though, kids today are a cost, not a profitable resource. And so people have don't have large families the same way they don't have livestock anymore. They have kids like they have pets, as small cutesy things that give them company. Things to watch and enjoy. People actually use the same vocabulary to refer to both children and pets the same way. Some people actually call their pets "children"!

The children market, such as it is, is determined by the demand of pets. Having the government socialize the costs of childrearing might help a bit on the margin, but it won't shift the fundamentals of the market. The fundamental issue is that children aren't profitable, and there's no market incentive for having large families.

Social Matter had a characteristically childish post[65] where they made a more or less accurate assessment about why present policies are wrong, but remained completely clueless about what could possibly fix the issue. "It's not about money". Indeed it's not about the money. Children don't make money and people have internalized that over the last 100 years. And that's why people don't have more than 1 or 2 children; the same way people don't generally have more than 1 or 2 cats. To create incentives for people to have large families there's only one way to do it.

Make it again about money. Change tax incentives so that childless people get their tax burden tripled, while large families are tax free. Make it profitable. Bureaucrats, East and West, are obsessed with socializing anything. But we have decades of experience with market incentives. People like money more than they like kids. At some point somebody is going to have to say it.

---

[65]   https://www.socialmatter.net/2016/03/01/throwing-natalist-benefits-at-women-wont-fix-low-fertility-rates/

Natural Selection

2016-02-26 // cucks, demographics, women

I believe myself that romantic love is the source of the most intense delights that life has to offer. In the relation of a man and woman who love each other with passion and imagination and tenderness, there is something of inestimable value, to be ignorant of which is a great misfortune to any human being.

Said Bertrand Russell. He had 4 wives, 3 children.

The greatest pleasure is to vanquish your enemies and chase them before you, to rob them of their wealth and see those dear to them bathed in tears, to ride their horses and clasp to your bosom their wives and daughters.

Gengis Khan. Had thousands of wives, thousands of children.

Love

2016-02-29 // women, rationalists

I have a couple of long posts ready, but I take it that everyone's attention is on Trump and Super Tuesday, so I'll post something lighter for today.

As per my last post, it's amusing that while Genghis Khan and his pals were banging the daughters of kings and utmost beauties of all the kingdoms from China to Iran, the great romanticist Bertrand Russell was singing the sublime pleasures of romantic love while banging this:

Now, Russell was no fool. Some of you will remember my being shocked[66] at Scott Alexander and other MIRI cultists being "polyamorists", which is a thing I didn't even know existed. It didn't took long for me to realize that "polyamory" such as it is, can only make sense if the people involved are unattractive, such as that sharing sexual partners doesn't feel so bad. Nobody wants to share a good thing, but sharing a lousy thing, having the vague chance of trading up, is not such a bad deal. And variety itself is appealing to men. Apparently the whole idea goes back to Bertrand Russell himself[67]:

As for Dora Russell, the story is incredibly perverse. Their marriage was, at first, designed by both of them, to allow for liberal bouts of adultery. Bertie became infamous, in the 1920s, for various writings, promoting their concept of the "marriage

---

[66] https://slatestarcodex.com/2013/04/06/polyamory-is-boring/

[67] https://www.larouchepub.com/eiw/public/2000/eirv27n45-20001117/eirv27n45-20001117_058-new_insights_into_a_20th_century.pdf

of the future." The problem is, when Dora took the matter to heart, and started having children with another man, Bertie went berserk, and began a lifelong campaign of hatred and revenge against her, the which included an about-face, against his former "liberal" views on marriage. Monk's descriptions, of how he dealt with Dora, from the late 1920s, on through the rest of his life, make for gruesome reading.

Read as: get a homely broad, with the advantage that she will let you screw other women, which he of course was eminently able as a celebrity aristocrat. He didn't feel so bad about his homely broad banging outside, or perhaps he thought she wouldn't be able to. But oh, that's only male projection. Women are always able to find a mate, and she did, so much that he cuckolded him 2 children! Then Russell stopped finding the whole thing so amusing, and went total asshole on her and his children with her.

Gengis Khan on the other side, was attacked by a rival tribe on his young days, and his wife kidnapped. He eventually raised an army and beat the rival tribe, recovering his dear wife after 8 months or so. She was pregnant, and soon gave birth to a boy, Jochi. He owned the boy, as the timing was barely plausible, but doubts about the boy's parentage never disappeared. He didn't allow them, though, he owned the boy as his eldest son, and he grew to be a great general, his house eventually founding the Golden Horde. As fond as he was of the kid, though, he didn't have him named his heir; his other children just wouldn't have accepted that. But he did care and respect his first wife as his empress for all his life. You can see there he was a better man than Russell.

That sex is about power, and not about pleasure, is an old feminist trope, but there's a nugget of truth in there. The pleasure of sex is fleeting, and women generally just aren't that interesting. Sex is a natural urge, just as hunger, but the same way hunger can be satisfied properly, or can be indulged with gluttony, sex can be satisfied properly inside marriage, an institution which sanctions power of men over women, or it can be indulged with lust. Gluttony produces sick and disgusting fat people, and lust produces vapid and evil men.

Trump and the GOP

2016-03-03 // cucks, democracy

A short reminder that the GOP would obviously prefer to lose the election rather than have Trump win. It's an obvious principal-agent problem.

By "GOP" I mean the GOP Establishment, Conservatism Inc., the pundit and election consultant industry, etc. All those people have cushy jobs, good incomes, fancy lifestyles and some degree of mainstream respect (or at least, toleration) from the Left.

Trump winning the election will give them absolutely no personal benefit. The politicians would have to deal with a brash and aggressive outsider, which is annoying. But think of the pundits and consultants. They are livid, and for good reason. Trump is obliterating their business model. He's winning the primary without spending a dime on them, and saying exactly the opposite of what they get paid for saying. Jeb Bush spent 150 million dollars on them, and he went to hell. Now think about that for a minute. 150 million dollars. That's a lot of money. That money went somewhere. It paid for lots of houses, cars, clothes, school tuition, restaurant fees, etc. Thousands upon thousands of people live off that sort of money.

Trump may be nominally part of the same thing, i.e. the "Republican Party", but what's in a name? Trump is a direct threat to all these people, and a not trivial threat to politicians who have made a career of being the tolerated opposition of the Progressive Soviet. If Hillary wins the election, these people will suffer nothing. Well, some of their donors may find it harder to get things done, and their donations may decrease a little. But probably not by much. Trump, on the other hand, is aiming for their throat. If Trump wins these people will suffer very real damage. Their family's lifestyle will be in jeopardy. So of course they'll sabotage anything Trump does.

Either Trump runs divide and conquer and plays one against the other, or he brute-forces his way to power by bringing enough new votes to compensate the loss of the upper-middle class vote. Average turnout in American elections is low enough for the latter to be possible, but it won't be easy.

Muh Faith

2016-03-04 // cucks

https://www.nbcnews.com/id/22273924/ns/meet_the_press/t/meet-press-transcript-dec/

MR. RUSSERT: You, you raise the issue of color of skin. In 1954 the U.S. Supreme Court, Brown vs. Board of Education, desegregated all our public schools. In 1964 civil rights laws giving full equality to black Americans. And yet it wasn't till 1978 that the Mormon church decided to allow blacks to participate fully. Here was the headlines in the papers in June of '78. "Mormon Church Dissolves Black Bias. Citing new revelation from God, the president of the Mormon Church decreed for the first time black males could fully participate in church rites." You were 31 years old, and your church was excluding blacks from full participation. Didn't you think, "What am I doing part of an organization that is viewed by many as a racist organization?"

GOV. ROMNEY: I'm very proud of my faith, and it's the faith of my fathers, and I certainly believe that it is a, a faithwell, it's true and I love my faith. And I'm not going to distance myself in any way from my faith. But you can see what I believed and what my family believed by looking at, at our lives. My dad marched with Martin Luther King. My mm was a tireless crusader for civil rights. You may recall that my dad walked out of the Republican convention in 1964 in San Francisco in part because Barry Goldwater, in his speech, gave my dad the impression that he was someone who was going to be weak on civil rights. So my dad's reputation, my mom's and my own has always been one of reaching out to people and not discriminating based upon race or anything else. And so those are my fundamental core beliefs, and I was anxious to see a change in, in my church.

I can remember when, when I heard about the change being made. I was driving home from, I think, it was law school, but I was driving home, going through the Fresh Pond rotary in Cambridge, Massachusetts. I heard it on the radio, and I pulled over and, and literally wept. Even at this day it's emotional, and so it's very deep and fundamental in my, in my life and my most core beliefs that all people are children of God. My faith has always told me that. My faith has also always told me that, in the eyes of God, every individual was, was merited the, the fullest degree of happiness in the hereafter, and I, and I had no question in my mind that African-Americans and, and blacks generally, would have every right and every benefit in the hereafter that anyone else had and that God is no respecter of persons.

2012

https://twitter.com/MittRomney/status/415569809267384321

https://twitter.com/mittromney/status/548152903085457408

Muh Faith, 2

2016-03-06 // cucks, religion

Let me first say that my previous post[68] wasn't about shitting on Mormonism or on Mormons as a whole. I have many Mormon readers, and they have been kind to me. I'm a great fan of Mormons and I wish more people were like them.

That said, I think Mitt Romney is an evil profiteer and a dishonest hack, "weeping" when his church finally kneeled to Leftist pressure and accepted blacks in their church. Aren't you supposed to follow your church leadership, whatever they say? Why do you weep when they say something which just happens to be good for you? You'll note that Mitt Romney's father was the man who presided over the Detroit riots, and made a career of his "moderate" conservatism, i.e. swimming left and dragging his church with him.

Rumor has it the GOP establishment wants to nominate Romney again. Which again shows they don't really want to win[69]. If all they want is to lose, they could nominate Cruz and lose even worse. Butwhat they want is to send a message[70] about what is tolerated. People like Trump will be crushed; people like Cruz aren't tolerated either. People who weep when freedom of association is abolished in favor of blacks are to be favored and lionized.

A common theme of this blog is that people using religion for their personal benefit is not only possible; it's to be expected. People tend to take religion seriously only to the extent that interests them. See an even more jarring example.

The Pope, Francis I, had this to say[71] in a recent meeting with a group of "French Social Christians". I take it there are other French Christians which aren't social. There he said[72] (Google Translate works well with Italian):

---

[68] https://spandrell.com/2016/03/04/muh-faith/

[69] https://spandrell.com/2016/03/03/trump-and-the-gop/

[70] https://www.overcomingbias.com/2016/03/cant-stop-lecturing.html

[71] https://www.bloomberg.com/news/articles/2016-03-04/pope-francis-refers-to-arab-invasion-as-a-social-reality

[72] https://www.osservatoreromano.va/it/news/il-papa-e-i-pesci-rosa

"Emmanuel Levinas bases its philosophy on the meeting with the other," sums up Francis. "The other has a face. We must go out of ourselves to contemplate."The adventure of the caravels would therefore something metaphysical? "From Magellan onwards, he has learned to look at the world from the south. That's why the world is best seen from the periphery to the center and I understand better my faith from the periphery, but the periphery can be human, linked to poverty, health, or a feeling of existential periphery". We understand well the importance of this issue has taken on in the preaching of Francis.

Emmanuel Levinas being some Jewish ~~philosopher~~ bullshit artist who made a killing in France, the mecca of all bullshit artists. Apparently the Pope takes his insight from Jewish philosophers, instead of the Catholic catechism.

"There's something that bothers me," the Pope said. "Of course, globalization unites us and thus has positive aspects. But I think there are good and less good globalization. The less good can be represented by a sphere: every person is equal distance from the center. This first scheme separates man from himself, uniformizes him and eventually prevents him to express himself freely. The best globalization would be quite a polyhedron. All are united, but every people, every nation, retains its identity, its culture, its wealth. The stakes for me is this good globalization, which allows us to keep what defines us. This second vision of globalization allows to unite people while preserving their uniqueness, which favors dialogue, mutual understanding. So that there is dialogue, there is a condition *sine qua non* : starting with his own identity. If they are not clear with myself, if I know my religious, cultural, philosophical, I can not turn to another. There is no membership dialogue".

Got it? Me neither. That's the crap the Catholic Church is selling these days. The global polyhedron.

"The only continent that can bring some unity to the world is Europe," the Pope added. "China has perhaps a more ancient culture, more profound. But only Europe has a vocation of universality and service." Francis returns then on the theme of his speech in Strasbourg, on 25 November 2014, when he compared Europe to a grandmother a little 'tired. "But here is the mother became a grandmother" sorridecon a hint of irony. I think of the biblical stories, the old Sarah who laughs when he learns that gets pregnant. The question may seem strange, but I can not not do it. It's too late? Grandma can once again become a young mother? "A head of state I have already asked this question," replies the Pope. "Yes, it can. But under certain conditions. Spain and Italy have a birth rate close to zero. France gets along better because he built a family policy that encourages the birth. Being a mother means having children."But the renewal is not only quantitative. "If Europe wants to rejuvenate, he must rediscover their cultural roots. Of all the Western countries, Europe has the stronger and deeper roots. Through colonization, these roots have even reached the new world.

But forgetting its own history, Europe weakens. It is then that risks becoming an empty place."

Don't get it? It doesn't make a lot of sense. Europe having "a vocation of service". The grandmother becoming a young mother. Rejuvenating by rediscovering cultural roots. Come on Francis, what are you talking about? Spell it out.

"We can speak today of Arab invasion. It is a social fact,"he says with detachment, as if observed that the weather is cold. But he immediately added - and theorists of the "Great Replacement", dear to the far right, would remain disappointed - "how many invasions has experienced Europe in the course of its history! But he has always been able to overcome herself, go ahead then they find themselves as increased by the exchange between cultures."

Now I get it. He finally said it, Francis. We are under an Arab invasion. That is a fact. But it's no big deal! We have been invaded before, amirite? And we're still around, amirite? What, untold numbers of people were killed, mamed, raped and kidnapped during those past invasions? The Arab invasions of the past were only repelled by physically expelling the Arabs after centuries of fighting? Details, details. The Pope doesn't bother himself with details. He has more important things to care about. The Big Picture. The Polyhedron. The Other.

A while ago I quoted Scott Atran[73] on religion being a coordination mechanism based on preposterous assertions (as I had put it previously, unfalsifiable crap), which are useful to check out who is loyal and who isn't. Turns out it doesn't really need to be preposterous or unfalsifiable. You can say obviously false things and still get away[74] with it as long as your frame is strong enough. Or as long as you have power.

---

[73] https://spandrell.com/2015/03/09/religion/

[74] 2012/06/21/the-fragility-of-logic/

Quotes

2016-03-10 // redpill, history, anglos, hbd

Sailer quoted Disraeli (d'Israeli, originally) saying "all is race". I got curious and Googled the guy, and damn.

I don't know if England has lost 15 IQ point on average since that time, as Charlton says. But Parliament speeches have lost even more than that.

Some samples from en.wikiquote.org/wiki/Benjamin_Disraeli

The noble lord in this case, as in so many others, first destroys his opponent, and then destroys his own position afterwards. The noble lord is the Prince Rupert of parliamentary discussion: his charge is resistless, but when he returns from the pursuit he always finds his camp in the possession of the enemy.

Speech in the House of Commons (24 April 1844), referring to Lord Stanley; compare: "The brilliant chief, irregularly great, / Frank, haughty, rash,—the Rupert of debate!", Edward Bulwer-Lytton, The New Timon (1846), Part i.

Heh. Prince Rupert being famous for being the best general to lose the English Civil War.

London owes everything to its press: it owes as much to its press as it does to its being the seat of government and the law.

Probably true. Not a good thing though.

Sir, it is very easy to complain of party Government, and there may be persons capable of forming an opinion on this subject who may entertain a deep objection to that Government, and know to what that objection leads. But there are others who shrug their shoulders, and talk in a slipshod style on this head, who, perhaps, are not exactly aware of what the objections lead to. These persons should understand, that if they object to party Government, they do, in fact, object to nothing more nor less than Parliamentary Government. A popular assembly without parties500 isolated individualscannot stand five years against a Minister with an organized Government without becoming a servile Senate.

It did eventually become that anyway, though.

First, without reference to England, looking at all countries, I say that it is the first duty of the Minister, and the first interest of the State, to maintain a balance between the two great branches of national industry; that is a principle which has been recognised by all great Ministers for the last two hundred years...Why we should maintain that balance between the two great branches of national industry, involves political considerations—social considerations, affecting the happiness, prosperity, and morality of the people, as well as the stability of the State. But I go further; I say that in England we are bound to do more—I repeat what I have repeated before, that in this country there are special reasons why we should not only maintain the balance between the two branches of our national industry, but why we should give a preponderance....to the agricultural branch; and the reason is, because in England we have a territorial Constitution. We have thrown upon the land the revenues of the Church, the administration of justice, and the estate of the poor; and this has been done, not to gratify the pride, or pamper the luxury of the proprietors of the land, but because, in a territorial Constitution, you, and those whom you have succeeded, have found the only security for self-government—the only barrier against that centralising system which has taken root in other countries.

Again, it only took a couple of wars to centralize power anyway.

I say, then, assuming, as I have given you reason to assume, that the price of wheat, when this system is established, ranges in England at 35s. per quarter, and other grain in proportion, this is not a question of rent, but it is a question of displacing the labour of England that produces corn, in order, on an extensive and even universal scale, to permit the entrance into this country of foreign corn produced by foreign labour. Will that displaced labour find new employment? ... But what are the resources of this kind of industry to employ and support the people, supposing the great depression in agricultural produce occur which is feared—that this great revolution, as it has appropriately been called, takes place—that we cease to be an agricultural people—what are the resources that would furnish employment to two-thirds of the subverted agricultural population—in fact, from 3,500,000 to 4,000,000 of people? Assume that the workshop of the world principle is carried into effect—assume that the attempt is made to maintain your system, both financial and domestic, on the resources of the cotton trade—assume that, in spite of hostile tariffs, that already gigantic industry is doubled...you would only find increased employment for 300,000 of your population... What must be the consequence? I think we have pretty good grounds for anticipating social misery and political disaster.

Talk about modern relevance.

But this principle of race is unfortunately one of the reasons why I fear war may always exist; because race implies difference, difference implies superiority, and superiority leads to predominance.

Yes, yes, yes.

The movement of the middle classes for the abolition of slavery was virtuous, but it was not wise. It was an ignorant movement. It showed a want of knowledge both of the laws of commerce and the stipulations of treaties; and it has alike ruined the colonies and aggravated the slave trade...The history of the abolition of slavery by the English and its consequences, would be a narrative of ignorance, injustice, blundering, waste, and havoc, not easily paralleled in the history of mankind.

It took a Jew to say that.

All is race there is no other truth.

Ditto.

The Jews represent the Semitic principle; all that is spiritual in our nature. They are the trustees of tradition, and the conservators of the religious element. They are a living and the most striking evidence of the falsity of that pernicious doctrine of modern times, the natural equality of man. The political equality of a particular race is a matter of municipal arrangement and depends entirely on political considerations and circumstances; but the natural equality of man now in vogue, and taking the form of cosmopolitan fraternity, is a principle which, were it possible to act on it, would deteriorate the great races and destroy all the genius of the world. What would be the consequence on the great Anglo-Saxon republic, for example, were its citizens to secede from their sound principle of reserve, and mingle with their negro and coloured populations? In the course of time they would become so deteriorated that their states would probably be reconquered and regained by the aborigines whom they have expelled and who would then be their superiors.

Tears in my eyes. The last 170 years have been completely lost.

The characteristic of the present age is craving credulity.

It got worse, my lord. Much worse.

In a progressive country change is constant; and the great question is not whether you should resist change which is inevitable, but whether that change should be carried out in deference to the manners, the customs, the laws and the traditions of a people, or whether it should be carried out in deference to abstract principles, and arbitrary and general doctrines.

He could've given a bit more punch to that. Change it to "in deference to the traditions of a people, or in deference to obscure, unfalsifiable and preposterous abstract claims made by idle people to signal their empty virtue.

King Louis Philippe once said to me that he attributed the great success of the British nation in political life to their talking politics after dinner.

As opposed to before?

The Informed Position on Tibet

2016-04-06 // china, history, monarchy, religion

Years ago I used to read a lot View from the Right, the blog of Lawrence Auster. Auster was a very peculiar guy. A Jew convert to Christianity, chanting the joys of social conservatism when being single (and most likely gay), he spent half his time criticizing progressive ideology, and half his time criticizing fellow critics of progressive ideology. His criticism was vivid, sharp and often accurate. Some of his criticism of rightist pundits was very good (Auster's law of race relations is brilliant and more relevant than ever), in many ways anticipating what today is called *cuckservatism*. Much of his material wasn't that good though, especially his awkward attacks of Steve Sailer for not defending Israel. The best part of his blog was how often he updated it (I was bored at college and appreciated the entertainment), and the comments by Jim Kalb. I wonder what Auster would've thought of Trump.

Auster was also quite obviously a man of the right, but he wasn't part of anything. He wasn't a paleocon, he wasn't a white nationalist. He was his own man. Being your own man is underappreciated. See this blog. It started as a neoreaction blog. At times I wrote quite actively about the "movement". Then the Eternal September happened and hordes of retards fell into neoreaction, driving the level of discussion down to the left half of the bell curve. Is this still a neoreaction blog?

See, I studied linguistics, and this sort of questions always interested me the most (though not my fellow linguists). What's in a name? What is the definition of "neoreaction"? What's the definition of anything, really? What's the definition of "race"? What's the definition of "rape"? The classical theory is that words have definitions, much like dictionaries do, and people have a "mental lexicon" which harbors dictionary definitions inside every individual brain. But the empirical evidence shows it doesn't work like that. People don't have mental dictionaries. People never agree on definitions. The definition of a word is whatever that word evokes in your mind, and that mental effect depends on a whole lot of cognitive and social factors. People say race is a social construct. No, the word "race" is a social construct. As are all other words. That's how language works.

That's why "racist" doesn't mean "person who is prejudiced against people because of their racial affiliation". The effective meaning of the word "racist" is whatever the word "racist" reminds you of; the Left has taken care that the word "racist" reminds you of evil white men, so the words "racist" effectively means "evil white man". QED. The word "race" for many reasons reminds most people of humans of different innate skin tones, which is why Bantus and Somalis are both regarded thought as "black", even though people with a better understanding of human genetic history know that's not a very useful way to put it. But it works, so the word stays in the language.

Once you understand this, (which you really should, nominalism in various forms is thousands of years old), I can ask, what is neoreaction? In actual fact, not what I'd like it to be. Neoreaction is whatever people are reminded of when they hear the word. 3 years ago, the word "neoreaction" reminded me of Moldbug, Foseti and Jim. That was a pretty cool thing. I was happy to join that boat. Today, however, "neoreaction" reminds one of Twitter and Social Matter. And I'm sorry, but that's not my thing. I can't say for sure if it's just them being boring, or it's just that my thinking has changed, while they remain faithful to the project. I get slightly embarrassed every time I browse my archives. At any rate it could be both. The point is, as the word "neoreaction" stands today, it has little to do with me. So I feel free to be like Auster and criticize them without restraints.

I mention this because of an article published a while ago at Social Matter, titled "What is the Neoreactionary position on Tibet[75]"? The title itself triggered me so slightly. I happened to know something about the history of Tibet and China, and I was worried that some Eternal September neoreactionary intellectual was going to say something stupid yet again about something he knows nothing about. I was relieved to see that no, the article made a fair point that neoreaction has no position about Tibet because it doesn't give a shit about Tibet, as it doesn't give a shit about Trump, nor about politics in general.

Now, quietism is cool, and I would indeed prefer that more people went quietist and stopped blabbing about what they know nothing about. 99.99% of people with a firm opinion on Tibet know absolutely nothing about Tibet. Why do they like to blab about Tibet? Because they're signaling something, of course, generally some edgy variant of progressive bona-fides. I'm all for people stopping to signal things that make me angry, as people blabbing about some topic in which I am knowledgable does to me. Gell-Mann Amnesia is preceded by Gell-Mann anger.

---

[75] https://www.socialmatter.net/2016/03/11/whats-the-neoreactionary-position-on-tibet/

Source:Dharmastation.com. How funny is that? "Dharmastation". Hah.

But wait a minute. This blog has been writing for years already about how politics is precisely about signaling. There's little else. Social life itself is about signaling. Social Matter saying they refuse to signal things about Tibet means they are refusing to do basic human sociality. Why do you have a blog if it's not about signaling? To have an opinion about something which doesn't affect your livelihood is signaling, by definition. To have an opinion about the benefits of not having an opinion is... yes, signaling. That's how human cooperation work. You say something, people agree or disagree, you make friends by signaling the same things, and next thing you know you got a big fat army to conquer your opponents. So saying that neoreaction doesn't have an opinion on Tibet because neoreaction isn't about having opinions doesn't make sense at all. If you don't have opinions, if you are a good quietist, you don't run a blog. Much less a group blog.

The real reason that neoreaction has no opinion on Tibet is that it knows nothing about Tibet. And the reason neoreaction knows nothing about Tibet is because Tibet is not a very compelling story for a reactionary. One of the most entertaining periods of Larry Auster's blog was when he blasted Moldbug for arguing that Britain had "chronic kinglessness", and that we needed a strong king like Henry VII. That never made much sense. Yes, if progressive ideology disgusts you, going back to the Birchers is a gush of fresh air. I just posted about how Disraeli could speak like an intelligent person in the British Parliament 150 years ago, while today you get thrown in jail for half that. And yes, the kings of yore obviously understood the realities of power because they had skin, limb and neck in the game, and they could afford to speak their mind to a much higher degree than the vapid potheads we have at Davos every year[76].

<hr>

[76]   https://www.weforum.org/agenda/2016/01/36-best-quotes-of-davos-2016

So yes, if you want to minimize the brain insults of stupid propaganda, absolute monarchy is not a bad idea. I write a lot about Chinese history, and the Chinese invented absolute monarchy a whole 2300 years ago. And their political philosophy is, in general, more realistic and down-to-earth than the Christian-descended sweet talk we peddle here in the West. It's a joy to read, and I enjoy writing about it. That said, ancient China wasn't pretty. It was a nasty and brutish place, where the court had absolute power to use and abuse its people without any legal recourse. The aristocracy had explicitly no say in government. The European feudal notion of gentleman's rights and limited power of the king didn't exist in China; and you could and often did get killed alongside your whole family just because it was convenient for some factional dispute.

And if China was bad, you know nothing about Tibet. I wrote once that the history of Japan is funny because it is short. Well Tibetan history isn't much longer. In fact Tibet appears in history just a bit later than Japan, in the 7th century AD. Both the first Tibetan and Japanese states were clients of the huge, prosperous Tang empire. As Peter Turchin or Christopher Beckwith wrote about, it often happens that the unification of great agrarian empires results in the unification of pastoralist empires on their frontier; for the obvious reasons. The rich Tang China had lots of stuff moving around, which means that pastoralists needed to gang up to raid or to extract good trade concessions.

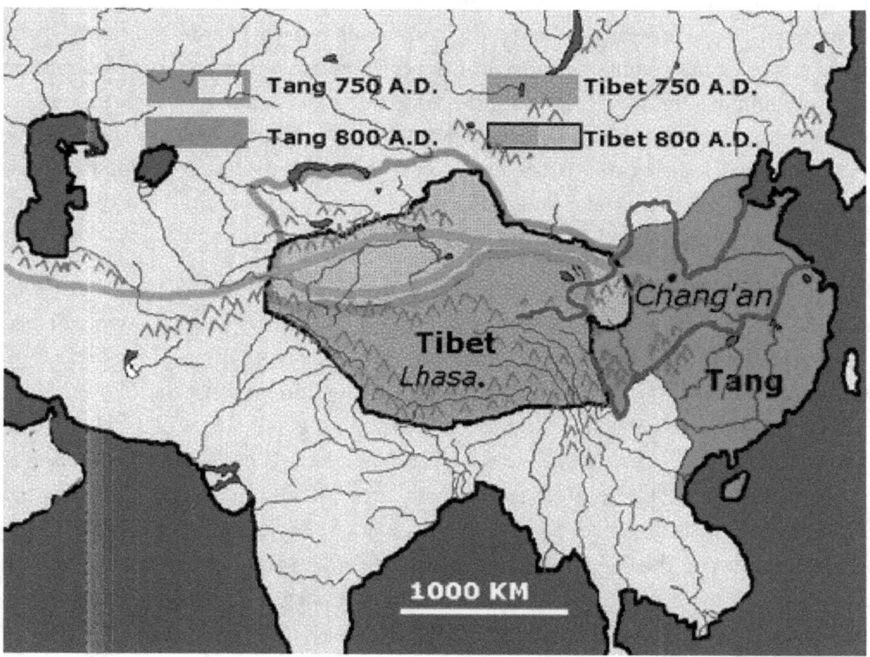

Tibet is the unlikeliest place to build a strong state; it's an arid, cold, sky-high plateau, with a thin population of livestock herders, and some little farming in the river valleys. But for some reason the first Tibetan Empire (618-842) was a very strong state, eventually invading the Chinese capital Chang An once, taking over the whole Tarim Basin, Yunnan, invading India every now and then, and having a strong presence in Central Asia. After the Tang declined, the Tibetan empire declined with it, eventually disappearing a few decades before China.

The early Tibetan Empire was not Buddhist; that came later, during the last half of the empire. And the power of the Buddhist establishment only grew into dominance after the empire fell; in a somewhat similar development to what happened in Western Europe after the fall of Rome. What happened after that is that Buddhist Monasteries ended up owning most of the good land in the realm, and basically ate up the whole society[77]. Monasteries owned the land, which was worked by serfs. Monks were recruited semi-forcibly from the peasantry, but who didn't want to be a monk before a serf? Monasteries merged and split, forming different schools (factions), who were constantly fighting each other. That means actual war. The whole thing sucked very badly; but it's hard for Tibet not to suck. It's just very bad real estate.

---

[77] https://www.michaelparenti.org/Tibet.html

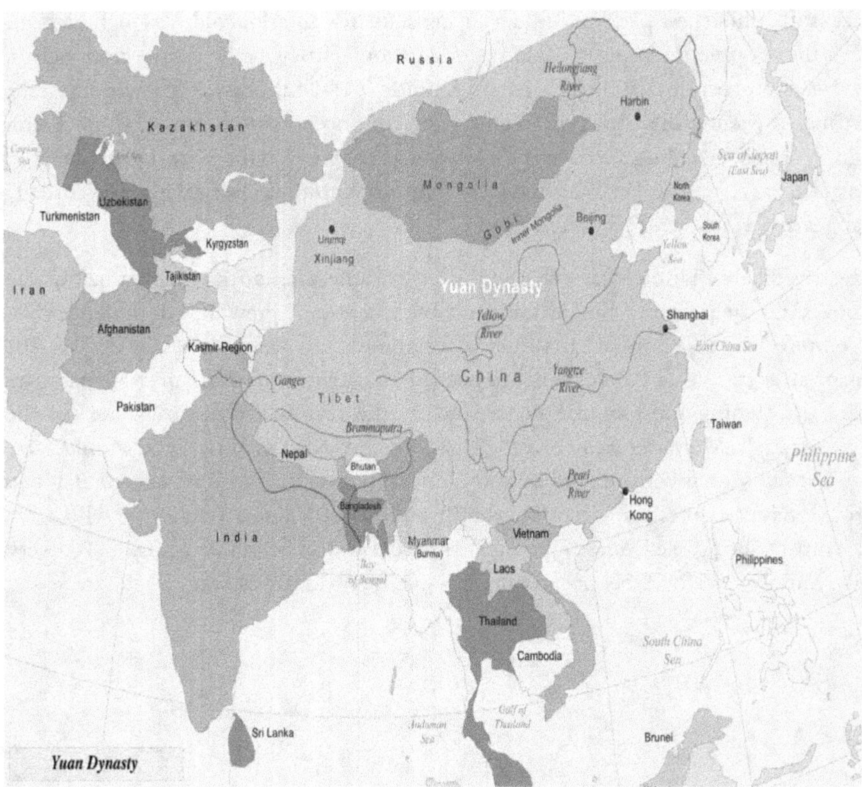

Eventually the Mongol Empire conquered Tibet, and from there onwards Tibet was the Mongols' bitch. Mongols of course being also pastoralists, and living close by, all they had to do is ride south and they had plenty of pasture to take over. That they didn't actually exterminate the Tibetans and replace them is perhaps a function of the genetic adaptation that Tibetans seem to have to living in 4,000m+ altitude, which the Mongols lack. Tibetans lived under the Mongol yoke until the Yuan Dynasty itself fell in 1368. After that the Mongols were divided and in no position to dominate Tibet, which achieved independence and returned to their rule by monastery. China, by then the Ming Dynasty, tried to conquer all the territories that the Mongols had controlled, even if they hadn't been Chinese before then. They conquered Yunnan, sent expeditions to Jurchen territory, and claimed suzerainty over Tibetans too. The Ming never actually sent an army and conquer the place, nor had any actual administrative control over Tibet back then, but they did "appoint" (i.e. sent a fancy seal every couple of decades) their leaders as being good subjects of the Chinese Lord of Heaven, which the Tibetans were happy to accept. They were cool looking seals.

Time passed, and the divided Mongol tribes started to get strong again, raiding into China, capturing their emperor once, and flexing their muscles around as much as they could. Eventually the Mongols again started getting involved in Tibet. You know the Dalai Lama, that guy who is supposed to be the epitome of all holiness? Well that's not a Tibetan title. That's the title that Altan Khan, khan of the mongols, gave to Sonam Gyatso, the leader of some Tibetan monastery. Altan Khan was the strongest tribal leader of the Mongols back then, but he wasn't directly descended from Genghis, so he was never accepted as the great leader he wanted to be. Altan then saw that these Tibetan guys had this weird religion thing going on, and they had mastered how to made their people more obedient to authority. So he got this monk, called him the Ocean Lama, and made him convert his people to Tibetan Buddhism. It worked, and the Mongols became pious Lamaists until the Soviets invaded. Then they became pious Communists.

In 1642, the Tibetans started fighting again, got the Mongols involved, and Gushi Khan conquered the whole thing, founding the Khoshut Khanate. All in the name of the holy lamas, of course, but the Mongols owned the place. Eventually the Qing Dynasty (1636-1911) conquered the Mongols, piece by piece, and by 1720 they invaded Tibet to take it over. Tibet kept being what it was; a miserable wasteland administered by feudal monasteries lording over serf masses, while a Chinese overlord took care that the monasteries didn't fight each other, and especially that they didn't bring any foreign powers in. Which for the most part they did. In 1788 the Nepalese invaded, which the Chinese repelled. In 1848 the Sikhs invaded, and again the Chinese took care of that. Then for some stupid reason the British invade in 1904.

Well, it was more some bored British elite boys deciding to do something fun for the kicks of it. It was a good time to be a white man in 1904, and Francis Younghusband knew how to have fun. Under some lame excuse (contain Russian ambitions! The Great Game!) they went over with machine guns and occupied Lhasa for a couple of weeks, then went back to India with a lot of pictures and stories to tell to their pals in London. They also extorted trade concessions and a big pile of money.

The stories did get through, and the invasion was a hit in London, i.e. the Cathedral of the day. Everybody was fascinated with this remote land of buddhist monks who lived in (forced) peace and (theocratic) harmony. Soon afterwards the Qing Empire collapsed in 1911, and the Tibetans know found themselves without a reliable overlord. China fell into civil war. And Chinese warlords are notoriously fickle and brutal. The Tibetan elite remembered that the Brits were close, so they tried to make friends, running a PR operation to gain favor of the British elites[78]. It didn't quite work out; Britain never committed to Tibetan independence, and once the Chinese civil war was over, with the Communist victory in 1949, Mao soon invaded Tibet and took it over in 1951.

The eternal question is what right had Mao to invade Tibet. The answer to that question is your "position on Tibet". The opposition to the Chinese invasion of Tibet comes mostly from the British invasion by Younghusband, which made Tibet a fancy

---

[78] https://en.wikipedia.org/wiki/Four_Rugby_Boys

topic of conversation by London housewives, followed by the Tibetan leadership PR campaign in the West, followed by the Dalai Lama becoming a CIA-funded celebrity used to have leverage to fuck with China. All that worked because, well, the English, and then American Empire's media apparatus (what we call the Cathedral) is very good. But the best salesman can't sell what doesn't sell. And Tibet sells. Tibet has fairly striking art, awesome architecture, and a very interesting culture. Tibet is a very good narrative, and the Cathedral know how to use a good narrative.

Now, the narrative they sell is that Tibet was a peaceful land of Buddhist monks, which spend their time in meditation and contemplation of the Buddha. Then comes Mao and kills them all. That sounds evil, and it's not exactly false. Tibet was, indeed, run by its monasteries for at least one thousand years. But what does it mean for a country to be run by monks?

Monks are, by definition, celibate. Monks don't have children. Where do monks come from, then? Monks were taken, forcibly or not, from peasant families, taken to monasteries, where they did their monk thing. They recited their sutras, they meditated, they discussed theology, they wrote books on it. They made art, lots of it, and pretty nice. Who did all the work? The peasants, which were serfs to the monasteries. The monks were monks, of course, but they were also gangs of single men. Gangs of single men tend to be... not very nice. And the Tibetan monks weren't very nice to their serfs, men or women. Or to themselves. While monks couldn't marry, they still had balls, and odds are they liked to use them once in a while. Tibetan monasteries weren't like European, or Chinese monasteries, were people who weren't interested in the physical world could opt-in to join. Tibetan monasteries were the ruling class; it just happened that the ruling class was made of single men. I imagine that it was the closest thing to a permanent fraternity, but one ruled by old men. There are records on how the hazing, beatings and all manners of physical and sexual assault were fairly brutal. Of course they were.

Besides that, having a placed where the highest status is achieved by gangs of single men has interesting demographic consequences. According to some estimates[79], Tibet had 3 million people in the old days of the 8th century Empire, but by the 19th century it barely had 1.2 million people. Well of course, the monks weren't reproducing themselves, and around 30% of the male population were monks. Serfs had children, but no great incentive to have a lot. Tibet is one of the few places on earth attested to have polyandry, i.e. men (usually brothers) sharing a single wife.

Tibet being very, very bad real estate, losing population was perhaps not a bad thing. The article in the link argues that Tibet, being the wasteland it is, was able to produce its highly sophisticated culture because its demographic system staved off Malthusian pressure, allowing for surplus wealth to go for the monasteries, which created a very striking religious package. Religious package which after being exported to Mongolia

79   https://mp.weixin.qq.com/s?
__biz=MjM5NzQwNjcyMQ&mid=403445329&idx=1&sn=70080fd5344b5a588
370f4c6d2f0ca67&scene=5&srcid=0401pJhUp8fILTLI60FY9ytT#rd

also reduced its population, and completely changed Mongolia from being an overpopulated land of bickering riders into a fairly urbanized and literate society.

Anyway, to the point: was China right to invade Tibet? The question is: how could it not invade Tibet? China had good reason to think that Tibet would become an Indian, and indirectly a British, or at least Western vassal. Why would China not grab a huge swath of land populated by a handful of people, which could perhaps contain some natural resources, but most importantly, was a hugely useful strategic asset? Of course Mao seized Tibet. That's how the world works. Do you know both the Yellow River and the Yang-Tse both start in Tibet? And the Mekong, and the Indus, and the Bhramaputra, and the Salween. China is supposed to leave that alone? Come on.

Is the world worse off without Tibetan Buddhism having a sovereign state of their own? That I don't know. As for the religion itself; I find it all to be pointless drivel, to be honest. Probably better than Chinese Communism, which is positively toxic. But Tibetan culture was pretty crappy, all things considered. It suited them well, for a thousand years, until it didn't, because we entered the industrial age, and the military equilibrium changed. You are not allowed to have your own idiosyncratic culture and do your thing these days. Everybody is on everybody's nerves, and looking for ways to take advantage and fuck with you.

Personally, I think it's probably for the best that China was able to seize Tibet and achieve a better strategic position as a sovereign nation. China is very, very Westernized these days, more than I like, but it's an independent state, one of very few on Earth today. If Tibet had to be sacrificed for that, well tough luck. Their culture was ok but not that interesting really, and at any rate that's the world we live in. And there's always pleasure in sticking it to USG and that insufferable contractor of theirs, the Dalai Lama.

Moldbug talked of the Patchwork of neocameralist nations. Pope Francis (!) talks of a Polyhedron of independent nations, all doing their thing. I think Scott Alexander had something similar. The idea of letting the hundreds flowers bloom, having a myriad cultures all doing their thing is of course a good and noble one. I'd rather we had more different cultures competing on this planet, instead of the rapidly declining death-cult of the modern Progressive state. I do feel Tibetans should be allowed to keep doing their monastery thing, dress in yellow, rape young monks and call Mongol mercenaries to burn rival monasteries. I find the Tibetan script to be very beautiful, even though they only use it to write pointless drivel. So I'm a little bit sorry that Tibetan culture couldn't survive. And most Chinese I know would rather Tibetans stayed home. Tibetans are rough, high-T, low IQ people. The gypsies of China, in a sense. They're also smooth with the ladies, good singers, dancers, and all that. They are a really, really bad fit in China. For everyone's benefit they should have their own country and stay there.

Alas, this is the world we live on. There's this thing called politics, and yes, foreign policy too. Bad people exist, they do bad things, and they force others to do bad things, sometimes preemptively, lest they do bad things to them first. Often it's not very clear what is bad or whether it's going to actually happen. Often foreign policy is used just as a way of achieving internal power. Shit happens. It will always happen. We can't wish it away. All we can do is study it.

Brussels

2016-03-22 // europe, islam, cucks, bureaucracy

Dozens of killed in multiple terrorist bombings in Brussels. Under the very nose of the EU headquarters.

The common response of European politicians has been that they are "united", in "solidarity" with Belgium, and "defending the values of democracy and freedom".

Think about it. What does "united" mean here? Who is united, and for what purpose? What about this solidarity? And what does democracy and freedom have to do with Muslim terrorism?

Was there a danger of European nations not being united and in solidarity with each other? How would it look like if they weren't? Could, Italy, say, or Poland, claim solidarity with the terrorists and say Belgium deserve it? That they're happy Brussels got bombed? That's absurd. It's just not in the realm of possibility. European nations of course dislike Muslim terrorism and everybody feels sympathy with Belgians.

The only way that those statements by European politicians is to understand them in political partisan terms. European politicians aren't speaking for their countries. They are speaking for themselves, and their parties. "United" means that they, as politicians, stay united with their friends in Brussels, their fellow politicians and bureaucrats. They stand united with their friends against their enemies, the far-right. "Solidarity" means they feel bad about their fellow Belgian politicians, and will keep on fighting the far-right so that the far-right can't take advantage of their reasonable proposals against immigration and take power from their Belgian bureaucrat friends. "Defending our values of democracy and freedom" is not meant in contrast with Muslim terrorists, it is meant in contrast to the far right, who don't share "our" (i.e. the EU elite's) values.

So what is happening right now is that Muslims have killed dozens of people in Brussels, and politicians across the country are going on TV and print media to declare that whatever happens they will never agree with the far-right, and keep on enforcing the present leftist consensus. They came out to proclaim that they have no interest in solving the issue and prevent more terrorism; they have an interest in staying in power and keep the opposition, their competitors, out of power. The Muslims are not a threat to the EU. They can put a bomb now and then, kill more or less commoners, but they don't have the capability of threatening the EU institutions, or any individual country.

The far-right, though, is a real and growing threat to the EU. They are aiming for the throat. A EU politician interested in keeping his job has a much bigger incentive for cracking down on the far-right, than he has for cracking down on Muslim terrorists. That's why politicians across the EU now are "united in solidarity with our Belgian friends". That's not a figure of speech. They mean it literally. They are united in solidarity with their actual pals in Brussels, and will keep supporting their policies against the proposals of the far-right, whatever the actual results of those policies. Even if the present policies enable more terrorism. And obviously bringing 1 million Muslim immigrants per year doesn't help.

That's what it all means.

Abortion

2016-04-04 // women, rightwingers

The most recent brouhaha is on Trump allegedly hinting that if abortion is murder, if it's a crime, well then we gotta punish abortionists. Criminals are punished, right? I think I've never written on abortion on this blog, so let me put my two cents.

It's hard to tell whether Trump is trolling or he actually means what he's saying. I mean, the point should be obvious. Criminals are punished. If abortion is to become a crime, we should punish abortionists. If abortion is murder, we should condemn abortionists of murder.

Alas, nobody really wants that. Because people don't really think abortion is murder. People *say* abortion is murder. People talk of abortion being murder as part of their signaling game. In modern America, and really America only, there's a signaling game where two sides, *pro-life* and *pro-choice*, battle each other in the political arena about the morality of abortion. Everybody in America is supposed to pick sides and join the fight. The whole thing is wrong, very, very wrong. Completely messed up. Human is a political animal. Politics is about signaling. Humans will choose random topics and form teams to battle each other. That's what humans do. But abortion is the last topic you should choose to have a signaling battle. Especially if you are in the weaker side. Now that Moldbug is back in the news cycle, I'll use his authority to remind you all: the right can't win by agitation. You just don't.

Apparently the whole abortion debate started from the right, with Christian groups mobilizing against the legalization of abortion during the 1960s. So this is the rare rightist movement fighting against yet another move to the left. Well, let me remind you: the right is weak. The right is always weak. The right can't win. Cthulhu always swims to the left. Picking a fight on abortion only caused the left to get serious on it, and escalate, coming up with the Pro-Choice movement in order to fight the right, and as it always happens in political movements, it has steamrolled the opposition, and spiraled into a huge international movement causing havoc everywhere.

Is abortion evil? When I read about how the Roman nobility became a bunch of decadent hedonists, that noble women in Rome engaged in abortion and infanticide in order to keep on having affairs all the time, I think it's messed up. That people would rather kill a fetus, let alone a child, in order to keep on having casual sex is indeed rather evil. Sex shouldn't be about fun. Less even about harnessing one's attractiveness in order to gain status by sleeping around. Sex is about procreation. Children in civilized societies require parents which stick together; stable marriages require spousal loyalty.

It's very simple. Should women abort in order to save money (to spend in some frivolous crap), or in order to engage in casual sex without fear of consequences? Hell no. That's messed up. The sort of woman who would rather undergo surgery to kill a fetus in order to ride the cock carousel should be tarred, feathered and shamed for years.

That's one thing. But is abortion evil per se? Say you have a normal, decent family. They have a daughter, who's 17 years old. She becomes attracted to some jock in the football team. Good looking alpha, dumb as a brick, a sociopathic asshole but all the girls like him. They sleep together and the girl gets pregnant. What should she do? In an ideal world the father would grab a shotgun, force the guy to marry, and they shall be happy ever after.

But this is not that world. The alpha jock is going to run as fast as he can. He won't be there for the child. Even if, like often happens in Japan, you could get the guy to marry the girl, odds are they'll divorce down the road, leaving a fatherless kid and an unhappy family. The right thing to do as a father, given the world we live on, is to grab the jock, punch him in the jaw, knock a bunch of teeth, and rush your daughter into the abortion clinic and do away with the fetus. As soon as you can; first trimester. Discipline your daughter as you see fit, and try to get her to forget the whole thing. Hopefully she'll grow up, get some sense, and eventually marry some suitable man at a more suitable age. Say, 25. Then she can have babies.

I have a daughter. Many of you have daughters. Odds are she won't be the sort of dumb bitch to get pregnant by some teenage alpha. But boys will be boys; and girls will be girls. Plenty of girls from good families end up fucking black drug dealers and getting pregnant. I don't like abortions; I don't like feminism. But you're trying to tell me that a girl shouldn't abort in that situation? Give me a fucking break.

The overwhelming majority of abortions being performed today are done to correct this sort of mistakes. And that is a good thing. You want to make a point of denying abortion because of "the sanctity of human life". Fuck that, and fuck you. You wanna oppose the left; good for you. But choose something else. Roosh and his fellow[80]"masculine" activists posted a video on how abortions are actually done. Gruesome stuff. Bloody baby parts all over the place. The whole procedure is pure evil. Should I show this to my daughter? Hell no. I'd rather keep the option to abort a stupidly conceived child, instead of imprinting her the picture of a baby torn apart.

And do you really wanna oppose the left here? You can't win. Women are adamant in favor of abortion; and not because they are all rabid leftists. They instinctually understand that girls do stupid things, and abortion can help them fix it. If you forbid

---

[80]   https://www.returnofkings.com/81542/the-ugly-truth-about-abortion-from-a-doctor-who-performed-them

abortion tomorrow, girls won't magically stop fucking the dumb jock or the black drug dealer. Of course women are for abortion. They don't like killing babies. It's gruesome stuff. Women like babies. Much more than men do. But women rather like having the chance to correct a stupid mistake they did because of a gina tingle they couldn't control. Men in those situations are very much in favor of abortion too.

Making a political movement opposing such a thing which women instinctually favor only makes them entrench themselves and move farther to the left. Again, nobody likes abortion. But if you force leftist women to justify abortion, they will. The left has the upper hand in any PR battle, and see how they came cracking down with all their might with their "Pro-Choice" answer. The whole pro-choice rhetoric is evil, but what do you expect? Pro-Life doesn't provide any nuance, why should the left provide any? By opposing the left in something they can't possibly concede, you make them take the offensive. And when the left comes up with something, it always by definition spirals out of control. So we got pro-choice feminists arguing how Abortion, i.e. killing babies is awesome and inspiring.

No, abortion is gruesome, nasty business. It's bad for you, it's bad for everyone, but sometimes it's necessary. A sane society recognized that, and chooses to taboo the topic and not talk about it, the same way you don't talk about nasty and gruesome things in general. Abortion in Japan is illegal, but tolerated, practiced by young single women, prostitutes, or women having affairs. There is no political movement in favor, or against. Nobody talks about them, it's a shameful act, which produces nothing but scorn when revealed, so people choose not to. For good reason. The local literature is full of women traumatized by the act, then leaving society in shame. That's the sane way of depicting it. In Europe it used to be like that until American leftist filth was exported, now it's a political point for leftists to use to humiliate the little conservatism left.

I'd rather people didn't have to do this. I'd rather abortion didn't exist. I'd rather we were all like the Mormons living in sane, decent communities, and nobody's daughter got pregnant by dumb irresponsible jocks. But that's not the world we live in. Men do stupid things for sex all the time; women also do stupid things, and get pregnant by evil men. If you wanna do politics, if you wanna oppose the government (which you probably shouldn't), choose your battles wisely. Opposing abortion is just the wrong way to do it. Choose something else; there's plenty of stuff.

EDIT: Abortion policy in Israel, as expected, is quite reasonable:

Abortion in Israel is legal under certain circumstances, with the approval of a committee for pregnancy termination. Approval for an abortion[81] in Israel[82] by a termination committee is given if the woman is unmarried, because of age (if the

---

[81] https://en.wikipedia.org/wiki/Abortion "Abortion"

woman is under the age of 18 - the legal marriage age in Israel - or over the age 40), the pregnancy was conceived under illegal circumstances (rape, statutory rape, etc.) or an incestuous relationship, birth defects[83], risk of health to the mother, and life of the mother

---

[82] https://en.wikipedia.org/wiki/Israel "Israel"

[83] https://en.wikipedia.org/wiki/Birth_defects "Birth defects"

Tibet and Tradition

2016-04-09 // religion, bluegov

Speaking of Tibet, the Dalai Lama just gave a long interview to the BBC. He went out of his way to make it easy for reactionaries to have an opinion on his country.

For some reason, the interview isn't published in the English website, which shows only a small lame news article[84].

The BBC Chinese version[85] though has a long and juicy account. Dalailama.com[86] also has a longer account.

What did the Dalai Lama say? He said he is in favor of abolishing all traditional Tibetan culture and formally become yet another NGO in the payroll of the US State Department.

As the Chinese headline says: "Dalai Lama claims reincarnation system is obsolete, must to adapt to Democracy.

The way the Dalai Lama institution works is that Buddhism, as most Indian religions, claims that souls are reincarnated after death, so after someone dies, it's soul goes into some baby. That needn't mean anything in particular; but of course Great Men are Great Men, so when a Great Men dies, his soul goes to some baby, then that baby by definition becomes a Great Men.

Tibetan monk leaders thus are not chosen amongst the monastery; instead some baby is brought up from the middle of nowhere, claimed to be the reincarnation of the old Boss, and made Boss himself. It sounds weird, but the Tibetan monasteries already had plenty of practice with kidnapping little boys, and it's probably not a bad way of avoiding succession wars inside the monasteries. Just bring some complete outsider and get done with it. Although in practice it necessarily was more complicated than this.

In the 18th century the Chinese emperor decided to reign on the selection process, and put the names of several candidates in a Golden Urn, after which a lot was taken; the Buddhainspired (under close watch of the Emperor) lottery decided who became the

---

84 https://www.bbc.co.uk/news/world-asia-35997625

85 https://www.bbc.com/zhongwen/simp/china/2016/04/160408_dalai_lama_tibet_reincarnation

86 https://www.dalailama.com/news/post/1381-his-holiness-the-dalai-lama-speaks-at-the-american-embassy-school

Big Fish Lamas in both Tibet, and by then heavily Lamaist Mongolia. This system continues to this day, although of course the Golden Urn is watched by the Communist Party of China.

Well, the present day Dalai Lama, which is of course in exile after he staged an uprising against China in 1959 and failed, has decided not only that the Golden Urn is a travesty; but that the very idea of reincarnation is "obsolete". "A remnant of feudalism", he says.

"I am committed to democracy," he said, "while many of our religious institutions, such as reincarnation, are remnants of feudalism. Today we need to act appropriately to the new reality in which we find ourselves. The future of Tibetan Buddhism doesn't depend on the institution of the Dalai Lama. It's the 10,000 monks and nuns now studying in Tibetan centres of learning, mostly in South India, who will ensure the preservation of the Nalanda tradition."

Well, I'm sorry Mr. Lhamo Thondup, but your whole religion is a remnant of feudalism. But you aren't supposed to say that. You are supposed to say that the theology of the Gelug School is the eternal truth discovered by sagely monks inspired by the Boddhisattva of Wisdom, or something. If "adapting to the new reality" means giving away all your theology and institutions, why do you even exist? What are your values? Some snippets from the Chinese version:

"I am committed to democracy."

"The next Dalai Lama could very well be a woman. Women have higher ability for empathy and feeling."

"If a female Dalai Lama were to appear, she would have a very attractive face."

There you go, progressive values. All he's doing is surrendering his tribe to the West; effectively dissolving the Tibetan people as a coherent unit.

Meanwhile in China, Tibetan Buddhism is booming, its monasteries full of people, running a constant confrontation against the Communist government. Thousands of Chinese across the country are converting to Tibetan Buddhism as they find it the only serious religion that keeps its discipline and hasn't sold out to modernity.

The only reason it hasn't is because China invaded the place, creating the ethnic tensions that Peter Turchin says are the origin of social order. Meanwhile the Tibetan government in Exile has become a progressive QUANGO funded by the US taxpayer to promote feminism in the Himalayas. And exhorting European countries[87] to accept the Muslim immigration.

---

[87] https://www.bbc.com/news/uk-34316578

So I think we can settle that the correct opinion on Tibet is to be glad Mao invaded, and only be sorry that the Dalai Lama managed to escape.

The Law

2016-04-14 // china, history, Song Dynasty, series, power

A while ago I wrote some posts on the classical Chinese novel, the 14th century *Water Margin* 水滸傳. The *Water Margin* is the story of 108 outlaws, in the original 英雄 好漢, which literally translates as hero 英雄 *yīngxióng* and ... 好漢 hǎohàn is very hard to translate. 好 means good, that one's easy, but 漢 means, well, Han, the Han Dynasty, the Han race we know today. It also means man, today normally expressed as 漢子 hànzi. But not just man, that's 男 *nán*. A 漢 is a real man, a strong, manly man, respected by his peers. You call someone a 漢子 *hànzi* as a compliment, to mean he's a real man. Add 好 to that, and you have a good+real man. I'd translate it as dude, for lack of a better fit, and also because it fits with the whole LARPing atmosphere of the men in the *Water Margin*.

They're just a bunch of outlaws, some with good reason, fleeing from the injustice of tyrannical government, some who lost their families to evil but connected people. Others though are just punks and hooligans; small time robbers, mountain bandits, drunkards, smugglers, that kind of people. That they spend the time calling each other great heroes is quite hilarious. Still, China has a long tradition of vagrancy and men doing their own thing, i.e. learning martial arts and forming gangs of bandits. Not everyone could pass the mandarin exam, you know. And those mandarins in the government didn't have the resources to police the whole country, so there was always very easy to hide in the mountains and make a living of highway robbery. If you got very big, chances were the government would give up on arresting you, and would rather take it easy and give you an official position in the army or government. Once an outlaw became a Mandarin he was way easier to arrest or even assassinate as expedient. Never bet against the government.

There are tons of great stories in the *Water Margin*, and one of the most interesting is the story of Chái Jìn 柴進. Mr. Chai, or Lord Chai as he is usually called, is a very rich guy, who gets into the novel because he becomes the patron of many of the outlaws in the novel. He says he enjoys "meeting hero-dudes", whom he houses and feeds in his compound for months at a time, while having them fight each other. Kinda like patronizing wrestlers in your house and have them put a show for you every now and then. Mountain banditry is fun, but there's not always enough to rob, and the government is always trying to kill them, so they tend to look for wealthy patrons who can feed them during bad times, and protect them from the police, who won't dare disturb wealthy aristocrats. Wealthy aristocrats also find it useful to have a bunch of goons at their disposal.

Lord Chai in the novel appears as a very high class, cultured man. He owes his position as his being the direct descendant of Chái Róng 柴榮, the last emperor of the Later Zhou Dynasty. The history goes like this. Remember that the *Water Margin* is based in the 1100s. Centuries earlier China had the Tang Dynasty, glorious apogee of imperial China from 618 to 907. After the Tang empire collapsed, China fractured in a dozen or so little kingdoms, constantly fighting each other, in an era called the Five Dynasties and Ten Kingdoms period.[88] At the end of that big civil war, one of the big warlords started to get the upper hand, and founded the Later Zhou Dynasty. It's second emperor was this Chái Róng, and he managed to conquer almost all of North China. Here's a little map.

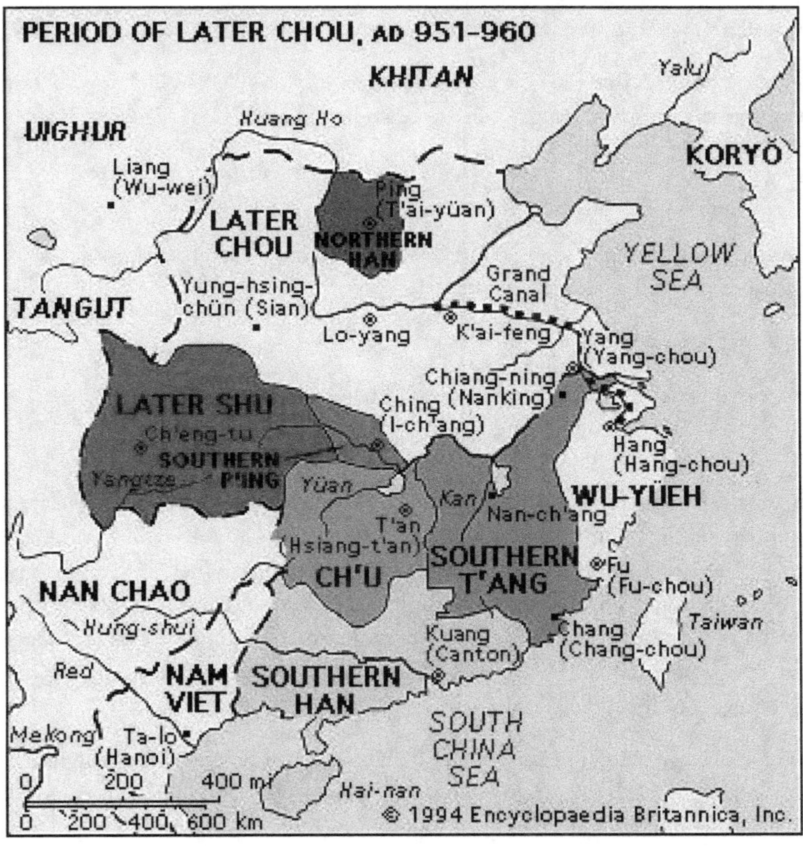

Chái Róng was a military genius, a real leader of man, and he appeared poised to conquer the whole of China and restore a unified empire. But then he died. 38 years

---

88 https://en.wikipedia.org/wiki/Five_Dynasties_and_Ten_Kingdoms_period "Five Dynasties and Ten Kingdoms period"

old. Damn. He left a heir, a 6 year old boy, who of course had never left the palace, and was under the control of his mother and a bunch of ministers, eunuchs, sycophants and all that. The army wasn't happy with having a bunch of bookworms and women running the show. Especially because the first thing that the new government did was send the garrison at the capital out to the war front, with the obvious intent of having them killed, so they could purge the capital and put new, loyal men in their place.

The head of the palace garrison, Zhao Kuangyin[89] 趙匡胤, was of course very close to the late emperor Chai Rong, which is why he was in charge of the palace troops. The new regent government sent him out to the front to fight the Khitans, the Mongols of the day. He of course marched on, but on crossing the first bridge out of the capital, his troops mutinied. It went something like this, I translate very liberally:

"My general, it's obvious that the new government wants you killed. Which is cool, but that means that all of us have to get killed too, and we'd rather not die, if you don't mind."

"What do you suggest then."

"We got you a yellow imperial robe, so put this on and let's go slaughter those eunuchs in the palace and put you as emperor."

"Wow wow wait a minute. What?"

"Look, you can do it, or your brother will. He's rather keen on the idea."

"Mmm ok."

And so General Zhao got his army, run back to the capital, staged a coup, and declared himself emperor of the Song Dynasty, which was to (mostly) reunify China, and last 319 years, 960 to 1279. Note that the events of the coup at Chen bridge are my personal interpretation. Officially he was drunk, his officers put the robe on him by force, he was reluctant but his officers didn't leave him much of a choice. His brother is said to have "persuaded him". I wonder how. He eventually murdered him and became the second emperor of the dynasty, by the way.

Anyway, General Zhao starts the Song Dynasty, which is the dynasty under which the events on the *Water Margin* unfold. Usually in China the founding emperor of a Dynasty leaves a set of ancestral rules, to be followed by all his descendants. One of the rules the first emperor of the Song Dynasty set was "Be nice to the Chái family." Zhao Kuangyin owed all he had to the patronage of Chai Rong, but he had just usurped the throne from his 6 year old son. He had good reason to do so; but he understandably felt guilty about it. So he left it as Ancestral Law, that the Chái family were to given

---

89 https://en.wikipedia.org/wiki/Emperor_Taizu_of_Song#Coup_d.
27.C3.A9tat_at_Chen_Bridge

privileges in all eternity. They were given an Iron Plate, which basically said that government officials had no right to enter their house premises, nor could they be put to death or torture under any circumstances.

And 5 generations or so later we get to Chái Jìn, who is the holder of the Iron Plate, and uses it to make hero-dude friends, who love the extraterritorial privilege of their house. Ostensibly, Lord Chai uses his privilege to make friends with good, virtuous men, who have been oppressed by evil government. So his house is a refuge for good men, and eventually becomes a base for the virtuous movement against corruption and tyranny. Which is the point of the whole book, our 108 herodudes rebelling to clean the government from evil and corrupt ministers, and restore power to our great Emperor, who of course knows nothing about it. Nothing at all.

Anyway, eventually the uncle of Lord Chai gets into a fight with some punk in his town, and eventually dies of his injuries. Lord Chai gathers up his herodudes and goes beat the guy who killed his uncle, and they beat him to death too. But apparently that punk was no ordinary punk. Else he wouldn't have dared touch the uncle of Lord Chai, of course. It happens that punk was the brother in law of the county governor. The county governor was of course livid at a relative of his beating beat to death. He mobilized the whole government forces, and went up to Lord Chai's house with an arrest warrant.

But wait, doesn't Lord Chai have the Iron Plate? Given by the imperial house itself? You can't touch the guy. It's against the law.

Well, as it happens the county governor was the cousin of Gáo Qiú 高俅, an imperial minister and very close friend of the emperor himself. Whatever the Iron Plate says, the county governor had a relative in high places. That means that he could do as he pleased. Yes, Lord Chai had the Iron Plate. But so what? News of his attacking an Iron-Plate holder will never get to the emperor, he'll take care of that. And in the event that the emperor does get to know, what is he going to do? Go against his best friend because of some 200 year old law? To defend some guy he doesn't even know about? No chance. Lord Chai was arrested and tortured alongside his whole family, and his large estate taken from him.

Of course the herodudes on knowing of this event rushed off to his rescue, conquered the whole county and killed all the evil officials they found, and then some. Lord Chai was rescued and joined the herodude fortress base at Liang Shan, where he realized how The Law works.

And how does the law work? The law is just a piece of paper, or in this case a piece of iron. It does nothing by itself. It's power depends on people enforcing it, people with weapons. But why do people enforce it? Because it's their job, you'll say. But that's not how it works, is it? Your job description is yet another piece of paper. Your real job, in any organization, is to keep your boss happy. To do that you're often supposed to do what's written in your job description. But it doesn't necessarily need to be so. Sometimes your boss wants something else, and if you wanna keep your job, you better do what he wants.

That people generally are asked to do their job descriptions and not something else, depends on the fact that your boss likely has another big boss on top of him, and other fellow bosses alongside him, who compete with him on getting favor from the big boss. If your boss asks for you something that you're not in theory supposed to do, some other middle-boss may tell big-boss about that, and then he's in trouble. Unless big-boss is in league with the whole thing too, in which case it's the squealing middle-boss is in trouble.

The law gets enforced because the people in power want in enforced. If they don't want it enforced, it doesn't. Border security is the law. It's not enforced. Firing employees for being opposed to gaymarriage isn't in the law. But it does get enforced. As Moldbug said of the Constitution, either a law reflects the will of the powerful, and it's thus superfluous, or it doesn't, and is then deceitful. It's not that simple in practice:

putting things to writing is not superfluous. It creates a small milepost, a Schelling point, which people can point at in order to use in their status competition. But it only works so far as people in power find it useful, or there's a culture which upholds respect for agreements beyond their actual use.

China never developed any tradition of jurisprudence, because they understood this very principle of politics. I sometimes think that the Chinese were too smart and realistic for their own good. Delusion can be good. The rule of law is pretty great if it works. Europe conquered China, not the other way around. But again, delusions only last so long, and in the end reality always asserts itself. The rule of law is dying in a way that wouldn't surprise the author of the *Water Margin*. Meanwhile China keeps being China. As Aldous Huxley wrote in one of his travel diaries:

I have seen places that were, no doubt, as busy and as thickly populous as the Chinese city in Shanghai, but none that so overwhelmingly impressed me with its business and populousness. In no city, West or East, have I ever had such an impression of dense, rank richly clotted life. Old Shanghai is Bergson's elan vital in the raw, so to speak, and with the lid off. It is Life itself. Each individual Chinaman has more vitality, you feel, than each individual Indian or European, and the social organism composed of these individuals is therefore more intensely alive than the social organism in India or the West. Or perhaps it is the vitality of the social organism - a vitality accumulated and economised through centuries by ancient habit and tradition. So much life, so carefully canalised, so rapidly and strongly flowing - the spectacle of it inspires something like terror. All this was going on when we were cannibalistic savages. It will still be going on, a little modified, perhaps by Western science, but not much-long after we in Europe have simply died of fatigue.

The Song Golden Age

2016-04-21 // china, history, Song Dynasty, series

People are asking for more Chinese history. I agree. Chinese history is great. It's long, it's well documented, and it's documented in explicitly moralistic terms. Chinese thought has been always focused in how to achieve good governance, and histories are written as to contain parables of what good government is, and what bad government leads to. The most valued history book in China, the *Zizhi Tongjian* 資治通鑒, written by Sima Guang in 1084, again explicitly states that it is to be an aid for emperors and mandarins to achieve good governance. Good government leads to nice things. Bad government leads to death and misery. That's all Chinese intellectuals have ever cared about. I think it's a good priority to have.

Sima Guang was a brilliant scholar, and it's a huge pity that he finished his book just before the best story in Chinese history happened. The Jingkang Incident of 1127. Oh man, that's such a great, great story. There should be more books about it. It's perhaps the most compelling story in the history of mankind. It's just so unbelievably simple, yet dramatic. It's so good it seems fiction. But no fiction is this good. Anyway, let me tell you this story. It'll probably take several parts.

So again, the time is the Song Dynasty, 960-1279. If you've been reading my posts on the *Water Margin*, you have some minimum background. The Song Dynasty was under many accounts the most wealthy and successful of all Chinese dynasties. Not to date; the best dynasty, period. Better than anything than came later. Richer, more urbanized, and arguably with better technology. The Song Dynasty had machinery that the Qing Dynasty didn't have in the 19th century. The Song economy had huge foreign trade links, and the Song government in 1000 again had higher revenues than the Chinese government in 1900.

Some argue that that was the result of better governance. As seen in the previous post, the Song had solved an eternal problem of Chinese governance: how to deal with the military and the aristocracy. The solution they took was to screw them both, and put the government completely in hands of the bureaucracy. They set up their model civil examination system, reduced the number of eunuchs to a minimum, took care the armies in the provinces didn't get too big, kept most of the imperial family in the capital so they didn't develop territorial power. I wonder if urban life was also meant to keep them busy having fun while depressing their fertility. Not a bad research idea.

Anyway, of course the obvious result of all that is that the army sucked balls. The Song army sucked really badly. How badly? Well compare a map of the dynasties of China.

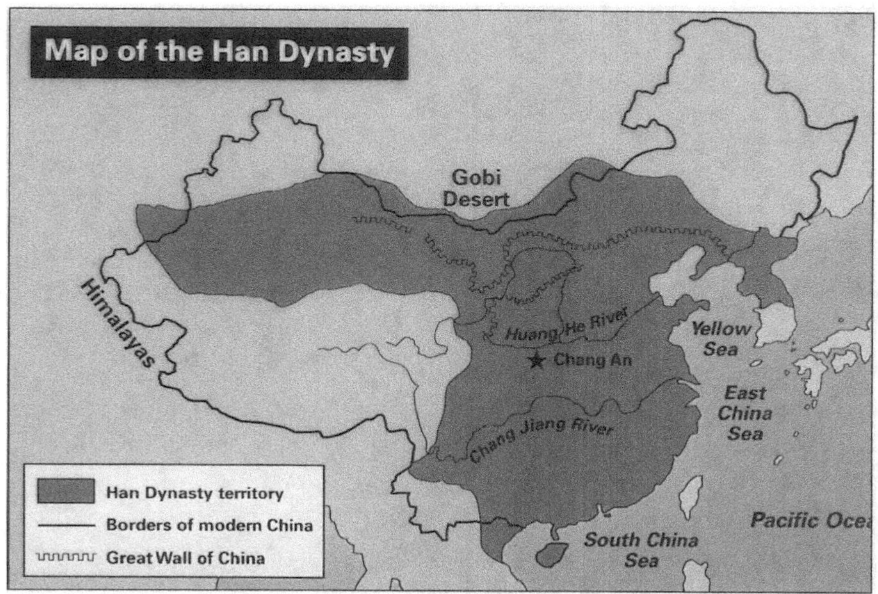

This is the first big Chinese dynasty, the Han dynasty, 202 BC - 220 AD. See it owns most of China proper, it also includes north Vietnam, north Korea, and the Tarim Basin, i.e. the Silk Road oases where today the Uyghurs live. It didn't start like that; the imperial territory was extended mostly by one guy, the emperor Wu (156-87), who was a truly amazing individual. I should write his story some day, but you could also watch 漢武大帝 which is an awesome show.

Anyway the Han Dynasty fell mostly when the Roman Principate fell. Like Rome too it kinda recovered once, but then they started fighting each other and the northern barbarians took over one half of it. Oh, parallels. And people say there are no patterns in history.

Anyway, Rome never recovered its glory, but China did unite again. It took a while, until the Sui Dynasty, but the whole thing didn't start working properly again until the Tang Dynasty (618-907). The Tang's peak territory looks like this:

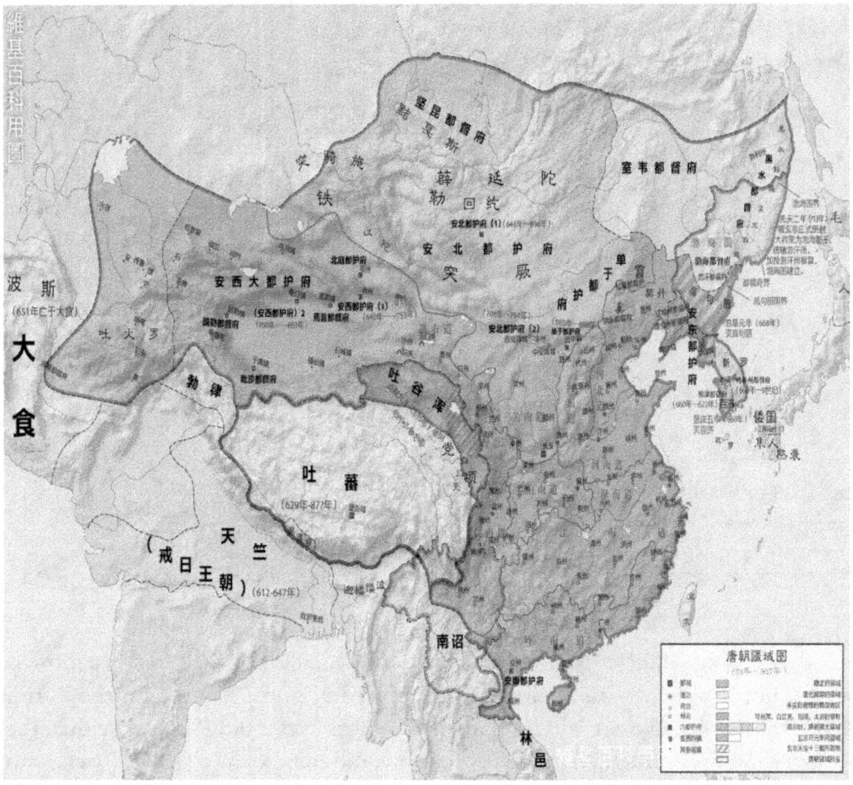

Look at that. The Tang owned all the Han did, and then some. The Tang owned the whole Mongolian steppe, Central Asia well up to the borders of Persia, not only north but a big chunk of South Korea. Now all that is, well, theoretical. The core Chinese land remained the same, everywhere else was populated by foreign peoples. But the Tang had beaten them militarily, every single one, and forced them to swear allegiance. It didn't take much for that allegiance to disappear; in about a century the Tang lost of all of Central Asia, the Tarim Basin, Mongolia and Korea. But the Tang had managed once to crush everyone, fair and square. The Chinese still love to read about the great Tang Taizong and how he led the best Chinese armies ever to beat everyone up to Persia.

Let's look now at the Song then.

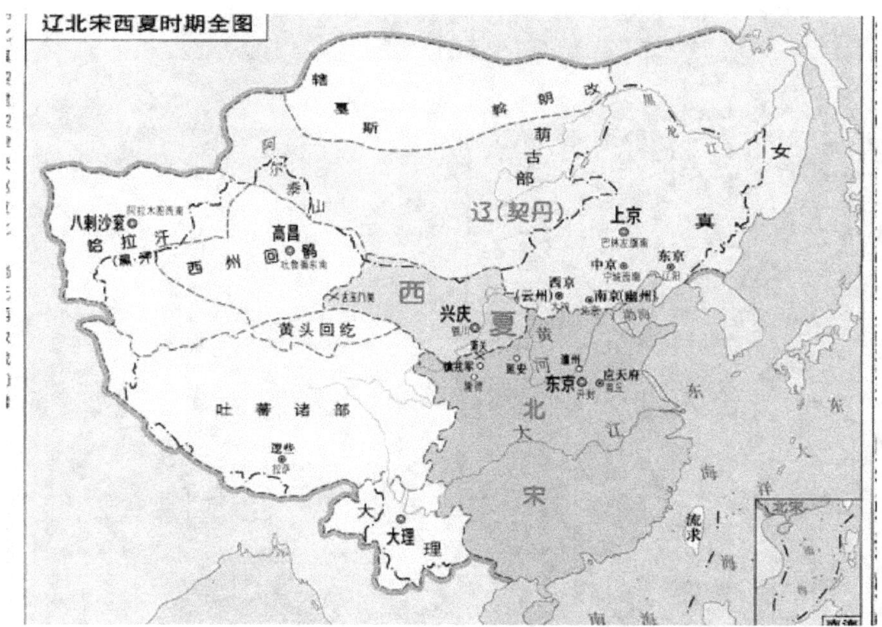

The Song were beyond small. They were by far the smallest dynasty in Chinese history. They lost Vietnam, which is still around by the way. They let a bunch of quasi-Tibetan herders, the Tanguts, grab the Northwest, the path to the Silk Road, land that had been Chinese for a thousand years. And they even lost the northern edge of the Chinese heartland, the land around Beijing today. Look at this topographic map.

You see that Beijing is at the edge of a huge plain. That's why the capital is there, to watch the mountain passes which divide China proper from the steppes at the north. You must control those passes, else the nomads come raiding whenever they want. Well, to be fair, the Song hadnt lost it, nor it lost Vietnam or all the others. All those lands were taken during the civil war after the Tang collapsed. The Song just failed to recapture them. The area of Beijing was taken by the Khitan, a dynasty of Mongolic herders, which as you can see in the previous map, was big, very big, and very very strong. The Song tried dozens of time but they couldn't dislodge them, nor could they beat the Tanguts, who were at most a bunch of ten thousand of herders. The Song was by far the smallest and weakest of all Chinese dynasties.

They didn't care though: they were swimming in money. Losing access to the Silk Road forced them to trade by sea: and surprise, maritime trade is much more profitable! The Song Dynasty had higher revenues in 1000 than the Qing dynasty had in 1900. Their technology boomed: by some accounts the Song had better machinery than the Qing 800 years later. Urbanization rates were also the highest China ever saw until the 20th century.

The Song were weak, but they were rich: they decided it was cheaper to pay off the barbarians than to keep an army to fight them. And it was true. What were the barbarians going to do with all that silver anyway? They naturally spent it in buying stuff from China. So the silver went away as tribute, and came back as trade. Better than to keep an army of uppity generals and risk that they stage a rebellion or blackmail the court every now and then. While a section of the bureaucracy was against such a dishonorable treaty, the smartest Mandarins knew that in order to keep running the government they'd better pay off the barbarians and keep the military from having any influence at court.

It was a massive diplomatic coup. It worked brilliantly. The Khitan were actually fairly civilized people. They were literate in Chinese, developed their own script based on it, run a fairly sophisticated state apparatus. The problem between nomadic herders and settled farmers is that nomadic life is hard. It's hard to live off animal products only. Nomads also want grain, cloth, paper, tea, you know, nice stuff. The only way of getting it is to trade or to take it by force. But the Khitan managed to invade a small bunch of Chinese land. It was enough for them; they got their small territory of Chinese land, full of Chinese farmers to make grain for them, Chinese scribes to run their government for them. The Khitan kept their capital north of the mountains, enjoyed their hunting and herding, and as long as the Song kept sending silver and silk, they respected a peace that lasted a 100 years.

The weakness of the Song solved the Mongol problem, allegedly for the price of the tax income of a single province. The army didn't like it, but the army could go to hell. At the Song it was the mandarins who run things. And they were doing a mighty fine job. The population doubled to more than 100 million people. Printing was invented and developed into a national industry, as well as gunpowder. Art and literature also developed beyond anything previous. It was a Golden Age. Some people say the Song were on the breach of undergoing a capitalist revolution.

And so we come to the reign of Huizong, the year 1100.

Huizong was a very refined man. Look at his face. He was a very skilled artist, and his paintings and calligraphy[90] have survived to our time. Take a look at the link, they're very impressive. His handwriting is regarded as one of the best in Chinese history, and I'm particularly fond of it. It must be fun to be able to write like that. I'd be writing stuff all day.

---

[90] https://www.google.com/search?site=&tbm=isch&source=hp&biw=1276&bih=705&q=%E5%AE%8B%E5%BE%BD%E5%AE%97+%E7%95%AB&oq=%E5%AE%8B%E5%BE%BD%E5%AE%97+%E7%95%AB&gs_l=img.3...
774.13381.0.13714.50.30.12.0.0.0.295.3979.0j10j10.20.0....0...1ac.1j4.64.img..20.28.3242.6H8TvB7dum0#tbm=isch&q=%E5%AE%8B%E5%BE%BD%E5%AE%97%E7%9A%84%E7%94%BB&imgrc=1F9uiMksIVZTrM%3A

Being an artist and all that, the emperor wasn't very much into government stuff. He was more into the joys of life. He liked painting, writing poetry, drinking with friends, playing football (they played Cuju[91], which sounds incredibly hard but apparently was very popular back then). He was into women too. He famously didn't like the uptight hookers that got sent to his palace, so he had a tunnel built to go from the palace to the fanciest brothel in the capital so he could have fun like just any other aristocrat.

He was also into gardening. He had the fanciest stones in the realm be sent to him to decorate his garden. Stuff like this.

---

[91] https://en.wikipedia.org/wiki/Cuju

South China is full of this weird porous stones, and our emperor had a fancy for them. He had them brought from everywhere, and sent to the palace, rewarding who brought them with lots of gold. The thing is some of these stones were huge. China had canals all around its territory, so they could be relatively cheaply transported by water. But canals have bridges over them, and some of this stones just didn't fit below the bridges. So what did they do? These are Imperial Stones we're talking about. Rapacious bureaucrats who wanted to look good with the emperor had bridges demolished just so they could push the stones through to deliver to the emperor. The historical record is full of commoners wailing at the injustice. This is of course the time of the *Water Margin* and its peasant rebellions led by herodudes.

Huizong was also fond of weird animals. He had a part of his garden set up as a zoo, full with tigers, elephants and giraffes he had sent from Africa. In summary you'll have noticed that the emperor of the Great Song after 1100 AD is a fairly extravagant fellow. But hey, the Song is rich, they could afford a fanciful emperor. What they could not afford though is a stupid emperor. Because just as Huizong was having fun watching pandas battle with giraffes for bamboo at his home zoo, probably accompanied by some hooker, at this very moment his Khitan neighbors were in trouble. Very serious trouble.

The distribution of power

2016-04-19 // china, history, Song Dynasty, series, power

Another Chinese story.

Royal absolutism was invented by Shang Yang in the Chinese state of Qin, 360 BC. Of course absolute rulers had existed before, in the Middle East obviously you had plenty of god-kings; but Shang Yang's governance was recognizably modern. It was planned on secular terms, it had a central bureaucracy, and it explicitly took power from the nobility in order to strengthen the authority of the central government. The way it was framed is that the King deserves to have all the power, that's why he's the king; and that the king having all the power will result in more Order and better government, as the people will have no power to resist and create Chaos. Later Chinese political thought changed a lot: Confucianism was explicitly against Shang Yang's ideas (what came to be known as Legalism). In fact one could think of Confucianism as the revolt of the upper middle class against the centralizing legalists. A sort of English or French revolution dynamic. Happens they lost; Confucianism only somewhat won in a very, very diluted way 300 later under emperor Wu of Han.

But the idea that the power of the Ruler should be absolute absolutely carried the day in Chinese political thought. That contrasts a lot with the Western tradition which since the Greeks is obsessed with Tyranny and Despotism and basically makes it hell to run a cohesive government. Power has to be shared or else Tyranny! Much of that was the spillover from the propaganda war on the Persian wars, where Greece was the Beacon of Liberty against the Persian Tyrant. Henceforth to be Greek meant to be against tyranny, because Persians. Then the Romans take over and the Romans were even more paranoid about central authority. They also had this trauma about the foreign Tarquins. The Romans really went the whole way by having two consuls which changed every year! That's crazy when you think about it. How can you get anything done? The only way the Roman state was able to remain cohesive is that the plebs were constantly agitating and salivating for the chance of slaughtering all the patricians, so the Senate must have been pretty cohesive.

An idea of the Western tradition of Liberty is that it was passed down from the old Indo-Europeans, who were a martial people. All men were soldiers, and men of arms tend to be very zealous of their honor and autonomy, if only in exchange of surrendering every time there's a war. I don't know how much that follows, though. The Chinese had their own martial tradition too; the Zhou order was a feudal order which started after the Zhou king distributed the empire's lands to his army buddies.

Maybe it has something to do with pastoralism; but look at the Mongols. Then again the Mongols had been surrounded by China for centuries so maybe they got absolutism from there. It certainly didn't come naturally.

Anyway, China invented central bureaucratic government in 330 BC, but it only refined it in a strikingly modern way during the Song Dynasty, 960-1279. As I wrote in a recent post, the Song Dynasty was founded by the general of the palace troops, who staged a coup against his lord, presumably forced by his own troops. The first thing he did after assuming the throne was to gather one advisor of him and talk of the future. He asked him: "Since the great Tang Dynasty fell, we've been through 8 emperors already. Wars all over the place, the people suffering misery and death. Thing's messed up, how did all this happen?"

Actual portrait of Zhao Kuangyin, founder of the Song Dynasty

Minister said: "Oh man I so love that you asked that question. You're awesome my lord. The answer is quite simple: the problem is that the ruler has no power, but his subordinates have too much. The provinces are too strong. Take away their power, their funding, their best troops, and the very next day the realm will be in Order."

So the great founder of the Song Dynasty gathers his generals, who remember had semi-forced him to stage a coup and become emperor. He stages a sumptuous banquet and tells them:

"Gentlemen, if it weren't for you I wouldn't be here as emperor. Thing is, I kinda miss being just a general. Since I become emperor I haven't slept a good night's sleep."

His general buddies are startled, and ask: "Oh your majesty, how can you say that?".

The emperor responds: "Oh come on. It's obvious. Who doesn't want to take my place?"

The generals stand up, befuddled: "But, the Mandate of Heaven is yours, the realm is in peace, who could possibly even think of betraying you?"

The Emperor put a stern face and said: "Who doesn't want to enjoy glory and riches? Come on. Even if you didn't want to; if someday *your* troops come up, put a yellow robe on you by force, could you even refuse?"

That's of course exactly what happened to him. The generals were now speechless. Couldn't come up with anything to counter that. That's just obviously true. They got the message, started crying, kneeled down, and with their heads down shouted, sobbing:

"We are stupid for not thinking of that. You are right, please tell us how to solve this problem. Please let us live."

You might have asked yourself why they were crying. Thing is, the traditional way of solving this obvious problem had been to execute the new emperor's buddies one by one. The Han Dynasty famously did that with every single one of the generals who had conquered the empire for Liu Bang. The Song founder telling them this was not just logical argument. In normal circumstances this was the prelude for the emperor's pretorian guard rushing in and beheading them all on the spot.

The Song emperor wasn't that kind of guy, though. He told them:

"Life is short and hard as it is. Why not just grab some money, some land, fancy real estate to leave your children and grandchildren; get some fancy dancing girls to enjoy your old age. Spend the rest of your days drinking and laughing, without fights and grudges, isn't that the best?"

You damn bet it is. The generals took the offer and spend their rest of their lives enjoying the pleasures of life. The Song emperor then established the most rational and orderly central government in China. The civil service exam was set as the only path to officialdom, it's standards were raised, corruption was crushed. Exams were long, and hard. The answer sheets were anonymized; an army of scribes copied every exam by hand, so that the examiner couldn't recognize the handwriting. The imperial relatives received no privileges, the emperor intermarried with mandarin families. The army was crushed and rearranged so that no single general could mass any amount of troops nor spend enough time to develop any feelings of loyalty with them. Chinese history had been plagued with military rebellions. The Song Dynasty solved that problem for good.

As a result, the Song army kind of sucked. But that's a story for another day.

The Song Dynasty's Decline

2016-04-23 // china, history, Song Dynasty, series, power

So we left the story at Song Huizong. Huizong was as I wrote a consummate artist and a famous *bon vivant*. He knew how to enjoy himself. That means he generally wasn't interested in politics. Politics is generally very boring, pushing paper around, taking decisions about stuff you know nothing about. However Huizong was very willing to do politics if the topic at hand was interesting enough; interesting enough for such a consummate artist, that is.

There is one topic he did like to discuss, which was *war*. Artists tend to like war. The glory of fighting, thousands of men armed to the teeth and killing each other in mass pitched battles. There's something aesthetically very striking about that and artists across the world tend to be very attracted to it. Huizong was no exception, he was very much into war.

The thing is the Song dynasty had been founded explicitly as a peaceful state. The Song founder had decided the army was more trouble than it was worth, so he instituted a meritocratic bureaucracy and let it run the state more or less unimpeded for 100 years. That results in unprecedented prosperity, the reign of the 4th emperor Renzong being regarded as the historical peak of Chinese government. That produced its own set of problems, though. While you may not be interested in war, war is interested in you. While the Khitans in the Northeast were quite honorable, the Tanguts caught notice that the Song had no army to speak of, so they started to harass the border in order to extract more money. The Song had to keep 1 million soldiers in the frontier, which weren't easy to pay. And the tax revenue wasn't getting any better. The commercial economy grew with the typical effects: rich getting richer, using their wealth to buy tax exemptions, the poor getting poorer, rising in rebellion every few years.

Things started to change when Huizong's father, Shenzong ascended to the throne in 1068. The guy was 19 years old. If 3000 years of Chinese monarchy have produced any lesson, the lesson is that young monarchs are trouble. They always are. Young people are by definition inexperienced, so they tend to do stupid stuff. And generally, young men like to fight. They are eager to fight. It's in their blood. Sometimes that turns out well, as Han Wudi who basically tripled the territory of China in 30 years and crushed every single army around it. But usually young emperors pick fights without thinking, and the outcome is catastrophic.

News of the Khitan troubles got to China's capital. Our artist emperor was of course ecstatic. At last! We should take advantage of that. All the sycophantic ministers proposed making an alliance with the Jurchens. Let them take all the barbarian land they wanted, in exchange of the Song taking back the northern edge of the Chinese plain and the mountain passes. The Jurchens agreed, but stipulated that the Song had to take the land they wanted by themselves. The Jurchens weren't going to do the job for them. Thus a formal alliance was achieved.

The whole thing stunk. For better or worse, Song China and the Khitan Liao Dynasty had been in peace for 100 years. The Khitans could've kicked Chinese ass any time they wanted, but they respected the treaty. Now that the Khitans were in trouble, the Chinese didn't wait a minute in betraying the treaty and stabbing them in the back. That wasn't a very nice thing to do. It wasn't very smart either.

Nobody told Huizong that, though, who was still having fun playing soccer and visiting hookers through his secret tunnel. In 1121 He ordered his closest eunuch, Tong Guan, who is famous as the only bearded eunuch in Chinese history, to command 150,000 troops and go straight to the southern capital of the Khitans, what is today Beijing. The Khitans in their steppe homeland were running from the Jurchens as fast as they could; surely they wouldn't hold in the south very long either.

But the Chinese were still just no match for the Khitans. The Khitan commander in the south, Yelu Dashi, who was also perhaps the most incredible heroes in this story, held the walls, struck back at the Song forces, and destroyed the whole army. 150,000 men, gone. The whole Song army vanished in what was supposed to be a cakewalk. The eunuch commander panicked. He couldn't just go back and say he didn't take the land! They execute you for that stuff. So he sent an envoy to the Jurchens, saying: "Hey, we're having some trouble here conquering the city. Why don't you come down yourselves and take it, in exchange you can have all the booty: the gold, the women, the children, take them all. We'll pay for all supplies you need. After you're done you leave and we'll take the land as agreed, right?".

Well, why not. The Jurchens found it to be a good deal, so they came back through the mountain passes, and conquered Beijing in a week. Grabbed the gold and valuables, took the local women as concubines, took the children as slaves, sent them back to the Jin capital, close to today's Harbin. Just in case you don't know, Harbin isn't a very comfortable place.

It was probably colder back then, and at any rate it was a wooden village. No gas heating. All the virgins of Beijing were going to be enslaved there thanks to the ineptitude of the Song armies. Ineptitude that didn't go unnoticed by the Jurchen armies on the ground. Remember they were supposed to hand the land over to the Song authorities. The Jurchens started discussing among themselves. "This guys suck, they couldn't take a single city that took us a week". But the Jurchen emperor, Aguda, was a man of honor. "We had an agreement, we'll stand by it. I'm not the kind of man that takes advantage of the weakness of others".

But then he died.

Signaling spirals

2016-04-23 // signaling, cucks, religion

1800: Oh, you still have slaves? I freed all of mine.

1860: Did you know they still have slaves in the South? My sons have enlisted to kill those evil slavers.

1920: You listen to classical music? I go to a Jazz Club, there's a black musician who is so awesome.

1950: I have a black secretary.

1970: I have a black friend.

1980: I have many black friends. I even slept with one.

1990: I have a black child. Well, half black.

2000: I adopted a fully black child. Straight from Africa. Zero white admixture.

2010: I adopted two black children. One from West Africa and one from East Africa.

2016:

This past Sunday, my gorgeous wife – a white evangelical, like me — gave birth to our beautiful African-American triplet daughters whom we adopted as embryos. These sweet girls will hopefully soon be coming home to meet their 3-year-old African-American brother and 2-year-old biracial sister, both of whom we adopted as infants.

People forget that Christians invented holiness signaling.

As a friend said, hopefully liberals will see that they can't compete with evangelicals and will move to the other side. If that happens I'll salute Mr. and Mrs. Halbert for saving civilization.

The Song Dynasty's Fall

2016-04-24 // china, history, Song Dynasty, series, power

So let's continue the rise and fall of the Song Dynasty. Let me digress a bit and let me talk about the capital of the Song.

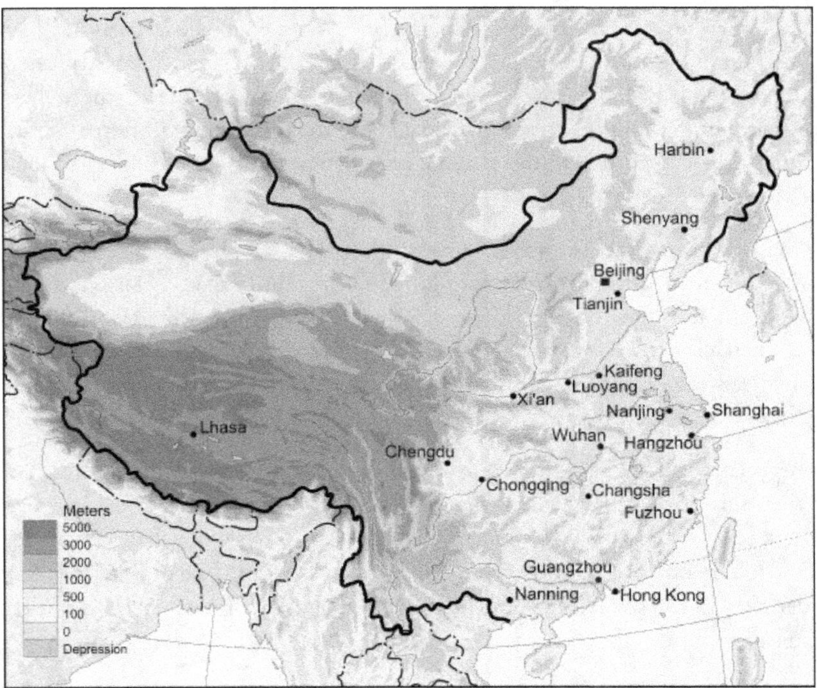

The borders of this map are contemporary China, but look at the topography. The Song Dynasty's capital was in Kaifeng. Kaifeng is probably the most retardedly located capital of all 3,000 years of Chinese history. Up until the Song, the capital of China had been alternating between Xi'an and Luoyang. Xi'an is in the Wei river valley, which is fairly narrow and easily defended if you control the mountain passes that surround the valley. Luoyang is just east of the mountains from Xi'an, in the North China plain proper, surrounded by mountains and a large river. Southern Dynasties had their capital at Nanjing, which is just south of the Yangtze river which is huge and completely impassable without a navy. And of course Beijing has been the capital for long due to its strategic location at the northern edge of the central plains.

But Kaifeng? It's in the middle of the damn plain! It has no natural defenses whatsoever. The only reason the Song capital is there is because the warlord who destroyed the Tang Dynasty 100 years later had his base there. Kaifeng is close to Jiangnan, the Nanjing-Shanghai area which is by far the wealthiest of the country, and the Grand Canal goes through there, so Kaifeng is well located to extract tax revenues from the rich areas. As such it had naturally grown to be a huge and immensely wealthy city, with over a million people. But military speaking it's a complete failure.

The emperor Huizong hadn't realized that, though. He was busy with his paintings, his zoo, his big fancy stones. His habit of bringing fine stones from the countryside had wrecked such havoc that just when the Jurchens were conquering the Khitan empire to the north, the Song had the huge Fang La rebellion which conquered the richest provinces south of the Yangtze. In fact the Song got to the invasion of the north 2 years later because they had to deal with so many peasant rebellions, all due to the fancy habits of our artist emperor.

Starting the war against the Khitans didn't help that. The state had to raise taxes and confiscate supplies in situ to feed the armies going north. That also started several rebellions in the northern countryside, which again also required military force to suppress. When all that was over, the Song army finally attacked the Khitan, and puff, 150,000 soldiers disappear in a single night. When the Jurchens came down to help out, the Song had virtually no army to speak of.

And so negotiations begin. The Jurchens declared that given that the Song had not fulfilled their side of the bargain, that they would't be giving away the whole territory they had agreed to. They gave to the Song about half of that. But well, what can you do. It's not like China was in a position to argue. A treaty was signed according to which the border was to be sealed, and any fugitive that crossed it was to be returned immediately.

Remember that the Jurchens were at most 2,500 cavalry men. That they had been able to conquer the Khitan was because they had taken over most of the Khitan armies, especially those made by minority groups. When invading the Chinese parts, most Chinese soldiers and officers employed by the Khitan surrendered to the Jurchen. One Chinese general who had surrendered to the Jurchen, on seeing the Song army occupying his neighboring county, decided to rebel against the Jurchen and declare his allegiance to the motherland, Song China. The Song commander was stupid enough to accept it.

The Jurchens were livid. They immediately sent an army to reoccupy the county, and the Chinese general fled to the Song controlled land. The Jurchens then demanded that the Chinese hand over the guy. The Song commander then, taking pity on his countryman, beheaded him with a clean blow, and sent the head over to the Jurchens.

The whole thing was a PR disaster. The Chinese were dismayed at how weak and dishonorable the Song army had been, giving away one of his countrymen after accepting his allegiance. The Jurchen swore that the Chinese would pay their breach of the treaty. You don't mess with Jurchens.

In 1123, the founder emperor of the Jurchens, now the Jin Dynasty 金朝, or Gold Dynasty, Wanyan Aguda died. The guy had had his glory, defeating his enemies the Khitans and taking over their empire; so he didn't press on the Chinese too much. But his successors wanted glory of their own. The Khitan empire was nice, but it was still a steppe empire. Not that much stuff in there besides sheep and horses. China, though, was rich and warm. And the Chinese were a bunch of lying bastards who deserved a lesson. The Song dynasty had been paying annual tribute to the Khitans in exchange for peace; the alliance treaty with the Jurchens stipulated that the Jurchens would inherit that tribute. When the Song failed to pay up in time, the Jurchens had had it. They decided to invade China.

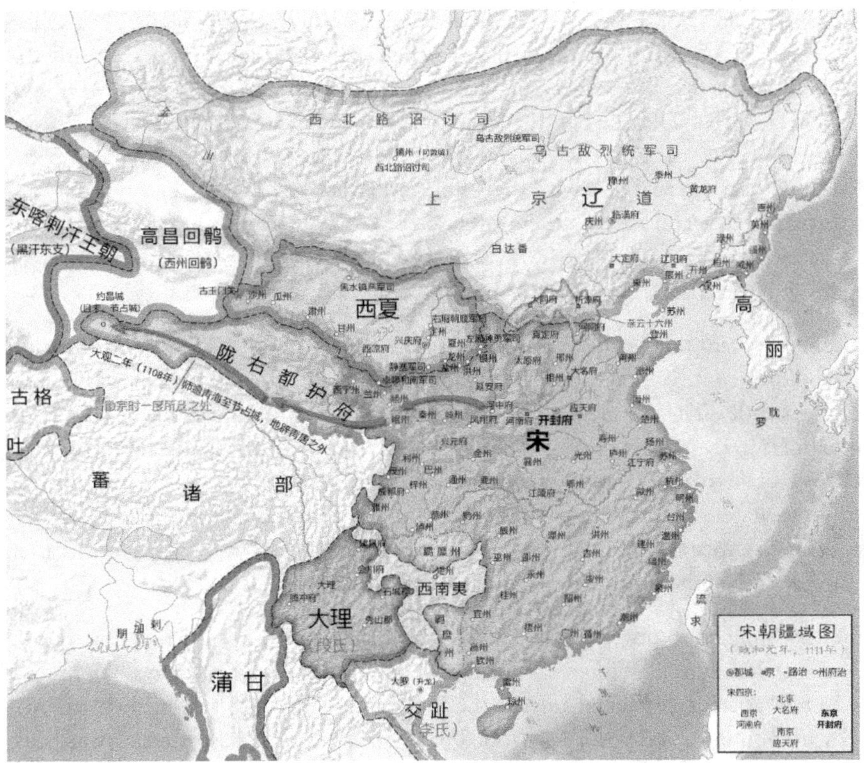

This map reflects the situation in 1111, the Song in orange, the Khitans in green-blue. It's 1125, and the Jurchens have effectively taken over the Khitan territory. In October

1125 the Jurchens rush south, and by February 1126 they are at the doors of Kaifeng. On their way they destroy everything they find, devastating north China. They reach the walls of Kaifeng and demand that the emperor, this Huizong they've heard about, respond for his treachery and breach of contract.

Now imagine our artist emperor must have felt. The guy had spent a life of carefree enjoyment of the most refined pleasures the earth had ever known. The best food, the finest silk, the best women, a personal zoo. Suddenly an army of savages from the forests of Siberia, two thousand miles to the north, is at the gates of the city asking for his head. Huizong panicked, wrote an edict blaming himself for all this problems... and abdicated on his first son. Then he made his luggage and fled to the south, where his ministers had promised he would be safe and could continue painting and playing soccer.

The son of Huizong, the new emperor, Qinzong (pronounced Cheen-tsong) apparently hadn't realized the gravity of the situation. 80,000 smelly barbarians at our gates? Nothing to worry about. Let's assault their camp during the night. And so the Song launched a massive assault to the Jurchen camp outside the gates. With the predictable result that the whole army was destroyed by the Jurchens. Who were now pissed. Very pissed. They demanded 5 million taels of gold, 50 million taels of silver, and the cession of the 3 border fortresses the Song had in the north. The emperor ordered the palace guard to search the whole city, house by house, for any valuables, put them together and handed them over to the Jurchens. They didn't even have to sack the city: the government did it for them. The Jurchens were running short of supplies, and lifted the siege in early March.

The Jurchens went home, and the Song decided to hurry and build up defenses so that they wouldn't come back again. Which sounds like the obvious thing to do. But you gotta be subtle. The Chinese were too damn obvious. First of all, the Chinese commanders in the border fortresses refused to surrender. They held up and forced the Jurchens to take over by force. The Song raised a new army and sent it up north to build up new defenses; meanwhile they sent diplomats to the remnants of the Khitan aristocracy to entice them to rebel against the Jurchens. All that in the few months after the Jurchens lifted the siege.

While the Song were obviously in a hurry to weaken the Jurchen; they just didn't understand that they were too weak for that. The Jurchen took the fortresses by force. The Khitan aristocrats weren't buying the Song offer of alliance. Those bastards! We allied with you once and you backstabbed us the moment we most needed your help. The Khitan handed the Song letter to the Jurchen emperor, which burst in rage. Those treacherous evil Chinese. These settled people have no honor. We'll show them. In October 1926 the Jurchens marched again south against China. By December they were at the gates of Kaifeng.

The Song sent armies from all across the empire to lift the siege; they were destroyed one by one. After 40 days, in February the capital of the Song Dynasty fell to the Jurchen armies. They sacked it with abandon. Took all valuables, burnt whole quarters, raped all the women they found. They entered the palace city, and captured the whole imperial family. The emperor, Qinzong. His father, Huizong, was found on the way to his escape. All the princes, dukes, earls. Their mothers, sisters. The princesses, concubines. Everyone was taken. 15,000 people in total. Every single descendant of the second emperor, along their wives and servants was captured and sent to the Jurchen capital, one thousand miles to the north, in the freezing forests of Manchuria. Remember the climate chart? Huizong was going to live there.

Just so you get a picture of the whole thing. They went from Kaifeng to Harbin by foot. 1,500 of the prisoners died on the way. On arriving to the Jurchen headquarters, the women were auctioned by the Jurchen army. 11,000 women were taken. The emperors' wives, daughters and sisters were given as concubines to the Jurchen generals. The others, if good looking were taken to the Laundry House, the public brothel of the Jurchen state, where they were put to service the Jurchen soldiery, day and night. The servants, the children, the ugly and the old were sold as slaves in public auction. We have good records of all these because plenty of court mandarins were taken prisoner too, and they kept detailed diaries of the whole process.

So our dear emperor Huizong, the brilliant artist,the *bon vivant*, the most consummate hedonist in the history of China, ended up the prisoner of smelly barbarians in the frigid forests of Manchuria. He spent 8 long years shivering at -20C temperature, while the smelly Jurchens, who 20 years before were just a small tribe of hunter-gatherers, spit on his face and laughed at him on sight, reminding him they were fucking his wives and daughters. Huizong died a broken man in 1135. His son Qinzong was not so lucky, he lived in ignominy until 1161. He died at 51 years old, of which he spent 34 in captivity, again watching his wives, sisters and daughters ravaged by his enemies.

And so the Northern Song Dynasty was destroyed. The war continued for some years, and eventually the Jurchens conquered the whole North China plain.

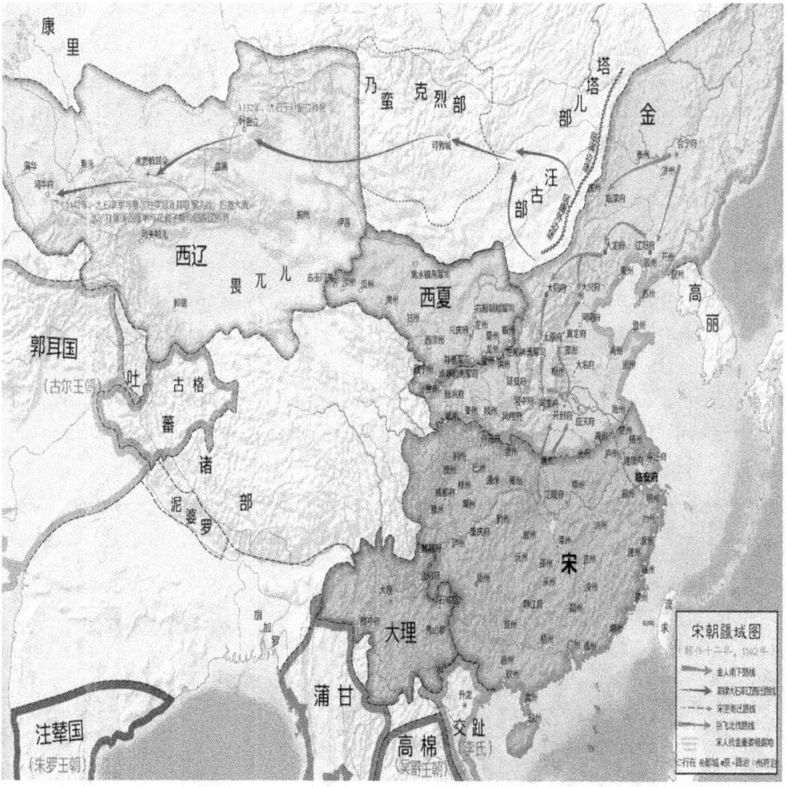

The Song managed to survive in the South. Their greed took them to betray their ally of 100 years to take a small piece of land in the north. They ended up paying with the destruction and loss of half the empire, and the lives and shame of the entire imperial family. All except one single man.

Reaction and the Bullshit Industry

2016-04-25 // cucks, nrx

Now that Ross Douthat has run an article on neoreaction[92] (no hyphen!) in the august New York Times, perhaps I should take back my previous statements[93] about disassociating with neoreaction because they're a bunch of retards of late. Bad timing! Before Anissimov comes back from his night job at a San Francisco bath-house, I shall proclaim myself Leader of Neoreaction and as such will negotiate with Mr. Douthat for any lucrative deal as the new edgy domesticated right. I have Catholic family too so I'm eminently qualified to deal with Mr. Douthat. He'll need my friendship when God-Emperor Trump comes down to ask him to respond for his articles against the Trump candidacy.

Jokes aside, Ross Douthat is really missing the point. His article argues that neoreaction is racist and evil, but we are often right about many issues and so mainstream conservatism should listen to what we say in order to have something real to say once in a while. He brings up Nicolas Gomez Davila aphorisms as an example of non-evil reactionary wisdom.

But reactionary wisdom like that used to be quite common. Did mainstream conservatism listen to it back then? No. The insight of neoreaction isn't that modernity and leftism sucks. Plenty of people have noticed that since before modernism even got running. Neoreaction explains why modernism happened even though it sucks. Why leftism gets progressively worse, and why conservatism, like the one Ross Douthat represents, is a complete joke. Mainstream conservatism are those few ideas which the left can't outright prohibit at a given moment, because the leftist consensus hasn't moved far enough. Mainstream conservatism was against gaymarriage because the Left hadn't reached an agreement within itself. Once the Left decided on gaymarriage, opposition was outlawed, and mainstream conservatism summarily dropped the issue. The moment that a conservative takes even the slightest hint of reactionary ideas the Left will make sure he is not allowed to speak in public. Journalism isn't about facts. Journalism is the state-run bullshit industry. And the left runs it very tight.

Mainstream conservatives themselves are part of the Left's censorship apparatus. They volunteer to police their own because they want to keep their jobs. See like Douthat

---

[92]   https://www.nytimes.com/2016/04/24/opinion/sunday/the-reactionary-mind.html?_r=0

[93]   https://spandrell.com/2016/04/06/the-informed-position-on-tibet/

himself has dealt with Donald Trump, even though it's increasingly obvious that Trump is a liberal fraud[94]. See what National Review has become. Douthat is of course right that people are increasingly disaffected from mainstream conservatism, as it has moved to the Left much faster than the common people have.

Douthat complains that reaction on top is a set of piecemeal complaints about democratic politics, which the bottom it's yet another nationalist movement based on racial grounds. The reason is obvious. The people on top have read their history and know that going back to the past is neither feasible nor desirable, that there are systemic reasons[95] why the Left always wins, and that the signaling patterns that move modern politics are likely to spiral into complete madness until the whole thing collapses.

The bottom has neither the expertise nor the leisure to engage in historical and sociopolitic analysis. If all politics are signaling, the bottom needs to find a good signaling post to rally around and to fight back against the modern leftist establishment that is destroying the middle class and using foreign barbarians to intimidate them with state-approved violence. And for better or worse, the only set of ideas that can fight leftism today is fascism. Good old secular ethno-nationalism. That works. It's working in France, it's working in Germany, it's working in Hungary. It just won the election in Austria[96]. It may very well make Donald Trump the president of the United States.

If Douthat wants to keep his job in the bullshit industry he better listen to those fascists on the bottom, not to the highbrow reactionaries. Reading me or Moldbug won't get you a job. Being friendly to the God-Emperor might. He doesn't like it. To be honest I don't like it either. But that's the way things work. That's the real message of the reaction.

---

94   https://www.witn.com/home/headlines/TRUMPNorth-Carolina-leaders-wrong-to-pass-bathroom-bill-376559851.html

95   https://spandrell.com/2015/03/01/leftism-is-just-an-easy-excuse/

96   https://www.dw.com/en/presidential-election-exposes-austrian-angst/a-19207311

The Song Dynasty's Surrender

2016-04-26 // china, history, Song Dynasty, series, power

So we left as the Jurchens conquer the Song capital of Kaifeng, empty the city of all its valuables, butcher most of the population, taking around 100,000 people as slaves. Among them the whole imperial family, 5,000 people in all, plus all their servants. The wives, mothers, sisters and daughters of the emperor and all the nobility were taken as wives, concubines, or put to work as whores in the Jurchen official brothel. Those who made it alive to the Jurchen homeland, that is. Many died on their way.

Once the Jurchen destroyed the city of Kaifeng, they grabbed one Song minister, Zhang Bangchang, gave him some of the imperial regalia they had grabbed from the Song palace, and put him as emperor of the Great Chu. Zhang was supposed to set a court at Nanjing and rule as the puppet of the Jurchens, who annexed all land north of the Yellow River, but left most Chinese territory to this puppet court. The Jurchens had no intention of ruling China at all. They had invaded to punish the Song court for its treachery and to extract some booty to share between the Jurchen generals. They achieved those goals, and then some. Setting a government in China and finding a way to rule the peasants sounded like a lot of trouble, trouble the Jurchens weren't interested in taking at all. The destruction of the Song Dynasty had also erased all public order in north China. Gangs of bandits roamed the countryside, killing landlords, public officials, Jurchen detachments and anything they could find. The Jurchen had enough men to destroy any Chinese army but it most certainly didn't have the manpower to police the whole empire. So they were happy to leave that job to that wimp Song minister, and go back home to enjoy screwing the myriad imperial princesses they had kidnapped from Kaifeng.

Mr. Zhang wasn't thrilled about this arrangement. Usurping the throne is the worst crime a Chinese minister can commit. It's tantamount to death by one thousand slices together with one's whole family. But what could he do? The entire imperial clan, thousands of men, had been taken prisoner by the Jurchens. Or not. There were rumors of a single imperial prince who was free, and had raised an army of 10,000 somewhere in the north. Prince Kang.

Huizong, our artist emperor, had had 143 wives, who had produced 38 sons and 34 daughters. Huizong didn't know them all. If Dunbar is right he barely even knew most of his women. The thing with polygamy, that some overzealous manosphere bros tend to forget, is that in traditional society sex was only allowed inside marriage. If an emperor wanted to have sex with a woman, he had to made her his concubine and take care of her for life. That means giving her proper status as the woman of that man. You can't just find her some smelly apartment in a project and give her 500 bucks alimony every month. The concubine of an emperor had to be treated as an imperial princess, and that didn't come cheap.

Prince Kang was one of the 38 sons of Huizong. In 1127, when the Jurchens invaded, he was 20 years old. He was the only child of his mother, who Huizong apparently slept with once or twice and never bother seeing again. Prince Kang though was a talented kid, tall, strong and good at the classics. But his father never met his mother, meaning his father never got to know him. The only way most Chinese emperors got to know their sons was when imperial concubines gave their pitch after having sex. "You know our son? He can write 100 letters already!" If your mother was out of favor, a prince didn't really exist. Of course he had his income as an imperial prince, and all the perks that entitled. Prince Kang at 20 years old had 4 wives, 1 son and 5 daughters.

When the Jurchens invaded China, they demanded the Song court sent an imperial prince as an envoy to discuss terms. Huizong discussed among his family, but of course nobody wanted to go. Prince Kang alone volunteered. He made quite an impression with the Jurchen generals; allegedly he was able to shot a bow so straight that the Jurchens thought the Song had tricked them. No way a Song imperial wimp prince could shoot a bow straight, this is a fake prince! Send us a real one! Prince Kang went back home, but later was sent again as an envoy during the second invasion.

While on the road to his diplomatic mission, a regional official told Prince Kang that the Jurchens weren't joking his time, and persuaded him to abandon his mission and take refuge in the countryside. He did, but then a huge mob of local peasants came up to see what was going on. While doing so they found it was Prince Kang, alongside the Minister of War. The Minister of War yelled at them, telling them they were an imperial envoy. People found out who that guy was. They remembered it was him who had ordered to use scorched-earth tactics against the Jurchens. This guy had burnt their homes and harvests. Now he was here as a diplomatic envoy? What, he's going to sell us out to the Jurchens? The peasant mob grabbed the Minister of War of the Song Dynasty and beat him to death right there. Prince Kang, 20 years old, barely escaped with his life.

Eventually Prince Kang raised a small army, and went around avoiding the Jurchens who had just conquered the capital and taken the whole imperial clan with them; including his mother, his infant daughters and most of his wives. He only had his son and the mother of his son with him. Some time later an envoy arrives from Zhang Bangchang, the puppet minister, who wanted out of that gig and offered him the crown. So Prince Kang went over to Zhang Bangchang's fake court, and was enthroned as new emperor of the Song Dynasty, Gaozong. First order of business was to execute

Zhang. He usurped the throne! Gaozong was nice and let him kill himself, and didn't punish his family.

The Jurchens, sometime after or during the wild orgies they were having with the imperial princesses up in Harbin, heard that their puppet emperor had abdicated, and that one imperial prince had escaped capture and had been enthroned as new emperor of the Song Dynasty. They were furious. They had destroyed the Song Dynasty. They had no right to start again. The Jurchens again amassed their armies and sent a massive punitive expedition, codename "Search the top of the mountains and the bottom of the sea to capture Zhao Gou (the personal name of Gaozong)". Using someone's personal name in old China is tantamount to call him a smelly bastard.

Gaozong could only flee. Flee south. He fled to the Yangtze, stayed a while in Nanjing. The Jurchen armies rushed to catch him, and he had to flee further south, to Hangzhou. I guess I might as well put a map again.

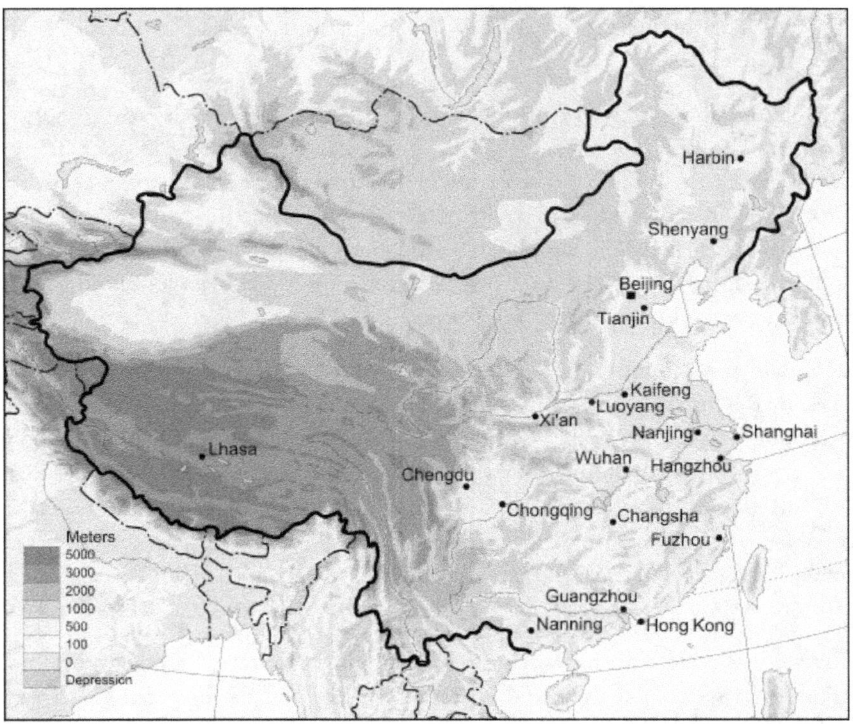

During this time there was a military coup on his side, which lasted only short while, but in the process his only son, 2 years old, died. Soon afterwards the Jurchen armies crossed the Yangtze, captured Nanjing, and were soon to get to Gaozong's court at Hangzhou. He had to get on a ship and flee south by sea. He spent weeks at sea avoiding the Jurchen armies, fleeing for his life. The whole escape was so sudden and traumatic that Gaozong had daily panic attacks. Apparently he became infertile. Traditional accounts say the Jurchen attack on Hangzhou scared him so much he became important for life. He never produced an heir.

So it's 1130 now, 3 years after the fall of Kaifeng. Eventually a Song army beat the overextended Jurchen armies, who retreated north of the Yangtze, and Gaozong returned to Hangzhou for good. He established his court there, and rebuilt the Song state apparatus in the south. Some great generals such Wu Jie, Han Shizhong and Yue Fei built strong armies who were soon able to beat the Jurchens in open battle. The Jurchens responded by retreating and setting a new puppet state in north China, headed by an old Song minister who had surrendered, Liu Yu. This guy actually liked the job, and put some effort into raising armies to fight the Song. Meanwhile the Jurchens focused on fighting in the West. China has always been unified the same way: a northern army invading Sichuan from the Xi'An area, and from there sailing down the Yangtze. The Jurchens tried hard but the Song armies held fast and blocked the Jurchen advance.

Meanwhile the Song armies were beating the puppet Chinese armies to the north. General Yue Fei was especially strong. His armies had found a way to counter the massive charges f the Jurchen heavy cavalry. He put his Chinese infantry in a sort of phalanx, with very long pikes, and had them cut the feet of the Jurchen horses as they run towards them. Now I'm simplifying a lot, but by 1140 Yue Fei was recovering more and more territory, and was close to recovering Kaifeng itself. But then his emperor Gaozong told him to stop it right there.

Gaozong had put a minister called Qin Hui as prime minister. Qin Hui had been captured by the Jurchens, and spent some time in the north. Nobody else ever escaped from capture, so there were always rumors that the Jurchens had sent him back on purpose as a spy. At any rate Gaozong was fond of the guy. Qin Hui's position was that the war was hopeless. The Song had to reach an agreement with the Jurchens and make peace as fast as possible. The Jurchen emperor had just die, and the new guy was favorable to a peace agreement. Qin Hui would make it happen as long as Gaozong gave the order.

So Yue Fei was there with his ever victorious army at the feet of Kaifeng, ready to march, when a special convoy comes directly from the court with orders to retreat, immediately. Yue Fei couldn't believe it. The work of 10 years lost in an instant! He argued once and again that they couldn't retreat, victory was at hand! But the emperor wouldn't have it. Yue Fei could only obey and resign his post.

Yue Fei is perhaps the most famous hero in Chinese history. He was the perfect man. Strong in arms, yet well educated. He was courteous, frugal, loyal and focused on his mission. He famously had a huge tattoo in his back with the letters 精忠報國, "utmost loyalty in service of the country". Mandarins from the court sent him gold, women, presents of all kind, yet he never accepted any. He had a single wife, which is unheard of in important men in China. He disciplined his army sternly and without failure, making it by far the best army in China. But he was just too perfect. In China the way to make friends with the elite is by grabbing each other's handle, sharing money, secrets, women, bad things. That way you know they will be loyal to each other; else they have something to use against you. Nobody had anything to use against Yue Fei. He was the perfect man.

That didn't save him, though. While on an audience with the emperor, Yue Fei had the nerve to ask the emperor to choose an heir. Gaozong was predisposed against the army. A military coup had killed his only son. He then became sterile, so he couldn't produce children. That indeed was a problem; what if he were to die? Yue Fei had good reason to ask him to resolve that problem. The whole imperial clan had been captured by the Jurchens, Gaozong should look for some other farther imperial relatives and create a new imperial clan. He eventually did, but that was no business of Yue Fei to ask. He was a damn general, and generals had no status in the Song Dynasty. Gaozong never forgot that slight.

Yue Fei also had the habit of saying he was fighting to expel the Jurchens from sacred Chinese territory, and push into their homeland to recover the two captured emperors. Well Gaozong wasn't very eager to recover the two captured emperors. His father made him the favor of dying in 1135, but his brother and lawful emperor was still around. The Jurchens used to threat that if the Song didn't stop winning battles, that they'd send the captured emperor on a boat straight to the new Song capital. How awkward would that be?

After Gaozong ordered Yue Fei to retreat in order to negotiate the peace treaty with the Jurchens, Qin Hui eventually trumped up charges of rebellion against Yue Fei, put him in jail and poisoned him. Other generals were furious against Qin Hui. One famously asked him:

Yue Fei was about to rebel? Nonsense! Is there any proof?!

To which Qin Hui laconically responded:

莫須有 (There doesn't need to be)

So Yue Fei, most talented, loyal and virtuous man in the empire, was killed on trumped up charges. And the Song and the Jurchen signed the peace treaty. The treaty was beyond horrible. It was the most shameful thing any Chinese dynasty had ever signed. It stipulated that the Song emperor was to refer to himself as "your servant". The Song emperor's title was to be "granted" by the Jurchens, not self-declared. The border established was also a disaster. The Song had control over much of the central plains. They could have pushed to retain the Wei river valley (the Xi'An area) and much of the central plains. But Gaozong didn't care. The border was set over the Huai river, a bit further north from the Yangtze, and that was that.

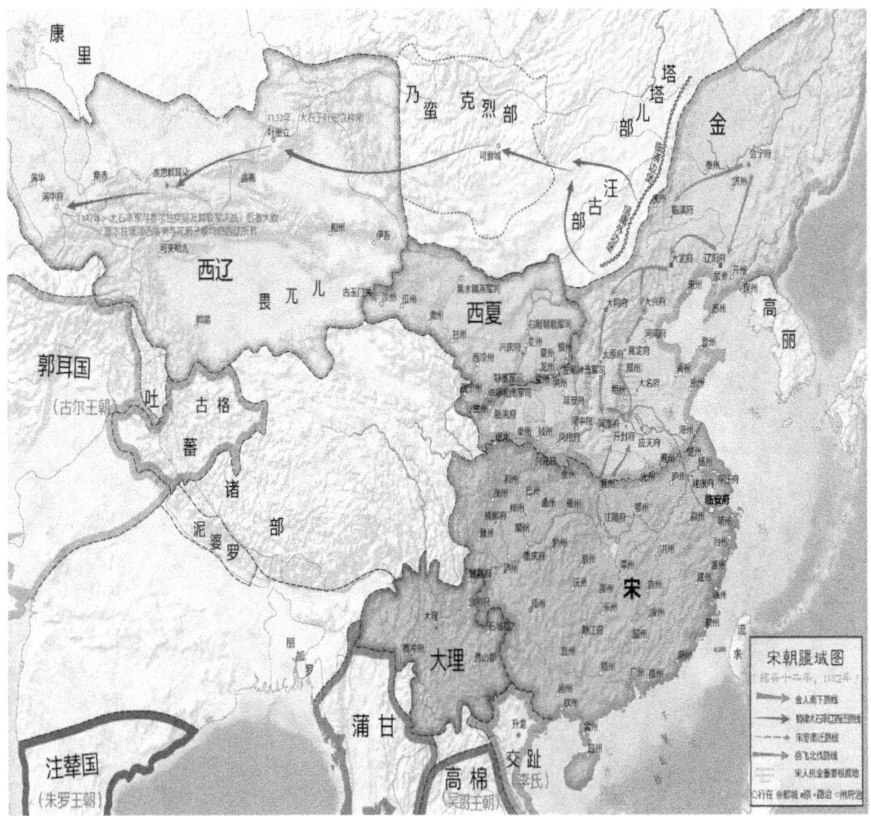

Millions of peasants who had been aiding the Song war effort were sold out and left in Jurchen territory. Many left all they had and rushed to escape into Song territory. Many didn't make it. The Jurchens didn't take it lightly.

Many wondered why the Song emperor hadn't pushed further and tried to get a better deal. In 1141 everybody understood why. The Jurchen's sent a carriage to the Song border. There was Gaozong's mother, empress Wei. While Gaozong (then prince Kang) had evaded capture, his mother, wives and daughters were taken by the Jurchens to their homeland. Gaozong's mother was 38 at the time. She was put in the Laundry House state brothel, where allegedly she was made to serve dozens of Jurchen soldiers every day. Allegedly she bore two children in the north. Gaozong had the records change to make her 10 years older, so that she would have been 48 at the time of her capture, thus officially unable of making Jurchen children. She died in 1159, officially 90 years old. Which isn't very likely. Still, living to 80 years old was quite a feat given the time, and what she had been through.

Qin Hui had secured her release by the Jurchens, in exchange of which Gaozong gave away half his empire, the best army he had, and his reputation for all posterity. Gaozong is today regarded as a despicable traitor, a coward that shamed China for centuries. Yue Fei was made a folk idol, the patron saint of all Chinese armies since. Qin Hui was made into an iron statue along his wife, which became a tourist attraction. It is customary for people to visit and spit on it.

Gaozong also lived to old age. He died in 1187, 80 years old. To choose an heir he had to find a commoner which was a descendant of the founder of the dynasty. Remember that guy[97]? The palace commander who rebelled, and then made sure his generals didn't rebel against him? His younger brother murdered him some time later. Henceforth the imperial throne was transmitted through this brother's line. Some people said that the first Jurchen emperor was the first Song emperor reincarnated, taking revenge on the descendants of his brother for murdering him. He certainly extinguished the whole line.

Gaozong's successor, Xiaozong tried to fix all the damage his adoptive father had done. He killed Qin Hui, repealed the peace treaty, raised armies, and tried to get back the lost territory. It didn't work. It never worked. The Jurchen ruled north China until 1234, when Genghis Khan destroyed the Jurchen state. When the Mongols started attacking north China, guess what, the Song made an alliance with them! And guess what, the

---

[97] https://spandrell.com/2016/04/19/the-distribution-of-power/

Song breached the terms of the alliance, and the Mongols took that excuse to invade and destroy the Song. This time for good. To their credit the Song Dynasty held until 1279, until Genghis' grandson, Khubilai, managed to conquer them. The Mongols ruled all China for 90 years.

And that's the story of how the Song Dynasty fell and how it came back to life in the South, mostly because the emperor put more value on his mother than on 20 million of his subjects. When people like Hoppe say that Monarchs tend to govern well because they have a stake in their property, they don't know what they're talking about. Not everyone places much value on their property besides the minimum to keep their personal status. There's an old saying, which I've heard in China and Europe too: "wealth lasts but 3 generations". What the grandfather builds, the grandsons brings to the ground. Honestly I'd probably change 20 million people for my mother, too. And I'd be glad to have a sociopath like Qin Hui to help on that. Although personally I would have done something to save my wives and daughters too. Gaozong never asked for them. 2 of his daughters survived and were married off to Jurchen men. But Chinese culture was about filial piety, children were an afterthought.

As a bonus, let me finish by telling the story of Yelu Dashi. You may have noticed that there's a light green blob in the map, way to the West of China, around what's today Xinjiang and most of Kazakhstan. You know who that is? The Khitans! The Khitan commander who held Beijing against the Song invasion, Yelu Dashi, was eventually captured by the Jurchen once they came south to help the Song out.

Yelu Dashi was not only a great general, he was a very cultivated man. He spoke Khitan and Chinese, had studied the Confucian classics, and was in charge of the administration of the Chinese areas of the Khitan empire. Shortly after he fell to the Jurchen army, Yelu Dashi escaped with his retinue. He rode fast, evading the Jurchen pursuers, and reached what's today northern Mongolia, which the Jurchen never controlled, and the Khitan had old ties of vassalage. This Khitan noblemen then raised a big army and rode to the West, conquered the Dzungar steppe, the Tarim Basin, went further West and built a huge empire that reached the Aral Sea! This new empire of Yelu ashi controlled for decades most of Central Asia, exerting its influence well into Persia. Imagine the life of this guy. He tried to raise armies to ride back east and attack the Jurchens, but it never worked out. He eventually learned to enjoy his new empire.

This new Khitan empire, called by historians the Qara-Khitai[98], is regarded by Chinese historians as a Chinese dynasty, the Western Liao. That's why it's painted in full color in the map. While it was a steppe empire ruled by Khitans, they kept the old Chinese-inspired administration, taught the Confucian classics, and kept many Han Chinese in the state bureaucracy. The Qara Khitai ruled Central Asia until... yes, Genghis Khan.

---

[98] https://en.wikipedia.org/wiki/Qara_Khitai

Lies

2016-05-01 // power

Moldbug was about formalism. Which is funny because I associate "formalism" with Chomskyian linguistics. The idea that language can be modeled in a quasi mathematical form. Let's say that didn't really work out.

Moldbug's was political Formalism. Give everyone an official title of what he already owns. Let us say it how it is and not lie anymore. Good idea. I wonder how you formalize this?

Sailer writes how[99] New York City is not actually run by its mayor; there's a sleazy bunch of "consultants" with a pipe to rich donors, who force any political candidate to hire this consultants in exchange for their donations. This includes the mayor, attorneys, and everybody who needs money to run a campaign in NYC. Guys like this.

Officially there's a mayor, who's supposed to run things, but he's not very smart, at any rate he needed money for his campaign and he wasn't very good at getting it. So he outsourced that to the free market, and the free market provided. Now there's a bunch of sleazy middlemen trafficking with influences from here to there.

How do you formalize this? Who's in charge? Who will be in charge tomorrow?

---

[99] https://www.unz.com/isteve/mayor-de-blasio-in-trouble-over-consultants/#comments

Not that this is somewhat particular to NYC, but not necessarily so. Is Obama in charge? Not really. He is the puppet of some conquistador consultant? Probably not. Who is? That's a good question.

Ancient China was very adamant that there should be one guy in charge. The Emperor. "The realm cannot be one day without a ruler". The theory was good, but the Emperor had a mother. And Ancient China was also very adamant about sons being obedient to their parents. So the Emperor Must Rule, but he must be obedient to Mom. Which is why there so many Empress Dowager.

The Western conception of power is different. We have people on top of the pyramid, and they're "responsible". Which means when something we choose to remove them when something goes wrong, even when the guy wasn't really involved in the process. But the process is very complicated. How to formalize that? It isn't any easier than formalizing language, like Chomsky. And that didn't work out.

The Evolution of the Sexual Marketplace

2016-05-06 // women, japan

I always say that I find East Asians to be much more realistic in general. They're less likely to comment about what they know nothing about, less likely to engage in empty virtue signaling, less likely to make up stuff in general. Less full of shit. Of course this is a relative term, there's plenty of Asians which are full of it, especially those in the media, politica or academia. But the amount of shit in circulation is an order of magnitude smaller than in the West.

Personally I believe that is because of the lack of organized religion for centuries, and because of widespread poverty up until very recently. Life in Asia has always been harsh. Every few decades you got a widespread famine. And lacking a religious establishment, being holier-than-thou didn't get you fed. So the penalties for noticing things were much smaller than in the West. This has changed a bit since the late 19th century, when European empires invaded the area. Democratic politics and mass media by definition promote form over substance. But the lack of a general tradition of generating feel-good nonsense has limited the damage.

See this very nice graph that is going around the Japanese internet. How the Sexual Marketplace has evolved since the 1950s. Forgive the awkward captions, but I'm busy with the book.

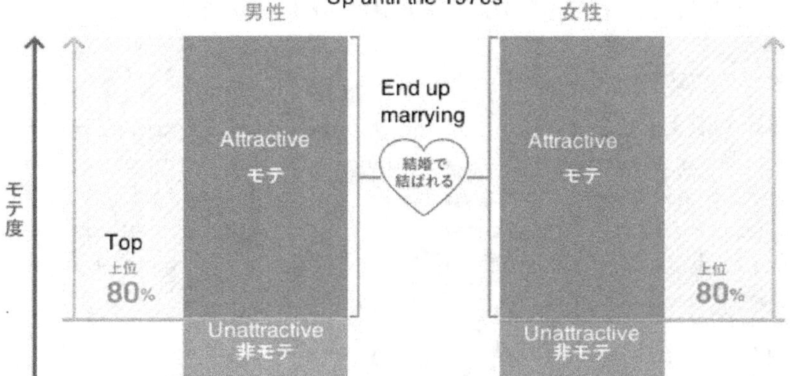

The Sexual Marketplace changed after the sexual revolution
自由恋愛主義が広まり恋愛市場が変化した

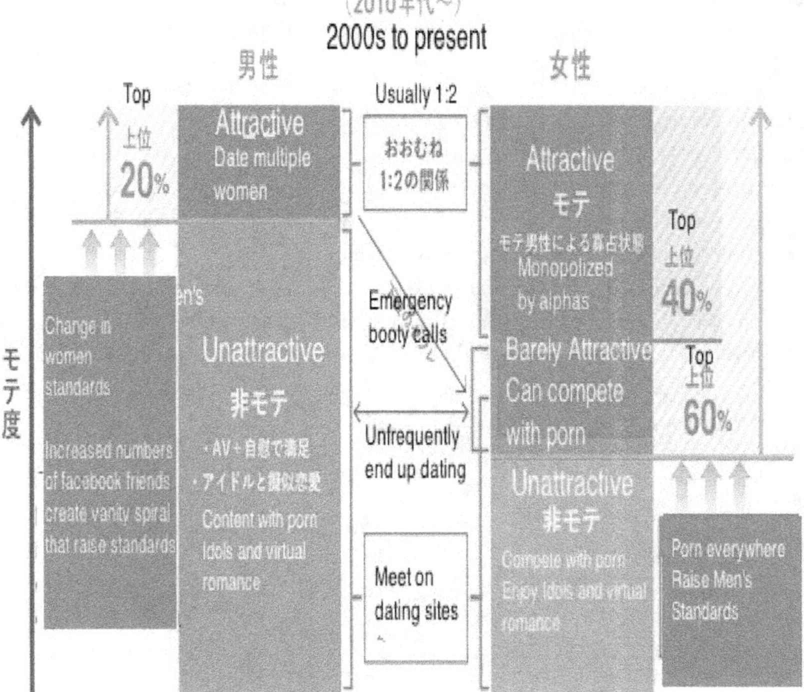

So in the old days, the top 80% of men and women got married, the rest became omegas and spinsters, and that was it. Then Free Love (the Japanese term for what we call the Sexual Revolution) happened. The top 40% of men started dating the 80% of women, leaving the rest of men shafted, but in the end women got bored of the carousel and ended up marrying men of their league, so 80% of men kept getting married, as well as 80% of women. Today, though, 20% of men fuck 60% of women. The rest of men occasionally date the 40 to 60 percentile of attractiveness (4s to 6s in redpill speech), but mostly subsist on a date of free and high quality porn, idols and romance videogames. 40% of women also get no action whatsoever.

Note that Japan has had no Roissy. No manosphere. No red pill. These people can't read English nor are interested in the American blogosphere. This is just regular Japanese people noticing things and discussing them freely on the internet. And the conclusion is accurate, concise, and very fair. Note how there's no attempt at blaming women for being all bitches, or blaming men for being all children. They understand that it's both. Men are so addicted to porn that it has raised the floor of minimum beauty that women need to have to get men interested. And that social media has made women expand their areas of gossip, so are know subject to attack by more vain women, making them insist in only fucking the top men, lest they get shunned out of female society by fucking normal men. I like the idea of the vanity spiral.

The analysis isn't perfect; e.g. no mention of the effect of women's entering the labor market. And some factors are peculiarly Japanese, in particular the "idol"[100] market and the pervasive romance videogames and comics. But the general situation isn't that different from Western countries. There's lots of articules and TV programs about how the Japanese "aren't interested in sex". Like the West isn't fully packed and bursting with incels of every sex and color. Again, the difference is that the Japanese notice, and talk about it, while in the West no one is allowed to notice anything that contradicts the narrative that we live in the best of all possible worlds, and we are making progress at every front. The few that do notice that something wrong end up forming internet groups blaming 100% of the problem on a single sex, as if the whole society wasn't rotten from the root.

---

[100] https://en.wikipedia.org/wiki/Japanese_idol

Secession

2016-05-11 // WNANR, blackpill, europe, leftism

One big idea out there is that what we need is Exit. We need to allow secession, for different people to go their own way. We obviously can't get along. Some people want homosexuals teaching sex education in kindergarten. Others want to put statues to Hitler and Genghis Khan. Others want the liberty to do drugs, own guns, preferably at the same time. Others want soda taxes enforced by a mercenary army. Many want sharia law.

That's what other countries are for! Give us borders. A patchwork, a polyhedron of independent countries free to develop their own culture. That's a fine idea. Autonomy is a fine thing. Surely better than having faceless bureaucrats ruling from thousands of miles away.

Well ok, let's say we all get secession. What happens then? Fortunately Europe is experimenting with the idea. Plenty of secessionist movements going on in Europe. Scotland is one of the most advanced. Soon Scotland may be able to become free, and the Scots can do their own thing. So what are the Scots up to?

They are arresting people for making videos of dogs doing the nazi salute.[101]

They are arresting people for complaining about "syrian refugees" on Facebook.[102]

They are basically running the mother of all censorship campaigns by arresting anyone who says anything non-PC on the internet. Hate crimes, you see. Even the Chinese Communist Party isn't this blatant.

---

[101] https://www.dailymail.co.uk/news/article-3580951/Call-centre-worker-arrested-online-footage-Nazi-dog.html

[102] https://www.theguardian.com/uk-news/2016/feb/16/man-arrested-facebook-posts-syrian-refugees-scotland

It is often said that the secret of European dominance after the 16th century was that Europe was divided in many small states, which created a competitive pressure which resulted in, well, massive advances in shipbuilding, weaponry, science, and eventually the Industrial Revolution. I buy that. But you'll note that for all the political division of Europe there is such a thing as European culture. European countries had different governments different languages.Yet they dressed mostly the same, had similar economic systems, basically the same religion. The elite intermarried profusely, and intellectual life was international. Many linguists will tell you that European languages, for all their differences, are basically the same; vocabulary and other grammar patterns having diffused so much that automatic translation actually works! Try to run Google Translate to any slightly exotic language and it breaks down very fast.

Even if the Western elite were to go mad tomorrow and allow widespread secession; even if Europe and North America were tomorrow to divide in 500 sovereign countries; who says that the common culture would necessarily fracture? The Irish fought valiantly for decades to gain their freedom from the British, only to use their sovereignty to fill Dublin with African immigrants. The Scots are likely to use their newly gained sovereignty to pass a law giving 10 year jail sentences to those who oppose bringing 100k male Afghan immigrants per year. Which will make the British then bring 120k, to spite them. The same way Voltaire was a celebrity in both the Russian and Pussian courts, or Confucius roamed the Chinese heartland working for different lords, Sadiq Khan may end up as mayor of Berlin after he's finished with London.

I don't want to oversell this argument. Of course sovereignty does matter at some level. I'm glad that Slovakia or Hungary are sovereign and can refuse to open their borders to barbarians. If the EU could it would have forced the distribution of migrants across European territory. Still, sovereignty only gets you so far. The EU could plausibly engineer a regime change in some country in Eastern Europe in the middle term, and put some Harvard grad to implement EU policy.

The issue here is culture. Politics of course influences culture to some extent, but the arrow goes the other way around too. Any patchwork, no matter how sovereign, will result in the same insane liberal monoculture if trade dynamics stay the same, everybody learns English, the global elite all goes to American colleges, and everybody is discussing politics on Twitter. Sovereignty doesn't mean anything if the sovereign(s) doesn't want to use it. I've made that point about monarchy several times. It applies to republics all the same.

What we[103] need[104] is...[105]

---

[103] https://spandrell.com/2011/11/09/we-need-a-new-religion/

[104] https://spandrell.com/2011/11/25/we-need-a-new-religion-2/

[105] https://spandrell.com/2014/07/07/we-need-a-new-religion-3/

We need a new religion, 4

2016-05-15 // WNANR, history, religion

We need a new religion. We sorely need one. And we will likely get one. But we might not like how it turns out.

In 200 AD, the Roman Empire was the largest, richest and most powerful empire on Earth. Roman civilization extended from Britain to Mesopotamia. Vast trade networks allowed for large and advanced industries that provided a very high standard of living, far above anything in the past. Rome was so great it seemed it would last forever.

Then a couple of substandard emperors, a military setback and a mutiny suddenly saw the Empire fracture into 3 parts, hundreds of thousands of barbarians entering the borders, plundering and murdering as they pleased. It took 50 whole years until Aurelian rebuilt the army, expelled the barbarians, and reunified the realm. But it was never the same. Too many people had died. Cities now had to build high walls to defend themselves, trade routes had been destroyed, the whole administrative apparatus had to be rebuilt from scratch.

All that was taken care of, especially by Docletian, who was very much interested in how to run a government. But still, as much as Roman emperors reformed the army and the administration, the virtue of the empire, the real power of Rome, the roman people, that was over. Any Roman of learning knew that. And they all wanted to do something to get it back. To fix Rome, to bring it back to its golden era. Romans used to be virtuous, strong, hard-working, just men. Not anymore. The Romans of the late empire were a fickle bunch, interested in frivolous sex, in sodomy, in spectator sports. We have almost no literary works from the late Empire; the Romans appeared to be uninterested in learning. Nor they cared to breed and form families. The whole society was a wreck.

The few virtuous Romans who noticed that must have wanted to fix this desperately, to use the power of the state to bring the Romans back to their virtuous, frugal and wise past, when men fought for their country, cared to learn about the mysteries of human existence, and took care of their wives and children. But none of those efforts worked.

What happened? A weird cult from the obscure province of Judaea, where people worshipped some countryside carpenter son of an old man with a teenager, who apparently got pregnant without having sex. Then the man started to preach about loving your enemies, rescued whores from stoning, made wine from water, told the poor that after death they'd lord over the rich; and other absurd stuff. The guy was justly executed by the Roman governor as an agitator but his followers believe he then came back to life and ascended to heaven with his mother.

The cult grew by preaching to women, to the poor, to slaves, to all manner of disaffected people. They formed local communities where they read this weird compendium of miracles of this Jewish lord of them. The Roman authorities killed some of them ever now and then but the guys appeared to like it! They called the dead "martyrs", and some of them appeared to actively seek martyrdom, as they believe it would pay off with privileges after dead. Bunch of provincial weirdos. Even weirder than the Jews they splintered from. That the Empire has declined to such an extent has much to do with this and other weird sects who are fooling the commoners, and even some women of good families! Scandalous.

No offense intended, early Christianity was in many ways a superior lifestyle compared to mainstream Roman life, which had plenty of weird stuff in it. But to any good old Roman patrician, the growth of Christianity, Manicheism and other assorted sects must have looked incredibly weird and threatening. As much as the Empire needed reform, nobody desired this kind of reform. To replace the classics of Greece and Rome with the made up history of some desert goat herders, to give rights to women and slaves, to encourage death and meekness instead of the classical warrior ethos going back for millennia. This is madness.Rome has to wake up. We can't let this happen.

But it happened. Rome never woke up. Classical civilization kept on with its decline, and eventually Constantine, a pragmatic man who just wanted a stable empire that obeyed his commands, made Christianity into the state religion. It replaced Roman civilization, little by little. Half the Empire died on the process, by the way. The invaders became Christians too, but never Romans.

The Romans of its golden age often said that the secret of Roman success was its *religio*, by which they mean their piousness, how their discipline was so tight they followed the old religious practices of paganism to the letter, no matter how useless they might have seemed. Worried Romans of the late empire must have thought all the time that Rome needed its religion back. They never got it back. They got a new religion. A pretty horrible one, for anyone who appreciated old Classical civilization. But a religion they got, and it wasn't that bad. Most of the Western empire still speaks Latin to this day. The Eastern half even kept calling himself the Roman Empire for a thousand years.

You might have noticed the parallels with our situation. We want to go back to the old days when Europeans were virtuous, frugal and strong. That's not going to work. It never works. I say we need a new religion. I say we'll get a new religion, because nature abhors a vacuum, and a vacuum is what we have right now. But the new religion we end up getting may not be nothing we like. It might very well something horrifying, something which denies all the values we hold dear. But as horrifying as it may be, it may end up winning.

Christianity had to be horrifying for a Roman patrician. But the Christians had children. They had stable families. They didn't do infanticide, did less drugs, less drinking, less sodomy, less idle watching chariot races or gladiator matches. The messianic wannabe Jews were a bunch of meek underclass pussies who hadn't read their Homer. But they won. And by winning, they destroyed Roman civilization. But they also tamed the Germans, and so a new hybrid civilization was born in Europe. It was poor, dark, brutish and nasty compared to the golden days of the Pax Romanica.

But at least the Roman peoples physically survived, and eventually developed a new civilization which was the most advance the world has ever seen. If Diocletian, Julian and the good old Romans had succeeded in crushing Christianity, pagan Romans would have probably continued in their hedonist ways, choosing drink and fun over reproducing; eventually the Huns would have come and destroyed the whole Empire, reducing half the land to pasture and physically replacing the Roman people. Even if by some miracle, the Roman empire had succeeded in integrating the Germans and the Huns into Romanitas, and they all started killing their infants while they devoted themselves to sodomy and gladiatorial matches; in a couple of decades some other northern tribe would have raced to the border and kill them all. It happened in China all the time.

You have probably guessed where I'm going. I won't repeat myself[106]. Europe now is in decline and all Europeans of good faith are trying to find a solution. We are being invaded by Islam, and nobody likes it. But the problem we have is not Islam. Is not Islamism. As bad as it is; which is horrible indeed. But ideas come and go. What doesn't come and go is the people. The gene pool. The problem we have is not Islam, it's foreigners. Arabs, South Asians, Africans, etc.. Most happen to be Muslim, many are not. The problem is not their ideas, as bad as they are. The problem is HBD. They're dumb. They're impulsive. They have different genes, going back tens of thousands of years.

Even if we could fix their culture, their family structure, the clannishness; which we can't. It still wouldn't matter. You could convert them all to Lefebvrism tomorrow and they would still destroy European civilization, and physically replace European people, who are busy watching football, binge drinking and wasting their youth studying socialist history.

But you can't say that. One can't object to the immigration of foreigners into Europe and North America on genetic grounds. I can't object to Arabs being dumb; because

---

[106] https://spandrell.com/2016/02/04/the-easy-way-out/

there's plenty of Europeans who are just as dumb, and they don't appreciate that we discuss population policy in terms of intelligence or other personality traits. Any rational, utilitarian discussion of population policy is a complete dead end because there is no workable Schelling point for proposing eugenics in a democratic society. It benefits no one. For one, we don't know that much about the genetics of behavior. Second, meritocracy is an excellent Schelling point. It's completely fallacious, but it works. The elite can justify their privilege because they have earned it, they have "merit", not just genetic luck. And the dumb can console themselves that there's nothing physically wrong with them; it's just tough luck, which could change any day. All human societies, every single one, believe that human behavior and performance depends on proper education. Of course they do.

And so we are left without sellable arguments against the invasion of Europe by fertile foreigners with a set of innate traits which make modern civilization impossible. We are left without arguments against Europe developing the demographic profile of Sudan, which implies the living standards of Sudan. So if we can't use this argument, what can we do? We can adopt a new religion. It doesn't matter which. As long as it ensures the physical reproduction of European peoples. As of now, Islam is a fix, if a bad fix. I hope we find a different one.

I have a reputation as a gloomy pessimist, but there's a different way of looking at this. Think of this post as a way of prodding you into action. We better come up with something damn fast, because there are only two alternatives. White Islam, or the physical disappearance of the European peoples.

Holiness Escalation

2016-05-19 // cucks, religion, signaling, bioleninism

Remember this? The lily-white couple who implanted 100% black embryo and gave birth to black triplets? They were so happy of themselves. So proud of it. The holiest people on earth. Surely nobody could be holier than us!

Oh boy.

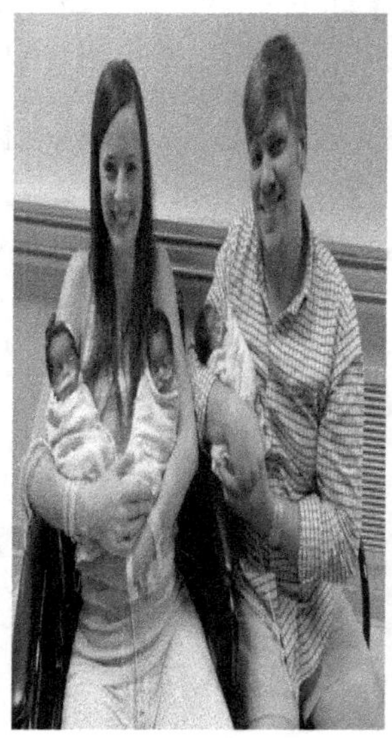

There's a Japanese saying, 上には上がある (ue ni wa ue ga aru). It means that as high as you get, there's always somewhere higher. As good as you think you are, there's always someone better. The world's a big place. And humans can be so annoying.

Another white American Evangelical couple are on the news. They have a black adopted child, but that's obviously old fashion, don't get points for that. So they had to do something. Now they have adopted a baby with no brain. That's right. No brain. And they made a video about it! Take *that*. The black embryo-couple only had some boring picture of themselves holding three babies. But we have a *video*. On Youtube.

https://www.youtube.com/watch?v=hN-1O_nVZzY

Besides, the black implanted babies have brains. How 2015 is that? You don't go to heaven by adopting babies with brains. That's just like, racist. Are you IQ-worshippers or something? Why do you need a brain for? We have faith. It takes real faith is to raise a brainless child. Don't need a brain if you have the Grace of God.

Here's counting until someone makes a video about adopting a black brainless kid. And after that, someone implanting an already defective embryo knowing that it would develop no brain. And eventually, the inevitable woman who actively provokes a disability in her baby, perhaps through heavy drinking.

In Brave New World, Huxley wrote of a future where different castes of human are deliberately manufactured by dumbing down developing fetuses with alcohol, so as to make them obedient workers and sustain the easy life of the alphas. We still don't have artificial wombs, but with a little bit of luck we might be able to outsource the problem to actual people! Now that's a Brave New World.

Seriously now, I shouldn't be snarking at some of the few white people who actually bother making white babies. And they didn't actually go seek a completely unviable baby, they were told at the last moment, and given their social standing they couldn't just renege on the deal. I think making a schmaltzy video signaling the joys of brainlessness is pretty fucked up, but perhaps it was some overzealous women at church that came up with the idea and talked them into it, and again they couldn't just refuse. The guy has that look in his face, the look of a man who is constantly out-talked by his wife and the old hags at church and is actually pretty pissed about it, but what can you do.

Still, the whole thing is a fairly good reflection of the twisted values of our society. File this under "we might not like the new era of religion".

Between a rock and a hard place

2016-05-20 // ethnicity, leftism, Top Post, hbd

This is on the news:

Who's this bitch? Nobody knew until today. Before the Internet nobody would have ever known and nobody would have bothered to check. But now we have Wikipedia, which knows everything. And apparently this bitch is Yuri Kochiyama, a Japanese-American psycho-bitch whose father was killed by the FBI after interrogating him about Pearl Harbor. As the good daughter of a samurai, she swore vengeance against the United States.

She is notable as one of the few prominent non-black Black Nationalists. Influenced by Marxism[https://en.wikipedia.org/wiki/Marxism "Marxism"], Maoism[https://en.wikipedia.org/wiki/Maoism "Maoism"], and the thoughts of Malcolm X[107], she was an advocate for many revolutionary movements, which extended to support or admiration for communist dictators and designated terrorist organizations.

In 1971, Kochiyama secretly converted to Sunni Islam, and began travelling to the Sankore mosque in Greenhaven prison[108], Stormville[109]"), New York, to study and worship with Imam Rasul Suleiman. (...) She also confessed her admiration towards Osama Bin Laden in 2003.

---

[107] https://en.wikipedia.org/wiki/Malcolm_X "Malcolm X"

That's a quite hardcore, thorough psychotic terrorist. Kudos to her. You don't mess with a Japanese commies. While Japanese people are extremely mild and polite, Japan also has its fair share of complete wackos, including Communist wackos. Japan had a Socialist Parties which openly went to North Korea to celebrate the birthdays of Kim Il Sung, hero of the proletariat. And Japan has a Communist Party today which is not half bad. Lives off basically off the support of the teachers union. Yes, the teachers union (one of them, anyway) in Japan is batshit crazy communist. The teachers tend to look exactly like this women in the doodle.

All of this is very fun and all, but why is this completely obscure batshit crazy psycho Japanese bitch in the frontpage of Google? That's a good question. My guess is that some Asian woman working at Google put her there. She had to put her there, no matter the cost.

I'm not Asian, and I'm not American. But I know many of Asian Americans, some of them good friends. Being Asian American (I'm talking of Americans of East Asian descent here, this may or may not apply to South Asians) is harsh. It's a pretty bad deal. You live in a country where bashing whitey is the national religion. Whitey is evil, whites are the cancer of the world. Every single bad thing that ever happened in history is whitey's fault. They teach that at school and Asians pay attention at school.

So if whitey is evil, then we Asians can shit on whitey then! Sounds fun. Let us then shit on whitey at every chance, while we do our thing, study a lot, make awesome grades, go to the best colleges and work at the best companies! We'll replace whitey at this rate and become the ruling class! After all we do everything right. We are good students, commit few crimes, work hard, and we haven't done all those bad things that whites did in the past. So we can just do our thing and let whitey pay for their crimes.

But no, sorry. It doesn't work like that. Yes, whitey is evil. And that's supposedly because whitey has done bad things. But you're not getting it. The way race works in USG was best described by Lawrence Auster:

1.	The worse a designated minority or non-Western group behave, the more they are praised and their sins covered up.

2.	The worse a designated minority or non-Western group behave, the more racist it becomes to speak the truth about their behavior.

---

[108] https://en.wikipedia.org/wiki/Green_Haven_Correctional_Facility "Green Haven Correctional Facility"

[109]   https://en.wikipedia.org/w/index.php?title=Stormville&action=edit&redlink=1 "Stormville (page does not exist

3. The worse a designated minority or non-Western group behave, the more their behavior must be blamed on white racism." (source[110])

4. The *worse* the behavior of minorities and non-Westerners, the *more* the behavior must be covered up or excused, and the *more racist* a white is for noticing it and thinking about it.

Bashing whitey is not the point. The point is to privilege minorities. But minorities are only to be privileged in so far as they don't behave like whitey. Which is the point, of course. If minorities behaved exactly like elite whites, had the same ability and disposition, they wouldn't need preferential treatment. They'd pass the exams and that's it. But the fact is that, on average, NAMs aren't capable of behaving like elite whites, and so they need preference. Giving them preference is the supreme, the most holy behavior in progressive society. And so it follows that the bigger the preference, the more holy the act, the more holy the people giving the preference.

And so it follows that the more backward, the more barbaric the person is the better. You only need to bend the rules a bit to give preference to a relatively well behaved Mexican, say. But to legal privileges to a 70 IQ serial felon Somali, that requires huge levels of preference, huge levels of holiness! And the worst, the more barbaric the recipient, the more likely white people will have contrary reactions. So you have more white people to chastize about their racism! Win-win-win. We need barbarians, lots of them, and the more barbaric the better. That's how the holiness economy works.

Where does this put Asian Americans? Asians are very well behaved. In all indexes of civilized behavior they score higher than whites. They're better students, harder workers, commit less crimes. Yes they tend to be quite boring, but that's the whole point. Latinos find whites boring. Blacks find latinos boring. Civilization is boring. Singapore is horribly boring. But it works. Unfortunately, Western culture today isn't interested in what works. It's interested in virtue signaling, praising bad people just to spite you. Getting ass-raped by a Somali and then publicly apologizing for his deportation.

The whole holiness economy works because elite whites don't really take NAMs seriously. They're just animals, things without agency that you can use to score holiness points against others. They don't hold them morally responsible for their actions. They're not their competition anyway. It's not like they're going to take their jobs or something. They commit crimes downtown, get lowly paid jobs that crowd out poorer whites, but who cares about them? The crime waves sometimes get a bit out of hand when people start virtue signaling against the police, which wasn't part of the plan (!!). But anyway, they're no threat.

---

[110] https://www.amnation.com/vfr/archives/008576.html

Asians though, those are a threat. A real damn threat. Those do take high paying jobs, jobs in the bureaucracy, jobs in law, in tech. All the good jobs that whites enjoy doing, Asians can do too, often better. That ain't funny. And so Asians are openly discriminated against. They get blocked out of elite colleges. They get mocked on TV, laughed about on daily life. Say something about blacks having big dicks, you get in trouble. Say something about Asians having small dicks, you get everyone laughing.

This may not be the case in the US, I don't know, but it's absolutely the case in Europe. Say something about Syrian refugees, nobody talks to you again. Say something about the Chinese taking over the retail business, and everybody gets riled up. It's an invasion! Those perfid Chinese, they have their wives working with them! Arabs do too, of course, and force the women to cover themselves and never go out by themselves. But you can't say that. Asians, though, are fair game. Something similar happens in the UK with Polish migrants. The UK has millions of Arabs, Africans and Pakitanis doing every kind of evil, of which the Rotherham rape racket is just a sliver. But you don't dare talk about them. Polish migrants, though, the horror! Too many immigrants!

Anyway, Asians in the West are between a rock and a hard place. They're supposed to be celebrated as being diverse and all that. But they're not. Nobody likes them. Europe is, well, in deep shit, likely to become a Muslim continent in a few decades. The Chinese have noticed, and they're talking within themselves. If Muslims win, the Chinese are in deep shit, they'll be targets of Muslim thugs until they lose everything they have. If Europe reacts and a white nationalist movement wins, the Chinese are in deep shit too, as Nazis don't like the Chinese a little bit either.

The same things applies to the US. The Chinese are freaking out about Trump. They know the US is in real danger of declining into the Third World. And they don't like that a bit, the US is the most popular emigration destination for rich Chinese; they're really invested in the US remaining a nice place to live in. But it won't at present trends. So Trump rises, wakes up the white population of the US, and wins the presidency. What are the Chinese to do? They're now discussing that. A faction says that the Chinese should support Trump: Chinese interests are aligned with White interests. We all want fairness and order.

Others say that won't do. Trump doesn't like China. The Trump supporters don't like Asians, period. They're foreign, and they're competition! No way that a reinvigorated White people are going to help the Asians out. So what to do?

Double down on progressivism. Go batshit crazy Tumblr Commie Islamist. Whatever, just burn it. Pull a Kochiyama and claim the leadership of the antiwhitey coalition, at any price. If white nationalism won't be nice to Asians, the best strategy is to help destroy the whole racket and try to pick up some of the pieces.

That must be what the Googler who made that Doodle is thinking. It's a hard problem, indeed. I wish we could all get along; we have much in common, and much to learn from each other. But conflict happens. Perhaps the best bet is to move to Canada, where there's so many of them that they can actually end up dominating at some level.

The Bow of the King of Chu

2016-05-21 // china, history, signaling

Google openly praises leftist terrorist supporters, Obama forces schools across the US to allow transexuals to choose the toilets they use. The West is fucked up. Yes, I know. The mission of this blog has been to explain in plain language why the Left exists, why it's so crazy, and why it gets even crazier over time.

Part of that mission is to find similar instances of crazy political ideas in non-Western cultures. Sir John Glubb spent some time in the Arab world, and he seemed to have the same interests, so he produced a very interesting account[111] on political madness in the Abassid empire, which looked fairly similar to contemporary leftism. I live in East Asia, and so I write a lot about East Asian history. I may end up making some money by selling my readers a fancy book with some stories. In the meanwhile, let me share another interesting anecdote.

The most fertile era of Chinese intellectual culture coincided with what came to be called the Axial Age. In China is the era between 550 BC and 200 BC, more or less. That's the era of the Hundred Schools of thought. China was divided in many kingdoms, who each wanted a piece of each other. It was if anything more violent and chaotic that Classical Greece, which had similar dynamics; division, constant warfare, and amazing intellectual life.

---

[111] https://www.isegoria.net/2014/07/the-effects-of-intellectualism/

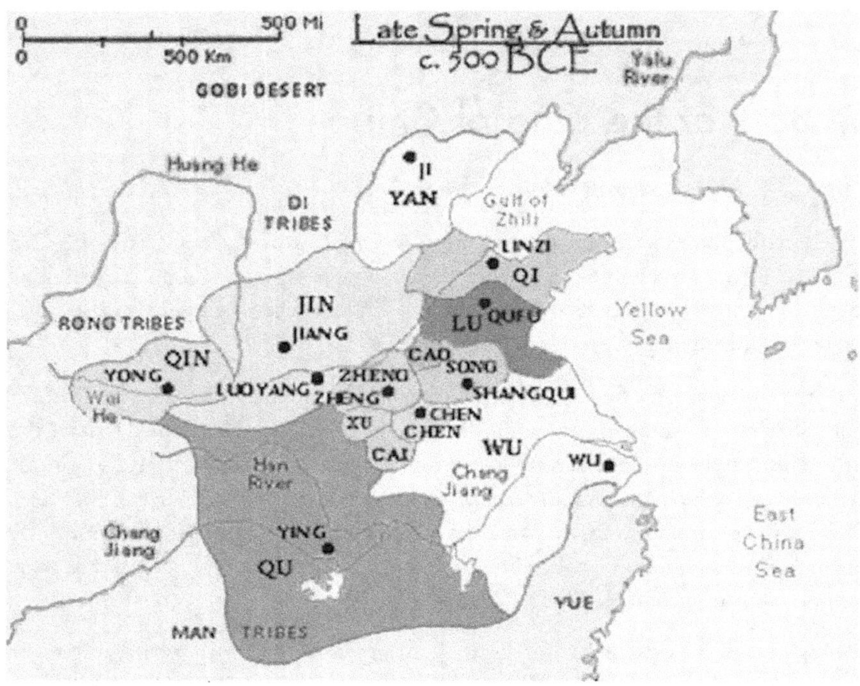

This is of course the era of Confucius, Laozi, Sunzi and all that. Some of you may have some general idea about classical Chinese thinkers, but it's also important to understand what was going on there. What kind of intellectual climate existed in that time. What happens when everyone is coming up with new ideas all the time? Think about it in contemporary terms. What happens when everybody and his grandma has his own ideas is... a whole lot of signaling spirals. See a small example. There was an old story about a king of Chu (Written wrongly as Qu in the above map, it's the big brown blob in the south).

聞楚王張繁弱之弓，載忘歸之矢，以射蛟兕於雲夢之圃，而喪其弓。左右請求之。王曰：'止。楚人遺弓，楚人得之，又何求乎？'

A King of Chu was out in the country on a hunting trip. He had a world famous bow, and the best arrows in the realm. So he was out there hunting dragons and rhinos (real story), when he dropped his bow. Lost it. The precious bow! His retinue was looking for it like crazy, but then the King told them to stop. "Stop looking for it. A Man of Chu lost his bow. A Man of Chu will find it. No need to search for it."

To European ears this sounds like a pretty awesome king. A great loving king who cares about his subjects. He lost his precious, world famous bow. But it doesn't matter, because he lost it in his territory. One of his subjects will find it, and use it for the good of his country. King or subject, we are all men of Chu, so who cares? What a great King. The stuff of legend.

The story soon became a cause of commentary across the other kingdoms in China. Every single one of the Hundred Schools had to publish their official stand on this story. What do you think of the King of Chu and his lost bow? It's kinda like modern journalism, where everybody has to rush to publish their stance on every item of the news. Psychologists call this "common knowledge", the social phenomenon where everybody is compelled to comment on something precisely because everybody else is doing so. This creates evolutionary pressures to reduce the total amount of information in society so that everything can be common knowledge and thus become efficient gossip, the fuel of human sociability. But I digress.

A modern nationalist would say that the King of Chu was an awesome king. But what did Confucius say about it?

'楚王仁義而未遂也。亦曰人亡弓，人得之而已，何必楚？'

'The King of Chu is a humane king, but he's still half-way. He could have said "a man lost his bow, a man will find it". Why specify "A man of Chu"?'

The King of Chu wasn't good enough in Confucius eyes because he dared put priority on his subjects, and not be equally nice to all humanity. Because Confucius, of course, was a humanitarian. A universalist. The King of Chu was a petty man who cared about his subjects, not about the entire humanity.

So basically, Confucius today would approve of Angela Merkel and Bryan Caplan. Thanks dude. No wonder he was never taken seriously by any of the dozens of kings of his time, and died a low-class civil servant. His universalism however was catnip for the nascent class of non-aristocratic bureaucrats, who developed it for centuries after his death. They loved this "we are above armies, borders, and that gruesome stuff. We care about righteousness and love, about what is right for all humanity". This in 300 BC. Do you see now why the First Emperor burnt their books and buried the scholars alive after he unified the Empire?

As a bonus, guess what the Daoists had to say about the King's bow.

老聃聞之曰：「去其『人』而可矣。」故老聃則至公矣。

"Why mention people at all?" That's right. A bow was lost. A bow was found. It doesn't need to be a man of Chu. It doesn't need to be a man at all. It can be a snake, or a frog. Or a tree. We are all part of nature, maaan. Want some more weed?

This is explicitly recorded as the Confucians being more 公, more public minded than the King, and the Daoists being more public minded than the Confucians. If this is not a virtue signaling spiral, I don't know what is. And again, this was going on 2200 years ago.

Names

2016-06-07 // language, nrx, china, philosophy

This has been going around.[112] Guess I should say something. I really don't know how to comment on that pile of nonsense. I might as well let the sages do it for me.

子路曰：「衛君待子而為政，子將奚先？」

子曰：「必也正名乎！」

子路曰：「有是哉，子之迂也！奚其正？」

子曰：「野哉，由也！君子於其所不知，蓋闕如也。名不正，則言不順；言不順，則事不成；事不成，則禮樂不興；禮樂不興，則刑罰不中；刑罰不中，則民無所錯手足。故君子名之必可言也，言之必可行也。

Confucius and his disciples were gathered at the master's house. One of his disciples, Zilu, asks the master.

Zilu: The Duke of Wei has asked for your opinion in how to rule his realm. He'll call you for an audience any time. What will be the first thing you tell him?

Confucius: Oh, that he must fix the names.

Zilu: What? That? Oh come on, master, what does that even mean. "Fix the names". I don't get it.

Confucius: Shut up, you stupid brat, and listen. It is like this. If the names aren't correct, what you speak becomes nonsense. If you speak nonsense, you can't get things done. If you don't get things done, you can't get the rituals to work. If the rituals don't work, the law isn't applied as it should. If the law isn't applied as it should, the people can't make a productive living. When a ruler names something, he must be able to make sense when talking about it. And when talking about it, he must be able to do what he means.

My translation. Philosophy of language was a hot thing in China in those days. The topic was "names", not "words", but of course it's the same thing. Words are just names we put to things. Names we put to things for a reason. That reason should be to make communication more smooth, to make society work better.

---

[112]https://marginalrevolution.com/marginalrevolution/2016/06/
what-is-neo-reaction.html

Alas it works the other way around too. If you mess with words, if you use them in ways which don't make communication more smooth. If you lie and manipulate and make up bullshit constantly; well society goes to hell. But making society go to hell through the purposefully wrong use of language is a common profession in our days. Certainly it's the bulk of the work done by most of the academic establishment.

Divide et Impera

2016-06-18 // islam, women, men, ethnicity

Half Sigma posted this video, and it made me think.

https://www.youtube.com/watch?v=8Mehk5eWcZA

Yes, damn Muslims. Damn them all. They're out to get us. Yes, they are indeed. But think about it for a second.

Obviously the Cathedral would want Muslims to convert to progressivism. Either outright, by becoming good atheist communists as good white people. Or either by watering down their religion, becoming the brown equivalent of white cuckservatives, who many are still Catholic or Protestant, but still accept every tenet of the Progressive faith with a lag of 2 or 3 years. You can be a Muslim as long as you accept gaymarriage, as a progressive activist boasted years ago[113] at Larry Auster's blog.

But look at those Muslim men in the video. Do they want to be progressive? Do they want to become good feminist men? Hell no. They aren't buying that. But why not? Being good Muslims in their banlieus isn't doing them any good. Our good progressive bureaucrat overlords apparently really don't get why these Muslims are so obstinate.

Surely part of it is that they're tribal, hostile, aggressive men, who like to fuck with Europeans and show their hostility because it's fun to fuck with foreigners. That's what men have done since time immemorial.

Surely part of is that they're Muslims, and Islam has its jihadi tradition. It is a noble thing to fight for Islam and kill infidels. You get status points just by claiming to want to kill infidels, even if you don't really have the guts to do so. There's the signaling spiral aspect to it.

But none of that would matter if there were good incentives for them to assimilate. If it was crystal clear that they would enjoy a better, richer, more fulfilling life by becoming good progressives, well by definition they would.

But if you're a young, tribal, hostile, Muslim young man, you see around you at your European neighbors. And do you want that? Do you want to marry a feminist that can divorce you at whim? Do you want to have women in the office who you aren't allowed to make fun of? Do you want to spend the rest of your life working some lame office job in which you can't promote your family and friends, send your kids to some lame

---

[113] https://www.amnation.com/vfr/archives/024197.html

progressive school where they will be taught to be disobedient and whom you will seldom ever see after they graduate? Hell no. Modern European lifestyle is a bad deal.

Muslims in Europe have no qualms about breaking Sharia when it's good for them. They have no qualms about drinking alcohol and harassing white women in the street. They'd very gladly forget about Islam if they got to drink fuck and be merry. But that's not what progressivism offers. What if offers is constant temptation of scantily clad women around the street, and yet at the same time the threat of complete destruction if you ever fall into that temptation and the woman happens not to like it.

What is now known as the "alt-right" is a composite of many different movements. I once wrote about a very diverse bunch of how Christian traditionalists, outright fascists, libertarians aware of human biodiversity, futurists and pick-up artists all started to become friends in the internet, and nobody really understood why. The only common is the realization that modernity is a bad deal for men. Progressive honchos have started to understand that, and now openly attack men as "brutes"[114], and blame Islamic terrorism on "toxic masculinity".

They have a point. The basic thing that keeps Muslims attached to Islam is their toxic masculinity. Because they realize that Islam is a better deal for men. It's not a good deal in general; Muslim countries are in general basket cases, and Islam itself is in some part to blame for it. But at any rate, for the average men there's absolute no good reason to abandon Islam, even nominally. Becoming progressive will only get you called a "brute" and openly discriminated against, likely killing your chances of reproducing and much social status. Of course second and third generation Muslims are more religious than their parents.

Michel Houellebecq noticed this and it led him to write Submission, where he trolled modern progressives by arguing that Islam is a good deal for people like him. I wrote something similar myself, if from another angle. But of course it likely won't happen, because Muslims don't want it to happen. Any political conflict has a racial angle; Muslims very much enjoy their hostility to white men. And the more hostile Muslims are to white men, the more white men fall into the trap of considering modern progressive culture as their turf. See how White nativists are using slogans about Islam being bad for women and gays. Or Gaving McInnes making out with Milo Yiannopoulos.[115] I don't know if it's NSFW but it's frankly revolting.

The more hostile Muslims are against Europeans, the more progressive can get away with, the farther left the leftist singularity can advance, as White men close ranks around the only thing they're allowed to close ranks around: progressive denigration of

---

[114] https://marginalrevolution.com/marginalrevolution/2016/05/what-in-the-hell-is-going-on.html

[115] https://www.youtube.com/watch?v=dbUHEpmX2lA

men. Which again drives Muslim men into further hostility, as they see what assimilation would require of them. This means the Left has absolutely no incentive to crack down on Islamic extremism. Until it gets out of hand. If it ever does.

The Spectre of Nationalism

2016-06-30 // Top Post, nationalism, history, theory

After some lazy Youtube pastes, I guess it's time to write something interesting about Brexit. You'll have to forgive my delay as I was too busy getting drunk in celebration. Or in despair. I don't know.

The ghastly forces of nationalism are sweeping now across Europe, liberals say. "Racism is out of the bottle", they say. The European project, the liberal world order is in danger, they say. Oh yes, yes it is. And they are right to be frightened.

Perhaps people out of Europe don't know, but in Europe, at least in academic circles, the EU is talked about as an almost godly institution. The most successful piece of institutional engineering in human history. A professor of mine had almost tears in his eyes when he talked how the EU "went against entropy", fighting all odds in integrating all European states into a superior, sacred institution of peace and prosperity. And then some Nigel Farage with goofy shoes comes and takes 60 million Britons out.

Naturally all the bien-pensant are horrified. Truly, really horrified, horrified as if a zombie just showed up at your window. The EU in Europe is worshipped in a way probably similar to how the early Catholic Church was worshipped in the early Middle Ages. It must have looked like a miracle that while myriad Goths and other barbarians completely destroyed the Western Roman Empire, the Church not only survived, but thrived with a very sophisticated organization across the whole of Europe, North Africa and the Middle East. That the Christian Church was able to conserve some modicum of civilization in those times was truly a miracle. It must have seemed that truly God was with them.

God thus appeared to be with the EU in the decades after WW2. 70 years of peace. Increasing economic and political integration. If you've read your European history it's certainly nothing short of a miracle. Of course the 70 years of peace might have something to do with the US Army garrisoning most of the continent, but you're not supposed to notice that much. The key to becoming a leading scholar in human society is selective noticing. It's more important to figure out what not to know, than what to know.

But anyway, indeed the EU was an impressive enterprise. Whatever model of government you have, everyone agrees that people in general don't like to give away power. Whether you think parliament rules, or the people rule, or the permanent bureaucracy rules; it doesn't matter who calls the shots, whoever does it is supposed to like doing so, and on principle wouldn't want to give it away. But in Europe they did. Little by little European nations were stripped of their power and they all celebrated it.

While the actual integration followed a very complex set of carrots and sticks; it helped that the EU project had a very good rationale. Europeans had been slaughtering each other for centuries. That had some good things; it gave incentives for research into bigger ships and stronger cannons. That research trickled down into the civilian economy and eventually gave us the industrial revolution. China invented gunpowder, but by the 1500s it had to rely in Portuguese cannons to defend itself, because in China research into cannonry just didn't pay. The huge Middle Kingdom didn't fight wars, only rebellions every many decades, and those didn't require cannons. China was into gun control, and they were pretty good at it. Europe wasn't into gun control. In Europe it was war all the time, for whatever reason. Eventually the slaughter got so out of hand during the 30 Years War that the Peace of Westphalia was signed.

Henceforth European states were to respect sovereignty. That is, you don't wage war because of what some other king has done in his country. You don't do that. Kings have the right to do whatever the hell they want inside their country. Even religion doesn't matter. The idea was good. But it still didn't work; European countries kept finding excuses to slaughter each other and went on developing more advanced weaponry all the same. Eventually Europe invented the mother of all weapons: Nationalism.

Academics recently like to talk about "institutions". Others like to talk about more abstract cultural traits. "Social technology" as some call it. If someone is still around in 200 years to write a World History of Technology, Nationalism will be there written as the foremost political technology ever invented by humankind. Nationalism destroyed the Ancien Regime. It revolutionized politics and war. It changed the world forever.

In the tribal, pre-state era, a "band of brothers" would ride to some foreign area, fight the local men, grab their gold and women and share it amongst them. If for some reason the bros didn't want to go back, they'd go to some area, kill the local men, and take their land (and gold and women, if any). This went on forever. Analysis of ancient DNA is just telling us the story of how many populations have been completely replaced repeatedly over time. When states formed, however, this dynamic changed. A king doesn't mind beating a neighbour and taking its gold, or perhaps the land. He's likely not that much in need of taking their women. But at any rate he has no interest in emptying the land. A king wants taxes; he doesn't care who pays them, whether his tribe or someone else's. In fact a king is, more likely than not, not of the same tribe as his soldiers. So it's not in his interest that the tribes that he rules over gain more land and thus more power. Eventually some tribal lord might rally his tribesmen against the king.

No, no. The way for a king to secure his place on the throne is to play divide and conquer on his own subjects. Ideally there will be no tribes whatsoever; the people will be separated into nuclear families, forbidden from worshipping ancestral gods. Their only social obligations will be with the state, i.e. the king. That was the gist of the Shang Yang reforms in 360 BC, what Solon did in Athens, what the Roman Senate did to its people, shuffling the tribes every few years. The Catholic Church did mostly the same to the Germanic kindreds in Western Europe. It was wildly successful, and produced what we understand as Civilization. Which is good.

So when a King has to fight a war, he pays for his soldiers, in hard cash. If he can't he doesn't go to war. No more bands of brothers, no more fighting for the tribe. No more exterminating neighbors. That's bad for business. Of course it still happened, if the foreigners were uncivilized themselves and one couldn't expect much tax from them short term. Still, the incentive was to take the land with the peasants untouched.

Nationalism was in essence a return to the emotional state of pre-state tribesmen. Soldiers weren't expected to fight for cash, or for traditional bonds of vassalage. Soldiers fought for their country, for the homeland. For the tribe. A pretty massive tribe, tens of millions strong. Pretty weird tribe if you ask me; but people ate it up. Nationalism was wildly popular. It of course didn't come out of a vacuum; the printing press, universal schooling and improved transportation did change cultural interaction so that people inside the same country ended up having the same degree of cultural uniformity as a 1,000 BC tribe.

But of course Nationalist War has the same incentives as Tribal War: kill off the men and take their land for good. We call that now *ethnic cleansing*. Nationalist people are committed to their nations. They won't pay tax to a foreigner; not as much as a countryman would. Remember French rule of the Ruhr? And besides, industrial economies make turnover much easier: you can ship millions of your own people to the vacated territory in months, and they'll start producing right away. So there's no downside to removing the foreigners.

Nationalist War was gruesome stuff. The Napoleonic Wars, the American Civil war, the Franco Prussian war, World War 1. Of course the scale of these wars weren't just due to nationalism, much of it was just superior technology; better weapons, better transportation. And bigger populations. World War 1 gave us machine guns, gas and air bombing, killing millions in months. After World War 1 there was an attempt to blame nationalism and stop it right there. But it didn't work. The opposite happened: Mussolini perfected Nationalism, and then Hitler took it to its logical conclusion. Total, industrial tribal war. With ethnic cleansing of enemies as its explicit mission.

We all know how that ended. The conclusion was that Nationalism was bad. And it wasn't an unreasonable conclusion. It makes a lot of sense. Nationalism had, if not caused, certainly aggravated World War 1. Why did all those millions of young men volunteer to be slaughtered by machine guns in Northern France? For the glory of their nations. Why did Germany wage war against the first, second and third most powerful nations on Earth at the same time? To gain lebensraum for the German nation. Why did Italy, of all people, dream of taking Dalmatia, Albania, and run a colonial empire in Africa? Certainly not for the juicy tax revenue that those territories would bring to the state! It was all because of a stupid nationalist signaling spiral where the most popular kids were those who came up with the wackiest plans for the glory of the nation.

And so it was deemed, again not unreasonably, that Nationalism was bad. After World War 1, when the same conclusion was reached, the popular idea among the elite was that we needed World Government. No small part of the impetus behind the global communist movement that consumed the elite of the Anglosphere was the idea that communism was a good path in order to achieve World Government: communism could out-compete nationalism for support of the working class masses. Read on that time, H.G. Wells, Keynes, all those were really into World Government.

Alas, again, Nationalism won that battle by morphing into its more evolved form, Fascism, that great innovation of Benito Mussolini. Mussolini was an old school socialist who after WW1 found out that the post-war evolution of socialism into a World Government cult wasn't going to fly. He had been in the war, he had seen the power of nationalism. So he invented nationalist socialism, and man, he hit the jackpot. Fascism swept over most of Europe in no time.

The elite, i.e. Western governments and their financial elites kept holding their World Government dream, though. Even F.D. Roosevelt, who borrowed a trick or two from the fascists, appeared to have been a very devout member of the World Government cult. After WW2, however, the Anglo-Soviet split made all dreams of World Government impossible. I guess we have Stalin to thank for that.

The dreams of World Government shattered, the only feasible alternative was to do try a local implementation in the US-occupied part of Europe. And so we got the EU. European nations were to disappear and integrat into something bigger, so they would stop waging war against each other. Again this was a good idea. War is bad. World War 2 was horrible. But dismantling the nations is easier said than done. By any account, in pure Marxist theory, the Soviet Union should have dismantled all its constituent "nations" and run a purely communist paradise of the workers. And yet what we got was Lenin's "theory of nationalities" and a hodgepodge of national republics. In fact some backward tribes which could have been easily dissolved had instead Soviet anthropologists and linguists sent to standardize their languages and document their culture. Even abroad, the Soviets didn't dismantle East European nations, they just occupied them, defanged them, but kept the nations neat and separate.

The thing is, European integration is a very dangerous idea; more dangerous than the original founders perhaps ever thought. In theory the EU was supposed to abolish all legal borders, dissolve national governments and rule the whole continent from a unified government. Ideally all Europeans would speak one language and follow one set of rules. You certainly can't have a common market if the local bureaucracies can't communicate with the center, and workers aren't willing to move to different regions because of language barriers.

But imagine that: a truly unified Europe. I used to like the idea, and that should tell how utterly dangerous it is. For better or worse, the apparatus of modern nations was built by nationalism. It presupposes nationalism. Modern states have unified laws, unified school systems, unified media industries. Modern states, by purpose or by accident, unify the culture of their subjects. Modern states create nations. A unified Europe would create a unified European nation. And what would that European nation be about? What do Europeans have in common? Their biological heritage and their history. That is, the white race and Christianity.

Wow wow, wait a second. The mere thought of a unified Europe of 800 million people, organized around its common bonds of Race and Christianity is... dangerous. It's dangerous to particular peoples who I will not name to avoid my comments section filling with retards. And it's dangerous to the whole world, really. The last time Europeans were proud of their race and religion they went on a rampage across the whole world, where not a square mile of territory was left undisturbed. You could say European colonization was good for them; that we brought them civilization. Well, the locals are apt to disagree, and even if it were true, the locals today would rather not have the process repeat itself again. Susan Sontag said the white race is the cancer of human history. A cancer it's not, the other races are still around. But the white race no doubt was a straight, strong, painful punch in the face for other countries.

And so European integration can't happen. It can't work, because we don't allow Europeans to bond around the only thing they have in common. Instead we feed them a diet of bullshit about how Europeans are bounded by European values of tolerance and human rights. Which doesn't make any sense. Europeans went along for thousands of years without any appreciation for tolerance and rights for women and minorities. Our very parents weren't into all this tolerance and rights stuff. Were they bad people?

Any ideology is going to produce winners and losers; if only to the extent that an individual's nature fits the ideology better or worse. If you're into the quiet contemplation, any society that gives high status to monks is going to be a good deal for you. If you're into booze, feasting, fucking and fighting; you're gonna become very fond of Viking society. If you're into tea, poetry, war and can't stand women, you're probably going to enjoy Islam. Ideally any ideology is going to evolve into a set of memes that give status to productive and upright people who help in the upkeep of civilization, and give low status to harmful people, but not so low they rise in violence.

Europeans today are supposed to base their identity on their tolerance and support of human rights, i.e. their obedience to the latest academic fad. Who wins from this arrangement? People who are by nature into tolerance and obedience to the latest academic fads. Those get to be elite. If you're not into tolerance and have no inclination to support the latest academic fad no matter how absurd; and you can't fake it well enough, well you're not going to be elite. Who's going to be elite? Women. Phonies. Clintons. Those are doing ok.

But what about men? Normal, average men, who like booze, like fighting, like competition, have no appetite for intellectual bullshit and little ability to fake it? Well modern Europe doesn't like you. No status for you. And no status doesn't mean what it used to be. In the old days you could be a brute, despised by the Church and by polite society. But you had your society, you could be a brute peasant with a peasant job and a peasant wife and kids. Not anymore. We don't have classes now. Peasant women go to the city to try to get into polite society. There are no peasant jobs anymore; and to the extent that they are, they are done by actual Asian peasants in their homelands or in yours.

For the average men it is beyond obvious that Nationalism was a better state of affairs. Yes, you were likely to be sent to Northern France and be killed because your stupid generals had decided you were to be sent as cannon fodder until the enemy machine gun run out of ammo. Which it never did. But still, you had status. You had dignity. You had a society which told you you were awesome; a society where your natural inclination for typical manly stuff: loyalty, bravado, physical exertion, absurd penchant to fight because of stupid differences, were deemed to be noble and sacred virtues.

But not now. A woman uses her natural inclination for nagging her husband to no end; and she's a great woman exercising her rights and using her intellect. A phony uses his natural inclination to make up some arcane bullshit about human rights; and he's a great intellectual. A normal person uses his powers of reason to notice something obvious about human nature; and he's a heartless bigot.

Nationalism evolved as an ideology in the era of mass politics. In those days, power was decided by who could assemble the biggest mob, the biggest army, the biggest electoral coalition. Nationalism was organic marketing. It was a very good sell. Progressivism isn't a good sell. It was a relatively good sell when World War 2 had killed so many millions that Nationalism didn't sound such a good idea; and when the economy was growing so much that a life of endless hedonism and pandering to every whim sounded completely feasible. People don't notice their social status while life is getting better.

But life isn't getting better any longer. And nobody remembers World War 2. Progressive society is rigged against native men; is it any surprise that they're turning back to Nationalism? Progressives believed their own lies. They were too slow. The old European nations had to be destroyed before this happened. But they couldn't pull it off. The EU as this sacred, precious project of order created out of entropy; but the old national states had their own bureaucratic elites, and surprise surprise, they haven't really surrendered that much power. Most importantly they haven't surrendered their money. To this day the EU budget is 1% of Europe's GDP. Yes, EU nations were trolled into joining their currencies into the Euro; but they've been haggling between each other ever since about every single issue of economic policy.

The only way to get the Euro to work was for Germany to pay everyone off; make the local bureaucracies of every single country of Europe be better off by taking German's money that by holding on to their national turf. Pull a Song Dynasty[116]. But stingy Germany wouldn't do it. Germany couldn't do it. The German electorate just didn't want to. And why would they? Germany is perhaps the most anti-nationalist nation in Europe. Kids are taught untold times how evil the German nation has been and how nationalism is the worst thing ever. Holding the national flag is a semi-criminal act.

And for good reason! World War 1 was stupid and it wrecked the whole continent for good. World War 2 was even stupider and it basically wrecked Germany forever. Nationalist spirals are a bad idea and Germany shows it better than anyone else. But you can't dissolve a nation by telling her so. You have to actually dissolve the nation. And the EU didn't do that. Germany is still Germany. It has 80 million Germans who speak German and have a common culture. You can tell them that their culture is tolerance and human rights; but it's not; their culture is the German language and the myriad little German habits that they have in common. And to destroy that you have to stop teaching the German language and physically dissolve the people among others. Like Stalin did when he sent the Koreans and the Chechens to Kazakhstan. Heck, even that didn't work, as his successors reversed the policy.

Bureaucratic inertia has allowed the European nations to subsist way beyond the expiration date of Progressivism. Progressivism only works when the going is good. Now it isn't that good anymore, and people can fall back into their good old Nationalism. Yes, Progressives have the state apparatus. They have modern technology that makes preventing and crushing riots much easier than before. They have their massive unproductive schooling apparatus that keeps young people loyal to

---

[116] https://spandrell.com/2016/04/19/the-distribution-of-power/

Progressivism until well in their mid 20s. And they have tens of millions of foreign barbarians in European soil paid to defend the state.

But as I pointed out[117], those foreign barbarians are a double-edged sword. Yes, they will fight Nationalism. They have nothing to gain from a nativist restoration. But Progressivism isn't being that good for them either. They came here too late. The economy isn't good anymore; so all progressivism has to offer them is taking their women and children out of their authority. Given that offer they might as well fall back into their tradition, i.e. Islam. Which is backward, not very fun, and likely to get them killed if they take it seriously; but it at least gives them status as men.

Neoreaction, the alt-right, the manosphere, religious traditionalism; all we have in common is the realization that contemporary society is rigged against the average man; and if men withdraw from society there is no way to maintain civilization. Which is why civilized people do not have children. Why the economy is declining. And why old ideologies are rising back all across the world. China just sent a warship into Japanese waters. Muslims are fighting their enemies across the world. England just voted to leave the European Union. Donald Trump might become the President of the United States.

I'm not into Nationalism myself. I know the history and it's all pretty stupid. I assume that the smarter Muslims aren't into Islam that much either. But we're not given the choice of a perfect thing. Politics is the art of the possible. And all the possible alternatives aren't looking very good these days. Interesting times ahead.

---

[117] https://spandrell.com/2016/06/18/divide-et-impera/

Brazilification

2016-07-05 // blackpill

Given present demographic trends, that is immigration and the birth rates of different ethnic groups, the data clearly points towards what I call Brazilification, i.e. Western countries eventually getting the demographics of Brazil.

Now, Brazil as a country has a lot going for it; that with nice beaches and hot girls. But its demographics and its politics aren't precisely one of its strengths. Nor its murder and mugging rate. For some reason Rio de Janeiro was chosen to host the 2016 Olympics, and man, the thing is not looking good.

I had thought that the Brazil government wasn't that stupid, and that the armed forces, if only them alone, had to enjoy high status and good pay. But no, apparently the Brazil government really is that stupid. How does that look for Brazilification of the Western world?

https://twitter.com/rcallimachi/status/750129507420495872

Who knows, who knows. The French are quite fond of striking too! Right now I guess this troops are well paid; but hungry and unpaid French troops holding machine guns in central Paris; well that would be something. France doesn't have a tradition of military coups; not since the great man. But one's gotta eat.

Brexit has made a lot of people write about how it symbolized the end of an era of ever greater integration and trade globalization. Now the trend is broken. The Olympic games are also a very powerful symbol of globalization, and the recent games have shown also signs of breakdown; billions stolen by corruption rackets; countries left with tons of debt and useless buildings left to decay. It won't be long until some Olympic Games really bomb it, and the whole thing is abolished for good. Now that would be a fine symbol of the end of an era.

Toxic Arab Masculinity

2016-07-16 // islam, men, women

I was mildly surprised to see that I was getting hits from the Inthenews subreddit.[118] Apparently a very nice reader posted a link to my recent post[119] on how Islam in the West creates perverse incentives for the Establishment to double down on feminism and other progressive articles of faith, knowing that the native white population will back them as a convenient Schelling point against the tribal enemy, Islam. He says my post predicted exactly the sort of psycho who killed 84 people in Nice in July 15th, and I must say that I did.

Let's take a look at the murderer, Mohamed Lahouaiej Bouhlel. Apparently he drunk alcohol like a sponge, smoked pot, went to nightclubs, ate pork, and didn't give a shit about Ramadan. He was a classic low IQ hoodlum who was more than happy to enjoy the hedonism that French culture offers to all men. His close acquaintances called him a "piece of shit". And yeah, that's a piece of shit if I ever saw one. And I've seen a lot.

As tends to happen with low IQ hoodlums he did have some luck with the ladies, and was married. With three daughters. I expect having three daughters, no sons, didn't exactly please him. Having a wife also can't have been very fun, given his penchant for booze and nightclubs. So again, as tends to happen with low IQ hoodlums, he often beat his wife. He also couldn't hold a job, so his wife recently divorced him.

So now you have this low IQ hedonistic hoodlum who finds himself divorced by his wife, with three daughters, who will take a large part of whatever meager income he can make as a truck driver or whatever job a low IQ hoodlum is capable of doing. Which isn't a lot. If you're into having fun, and Mr. Lahouaiej (French spelling really is retarded) seems to be very much into having fun, seeing yourself in debt bondage for at least two decades to a family which you can't even enjoy; well that sucks. That sucks very much. So he went postal.

Is Islam to blame? Well, yeah. The guy did shout Allahu Akbar while running over and shooting 84 people in Nice. The equivalent low IQ hoodlum, were he a white Frenchmen, which does happen, would have probably just shot himself, in extreme cases maybe shoot his wife and then himself. Were he a Christian he most certainly wouldn't go kill innocent people shouting Christ is Great, or Richard Dawkins is my Hero, if he were an atheist.

---

[118] `https://www.reddit.com/r/inthenews`

[119] `https://spandrell.com/2016/06/18/divide-et-impera/`

But low IQ hoodlums who happen to be Muslim have a different way out. They can get to the mosque, meet some of their buddies, get an intensive jihad session by some 105 IQ Arab nerd, and suddenly realize that indeed his life sucks, that he's fucked for life, that it's all the fault of those damn infidels, and that Allah is merciful and provides him a way to die like a hero. Just get a weapon of some sort and kill a big bunch of people. Allahu Akbar.

So yeah, Islam is to blame. Islam is a necessary condition. Is it a sufficient condition, though? Certainly not. You need to be a low-life good for nothing kind of asshole to get yourself in that sort of situation in the first place. The trick is that, as it happens, Muslims tend to come from low IQ, high-impulsiveness populations who are way more likely than native Europeans to become a low IQ hoodlum. And modern European culture produces huge amounts of low IQ hoodlums. It provides them easy sex, cheap booze, drugs of all sorts, and an individualistic and hedonistic culture that pretty much *dares* you to not be a hedonistic fuck. Especially France, if I may say so.

So yes, it's complicated. But not that complicated. At any rate having Muslims around in our culture just makes it inevitable for these things to happen. And blaming Islam is a perfectly reasonable conclusion.

Shifting Right

2016-08-04 // japan, cucks, power

Just in case anybody was concerned, no, I wasn't killed at any of the recent Islamic murders in Europe in the last few weeks. And I really didn't have much to say about it. My last post[120] stood as an almost miraculous oracle of why Islamic murders happen, and why they will continue to do so. And voila, they continued to do so. And of course, as I said, European governments did nothing of importance to address the problem. Because they can't.

But now some days have gone on without further incidents, so it's time to change topics. I could write about Japan, which has gone through two very important elections, elections for the Senate in July 10th, and elections for the governorship of Tokyo in July 31st. The Senate elections gave a large 2/3 majority to the right, which in Japan it's defined as nationalists who want to change the constitution, apparently to, among other changes, delete the clause that "The Emperor has the responsibility to uphold the constitution". So they want nominally absolute monarchy. Nominally, of course, Japan's emperors haven't counted for shit for thousands of years[121], and the next emperor in line is known to be a wimpy liberal whose wife spends more time shopping in Paris than attending Shinto rituals.

Some say that Japan will go bankrupt before any constitutional change can be decided on; but financial crises do not stop political change: they accelerate it. Usually in a bad way. As things stand, Japan is on course to enter a rightist singularity[122] of ever accelerating nationalist madness. And lack of money will only fuel the fire. Interesting times.

The Tokyo election was somewhat different: the incumbent, recently elected (2 years on the job) governor of Tokyo, Masuzoe, was busted because of misuse of government funds. The dude was spending big money travelling first class, spending weeks on a time on pointless foreign trips. But that's a long standing Tokyo tradition, his predecessor was even worse than him. The guy was completely busted by the media, and he didn't get it. What have I done wrong? The Tokyo bureaucracy obviously loved the guy, who was never around, so they had free hands to do what they pleased; another long standing Japanese political tradition.

---

[120] https://spandrell.com/2016/07/16/toxic-arab-masculinity/

[121] https://spandrell.com/2013/10/18/monarchy/

[122] https://spandrell.com/2013/05/25/the-rightist-singularity/

The guy did get it coming in many ways. He was a textbook sociopath, narcissistic fuck who has published dozens of inane books about how awesome he is; multiply divorced, is known to have multiple mistresses, all of them with his children, whom he refuses to support. A nasty piece of work he was. But that isn't immediately disqualifying for office; and in any case everybody knew that before the election, and he got the job anyway. So there's no good theory about why suddenly the establishment went against him. As I am a great believer that the face is the mirror of the soul, please take a look at the guy.

The only plausible reason I can think of is that he was in cahoots with the Koreans. Tokyo has a famous issue with a lack of daycare centers; and the guy canceled a daycare center building in order to sell the land for cheap for the construction of a Korean school. Koreans don't have children; nobody has in Tokyo, there's no good rationale for a second Korean school. Obviously this was about money and patronage; first thing the guy did in office was go on a trip to Seoul and bend his back to the Korean president. And that looks bad. Baaad. Bad! in Japan. So powerful forces started to conspire against him; his arrogance made him look bad in the media, who realized that shitting on the guy got them better ratings; one thing led to another, and the guy got busted. Oh well.

So they held new elections a week ago. And it got interesting because the ever-ruling party, the LDP, i.e. the right, the party of Abe, couldn't agree on a candidate, and thus split. The LDP is the ever ruling party of Japan, running the place almost uninterruptedly since 1945. But like I always say about monarchy, the nominal power structure doesn't mean anything. If there's many parties competing for power, people will organize themselves around that. If there's a single party running the place, people will form factions and bicker inside the single party. The amusing thing about the

Japanese LDP is that the faction system is formalized: there are nominal factions, which call themselves "factions", which openly meet in congress centers and conspire for their benefit in front of everyone. It's pretty funny.

The divide lines among the LDP are pretty obvious; especially so in regional centers such as the Tokyo council. Basically it seems that the Tokyo legislature is run by this big old corrupt ogre, which runs a huge pork machine which basically controls the whole of Tokyo. Again tell me if he just doesn't look like a big old corrupt ogre.

Well this guy has been running Tokyo for a decade or so, and for this new election he of course wanted to run his own candidate, somebody who was willing to allow him to run his pork machine for a small commission. And so he got some boring old ex-minister, Masuda. What's funny is that this Masuda guy had been Minister of the Interior years ago; and one of the things he did was send huge amounts of money out of Tokyo out into the provinces, in order to help the struggling countryside. "How can you put this guy to run Tokyo? He's the enemy!"

But that was missing the point. The guy as Minister of the Interior did what the Minister of the Interior bureaucrats wanted him to do: get them bigger budgets. And as Governor of Tokyo he presumably would do what the big old corrupt ogre wanted him to do: get him bigger budgets, and help him come up with new bullshit projects with the excuse of the 2020 Olympics, which have already become an obscene money drain.

But surprise, surprise, some other faction of the LDP decided that his couldn't go on. While this big old corrupt ogres go on wasting money on pork, at this rate even Tokyo is going to go bankrupt. No, we need Reform™. We need to cut on bureaucratic waste and entrenched interests. And so this lady, also from the LDP, declared her candidacy. Ms. Koike.

Big old corrupt ogre went batshit crazy. He threatened with firing her from the party, announced that she would get no electoral support. And he sent a memo to all Tokyo party members, saying that if any party member, including their families, supported Ms. Koike, they would be immediately fired. Including family members! Yes, Japan is going back to the middle ages.

The first news reports were that Ms. Koike had effectively committed suicide; she had no party machine, no voter pool, no support from the party. She would lose badly, get expelled from the party, and die the lonely death of a traitor spinster. And those news got the left excited. Because yes, I haven't mentioned it, but Japan does have a left. And as the right is getting righter, the left is getting lefter.

Japan used to have a Soviet-aligned Socialist Party during the Cold War; whose party leaders went to North Korea to celebrate the birthdays of Kim Il Sung and stuff like that. That's besides the official Communist Party, which is still around. The Socialist Party never managed to win an election, and after the Cold War it slowly disintegrated. For a while the remnants formed the Democratic Party, which was supposed to be a modern, Blair-Clinton kind of thing. They never managed to amount to much, but they did win the 2009 election, just in time to preside over the big 2011 Tsunami.

Besides the Tsunami they botched everything they did; basically they were dumb, and the bureaucracy sabotaged everything they wanted. So since 2012 the Democratic Party has been dead, completely suppressed by the amazing Abe charisma.

The solution the Democratic Party chose since 2015 was to... ally with the Communist Party. Yep. I've no idea who convinced whom but this madness actually happened, with predictable results. The Democratic Party went full retard on leftist insanity, arguing for increased immigration, voting rights for foreigners, new feminist laws, gaymarriage, abolishing nuclear power, that sort of stuff. Stuff which is not exactly popular right now because Japan is undergoing a rightist singularity as we speak. But the Left is the Left is the Left, and their solution is always to move lefter. So they made an alliance with the Communist Party, and given that the right had split before the Tokyo elections, they thought they stood a chance. So they selected as a candidate this guy, Mr. Torigoe.

Now you can see from his hairstyle, that this guy is a complete douche. He's also a leftist douche. 75 years old, he's a remnant of the old Soviet aligned left, those who were students in the 1960s. He made his living as a leftist journalist, so he had plenty of brand recognition. But the guy also happens to have multiple cancers, and show clear signs of dementia. He's 76 after old. Also, being a leftist douche, he was found to have harassed dozens of young women. Kinda like Sartre and all other famous leftists have always done. I mean, what's the point of being a leftist celebrity if you can't get young pussy through it? That's the actual motivation, ideology is the means to an end.

Anyway, the Democratic and Communist parties thought they could pull a Tokyo governorship with this guy, but the election was so completely inept that they botched it spectacularly. And I mean spectacularly. Mr. Leftist Douche came in third place. The puppet of the Tokyo pork machine came second. And... oh yeah, Ms. Koike the outsider won the election. Reform won the day.

It's unlikely she will be allowed to get away with much; the governor doesn't have that much power. But I don't know; perhaps there are sectors of the Tokyo bureaucracy that she can use for her ends. Bureaucrats play divide and conquer with politicians; a skilled politician has to play divide and conquer with his bureaucrats. Structurally speaking bureaucrats are usually better able to run tight loyal ships to avoid that kind of attacks, while politicians are more vulnerable to it. But Ms. Koike has a reputation for being tough as nails. And yes, she is also hard-right. "Let's change the constitution and have an army"-right.

That shouldn't matter much, but as thing stand today, being a "let's have an army" politician is a fairly good way of gaining support from a wide set of people. There's lots of conspiracies about "secret sects" like Nihon Kaigi that are conspiring to get Japan back into the Middle Ages, which is driving the US foreign policy[123] circles crazy right now; and while it can't get that simple; the fact is that being on the right in Japan pays. So people move to the right. It doesn't pay to go crazy Nazi; there's plenty of those, and they are very unpopular. But a smart degree of rightist signaling gets you a long way. And that's not thanks to media support. The mainstream media is, generally, batshit leftist, and they overwhelmingly supported the rapist leftist douche. What is rightist though, is the internet, and some more fringe sectors of the media, such as news weeklies and the like.

The funny thing is that Schelling points right now, while still functioning as Schelling points, are all slowly shifting in different directions. And that is a worldwide trend. Interesting times.

---

[123] https://www.nationalreview.com/article/437950/japans-new-fascism

Social Constructs

2016-08-06 // theory, language, philosophy

Razib Khan recently wrote a good post[124] about how retarded the whole tirade on "social constructs" can be. Gender is a social construct! Sports should be integrated! Come on. As a scientist it's natural he gets pissed at the whole thing.

I commented there a while ago about how, you know, leftists are actually right. Race is a social construct. Gender is a social construct. They got that exactly right. It's a rather profound point, and I've been thinking on exposing my argument a bit better. It's a linguistic argument, but that's what I do.

Let's put it more precisely. Race is, obviously, not a social construct. But "race" is a social construct. As "gender" is a social construct. The same way "car", or "moon", or "democratic republic" is a social construct. Words are social constructs. That's how language works. Word meanings are social conventions. There's nothing else to it. If you raise a child in a community where the word "car" is used to refer to a certain subset of vehicles, then that's what a "car" is. If you raise a child in a community where "fascists" is used to mean a certain subset of low-status people, that's "fascists" are.

Of course there's a lot of details about how children adopt the usage of words. Sure, language, as so much else, is a social convention. Most human behavior, indeed the behavior of most social animals is conventional. People from different places walk in different ways. Samurais pre-1860s famously had to be trained by French officers to run properly, as samurai practice was to lower your back and run in small steps like a 6 year old kid after shoplifting. Language works the same way. A sensitive person can tell accents and little quirks of speech at the village, even the family level.

But why would people adopt those conventions? That's the real question. Why do people in villages adopt every tiny little intonation quirk? Part of it is just human instinct: people are mimetic creatures, as the late René Girard liked to say. But instinct evolved for a reason. To put it simple, adopting conventions is useful. It helps you get by. It gets you more status than you would get by not adopting the convention. Humans adopt behavior which is useful to them. Humans are pragmatic.

And so language use depends on its pragmatic nature. Race is, certainly, not a clear cut category. Humans can mix. There are continuums of genetic clusters. But humans, at least since the modern era, have classified humans in different races; often according to

---

[124]   https://www.unz.com/gnxp/the-lack-of-progress-in-science-sex-differences/

very crude markers such as skin color. Andaman Islanders aren't at all African; no genetic test will cluster them with Nigerians. But if you found one at your local grocery store you would most likely call him black. Why? Because it's useful. If Andaman Islanders were all incredible geniuses who gave you 10 bucks every time you met them, soon enough people would find a way of telling them apart from other dark skinned, kinda African-looking people who don't give 10 dollar bills at first sight. But in real life, dark skinned, kinda African-looking people tend to behave in similar ways; so there's no particular necessity to notice their little differences and tell them apart. Nigerians, Jamaicans, Kenyans and Somalis are interchangeable for most purposes. The same way people don't care to tell apart Irish from Italians from Swedes in America. They do in Europe! Because it's useful to do so. Not in the US: so they're all white.

Wittgenstein made himself famous by basically destroying the whole academy of philosophy by pointing out the, on hindsight, obvious point that Philosophy is based in a misunderstanding of how language works. How people use language in daily life. Words don't have definitions, they don't have essences. Writing books about single words is completely pointless. Words are things we use in particular contexts; the use changes all the time. It's all convention, and conventions are dynamic, pragmatic affairs.

Everything is a social construct; because society is very important for human life. Many people, in particular the sort of person who would read this blog, often can't understand why most people believe common progressive ideas. Surely humans aren't all equal! Surely open borders doesn't make sense! Surely spending millions on transexual toilet rights is pointless! Why does anyone take all this seriously? Well, because it's useful. Because not doing so brings very concrete social consequences.

If you put your finger in a fire, it burns. It hurts a lot. If somebody comes later and tells that you that fire doesn't burn, to put your finger in the fire; you are likely to protest. Of course it burns. It hurts like crazy. But most things in life aren't like that. Nobody has ever got burnt due to global warming. Most ideas don't have immediate consequences. If somebody tells you that "Muslims belong in Germany", unless you have been stabbed by a Muslim recently, the proposition doesn't have real consequences for you. It's just a set of words. Your reaction to that proposition doesn't depend on your memory of getting your finger burnt. The only real consequences to that conversation is the opinion that your peers will have about you. So if your memory about talking on Muslims belonging in Germany is that any contrary opinion gets your peers mad, and results in you having lower status; well your reaction will be "sure, Muslims belong in Germany. Merkel is awesome".

The vast majority of ideas don't have physical consequences; all they have is social consequences. They are status markers. Whether Muslims belong in Germany or not won't get your finger burnt immediately. It may over the long term, but human brains don't work like that. You learn behaviors to avoid danger and earn pleasure. And social disapproval by uttering non-progressive opinions are as harsh and immediate as a burnt finger in a fire.

So the reaction of most people to any abstract proposition like that will rely on their calculation of the social consequences of their particular reaction to that proposition. As it happens, being a good progressive gets you status and approval; not being a good progressive gets you low status and disapproval. So of course most people will do whatever gets them status and approval. The few contrarians like us who disagree, do so because of different experiences, because they don't see the point in earning that sort of status, or, in many cases, because they are like the philosophers who Wittgenstein made fun of, and are just not getting the point. Taking stuff literally when you're not supposed to. That's not how language works.

You could make a meta point about "social construct". It of course means that definitions are social conventions, which is a completely accurate point. But how is the string "social construct" used in actual language usage? A mere frequency analysis would tell you that "social construct" is a string that leftists use in order to crack down on bad people. You could perfectly define "social construct" as "a word whose definition is set by the Cathedral, and which denying it would get you in real trouble so shut up already". When people come out of their way to state that "race is a social construct", that's not a scientific point. All they mean is "race is what I and my friends say it is and shut up you fascist".

Note that they don't really need to be aware of the difference. Surely some people understand that "social construct" is supposed to mean a concept deriving its meaning from social convention. But plenty of people just have picked up "social construct" being used in leftist agitation, got what's used for, and imitated that usage themselves. You don't need to be aware of the origin of words; only how they're used. That's the etymological fallacy at the micro level.

I've had hour long conversations about how to define "racist". But "racist" in common usage means "bad person who I can easily accuse of disliking black people in order to ostracize him". That's how the language game is played. You can contest that kind of usage, and word usage indeed changes a lot all the time. But changing social conventions requires power. Political power. Because, of course, everything is politics. That's a point the left understood a very long time ago. Even if they won't say so.

The Will To Not Power

2016-08-16 // japan, monarchy, power

I've written[125] extensively[126] about[127] monarchy[128]. And for good reason. We're all here in great part because we share our criticism, or at least disillusion about democracy. Some critics of democracy come from the long reactionary tradition, going back to the De Maistre and the opponents and the French Revolution. But most of it today, at least on this corners of the internet, derives from libertarians figuring it out that democracy isn't quite conducive to liberty. Certainly not in a theoretical way. Hans Herman Hoppe put it best, wrote a whole book about it, saying that if economic theory made any sense, monarchy was the best system of government. Moldbug run his whole blog on that. He used to troll Larry Auster in that the modern world suffers from "chronic kinglessness", then went away praising Henry VII Tudor.

My answer to that is that if you know your history you know that monarchy doesn't work like Filmer or Hobbes said it did. The theory was good; but an absolute ruler is just that, a theory. In practice power gets exercised by the people who seek power. And a king won't necessarily seek power. He may be a shy man; or a dissolute hedonist. Or have a strong mother who won't let him. Or have powerful ministers who craftly dodge his attempts at exercising him his royal prerogative. Modern governments are a mess. Old royal courts were also a big mess. And it's all written down.

Still, some people keep on not getting the joke. Mostly because they don't want to get the joke. It's convenient for them to keep on theorizing in how awesome monarchy is. Filmer and Hobbes were amongst those. The modern Japanese right[129] is also like that.

As I said the modern Japanese right has been organizing for some time around the need to reform the Constitution. Or more frankly, to scrap the present one and come up with a new one. They just won the election and they're getting to it, but they've been planning for some time. In 2012 the LDP, the perennial ruling party, or more specifically the right wing of the LDP, announced their draft for a new constitution. It

---

[125] https://spandrell.com/2013/10/18/monarchy/

[126] https://spandrell.com/2014/02/08/monarchy-and-monarchs/

[127] https://spandrell.com/2014/01/13/chinese-monarchy/

[128] https://spandrell.com/2014/01/16/chinese-monarchy-2/

[129] https://spandrell.com/2016/08/04/shifting-right/

scraps article 9, which forbids Japan from (nominally) having military forces. And it changes article 1. Article 1 right now says:

Article 1. The Emperor shall be the symbol of the State and of the unity of the People, deriving his position from the will of the people with whom resides sovereign power.

And this they want to change into:

Article 1. The Emperor is the head of the State and shall be the symbol of the State and of the unity of the people, deriving his position from the will of the people with whom resides sovereign power.

You can see the total list of changes here[130], in very good English.

So anyway, the change isn't very big. But the whole thing of the "head of state" has the internet right, which like the Western alt-right but 100 times bigger, very excited with talk of having a proper monarch and all that. And all that's very cool, but they seem to have forgotten to actually ask the emperor. And he's not playing ball.

In July 13, the whole country was startled when the public broadcaster, NHK, announced that the emperor had the intention of "abdicating"[131]. The wording was pretty ominous, "生前退位", "abdicating in life", but the actual wording is "giving away the throne". The proper wording would be 譲位 "passing the throne to". The wording kinda meant the emperor was abolishing the institution. That mostly was just a careless journalist not knowing his imperial vocabulary, but still. The very fact of rumors coming out of the imperial household was completely unheard of. And to make it worse, later in the very same day, the Imperial Household Agency, the government bureaucrats who run the palace, denied the whole thing. Nothing to see here!

So not only rumors were coming out of the imperial palace; but there were conflicting rumors. That's even worse. Something was seriously amiss here. But for weeks nothing happened. Until last week, the Emperor gave a press conference.

https://www.youtube.com/watch?v=jW9ObpFgCP8

First of all, the Emperor is not supposed to do that! He shouldn't be talking to the people besides any predetermined royal business of his. But he had something to say, and he said it. And what did he say? That he's old, that he's busy, that there's a lot of stuff to do, he's not able to do it, so he thinks it better if he leaves the throne so that the tasks of the emperor don't suffer.

---

[130] `https://www.voyce-jpn.com/#!ldp-draft-constitution/px2wu`

[131] `https://www.theguardian.com/world/2016/aug/08/japans-emperor-akihito-health-abdication-rare-tv-address`

The whole thing was weird. Weird in the eyes of monarchists. The Emperor is the royal person. He can do what he wants. He's not a bureaucrats with tasks to do. That's secondary. But the Emperor doesn't see it that way. He mentioned the word "symbol" 8 times. Because that's his job under the current constitution, to be the "symbol of the nation". Apparently he feels very strongly about his job as a symbol, and wants someone to do it if he's unable to. But that's not the idea of the monarch that people have these days. He's to be the head of state! The symbol thing is just some word. But he doesn't see it like that. He feels he has a job. He feels like the right wants to change his job. And he surely doesn't want to do it. He doesn't even want to be there when the whole thing happens.

The left has rushed to argue that this is the Emperor's way of protesting against the rightist shift. And they have a point. Imperial sovereignty in pre-war Japan led to the military declaring war to the whole world in the Name of the Emperor. And the Showa Emperor, Hirohito, the present emperor's father, grew to resent that. When the famous Yasukuni shrine went fascist and declared that the war criminals punished by the US in the Tokyo trials were also enshrined there, the Emperor never again visited the shrine. His son, the present Emperor, has never gone himself. The Imperial Household is not amused by rightist nostalgia of pre-war Japan. They are in the left.

And if the present emperor is in the left, you haven't seen his son. The crown prince, Naruhito, is married to a Foreign office bureaucrat, who is always sick, unable to do her princess duties, unless she has to go to Europe. Then she's always healthy and stays long periods of time shopping in Paris. She hates the imperial bureaucracy, and they hate her back. And the crown prince is fully on her side. He has protested several times on how the imperial bureaucracy treats women badly. You know where this goes.

And, to make matters funnier, the crown prince has one only child. A daughter. Which under the present imperial household regulations, can't inherit the throne. There was some attempt at reforming that, and allowing a future empress. But then the crown prince's brother had a baby boy, and he became the next in line. But once the crown prince becomes the Emperor, he will most certainly push to reform the law to get his daughter on the throne some day. And he will have the full support of all the Japanese left.

So you have a monarchist right, which dreams of traditional monarchy, fighting a leftist royal house who wants nothing to do with it. They want to be fancy bureaucrats on a salary doing a "symbol" job. But the right doesn't care. Their monarchism isn't about the monarch. It's just some convenient Schelling Point they got to make friends amongst themselves and sell bullshit to the populace. Which is what politicians do.

And you could say that of any political idea. The content is secondary. The consequences are completely besides the point. What counts is what works in the political arena. What gets retweeted. What gets you votes. How ideas develop depends on that, not in actual internal logic or likely consequences.

Correct Naming

2016-08-25 // china, history, philosophy

Master Xun (荀子 Xunzi):

夫民易一以道，而不可與共故。故明君臨之以埶，道之以道，申之以命，章之以論，禁之以刑。故民之化道也如神，辨埶惡用矣哉！今聖王沒，天下亂，姦言起，君子無埶以臨之，無刑以禁之，故辨說也。實不喻，然後命，命不喻，然後期，期不喻，然後說，說不喻，然後辨。故期命辨說也者，用之大文也，而王業之始也。名聞而實喻，名之用也。累而成文，名之麗也。用麗俱得，謂之知名。名也者，所以期累實也。辭也者，兼異實之名以論一意也。辨說也者，不異實名以喻動靜之道也。期命也者，辨說之用也。辨說也者，心之象道也。心也者，道之工宰也。道也者，治之經理也。心合於道，說合於心，辭合於說。正名而期，質請而喻，辨異而不過，推類而不悖。聽則合文，辨則盡故。以正道而辨姦，猶引繩以持曲直。是故邪說不能亂，百家無所竄。有兼聽之明，而無矜奮之容；有兼覆之厚，而無伐德之色。說行則天下正，說不行則白道而冥窮。是聖人之辨說也。詩曰：「顒顒卬卬，如珪如璋，令聞令望，豈弟君子，四方為綱。」此之謂也。

Which translates as:

The people can easily be unified by means of the Way, but one should not try to share one's reasons with them. Hence, the enlightened lord controls them with his power, guides them with the Way, moves them with his orders, arrays them with his judgments, and restrains them with his punishments. Thus, his people's transformation by the Way is spirit-like [i.e. religious]. What need has he for demonstrations and persuasions? Nowadays the sage kings have all passed away, the whole world is in chaos, and depraved teachings are arising. The gentleman has no power to control people, no punishments to restrain them, and so he engages in demonstrations and persuasions.

When objects are not understood, then one engages in naming. When the naming is not understood, then one tries to procure agreement. When the agreement is not understood, then one engages in persuasion. When the persuasion is not understood, then one engages in demonstration. Thus, procuring agreement, naming, demonstration, and persuasion are some of the greatest forms of useful activity, and are the beginning of kingly works.

When a name is heard and the corresponding object is understood, this is usefulness in names. When they are accumulated and form a pattern, this is beauty in names. When one obtains both their usefulness and beauty, this is called understanding names.

Names are the means by which one arranges and accumulates objects. Sentences combine the names of different objects so as to discuss a single idea.

Persuasion and demonstration use fixed names of objects so as to make clear the proper ways for acting and remaining still. Procuring agreement and naming are the functions of demonstration and persuasion. Demonstration and persuasion are the heart's way of representing the Way. The heart is the craftsman and overseer of the Way. The Way is the warp and pattern of good order. When the heart fits with the Way, when one's persuasions fit with one's heart, when one's words fit one's persuasions, then one will name things correctly and procure agreement, will base oneself on the true disposition of things and make them understood, will discriminate among things without going to excess, and will extend by analogy the categories of things without violating them. When listening to cases, one will accord with good form. When engaging in demonstration, one will cover thoroughly all the reasons. One will use the true Way to discriminate what is vile just like drawing out the carpenter's line in order to grasp what is curved and what is straight. Thus, deviant sayings will not be able to cause disorder, and the hundred schools will have nowhere to hide.

One kind of person is brilliant enough to listen to all cases, but has no combative or arrogant countenance. He has generosity enough to extend to all sides, but does not make a display of his virtue in his appearance. If his persuasions are successful, then all under Heaven is set right. If his persuasions are not successful, then he makes clear his way but lives in obscurity—such are the persuasions and demonstrations of the sage. The Odes says:

Full of refinement and nobility,

Like a jade tablet or scepter is he,

So lovely to hear and lovely to see.

The contented and tranquil gentleman

Serves as a model universally.

This expresses my meaning.

Translation from Eric Hutton's Xunzi[132]. Pretty good translation, I must say.

And yes, Classical Chinese writing really is that short.

---

[132] https://www.amazon.com/Xunzi-Complete-Text/dp/0691161046/ref=sr_1_2?ie=UTF8&qid=1472121129&sr=8-2&keywords=xunzi+hutton

The Great Ming Emperor Admonishes his Troops about Women

2016-08-30 // china, history, women, redpill

So some people are saying I'm just some rootless cosmopolitan who speaks Chinese. How can I be alt-right?

此言差矣. It doesn't work like that. I have insight precisely because I've been around, and I've read around. Let me prove my alt-right bona-fides by quoting Zhu Yuanzhang, the great founder of the Ming Dynasty, the Empire of Brightness.

Zhu Yuanzhang is the greatest rags-to-riches story in the history of mankind. He was some minor son of a landless peasant, born during the period of Mongol rule in China. Mongol government in China was quite horrible; infrastructure decayed, bandits were everywhere, and all manner of natural disasters happened all the time. One of those disasters killed our hero's whole family. Starvation. Every single one of them. Our hero had to go to the closest Buddhist temple to beg for some food; and all he got was an old wooden pan, and an order to beat the crap out of the temple and beg some food outside. Which he did for years. Beg for food. Around the country. For years. Until he met some band of bandits. Heaven had it so that his best childhood friend was a bandit chief; so he soon joined them. Our hero then slowly but steadily climbed the bandit meritocracy ladder; next thing you know he is leading the best rebel army in China, expels the Mongols to the steppe and reunifies All Under Heaven.

There's something to say for the tradition, the slow accumulation of knowledge in society. But some things just don't require an education. Just razor-sharp smarts. And industrial amounts of cruelty. And Zhu Yuanzhang had those. He was an illiterate beggar, and yet he built and commanded the armies that beat the Mongols and founded the Ming Dynasty. Not unlike Genghis Khan; he also didn't need to go to school to command the best run armies in the history of mankind. Politics really isn't that hard.

Anyway, one of the most fun things of the founder of the Ming is that he was illiterate. Which in China is a problem, as elite people were supposed to be able to write in Classical Chinese, which is kinda like Latin in the West. Obviously he couldn't do that, so many of his edicts are written in plain vernacular language. So he would sent imperial decrees to his troops saying "grab those damn Japanese pirates and slit their fucking throats on the spot. This is My Command". He was very fond of sending commands, edicts and decrees to the whole country. China is a big country; and the guy, for all his illiteracy, had many ideas. He had built and run the army who conquered the country. Surely running the country in peace couldn't be that hard? All you need is order and discipline. And he knew something about that.

Anyway, this is one small snippet of his views on women and sexual propriety:

男子婦人必要有分別。婦人家專一在裡面，不可外出來。若露頭露臉出外來呵，必然有惹淫亂的事。而今有等愚夫愚婦好生部不守道理，把風俗壞了。便如曲靖衛指揮牛麟，他在雲南討一個婦人做妾，每日與同僚官喫酒，便着這婦人出來同座喫酒。因此上被指揮柳英誘引私通，教本婦將毒藥毒死牛麟。有這等無知的，婦人家如何着他與男子漢喫酒，喫一會酒了，自家的性命也被人害了。若是有分別呵，那裡有這等事。指揮柳英與那婦人，都將殺了。今後再有這等的，拿住一般罪他。

Which translates as:

There must be a separation between men and women. Women must be always inside the house, must not be allowed to come outside. If they go out of the home revealing their head or their face, that will inevitably result in lewdness and debauchery. But these days there are some stupid men and stupid women who can't reason properly and make a mess of proper morality.

See for example this the Commander of Qujing, this Niu Lin guy. While he was in Yunnan he got some woman as a concubine, and when he went to drink with his comrades, he would take her to drink with them! So of course she ended up being seduced by another commander called Liu Ying, who then had her poison her husband Niu Lin.

Just how dumb was this guy? He brought his wife to drink with other men, drunk for a while, next thing you know he got killed. If he had kept a proper separation between men and women, nothing like this could have happened. I had Liu Ying and that woman killed. If something like this ever happens again, they'll get the same treatment.

Real News and Fake News

2016-09-12 // media, capitalism, bluegov, democracy

Look at this page: https://www.reuters.com/article/us-austria-election-idUSKCN11I0NA

Two important pieces of news here.

One is that the Austrian presidential elections have been postponed. These elections are the repetition of the elections done in May. Why are they repeating them? Because of massive electoral fraud. Electoral fraud done to give the election to a leftist candidate, against an anti-immigrant rightist one.

This sounds trivial but it's the first time in... a 100 years? That fraud is a thing in European elections. This is how bad things have got.

And they're worse still, as the elections are being postponed because of tampering with postal votes! This is how bad things have got. If something happens to democracy it won't be because of the persuasive powers of reactionary writers. It'll be because the left realizes it's not in its interest anymore. Kinda like the fall of the Soviet Union.

This other piece of news is also interesting. Stop your Ad-blocker for a minute and look at the bottom right corner.

SPONSORED **TOPICS**

Climate change is the biggest single threat facing the world economy *STOXX PULSE ONLINE*

Introducing a Multi-Asset Dynamic Allocation *STOXX PULSE ONLINE*

Top 10 reasons to invest in income *MarketViews*

Weekly update on the financial markets *MarketViews*

Expert financial and political views on Latin America *MarketViews*

In this world of today, where all print media is effectively bankrupt, and surviving only due to public subsidies or the whims of billionaires, Reuters is still honest enough to relegate its sponsored content, i.e. it's corporate propaganda to a small corner of its website. But look at the first article. Climate change is the biggest single threat facing the world economy. That seems like a fairly normal headline, doesn't it? I've seen that on actual newspapers all the time. But we of course know what the deal was all along. Now Reuters is nice enough to make it explicit. Sponsored Content. Of course it is.

The Loudspeaker

2016-10-09 // islam, men, religion

Well it's been a while since I wrote a post. I apologize, but I have been busy, and everybody's attention is on the American election, Trump or not Trump. That is the question. Quite predictably the Cathedral has focused all its resources in fighting Trump with every tactic on the books, and then some. Twitter is banning thousands of people, every single newspaper in the US has openly abandoned any pretence of unbiased reporting. Some people on the left have hinted that democracy may not be such a good idea, given that someone like Trump could possibly win.

I like the train of thought; but they've managed to probably knock Trump out of the race. How? With a tape where he spoke like 80% of men do in a normal country. Where he talked about pussy and how much he likes it. That is the true fault line of Western politics. Feminism is the strongest Schelling Point of the progressive system, the indestructible idea that will bury us all. Again Houellebecq is provided right all along.

Anyway, let me do what I do best and introduce a funny story I saw in a Chinese website. It's unrelated only if you want it to.

I was born and raised in a small village in Henan, in central China. In some of the neighboring villages there are some Muslims (the Hui people, Chinese-speaking Muslims), and since I was a kid the adults in the village always told us kids the we should never go to Muslim villages, as the Muslims liked to beat up Han-Chinese kids. I was a small child and didn't really understand what that was all about.

I remember when I was in first grade, in the spring, I went to the hills to get some edible wild herbs (when I was a kid I loved eating wild herbs with noodles), and I bumped into a Muslim herding his sheep into the wheat fields of our family. His sheep were eating up all our wheat! I was furious, I went up there to tell him to stop, but the Muslim herder beat me up very hard. Then he just said he was going to get his sheep to eat all our wheat, and that if I tried to stop them again he'd bring his buddies from his village and would beat up our whole family.

I went back home and told my parents. They were really scared, they didn't dare go confront the Muslim herder. I asked my parents: "why are we so scared of the Muslims?". My father answered: "Because when a Muslim gets into a fight with a Han, he goes into his mosque, the imam from the mosque then grabs the loudspeaker in the mosque and calls up all the Muslim men in the village to go beat us up. We have few men in our family, we can't possibly beat them in a fight. So all we can do is give up and let their sheep eat up our wheat."

I remember that this kind of things happened quite often in the village, and it often ended in Muslims and Han fighting. But most often it was the Han who lost, because they had less men to call up for help.

The balance of the natural and social world

2016-10-09 // history, religion, men, signaling, leftism, WNANR

Apparently I missed this kind post by Jim[133] where he calls me clever but pessimistic. Guilty as charged. I agree with his point though. Irrational optimism works. I'm just not very good at it. Which is why I've been reading and writing on how to generate it exogenously, i.e. for people like me.

The discussion there at Jim is uncharacteristically good. The main issue people ask is that you can't just make up a new religion. That's a good point. It's also a bummer, given that my shtick for 5 years has been that We Need a New Religion (see 1^{134}, 2^{135}, 3^{136}, 4^{137}, 5^{138}). But once you understand what religion is about, what it is for, it's obvious that you can't just make one up from thin air. Any coordination mechanism for groups, any set of ideas to generate loyalty is more likely to work if it feeds upon previous ideas which are out there, preferably for a long time. If only to make people not feel inadequate about their past ideological stances. If you want Christians to join your group you should make them feel good about having been a Christian; at least parts of it. Ever read the Quran? The writer was very, very familiar with Christianity and Judaism. Christianity was of course also based on Judaism. And Judaism on ages old tribal traditions of the Hebrew tribes. Hardly any religion has ever been produced ex-nihilo. Japan tried to make a religion[139] out of the (purported) tribal traditions of the Japanese people but they just couldn't beat up centuries of Buddhist faith.

It follows that the solution would be to come up with a slightly modified version of Christianity. It would make it easier to get our natural allies on the right side of the Christian community to join the institution of a reactionary society. The problem is, as many correctly argue on the comments at Jim's, that Christianity is a leftist cult. The teachings of Jesus are pure and simple leftist agitation. The rich go to hell. The poor

---

[133] `https://blog.jim.com/war/deus-vult/`

[134] `https://spandrell.com/2011/11/09/we-need-a-new-religion/`

[135] `https://spandrell.com/2011/11/25/we-need-a-new-religion-2/`

[136] `https://spandrell.com/2014/07/07/we-need-a-new-religion-3/`

[137] `https://spandrell.com/2016/05/15/we-need-a-new-religion-4/`

[138] `https://spandrell.com/2015/03/09/religion/`

[139] `https://spandrell.com/2014/11/26/shinto/`

will inherit the earth. Prostitutes are as noble as any of you. If some white guy wrote a Medium long-form post talking on his experiences touching and healing lepers we would all call him a holier-than-thou virtue signaller.

Many argue that the teachings of the Church (whichever you fancy) are distinct from those of Jesus alone, and we just need to follow those instead of just reading the bible. And there's a point to that; but the teachings of the Church aren't particularly reactionary either. They haven't been for ages. There's plenty of exhortations to respect women and give to the poor and be a general Nice Guy. A guy like Donald Trump using his fame to grab hot pussy would have been busted in any Christian community in any time and space. Christianity just doesn't do that. It's a nice cult. The Romans knew that: plenty of Roman writers wrote about these meek Christians who sold feminism to their women, messing with good old classical mores.

So yeah, Christianity is leftist by nature. At least leftist indeed to not be very conducive to a hard move to the right as the West is sorely in need of. But... Christianity did beat the Romans, didn't it? And it's had a pretty impressive track record at least until 1965. Plenty of Christians do remind us that Christianity is the West, and we can't save one without the other. They have a point. What made Christianity so successful?

Well first of all Christianity wasn't successful everywhere. It certainly was in Europe. But not in the Middle East. Islam surely beat it there. And the few Christian communities that remained since antiquity until the 2003 Iraq War weren't anything to call home about.

It seems to me that Christianity as a mildly leftist, i.e. socialist and feminist cult, it had an important role to play in the ancient and medieval world. Especially the medieval world, where barbarians roamed Europe at will. The world of a barbarian is the complete opposite of a modern one. Barbarians are manly. Very much so. There's this Jack Donovan guy pulling a Yukio Mishima and translating his gayness into poetry about how cool the barbarian Way of Man is, how awesome are the men it produces. Which it is. We all love Conan. It's cool. It looks like tons of fun.

It's still messed up in many ways. In modern parlance, the barbarian world is a world of toxic masculinity. It's a world where men do whatever the hell they want. In my parlance, it's a world of bro signalling spirals.[140] Which is a lot of fun for men. But it produces pretty crappy societies. It's stupidly violent. It despises menial, boring work. It despises family life for the pursuit of vainglory and pussy. It's nasty, brutish and short. That's what you get when men do what their feel like.

---

[140]   https://spandrell.com/2015/12/30/men-doing-their-own-thing/

In that kind of world, having Christian institutions trying to get men to stop hunting for a while and just fucking till the land and feeding their children, is actually a pretty good idea. Shaming a man to sticking with his ugly and nagging wife even though she's a total bitch is a pretty good idea if you want children to survive and food surplus to get grown. Getting elite men to not shoot each other over stupid slights, to not drink too much and moderate their appetites, to don't spend their inheritance in women and parties... was pretty much hopeless for the most part. But to the extent it succeeded it had a civilizing effect.

So to speak in modern terms, if you have a society which is, due to its historical background or its technological level, naturally shifted to the right, having a pole of lefty ideas produces a pretty healthy balance, one where men get a bit of what they want, women get a bit of what they want, and we're all better off thanks to it.

That's obviously not what we got today. The situation in 2016 is one where feminism is the law of the land, men doing what men do by nature (cf. Trump) is illegal and strictly punished, and every single institution with some power just pushes the same leftist ideas. Women are better, open borders is good, everybody has the right to organize and fight for their selfish interests except white men. In this circumstances if we want to restore some balance, if we want civilization to work, we need the complete opposite of what Christianity was. We need a big fat magnet of rightist ideas, a rightist pole to exert the same influence on our feminized society that Christianity had on the manly society of the Middle Ages.

It seems to me that Christianity can't possibly be that. What could be? Your guess is as good as mine. If you've been reading this blog you probably know one answer. But again I like it as little as you do. For all purposes I'm still for a New Religion.

Faith

2016-11-07 // religion, wat do

Every time I get more Twitter hits than usual I run a Twitter search to see what are people blabbering about me. It's usually quite interesting. See here:

https://twitter.com/28ShermanSOBL1/status/795426241641934849

Heh. See also Alfa NL, who perhaps should call himself Maurice of Orange-Nassau or any cool soldier from Dutch history, wrote a post where he very kindly called me his Final Boss[141]. I kinda like the attention. He writes how I'm a very compelling advocate of atheism. But he believes in God, and he wants to make God's will a part of my theories.

He is misunderstanding me, as many do. I actually get quite a lot of correspondence by sympathetic Christians telling me that I could accommodate Christianity in this or that way. The very fact that I get sympathetic Christians reading my blog should tell you that I'm no atheist. I've explicitly said so myself long ago[142]. And I've said so with the very same argument that Alfa NL makes in his post. There's no point to atheism. It's completely self-defeating. I totally get that. I've always got that, and over the years I've learned what I think is the exact mechanism that makes atheism useless and religion useful.

So why be an atheist? I'm certainly not. But as a writer I can't be a theist. Thomas Huxley was in the same conundrum when he coined the word "agnostic", which I think is a brilliant way to put it. Being a theist would destroy all my work. It's cheating. I want to explain things with the available evidence. Inserting god here or there while I write about history or about theories of social behavior would be just too easy. So I don't, and I never will. No good historian does.

But if you want to believe in God, but all means don't let me stop you. If you want to believe in the coming race-war, by all means keep on believing that we will win. Don't let my pessimism discourage you[143]. Incidentally titled my blog "we shall drown and nobody will save us" after a funny page on a 1930s English textbook that I found at my grandfather's, where they taught the difference between the usage of "will" and "shall".

---

[141] https://alfanl.com/2016/09/28/final-boss-spandrell/

[142] https://spandrell.com/2012/01/29/on-mystics/

[143] https://spandrell.com/2016/01/31/blood-is-thicker-than-water/

I thought it was a pretty accurate reflection of my views. I stand by those views. I do think we're likely going to hell. But I don't want you to agree with me. I probably did back in 2011, but I don't now, now that I know, and have extensively written about[144], what religion and ideology, and most social behavior is all about.

Razib Khan has had a similar epiphany[145], his one apparently being caused by his inside exposure to academic politics in the US. Razib Khan is an awesome blogger who's been writing on history and human biodiversity for a decade already. If we were Chinese I'd call him 師傅 *master* and would have to be extremely polite with him. Razib knows his facts. He knows a whole lot of them.

But nobody likes facts. Well of course some people do. Razib Khan certainly does, as I do. But why? Because we're good at it. We're so much better than everyone else we know that we use the comparative advantage to try go get status. But people aren't interest in the facts I give them. Why? Because being interested will make them lose, and me win. And they don't want me to win, of course. Well my mother does (sometimes). But some people want me to lose, they want to win themselves. In this status struggle, the facts aren't very important. They're only a factor inasmuch as I make them a factor because I'm good at them so I use them to get status. But if my conversation partner is adamant at being hostile to me, he'll deny the facts with extreme ease. All of them. You've all seen that happen. Especially on the internet.

The old Conquest's law argues that everybody is conservative (sticks to the facts) in what they know best. But that doesn't necessarily imply that they *talk* conservative. They must *act* conservative, *behave* conservative, basically because it's the only way to get things done. But they don't need to talk conservative. Many around here are constantly bemused about how high IQ, high conscientiousness, by any measure high performance people can be braindead liberals when you talk to them. Well of course they are; they must be, because it's the way to get status. Talk is also a kind of behavior. It's social behavior. And the point of social behavior is to maximize social status. So if talking progressive is the shortest path to social status, people are gonna talk progressive. They might even act progressive; but you might have noticed that people tend to do the talk but not the walk. They proclaim the equality of all races but live in white enclaves. They proclaim their love for public education but send their kids to private schools. Hypocrisy? No, just rational behavior.

Now the question of course remains; why is progressive talk the path to social status? The assumption in the right tends to be that the left is in power so they get to write the

---

[144] https://spandrell.com/2015/03/09/religion/

[145] https://www.unz.com/gnxp/winning-isnt-everything-winning-your-team-is/

rules. 成王敗寇. The winner gets called the king, the losers get called rebel scum. And there's something to that; but that begs the question: how did progressives get to power? There's something to progressivism itself that gave them an advantage, an edge.

I've written extensively myself; perhaps my oldest and most long-lasting insight is that the particular beliefs of progressivism aren't contingent. They aren't just some random stuff that got in there. The progressive memeplex evolved because it's fit[146]. For better or worse, talk about human equality is good social glue. It makes it easy to make friends and keep them. It also makes it easy to virtue-signal; and people like that. It makes it easy for women to claim for power; and as S.A.M. Adshead pointed out, the history of modernity is the history of the feminization of civilization. So the memes that progressives talk about (not necessarily act upon), are, in a sense, just good manners.

Note that evolution works in the margin; it doesn't follow that good social glue necessarily results in Bruce Jenner getting his dick chopped off using taxpayer's money. But human equality, feminism, anti-racism, all those are evolutionary fit memes; the perfect cultural viruses that Richard Dawkins suspected were behind much of human history. He didn't quite understand the mechanism; but then again he's no sociologist. Human society is complicated; and mere discussion of it is a social bomb. He's finding that out recently.

If progressive bullshit, if completely absurd beliefs work because they are good social glue; do facts matter? Does the cold, sharp truth that I write about count for nothing? No, it doesn't. It hasn't made me any friends. Search for my name in Twitter: you'll find everyone is saying the same thing: I'm too negative, I don't get religion, I give people no hope. And they're right in the general point. But I do get religion. I don't do religion; not in this blog. But I very much get it. I'm the one who's been telling everyone that we need a new religion. I'm just least suited man in the world to come up with one. But I'm telling you it's a good idea.

So again; don't let me discourage you. You wanna believe in God's Will: go for it. You wanna believe in Kek: I think it's a great idea. Just don't expect me to do Kek theology or to theology about God's will in this blog. It's not my strong point. I don't do bullshit. I just don't; I'm awfully bad at it. What I'm very good at is cutting through bullshit. Which I understand is counterproductive if you're trying to build a cohesive political group, but chill. My focus is and has been to cut through progressive bullshit; and I will continue to do so. If and when the cult of Kek or something more suitable to my purposes and those of my family and people achieves power: I for one will be the first to worship our new God and shut up all this negative truth speech.

---

[146]   https://spandrell.com/2015/03/01/leftism-is-just-an-easy-excuse/

So get working in your theology. And if you want to think of me as the enemy; be my guest. Any workable religion will have to answer all the questions I'm posing here. Think of me as a friendly sparring. But I am friendly. No enemies to the right. Not until the new dynasty is founded, of course.

And incidentally: my last post about the founding of the Ming Dynasty got people excited and all that. But do remember: the first thing Zhu Yuanzhang did after consolidating power was forbid all cults across the whole empire, and torture and murder everyone who disagreed. Manicheanism and all these Lotus Societies pretty much died forever. Oops, here I am again with my negativity. But hey, I didn't write the history books.

Where did the Samurais go?

2016-10-25 // japan, men, women

tl;dr: They were killed by their women.

There's been news of a very rare occurrence in Japan. A bombing. In a provincial city, at that. Utsunomiya, a town nobody knows about and nobody should really know about. Nothing going on there.

This week though, there was a big bombing. 1 dead, 3 injured. A car exploded in some park.

The media and the Internet were all talking about it. Terrorism! Must be, right?

Wait, terrorism? In Utsunomiya? No way. No fucking way. Of course it's not terrorism. So what is it? Who did this?

This guy:

And who is this guy? A Samurai. A pissed off Samurai.

An old Samurai too. Retired. 72 year old ex officer of the Self Defence Forces. He had worked his whole life for the defense of his country. Alas, his country didn't pay back the favor.

Kurihara Toshimasa had a schizophrenic daughter. She was going insane all the time at home, making a mess of herself and everything around her. He tried to control her anyway he thought of; to no avail. Eventually he forced her into an asylum.

His wife though had other ideas. A local cult sold her that her daughter wasn't ill, she was just possessed or something, and they had this magic potions and rituals and stuff that could cure her of those possessions. The wife ate the whole thing up; eventually spent 500k dollars in whatever scam the cult came up with. The totality of Mr. Kurihara's savings. A lifetime of savings. Including the retirement allowance that the army had given him. All gone.

Well eventually an argument ensued. The wife responded by suing our samurai for domestic violence. Everytime her daughter went batshit and he came to physically restrain her? Domestic violence. Sending her to the asylum against her schizophrenic will? Domestic violence. Arguing with the wife about money? Domestic violence. Evidence? None. The wife's word.

Thing is our samurai was a bit old fashioned. He didn't lawyer up. Why would I need a laywer? I'm in the right. Surely our legal system will recognize there is no evidence against me. Oh man. The judges gave his cultish wife everything she wanted. Divorce. Money. Property. Even the car. All to her. Our Samurai protested. "My wife tried to kill me. She assaulted me with a knife! Surely I had to restrain her". The judges laughed. "Well if you had died we'd recognize that".

Our Samurai had lost everything. His family. His property. His dignity. What could he do? It's not like he didn't defend himself. He run a Twitter account blogging about his trial. He started a blog. He went every day on 2ch (like reddit, sorta) trying to gain sympathy and attention. It didn't work. Nothing work. Modern society is not kind to a samurai. It is however very kind to women. Even insane women.

And so he decided. He had lost everything. He was not allowed to live like a man. Then he will die like a man. On the morning of the 23th of October, he burnt down his (now his wive's) house. 20 minutes later he sat on his car, and made it explode. His wife wanted the house and the car. Well, she won't have them. That's the least he could do.

People talk a lot about what a bunch of sexless wimps the modern Japanese have become.

https://twitter.com/thelateempire/status/788137373909614592

Now you know why. Humans are rational. Everything is rational. Gnon is always there.

Nobody rules alone

2016-11-02 // theory, power, democracy, korea

https://www.youtube.com/watch?v=rStL7niR7gs

So this video has been doing the rounds. You should watch it. It's very well done. And the book it refers to, The Dictator's Handbook, is also a great book. I read it a while ago. Hell, I should have done a book review. It's a really good book. It's analysis of government in general, and how dictatorships work, is brilliant.

Alas, the book flounders when it talks about democracy. Which it basically posits as the Great Solution, the final End of History where everyone is happy because the selectorate is big and blablabla. Well of course you'd expect a book by an American academic to say that democracy is awesome and magical and sacred. How else would he have a job? But it's quite a shame, as the book is really good. And he could have analyzed democracy quite well using the very same theory he created. He just needed to get his hands a bit dirty. Talk about ruling classes, political factions, networks of connections, pork barrel and all that stuff. But of course he didn't. He couldn't. He has an academic job and he'd rather keep it.

Well I don't have an academic job, so I'll do it myself. And I have a blog somewhat focused on East Asia, so let me refer to this piece of recent news. The finding that the President of South Korea, Ms. Park Gyun-Hye (pronounced Pak Kune), is a "puppet" of a sleazy bunch of con artists who clame to be shamans with spiritual powers[147]. Those sleazy shamans have been caught trafficking in state secrets, writing up her speeches, and extorting every single business in the country for zillions of won in name of the president. The most funny anecdote is that the President gave this conwoman her whole presidential budget for clothes, and what she did is give her some lousy second hand clothes while she embezzled the rest of the money. Some shaman.

But hey. Wait a minute. South Korea is a democracy, right? How did that happen?

Apparently I'm the only one asking that question. The Internet is full of news stories about how the South Korean people are shocked, shocked! about this news. Ms. Park is the daughter of Park Chung-Hee, the awesome right-wing dictator that raised South Korea out of its postwar misery and set the basis of what became their economic miracle. What many don't know is that Park Chung-Hee saw his wife assassinated by

---

[147]   https://www.unz.com/isteve/president-of-south-korea-is-a-puppet-of-her-shaman-fortuneteller/

North Korean agents, and years later he himself was shot in the head by the chief of the intelligence agency, amusingly called the KCIA.

That is its own piece of interesting history, but the point here is that Ms. Park is an orphan. And a fairly dramatic one. Have both your parents shot in public at different times must be shocking. Steve Sailer claims that it's understandable that she fell under the spell of some conmen given the circumstances. And yeah, I'll grant that point.

But still. The question that nobody is asking is: did nobody know about this? Yeah of course the people at large didn't know. But watch the video on the top again. No man rules alone. No man gets elected alone. Ms. Park is the head of her party. She was nominated to that place by people who knew about her, and thought she'd be a good deal for them. Ms. Park had to play politics in a very complex environment, in multiple layers. At the very least her party and the country at large. Did nobody know?

Obviously the insiders must have known. And yet they nominated her to lead the party. In fact Wikileaks points out that part of the story leaked years ago, and the American embassy had a long comment to do about it. Plenty of people must have known. Did nobody tell her? "Hey, this shaman friend of yours. She's no good". The whole thing makes little sense. Of course there's a huge media brouhaha going on right now, but we folks know very well not to trust the media about anything. Gell-mann amnesia and all that.

There's two possible answers here. Either the President is no puppet; she's just a crook with crook friends, everybody knew about it but they chose her anyway because she was good for business. Or she is a puppet, and everybody knew about it but they chose her anyway because she was good for business.

Little difference it makes, of course.

For some reason the conwomen shaman woman, Choi Seonsil, is being singled out as some mastermind of evil and corruption. But she was put there by someone, by many people, all of whom to some extent knew what was all about. But they chose her because they are as much of a crook as she is. And the President herself may or may not be a crook, but she most certainly is the nominal top of a gang of crooks who has been robbing the Korean people for years.

Who is to blame? The question is meaningless, in philosophical terms. Every effect has a myriad causes. You can never pin-point a single one. But that's not the point of blame. The point of blame is to produce a result. If you blame the president, and throw her away, you have a situation in which you need to choose a new president and everybody starts fighting and the whole thing can get messy. If you blame the shamaness, well you get a situation where the President looks like a fool and the religious landscape of Korea becomes the center of attention of the press for years. If you blame the whole party, you create a situation in which the opposition parties will most certainly win the new election. So "who is to blame?" is a very important question.

And that's the actual point of having a different political systems. You'll have noticed that Ms. Park had a cabinet full of conmen and crooks. Steve Sailer calls her a "Rasputin-like figure". But Rasputin was the confidant of the wife of the Russian Czar! An absolute monarch! Isn't democracy supposed to prevent this kind of thing? It obviously doesn't. Look at the Clintons. I thought Bueno de Mesquita has been quiet for some years, but I guess watching the increasingly open corruption of the American elite has made him a bit ashamed of his apology of the structural benefits of democracy.

Democracy or monarchy don't change the fundamental rules of politics. Crooks happen, advisors get power they shouldn't have, people in power do good or bad things or do nothing at all according to their disposition. Chains of crooks linked by personal connections will always run things. None of it matters. What matters is who we blame. In a monarchy we have a set of taboos that say that it's always the ministers who are wrong; and by blaming the ministers and never the king we keep the levers of power in a more or less stable way; which can be good or bad. In a democracy we have another set of taboos, which result in every link of the chain of corruption being interchangeable, but the very existence of the chain being unmentionable; everything else would be Endangering Our Democracy. This can be good... or bad.

You'll have noticed we don't have very good vocabulary to discuss this kind of matters. Imperial Chinese political theory has its biases, but it has insight we don't have. The Japanese in their insularity also have their insight. I'm sure the Ottomans and the Arabs have their own. As the US world police declines so evidently that the Philippines calls Obama openly a son of a bitch and Malaysia [148] tells the West to take a hike, we might as well stop believing our own crap and try to refine our theories on how politics work by looking at what is going to be our future.

---

[148] !

Trump needs Friends

2016-11-06 // trump, power, loyalty, religion

Say Trump wins. Trump may very well end up winning next week.

So say he wins. He'll then be at the top of the Federal Government. A lair of snakes if there ever was one. Every single agency of government, and every single unofficial agency of government (Academia, the Press, all those QUANGOs, basically every organization which belongs to the Cathedral but is not technically part of USG) is against him; against him to the point of willing his assassination.

This is going to be tough. Trump needs friends. Lots of friends. He needs to purge the whole establishment and put people he can trust on their place.

But who can he trust? Who are his friends? It's not that he has no friends. He has plenty of supporters and sympathizers. Even inside USG. But how can he find them? Of course he could ask them to stand up; but plenty of evil entryists would stand up too and try to destroy his projects from within.

So Trump has a big problem here. He needs to find loyal people and he needs a good way to identify them. How can he do that?

If you've been reading this blog for some time, you may have some hint at the answer. But let me do some historical analogy. Of China, of course. It's not a very good one; but it's what I'm reading right now so I might as well write about it anyway.

The Mongols conquered China in two stages; In 1234 they destroyed the Jurchen-ruled Jin dynasty, which controlled North China, and in 1279 they conquered the Southern Song dynasty, which ruled the South. It didn't take a long for Mongol rule to break down. China is a huge country; it took a lot of very fine administrative finesse to keep the whole thing controlled under a single government. And the Mongols weren't very good at administrative finesse. Once the Mongol armies stopped being awesome the whole thing unraveled pretty fast. By 1330 the whole thing was disintegrating fast. By 1350 the Mongol court barely controlled the capital area.

While public order disintegrated, dozens of warlords arose, each controlling some part of the country. Some were Mongol generals themselves. Some were organized crime, mostly smugglers, who had money and armed people at their disposal. Some were just local rich guys who were good at raising an army. And others were wacko millenarian cults who preached the coming of some new awesome godly world were food and babes fell from the sky, dressed up in a mix of Buddhist and Manichean jargon.

These warlords then of course started fighting each other, in a huge and devastating civil war that lasted until 1368. The Mongol generals first had the upper hand; they had seasoned troops and the old administrative apparatus on their hand. The smugglers were also pretty strong; they had long experience at running armed operations, and they had money to burn.

But you know who won in the end? The Ming Dynasty. And do you know what 明 Ming means? Brightness. Ming was the name of the Bright Cult, Manicheanism. Zhu Yuanzhang, the founder emperor of the Ming Dynasty, was a beggar monk who the joined one of the myriad cultist armies around the country. He is the biggest rags to riches story in human history. He was literally begging for food 10 years before he was the absolute ruler of the largest country on earth. And how did he do that? By joining a cult. Obviously the wacko cultist thing had some sort of advantage that made them win against unsurmountable odds, beating the best armed organizations in China.

How did they do it? By being better friends. The Mongol generals got backstabbed by their own imperial court; which they had ties to. Jealous eunuchs and princesses and rival ministers conspired to unseat those big Mongol generals who had too much power. The smugglers also fell to a similar fate; you've all seen the Sopranos. Organized crime is a dangerous world. Smugglers aren't the most reliable people. But the wacky Manicheans, with their absurd tales of the coming of Maitreya or whoever, and those weird rituals and songs and dances; those guys won the game.

Just saying. Those kek guys might be onto something.

Inscrutable are the ways of the Lord

2016-11-09 // trump, lol, drunkpoasting

In 1944 Jorge Luis Borges, the best writer that the American hemisphere has ever produced; wrote a short story called "Three Versions of Judas". The gist is that Judas should be our object of worship, because only by his treason of Jesus he made the crucifixion possible; and it was that which saved humanity. So no Judas, no salvation. Blessed be him.

Well, by that logic God Emperor Trump was made possible only by the treason of Anthony Weiner. So blessed be Weiner. Praise Weiner. Praise Kek.

Does anybody have a picture of Anthony Weiner with a green froggy face? I'll print it out and give offerings every Tuesday.

Let's start the new religion

2016-11-10 // trump, lol, WNANR

I want to build a virtual altar to worship these two figures:

Kinda like a Chinese temple worshipping Guan Yu and stuff like that.

Those with mad Photoshop skillz who pull it off will be highly rewarded. Praise Kek.

Schadenfraude and Reflection

2016-11-10 // trump, leftism, power, status

https://twitter.com/arthur_affect/status/796420056544641028

https://www.youtube.com/watch?v=NNi1hKi9Z5c

https://www.youtube.com/watch?v=NXUaQe3ziEY

You might remember that I called leftists "psychopathic status maximizers"[149]. Look at these people. Look carefully. Do you think they "believe" in some set of values?

No. It's all crap. We know since David Hume. We humans don't really know anything. You can't. You only get to be quite certain after a lot of trial and error about a very narrow area that you are good at. Everything else is signaling. And signaling is done to gain social status. Everything is crap that people say to get at you, to gain some advantage and fuck over others.

Moldbug said it well too: journalists love power. Journalists in Elizabethan England didn't care about human rights, they cared about the Great Virgin Queen. Who was widely hated, by the way. But you'd never know because those psychopathic status maximizers just did what they had to. And all these upset leftists who are uploading their narcissist signaling to Youtube will come around if the state religion ever changes. If Trump stays in power; they will adapt. And soon enough you'd be seeing the very same people, often the same individuals saying the complete opposite things, but in the same tone of voice and with the same insufferable attitude.

---

[149] https://spandrell.com/2015/10/09/the-social-module/

It's Happening

2016-11-11 // trump, lol, WNANR

The thing with Divine Revelation is that it is hard to notice. But sensitive people of all stripes can and do notice what is going on. Those with heartened hearts do not see what is happening even if its in front of their noses. But those who understand the ways of the Gods can sense it even thousands of miles away.

The Minister of the Interior (!) of Israel had this to say about the American election.[150] (H/T Vladimir)

Shas chairman and Interior Minister Arye Deri said Thursday that Donald Trump's election could herald the coming of the Messiah due to the blow he expects the next president will strike against the "non-Orthodox Jewish hold on the US government."

"There is no doubt that one can give thanks to God that all those who have damned the [Jewish] covenant and would wipe out Judaism, thinking they could take control over the Land of Israel here and lead reforms in order to cause destruction received their blow," Deri said during an address to the local religious council of Ashdod.

"Their influence and the great threat they posed to us because they held [control over] the US government...They understand that this power has disappeared and we can continue, God willing, to strengthen traditional religion and Judaism, transmitted down to us from generation to generation."

---

[150] https://www.jpost.com/Israel-News/Trumps-election-heralds-coming-of-Messiah-says-Deri-472282

Trump's election, he added, presages the coming of the Messianic Age.

"If such a miracle can happen, we have already reached the days of the Messiah. Therefore, we are really in the era of the birth pangs of the Messiah when everything has been flipped to the good of the Jewish people."

Now of course, when you have a hammer everything looks like a nail. To an Orthodox Jew, every hint of Divine Intervention looks like the coming of the Messiah. Different religions saw the Flood or the birth of Jesus in different ways; it's natural that each have their own interpretation. But only one is True. And of course, we all know that what happened on Tuesday was not the Jewish Messiah. It was the prophecy of Kek.

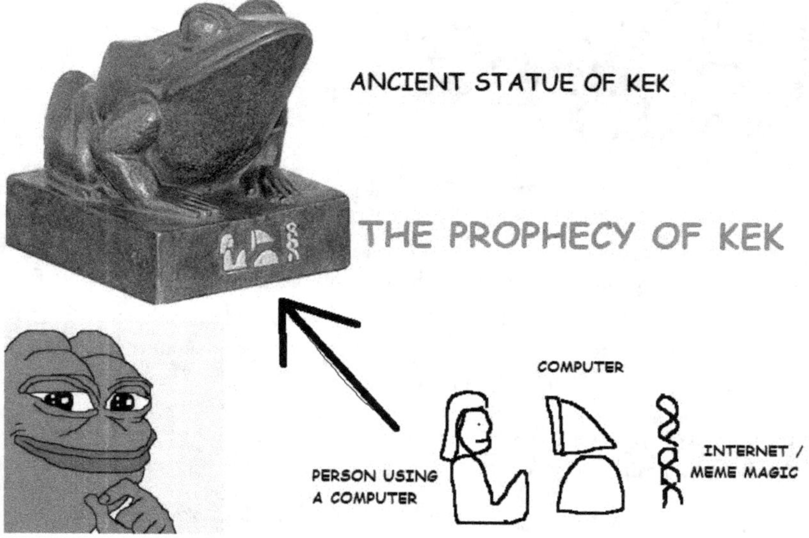

And the works of Kek were done through the phallic avatar we call Anthony Weiner. Who incidentally is Jewish, so perhaps Mr. Deri has a point. But anyway.

These are minor details. I'm happy for Israel's Minister. Let us all rejoice. Praise Kek.

www.alamy.com - CWD045

Keep up the pressure

2016-11-15 // trump, rightwingers

Twitter these days is a joy to see. Liberals crying and moaning. And our people gloating and keeping up the pressure. Never let down people. In a war initiative is everything. Never give the enemy any breathing time. Break their morale.

Some examples.

https://twitter.com/paxdickinson/status/798191723776122880

https://twitter.com/nntaleb/status/797968450429693953

https://twitter.com/ramzpaul/status/797919224320565248

And then of course there's stuff like this:

https://twitter.com/ESYudkowsky/status/796376195088551938

The smarter leftists are deep in self-reflection, constantly wondering "how did I get this wrong? How did we all miss this?".

I thought a new slogan to say to these people.

Check Your Signaling.

Yes, Shlomo. You lost your bets because you were busy signaling. Every time you say something stupid we'll be there to tell you: Check your signaling. Because we know. We know you're full of shit. And the thing is, we know you know it too. You're a smart guy. You just need somebody to remind you. To shame you on your fawning to the elite. To shame you on your greedy status-seeking. To shame you on your signaling.

The Left is getting ready to spend 8 long years signaling how "people are afraid", shitting on Trump day and night signaling how they are the protectors of blacks, mexicans, sexual deviants and every kind of fucked up people. They are not doing this because of any belief they hold. They are doing this because they want status. They signal holiness in order to make money and get attractive mates. That wouldn't matter if that's all they did; but then every once in a while they get in a position of power and they have to make good on their signaling by implementing leftist policies; leftist policies that are harmful to everyone; even themselves. Do white leftists really benefit from all the leftist policies of the last 50 years? Of course not! They are wrecking Western civilization as a whole. Matt Yglesias got beat up by black thugs and sent to a hospital. Plenty of leftist women have been raped and assaulted. Look at Germany!

They don't do it because it's good for them long term. They do it because it makes them look good short-term.

Behavioral economics is some academic claptrap that leftists came up with to justify arbitrary government intervention. The gist is that humans are stupid, full of biases, and government needs to help them for their own good. And you know, they have a point. Humans have a bias to signal holiness, even when its harmful for them. Well, we, out of charity and love for humanity, will help them out of it. We will help them Check their Signaling, making them shut up, so that they don't hurt themselves down the line.

Remember, this is very important. Don't think it's just talk. Talk is very important. Stop the signaling and soon enough they'll stop their evil-doing. Call them out. Every single time.

Branding

2016-11-24 // wat do, rightwingers, nrx

So there's a stampede of people trying to disavow and disassociate from the alt-right because Richard Spencer has gone full-Nazi. The speech is out there. It's pretty lame. Not a fan myself. But hey, works for him. I'm sure he's having the time of his life. Getting laid like a champ, if he's into ladies. I'm happy he's having fun, instead of blue-haired fat Hillary supporters having fun.

Jim has done an eloquent argument for having no enemies to the right.[151] I have little to add to it. What I will do is talk what I know about, language. See, the alt-right isn't a thing. "Alt-right" is a word. A word with no clear owners, no set definition. I actually recall it starting with Spencer himself; then it got a big bigger, then Hillary made it famous in her speech, with even Bannon putting it to good use. I myself too jumped into the bandwagon, if only to make a linguistic point.

But the thing with words is that you don't get to control what their usage. People are getting out because they're afraid that "alt-right" will be used as a buzzword for Sieg-Heil-ing Nazis, and they don't want to be associated with that. That's a reasonable point. Leftists in the USA call themselves "liberal", because the word "socialist" became associated with bad things. That never happened in Europe where there are proud Socialist Parties in almost every country. Perception matters, language usage is mostly a function of habit, if the mainstream press succeeds in associating the word "alt-right" with Spencer's LARPers through sheer repetition, the thing will stick.

So people may need a new name. But don't forget that you won't get to control the new name. Neoreaction was a cool name until Eternal September happened and it soon enough became associated with depressed medicated millennial monarchists. Nick Land has had more success using his fame and charisma to basically own the "NRx" brand. He gets to define it; good for him. Ownership is good. There's a reason why intellectual trends always happened on a personal master-apprentice basis. The extreme left is always splintering into different parties, all named by some variant of Revolutionary Trotskist Democratic Action Communism or whatever.

We all need a name. "Alt-right" was a good name, and it was useful as a marker for the non-cucked right during this election. But of course a name without an owner is always going to cause the same problem: somebody stupid and vain is going to use it to do

---

[151] https://blog.jim.com/politics/no-enemies-to-the-right/

something that you'd rather they didn't do. There's millions of people in this earth; you just can't stop this. Somebody will do something stupid sooner or later.

You have two options: you can not care; ignore the criticisms of your enemy, be overtly accepting of everybody to your right. Or if you do care; then you need to get a new name and own it. You need authority; a school, a school master, and a chain of command so that you can ensure that nobody does anything stupid.

And by the way some people are saying that Nazis aren't "to our right". But of course there are. You see, humans are pretty smart. There's hidden wisdom in the categorization of "extreme left" and "extreme right". Sure, the actual policy proposals of communists and Nazis (national socialists!) are fairly similar. But that's not the point. Politics isn't about policy. If you've learned anything in this blog is that people's overt statements are just signaling positions in a personal game of status struggle.

What "extreme" means is willing to use extreme means to gain status. The extreme left is batshit communist, feminist lesbians who argue for the extermination of men, people who are willing to use violence to get on top. The extreme right is batshit Nazi, people claiming the white race is genetically superior to all, that white men are all by birth natural conquerors and crusaders, willing to argue for the extermination of other races, people who are willing to use violence to get on top.

Character is inborn; your politics are just an avatar of that. Some people want status very very badly. Some don't care that much. Your politics generally is a function of that and your particular identity, which drives to the camp which you find more likely to bring you status. As of me; I wouldn't mind that Richard Spencer and his folk gained some status; I sure prefer it to blue haired lesbians and black gay men gaining status. So I won't have enemies to my right. Just don't ask me if I agree on what they say. I don't think the question even makes sense.

By the way, you can find me on Gab:

https://gab.ai/Spandrell

Epistocracy and Moral Intellectualism

2016-12-12 // theory, democracy, power

Ever since it became obvious that Trump had a chance of winning, the junior minions of the Cathedral, those mediocre status-seekers waiting for breaks on the status hierarchy so they could scavenge some point for themselves, started to come up with some long-winded arguments against democracy. Which was a lot of fun to watch.

Less fun to watch was the particular argument that they came up with. We need "epistocracy". The rule of those who know. That's mean to exclude those Trump voters. Those are ignorant. Shouldn't vote. Only those who know, those who are not ignorant, should vote. Hence epistocracy.

This is a fairly old idea, obviously, and it reflects a very old and basic misunderstanding that the Western philosophical tradition has about knowledge. We tend to think that knowing more stuff makes you a good person. Socrates used to say that evil people were just ignorant of the good. If we only could teach them, have them understand, they will quickly and resolutely change their evil ways.

But that's bogus. Knowing a lot doesn't mean shit. If you can even measure that properly. The question is what you do with your knowledge. Of course ceteris paribus it's better to know stuff than to be ignorant. But we're talking politics here. The wise guy isn't necessarily the good one. Evil is not about ignorance, evil is about evil. Lack of empathy, selfishness, impulse control, whatever. Evil is a personality trait, most likely inborn or socialized in early infancy, and very hard to change. Only changeable through constant social pressure to make sure the guy can't do evil even if he wants to.

The same goes for meritocracy. Yeah, we have the smartest guys on top. We have exams to guy to elite universities, to get to high places in the civil service and the top companies. So what? Are smart guys better people? Look at Wall Street. Look at China. They invented meritocracy. I've written about some examples of the top mandarins at the Imperial court. Were they good people? Surely some were. But many others weren't. And an evil smart guy is a formidable man. Look at the crap Google or Starbucks is capable of coming up to justify anti-white discrimination or tranny rights. Smart guys all of them.

Which is precisely the problem. Dumb people have weaker imaginations. They only have cognitive capacity to see the real world around them and barely deal with it. Smart guys can signal their social desirability by coming up with long and convoluted chains of utter and complete madness, and still survive, leading normal lives. You don't necessarily want those guys playing politics.

The real issue in running an organization isn't smarts, or knowledge. It's competence, loyalty, and commitment. Skin in the game. All those journalists have neither competence, nor loyalty, nor commitment. Their skin is in another game, the con-game they've been running since they invented the newspaper and started agitating against the traditional order in old Europe. No, we don't need epistocracy. We need the rule of the good, the competent, the loyal.

2016

2016-12-30 // links

So the year is near its end. It's been an eventful year. A good year, perhaps. A year of hope. Trump won. The UK voted to leave the European Union and the government is willing to enforce that. Millions of hostile Muslims are roaming Northern Europe, stealing and raping at will. Fortunately I'm not in Germany. But I might come back to Europe during next year. Asia haters can rejoice. I'll have some skin in the game shortly.

2016 hasn't been the most prolific year for this blog, nor the most insightful, but my readership has exploded. What had a slowly rising readership from 2013 to 2015 more than doubled in 2016. And I've been getting a lot of praise around. So thank you everyone. Or I guess I should thank Donald Trump. 2016 for has been the year of the alt-right, and I'm glad of having been part of it, if only marginally. But I like marginal. I like being in the right edge of the Bell Curve of nuanced thought and careful look at the facts.

Incidentally my most popular posts for this year have been the following:

-The conflict within Asian Americans between allying with Whites for Trump or doubling down on anti-white leftism.[152]

-Nationalism [153] is back because post-nationalism, i.e. global liberalism is a bad deal for men. Nationalism is tribalism, a war ethos, and men can find status there. There is no status for men in managerial globalism.

And of course my series elaborating on Houellebecq's Submission. Europe might turn Islamic, and that may not be a bad thing[154], considering feminism and present demographic trends. There is a reason that second-generation Muslims in Europe are more devout than their immigrant parents; and that's a reaction to feminism.[155] Which is also what drives many terrorist attacks[156]. At any rate, we need a new religion, and Islam is already here and pretty healthy, so odds are they might win out. You don't like

---

[152]   https://spandrell.com/2016/05/20/between-a-rock-and-a-hard-place/

[153] i.e. the alt-right core

[154] https://spandrell.com/2016/02/04/the-easy-way-out/

[155] https://spandrell.com/2016/06/18/divide-et-impera/

[156] https://spandrell.com/2016/07/16/toxic-arab-masculinity/

it, I don't like it, but neither did Romans liked that weird cult from Judaea, and yet they ended up embracing Christianity[157] and exterminating Pagan culture in a few decades.

I didn't make many friends by saying this, and unlike Houellebecq I didn't make any money either. But it needed to be said. Now that I might be back in Europe I'm likely to stop saying it as I confront the reality of having dumb Muslims around, so my disgust prevents me from entertaining historical abstractions. But the trends are there for everyone to see.

What did make me friends were my posts on Chinese history. Here's a post on why Tibet belongs to China[158]. The Great Ming Emperor on why women shouldn't leave the home.[159] An anecdote on how the golden age of Chinese philosophy was in part pretty much a holiness signaling by Confucius and his pals[160]. The great story of how the Ming dynasty fell and the Manchus took over[161] with the enthusiastic help of Chinese generals. And of course my series (1[162], 2[163], 3[164], 4[165], 5[166])on the Northern Song Dynasty, and the story of how it spectacularly fell to the Jurchens who took the entire imperial family 2,000 miles to the north, and put all the imperial princesses in a smelly wooden brothel, where they also made to wash their smelly leather clothes.

People asked me if I could write a book, and I considered it for a while; but I just didn't find the time this year. I apologize for that. But I did prepare for a while, and jointly

---

[157] https://spandrell.com/2016/05/15/we-need-a-new-religion-4/

[158] https://spandrell.com/2016/04/06/the-informed-position-on-tibet/

[159] https://spandrell.com/2016/08/30/the-great-ming-emperor-admonishes-his-troops-about-women/

[160] https://spandrell.com/2016/05/21/the-bow-of-the-king-of-chu/

[161] https://spandrell.com/2016/02/04/choices/

[162] https://spandrell.com/2016/04/19/the-distribution-of-power/

[163] https://spandrell.com/2016/04/21/the-song-golden-age/

[164] https://spandrell.com/2016/04/23/the-song-dynastys-decline/

[165] https://spandrell.com/2016/04/24/the-song-dynastys-fall/

[166] https://spandrell.com/2016/04/26/the-song-dynastys-surrender/

with some friends we have a project ongoing to start a new site to write Chinese history in a more dedicated way. Heaven willing that might get started early next year. Please stay tuned. And if somebody wants to help out, either with writing or website design skills, by all means send me an email.

Not that this blog is going anywhere. But the theme of this blog has never been history, as much as I like to illustrate my points by coming up with stories from the old days. The theme of this blog is the analysis of human politics, especially the most bizarre parts of it, such as religion, ideology, self-destructive leftist politics, democracies where people happily go to vote to parties who cheat on them every 4 years, and that kind of stuff. I could never understand any of it; until last year when I finally had my epiphany[167], thanks to Scott Atran[168] and the basket of mangoes[169] that Pakistan sent to Mao Zedong. Now I understand what leftists are all about. They're about screwing the social order[170] so that they can come up higher up after the revolution. And they don't care about facts because nobody cares about facts. Certainly not as much as their personal status.

That said, I haven't run out of things to say. There's still a lot to explain. Trump won! And he did so in a democratic election. The foundational theory of neoreaction, Moldbug's argument that leftism was unhinged because the Cathedral rules the world and democracy makes it worse can't quite account for what we are seeing. We have a pretty decent theory of leftist victories, but we don't have one of leftist defeats. Next year we should have time to discuss that. I also hope to refine my methodology by introducing some very needed Chinese philosophy of languag[171]e over here. People throw words around like it's nobody's business. Well this blog is about calling a spade a bloody shovel. Language is a very technical skill; but it's not about quantity. Trump is pretty inarticulate, but look at him. So expect more linguistics (traditional, not the modern academic trash) for next year.

---

[167]   https://spandrell.com/2015/03/01/leftism-is-just-an-easy-excuse/

[168]   https://spandrell.com/2015/03/09/religion/

[169]   https://spandrell.com/2015/02/19/explaining-the-cultural-revolution-signalling-arms-races-as-bad-fiat-currency/

[170]   https://spandrell.com/2015/10/09/the-social-module/

[171]   https://spandrell.com/2016/08/25/correct-naming/

And of course the other main theme of this blog was that We Need a New Religion. I've been fleshing out the reason for why we need one, and what kind of religion we should get. This was an approximation[172], expect more of this to come.

Happy New Year.

---

[172] https://spandrell.com/2016/12/27/gnon-theology/

Self-Deceptive Status Filters

2016-12-21 // status, signaling, leftism, theory, psychology, philosophy, chechens

People call me cynical because I say ideology is crap. It's just stuff people say to look good to their peers. Signaling, that is. And I support this claim by pointing out that people just don't know shit. David Hume proved that. We don't even "know" the laws of nature with any certainty. Yes, we're used to some things happening after certain things. There's chains of events that strongly hint at causality. But you can never know for sure.

Of course that kind of fuzzy knowledge is good enough for human purposes; people do get by in their lives, do things expecting consequences to occur, and they almost invariably do. But the strength of that knowledge depends on the frequency of their repetition. So people only really know what they're very familiar with. Their job, generally. This maps to Conquest's Second Law: everybody is conservative about what they know best. People are not conservative (i.e. they are leftist) on the things they don't know. Why would they be? They don't know much about it. And yet they have an opinion about it. They talk about it. Why would you talk about something you don't know about? Signaling, of course.

Signaling doesn't exactly equate leftism, but it kinda does. Signaling is about gaining status. That's why you signal, that's what living in society is about. If you were a tiger you'd be in the jungle eating animals and looking for females to rape; as it happens humans are social primates, and we need to get along with other humans. We want other humans to help us for the lower cost possible; getting what you want in society is the definition of having status. Of course everybody wants to get their way; everybody wants status, but it's physically impossible for everyone to get what they want. Basically food and pretty women. You need people to help you out, to work for you, and there's only so much work available. Status is scarce. So people compete for it. Compete all the time. Animals do all the time too; see all those deers and goats and bulls jousting for access to females. Humans do that all the time too, but human bands need common labor so they evolved ways to try to avoid ingroup violence. You can't just beat and kill your status-rivals; you need them to grow crops with you. And humans can make weapons so there's no obvious hierarchy of strength where the biggest dude gets to rule forever, as in lions.

So you gotta status-jock without violence. So you signal. I guess women started that; they can't just beat up other women by sheer physical strength, and odds are the woman you wanna beat up is some dude's bitch, and as a woman you don't wanna cross him. Or maybe it's sexual selection of men just not being into murderous women. At any rate, civilized society is about signaling. And it's much better than constant jousting. Civilization is nice. Not having to kill or maim all your rivals for access to food and women is nice. But signaling has its own problems. For one you gotta make up stuff. You gotta get used to lying, having an opinion on no grounds, repeating high-status opinions like they were your own. Civilization requires constant bullshit on a massive scale.

Of course this implies that humans, or animals in general are wired up to accurately perceive reality. But that's a pretty baseless assumption. Living beings evolve so that they can survive and reproduce. They are wired up to find food, avoid danger and mate as much as possible. That's all there is to it. Their reality-perception abilities will only develop to the extent that they improve survival and reproduction, i.e. fitness. For solitary animals one would assume that they gotta be pretty accurate at analyzing their environment. They're busy enough finding food and females to entertain bullshit. At most nature may favor some amount of baseless optimism so they don't get discouraged. But social animals are different. You need to get along. You need to interact with others to get your way. A good way of getting your way is lying your way. Cheating your peers so that they give you stuff. Of course this creates incentives to avoid being cheated yourself. So you wanna be able to notice if someone's lying to you. You need to find signals that your friends are lying. Tone of voice, twitching of the eye, posture. There's always ways to tell. But this detection-race of course creates the ultimate incentive. Bullshit without lying. Believe your own bullshit so that you don't produce any sign of cheating. That way you can't be detected.

Some people may have noticed this is the argument of the great evolutionary biologist Robert Trivers in a series of papers on Self-Deception. Let me paste some quotes from his 2000 paper, The Elements of a Scientific Theory of Self-Deception.[173]

(...) the argument for self-deception is not so obvious. For a solitary organism, the prospects seem difficult, if not hopeless. In trying to deal effectively with a complex, changing world, where is the benefit in misrepresenting reality to oneself? Only in interactions with other organisms, especially con-specifics, would several benefits seem to arise. Because deception is easily selected between individuals, it may also generate self-deception, the better to hide ongoing deception from detection by others. In this view, the conscious mind is, in part, a social front, maintained to deceive others —who more readily attend to its manifestations than to those of the actor's unconscious mind.

My bolding. This maps pretty well with Randall Collins' theory of people's behavior being formed by interactional rituals, where you learn what to say and do while

---

[173] https://roberttrivers.com/Robert_Trivers/Publications_file s/Trivers2000.pdf

watching your peers do it together. Note that speech is also a form of behavior. In the rationalist West we assume that speech this special power that reflects the content of the mind, but there's no evidence for that, nor can there be. Speech is like gestures or grunts; things you do to communicate with others. There's nothing magical about it.

there are also situations in which your dominant activity (say, lecturing) is honest, but a minor activity is deceitful (stealing the chalk). These can be thought of as directed by unconscious modules favored by selection so as to allow us to pursue surreptitiously strategies we would wish to deny to others. Naturally these will often remain unconscious to us.

I will shortly describe in detail a deceitful little module in my own life which I have discovered primarily because my pockets fill up with contraband: hard, concrete objects that others may soon miss. What is the chance that I perform numerous unconscious selfish modules whose social benefits do not pile up in one place, where I can notice them (and others confirm them), e.g., ploys of unconscious manipulation of others (including, of course, as an academic, expropriating their ideas)?

I have discovered over the years that I am an unconscious petty thief. I steal small, useful objects: pencils, pens, matches, lighters and other useful objects easy to pocket. I am completely unconscious of this activity while it is happening. I am, of course, now richly aware of it in retrospect, but after at least 40 years of performing the behavior I am still unconscious ahead of time, during the action, and immediately afterwards. Perhaps because the trait is so unconscious, it appears now to have a life of its own and often seems to act directly against even my narrow interests. For example, I steal chalk from myself while lecturing and am left with no chalk with which to lecture (nor do I have a blackboard at home). I steal pencils and pens from my office and, in turn, from my home, so if I download my pockets at either destination, as I commonly do, I risk being without writing implements at the other end. Recently I stole the complete set of keys of a Jamaican school principal off of his desk between us. And so on.

In summary, noteworthy features of this module are that: (1) it is little changed over the course of my life; (2) increasing consciousness of the behavior after the behavior has done little or nothing to increase consciousness during or in advance of the behavior; and (3) the behavior seems increasingly to misfire, that is, to fail to steal useful objects.

What is the benefit of keeping this petty thievery unconscious? On the one hand, if challenged, I can act surprised and be confident in my assertion that nothing like this was ever my conscious intention (see below). On the other hand, unconsciousness ensures that my thievery will not interfere with ongoing behavior, while the piece of brain devoted to stealing can concentrate on the problem at hand, i.e., snatching the desired item undetected. Part of its consciousness has to be devoted to studying my own behavior since integrating its thievery into my other behavior will presumably make this harder to detect by others, including myself.

Lol. This guy's a piece of work. But hey, insight comes from the unconventional. Anyway, I digress.

Self-deception as self-promotion. Another major source of self-deception has to do with self-promotion, self-exaggeration on the positive side, denial on the negative, all in the name of producing an image that we are "beneffective," to use Anthony Greenwald's apt term, toward others. That is, we benefit others and are effective when we do it. If you ask high school seniors in the United States to rank themselves on leadership ability, fully 80% say they have better than average abilities, but for true feats of self-deception you can hardly beat the academic profession. When you ask professors to rate themselves, an almost unanimous 94% say they are in the top half of the profession!

This is a good example. Somebody asks you where are you in a ranking in your profession. But how the hell would you know? Have you met all of your fellows? Do you even know yourself that well? Of course not. When asked a question like that people aren't processing information stored in their brains. What they do is look very well at the interviewer, figure out that they have a chance to gain some status by signaling their awesomeness, and they do so. Of course they do. Incidentally in Japan, where humility is traditionally seen as high-status, people would answer the other way around. Oh, I'm a very bad leader. I'm just some guy. Of course that's changing thanks to MBA culture exported by the US.

The construction of biased social theory. We all have social theories. We have a theory of our marriages. Husband and wife, for example, may agree that one party is a long-suffering altruist, while the other is hopelessly selfish, but they may disagree over which is which. We each tend to have a theory regarding our employment. Are we an exploited worker, underpaid and underappreciated for value given (and fully justified in minimizing output and stealing company property)? We usually have a theory regarding our larger society as well. Are the wealthy unfairly increasing their own re-sources at the expense of the rest of us? Does democracy permit us to reassert our power at regular intervals? Is the judicial system systematically b ased against our kind of people (African-Americans for example)? The capacity for these kinds of theories presumably evolved in part to detect cheating in our relationships and in the larger system of reciprocal altruism.

Social theory is easily expected to be biased in favor of the speaker. Social theory inevitably embraces a complex array of facts and these may be very partially remembered and very poorly organized, the better to construct a consistent self-serving body of social theory.

Social theory being a nice sounding name for ideology. You gotta give it to Trivers that he was an honest and insightful guy. He personally was best friends with the Black Panthers and spent decades as an activist for black power in America. And yet look at him: here he is confessing it's all bullshit he made up, biased in favor of him and his friends.

Alexander was, I think, the first person to point out that group selection thinking—the mistaken belief that natural selection favors things that are good for the group or the species—is just the kind of social theory you would expect to be promulgated in a group-living species whose members are concerned to increase each other's group orientation.

Touché, group selectionists. What else is there to say? Just look at E.O. Wilson and tell me he doesn't look like a Puritan pastor.

Fictitious narratives of intention. Just as we can misremember the past in a self-serving way, so we can be unconscious of ongoing motivation, instead experiencing a conscious stream of thoughts which may act, in part, as rationalizations for what we are doing, all of which is immediately available verbally should we be challenged by others: "But I wasn't thinking that at all, I was thinking such-and-such." A common form in myself is that I wish to go to point C, but can not justify the expense and time. I leap, however, at a chance to go to point B, which brings me close enough to point C so that, when there, I can easily justify the extra distance to C, but I do not think of C until I reach B. We may have much deeper patterns of motivation which may remain unconscious, or nearly so, for much longer periods of time, unconscious patterns of motivation in relationships, for example.

This is a similar argument to Scott Alexander's "Schelling fences on slippery slopes"[174] post. If Less Wrongers wanted to really understand cognitive biases they could just read Trivers work, which is shorter and to the point. But of course what they really wanted is to follow Shlomo and make money scamming the government through their institute while enjoying in easy sex. But I digress.

In summary, the hallmark of self-deception in the service of deceit is the denial of deception, the unconscious running of selfish and deceitful ploys, the creation of a public persona as an altruist and a person beneffective in the lives of others, the creation of self-serving social theories and biased internal narratives of ongoing behavior which hide true intention. The symptom is a biased system of information flow, with the conscious mind devoted, in part, to constructing a false image and at the same time being unaware of contravening behavior and evidence. The general cost of self-deception, then, is misapprehension of reality, especially social, and an in- efficient,

---

[174] https://lesswrong.com/lw/ase/schelling_fences_on_slippery_slopes/

fragmented mental system. For a deeper view of these processes we must remember that the mind is not divided into conscious and unconscious, but into differing degrees of consciousness. We can deny reality and then deny the denial, and so on, ad infinitum. Consciousness comes in many, many degrees and forms. We can feel anxious and not know why. We can be aware that someone in a group means us no good, but not know who. We can know who, but not why, and so on.

We can also know things and not know quite how to put them into language. You get hunches. That happens because language is a tool to make up excuses with your friends. Practice breeds mastery; if something happens which you understand but it doesn't serve as an excuse for anything you most likely won't even know how to talk about it. Because you never have.

Prayer and meditation are two widespread examples of people wrestling with their phenotypes, some of which may have been favored by selection to suppress negative phenotypic traits, including the negative phenotypic trait of self-deception! Many famous passages from the world's great religions, as well as rituals of prayer and meditation, are directed against self- deception, as in this loose translation of Matthew 7:1–5 in the New Testament of the Bible: "Judge not that ye be not judged, for you are projecting your faults onto others; get rid of your own self-deception first, then you will have a chance of seeing others objectively."

Might be why I've never been into meditation.

Positive illusions? Another important possibility is that self-deception has intrinsic benefit for the organism performing it, quite independent of any improved ability to fool others. In the past twenty years an important literature has grown up which appears to demonstrate that there are intrinsic benefits to having a higher perceived ability to affect an outcome, a higher self-perception, and a more optimistic view of the future than facts would seem to justify. It has been known for some time that depressed individuals tend not to go in for the routine kinds of self-inflation that we have described above. This is sometimes interpreted to mean that we would all be depressed if we viewed reality accurately, while it seems more likely that the depressed state may be a time of personal re-evaluation, where self- inflation would serve no useful purpose. While considering alternative actions, people evaluate them more rationally than when they have settled on one option, at which time they practice a mild form of self-deception in which they rationalize their choice as the best possible, imagine themselves to have more control over future events than they do, and see more positive outcomes than seem justified. What seems clear is that they gain direct benefits of functioning from these actions. Life is intrinsically future-oriented and mental operations that keep a positive future orientation at the forefront result in better future outcomes (though perhaps not as good as those projected). The existence of the placebo effect is another example of this principle (though it requires the cooperation of another person os- tensibly dispensing medicine). It would be very valuable to integrate our understanding of this kind of positive self-deception into the larger frame- work of self-deception we have been describing.

Irrational confidence works. Ask Roissy about it. Fake it till you make it. You never know, right? So if all knowledge is uncertain, might as well make it look like you are capable of anything. You're awesome, you can get anything done. I mean you could potentially get it done. The possibility might be small but it's still possible. You might always get lucky. So why be negative? And of course people are attracted to conmen of this sort. What if it's true? Might as well be his friend. Might as well sleep with this guy.

I also like this theory of depression. If you can't shit-talk your way into anything, if you're certain of that; well might as well take a break.

Self-deception appears to be a universal human trait which touches our lives at all levels —from our innermost thoughts to the chance that we will be annihilated together in warfare. It affects the relative development of intellectual disciplines (the more social the content, the less developed the discipline: contrast physics and sociology) as well as the relative degree of consciousness of individuals (generally, more self-deceived, less conscious). An evolutionary analysis suggests that the root cause is social, including selection to deceive others, selection on others to manipulate and deceive oneself, and selection on competing sections of one's own genotype.

So to summarize: consciousness is just a social front, a social-facing program you make up so you can manipulate your peers to do your bidding. I'll add that language is just the main (though not only) tool of this social front, and its purpose is of course to manipulate others to do your bidding. It's nothing else; it's not what your thoughts are made of. Is something you use to interact with others.

As such the output of this program we call consciousness is not necessarily the truth. That's just not part of the program. The program is designed to get you status. If a careful and accurate analysis of reality gets you status; well we'll use that. If parroting slogans about Global Warming or Black Lives Matter or Transexual Pronouns gets you status; well just parrot that shit.

Again don't get me wrong: I'm not saying everybody is a filthy liar. The definition of a lie is a misrepresentation of facts done with the conscious intend of deceiving someone. But that's not the argument here. The argument is that brains aren't built to represent facts accurately anyway. Animals gotta survive. They gotta reproduce. Slowly, generation by generation, they found ways to do that. In social species getting along with your friends and having them help you find food and mates is most important. So of course being able to manipulate your friends is more important than being able to accurately perceive reality. And self-deception is a pretty good strategy to achieve that.

Of course self-deception isn't a very accurate naming. Deception implies intend to deceive. And this stuff is unconscious. It's more like a status-filter. Your brain only processes the information that is good for you. That is useful for social life. For fitness. And again, that goes down to a basic epistemological problem. You can never be certain of things. Natural laws appear to exist, and high frequency makes you fairly comfortable of them. The way that brains work is that high frequency creates habits so that the behavior in reaction to that becomes increasingly fast and automatic. So there's that. But that's not certainty; that's habit. Who's to say that God isn't going to come down and cut the Red Sea in half? You never know. Remember that Al Ghazali basically killed Islamic science by saying that fire doesn't burn cotton; it's Allah who comes down and makes the cotton turn hot and black. Which implies some day he may not do so.

You could be pretty damn certain of things if you lived by yourself with nobody to challenge your memory; but living in society people are talking all kinds of bullshit all the time, which also distorts your perception. What if they're right? At any rate you gotta get along with them, else they might get pissed and sacrifice you to the Frog totem. So the evolutionary sound strategy for a social species isn't caring for the truth. Not even close.

To finish up, and for no good reason, here's a video of Chechens dancing.

https://www.youtube.com/watch?v=NAamfDx1DAU

Intellectuals

2016-12-20 // Jordan Peterson, democracy

I made the point in the last post that having smart people on top as a principle doesn't necessarily help things because they might very well be evil. Here Jordan Peterson makes the same point in a more forceful way.

https://youtu.be/QPxofHfffS8?t=2h39m16s

If you can, take a look at the whole thing. I think it's not hyperbole that this is the best interview ever. This guy is good. I think he's got a new religion in his head and he did it all by himself. What a man.

If any of you are reading this: Please, somebody set up a chat between Moldbug and Peterson. It would be epic.

Jordan Peterson on Truth

2016-12-22 // Jordan Peterson, philosophy

So I wrote this whole last post; and soon later I found that Jordan Peterson was saying pretty much the exact same thing but in more accessible language. So if you didn't quite get my last post, you can listen to him say it.

https://youtu.be/bjnvtRgpg6g?t=1h23m7s

 Start at 1h23m.

Some people, religious people usually, get angry when I make this pragmatic argument. Like I'm a toxic personality which is arguing for nihilism. Look, I'm no nihilist. But you don't need to be a nihilist to be depressed. Look outside. Read the news. See how Western Civilization is dying in front of our own eyes while the best and brightest are not only failing to stop it but actively aiding the demise. That's what depresses people. And for centuries, neither traditional religion nor "conservatives" have had a decent explanation for why the hell this is happening. Moldbug was the perhaps the first to make some sense. I think I've come up with a very good explanation.

Now I agree that relativism of this sort isn't exactly constructive. I know very well. Hell, I'm the guy who's been arguing for a new religion for 5 years already. I know very damn well, so stop telling me that. I know you can't run a cohesive army by telling your soldiers that their consciousness is a social front. I get it. But I'm not running an army here. I'm trying to make sense of reality. And I'm making a damn lot of sense.

But look again at Peterson. This guy is no nihilist. He's almost the least nihilistic guy ever. He's the boss of self-help preachers. He's a "deeply religious" guy who makes his living by telling people that life has meaning, convincing people to live socially conservative lives. And yet he understands and recognize the basic reality of human knowledge. He's making my exact same argument; and I swear I got there by myself before watching him. So it's pretty obvious that accepting pragmatic philosophy doesn't necessarily lead into nihilism. I'm not sure I buy this guy's framework, but at least he shows it can be done.

But at any rate; I'm not trying to make anyone feel inadequate. If you want to run a Christian army; by all means preach them the old Thomist trope. If you want to run a Jewish army you can preach them whatever the hell it is you guys preach. If you want to run a White-nationalist army you can preach them about Thor and Odin and Sumerians being Aryans and whatever. Do your thing, and I'll praise your courage and valor and donate money and hold a party for every victory of yours against the forces of progressivism. I'm your friend.

But if you're not running an army, and you just want to know what the hell is going on, well you better read my blog, because what those armies are telling you makes no sense. And now I'm going to make a point about the lack of a need for ideological coherence and will give an offering to Kek. Merry Christmas to everyone.

Gnon Theology

2016-12-27 // Jordan Peterson, theory, philosophy, history, religion, Top Post

I propose a short ritual for when reactionaries meet each other. You go to a church, or some nice old building. Emphasis on old, more than nice. You get there, and the master says the following string, which the apprentice is to repeat.

There is no God but Gnon. Kek is his avatar. And Jordan Peterson is a pretty good prophet.

Once that is done, the master shows a red pill to the apprentice, hands it to him. And the apprentice swallows it. No. He bites it. Munchs it. He chews it. It's hard. It's bitter. It's really hard to chew really. But at the very end it leaves an awesome aftertaste. Then Dark Enlightenment occurs.

Listen to this short clip (starts at 1:04:50), up to the end.

https://youtu.be/RcmWssTLFv0?t=1h4m57s

The Dark Enlightenment is based in evolution. This admits no discussion. Criticism of modernity on non-evolutionary grounds is just plain old reaction. Religious traditionalism. That's a thing. It's not my thing, but it's out there, even here on my comments, most often by a kinda annoying Jew. All in all it's a good thing that it's out there, annoying as it is. But there's a reason why reaction is a thing and neoreaction is another thing. Arnold Kling called Moldbug "neoreactionary" because he saw he wasn't just some plain old Crown Church and Country guy. Moldbug mentioned (not very heavily) HBD and that's about evolution. But there's more about evolutionary critiques of modernity than mentioning the biological heritage of humanity.

There's many ways that evolutionary theory shows the errors of progressivism. Let me mention 4 of them.

The basic one is that evolution shaped our brains as much as any other part of our bodies; our brains determine much of our behavior, and so much of observable behavior is inherited. See the above. Serotonin modulates animal behavior in lobsters, as much as in humans. You can't change that.

A corollary of these is that different populations evolved in geographically separate areas, adapting over tens of thousands of years to their different environments, producing basically different types of brains. And bodies, of course, but brains too. Evolution does not stop at the neck. So different human populations, and that includes what in popular speech is called races, have different types of brains. Different types of behavior. Different sorts of talents and dispositions. Steve Sailer called that HBD.

And of course a very important characteristic of life in earth, certainly of animal life, is that reproduction is sexual. There are two sexes who must copulate in order to reproduce. We call those male and female. The definition of male and female relies on the different size of the gametes. Males have small gametes: in animals we call it sperm. Sperm cells are tiny. Females have big gametes. In animals we call them eggs. Eggs are pretty big. That alone, the difference between the small reproductive cells of males and the big reproductive cells of females, already creates huge incentives for different behavior between males and females. Sperm is small, cheap to produce, easy to spread. Egg production is metabolically costly. It's basic economics. Sperm is cheap, eggs are expensive. Reproduction being extremely important; basically the whole point of DNA as a molecule, the very point of life; well having your reproduction mediated by cheap or expensive stuff is probably going to drive your evolution in different ways. To the extent that is possible (after all male and female DNA is mixed in every embryo), males and females are going to reproduce better if they evolve behavioral strategies that optimize how they use their gametes. And so males and females of all species behave differently. They must. Else evolution makes no sense.

This enough is very powerful. It goes against every single dogma of progressivism. Behavior has a strong genetic input. That implies races behave differently. Also that sexes behave differently. Which already by itself demolishes the very basis of progressivism. Of the Enlightenment really. Human brains aren't an blank slate. They are shaped by evolution, in different ways. Ways that matter. And ways that you cannot change.

But brains aren't the only thing that evolution shapes. And this is the fourth and most profound implication of evolutionary theory. Evolution is not only about life. Evolution is about existence. Well at it's core evolution is about conflict; evolution proves what happens when different things are in conflict and what strategies they take to win. And existence implies a conflict. Existence is in conflict with non-existence. Things that exist are here for a reason. Basically because they out-competed other things, which hence don't exist. Things exist because they work. Things that don't work cease, sooner or later, to exist. If you track how things came to exist, how they out-competed other things which used to exist, or things that might have existed; well you are doing evolutionary theory. This is of course more abstract than the very physical evolution of DNA molecules in living beings. But it is the same process all the same.

It is so abstract that can even be mapped to transcendental religion, which is why the term Gnon was coined. Gnon standing for Nature or Nature's God[175]. Nature being that which exists. And so that which evolved. Once you understand this point you must think that everything exists for a reason. Everything exists because it works, certainly it worked until the present day. Now you may not like it that some things exist. You might want to destroy them. But before you do so you should stop and think about the evolutionary process that made them exist in the first place. Because remember, that things is there because it worked. And if the evolutionary process that put it there on there first place remains in place, then that thing will come back. Gnon will bring it back, no matter how much you hate it. No matter how utterly you destroy it, Gnon will bring it back. And you can't do anything about it.

That doesn't mean you must like everything. Or that everything always stays the same. Nature changes. I mean, Gnon changes. Evolution is a process; that implies change. Life changes. Animals change all the time. Humans also change things, and sometimes the change sticks. Human sacrifice used to be a thing. The Carthaginians sacrificed their own children. Their first bon sons. That was a thing. It happened for a reason. It evolved. It worked for them. Then the Romans conquered them and destroyed that thing; and it didn't come back. It stopped working. That's evolution too. That is Gnon's will.

The Romans destroyed other things too. They destroyed the patriarchal family[176]. They'd rather have fun and be merry. They stopped having children. Roman hedonism was a thing. Then the Germans conquered them. Roman hedonism stopped being a thing. Rome itself stopped being a thing. Gnon brought back the patriarchal family. That one works. You can mess with it. You can destroy it for a while. Even a long while. But it will come back. Gnon will always bring it back.

So the point here is to tell what will come back and what will not. What works always and what doesn't necessarily do so. In theological terms, we must find out Gnon's will. I guess I'd translate it into Chinese as the Dao. Figuring out Gnon's will is not easy. Surely some Carthaginians might have protested about having to throw their first bon baby sons to die on the feet of Moloch. But the Carthaginian elite strongly believed doing so was Gnon's will. Turns out it wasn't. And they paid dearly for it.

And of course many Romans protested about the changes to paternal authority and general sexual morality in late Republican and Imperial Rome. But people thought that wasn't important, that Gnon's will was changing. Turns out it wasn't. And they paid dearly for it.

---

[175] `https://www.xenosystems.net/the-cult-of-gnon/`

[176] `https://blog.jim.com/economics/sarah-perry-on-the-economic-value-of-children/`

So you gotta be careful about every thing. And society is a thing. Culture is a thing. Every social ritual is a thing. You must understand Gnon's will if you want to survive. If you want to continue to be a thing yourself in the future. This means you need to understand why every thing exists. How it got there. How it evolved. You must understand it's history, in other words.

So in the above examples: the Carthaginians sacrificed their baby boys because many centuries back home people back in the old country in the Levant were doing their sacrifices. They had some problem, perhaps some weather problem, or some war with a neighboring tribe. Sacrificing bulls and goats as usual wasn't quite doing it; so some crazy guy. Most likely a woman actually, she threw a baby boy to the idol's altar. Then something good happened. It worked. Maybe the tribesmen saw the woman killing her baby to the tribal god, felt her strong commitment towards the tribe, which gave them courage, took them to battle, and made them win. Or maybe it was just some coincidence and it rained the next day. At any rate, the thing stuck, and ever since it became a mainstream signal of commitment to the tribe. An extremely costly, and hence strong, signal. Now signaling is also a thing. It exists for a reason. A very good reason. Signaling is important. You can't run a large human group without commitment. And you need costly signals to confirm commitment. But signals also tend to spiral for spurious reasons. Greedy people trying to gain status for themselves. Gnon doesn't like that. He doesn't care too much about it, hence peacocks. But every now and then he comes down to stop the spiral and restore order.

So child sacrifice died because it stopped working; it wasn't necessary to produce its evolutionary function of giving costly signals of commitment. Gnon came up with an alternative. The Roman error was more egregious. The Romans didn't get signaling wrong. They got something very fundamental wrong. They got family wrong. And there is no alternative for family. You can get everything exactly right and still perish because you got family wrong. The Roman Empire was a very great, long-lasting empire. It did everything right. They had the best military machine the world had ever seen. They had a very well managed urban culture that tribes all over the West eagerly adopted. They had a great bureaucratic and logistic machine. But they got family wrong. And Gnon made them pay dearly. Family exists for a reason. A permanently valid reason. Well perhaps not permanent, nobody knows the future. But certainly valid today, and likely to be valid for the foreseeable future.

The patriarchal family works. It evolved for a reason. It probably evolved separately a lot of times. There's this book called "The Inevitability of Patriarchy[177]" which makes the point at length. Basically for a country to prosper you need men to defend it. And why would men defend the country? What's there in it for them? Well they get paid.

------

[177] https://en.wikipedia.org/wiki/The_Inevitability_of_Patriarchy

Pretty well actually, soldiery was good job in Rome. But what do they want the money for? To raise a family. To have a wife and children. Emphasis on *have*. Have implies possession. Possession implies some degree of freedom of use. You have a wife so you can use her. So that she's nice to you and does things that you want. And of course the same goes for children. Children are the whole point. Children are everything. Gnon manifest his will through children. That's what evolution is.

But for some odd reason Gnon did not make men desire a wife and children in the abstract. The behavioral urges of men are somewhat indirect. Men need sex, the way they need food. A man without food for a sufficient lenght of time will stop whatever he's doing and go crazy until he finds something to eat. A man without sex will stop whatever he's doin and go crazy until he finds a suitable woman. If the woman is nice to him he'll stick around. That is the way Gnon made it. In the old days that fairly reliably resulted in surviving children. Gnon saw it and saw it was good; and so that is what men do. A man with an obedient wife and well behaved children is a happy man. A man that will fight to defend it.

Well take that from a man and he will not defend his country. Why would he? Not to say that often it isn't man that takes it from himself. Many a man would rather not stick by his wife nor care about his children; seeking random women instead. That man, if successful, might be quite happy. Happier than a married man indeed. But he won't fight for his country. He has no reason to. Which is why that man, the sneaky fucker man, is considered evil in most societies. This is a man who has no skin in the game. An unloyal man. Gnon had it so that healthy societies did not allow that kind of behavior. That's why we got fornication laws. Regulation of sexual behavior. Monogamy was one way to solve it, but not the only one. But as Gnon had it having sex with a woman who was not your legal wife or a prostitute was a punishable crime.

The Romans messed with all of that. They allowed women to not be obedient to their husbands. This destroyed the incentive for many men to stick to their wives. This destroyed their incentive to defend their country. Soon enough no Roman was willing to do so. What happens when the men of a country are not willing to defend it? Somebody attacks you; and they win. The inevitability of patriarchy. That is evolution. Gnon's will.

Let me recap. I have been writing about Epistemology of late. An important theme of this blog from the beginning was why leftists believe what they do. All that obvious crap. Are they stupid? Well they obviously aren't stupid. Look at Harvard. Those guys aren't stupid. But leftist they are. They believe obviously false things. Well why?

There's two parts to the answer to that. First is that you don't know what people believe. You know what they *say* they believe. That's different. You can't possibly know what's going on inside somebody's head.

Second is that most likely there's nothing going on inside that head. You can't possibly have definite knowledge on anything. And there's no reason why human brains will have evolve to capture objective truth. Brains are designed by Gnon so that you could be here. That means have you survive and reproduce. That's all they have to do. It's no easy task, of course, which is why are brains are so big and complex. But caring about objective truth makes no sense, either in philosophical or evolutionary terms. What's important is to be evolutionary fit. In human terms that means to have social status. So people who want social status will *say* whatever it is necessary, no matter how false. And they will *believe* whatever is expedient. That's all that *believe* really means anyway; you may define it is "to have whatever mental content necessary in order to produce some particular behavior". So most people today believe that homosexuals are born that way while transexualism is a free choice. It's logically nonsensical, of course. But the point is to say that when asked, and to be able to interact with the designated victim-privilege groups as necessary.

Rationalism equates language with thought; Chomsky famously said that language's primary function is as a vehicle of thought, not communication. That's completely wrong, of course, most of the computation your brain does to keep you alive doesn't use language at all. To the extent that a minority of people tend to have extensive internal monologues, that's just conversation practice. Talking to yourself; generally in order to be ready to talk with others.

Now of course language is a huge part of how we interact socially; and much of our knowledge is social. We learn from others how to behave, how to speak. To the extent that knowledge is mediated through language; well language is a social medium. There is no meaning to language but the correlation between the use of certain words and the behavior of the people who use them. You can learn that the sun comes from the same direction every day just by looking yourself. But you will only learn the meaning of the word "democracy" by hearing somebody talk about it. I made that point also here[178].

Now of course humans are social creatures, we learn most of our behavior from others, which includes the entirety of our language. But what determines what society does? One way of thinking about this is that Power does. Politics does. Societies have power hierarchies. People on top can change the behavior of others, either through violence or persuasion. This seems pretty obvious. Indeed it was at the core of Chinese classical political thought. Confucius talked about how a courteous and well behaved lord could "teach" their people to behave morally. Lord Shang talked how the state could make laws that killed or tortured those who didn't behave morally. Both work, to a point. Eventually they were integrated into Imperial Confucianism, the ruling ideology for 2,000 years.

---

[178] https://spandrell.com/2016/08/06/social-constructs/

Europe was under the spell of rationalism mediated by Christianity so we didn't really get this until the Communists came by. Or I guess Hegel stumbled upon this. Experts on German idealism can contribute in the comments. But Communists soon enough realized that people do and say what they're told; and they loved the idea. They'd grab all the levels of power and change people to do what they wanted. They'd change everything, even language. George Orwell made that point very vividly when O'Brien forces Winston Smith to say that 2+2 equals 5. There is no module in your brain which contains numbers when you're born. Some forager tribes hardly have any numbers at all. The way we count, our number system is a social construct. If the state applies enough force, they could possibly change that.

But of course the problem with Communism, as well as Chinese legalism is that they forgot about Gnon. Knowledge is socially constructed alright. Power can alter society alright. But power is inside society. The powerful are also people. The state is not an uncaused agent with freedom of action. Nobody has freedom. Everything is evolved. Everything is subject to the will of Gnon. Knowledge is socially constructed alright. But the precise way in that humans acquire their knowledge from society is an evolved mechanism. And it's fixed. You can't change that mechanism. That is Gnon's mechanism. If you want to play with it you have to understand it first. You can't just tell people that 2+2=5. Partly because that sort of stuff is taught to small children and once taught it's extremely hard to alter.

You can't tell people to look at a guy with a beard and call him "ze", because the basic constructions of language are learned as a small child and they're as much a hard habit as the way you walk or jump. You can force people to drop on their knees and *say* what you want them to say; but you can't change habits enforced by decades of repetition. And repetition is the point; the point of pronouns is that they're very frequent, and gendered pronouns have almost equal frequency, which is why they still exist. Evolution can be seen in the natural world but it is most obvious and easy to see in language. The grammatical patterns which do not work over time disappear. You won't get people to remember a pronoun they only use while in university and when meeting 1% of the student body.

So yes, everything is socially constructed. But social constructions are evolved. And evolution follows the rails that Gnon set up. It follows our innate brain structures. Which are themselves the product of evolution, if biological, on another timescale. The social constructions which work remain in place; those that do not work disappear. And often they take the people with them. You can play with language; but it will not stick. You can play with signaling; but you may end up killing your own babies. You can play with family; but you can kill a whole people if you get that wrong.

The only way to see which social constructions follow the Will of Gnon is to look at history. To look at what existed, where it existed, and for how long. What Moldbug called "slow history". Only there you can find the Old Truths (H/T AlfaNL). Which is why Gnon's church has no priests. Only historians and biologists. And motivational speakers on tour.

called "slow history". Only there you can find the Old Truths (H/T AlfaNL). Which is why Gnon's church has no priests. Only historians and biologists. And motivational speakers on tour.

Jordan Peterson

2017-01-23 // Jordan Peterson, philosophy

Last week Jordan Peterson went to Sam Harris' podcast. I had mixed feelings about it. I thought nothing good could come out of that. And as I had expected, Sam Harris trounced Jordan Peterson. Completely. The podcast got into a complete bog down on epistemology, where Jordan Peterson tried to define the word "truth" as "good", and Harris wasn't buying it, explaining 30 times how it's very useful to have a concept of truth which is separate from the concept of good. Peterson stood his ground and confronted with volley after volley of sheer logic, refused to concede the point. The guy is stubborn. Which would be ok if he explained his logic, which he fails to do.

Now, I'm no fan of Sam Harris. I find him a bit of a narcissistic douche. You can see that on his completely unhinged criticism of Trump. And of course his dumb promotion of atheism alongside some senseless mystic crap aided by Amerindian drugs or something. This guy wants to be a liberal with the status it brings, but he wants to make sense too. And he also wants to be a guru. He's trying to sell you the leftism of yesterday as it if were some new awesome deal. Well it doesn't work like that.

That said, Sam Harris is smart. He's very articulate, his thinking is fast and precise. The guy can do logic. All things which aren't Jordan Peterson's strong suit. So he got trounced. He didn't get trounced on ideology, mind you. Jordan Peterson has semi-overtly become a prophet of Gnon, mostly on grounds of his brave refusal to submit to Ontario's Social Justice Tribunals. Sam Harris would never confront the establishment openly like that. But, credit where it's due, he's no fan of the extreme left either, and he has been quite outspoken as a critic of Islam, which hasn't made him any friends in polite society. So the guys aren't that far away in ideological terms. But they're selling different stuff. Sam Harris is selling logic. Materialism. Science. Jordan Peterson is selling pragmatic psychology. But Sam Harris knows his stuff better than Jordan Peterson knows his own stuff.

https://twitter.com/jordanbpeterson/status/822928363258056709

Now not knowing quite well what he's selling doesn't stop him from making $15,000 a month on Patreon, which I'm sure Sam Harris isn't making. So maybe he knows what he's doing better than anyone in pragmatic terms. But still, I do like consistent and articulate ideas, so let me do some fisking of Mr. Peterson. I do think he's on the right direction, widely speaking. His stuff has more potential than Sam Harris. Atheism has been tried. There was this thing called objectivism. Doesn't work very well. Pragmatic philosophy is a more robust philosophical framework to understand how living beings actually work. And putting that in a wider Darwinian framework is exactly the way it should be done. But it's hard. It's really hard. So I don't blame Jordan Peterson for being confused. I do blame him for being so inept at arguing with Sam Harris. Getting emotional I guess works for a class full of 18 year old girls or to do clinical therapy, but it sure fails to work as robust pragmatic philosophy. It's a pity, because again he's on the right track. He has really brilliant moments. So I'll try to improve on some of his ideas myself, I believe I have an advantage. Jordan Peterson is trying to understand Wittgenstein while being monolingual. It doesn't work very well like that. As insightful as he is, he just lacks in worldly experience. And that comes pretty handy if you want to see things as they are and not just as your culture primes you to see.

Anyway, you can check out the podcast here[179]. If you have a long commute by all means check it out. Seeing Sam Harris come up with a very good thought experiment every 5 minutes is something to behold. He's really good at it. But all in all I found the whole conversation pretty infuriating. The two professors speaking of morality this, morality that, how we need to make science subordinate to morality, either through cold unbiased logic, or through wholesale reform of our definition of reality. I'm starting to hate the very sounds of the word "moral". I mean, please. Science is already subordinate to morality. To morality as it actually exists in the world: to politics. Try to make science against the establishment. Try to deny global warming, or HNU. Heck, Jordan Peterson himself is getting tarred and feathered and risking life and limb for fighting those who would subordinate science to social justice.

Yet again, Professor Peterson is a prophet of Gnon, of a sort, and he is a brave man, so he deserves the benefit of the doubt. I went through the whole set of lectures of this Maps of Meaning class he gives every year, and some other stuff. I've reached the point where he's repeating the same stuff all over again, so let me put some highlights and my comments on them.

https://youtu.be/07Ys4tQPRis?t=6m39s

The first few sentences. Brilliantly put. It doesn't work. Evolutionary thinking takes you to the dark side. The Dark Enlightenment. I don't agree that rationality is new, though. Language is new, but animals are plenty rational at following their goals. A good compromise is to say, indeed, that it hardly matters, but he should explain why. He should explain that behavior is what matters, and what we call "rational" behavior is a tiny subset of behavior which doesn't need any special rules to explain.

https://youtu.be/mJI0hVV-5Vs?t=35m17s

Watch until 39:30 or so. I don't know if he has read Roissy, but it wouldn't surprise me. Yes, sexual selection is very important. Natural selection is adapting to a changing

---

enviroment. Sexual selection on the other hand drives you back to a more fixed, ancient standard. That standard of course evolves, but slowly. So modern men still kinda like cavewomen and modern women most certainly like cavemen.

https://youtu.be/mJI0hVV-5Vs?t=1h7m11s

Watch until 1:14 or so. This guy has balls of steel. Here he's telling a psychology class, which must be 80% female, that conflict resolution requires violence, better still the complete destruction of the enemy. But women don't do that; and when men get an annoying women, it's really hard to know what to do. Because the way to resolve that would be to beat the hell out of her. But that's not proper in our society, so men will basically remove themselves out of society. Which to some extent is happening.

https://www.unz.com/isteve/white-women-drinking-themselves-to-death/

https://youtu.be/PcYLzW1B6cY?t=15m25s

The Yungian argument for immigration restriction. "Every place where the things that you expect to happen, happen, is your territory. You're at home whenever you know what to do". Yes, yes. Bringing people from foreign cultures into your land makes you not know what to do; because you learn what to do, you learn your culture when you're a child. Bringing foreigners, especially hostile foreigners, messes with the cognitive map of your environment. How many people in Europe say they don't feel at home in their own countries?

https://youtu.be/F7T5cg1a77A?t=1h49m0s

Yes, yes. It's behaviorism. Prof. Peterson is a smart guy to make that connection. But there's nothing wrong with behaviorism. You're the guy who said that you can't be a rationalist if you understand evolution. Well if you're not a rationalist you're a behaviorist. Or you should be. Now of course, Behaviorism with a capital B was a historical movement with people like Skinner, and yes many of those guys were blank-slatists, who though they could condition any behavior on any animal given enough time and food pellets. Then they were beaten by the nativist rationalism of Chomsky. But Chomsky and Fodor and all those were full of shit too, let us remember that. There is no necessary link between nativism (i.e. anti-blank slatism, the idea that the brain has an innate structure) and rationalism (or it's modern descendent cognitivism). Conversely there's no necessary link between behaviorism (the idea that the brain is organized to produce behavior and not to manipulate abstract information) and blank slatism. Surely we can all agree that the brain has an innate structure, and innate behaviors. We call that instincts. Surely we can say that some behaviors are hard coded, and others rather less soft-coded, and others very soft-coded, so that there are pathways that given certain experiences over time will produce broadly similar behaviors. That's all compatible with a behaviorist perspective while being perfectly nativist.

And please, let us stop with the Magna Carta nonsense (1:50:00). The Magna Carta wasn't about "the people" against "the monarchy". It was about the nobles vs. the king. The nobles had hereditary rights which the king couldn't invade. That happened in Hungary in 1222 too, by the way. It resulted in the complete destruction of the Hungarian state by the absolutist Turks, but anyway. The point was about how to share the spoils of state power, not about "the people". That came way later when the much expanded nobility fought a war against the English king in 1642, by which time demotism was a thing.

https://youtu.be/UGLsnu5RLe8?t=17m17s

So people aren't consciously computing what to do in every instance. Which is... behaviorism. Come on Jordan, don't fight it. Join the Dark Enlightenment.

The point of how wolves and other animals have evolved strategies to come up with a dominance hierarchy without having to actually kill their rivals is a good one. Humans of course do that all the time, with the highly ritualized wars of tribal people, where people basically just show up and shout to each other. Or the very limited wars of antiquity with those chariots and stuff. Then cavalry happened and proximity vs. diversity produced vicious war. Those guys just didn't get the joke. There's this story on the Mongol invasion of Japan. The early Samurais had this fairly lame form of warfare, where they would run to the battlefield, start reciting their ancestry. My father was Lord Fujiwara this my grandfather was Lord Fujiwara that, I am the lord of here and there, then they would have this jousting contest and maybe have their minions shoot an arrow or two. Then the Mongol army came with gunpowder bombs and shooting arrow waves on sight, killing thousands of people in minutes.

Now of course we've gone back to ritualized fights to minimize bloodshed. We call that democracy. You count the armies' soldiers, whoever has more gets to rule for some years.

Jordan Peterson has many little gems like this; you might have caught the general gist of his worldview. But then he goes into epistemology and moral realism and he gets confused. You can see that very clearly because he actually doesn't know what to say. He stops for seconds trying to find a way of putting it. I think he's trapped. He's pwned by his Christian rationalist substratum. Next time let's see if I can help him get out of his confusion. Hopefully I'll be briefer than Moldbug's depwning Richard Dawkins.

Making Virtue out of Necessity

2017-01-06 // europe, economics, signaling, stagnation

Or, making virtue out of lack of lack of other paths for upward mobility.

The most important topic in social science, the humanities or however you want to call it, is what drives cultural change. Things change, that is obvious enough, and humans have been discussing it since they ever started doing abstract thinking. We understand a lot of change now. Physics tell us why the physical world changes: by obeying the laws of physics. Biology tells us why living things change: through evolution. What we still haven't figured out is why societies change. Cultural change. You can define culture as behaviors inherited through non-genetic means. We still haven't quite figured out the laws of cultural change. It happens they're immensely complicated. We know it has a lot to do with politics. And it happens that the very act of trying to figure culture out is a political statement, so it's hard to get honest inquiry running. The stakes are too high.

But still, I've always been fascinated (I'd say obsessed, but the word is quite abused these days by all sorts of posers) by why different societies do different things; and how people do different things across history. Even the same persons end up having different opinions over time. Of course you could buy the Christian-Enlightenment paradigm and think that they've just earned new information over time. You see, they suddenly realized that gaymarriage is a human right. Or you may take my Darkly Enlightened behaviorist idea that they changed their behavior because behavior follows status and they figured out that the means to earn status have changed. That would be a good subdiscipline to focus on: the study on what societies regard as high-status and how it changes.

The Melian dialogue, perhaps the first red pill ever, said it quite clearly. The strong do what they can, the weak suffer what they must. You could rephrase that to say: the high-status do what they want, the low-status do what they must -in order to raise in status. Which in humans, due to the way our behavior is imprinted through social pressure, tends to trump even the survival instinct. The Melians famously chose death before surrender. They had been raised to expect dishonor would result in extremely low status. And death is rather preferable to that. While fighting for their freedom they must have felt rather happy, doing what, if they had been able to survive, would have brought them high-status for a lifetime.

So, different societies allow for different pathways to high status. Of course societies aren't exactly free to set a standard. Those standards have evolved over time. Gnon, you know. Evolution works through environmental constraints. Even in their absence there's always genetic drift; weird practices evolve kinda randomly over time in the absence of selective pressure against them. But most of the time environmental constraints on social evolution are quite obvious.

A couple of things I read recently reminded me of a think I've always thought, and written in this blog from the very beginning[180]. My most basic intellectual inquiry has been to understand why people have gone increasingly ideological over my lifetime. I remember people in the 80s being quite easygoing, then increasingly getting worked-up about quite absurd ideological points; which of course it's getting worse. Over the years we have now developed a good conceptual framework to explain is: signaling spirals. Which indeed explains a lot: but we don't write enough about what drives them. What makes them go slower or faster. My hunch has for a long time been that the economy is perhaps the biggest factor.

The Great Stagnation is here; the great era of worldwide economic growth is over. And it's not coming back. We won't invent another energy source that improves over oil as oil did over coal. We won't invent another method of locomotion which is faster than a car or a jet airplane.All that is gone; forever. Even Moore's Law is dead now. Some things are advancing: genetics, materials science. But that doesn't fix the most important. Much of the economic boom since 1800 has been a population boom of productive populations. The population of Europe multiplied several times, filling Europe and its colonies, much of what was empty land. Well that's not going to happen, ever again. And as it happens, we have state finances all over the world set up so that increased populations of productive people are necessary to keep the system going. Well that's not happening. The system is not going. The sheer mass of rent-seeking rot is collapsing before our eyes. Even if technology were still advancing we'd still be in deep, deep shit. And it's not, so you can imagine. For some time after WW2 it used to be very very easy to make money. Now it is very very hard.

https://twitter.com/janzilinsky/status/816880633045721089

If you live in a society undergoing an economic boom, well the easiest way to gain in status is likely to be to make a lot of money. Make money, drive a fancy car, buy expensive clothes, maybe some stupid overpriced Swiss watch, go on vacation to some fancy beach, that stuff. Watch some movies of the 60s in Europe or Japan. Go take a look at China today. The people there aren't ideological. They don't give a shit. They just want to make money. Tyler Cowen was in Nigeria recently, and he reports[181] the

---

[180]   https://spandrell.com/2012/04/08/sola-fide-2-the-enforcers/

[181]   https://marginalrevolution.com/marginalrevolution/2017/01/friday-assorted-links-94.html

Muslims and Christians get along well there. Because they're too busy making money to care much about religion anyway.

So when do people care about religion? Or ideology, which is pretty much the same. Well when that happens to be the best way to get status. If it's easy to earn status through money, you'll get a fancy watch. If there's no freaking way you're making any money, well you need something else. What else? Well you can always be holier-than-thou.

I saw a Tweet by a Japanese guy who noted how these days, the temples are brimming with people for New Year's. This is often toted as a Shinto Tradition. But he distinctly remembers how when he was a child the temples were always empty. Now they're not only full in New Years; there's people going all the time. And while back in the 70s and 80s people would just to there and bow randomly, now everybody comes and does a very elaborate ritual without fail. Two bows, one clap, one bow. Now it's common for people to have strong opinions on the soul of the nation, our sacred traditions and all that. Good luck trying to find that in old movies. TV is a very good example. Now half of the programming is history and stories about how awesome our country is. It used to be girls in miniskirts and fast cars. What happened?

Well the Japanese economy went to hell, that happened. Well it didn't quite go to hell. In nominal terms the Japanese have kept a pretty respectable GDP per capita. But economic growth has tanked, taxes are up, debt is up. It's just very hard to make money. You can get a job, ok. But not a job that gets you high status. So what do you do? You go to the temple a lot. And you bow very carefully. See? Now you're a Good Person. It's the least you can do.

I've always thought that the ideological spirals we are seeing recently have much to do with that. Why are American journalists so insufferably leftist? Because they aren't getting paid. The industry is in tatters, it's awfully hard to get a decent job. So they gotta compete in holiness. Why is Europe full of regionalist movements[182], some of them even threatening independence? Because the rural economies have collapsed. There's nothing out of the big cities anymore, except in Germany, and not for long. So what rural people do is make virtue out of necessity and ceaselessly brag about their rurality. Hey, we speak Scotts here. Yeah. Oh, and we eat Haggis. Yeah. With a bit of luck they can get a job in the Scottish Parliament. The public sector isn't stagnating.

How was the world economy doing in the 1930s, when all ideological hell broke loose in the whole world? You get the point. Of course this isn't the only factor affecting signaling spirals. But it's an important factor in how they trickle down into society at large. Elites are always playing signaling games to compete with each other. Money doesn't get you status when you have too much of it. Money does get you status when

---

[182] `https://spandrell.com/2012/01/20/platters-of-loose-sand/`

you don't have it. Well now there's not much money to be made by anyone: so signaling games it is. That's not going to change unless we get an economic boom; but rent seeking bloat, bad demographics and technological stasis have made that impossible. So the signaling spiral will go on. The only question is to which side it will swim.

Fighting

2017-01-17 // leftism, loyalty, rightwingers, status

The Dark Enlightenment is Dark. That's the whole thing about it. The more you know the truth the darker it gets. The very term was coined by Nick Land who is pretty much a Skynet apologist. He doesn't seem humans have it in them to get out of this shit. Now most people don't agree with that, but the term Dark Enlightenment has stuck, and there's a reason for that. Many understand that truth is dark, and that we're heading to dark times.

I also get called very gloomy and pessimistic myself. I think that's a bit unfair; I write more about history, which is plenty dark, and more abstract points on how human society works. There's always some room for uncertainty when you write in the abstract. You wanna see real dark? Real, concrete, visceral dark? Take a look at this guy.[183]

Now I don't know who this David Hines guy is. But he knows his stuff. He knows it really well. Some snippets:

https://twitter.com/hradzka/status/820107066933202944

https://twitter.com/hradzka/status/820107288459546624

https://twitter.com/hradzka/status/820107345695035393

https://twitter.com/hradzka/status/820107423683899392

https://twitter.com/hradzka/status/820107598234087425

Of course they are. The Left is about Power. The Left is where psychopathic status maximizers go in order to attain power, i.e. maximize their status. It follows that the Left will always have the upper hand in any political conflict (i.e. war), because they're more committed to gaining power. That's the whole point on being on the left. All the stuff they believe in, all that "progressiveness", that's just means to an end. The ideas change; the goal does not. The goal is to have crush your enemies having them driven to you and hear the lamentations of their women. The left is good at that.

https://twitter.com/hradzka/status/820110007572320256

https://twitter.com/hradzka/status/820110298237587460

---

[183]   https://storify.com/sphenoid/days-of-rage-pt-5-finale-what-does-it-portend

https://twitter.com/hradzka/status/820110368353779714

https://twitter.com/hradzka/status/820110508577656833

Yes, yes. The Left knows how to fight. The left is an army. What we call the left is the descendants of the dissenting mobs which destroyed the old state order in Europe. They destroyed the English monarchy, the French monarchy. That's no joke. Nobody ever managed to destroy the traditional order in China or the Islamic world. It's some pretty virulent virus that managed to destroy European states. Of course they had inside help; but that's besides the point. Once the tactics were created, once it was shown how effective political agitation can be, it could never die again. Every time a psychopatic status maximizers was born, all he had to do was to look back, see how it's done, and do it.

I could paste the whole series of Tweets; but go read the whole thing. His point is very insightful. The Left knows how to do violence; it has been doing it for centuries. They invented this shit. As I say, a better argument would be that the tactics come first; the ideas are accessory. They come up with whatever ideas are best in order to raise a bigger army, have it funded, and keep agitating. If the Right wants to survive, if it wants to fight back, it's not going to be easy. Having balls is important. Donald Trump has balls. Many of his people have balls. But balls is not enough. You need organization. You need logistics. And you need the will to power. You need the psychopathic status-maximizing drive to keep you from giving up. Remember Leftists died all the time for the cause. The Right doesn't want to die. That's the whole point of being on the Right! If the Left is about maximizing status whatever the costs; the Right is about being left alone and allowed to survive.

Well, in a fight, the guy without scruples always has an advantage over the guy with scruples. When the Jihadists in Europe go bust Rightist demonstrations, they shout "you will lose, you love life, we love death". It's hard to argue against that. The Samurais also said their edge was that they loved death. It's hard to fight against an army who doesn't mind being sacrificed. It's not impossible; especially if they're dumb Muslims who are a bit too eager to die. But Communists aren't suicidal, the get that point. They're just ruthless. They are willing to kill, and ostracize, and starve their enemies.

As David Hines point out; the Left is not a set of ideas; it's a set of optimized tactics for agitation. And the only way to win a fight against an optimized set of battle tactics is to adopt them yourself. That was Fascism was about. To use Communist tactics against them. Some retarded conservatives use this point to argue that "fascism was leftist". No, that's really dumb. That's like saying that a Republican army is monarchist because it has a chain of command. The words "left" and "right" are not about their proclaimed ideas. They're just fighting teams, you got two of them, and you gotta give them opposite names so that the idea gets across. If the Left is winning because it's doing something right, well the Right is going to do the same. So Mussolini and Hitler ran party armies harassing the populace, it run massive rallies, it assassinated political enemies. And yes, it adopted some ideas that made it easier to raise and fund an army. He had to if he wanted to get anywhere.

The thing is that to raise an army you gotta motivate it. The Left pays it people, but more than anything it has a very solid memeplex to sell. It sells equality. If you're below average, "equality" to you sounds like "raise in status", so by definition half the population is always on board for that. And if you're running the army you get to be pretty high in status, which is very attractive for greedy status-maximizers. The problem with the Left of course is that to deliver equality you have to destroy society. The whole thing. But society has this habit of reconstructing itself, because that's what social species do; so you need to become increasingly crazy and destroy everything that can support human life if you want to deliver equality. So you get a signaling spiral. Now they're denying that biological sex is real.

The Right really just wants to survive. The Right is by definition the reaction against the Left, whatever the Left is in a particular time and space. AlfaNL says that the Dutch Right are Left Libertarians.[184] He means they are what Americans would call Left Libertarians. But in Holland they are the Right alright, because the Left comes first, and the Right is whatever army can be raised to oppose the Left. If the Left becomes crazier and murderous, the Right will morph into whatever can effectively oppose the Left. When the Left was Jimmy Carter, the Right was Ronald Reagan. When the Left is Hillary Clinton, the Right becomes Donald Trump. If the Left is going to go back to the 1930s, the Right might as well have to do so too.

Nationalism used to be a Leftist movement against the traditional monarchies of Europe. Once they won, and Nationalist democracies became the establishment, the Left became Socialist internationalism. That was a winning strategy. It spread like wildfire. It destroyed 3100 years of Chinese monarchy, which was no mean feat. But as 20th century history showed, there was a way to counter act that. Doubling down on nationalism. Equality is effective. But tribalism is pretty effective too. Especially for men. If anything, this time it should be even more attractive for men, as the Left has gone much further on feminism this time around. Now of course tribalism is harder because every Western country has hordes of enemy tribes in their midst; so going racist is basically declaring a will to engage in ethnic cleansing war. Those are harsh. Being racist in 1933 Germany was pretty much harmless LARPing. Yeepee, Aryans are awesome. Trying saying that in Berlin right now. It takes balls.

---

[184] https://alfanl.com/2017/01/12/the-dutch-right-are-leftist-libertarians/

But the Right by definition doesn't have balls. It just wants to live. Nobody wants Civil War. The Left doesn't mind it, if that's what it takes for them to gain more power. So they might force it. Somebody else said that the USA today sounds like Spain before the Civil War. That was a textbook example of the Left forcing the Right into rebellion. I recall reading that the Army generals that rebelled said on the day of the uprising: Half Spain does not resign itself to die. The Right half. I think that really says it all.

The Strong Do What They Can

2017-01-19 // china, islam

This pic has been doing the rounds in the Chinese Internet. It's a parking sign in a mosque in Gansu province, Western China. There's a lot of muslims there, about a million, 3% or so of the province population. There used to be quite a lot more, until they rebelled in the 1860s[185]). Then Zuo Zongtang and his army came and massacred every muslim he could find.

---

[185] https://en.wikipedia.org/wiki/Dungan_Revolt_(1862%E2%80%93
77

Those days are long gone, though, and muslims are quite assertive in China today. Back to the sign. It's just a run-of-the-mill sign, telling people who go to park inside the mosque what they have to do. Drive slowly, follow directions from the staff, pay the ticket, watch your valuables, you know. Now take a look at rule 3. in the second section. It says:

凡装有易燃易爆，剧毒污染性物品的车辆，特别是凡有女人的车辆不得驶入寺内，否则后果自负

"All cars who are carrying flammable, explosive or toxic products, especially all cars which are carrying women, cannot drive into the mosque. Else they will face the consequences."

Doesn't say which consequences. But it can't be very good. I kinda like the "especially". Like bombs and poison is bad, man. But be especially careful about bringing women! That's even worse! That's just trolling. And successfully, now the sign is all over the Chinese internet. And the Chinese are pretty feminist. Women there almost universally work, nag and are often pretty annoying in general. Nothing like the modern West, of course, not even close. But stuff like this really gets them angry.

But still, muslims are quite assertive in modern China. As often, the bulk of political signaling is done in universities, this bizarre contraption where young people in the pinnacle of their narcissism and status-seeking instincts are put in a closed area for 4 long years doing nothing at all but listening to senseless bullshit. And men and women put together! Well, what many Chinese college students do is go on online forums to bitch about muslims. Those bitches with the hijab claiming discrimination. Those fuckers who get private halal canteens. Who always walk in packs and hit on our women; while if we hit on their women we get beaten up and nobody cares. I hear it's getting worse. For how long, I wonder.

What is True?

2017-01-27 // Jordan Peterson, theory, philosophy, language

So let me follow up on my last post on Sam Harris vs. Jordan Peterson, and what constitutes a solid epistemology. The podcast itself is quite painful to listen to, and Jordan Peterson doesn't do much of an argument there. I think the guy doesn't do debates well. He's best when you let him speak for hours. Just give him a mike and let him ramble. He'll get somewhere. You'll notice he doesn't use notes when he speaks, he improvises all the time.

That's impressive, but there's a reason why most good intellectual output, like for example this blog, is done on writing. We're kinda losing that, now with the popularity of podcasts and Youtube videos with men speaking in pseudoprofound voice tones. You can get away with being incoherent and contradicting yourself in speech if you push the appropriate emotional buttons frequently enough. But in writing you have to make logical sense, else people will stop reading. The Greeks realized that pretty soon; they'd go in the Agora and make some sophist speech, and they'd get famous, because even if people don't like what you're saying, they can't help hearing you blabber, and odds are you'll say some good line sooner or later, and people can't help remembering that one line that made sense.

Anyway, the reason I like Jordan Peterson is, besides because he has balls of steel and refuses to bow down to the latest bout of the leftist singularity, where a law has been passed in Ontario saying that self-styled transexuals can demand you to refer to them with whatever pronoun they wish, on punishment of a $100,000 fine or something. Now, I've been against leftists since way before this; if I were a Interview with the Vampire character I would have started opposing leftism around 1880 or so. But as a linguist, playing with language is a 是可忍孰不可忍 moment. You don't play with words. And you especially don't fucking play with closed-class words. That's evil. But I digress.

The reason I respect Prof. Peterson intellectually is because he understands evolutionary psychology, he understands pragmatic philosophy, and he's even read his Wittgenstein. Now that is quite something. Ever since he completely demolished traditional philosophy and linguistics in 1953, poor Wittgenstein has been totally ignored by the intellectual establishment. That's no wonder, philosophers like having a job, as do linguists, and understanding Wittgenstein basically means you should go home, shut up, and take a job in the private sector. It's much more lucrative to just keep going with the bullshit and pretending nobody has noticed that it's precisely that:

misunderstanding how language works and sounding arcane so that nobody actually notices what you're blabbering about. Nobody besides your fellow philosophers who, of course, have a vested interest in keeping the racket going.

The key insight of Wittgenstein is that speech is a kind of a game. You agree on a set of rules, e.g. that the word "apple" stands for a certain kind of fruit, and you agree to use that word to refer to that fruit. But games, like most human social interactions, are a local thing. There's no universal set of rules, and you can come up with a different set of rules with other people. Kinda like good friends sometimes may modify the rules of their card games just went playing among themselves. So you can use the word "apple" to refer to apples, but with some other group you can use the word "apple" to refer to the breasts of women, or whatever. The thing often gets out of hand, as in things like Cockney rhyming slang. The point being that words don't have "meaning", they only have patterns of use in certain contexts, governed by local sets of rules. Understanding those rules is a form of sociology.

If you can only watch one clip by Jordan Peterson, it should be this one. I'll say more: just watch this one clip, you can skip the others. Sorry Jordan, no disrespect, but you're making enough money. This video is by far the most insightful. Here he explains how human society is in fact just a collection of overlapping games, and what we call morality is just the rules of the game(s). This is not a new idea. Confucius didn't call it "game", he called it "ritual". Plenty of people, most infamously communists, have seized upon this idea to argue that political power can change the rules of the social game in order to change people's behavior. To some extent that is true, but game rules aren't completely arbitrary. A game to be a game has to be playable. And that puts severe limits in what kind of rules it can have. The game has to be playable. It has to work. There are natural limits to that. Which brings us back to Gnon's law. But do listen to him.

https://www.youtube.com/watch?v=RcmWssTLFv0

From 30:00 there's a fairly good, if rather unfocused, exposition of pragmatic philosophy. Humans have brains; brains have evolved in order to survive and reproduce. It follows that while your brain has to perceive external reality, it only has to do so to the extent that it allows you to survive and reproduce. Once it has gone to that level it's quite free to evolve in ways that make you completely oblivious of it. Or at least unaware of reality's details. Humans being a social species, survival and reproduction depends on your social status inside the group. So if for some reason the group has decided that that animal isn't edible, even though all evidence tells you it is, you better believe it's not edible, else the group is going to murder you, skin you and put your head in a pike. Hence groupthink.

That's one part. The other part, which necessarily follows, is that you can never be sure of your knowledge. You have some ideas in your brain, how do you know which are true and which aren't? David Hume said it well, you never know what's going to happen. All you have is some confidence that things that happened before with some frequency are going to happen again. What Hume missed is that there's a reason why habit makes you have that confidence. Kant kinda got halfway there, but the very reason why "custom" basically stands as knowledge is that, well, humans have evolved over millions of years that propensity to take habit of perception to stand for the laws of nature. And they have evolved that because it pretty much works like that. To put it in other words, you don't really "have ideas in your brain". Your brain is not a hard-disk. What your brain has is a proclivity to modify its behavior in order to expect that things that happened before on a certain sequence will happen again, which is a good approximation of causality.

Being skeptical of knowledge at this level is just being an ass (David Hume had good reasons for being an ass). All living beings understand causality at the behavioral level because causality is real. If it weren't, we wouldn't be here. We wouldn't have survived and reproduced. Causality is true because it works. That's what "true" means, as Jordan Peterson wants to put it.

But again, your human brain has also evolved so that if your tribe says you gotta put a lip-plate[186] or some ghost is going to snatch your husband's penis, well you're gonna put a lip-plate and make sure every single friend of yours does so too. So we're back to square one. Epistemology is hard. What is true? Is causality true, contra Hume? Well you bet it is. Is true the fact that failing to put a lip-plate will make your husband lose his penis? Well many Nilotic tribesmen say it is. Passionately so. Why? It works for them. By Jordan Peterson's argument, it is true. I don't think it's true.

Again, epistemology is hard. Given how brains work, and how the brains of social species work, there is just no way to set up a complete set of axioms. You can propose a One God that does that for you; but we don't have that, and even if we did, social factions would soon start to twist the definitions of things to fuck with their enemies. So we don't only need a One God, we need a One God which is constantly coming down to earth to make sure that we don't change the agreements we had on what is real. That we don't have. All we can do is make an agreement among ourselves, fallen humans, on what is true, what is not, and how to go find it. That's what we have right now, actually, with most scientific minded people agreeing that the best standard of truth is predictive power. You'll notice that is similar to the animal instinct of assuming causality after confirmation of predictive validity. It works pretty well.

---

186 https://www.google.es/search?
q=lip+plate&source=lnms&tbm=isch&sa=X&ved=0ahUKEwjC74-
YuOPRAhVBIMAKHTClBZUQ_AUICCgB&biw=853&bih=489

So we non-Sudanese lip-plate wearers, have this rule among ourselves, to assume an objective reality independent of subjective hangups, and to test the truth of theories according to experimentation, observability and predictive power. This rule is, again, a kind of game. It is a good game. A playable game. A very productive game.

So when Jordan Peterson says that the concept of "truth" shouldn't be just applied to objective reality, but should be modified so to aid the flourishing of human existence, whatever that means, he's proposing we change the rules of the game. Of this particular game, which we call the English language, in which the word "truth" is generally used to mean conformity to external reality. He makes it sound as if some cabal of scientists conspire together to change the meaning of the word so that it excluded subjectivity and religion and whatnot. Well, no, it wasn't like that. The word "truth" has always excluded subjectivity. In English and in all languages I'm aware of, which are quite a few. That doesn't mean some groups of people, like say Christian theologians, didn't have their local rules where they used the word to refer to unfalsifiable and honestly quite bizarre claims. But that wasn't about claiming a new sense for the word. They really meant that their stuff was also objective reality. If only to signal that they had the power to get away with any sort of absurd claim.

Even the Sudanese lip-plate guys actually think that ghosts are objectively real and they actually snatch the penises of dissenters. They don't think it's "true enough" for the purposes of tribal cohesion. So you can't change the rules of the "truth" game even if you wanted to. I get it that he wants to stop Communist scientists from crossing Ebola with Smallpox. But the way to do that is not by changing the rules of the language and epistemology game. To the extent that that's even possible; you can't mess with one word and expect the others to stay the same. Language is a self-referential network. You change one node and the other nodes shift too. Often in unpredictable ways.

Now, I'm a friend of Jordan Peterson. I agree with his dislike of modern society. I agree there's lots of problems. Lots of nihilism and mental illness and despair. Society is going to hell. Sure enough. But that's not because of the overzealous objectivism of the scientific establishment. Again, Prof. Peterson is being attacked by Gender Scholars. The problem with science is not that it insists in analyzing objective reality. The problem is that the scientific method only works when observation is reliable. Which worked well in earlier physics and biology. But the prestige of science made us come up with things which just can't be measured with any reliability. Economics. Psychology. Climate science. Much of medical science. It's just too complicated to take any reliable data on much of it. And we refuse to admit that we don't know much about it, and that we can't know much about it. It is not possible. There is only one ancient intellectual discipline which hasn't been made into a science: history. It can't be done. The data just isn't there. And historians always understood that. There was this healthy skepticism about "history is written by the victors". You had to take it with a grain of salt. But it has its value nonetheless.

Instead of understanding Economics, or Climate Science any other intellectual disciplines as being the same sort of intellectually dubious and politically charged discipline as history is, we have deluded ourselves into thinking they are epistemologically sound sciences such as physics or chemistry. No, they are not. And they can't be. And it's ok. We just have to stop spending billions on them and using them to justify public policy. Yet again history is used to justify public policy all the time.

That half, or 80%, or 90% of modern science is bullshit that doesn't replicate, and obfuscates more than reveals, is a problem of our modern scientific establishment, not of the scientific method itself. And most certainly not of the idea of "truth", which again, predates science by millennia, and is a very important foundation of human sociability. Even if Prof. Peterson were to get his way and change the definition; which would require Stalinist levels of social influence; people would soon invent another word to refer that stuff to that stuff out there which doesn't depend on our subjectivity: the Truth. That's a good game.

Let me finish with some Chinese history. I wrote about this before[187]. During the last stages of the Jurchen-Chinese war, in the 1140s. General Yue Fei, the most successful Chinese general, was arrested for plotting a coup against the emperor. One of his fellow generals, Han Shizhong, run towards the prime minister, Qin Hui, at court. He then asked him: "What is this thing about Yue Fei plotting a coup? Is any of this true?".

The prime minister, laconically answered: "It doesn't have to be".

By which he meant, the emperor wants him dead, so the hell cares anyway. Note that he didn't say "it's true enough".

Now after reading all this, you can listen to Prof. Peterson make his truth argument at length. Tell me what you think of it now.

https://www.youtube.com/watch?v=07Ys4tQPRis

---

[187] https://spandrell.com/2016/04/26/the-song-dynastys-surrender/

Behaviorism in Context

2017-02-02 // philosophy, theory, language, status

Let me explain what I mean when I call myself a Behaviorist. No, it's not about blank slatism, or being able to completely manipulate anyone at will. It's about not taking what people say at face value.

See this tweet:

https://twitter.com/DegenRolf/status/827054957329260544

No, no. Just, no. Please, somebody just close all the psychology faculties. Or close the whole universities while they're at it. But this is completely wrong. Nonsensical, really. "People believe that..." doesn't make sense. Look at this closely. It assumes that people have stuff inside their heads ("ideas") and that that stuff inside their heads has some causative effect in how they behave. This is an utterly wrong way of thinking about this.

I mean, you don't know what's going on inside people's heads. You just don't. Look at this study in particular. They ask people about their own eating behavior and that of others. The answer to that question is not the "ideas" in the people's heads. I mean, just look at the setting closely. You have:

1.   Some college students
Being asked some question by:

*   A professor or grad student
About their own behavior.

And surprise, surprise, they make themselves look good and make others look not so good. Why would they do that? Well... maybe they want to make themselves look good. Because they want to appear high-status because that's what people do.

Imagine this other setting: you are in Berkeley, and leftist thugs are running a Maoist style struggle session. They grab unpopular kid, who they think might be a Trump supporter, and they ask her what she thinks about heir own and the leftist eating habits.

What do you think she's going to say? If she doesn't want to get beat up with bats until she's unconscious and gets half her rib broken, she'll say her eating habits suck and that those of others are awesome. Why? Because she wants to survive. That's also something that people do.

If you want to know what drives people's behavior, you have to look at... people's behavior. What they actually do. Not just ask them questions. Questions are social behavior which follows social rules. It's all about context.

Modern social science still works on the rationalist paradigm, that people have "ideas" and that they "reason" about them. That is just a descendant of the Christian emphasis on "faith", i.e. that some people have "faith" in their "hearts", which makes them better people. Of course that was just a subterfuge to run a loyalty assessment on people. Making a good show of the "faith" in your "heart" was a very good costly signal to show your loyalty to the Christian team. Politics runs on this sort of misleading rituals. They work very well. I'll loudly proclaim my loyalty to Kek and prostrate in front of its image whenever needed. The more people think it's stupid the better a signal it will be.

But science should be about how things actually work. And the way things work is that you must look at what people do, not what they say. Or more accurately, you should understand what people "say" as a kind of "do". If all those "scientists" got out of their parochial WEIRD world they'd actually understand that.

Penis Envy

2017-02-13 // islam, women

I've meant for a long while to write a post about iconoclasm. The Byzantine Empire had been suffering defeats to Muslims for centuries. They lost 2/3rds of the Empire, and almost lost the whole of it too. It's no wonder that some emperors thought that maybe Muslims were doing something right. They certainly seemed to have God's favor.

The conclusion they reached was that God liked the Muslims because they did not have human figures in their mosques. Byzantine churches being full of icons, paintings, mosaics of Jesus and the myriad saints. Most of them pretty lame, too. Byzantine icons tend to be plain, dull, and often just badly drawn. It probably was the work of an endogamic caste of icon-painters who promoted each other for personal reasons unrelated to skill at painting, and flayed at any criticism by laypeople. How dare you criticize our holy art? You are just ignorant of God's taste in painting. Kinda like the argument that progressive academics use when called out on their nonsensical "research".

Anyway, Iconoclasm was attempted. The Byzantine state burned every human figure from their churches, which became as bare as mosques. It didn't do much to help out in the war against the Muslims. What it did was provoke a century-long civil war. The icon-painter guild was *very* stubborn. And the Byzantine state was a mess who couldn't impose it's authority. So the change did more harm than good. Rhomania kept declining and rising again and then declining for good. And that was that. I guess there's a parable here about cultural continuity.

Still, whatever the real world results of Iconoclasm, I couldn't help feeling for Leo III when reading this piece of news. Man, these guys are doing something right.

Who is this lonely looking woman? It's the premier of the Canadian province of Ontario. She went to visit a mosque.[188] See? All my multicultural subjects are my dear ~~subjects~~ citizens, I go around and they all worship me equally. That's an actual line by Yongzheng emperor when been asked by a Chinese minister about Muslim misbehavior, by the way. But I digress. The premier of Ontario goes to visit a mosque as part of her show of holiness, and what happens? The Imam tells her that the guys are praying, so she gotta wait. And out of the way, please. We guys are busy. Serious stuff. Oh, yeah, go sit over there in the corner. But don't you dare take off your veil. That's right, good girl. Now where were we guys? Allaaaaaahu akbar.

The funny thing is that the Ontario premier is a lesbian. "First openly gay blabla". A lesbian. A woman who wants to be a man. She probably wants to be there with the boys, praying to Allah. Dressing like a bro. But Allah won't have her. Look at that face again. Poor thing. All the power of her office is nothing against the rock-solid frame of the Imam. Damn, that must have felt good.

---

[188] https://linkis.com/com/HJV1X

Why do people go to class

2017-02-15 // status, education

Not to learn, certainly.

David Friedman says:[189]

I have long been puzzled by why lecturers were not replaced by books shortly after the invention of printing made books cheap. Video is just the latest incarnation of that puzzle.

Well if you've been puzzled for long, why don't you think about it? Come on, Mr. Friedman. You're a smart guy. If you don't understand something, just think a bit harder. Or better still: think outside the box.

Some guys out there put theories about humans being wired to pay attention to lecturers, more than to books or videos. I don't know. Certainly didn't work like that for me. A boring lecture is a boring lecture whether on video or in person. I'm not the most patient guy so your mileage may vary but I surely didn't pay much attention myself to my professors unless they were particularly good.

The answer to the question is obvious. I mean, come on. People don't go to college to learn. They go because it's the official way of attaining high status. That's what education is for. The guy who just wants to learn already reads the book and doesn't bother with the lecture. The fact that we still have lectures and pay lecturers, as some guy said over there, "pay thousands of professors to give exactly the same Calculus lecture", is not to satisfy the market of kids who want to learn. That's not the market that high education caters for.

Robin Hanson made what I consider the best claim: education is about making friends with high prestige people. "Impressive people", as he put it. He would know, as he's quite impressive himself, and he appears to understand that a lot of people try to be friends with him even though they aren't at all interested in what he has to say. So for any average kid, a math professor is a high prestige guy. He's smart. He's impressive. Being in the same room with the guy means you have something of the social standing of that guy. You may not be impressive yourself, but you're good enough to be in the same room as an impressive guy.

---

[189] https://slatestarcodex.com/2017/02/09/considerations-on-cost-disease/#comment-466256

You'll notice that's the same logic for why people follow celebrities all over the world. What's the freaking point in going batshit crazy over some singer, paying thousands and thousands of dollars? Why do people ask for autographs? Why do teenage girls go insane when some famous guy looked at them? Why the hell does every TV celebrity have millions of followers on Twitter? Because interaction is status. I have some connection with a high-status guy. Means I'm high status too. Sorta. It used to work like that in 100,000 BC. Not so much today in social media. But evolution is what it is. Gnon is lazy.

Dunbar Feminism

2017-02-13 // women, islam, status

I think I should stop selling "behaviorism". By which I mean, I should stop calling what I sell "behaviorism".[190] I shall call it "immediatism".

Basic points are: all politics are local. All cognition is local. Nothing is abstract. People behave so as to immediate conditions. Here's an example. Sweden.

https://www.government.se/government-policy/a-feminist-government/

Let me quote:

Sweden has the first feminist government in the world. This means that gender equality is central to the Government's priorities – in decision-making and resource allocation. A feminist government ensures that a gender equality perspective is brought into policy-making on a broad front, both nationally and internationally. Women and men must have the same power to shape society and their own lives. This is a human right and a matter of democracy and justice. Gender equality is also part of the solution to society's challenges and a matter of course in a modern welfare state – for justice and economic development. The Government's most important tool for implementing feminist policy is gender mainstreaming, of which gender-responsive budgeting is an important component.

Feminism gender gender feminism power gender feminism. And first. You get the gist. They also had this sort of battle picture:

---

190 https://spandrell.com/2017/02/02/behaviorism-in-context/

1486134179161

So you'd think these people will be very consistent feminists, and make a lot of policies to further the movement. And indeed, they are wreaking havoc in Sweden by doing retarded stuff like "feminist snow plowing", collapsing the whole transport system in the process. But then these feminists do things like this:

https://twitter.com/PeterSweden7/status/830579268027576321

https://twitter.com/PeterSweden7/status/830568651652730880

And so people start howling: you can't do this! What kind of feminist are you if put on a veil to pander to Muslims. Which is true of course, and this bunch of evil hags should be shamed as much as possible. But if you want to understand what is really going on, you gotta understand immediatism.

See, these Swedish middle aged women aren't feminist in the abstract. They are feminist in their local environment. Which means that there are in a power struggle against *their men*. Not men in the abstract. But Swedish men. Their husbands, their brothers and their fathers. It is them who they want to spite. And to spite them they adopt "feminism", i.e. they parrot feminist rhetoric, mostly imported from the USA. And the policies they adopt are tailored to fuck with Swedish men: like taking the snow out of the driveways that women walk, instead of the big roads that their men use to drive to work and transport stuff.

Iranian men just don't compute in whatever drives these people's behavior. Even the Muslim men who are slowly invading their country don't count for much. For all they care they aren't real people. They're just some abstraction you read about. Only the people in your Dunbar circle are real. So their "feminism" is about fucking with the men in their Dunbar circle. Anything else isn't actually there. It is often said that progressive rhetoric assumes that minorities don't really have agency. Everything is the fault of white men. Same thing. Progressives are in a power struggle against fellow white people: nobody else matters. "Agency" only exists in so far as progressives find it useful in order to achieve more power for themselves against their Dunbar-rivals.

And so when a Swedish prime minister goes to Iran, she puts the veil. Not because she's not a feminist: but because her feminism is an immediate concern, not an abstract principle. Far away from home, out of sight of her husbands, brothers and fathers who they want to spite, they can be themselves, and enjoy being in the company of real men who force them to behave like decent women. They actually enjoy this, obviously. But they will never admit so to their fellow men. There's two reasons for that. Often people say that is because their fellow men are beta, feminism is a shit test, the local people don't pass the shit test so women end up despising the men for it. But I don't think that's all the story. Point is, in the local environment, white women and men are rivals in a power struggle, and no quarter is given. No amount of alpha can solve that. Only alphas who are not part of the local power struggle can influence women. Of course the question is how to stop white women from being in a state of war against their men. But that isn't as easy as it sounds: Asian women give plenty of shit to Asian men, and even Muslim women are a pain in the ass in their own way. I guess only Afghans got that solved for good.

Find the Symmetry

2017-03-15 // theory, media, nrx

The liberal media won't shut up about the Alt-Right. They're even talking about Neoreaction. Apparently Trump has read Moldbug. Or at least Bannon has. The counterrevolution is happening. Or so you'd think if you believed the liberal press.

Funny thing is, the dark side of the Internet is a small, tiny little thing. Really. Neoreaction is, what, 1,000 people? Spread around the whole world. 75% in the US, maybe. And the alt-right, which has inherited much of good ol' national-socialism, is what, 20,000 people? I love those guys, I really do. Frog Twitter is hilarious. /pol/ is very funny. But come on. Even Steve Sailer, who has been writing for decades, who is a middle-class, 50+ old, utterly middlebrow guy who writes in very accessible language, who writes about sports! Steve Sailer has 13,000 followers on Twitter. Ezra Klein has 1.6 million. Ezra Klein, that doofus-looking doofus. Even Matthew Yglesias, whose picture is in English phrasebooks to explain the phrase "his face looks like a joke", has 270k followers. The alt-right is beyond small. Trump didn't win because of the alt-right. He won because he got 60 million Fox News watchers to vote for him.

But, the liberal press won't shut up about the alt-right. Why? Why aren't they writing about the actual Trump voters? Because this is not about numbers. This is a war of ideas. And even if ideas can adapt to people, more often than not people adapt to ideas. Ideas are the stuff of humanity. The stuff of social coordination. Ideas is what we use to get together and to stuff. Schelling points, remember? Well, for the first time, the left is scared. They're very scared. And why are they scared? The left are masters in ideas. They have come up with this steel-strong memeplex that even though it doesn't make any logical sense whatsoever, even though it wrecks every culture and civilization it touches, even though it makes men and women miserable and keep them from having babies; these guys keep winning. The left is good at ideas. And the left won't shut up about the alt-right.

Maybe they sense something? Maybe they're scared that they know that fascism is a good product. Not that it makes much sense. Slightly more than what the left sells, but fascism isn't about truth and logic. Fascism is about what it has to be about; about coordination. About power. What the left is also about, if only in a more cheating and roundabout way. Maybe the left is scared because they know what happens when good ideas get out of the bottle. First some guy like Bannon reads Moldbug. Then he becomes the Chief Strategist of the POTUS. Then the guy actually manages to have political power. They're trying hard to stop him. It's likely that they succeed. But say they don't. Say Trump and Bannon manage to stop the meddling of the US judiciary in the legislative process; say he purges the shuts down the CIA and consolidates the 16 intelligence agencies into a single one that actually follows orders; say he gets Paul Ryan to go home and work as a stripper for fat cougars.

If that happens, then whatever Bannon thinks will, slowly, become high-status. And then people who want a piece of that status will start to believe in the same stuff. And once some critical mass has been achieved, everybody will start believing in it. And once the ideas go mainstream, then they become a religion, a self-catalytic process where people start signaling and out-signaling each other and manipulating others into signaling too. That provided the ideas are a good sell at the beginning. Provided the ideas can get that critical mass. That means they must sound like a good deal, in abstract. But of course fascism sounds good. That's the whole point of fascism. It's catnip for civilized men.

Journalists are peddlers of ideological catnip. They're drug dealers. That's why there's so many. It's a nice job. I mean, it's not, it doesn't pay crap, but some people are irresistibly driven to it. And those guys who were driven to the Current Year Leftism, just can't stop writing about the alt-right. Part is tribal anger, of course. But again, the tribes are incommensurably different in size. There's no contest really. There's a million leftist writers for every alt-right Twitter account. And yet... they can't stop being curious. They see those Frog-Twitter kids, they see the drive, the passion, the brotherly manners. The asabiya. They know that's how ideas get started. And once they get started, they can get big very, very quickly. And once they do, the guys doing the street violence won't be Berkeley communists. They'll be Berkeley nazis. The same people, perhaps. Because people are just empty vessels, looking for a kick. They don't really care who provides it, only that it's good.

How to Figure out Gnon's Will

2017-03-16 // islam, psychology, men

A basic idea of this blog is that people don't choose ideas according to the merits or the logical value of those ideas. People have different personalities, different status-seeking dispositions, so to speak. Some people desire a lot, some people are content with less, some people are willing to go further in order to attain it, others don't. Given that basic foundation of personality, people *then* choose the ideas that think can better aid their status-seeking plans. Ideas spread or don't spread according to how well they fit the wider aggregate status-seeking dispositions of the population. Which of course is affected by the current idea landscape of the culture.

This is why rabid leftists become rabid rightists, or viceversa, while seldom becoming apolitical. They're just into politics, period, so they get behind whatever is fashionable or suits their background better. Understand this point and you'll understand much better how the ideological landscape in the West is going to change in the next few decades. For instance, take a look at this:

A tale of two white British brothers who took VERY different paths: One supports right-wing EDL - while the other has converted to Islam[191]

How can they be so different? Well it's quite obvious. The guys just aren't into mainstream crap. They're edgy, as brothers they share those edgy genes, they just happened to stumble into different edges.

But of course ideas have consequences. Not ideas themselves; but different ideas help different groups get together, and social circles have big consequences. Social circles are everything, really.

Another point of this blog, of course, is to look at human behavior from a biological perspective. Richard Dawkins was able to write his masterpiece The Selfish Gene, because he was a zoologist. Everybody should be a zoologist. Everything makes much more sense when you look at stuff like that. Gnon is a zoologist. He really is. Now let's look at the British brothers as zoologists. One looks happy, has two children, an obedient wife. The other has... his pub mates. Doesn't look very content, does he?

Now I could start with that and start with the sociological consequences of that... but you already get it, don't you? Again, I'm no apologist. I completely agree with this post

---

[191]   https://www.dailymail.co.uk/news/article-4317004/A-tale-two-white-working-class-brothers.html

by Jim[192]. This is the solution we don't want. But I'm not sure Gnon cares about what we want.

---

192 https://blog.jim.com/war/the-solution-we-do-not-want/

The Journalistic Mind

2017-03-15 // media, psychology, status

Yesterday I wrote that the leftist media (i.e. all of it) can't shut up about the alt-right because they're fascinated for finally having a worthy rival. They see the appeal.

Another possibility is that journalists basically spend all their lives in Twitter, and our Frog-Twitter friends are trolling them so hard that their Dunbar brains are just saturated with alt-right people. And so they react. And react, way beyond the real world importance of them. It's like high-school kids talking all the time about their classmates. Of course they do, it's where they spend their whole lives. But it's all absolutely trivial in hindsight.

Here's some evidence of how journalists work, and why they're brains are basically on drugs with Twitter. This is a passage from David Halberstam's *The Best and the Brightest*, a 1972 book detailing how the Cathedral back then, the media and the bureaucracy, botched the Vietnam War because they couldn't stop sucking each others' dicks. Basically because everybody wanted to suck JKF's dick.

David Halberstam was a fairly successful journalist, who took a long leave of several years in order to write a book. He writes how hard it was to quit his usual routine as a journalist for the lonely job of writing a book who would only be complete after years of work.

The hardest thing I had to do at the start was to take leave of my byline for the next four years. Ours is a profession built upon the immediacy of reward: We graduate from college, and our peers go off to law school and graduate school and medical school. They have barely started their first-year classes, and our names are bannered across the front pages of the nation's leading newspapers. They get their medical or law degrees, and start out in their residencies or as the lowest hirelings in a law office, and we are old-timers, covering the statehouse, or on our way to Washington, by now, we believe, the possessors of a well-known brand name. The byline is a replacement for many other things, not the least of them money. If someone ever does a great psychological profile of journalism as a profession, what will be apparent will be the need for gratification— if not instant, then certainly relatively immediate. Reporters take sustenance from their bylines; they are a reflection of who you are, what you do, and why, to an uncommon degree, you exist. It was hard enough to give so much of it up when I went to Harper's, where I would get only five or six bylines a year. But to go from the world of easy recognition, from the world of the Times and Harper's, to a world where I might get only one byline in four years, was a great risk. A journalist always wonders: If my byline disappears, have I disappeared as well? My friends, knowing my compulsions, my innate impatience, wondered if I could do it. Would I be able to resist assignments and stay with my project?

The Geopolitics of Empire

2017-03-22 // history, turchin, europe, russia

Cool title, huh? It always feels good to type this kind of stuff. "Empire". Pronounced with a 1900s British accent. Feels good man. Insert happy frog pic.

Anyway. The most interesting, shall I say "official" theory of historical geopolitics of the reaction must surely be Peter Turchin's theory of meta-ethnic frontier armies pumping up their asabiya and conquering the civilizational center.

The theory basically says that to run a civilization you need a strong army. To run a strong army you need cohesion, discipline, i.e. asabiya. To produce this cohesion and discipline you need your soldiers to feel its need. Discipline isn't nice. You'd rather slack off and drink beer and be merry. The kind of discipline an army runs off is produced by massive amounts of violence and unreasonable demands. You can only get people to do so if they feel is absolutely necessary. And they will only feel it's necessary if they get to the realization that either they behave like good soldiers, or they're dead, and they will lose everything they hold dear.

The way you get your soldiers to feel that is to stack them against a different civilization. People so alien to you that they you have nothing in common. If they win, everything you are accustomed to, all your life, all those little habits of behavior that form your identity: all that will be destroyed. And you don't like that. It's taken a while for you to adapt to that culture. Starting at birth. Your brain unconsciously produced a very fine set of motor sequences that make you able to gain some status inside that culture. If that culture were to change, because you got invaded by a different one, you're screwed.

I mean, most likely you'd be directly screwed, in that your wife and daughters will be raped and you and your sons will be put into slavery; but even if the invaders were nice, they are just alien sons of bitches. So you gotta be sure they don't conquer you. So you gotta be strong. So you join the army and you become a good soldier.

Once you are part of this strong army, you realize that all your fellow countrymen down below in the center are a bunch of pussies; you could easily conquer their asses in no time. Not that you need to, most of the time, but every now and then the center just collapses out of sheer dysfunction and runaway rent-seeking. So when the center collapses, the strong armies of the meta-ethnic frontier come down and restore order. That's the Ibn-Khaldun civilizational cycle.

It's pretty easy to understand, and it makes a lot of sense. Check your history and it fits quite mightily well I must say. And it also fits stuff that didn't end up happening but people used to think it would. See this quote that a commenter at Nick Land's[193] left some days ago:

"The oppression of Hungary has ratified the oppression of all our continent. Since she has fallen, Italy has been completely crushed, the moderate freedom of Germany has been put down by Austria with the support of Russia; lastly, the usurpation of Louis Napoleon has been made possible. Without the restoration of Hungary Europe cannot be freed from Russian thraldom; under which nationalities are erased, no freedom is possible, all religions are subjected to like slavery. Gentlemen! the Emperor Napoleon spoke a prophetic word, when he said that in fifty years all Europe would be either republican or Cossack. Hungary once free, Europe is republican; Hungary permanently crushed, all Europe is Cossack.

The political fragmentation of Europe is an obvious historical anomaly. The history of mankind is the history of great empires. China, surely. The Persian Empire, and it's Arab successors. The Roman Empire was the only one which didn't rise again. Of course there's a thousand theories about it; mainly Britain being a pain in the ass. But if you look at the map, it is pretty reasonable to conclude that Europe would end up a part of the Russian Empire. Russia is of course a perfect example of a meta-ethnic frontier, with White Christian Farmer Russians fighting for centuries against Asian Muslim Nomads. Now I know someone who is just going to come and write that the Russian army was a piece of shit, and that Russia only won because of sheer numbers and an Asiatic disregard for human life. But anyway. Those guys could fight. Hell, they conquered up to Alaska, the whole of Central Asia, and would've conquered Constantinople if not for British and French intervention.

So why didn't Russia end up conquering the decadent Europeans? Well, in great part because the fragmented Europeans weren't quite decadent. We could fight pretty well. France and Britain kicked ass everywhere they went. Which is weird, as neither of them are on a meta-ethnic frontier. Or are they?

Britain and France were huge colonial powers, which meant that their effective frontier was all over the place. By that argument Western Europe was the longest meta-ethnic frontier ever to occur in human history. They were out there fighting extremely alien peoples all over the planet.

But again that doesn't quite apply to Napoleonic France. Or to the German Imperial army, by most accounts the strongest and most disciplined army in the world, probably since the Mongols. And Germany was no colonial power. By no stretch of the word you could argue that Germany is on a meta-ethnic frontier.

───────────────

[193] `https://www.xenosystems.net/sentences-93/`

So what is it? The Napoleonic singularity should give you a hint. Nationalism is what fed the French army. And very much what fed the German army. Nationalism creates a meta-ethnic frontier from thin air, by changing the parameters of what makes an ethnicity. If you force people to become extremely anal about their group identity, the asabiya-production algorithms are much easier to activate. The Germans understood that was the basis of their strength; and so after losing WW1 they doubled down and came up with a Hitler.

Of course the asabiya-hacking ability of nationalism is a collective action problem. The point of asabiya is war. Of course it's useful for a lot of other things, namely to run a wealthy industrial economy. But, at the end of the day, the business of groups of men is war, and excess asabiya will end up creating the circumstances so that it can show itself in the battlefield. And so nationalism ended up creating meta-ethnic frontiers all over the place. Which created the most massive and coordinated armies ever seen by men. Which was complete overkill. Not a good idea.

But now that Europe has forsaken nationalism, maybe the old patterns will reassert themselves, and Europe will fall to the closest meta-ethnic power. That is kinda the situation right now, with the USA as the conquering power. But they didn't do so explicitly, and they are likely to leave in short term.

I never read him, but isn't this argument basically what that Alexander Dugin guy is always talking about?

Peterson vs. Harris, again

2017-03-23 // Jordan Peterson, cucks, philosophy

So, you might remember a series of posts I did about Jordan Peterson, now famous psychology professor from Canada, about his philosophy of life. I wrote about him here[194] and here[195] and here[196].

You might also remember that Jordan Peterson was invited to the podcast of Sam Harris, of which I wrote about here[197] and elaborated here[198]. That podcast made me very, very conflicted. Because I think that Peterson is right, and Harris is wrong. But Peterson makes absolutely no sense in the podcasts, neither the first or second; while Harris is eloquent and logical and just sounds smarter. Or at the very least easier to understand. Peterson just sounds like a broken record of a snake's oil salesman pitch. But make no mistake about it: Peterson is right. Harris is wrong. The problem is he isn't capable of explaining it in a way that makes sense so that he can win the argument. Now they made a second podcast[199]; and while it's better, it's still far from persuasive.

Well, allow me to win the argument for him. And I'll do it for 1% of his Patreon salary. Nah, I'll do it for free. Sam Harris deserves being proved wrong. That's the least I can do for his good cadence of speech and the clarity of his thought.

So the two men are basically arguing about ethics: how should human people behave in society. Peterson goes on his by now familiar shtick about evolution and lobster serotonin and archetypes and Horus and Set. Harris answers that all that's very good as biology or history perhaps; but not as ethics. We're trying to come up with a system of morals, with rules of behavior; an accurate explanation of human nature, to the extent that Peterson's explanation is accurate, doesn't help there. And that's because really existing humans have had, and some still have, pretty fucked up systems of morality. Read some ethnographies and you'll find out plenty of stone age tribes with unbelievably stupid religions (i.e. beliefs about ghosts and stuff) and appalling behavior

---

[194] https://spandrell.com/2016/12/27/gnon-theology/

[195] https://spandrell.com/2016/12/20/intellectuals/

[196] https://spandrell.com/2016/12/22/jordan-peterson-on-truth/

[197] https://spandrell.com/2017/01/23/jordan-peterson/

[198] https://spandrell.com/2017/01/28/what-is-true/

[199] https://www.youtube.com/watch?v=31Ud7-EkZEI

towards one another. My personal favorite are the lip plate wearers in East Africa. And of course, Harris is an outspoken enemy of Islam; and surely if you're an Enlightened, blue-pill, 1960s guy, Muslim societies today are in general quite appalling.

Harris' argument, which you can listen to from about 48:00 in the Youtube clip, is that appalling societies just have "failed science". Their religion is a way of figuring things out: but they're wrong. They're mistaken, and so they do bad things, and their societies suck. If they only knew the truth, the Scientific Truth as discovered by Western Civilization, their societies would flourish and they'd all be as nice as Scott Alexander at a gaypride parade.

This argument is, of course, as old as sin. It's moral intellectualism. That's Socrates' idea. People do bad things because they are ignorant. We should strive to know more so that we can be good. How do we know more? By asking questions and having a Socratic dialogue. Rince, repeat, then have Socrates executed for being annoying as hell.

It doesn't occur to Harris that, even granting the Whig theory of history, that humankind progressed from ignorance to wisdom on a straight line, and things get better that way, that truth needs to be sold . There's this thing in linguistics called diachrony and synchrony. Diachrony is watching the evolution of a language through time. Synchrony is watching to a language as it currently exists. You can take a synchronic look at the world today: and you'll see that while Western Civilization has used Science™ to get to this pinnacle of wisdom and morality, there are plenty of other societies out there who aren't buying it. They could buy it. Some even were buying it 50 years ago. But they're not buying it now. And they're right there, looking at us, kinda envying our technology and our wealth: but they're still not buying it. These guys are out there and they don't give a crap about we knowing the truth while they are suffering in falsehood.

And why aren't they buying it? Peterson should have explained this to him. I guess it's what he wanted to explain to him all along. The guy is a creative one and he very often finds it hard to put things into words. He should speak less and write more. He'd find it easier to make coherent arguments. Alas he gets paid infinite times more to speak than I get paid to write, so I don't blame him there. But the point is that the Scientific Truth does not matter when you try to arrange a society. Not only it does not matter; pervasive knowledge of truth quite likely is deleterious for societal harmony. You basically can't have a society, not a long-lasting one anyway, if the truth is widely known.

You may have noticed that after centuries of the scientific method; most people, i.e. 70% of the population don't give a crap. Homeopathy is still around. People believe in all sort of crap; and they're not even consistent about it. Why don't people care about the truth? Because, as Peterson said, what people care about is what their biological drives have them care about; and those biological drives have evolved over millions of years. What they tell us to care about is what people across age and culture care about; and you can discover that by reading their myths and stories. What they care about is the survival of the tribe as a unit, i.e. the resiliency of their society. What makes the group function. And sex; how to get those picky annoying women to notice you individually. Here, I spared you 20 hours of Jordan Peterson's Youtube clips. That is his argument.

Actually Sam Harris makes his own counterargument when he claims that the fact of human evolution has no place in a system of ethics, because if so anybody who understood Darwin would spend his whole life in a sperm bank so that he could have the maximum number of descendants. Yes, indeed. A society which placed high value on scientific knowledge would have people do exactly that. People want to win. Certainly guys want to win. But a society in which people understood in very clear terms that human females only mate with high-status men, and the status is a zero-sum game; well that wouldn't be a very cooperative society, would it. And so humans have evolved to put a lid over all that stuff, which is kinda obvious when you think about it. But seeing the obvious is not what human nature is about. We wouldn't be here if it were. Human nature is about coming up with bullshit, believing it and sticking to it, so that we can all get along.

Now there's a lot of ways of getting along. Some people put 10 inch diameter plates inside our lower lips. Some people have women wear burkas while they shove their dicks in the anus of 12 year old boys. Some give high public status to women, while actually paying money to high-IQ code monkeys, who then can't get laid, then dress like women so they can get the status, and allow this men to use the women's restroom, which women hate but can't complain because... I'm not really sure about that one.

Sam Harris wants a new system of ethics: well then he first must understand how systems of ethics came to exist. Peterson knows something about that. Then you can argue, indeed, that some ways of getting along are better than others. But the truth argument just doesn't make sense. You can't just drop the truth on a stone age tribe and expect they'll come out next day as Californian 140 IQ Jews. Two reasons for that. The present American culture that Harris finds so dear wasn't produced by the truth. It was produced by the Blue Pill. Which contains some truth, and a lot of made up unfalsifiable crap. That is, a lot of religion. And, as it happens, the society the blue pill produced is collapsing before our eyes. Peterson knows something about that too.

What we need is two things. One, ironically, is what Harris says he wants, but doesn't actually want. The truth. The red pill. The other is some other stuff, not quite true, to put inside the red pill and make it sweeter. Else people won't take it. People like sweet pills. That's how we evolved.

By the way it's the content of this second pill that Peterson wants to call "truth". That which works. And yeah, ok, you can put that on the package. That's probably good salesmanship. But first we have to make it. And you sure as hell shouldn't be telling people at this stage that what we call truth isn't really the truth.

How Menopausal Feminism leads to Islam

2017-04-02 // women, islam, demographics

I'm reading this book by a Japanese historian on how Neoconfucianism in the East unwittingly prepared the ground for the adoption in East Asia of Western progressivism as its logical conclusion. Really cool stuff. I'll have a review shortly.

But before that, let me anticipate you this kind of evolutionary argument with something more relevant to our day.

I've been writing a lot about how Islam has a big chance of taking over the West. Not because Muslims are strong or anything. They're a bunch of lazy low IQ pansies for the most part. But they have their shit together, and for various reasons they are immune (on average, of course) to adopting progressive ideology. One reason which I've written about a lot is that Muslim culture gives very high status to men. It's a patriarchy. And Muslim men very much enjoy that. So when they move to the West, where feminism gives pretty low status to men as men, well Muslim men see very clearly that assimilating to Western culture will lower their status.

And they'd very much not lower their status. So Muslim men cling steadfastly to their traditional culture, as dumb and dysfunctional as it is, with its clannishness and laziness and inshallah fucked up work ethic. None of that matters compared to the dire threat of losing status. You'll notice that the odd Muslim man which lands a high-status job, say Fareed Zakaria or Mohamed Hadid are quite happy with abandoning Islam for progressive. Feminism is pretty good for the high-status rich guy. But for your average guy, even a high middle class professional, feminism is a way worse deal than Islam. You'll note plenty of self-bombing jihadists have been doctors and engineers.

Anyway, this is one factor. The male side to the equation, which accounts for why Islam is so healthy, unlike Christianity. But there's this other side of the equation. The side which accounts for why the West is so weak. The female side. Take a look at this white lady.

https://twitter.com/reo_lowe/status/848533440458887168

This British woman, apparently some journalist or QUANGO employee or whatever, went on a cycling trip from Britain to Iran. Because she loves the Middle East or something. Now, if you know your geography you may have thought that she just cycled through Turkey and that's it. Which would be dangerous enough. It wasn't that long ago that a Japanese college student was raped and murdered in Cappadocia. But no, this chick is the real deal. Look at her route.

She went all the way down to Sudan. She's the real deal. She really likes them arabs. You may have noticed that on her Twitter picture she's wearing a veil of some sort. Now why would she do that? Why would she like Middle Eastern culture so much? This clip gives you a hint. (HT Sailer's[200])

https://www.youtube.com/watch?time_continue=2530&v=_8FvwoAZvVY

That's Omar Sharif. If anyone knew Arab women, it must be him. And he makes a really good point. Egypt is indeed becoming more piously Islamic than it used to be. The whole Muslim world is. This is Kabul in the 1970s.

---

200   https://www.unz.com/isteve/what-feminist-islamophilia-is-really-about/

And of course in Egypt, things like these[201] were going on. Nobody wore the veil well into the 1980s. Then they did. What happened? As Omar Sharif puts it, back in the 1950s and forward, you had this big baby boom, and the modernization of the whole Muslim world. Egypt had this huge showbiz industry, and the showbiz industry was run on more or less Western templates. Women in short skirts and all that. Young actresses, being young women, surely liked to show off.

But then this very same actresses got older. They weren't so pretty anymore. And so they made virtue out of necessity and started to cover up those wrinkles and saggy skin and unshapely legs. But they were still in showbiz; they started the industry, they still had some authority. Given that celebrities were wearing the veil, that surely must have trickled down. Not just out of imitation, but because they had a point. All those Westernized girls were getting older. Westernization hadn't brought the world of honey and spice that they'd thought. So they went Islamic. Once you go Islamic, the signaling went out of control. Next thing you know you ought to wear a Burka and let yourself get beaten by your husband. But, by then it was too late.

Western women like our British cyclist journalist aren't immune to that temptation. Look at that woman again? WYB? I don't think so. But man was she popular out there

---

[201] https://www.frontpagemag.com/fpm/48901/how-veil-conquered-cairo-university-jamie-glazov

in Turkey and Egypt. Must have felt nice. Not sure how many men she slept with. She won't say, she has a "boyfriend". But you and I know she didn't go all the way to Sudan just to see sand dunes. At any rate, during her trip she must have understood why the veil is a good idea. It hides you, but hides also everyone else. If you're not very good looking, it's a winning proposition in the zero-sum game of status competition.

Let's be honest here, Western culture is exhausting for women. For men too, of course. But sexual freedom means women have to be in their top game; and then again you can't help your genes. Sexual freedom expanded the field of conflict[202]). And that brings a lot of losers. Feminism is if anything a compensatory symptom more than a cause. If you're gonna shit on me because I'm ugly then I'll use feminism to paint you as an evil fuck. Which is, of course, why the most prominent feminists tend to be ugly and fat.

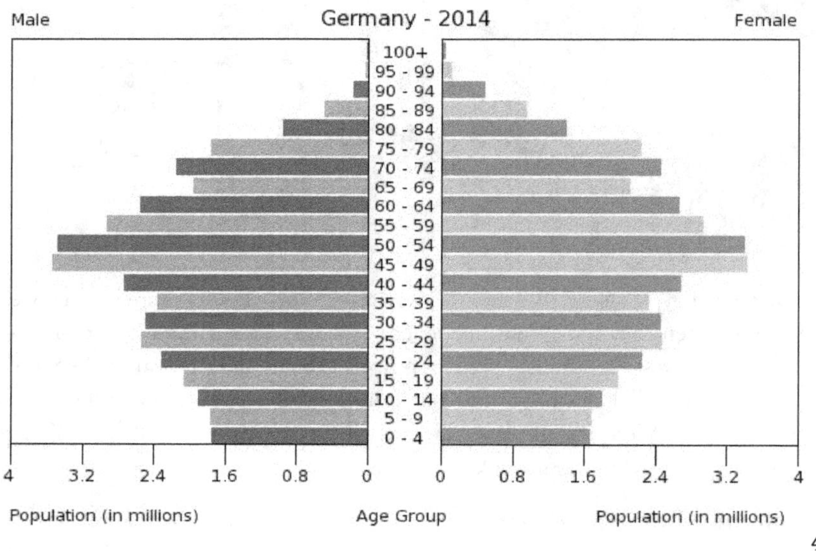

4

This is Germany's population pyramid. Not a lot of young ladies. A huge bunch of older ladies. And it's not getting any better. And so the interests of the older ladies have the upper hand. If there's something older ladies don't like it's hot young ladies. Having them cover up is perhaps not such a bad idea. Probably overkill in Germany, given that the men have been completely neutralized. It would be interesting to test this theory in Italy or France, with more of a culture of adultery.

So anyway, more to worry about.

---

[202] https://en.wikipedia.org/wiki/Whatever_(novel

The Economics of Democracy have Stopped Working

2017-04-17 // democracy, economics, power, theory, japan

Everybody reading this blog may have noticed that I was ecstatic about Trump's election. I was really happy. I went out that night and spent days giggling with a MAGA hat on watching the progressives melt down.

That was of course a tribal feeling. I used to look down on people who behaved like that when their soccer team won. "It's not your team, dumbass, it's just a bunch of overpaid foreigner jocks". But the same way that most middle class men in the West put their identity in sports, I've always put mine in politics, and having Trump, the closest thing in decades to be close to my thinking, win the election to the highest office in the world, was a huge, huge piece of validation. Progressives say that all politics are identity politics.[203] And it's true. Human is a social animal, said Aristotle. And the core of human social behavior is forming identity groups (i.e. tribes) and fight each other. And a guy who appeared to be of my own tribe had won. So of course I was happy.

I was also kinda confused. The core part of neoreaction's theory is that the contemporary political game is rigged so that our tribe just can't win. The game is set up so that the "Cathedral", the power base centered on the US bureaucracy and satellites and it's PR apparatus in the media and universities just control everything. And yet Trump won, with a platform set up by Steve Bannon who is by any account a true and faithful member of our tribe. How could this happen? I wrote shortly after the election that we needed to explain this. We needed a Theory of Trump. And yet for some reason I couldn't get myself to write one. The whole thing just felt odd. So I waited, to see if I found any clues to explain's Trump's ascent to power. To explain the Cathedral's weakness.

Well it seems I did well in waiting, as the Cathedral isn't weak at all. The news from the last few weeks is that the whole Trump platform is collapsing. The federal bureaucrat hiring freeze isn't happening. The wall isn't being built. The judiciary appropriation of legislative power in the US is untouched. Steve Bannon was publicly demoted. Goldman Sachs and assorted globalist bankstas run the show. And Trump just bombed Syria on the flimsiest of pretexts. Now, I don't want to commit myself too much on this. The bombing of Syria wasn't that big, and Trump isn't sending troops. The wall

---

[203] https://www.vox.com/2015/1/29/7945119/all-politics-is-identity-politics

may get built after all. The immigration ban may happen after all. But the signs don't look good.

So it looks like Moldbug wasn't wrong after all. There is a Cathedral deep-state running things completely impervious to the power of the presidency. It seems I wasn't wrong after all either. Leftism is a memeplex evolved precisely in order to achieve and hold power, its content contingent to whatever works to achieve power. As such, we are not supposed to win. Not that easily, at any rate. Being right, having a correct understanding about how the world works is emphatically not the way to achieve power. There is a collection of games that must be played in order to win. Trump was very good at playign the electoral game; but that's is just the outmost layer of the power onion. The inner parts are what actually gets you power, and nationalism, let alone HBD, patriarchy and neoreaction is just not very good at that game.

So all that said, I say it's time we stop caring about Trump and we keep on developing theory.

At its core, the Game of Power is about this:

https://www.youtube.com/watch?v=rStL7niR7gs

You might remember I wrote about this[204]. It's a very good video, based on a very good book. I also like the jargon. The ruler and the keys. Brief and clear. It has some problems, of course. The focus on "treasure", while quite accurate in practice and a good metaphor, is of course incomplete. A ruler doesn't necessarily have to grant cash. What humans seek is not money per-se, it's status. Again, money is more often than not a good enough proxy; but in civilized societies a ruler can sustain its power by granting status, not necessarily money, as Robert Locke so eloquently argued[205] in his apology of the Japanese economy.

But the biggest problem of this video and Bueno de Mesquita's analysis is how it analyses democracy. Like it's some end-of-history endgame where everybody is happy because the government gives away public good in order to buy votes from the people. Oh man, that's just so fucking wrong it's not even funny.

So the basic argument there is that dictatorships are run on the tight loyalty of a few important supporters (keys). Those keys come from a pool of potential keys, the "selectorate". They keys will cost more or less money to keep loyal depending on the ratio of keys to potential keys. If the potential keys are few, the keys are scarce, hence expensive. If the potential keys are many, the keys are expendable, and so they will cost less. So what a Ruler wants is to have few keys, but many potential keys. That's basic

---

[204] https://spandrell.com/2016/11/02/nobody-rules-alone/

[205] https://www.paecon.net/PAEReview/issue23/Locke23.htm

economics. A key works better when he has few ministers, but drawn from a vast aristocracy, instead of just a few nobles. Or better even, draw your ministers from the civil bureaucracy, who are dime a dozen. This is why historically aristocratic systems just don't last very long. The king doesn't like them. Their loyalty is too expensive.

That's easy so far: so what about a democracy? How does that work? Who are the keys, and who are the potential keys? The video starts talking democracy at 6:00. And the beginning is pretty good. In an electoral system, the keys are the people who get you elected; i.e. who give you power. In practical terms the keys are interest group leaders, the people who mobilize vote blocks on your way. In order to please these blocks, a ruler gives them treasure.

Well, not quite treasure. We're not talking kings anymore. The rulers for rulers aren't just for sovereigns; they apply to any power dynamics, no matter at any level. Politicians in a democracy aren't at the pyramid of the power hierarchy as a king or dictator would be. They're at a lower level; so the treasure isn't quite for them to take. Politicians in a democracy are quite easily replaceable themselves, so they gotta play by the rules, if only up to a plausibly deniable point. There's a Schelling point, slightly different in different countries, where a politician can deliver treasure to his keys without getting themselves replaced. We generally call that "corruption", and involves pork, tax loopholes, and that kind of stuff.

The video gets that alright, then notes that democracies tend to have lower tax rates. Which sounds counterintuitive if you're some form of libertarian obsessed with Scandinavia and public expenditure to GDP rates: but it is true. Tax rates in China are quite outrageous. Tax collection efficiency in dictatorships may be quite bad; but the size and autonomy of the private sector is generally very small. The state really dominates the economy more than in a democracy. Not overwhelmingly so, but it really does. So the point is correct. Politicians want to get elected and lower taxes are always a good incentive, even if interest group dynamics make it easier said than done.

Then at 12:00 the video talks about how democracies compensate for lower tax rates by investing more in public infrastructure to make people more productive! You gotta be kidding me. We've talked about how power works. We've talked about how democracies nurture interest groups because they are easier to manage and buy off. We've talked about tax loopholes and pork. All absolutely correct. And now you're telling me that democracies want people to be more productive so that they produce more wealth? What the hell? You think dictatorships don't? Ever been to China? Know of Tsarist Russia? Everybody wants more wealth.

Sure, higher productivity often entails giving people access to stuff that may make it easier to revolt, and to some extent some countries do not encourage productivity that much, especially if they can afford to, having natural resources or something. Stability is a very good thing if you happen to be at the top. You don't wanna change stuff. You wanna stay on top. But if you can be sure that revolt is not an issue, even the nastiest dictatorship tries to get his subjects to be more productive.

The reason that modern democracies invest a lot in public infrastructure, in hospitals and universities, is not because they want their people to be more productive. It's because the power dynamics of politician make outright spending of treasure to be forbidden, and thus ever more complicated forms of pork must be found. And the Schelling point for spending public money without being accused of corruption in the USG dominated world order is healthcare, education and public infrastructure. More or less in that order. Those are not about productivity. Spending in public goods in the West hasn't increased productivity since at least 1970. There's a good argument to suspect that investment in education has decreased productivity to a catastrophic degree[206]. But the money keeps being spent because it is a good way to pay treasure to key supporters.

There was a pretty obvious example of this last year in Japan. Now I'd like to come up with some example closer to my reader's concern, say something in America, but East Asian political culture is so honest and straightforward that it's much easier to come up with corruption cases which map well with this kind of straightforward theory.

So, the Ministry of Education in Japan in 2013 came up with this initiative called "Super Global Universities". Yes, Super. Not kidding. The idea was to have universities across the country come up with a plan to make them Super Global, say by promising to give more classes in English or getting to invite foreign students from India or whatever, and in exchange the Ministry would give them extra cash. And so they did, some were selected, some weren't.

Fast forward to 2016, and the Ministry of Finance is desperate to make spending cuts. There's just no fucking money. They ask around and nobody wants to make cuts. Then they figure out that they hate the most the Ministry of Education. Perhaps some personal vendetta of high-fly bureaucrats there. Whatever the reason, the next day the press is all talking about how the Ministry of Education sent retired bureaucrats to some universities to work as administrators or professors on high salaries. And who would've thought, the universities who accepted those retired bureaucrats were selected as Super Global, and got a shitload of extra taxpayer cash thanks to it. I'll put the guy's face because he looks so much like a corrupt asshole bureaucrat I think it's funny.

---

[206] https://devinhelton.com/how-many-jobs-require-college

That is the most classical form of corruption in Japan, the *ama-kudari*, the sending of retired bureaucrats to cozy sinecures paid on the public purse. That's just the Schelling point that Japan has come up in order to keep the bureaucrats from being at each other's throats. You promote one guy, the loser gets a cozy sinecure on double salary, everybody is happy. Except the public purse. But nobody cares about the public purse. It's public.

The Rules for Rulers guy would want you believe that Japan is investing in Super Global Universities because it wants the Japanese to be more productive. Give me a fucking break. You could've said that in the 1950s, when highways and railways and airports were getting built all across the world. But still, it wasn't even true that the point was higher productivity. Higher productivity was just a convenient Schelling point to get the bureaucrats to not fight each other and get behind the project, and conveniently skim some money for themselves and their cronies (keys). But note that once the higher productivity excuse ceased being true, once all modern countries were bursting full of highways and bridges to nowhere and marginal universities and useless hospitals full of 90 year old vegetables; they didn't stop building. They kept going. Building more and more without thinking much about it. They just had to pay some more to get the media and academia to justify the more and more obviously useless expense. No Child Left Behind! Like there was anyone being left behind to begin with.

Now a disingenuous liberal, say Scott Alexander, may argue that even if the causal arrow is confused, the fact is that the scattered power system of a democracy still results in more investing in public goods, even if they do it for spurious reasons. And they'd have a point. China started investing in getting their country more wealthy once Mao died and the power of individual Chinese bureaucrats become more unstable, so they had to spend their pork on ostensibly public minded projects. But that's not a point about democracy per se, it's a point about unstable bureaucratic systems. And the industrialised nations as a whole are way, way beyond the point of diminishing returns of public good spending. I'd really rather have politicians outright buy votes rather than send more money to universities to poison the minds of the young.

The cycle of politics may turn out to be just as the Greeks saw it: a cycle of monarchy, aristocracy and democracy, underpinned by the economics of the different systems, spending too little, then too much. Now we are spending way, way too much. Which means that we need a change. A change to less democracy. Whose turn is it now[207]?

Not Trump's at any rate. Sigh.

---

[207] https://spandrell.com/2013/10/18/monarchy/

The Role of Government

2017-05-04 // theory, power, nrx

So the Role of Government used to be to Establish Order. That's something the Romans and the Chinese could agree on.

The the English parliament stumbled itself into winning the English Civil War. So they decided the role of government was the Protection of Property. Not a bad idea, all things considered.

Now though we know a bit more about how society works. Let's say we become worthy and assume power. What's the role of government now?

Let me propose: to break malignant signaling spirals.

The Role of Government, 2

2017-05-14 // theory, power, signaling, nrx

A few centuries ago people in Europe discovered free trade. The market. They got the state to say: go make money, free of any guilds or regulations. I won't stop you. Go out there and make money. Compete freely. So people went to make money. Started businesses, factories, mines. In short order we got 2 industrial revolutions, the greatest technological advances in history, and vast, vast, amazing amounts of wealth. Pretty neat.

But. We also found the market isn't perfect. Yeah it produces wealth. A damn lot of it. But leaving people alone to make money also resulted in other outcomes which weren't so desirable. For some people, at least. You see, people compete to make money, and the competition can get ruthless, so people start doing bad stuff. These undesirable outcomes ended up being called "market failures". There's a whole literature about that. Externalities. Monopoly. Sweatshops. There's lots of stuff, it isn't quite clear what is and what isn't a market failure; but the consensus out there is that there are quite a lot. And that the government should use its power to regulate the market in order to prevent and/or fix market failures. Again, it's messy business, as tends to happen with government stuff, but that is how it works today. And it doesn't work that badly. We got clean air and stuff. Which is nice.

So let me do this analogy:

A few centuries ago people in Europe discovered civil rights. Democracy. They got the state to say: go, be free of all legal restrictions in status. No more nobility or medieval ties. You are all citizens, get into politics. I won't stop you. Go out there and say and read and assemble as you wish. Compete freely. So people went out there and started to do what they wished. Started newspapers, political parties, clubs. In short order we got a dozen liberal revolutions, the abolition of all hereditary privileges, universal suffrage, equality before the law. The first East Asian visitors to Europe in the late 1860s saw how cargo was transported by animal-drawn carts, never by people, and wrote: pretty neat. This white guys treat men like men, not like animals. The shock killed Confucianism in a decade.

I digress. And there is no but. Only a small minority of reactionaries ever protested against this. Civil rights only got bigger, deeper. The free market produced much wealth. Free societies also produced much good stuff. But surely free societies have also resulted in undesirable outcomes. You see, people compete in society, competition can get ruthless, and people do bad stuff. We might call that social failures.

Surely low natality is a social failure? The education bubble? Youth unemployment? High criminality? Ugly art and architecture? You name it. All caused by the same thing that causes market failures. Competition run amok; too little oversight. Too much competition makes ruthless people take the upper hand, and the little people suffer.

Libertarians have this dream about the market which self-regulates. The market is just Human Action. Well, to a point. The market doesn't care about what humans want long term. If it did there wouldn't be Capitalist accelerationists who openly cheer for Skynet. So it stands to reason that public force is to be used to correct some market outcomes produced by too much economic freedom.

Libertarians also have this dream about society itself, which self-regulates. Hayek pontificating against social engineering. Well, to a point. If society self-regulated perfectly no people ever would have gone extinct. And there's a ton of social equilibriums, which we may or may not like. Not sure if I want lip plates as standard fashion. So, it stands to reason that public force is to be sued to correct some social outcomes produced by too much social freedom.

The White Left

2017-05-15 // china, redpill

So this article[208] is doing the rounds. Chinese netizens have synthetized a very powerful compound which has the Cathedral in complete terror. What is it? The word 白左, the White Left. This means that some people in China understand that progressivism is a foreign conspiracy against the Chinese nation. And they see this is in overt racial terms. It's not "Western left". It's the "White left".

Now, don't get too excited. Nick Land is excited.[209] But he lives in Shanghai. And he just found out about this. Which means it's not anything mainstream going on in China. I found the word in my Twitter feed about the time of Merkel's boner, when she decided to bring 1 million hostile men into Europe.

The Chinese in Europe were livid. And for good reason. The Chinese went through a lot of hoops to get legal residence in Europe. The Muslims just got in for free. The Chinese are law-abiding and industrious. The Muslims are lazy and prone to crime. The Chinese live in low-rent areas where the Muslims flock to, and they assault the local Chinese all the time, while the police do nothing[210].

Now the Chinese have long had their problems with western style progressivism. There's lots of Chinese living in the West, many go back taking their newly learned progressivism with them. And of course China is poor, the West is rich, so there's plenty of people who consume Western media like crazy just because they think it smells of status. China even has SJWs; but they're almost always women. They have a word for them: 聖母婊, "saint whore", in that they claim to be as compassionate as a Catholic female saint, but are in fact mere attention-whores.

But it took the Muslim invasion of Europe for the Chinese to connect the dots. Feminist saint-whores are one thing: but ethnic pandering is a huge topic in China. China has plenty of Muslims and they hate them. Well, the people do, the Communist party is committed to diversity. The hates comes especially the college-grads who are likely to be into political discussion. Everybody has stories of Muslim minority kids getting affirmative action to get to college, making gangs inside school, picking up Han

---

[208]   https://www.opendemocracy.net/digitaliberties/chenchen-zhang/curious-rise-of-white-left-as-chinese-internet-insult

[209] https://www.xenosystems.net/%e7%99%bd%e5%b7%a6/#comments

[210] https://www.bbc.com/news/world-europe-37720780

girls, getting privileges for Halal food and shit. Say you're some Han college grad, who has been resenting this people for 4 years. You then get to go to America or England for grad school, and what do you find? Ethnic pandering squared. And Saint-whores cubed.

And then Trump happened. Trump started a big debate among the Chinese, both those abroad and those in China. Soon the consensus was that anti-Trumpism was a conspiracy of the "white-left", that coalition of feminists, pro-muslims and anti-chinese leftists that come from the West. China has a local left, the Maoists, which are called 毛左, the Mao-left, so this brand of very different leftism was called the 白左, the White-left.

But again, this is not something big in China. Your average Chinese citizen doesn't talk politics, doesn't read politics. If the alt-right is small, the Chinese alt-right is an order of magnitude smaller. This, if anything, is the ethnic-Chinese branch of the alt-right, here in the West, learning from the alt-right what is going on. These guys don't want China to beat the West. They want the West to be the nice hedonistic place they always wanted to live in, or copy their institutions. Now they're seeing that Eurabia and North Brazil are in progress, and they're not happy about it. Who are they gonna sell their crap to? If the West falls to Islam, then China is the last fortress standing. They're not happy about that prospect.

Occam's Butterknife

2017-05-16 // media, women

https://www.1843magazine.com/culture/the-daily/the-small-world-of-modern-thrillers

THE SMALL WORLD OF MODERN THRILLERS

Plots used to be driven by real-world conflict, but now they revolve around domestic drama. It's a trend that blights films and TV, from Sherlock to Bourne

I did like Steve Sailer and did a Control+F on "women" and "female". There was nothing to be found.

The elephant in the room, that men are playing videogames and only women are watching TV so plots cater to female tastes, i.e. domestic drama, cannot be mentioned. It is crimethink. It really must be exhausting to be a writer these days.

One Belt One Road

2017-05-17 // china, Cold War 2

So the Chinese government just had a huge party in Beijing, attended by 100 or so heads of government, where they announced the launching of the One Belt One Road initiative. They even had cute videos in English like this.

https://www.youtube.com/watch?v=M0lJc3PMNIg

But still, nobody has any idea what this is all about. And the reason is that Chinese public PR is utterly retarded. It just doesn't work. China's government has absolutely no way of reaching the hearts and minds of white people.

Part of it is racial hostility. Yellow men just aren't cool. I hate saying this, I've lived half my life among them, and personally I like them very much. But I gotta say the truth. They just aren't cool. Not even physically. They're not small, the average Chinese is probably taller than the average Italian by now. But they're skinny and awkward and just not very alpha. You just can't fight average T levels. There's plenty of cool guys in the right edge of the distribution, but alas. China will never be cool. Not even Japan is cool. Look at Cool Japan and other government initiatives. Only Anime and other stuff geared to 13 year olds is cool, because the Japanese never grow out of that age, as McArthur famously said. And the Koreans are basically prostituting their teenage girls all across the world for cheap (Korean dramas and K-pop shows are sold really cheap to get access) just in order to spite Japan getting more Western attention.

So now that I've established my impartiality by shitting on all of East Asia at the same time: what is the One Belt One Road thing? Well I don't really know; but what I know is why it sounds so weird. You see, Chinese has this thing where ideally any word or language unit must be 4 syllables long, in order to sounds good and be memorable. As it happens Chinese characters are all 1 syllable long, so it's also 4 characters, 4 words. It just has to. It just sounds good. It fits. It has been like that for 3,000 years. Even Confucius spoke in 4-word units. Mandarin today is about 30% 4-word idioms, some classical idioms going back thousands of years, some neologisms made by ad agencies, some political slogans made by the Communist Party Propaganda Department. That's how Chinese works. And it's beautiful once you get used to it.

So One Belt One Road is exactly 一带一路 *yidai yilu*, 4 words. Other famous slogans would be Mao Zedong's 造反有理 *zaofan youli*, "rebellion is justified", Deng Xiaoping's 改革开放 *gaige kaifang* "reform and opening", or Jiang Zemin's 三个代

表 *sange daibiao* "the three represents", which incidentally means the Communist party represents the peasants, the workers *and* the capitalists whether they like it or not.

So anyway, everything has to fit in 4 words, so 一带一路 it was. They couldn't just say "Land and Sea overseas infrastructure investment plan". That would be more than 4 words. So you get this weird "belt" and "road" thing, where the belt stands for land route and road stands for sea route, for the only reason that it sounds right. Apparently the Koran doesn't make any sense at all when read in translation but the Arabic just sounds so incredibly good, with rhyming and stuff that it became incredibly popular. Although it really doesn't make any sense at all. Well, welcome to humanity.

So anyway, a friend of mine just told me he'd been to a conference on One Belt One Road and that it was the most boring official speech he'd ever listen in his damn life, and that's saying something in China. Another friend though just sent me this chain-mail sort of stuff which kinda cheers on the whole thing. I assume it was made by the government, but I'll translate it here so you can also have the Chinese side. Or better put, what China's government says internally. Because remember, 90% of what the mainstream western press says is also, exactly, government made propaganda, we just don't call it that.

A lot of people can't quite get what One Belt One Road means. In fact it's quite easy if you make a simple metaphor: say infrastructure to a country is like a person who goes buy a house. For the vast majority of people, they do need a house, but they don't have the money on hand. Well, China here is like a developer, a construction company and a bank all put together. China has money it doesn't know what to do with, it has empty houses, and the construction companies have no orders either. So we have both demand and supply sides here with nothing to do. What can we do?

Easy, we make a mortgage. China lends money to all these countries, and then these countries use this very money to ask Chinese companies to build them infrastructure, paying back the money to China in installments in the next decades.

By doing this China can use it's foreign currency reserves in a smart way. We can avoid buying US treasury bonds like we're stupid; those give almost no yield. By lending out the money for interest, the yield is much higher. With this plan China can also put to use its industrial overcapacity, we get orders which reactivate our manufacturing base. And all these countries which would use China's money and rely on China to build infrastructure; their economies will grow eventually, they'll use money to pay us back, and they will also buy Chinese products.

So everybody wins, that's what One Belt One Road is all about. [This sentences rhymes in the original]

Also through this infrastructure we can achieve two roads to Europe, one by land and one by sea. If there is any war with the US, the US won't be able to encircle us. At the same time this would accelerate the speed of transport from China to Europe, lowering transport costs and increasing China's competitiveness.

All these countries would use Chinese products as the standard of their infrastructure. This means that in the future they would need to use Chinese products to service the infrastructure. This would exclude other countries' products, giving our manufacturers an advantage when competing with foreign manufacturers.

Of course inside all this there will be some loans which go bad. It's like a bank, there's always someone who can't pay back their mortgage or their car loan. But banks don't care about that, why? Because they make enough profit to compensate for it. And with China's One Belt One Road, China would profit twice. One through the interest on the given loans, way higher than the yield of US debt. And then again when these countries buy Chinese products, giving money to Chinese private businesses. In business terms this is a very lucrative process, if we can manage well the level of bad debt, we are sure to make a net profit.

Also if China gets to develop these countries' infrastructure, naturally these countries will become more friendly towards China. All these countries will be our friends. And as everybody knows, it is always good to have many friends. This applies to people and to states.

During this process, you may notice that China outright gives aid to some countries, without expecting payback. Some people don't understand this, how can we give stuff away for free? It's very easy. When you get some business from someone, you gotta give them some advantage. When shopping in a store, many shops give regular discounts, they'd give you coupons if you buy a lot, or even free products. Countries do the same. You're making money out of someone, if you don't give them something in exchange, well the business won't go anywhere. All these aid packages are in fact discount coupons of a sort. Because besides us there's also Japan or Germany giving loans, helping others build infrastructure. We have competition.

This kind of plan was in fact invented by the Americans. When the US wanted to open up foreign markets, they didn't do like other countries and use military force to conquer colonies and their markets. What the US did was use what they called "open-door policy", they used loans, the Marshall plan, etc. They gave loans to other countries, and these countries then used the money to buy American products. By doing so the US occupied these countries' markets without shedding blood, which helped America become wealthy, and the US dollar become the world's reserve currency. Thus the US became the world's factory and ultimately the boss of the world.

China is actually learning from America's path to greatness, growing through peace, and not force.

So, you see, One Belt One Road is a very farseeing policy, it is precisely the path for China's rising. If you have any friends who still don't get it, send this piece their way. Let everyone get it. The Great Renewal of the Chinese Nation is just around the corner!

Original below

很多人搞不清楚一带一路到底是什么意思？其实打一个最简单的比方，基础建设对于一个国家来说，就像一个普通人去买房买车，对于绝大多数的国家来说，需要，但是拿不出这么多钱。而中国就好像是房地产商，建筑商和银行的组合体，有闲置资金，有空房，同时建筑公司也没活干，两边都有需求，怎么办？很简单，按揭了。中国借钱给这些国家，然后让这些国家，用这笔指定的钱找中国公司去修基础建设，然后分成几十年慢慢地还给中国。这样中国的外汇储备就有了灵活的运用，不用傻乎乎的只能去买美国的国债，收益几乎为零，借给别人收利息，收益高的多。中国过剩的产能，就有人出钱来买，盘活了中国的制造业。

而这些用中国钱的国家，靠中国帮助修好了基础建设，经济就会发展，就会有钱来还中国的钱，同时还会买更多的中国产品。这样各取所需，就是所谓的一带一路。

除了这些，一带一路的国家接受美元贷款，可以用人民币还款，这样，这些国家慢慢就开始接受了人民币作为储备货币，人民币，慢慢就获得了和美元同等的地位。同时通过这样的基础建设，形成了从海上和陆路两条直达欧洲的通路，一旦发生和美国的战争，美国无法对我们进行完全的封锁，同时，另一方面也加快了中国到欧洲的物流速度，降低了流通成本，进一步增强了中国的竞争力。由于这些国家使用中国产品作为基础建设的标准，后续的配套自然也要使用中国产品，这样就产生了排他效果，让中国在和其它的制造业国家竞争时，占据了优势地位。当然在这个过程中，肯定会有一些坏账，就像是银行一样，总会有些人还不起房贷车贷。可是银行依然乐此不疲，为什么？因为它赚的更多。而中国的一带一路，实际上赚两次钱，一是借钱出去的利息，比买美国公债赚得多的多，另一方面，这些国家必须使用中国的产品，让中国的民间企业能受惠，所以从商业的角度来说，几乎是一个暴利的过程，只要控制好坏账的比例，肯定是利大于弊。同时，由于中国为这些国家发展基础建设，会增大这些国家对中国的友好度，让这些国家成为中国的好朋友，谁都知道，朋友多了好办事。做人是如此，国家也是如此。在这个过程中，你会发现中国会对一些国家进行无偿援助，很多人想不通，为什么会这样呢？很简单，你做别人的生意，就得送给人家优惠。商场也要定期给你打折，买多了要给你送优惠卷，免费的产品。国家也是如此，光赚别人的钱，不给人家点好处，生意就做不走，这些无偿援助，实际上就是折扣卷。因为除了我们，日本德国也借钱给别人，帮别人搞基础建设，我们是有竞争的。这个方式实际上是美国人最先发明，美国为了获得市场，并没有采用其他国家的办法，通过武力征服，获取殖民地来获得市场。而是通过所谓的门户开放政策，租借法案，马歇尔计划等等，借钱给其他国家，让这些国家回过头来买美国的产品，这样兵不血刃地就占领了这些国家的市场，促进了美国的繁荣，让美元成为世界储备货币，使美国成为了世界工厂，最终成为世界老大。中国实际上在学美国崛起的方式，通过和平而不是武力，实现崛起。所以，一带一路是非常有远见的决策，是中国崛起的必由之路，如果你的朋友中还有人不知道到底是什么意思？把这个转出去，让大家都明白。中华民族的伟大复兴，已经指日可待了！

The Future

2017-05-26 // demographics

Let us talk demographics. Because life doesn't suck enough as it does. Yes, had a bad day.

A while ago[211] I proposed the concept of "projected population". You get the total live births in a country, then you multiply it by 80, an approximation of life expectancy. So, assuming the level of births remains constant (which it won't), in 80 years a country would have that amount of people.

So to put an example. Japan today has a population of 127 million. Live births in 2016 were 981k, so if the birth rate remained constant, in 80 years, roughly 2100, Japan would have a population of 78 million. Now of course the birth rate will not remain constant, given the fertility rate, 1.4, the population will shrink way beyond that. But there's always a chance the birth rate comes up again. Some miracle. So projected population is only a way to understand how things stand right now. I'm not predicting anything. To the extent the projected population predicts anything it's a best scenario. A miracle scenario.

So right here[212] we got stats on birth rates across Europe. As of now, the 28 countries of the EU (including Britain), had a total of 5,103,165 births in 2015. Of course the EU isn't the whole of Europe. But it's close enough, and Serbia, Ukraine or Norway aren't having that many babies anyway. So get this number as a good proxy. In Europe right now 5.1 million babies are being born per year.

Multiply per 80 and you get 408 million total population. The population as of 2015 was 510 million, so that's a whopping 20% decrease. 100 million less Europeans at this rate. But wait. If you clicked the link you'd see there are stats on births "per country of birth of the mother". That's the total, this includes mothers born outside the EU. How many babies did foreign mothers have in 2015? 1,015,926 million. 20% of the total births. And this has been increasing at 25k per year. Babies from mothers born in the EU were just 4 million.

Interestingly enough the stats have data from Turkey. Over there in 2015 they had 1.3 million babies, of which only 22k were born to foreign mothers.

---

[211] https://spandrell.com/2015/12/20/demographics/

[212] https://ec.europa.eu/eurostat/web/population-demography-migration-projections/births-fertitily-data/database

So anyway, at this rate, the population of the EU in 2100 would be 408 total, of which 80 million would be foreign or half-foreign babies, 328 million native. But wait. There's plenty of ethnically foreign women in the EU having babies who weren't themselves born abroad. Second and third generation immigrants. These count inside the 4 million EU births. How many of them are there? The EU wouldn't say. If anybody has good data by all means put it in the comments.

I guess it's fair to assume they're somewhat above 10%. Perhaps not 25% yet, not EU wide. But again this is about mothers. Conveniently. Foreign fathers with native mothers are a pretty big part of the birth rate these days. So to say that 25% of kids born to "native mothers" aren't 100% native kids sounds reasonable. That would mean that of the 4 million total births to European born mothers, 1 million kids are either foreign or half-foreign. So that leaves 3 million white kids born in 2015. And 2 million foreign or kinda foreign kids. 40% of the total. As of now. And it's getting worse pretty fast.

So again, get that number into your head. As of 2015:

3 million White babies per year in Europe.

2 million White babies in the USA.

1.3 million Turkish babies.

17 million Chinese babies.

27 million Indian babies.

7 million Nigerian babies (!)

In 20 years, there will be just as many 20 year-olds.

This is the future we will live in.

Houellebecq on the new matriarchy

2017-05-29 // france, europe, women, redpill

A while ago I said that France deserves to die, if only to atone for the dozens of evil intellectuals that she has inflicted on the world, from Rousseau to Derrida. That's a bit harsh. France after all has given us Michel Houellebecq, and while he will never have 1/1000 of the influence of a crazy sodomite on drugs like Foucault, he is still the best writer in the whole world of the last 50 years, and that counts for a lot.

Apparently Monsieur Houellebecq went to Argentina to give some talks, and here's one which got uploaded to Youtube. The talk is in French, with Spanish subtitles, both of which are quite tractable on Google translate. He talks about the current intellectual landscape of France, where everyone even half interesting is a reactionary, haunted by the left, but they don't mind it, hold it as a badge of honor. Let me highlight the last 15 minutes.

https://www.youtube.com/watch?v=Ffd5wWuewIM

Let me quote Tocqueville:

I want to imagine under what new features despotism could present itself to the world; I see an innumerable crowd of similar and equal men who spin around restlessly, in order to gain small and vulgar pleasures with which they fill their souls. Each one of them, withdrawn apart, is like a stranger to the destiny of all the others; his children and his particular friends form for him the entire human species;g as for the remainder of his fellow citizens, he is next to them, but he does not see them; he touches them without feeling them; he exists only in himself and for himself alone, and if he still has a family, you can say that at least he no longer has a homeland [patrie].

Above those men arises an immense and tutelary power that alone takes charge of assuring their enjoyment and of looking after their fate. It is absolute, detailed, regular, far-sighted and mild. It would resemble paternal power if, like it, it had as a goal to prepare men for manhood; but on the contrary it seeks only to fix them irrevocably in childhood; it likes the citizens to enjoy themselves, provided that they think only about enjoying themselves. It works willingly for their happiness; but it wants to be the unique agent for it and the sole arbiter; it attends to their security, provides for their needs, facilitates their pleasures, conducts their principal affairs, directs their industry, settles their estates, divides their inheritances; how can it not remove entirely from them the trouble to think and the difficulty of living?

This was published in 1840, in the second part of Democracy in America. I found it breathtaking. In terms of ideas, this own passage contains the whole of my work. I'd only add one thing: the individual in Toqueville at least has a friend and a family; in my universe he doesn't anymore. So the process of atomization that he described has reached it's final conclusion.

This passage also contains almost all of the work of Phillippe Muray. Phillippe only added one thing: that that power he described isn't a fatherly power. He sees it as motherly power. And so the modernity announced by Muray implies the comeback of the matriarchy, in a new form, formed by the state. So the state keeps the people in a perpetual state of infancy; and the first enemy that modern society attempts to crush is virility itself.

In this sense, the evolution of France since Muray's death [in 2006], and in particular since the socialists won the presidency, have confirmed his prophecies to an amazing degree. So much that even himself would have been surprised by, for example, the fact that France was after Sweden the second country in Europe to criminalize prostitution. I think he would have had trouble understanding it.

If I tell you my opinion, I believe that banning prostitution amounts to abolishing one of the fundamental pillars of society. It means making marriage impossible. Without prostitution as a corrective, marriage collapses, family collapses too, and then society for demographic reasons. And so banning prostitution is simply one aspect of the European suicide.

So as things stand now we can predict a great future with a rather ancient formula, which comes from the Middle Ages, the 7th century. Salafist Islam. It's true that right now the events aren't quite agreeing with me. But I stand by my prophecy. Because jihadism will end, people always end up tiring of carnage and suicide. The proliferation of Islam is only on its early phases, because demographics are on its side. And Europe, by not defending itself, has a suicidal attitude. And we mustn't think it will be a slow suicide. With a fertility rate of 1.3 or 1.4, it will happen very quickly.

Given the circumstances, I think all those debates that French intellectuals are having on secularism, Islam, etc. are all completely pointless. For they ignore the only relevant factor, which is the present state of the couple and the family.

Gender inequality in fertility

2017-06-01 // demographics, europe, women

I've noticed people don't wanna hear this, but I still gotta say it.

I was doing some light research to follow up on my last post. Stumbled upon this:

JANUARY 2014

Fertility of Turkish migrants[213]

in Germany:[214]

Duration of stay matters[215]

The writing is incredibly bad. Purposefully obfuscating. But the figures are very illuminating. Take a look at this one:

Table 5: Total fertility rate and mean age at first childbirth by age at migration.

| | TFR | | MAC_1 | |
Age at migration	Male	Female	Male	Female
0-14	2.08	2.15	24.4	25.20
15-19	2.61	2.49	24.3	26.00
20-24	2.29	2.49	26.2	23.00
25-29	2.19	2.44	28.4	24.20
30-50	2.04	2.18	28.9	28.90
All Turks	2.28	2.35	25.7	24.9
All Germans	1.27	1.67	29.7	26.6

Notes: German GGS 2005/06, unweighted (own calculations).

TFR of German men: 1.27. That's low.

TFR of German women: 1.67. Huh? German women are having 30% more children than German men. With whom?

With someone besides German men, of course. That's how it works.

So now you know why:

---

[213] https://www.demogr.mpg.de/papers/working/wp-2014-001.pdf

[214] https://www.demogr.mpg.de/papers/working/wp-2014-001.pdf

[215] https://www.demogr.mpg.de/papers/working/wp-2014-001.pdf

Can't fight Darwin.

Fate

2017-06-12 // women, leftism, bioleninism

Years ago, when the alt-right was barely beginning to form, many Western patriots hang out at Lawrence Auster's blog. There was one very interesting guy, called Conservative Swede. Eventually he surrendered, and I don't know what is of him now. But he had a very interesting blog on Europe and Islam and all this stuff which now has been taken over by the alt-right and Frog twitter.

The best thing I ever read of Conservative Swede is when he wrote that Mecca will be nuked. Eventually. It just has to happen. If you had a computer simulation, and you had both Islam and nuclear power, the odds are that at some point someone is going to throw a nuke at Mecca. Islam just can't help being violent and conflictive. Mecca is the center of Islam. And so eventually someone is going to get pissed at them and throw a nuke there. It may not even be outsiders. It might be Shi'a. It may even be some crazy Wahabbi who follows the signaling spiral to the end, and the same way the house of Muhammad was destroyed by the Wahabbis, well Mecca itself is a physical relic, so let's burn it down. At any rate, Mecca will be nuked. It's the inescapable conclusion of the intrinsic logic of Islam.

I recalled this argument when I was looking at this woman:

https://www.youtube.com/watch?v=hdjmYJTnwfY

So Blair Imani is your typical black American Cathedral activist. She's 60%+ white, around 110 IQ, she's even kinda pretty. And most importantly, she's loud, energetic and relentlessly self-promoting. A psychopathic status maximizer[216].

It wasn't turning out that well for her, and so a couple of years ago she converted to Islam. Now you may think that's a shamelessly opportunistic thing to do. And yeah, that's precisely the point. But there's also the detail that she has curly afro hair.

---

[216] https://spandrell.com/2015/10/09/the-social-module/

So by wearing the hijab, she actually looks better than before. Or at least not much worse See, this girl is smart. She's playing many games at the same time.

My point is: the same way that Islam has an internal logic, which may or may not imply the nuking of Mecca. Progressive politics have an internal logic, which is a fall into identity politics and a war of all against all competing for victim pokemon points. Well this girl has it all. She's black. She's a woman. She is a "victim of sexual assault". And she's Muslim. And of course she's a loud and energetic self-promoter. And she looks ok.

I just don't see how she won't get to be president of the United States. Or maybe not her, but something eerily similar. That's just how the game works.

Fake Science

2017-06-19 // leftism, decadence, media

After Donald Trump won the election, the Central Politburo of the Free Media© came up with the official interpretation of their defeat: Fake News™. People on Facebook were pasting news from shady sites saying that the Pope had endorsed Trump, and that led to Trump winning. Or something.

Now, I don't know who came up with Fake News, but man, he struck a nerve. As a meme, Fake News is perhaps the biggest and most rapidly expanding one I've ever seen. It's everywhere, the Left uses it to shit on Trump; the right uses it to shit on the Left. And not only in the West; go on any Asian internet forum and everybody is talking about Fake News this and Fake News that, translated to every language.

Now there's a pattern to how memes expand. The same as words, really. They just serve a function. People adopt a new word usually because it fits in a mental pattern they already had, and it allows them to do something which is very useful. Some Cathedral honcho came up with Fake News for the sole reason to imply that Trump wasn't a legitimate president; but the fact is people all over the world were already starting to understand that the news media wasn't telling the objective truth. More often than not the media is just spinning facts in order to build a narrative for their own partisan political gain. Which is the very definition of the string "Fake News" as it is used today. CNN shits on Trump? Fake News. Fox News says something bad about the Democrats? Fake News. The NYT comes up with some corruption case about Xi Jinping's advisors? 假新闻. Koreans come up with yet another sex slave from 1940? フェイクニュース. Somebody saw the King of Thailand fucking a dog? ข่าวปลอม.

So now that people understand what the news media is all about, and have a word to express it, it's obvious that Fake News is here to stay. Which is a great thing; it's quite accurate after all, even if Fake News gets thrown around to everywhere the enemy tribe says. What I don't get is why the concept is yet to be extended to other extremely similar cases of content being sold as objective truth when it's obviously just some story spun for political purposes. I'm talking of course of the scientific establishment. 90% of which is Fake Science. Global Warming? Fake Science. Social psychology? Fake Science. Economics? Fake Science. All of it.

Usually when some media apparatus or somebody on social media came up with some lame scientific paper and used it to justify anything, people who actually knew something about it would caution about Gell-mann amnesia. Which is a great concept to have. But it lacks the punch and ready accessibility of Fake Science.So let me propose that when any scientific article which isn't about engineering or hasn't been replicated n times and resulted in an actually workable and useful idea be deemed Fake Science. Just throw it around on Twitter, I think it'll stick.

The Fall of Singapore's Monarchy

2017-06-20 // singapore, Lee Kuan Yew, monarchy, pozz, bluegov, women

It's been a while since I last wrote about Singapore. Now that the old man is gone it's seldom on anybody's radar anymore. But that has changed recently. Singapore is in the news. First there's this article by Nick Land[217] on Jacobite, where he quotes my coinage of Singapore Singapore as an IQ Shredder,[218] and notes how we don't yet have a fix to perhaps the biggest problem we have.

But there's a pretty big piece of news going on in Singapore. Big enough that the Prime Minister, Harry Lee's son Lee Hsien Loong, is out on a charm offensive to defend his honor. Hear him speak.

https://www.youtube.com/watch?v=cA9Xv7KSrh0

Now, I intend no offense. But man, this guy is goofy. Compare him to his father's speeches. Man, Lee Kuan Yew had an iron fist and a steel tongue. He could talk a crowd like he was Sulla on horseback. But then look at his firstbon son. Who by all accounts has a genius IQ, is tall, athletic and a very fine specimen. But he's just goofy. Look at his inaugural smile, the lame bow with the head. And his English. How the hell does he speak worse English than his father? The accent is pretty standard Singaporean English, not that he's bad at it or anything. But English is this guy's first language. And he's lived for years in the US. And yet look at him. This shows again my personal theory that language ability and IQ aren't at all correlated. And that for people with low language ability, bilinguism is just too hard. And so you get people like the Second King of Singapore, Lee Hsien Long, who speaks goofy English and lousy Chinese.

Again, not dissing the guy. He's probably 2 sigma smarter than I am. A legit math progidy. Just a pity that he was born in a royal household, where he has to do things that aren't his strong suit. As the Chinese poem，

吾本西方一衲子 为何流落帝王家

But anyway, what's going on in Singapore right now? We are witnessing a crisis of the monarchy. Lee Kuan Yew had 3 children. The eldest, now king (prime minister), a daughter, Lee Wei Ling, and a younger son, Lee Hsien Yang.

---

[217]   https://jacobitemag.com/2017/06/20/modernitys-fertility-problem/

[218]   https://spandrell.com/2013/03/26/lee-kuan-yew-drains-your-brains-for-short-term-gain/

The younger son is just a lame prince, spent some time in the military, then was an executive, now is Chairman of the Aviation Authority. Take a look at him. He's just your run of the mill , boring mediocre Chinese business cuck.

https://www.youtube.com/watch?v=DVCQZnCrLfE

Things start to get interesting when you factor in his wife, Lee Suet Fern. As it often happens, if some big shot is just some mediocre boring cuck, odds are its his wife who wears the pants in the household. And the young daughter in law of Lee Kuan Yew is exactly what you'd think she would be.

There you go, a good looking, well dressed, heavily jeweled up lady. She also happens to be a big shot lawyer in Singapore. And she just looks like a scheming witch. As she should be; she didn't marry that boring lame ass beta prince for nothing. She wanted power, status. And big earrings.

Why does this matter? Well this matter because there is another very prominent woman in the Lee royal household. The wife of the Lee Hsien Loong. The Queen of Singapore, Ho Ching. Now, go back to the top of the page and take another look at our goofy king. How do you expect his queen to be?

Everyone in Singapore says she looks like his mother. Which is a bit unfair. She's 64 years old, she looks like an average 64 year old before feminism. She doesn't need to look like a scheming witch covered with diamonds. But basically because everybody knows she's the mother of all scheming witches. She was, before marrying into the royal household, already a high ranking bureaucrat. And she is the leader of Temasek, the Singaporean sovereign investment fund, managing over 300 billion dollars in assets. She has the money. The Queen controls the purse, the huge purse of the very small country of Singapore. Many say she's the actual ruler of the country. She certainly looks more like it than her goofy husband.

Here's a video of her in her professional capacity:

https://www.youtube.com/watch?v=lnLO1fQNp7c

So well, right now you might imagine that this two households, the eldest and youngest sons of Lee Kuan Yew, just don't get along very well. Which they don't. But we'll get to that later. Now it's time to talk about the other child of LKY. His daughter. Daughter?

https://www.youtube.com/watch?v=0m1QW8SHBbU

Let me put some more pictures of Lee Kuan Yew's dear daughter. I'll make them smaller as I don't want anybody to choke.

There ya go. This is Lee Wei Ling, daughter of Lee Kuan Yew, royal princess of Singapore. She's 50 something. Unmarried, as you might have guessed. As it happens she's a talented neurosurgeon. Yes, she broke the glass ceiling into this traditionally male occupation. You might have figured out why.

Now, some might say I'm being nasty about her. Nothing wrong about being ugly. But no, sorry. I don't buy that. First of all because she needn't be this ugly. Not at all. She looked fairly pleasant while young.

And while some say she got this nasty disease or whatever, it's still no excuse. Being fat is, generally speaking, a choice. Looking bad is in the overwhelming majority of cases, a choice. She could just eat a bit more. She could let her hair grow a bit more. She could buy a decent pair of glasses. She could stop juicing on steroids to get thicker arms than 90% of Singaporean man. And more importantly, she could stop being a bitch and writing articles all over the state controlled media in Singapore saying that she's hot stuff. She's "eccentric[219]", is glad of "looking like a boy[220]", how she "chose" to be single[221], writes books about "being a woman" while doing everything she can to avoid looking like a woman. She just won't shut up[222] about how much of a victim she is because people think she got it easy by being the King's daughter. Poor little thing. She's the perfect example[223] of Steve Sailer's law of female journalism: everything a woman ever writes is advocating for social change so that come the revolution, the woman herself would be considered hotter. It just happens that she's, by far, the ugliest woman in Singapore; probably the ugliest woman in all East Asia. And yet she's the

---

[219]   https://www.asiaone.com/singapore/lee-kuan-yews-daughter-im-martian-anyway

[220]   https://everythingalsocomplain.com/2010/11/07/i-could-pass-off-as-teenage-boy/

[221] https://www.ngejay.com/?p=2457

[222]   https://everythingalsocomplain.com/2012/06/03/lee-wei-lings-child-like-friend-categorisation-process/

[223]   https://everythingalsocomplain.com/2011/12/04/lee-wei-ling-looks-like-her-father/

King's sister, so the state media better publish her crap. If she were in the US she would've been arguing for her own pronouns 20 years ago. Might have called herself zorg.

You'd think she at least would be thankful to his brother who lets her keep being the worst example possible of behavior by a royal princess? Oh no. She's been shitting on her brother publicly for years. And it all culminated last week when Lee Wei Ling and Lee Hsien Yang, brother and sister of the Prime Minister, issued a joint letter accusing the PM of using the state apparatus to harass them, to use the inheritance of the late Lee Kuan Yew to prop up the dynastic hopes for their son; and just being so much of a corrupt asshole, he and especially his wife Ho Ching, that they will go into exile right away. Here's the letter.[224]

The whole thing is just some lame family dispute about the house of the late LKY, which passed to his heir, but he was nagged into selling it to his brother, who wants it demolished but the government won't do it because they want to make a museum of it or whatever. It's pretty lame stuff. It gets pretty complicated because apparently there were 6 wills by LKY and the last one was quite different from the previous one. But you're probably bored out of your mind already. Who gives a crap? Well Singaporeans give a crap. This sort of mind-dumbing family disputes are the plot of 99% of SEA soap operas, including Taiwan and Hong Kong. These guys just eat up this stuff. It's pretty similar to South American soap operas; just without the hot chicks and the sex.

So anyway, this is perhaps the biggest scandal in Singapore in decades; all just a petty dispute by the very very petty characters in the royal household. For all those monarchists out there; that's what happened to traditional monarchies. Here we have the very son of Lee Kuan Yew playing Duke of Orleans, bringing down the monarchy out of spite. And most likely not even personal spite, but just spite between their wives.

As it also tends to happen, the people at large are quite sceptic of all the scandal, and majoritarily support the King against his evil brothers. So it may still happen that the Queen gets her way and the Lee Dynasty goes on for a 3rd generation. I gotta say the crown prince, Lee Hongyi, does look like a proper king, though he denies any interest.

------

224 https://drive.google.com/file/d/0ByodqaSLlpPIWHdRdFE2QlZYb zg/view

Or maybe it happens like countless previous times; the elite uses this scandal to dump the king, and follow up with what formally is already a Republic. So you'd get party politics and dissolve state controls on the media, and the typical signaling spirals of all democracies. The end of Singapore.

I did say that history wouldn't be kind[225] to Lee Kuan Yew's legacy. But I didn't think it would come down so fast. It is also no wonder that the old man looked so depressed in old age. What a bunch of useless brats. Especially his daughter, who lived with him until the end. He was pissed to no end at why she turned out like that. But I guess that, like so may men of action, he cared much more about his work than about his family. Reminds me of American Sniper, with Chris Kyle choosing Iraq over his family for many years. Why? Because he had a job to do. Domesticity was not for him. Well, we all reap what we sow.

---

[225] https://spandrell.com/2015/03/23/harry-lee-rest-in-peace/

Alt-psychopathic status maximizers

2017-06-24 // cucks, trump

https://twitter.com/Cernovich/status/877563552730562561

A while ago I called myself alt-right because hey, the God-Emperor got elected. Later, the elected has shown himself not to be much of a God, and certainly not an Emperor, and so I've lost my interest. And you would think everybody else had done so too, but then you wouldn't understand politics.

I haven't been following this very much, but apparently there's the alt-right, and now something called the alt-lite. What is the alt-lite?

How to answer this question? I could go on doing some reading about their positions, what they believe in. But that would be missing the point. If that's how you analize political movements then you haven't been reading this blog properly.

The point here is that the "alt-lite" is at the left of the alt-right; but their naming suggests that they want to contest the alt-right space. So by definition, the alt-lite are entryists who want to eat up the political space of the alt-right. And to do so, they will take whatever position, they will do whatever is necessary. Because the difference between left and right is not one of "beliefs". It is one of drive. The left are the psychopatic status maximizers. The right are those who are not. Relatively speaking, of course. So you can expect the alt-lite to be a psychopathic status maximizing version of the alt-right.

So what will they do? They'll keep Trump support, because there's a lot of money there. 60 million people voted for the man after all. They will tone down the Nazi stuff because there's little to gain there. You'll have a lot of women there. A lot of Jews. A lot of gays. A lot of fund-raising. A lot of media promotion. A lot of weird changing of positions according to what the media likes to hear at the moment.

There's a clip here which shows a good example to where this is moving:

https://www.youtube.com/watch?v=QLLPTxfm2G8

And you know what? They'll probably win. Because they have way more drive than your average chap on frog-Twitter. In a fight, the guy without scruples always beats the guy with scruples. The common thing to people who have achieved something in life is greed, the drive to achieve something at whatever cost and no matter how many people you should trample over in your way. These sociopaths genes exist for a reason. They work.

Until everything goes to hell and there's no more prosocial chumps to fool.

Uptalk

2017-06-30 // language, cucks, anglos

Chalupas Cowen interviews Ben Sasse. I had no clue who this Sasse guy was, but apparently he's a poster child of a well-adjusted American conservative. The uber cuck. Now this is a bit unfair. The guy does seem smart. And he seems like a good person. A healthy, down to earth family man. He's even written a book about education which isn't half bad.

The guy just seems like a very productive person. A german-descendend guy from Nebraska, when he commits to a job he does it well. Extremely well. And now his job is to be a Republican senator. To be a cuck. So he's a professional cuck. An extremely productive cuck. It's not his fault really, it's just the world we live in. If he had lived in Germany in the 1930s he would have been an extremely productive Gestapo commander. If he had been an Englishman in the 19th century he would have been an extremely efficient colonial conqueror. Alas, he's a Nebraskan in the current year. So he went to Harvard, then was a university manager, and now he's a proffessional Senate cuck.

By the way I wonder what it takes for a white evangelical kid from the Midwest to get into Harvard. Maybe things have changed since this guy's time. But the few non-connected white Christians who get into Harvard must be *extremely* tightly screened.

This post isn't about Ben Sasse himself; there's little I can say about him. I'm not an ornitologist. But I am a linguist. So I can talk about his way of speech. Now many of you might have heard of "uptalk". Most Americans don't notice it, the way fish don't know what water is. But for foreign learners of English, uptalk is just weird. They don't teach uptalk in English classes. I should talk about language teaching some other day, it's really broken. The only way to actually learn something is if you have the power to notice things by yourself. But that applies to most education. Anyway, I digress.

Uptalk is the relatively recent (last 25 years or so) trend of mainstream American speech, where the rising tone typical of question clauses gets applied to words in the middle of a declarative sentence.

I like traveling to foreign countries? Because I think that the culture? And the things you see? Are fascinating and fullfill me as a person?

The whole things doesn't make a lot of sense. But as always, there's two dimensions to language. There's language as a set of rules, which are made clear by prescriptive analysis. And then is what people actually do with the rules, i.e. change them all the time, and that's descriptive analysis. Uptalk started apparently with teenage girls in California. But now it's freaking everywhere. And you have a 45 year old man, a US Senator with 3 children, using uptalk 5 times per sentence. It's infuriating. But let's not have value judgment stop us from doing a good analysis.

Why do people do uptalk? We can define uptalk as the transfer of question marks into non-questions. Now why would people do that? There's a good thing that questions and non-questions are distinct in speech. But the common way of explaining questions vs. non-questions is, as tends to happen with all Western style social science, heavily restricted by a logical analysis of how language works. Questions don't only demand information. They're also a way of calling attention. Of showing epistemic humility. Or of being a pussy who doesn't stand by his opinion.

A statement implies certainty. I like traveling. Yes I do. That's my prerrogative. And now I let it known. That's how it used to work. But not anymore. Now every statement is suspect of fascism. Being too sure of yourself is toxic masculinity. Assuming that people talk to you because they want to know something about you is mansplaining. The correct way of having a conversation is to make it everything into a question. The implication is "I'm not very sure about this, if you think I'm wrong or a fascist or I'm guilty of having a penis please forgive me, I'll change my opinion sooner than you can say the word"cuck"".

... or that's what Roissy would write. Well, actually that's pretty much exactly what Roissy wrote some time ago.[226] I wrote the above before checking that out. The thing with language though is that one shouldn't read too much into it. At the end of the day, language is just a behavioral habit. People don't "generate" language according to some calculated inputs. I'm quite sure Senator Sasse isn't generating uptalk because he's a passive-aggressive cuck who actually wants to coerce your agreement after each freaking clause. He's just doing what everybody else in his milieu does; and him being a *very* well-adjusted religious German who does what his peers expecting him to do, he got a habit of uptalk.

Which is interesting in its own way: language is *the* window into human behavior, because it follows the same rules as every other behavior does, but it's orders of magnitude more frequent and easy to analyze. And a good rule that language analysis gives us, is that if you want to find the cause of some behavior, you shouldn't look at its present shape. The present shape is just a function of habit and people copying each other, especially higher status people. The best way of achieving some explanatory power is to loo at the evolutionary process by which a habit became common. In genetics I think they call that "achieve fixation".

---

[226] https://heartiste.wordpress.com/2015/10/25/lets-have-a-talk-about-uptalk/

In evolutionary terms, Uptalk started with teenage girls, and indeed it was an effect of modern Californian teenage girl society, which is a good approximation to a Hobbesian state of nature of all against all, where you must police your every single act, lest the sisterhood comes crashing down on you and throws you and your status into some ghetto in Oakland. So that's how teenage girls evolved passive-aggresiveness and high-frequence semi-questions as self-defence. The interesting thing is why that spread out of teenage girl life into wider society. This implies there's something about modern society which is similar to teenage girl total status war.

Uptalk can also be seen as the fusion of the colloquial tags "like...", "you know?" into the actual word itself. "Like" and "you know" are also a ways of holding plausible deniability about one's statement. You aren't just asserting something. You aren't really like, sure, you know, so you hold plausible deniablity lest your interlocutor be short of status in that particular moment and she uses the chance to throw you under the bus. Again, one way of putting this is epistemic humility. Another way of putting this is a complete breakdown of social trust so that conversation is pretty much... impossible?

Steve Sailer often says that it's a good thing we got this Tower of Babel thing; as different languages make the transfer of bad ideas extremely easy, and different languages act as a good barrier. Uptalk makes an excellent example of this. In a few decades it has conquered the whole US, and it's fast making inroads into Britain; while I've never seen anything like it in any other language. Parochialsm has its own problems, but avoiding Uptalk and other progressive memes makes it worth it.

Do check out the whole podcast. Not that the content itself is interesting; that would be controversial and problematic. Interestingly Tyler Cowen has its own slightly milder version of uptalk, but he uses it in almost every single end of clause. This follows Cowen's own style: he follows the mainstream, he's a well behaved true-believer; but he does it his own way; lest the wind changes some other way, then he can claim that he was always for war against Eastasia. Of course he was.

Liu Xiaobo

2017-07-14 // china, redgov, Cold War 2, leftism

Liu Xiaobo is dead. Who the hell is Liu Xiaobo?

A pyschopathic status maximizer from Northeast China. Or may I say a high-IQ status-greedy sociopath. Or a shameless self-promoter taking money from USG to undermine his own nation?

Or in one word: an activist. Liu Xiaobo was a student activist from the 1980s. The 1980s were a very delicate time in China. Mao was dead. Deng Xiaoping had opened up the country. The old order was shattered; and when a country is in disorder, the status-hunters smell weakness. They saw blood. And so they started agitating. Writing articles on how backward China was. How utterly rotten and corrupt and just smelly it was, compared to the utopia in the West. Western governments obviously encouraged the agitation. They gave money and resources. This agitation culminated in the 1989 Tiananmen protests. Liu Xiaobo was there, showing his teeth, ready to destroy the government and take their place. To gain the supreme status he knew he deserved. Everybody thought that the government would fall, and a new state would have to be built on Western standards. A new state led by themselves, of course.

But no, that didn't happen. The little old man had a pair, and he sent the tanks. Most of the psychopathic status maximizers fled. But Liu Xiaobo didn't. The guy isn't just some run of the mill leftist activist. He's a stubborn son of a bitch. He stayed, doubled down on his writing about how China is bad and corrupt and evil and nasty and everything Western is honey and spice and everything nice. He was sent to jail, again and again. And while he went abroad every now and then to pick up some Western money, he always returned to China. He just couldn't believe that China wouldn't bow down to his majesty and just hand him the status he deserves. Surely these evil pigs won't send me to jail again?! Not when I have USG behind me?

To jail he went. He was given a damn Noble Peace prize. To jail he went. China doesn't care. Well, China cares more than it should. China has signed all those bogus Human Rights Treatises. But they just wouldn't release Liu Xiaobo. This guy is evil. This guy wasn't just some prog activist; he was a traitor of comical proportions. The guy was just surreal. Even some Western leftists, at the Guardian no less[227], just couldn't believe how big a traitor this guy was. See some things he said:

In a 1988 interview with Hong Kong[228]'s *Liberation Monthly* (now known as *Open Magazine*), Liu was asked what it would take for China to realize ·a true historical transformation. He replied:

"It would take 300 years of [colonialism][229]. In 100 years of colonialism, Hong Kong has changed to what we see today. With China being so big, of course it would require 300 years as a colony for it to be able to transform into how Hong Kong is today. I have my doubts as to whether 300 years would be enough."[31][https://en.wikipedia.org/wiki/Liu_Xiaobo#cite_note-open2-31][33][https://en.wikipedia.org/wiki/Liu_Xiaobo#cite_note-open1-33]

This comment by itself just lost him all the local support he could have enjoyed just by being propped up by Western propaganda. How could you call for the colonization of your own country? 300 years! This guy is insane. Just how much of a Western stooge was he?

Known for his pro-West stance, Liu once stated in an interview: "Modernization means whole-sale westernization, choosing a human life is choosing Western way of life. Difference between Western and Chinese governing system is humane vs in-humane, there's no middle ground... Westernization is not a choice of a nation, but a choice for the human race" [24][230]

---

[227] https://www.theguardian.com/commentisfree/2010/dec/15/nobel-winner-liu-xiaobo-chinese-dissident

[228] https://en.wikipedia.org/wiki/Hong_Kong "Hong Kong"

[229] https://en.wikipedia.org/wiki/Colonialism "Colonialism"

[230] https://en.wikipedia.org/w/index.php?title=Liu_Xiaobo&oldid=787871064#cite_note-24

You'd have to go to Stormfront to find this kind of hyperbole even this side of the world. A Western life is a human life. Everything else is not barbaric; it's not even human. Ok dude, you're gonna make a lot of friends that way.

He also faulted a television documentary, He Shang, or River Elegy, for not thoroughly criticising Chinese culture and not advocating westernisation enthusiastically enough: "If I were to make this I would show just how wimpy, spineless and fucked-up [weisuo, ruanruo, caodan] the Chinese really are". Liu considered it most unfortunate that his monolingualism bound him in a dialogue with something "very benighted [yumei] and philistine [yongsu]," the Chinese cultural sphere. Harvard researcher Lin Tongqi noted that an early 1990s book by Liu contains "pungent attacks on the Chinese national character".

So China is wimpy and fucked-up, the West is this awesome utopia; but the guy was monolingual? What the hell? Oh wait. This isn't about logical consistency. This isn't about careful thought on the issues. This is a guy who just saw that the Communist Party had loosen his grip on Chinese society and wanted to crack a wedge into the system so he could come up with more status than he had. And he chose to worship the West because that was the zeitgeist: Communism was collapsing everywhere, and the West was way stronger. So odds are the West would sponsor him some time or another. And voila, USG gave him millions. For which the guy was grateful. 2,000 years of Confucianism don't go away so easily. Chinese intellectuals know to be loyal.

in his article Lessons from the Cold War[231]"), Liu argues that"The free world led by the US fought almost all regimes that trampled on human rights ... The major wars that the US became involved in are all ethically defensible." During the 2004 US presidential election, Liu warmly praised George Bush for his war effort[232] against Iraq and condemned Democratic party candidate John Kerry for not sufficiently supporting the US's wars:

[T]he outstanding achievement made by Bush in anti-terrorism absolutely cannot be erased by Kerry's slandering ... However much risk must be endured in striking down Saddam Hussein, know that no action would lead to a greater risk. This has been proven by the second world war and September 11! No matter what, the war against Saddam Hussein is just! The decision by President Bush is right!

---

[231] https://wangjinbo.org/archives/1390 "Liu Xiaobo: Lessons from the Cold War (in Chinese

[232] https://www.boxun.com/hero/liuxb/217_1.shtml "Liu Xiabo piece on Chinese language site"

Liu also published a 2004 article in support of Bush's war on Iraq, titled "Victory to the Anglo-American Freedom Alliance", in which he praised the U.S.-led post-Cold War[233]conflicts as "best examples of how war should be conducted in a modern civilization." He wrote "regardless of the savagery of the terrorists, and regardless of the instability of Iraq's situation, and, what's more, regardless of how patriotic youth might despise proponents of the United States such as myself, my support for the invasion of Iraq will not waver. Just as, from the beginning, I believed that the military intervention of Britain and the United States would be victorious, I am still full of belief in the final victory of the Freedom Alliance and the democratic future of Iraq, and even if the armed forces of Britan and the United States should encounter some obstacles such as those that they are curently facing, this belief of mine will not change." He predicted "a free, democratic and peaceful Iraq will emerge."[29][234]

Unwavering support for the War on Iraq. He the Noble Peace Prize winner. Why? Convictions? Or because Bush was paying his salary?

At any rate, the guy is dead. Inside China. All the Bluegov empire ("the international community") pressure didn't work. Now I don't know who coordinates this kind of operations, but guys, if you want to have influence in China. You're doing it wrong. Finding a complete asshole like this guy just won't get you any popularity in China. Or anywhere else, really. I mean just look at the guy and his... wife. Or something.

---

[233] `https://en.wikipedia.org/wiki/Cold_War` "Cold War"

[234] `https://en.wikipedia.org/w/index.php?title=Liu_Xiaobo&oldid=787871064#cite_note-epoch-29`

The US has the most advanced marketing PR apparatus in the whole world. They know how to promote stuff. Why are they so inept when it comes to political influence abroad? A hot teenage girl or a smooth homo could actually accomplish a lot of progressive agitation in China today. But nah, Bluegov keeps picking up these ugly sociopath nerds who offer themselves to them. Well, you reap what you saw.

What's killing the West

2017-07-25 // women, theory

https://twitter.com/hitehranhostel/status/889899796609290241

I wrote a long time ago that what unites the dissident right, the "glue" for lack of a better word, was opposition to feminism. The catholic reactionaries, the Moldbuggian neoreactionaries, the manosphere and all those other guys out there around 2013; we all had little in common. We thought most of the others were crazy or deluded. But we all shared a common idea that women don't belong to political society; and that women having equal or higher status than men was what was breaking the social fabric in the civilized world. It just breaks all incentives to mate and raise children, saps all motivation to pursue excellence and be contribute to society.

Now of course this reactionary sphere was quite small. And since Trump it has been completely overshadowed by the alt-right; if fortunately it hasn't died out. And it hasn't because the alt-right is basically feminist nazism. Essentialist Nationalism? Check. Down-with-the-plutocrats Socialist economics? Check. Gas all the Jews? Check. But hey, Ivanka is our Aryan princess! Laura Southern is so cool and smart! The French Front National is run by a woman. The German AfD is run by a woman. Having women commanding men just shows it to those evil mud Muslims.

You're doing it wrong. Aesthetics is important. It's an underrated motivation for men's actions. Yes, a 20 year old white woman with long hair can be a lovely thing, and it looks so much more worth defending than those ugly fat Muslim women in black bags. But that's not the point. The point is that Western men aren't actually doing anything to defend their civilization against an invasion by millions of foreign men. You might say it's because their governments won't allow them, and there's a point to that. But the vast majority of white men don't even show any will to resist. They still overwhelmingly support leftist politics.

Western men aren't actually doing anything to defend those cute white girls from being harassed by Africans or Muslims because they don't own them, and they have no prospect of ever owning them. So of course they don't fight. They just go on following the latest leftist fad, hoping for some mainstream status, so they can get some money and maybe some short-term sex relationship. Those who dislike leftism overwhelmingly choose to enjoy the decline poolside. Nobody is going to risk their skin in order to protect the right of their women go to Iran to take Instagram pictures larping on what used to be a most respectable male profession.

I've been writing a lot about rhetoric and why it's important. And yes, nationalism, even racism makes for better rhetoric, a better sale than The Patriarchy. But as important as rhetoric is in aiding coordination by synchronizing people's status signaling behavior; at a more basic level there are systemic incentives without which people just won't work. And men just won't work to defend feminism. They may say they will. But they won't do it.

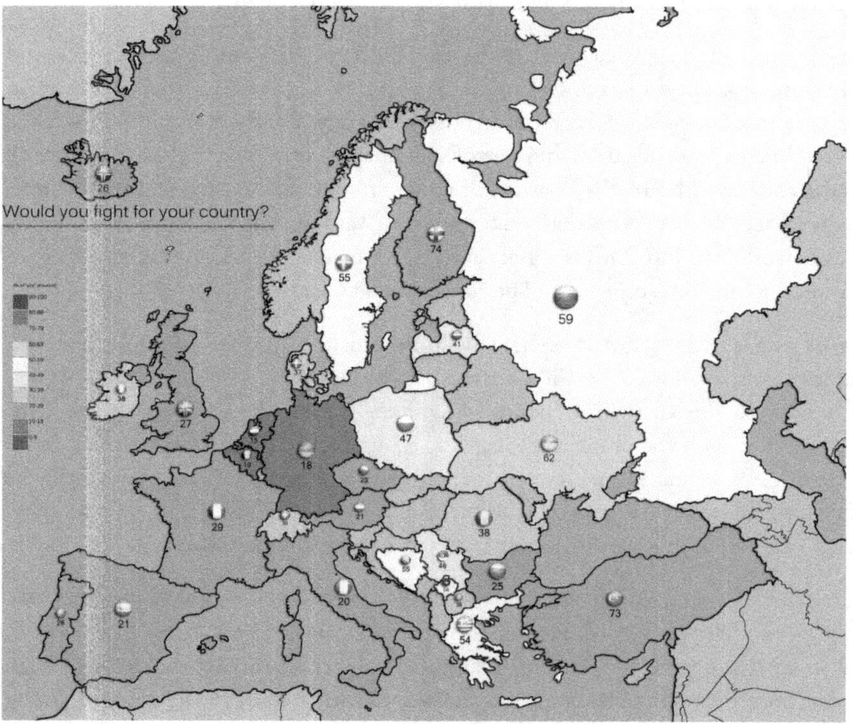

Trump is cool. Race is important. But sex is much, much more important.

Feminist Nationalism doesn't work

2017-08-03 // rightwingers, europe, women, demographics

So Viktor Orban gave a speech recently[235]. It's quite something. Let me quote.

A country the size of Hungary – not the size of Germany or the United States, but similar in size to us – can only be strong if there is robust majority national ownership in the strategic industries which determine its fate. This wasn't the case in Hungary before 2010. Now, however, we can say that there is clear majority national ownership in the energy sector, the banking sector and the media sector. If I had to quantify this, I would say that in recent years the Hungarian state has spent around one thousand billion forints on repurchasing ownership in strategic sectors and companies which had previously been foolishly privatised.

Mmm... yeah, that makes sense. So Orban has been buying back strategic industries from, I assume, foreign corporations. Well done, man.

For a country to be strong, demographic decline must be out of the question. At this point in time, this is Hungary's Achilles heel. A country which is in demographic decline – and, to put it bluntly, is not even able to sustain itself biologically – may well find that it is no longer needed. A country like that will disappear. Only those communities survive in the world which are at least able to sustain themselves biologically; and let's be honest with ourselves, Hungary today is not yet such a country.

Good point again. And extra points for honesty. This man is a consistent nationalist. He knows what he wants and he knows what needs to be done.

We must also admit that on demographic issues – the creation and growth of families – the hands of the government of the day are tied. This is because no policies of any kind can decide whether or not there will be children in a community, whether children are being born into families – and if so, how many. This is because only women can make such decisions. Things will be what women decide them to be.

And maybe that's the problem. Thought about that, Mr. President? He then goes on to brag about he's taking money from Soros to give it to Hungarian women. Who don't want it and refuse to breed nonetheless. Hungary's president knows what he wants; what he doesn't know is how to achieve it. He has absolutely no clue. He gives a great

---

[235] https://visegradpost.com/en/2017/07/24/full-speech-of-v-orban-will-europe-belong-to-europeans/

speech on why nations are good and how to make sure our nations can survive. What ethnic identity is and why it matters. And yet he openly admits his own nation is dying; he even mentions why it's dying, and yet refuses to do anything about it.

Mr. Orban, you're doing it wrong. None of that matters until you fix that little part I bolded for you. France will not be French, Italy won't be Italian, and even Hungary won't be Magyar if you don't stop giving women the power to decide how many and whose children are born. Physical borders won't fix that. Closing down Soros' propaganda racket won't fix it. And don't get me wrong, I strongly admire Orban for doing what he's been doing. But it will all be for naught if he doesn't go to the end. If you want nationalism to work, you need the whole package. And that means 1848 sexual mores too.

ETA: Just some background data to understand how bad the demographics are in Hungary.

Year	Population (x1000)			Births	Deaths	Population growth
	TFR					
1980	10 707	148 673	145 355	3 318	1.92	
1981	10 700	142 890	144 757	-1 867	1.88	
1982	10 683	133 559	144 318	-10 759	1.78	
1983	10 656	127 258	148 643	-21 385	1.73	
1984	10 619	125 359	146 709	-21 350	1.73	
1985	10 579	130 200	147 614	-17 414	1.83	
1986	10 534	128 204	147 089	-18 885	1.83	
1987	10 486	125 840	142 601	-16 761	1.79	
1988	10 443	124 296	140 042	-15 746	1.78	
1989	10 398	123 304	144 695	-21 391	1.78	
1990	10 374	125 679	145 660	-19 981	1.84	
1991	10 373	127 207	144 813	-17 606	1.85	
1992	10 369	121 724	148 781	-27 057	1.76	
1993	10 357	117 033	150 244	-33 211	1.68	

1994	10 343	115 598	146 889	-31 291	1.64
1995	10 329	112 054	145 431	-33 377	1.57
1996	10 311	105 272	143 130	-37 858	1.45
1997	10 290	100 350	139 434	-39 084	1.37
1998	10 267	97 301	140 870	-43 569	1.33
1999	10 238	94 645	143 210	-48 565	1.29
2000	10 211	97 597	135 601	-38 004	1.31
2001	10 198	97 047	132 183	-35 136	1.31
2002	10 165	96 804	132 833	-36 029	1.31
2003	10 129	94 647	135 823	-41 176	1.28
2004	10 108	95 137	132 492	-37 355	1.28
2005	10 088	97 496	135 732	-38 236	1.32
2006	10 072	99 871	131 603	-31 732	1.35
2007	10 056	97 613	132 938	-35 325	1.32
2008	10 038	99 149	130 027	-30 878	1.35
2009	10 022	96 450	130 350	-33 972	1.33
2010	10 000	90 335	130 456	-40 121	1.26
2011	9 985	88 049	128 795	-40 746	1.24
2012	9 932	90 269	129 440	-39 171	1.34
2013	9 909	88 689	126 778	-38 089	1.34
2014	9 877	91 510	126 308	-34 798	1.41
2015	9 823	91 690	131 697	-40 007	1.44
2016	9 790	93 100	126 900	-33 800	1.49

Hungary has been losing population for 37 years straight. 37 years. With no end in sight. It has lost a million people, around 10% of the population since 1981. And to add insult to injury, there's this little map over here:

Roma tanulók becsült aránya megyénként

százalék

0-5
5-10
10-20
20-30
30-

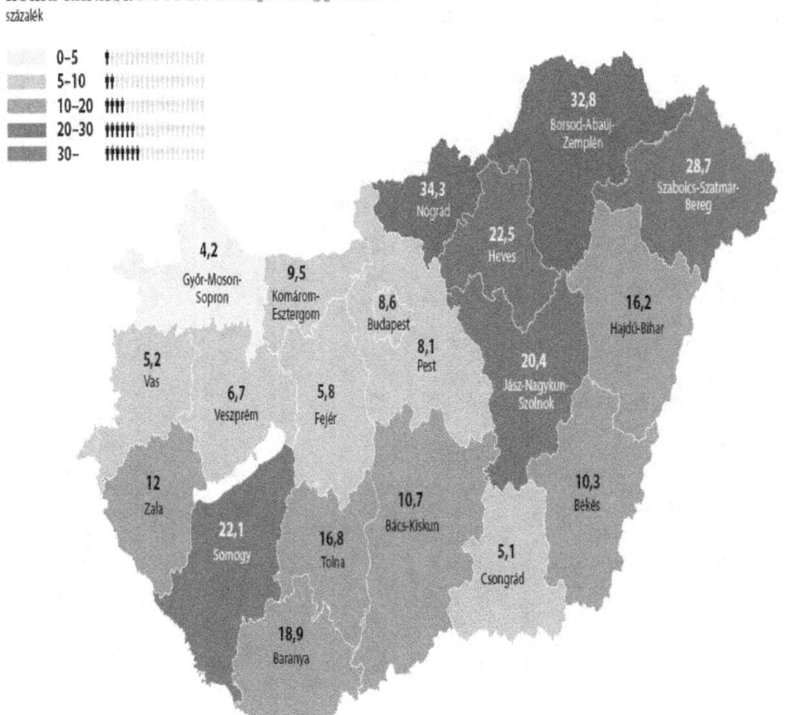

Forrás: HVG, Papp Zoltán Attila számításai az OKM 2013. évi telephelyi adatok alapján / MN-grafika

That's the Gypsy student population per province.

So this underscores a bit of the urgency that Hungarians feel about Third World immigration. They really can't afford even a little of it. The country is in very dire straits. And it will continue to get worse until they understand that surrendering the very core of their society to the whims of their women is the root of their problem.

Being a Conservative

2017-08-17 // cucks

This Tweet encapsulates perfectly the cuckservative mindset. Cucks are, by any account, more pleasant people than leftists. Usually smarter, or at least with way more common sense. I'd guess most of us have conservatives in our family. Many I guess have married one.

What makes them contemptible, though? What makes them cucks? Their cowardice. It's one thing to ignore the truth. To just not notice what's in front of you. It's another thing to be an evil liar and just spread falsehoods for your own benefit, as leftists do.

It's a yet completely different thing to be able to notice the truth, admit most of it, and just stop our brain working just when it starts to get interested. To be just that close, to be on reach of the truth, but then... crimestop engaged. That's what makes the cuck a cuck.

https://twitter.com/FukuyamaFrancis/status/898221254057934848

Don't be a cuck.

Oh, and incidentally, don't be alt-right either. Why? They are getting purged utterly from the Internet[236]. So let this be a lesson of functional semantics. The only valuable labels are those that work.

---

[236] https://www.vanityfair.com/news/2017/08/silicon-valleys-anti-nazi-purge-kicks-into-overdrive

Babies watch

2017-08-22 // demographics

Chinese media celebrate the success of the 2 Child Policy: 18.46 million births in 2016. 2 million more than 2015. Hurray. Long live the party and its core leader Xi Jinping. 萬歲萬歲萬萬歲.

Why the Chinese would want even more people escapes me. But given how modern economics (either through this Landian catallactic capitalist logic or whatever) hates demographics vacuums and tends to fill every empty spot with whatever human-like DNA it finds; well I don't blame them for wanting to take care of that. And who knows; the whole First World is depopulating, maybe there is a grand plan of colonizing the whole world once the Great Famine happens and all those "refugees" die of their own ineptitude.

At any rate, let's review the Baby production statistics worldwide:

China: 18.46 million Chinese babies (source[237])

Japan: 0.98 million babies (source[238])

US: 2 million white babies (source[239])

EU: 3 million white babies (source[240])

Greater Russia: 2 million white babies (source[241])

India: 27 freaking million babies (source[242])

Maybe some commenters can illustrate the breakdown between Hindu et al.

---

[237] https://www.guancha.cn/society/2017_08_22_423927.shtml

[238] https://en.wikipedia.org/wiki/Demography_of_Japan

[239] https://www.pewresearch.org/fact-tank/2016/06/23/its-official-minority-babies-are-the-majority-among-the-nations-infants-but-only-just/

[240] https://spandrell.com/2017/05/26/the-future/

[241] https://en.wikipedia.org/wiki/Demographics_of_Russia

[242] https://en.wikipedia.org/wiki/Demographics_of_India

I'm guessing caste-based dysgenics must be quite serious.

Subsaharan Africa: 37 damn million black babies (source[243])

---

[243] https://fred.stlouisfed.org/series/SPDYNCBRTINSSA

Bucolic Japan

2017-08-23 // japan, china

https://twitter.com/DissidentRight/status/900387460978532354

I'm guessing that Mr. Derbyshire's Chinese in-laws have been extremely mean to him; else I don't quite get his hostility towards his children's motherland. He should be happy that they'll get to choose to live in the world hegemon no matter what happens during this century. But no, he keeps criticizing the empire.

To his credit, he criticizes the other, as of now foremost empire, the USA. I guess it's this small-town conservatism thing. This dream of ethnically homogeneous, small countries, tied by very strict but widely shared cultural norms, and ruled through direct citizenship participation. Yes, it's kinda nice. There's this bucolic flavor to it; and if we look at revealed preferences, people all over the world pay big bucks to visit those kind of places (Switzerland, northern Italy) every year. To the point, tourists visiting Japan is a booming industry, with over 20 million visitors last year.

But as nice as homogeneous, peaceful towns/countries are; the logic of history doesn't care. Northern Italy was this collection of small sovereign city states. Then they consolidated into a few states ruled by the biggest cities, Milan, Venice. Then Napoleon came with his steamroller and it all went to hell. The fact that Switzerland still exists has all to do with it being a bunch of (back then) unproductive real estate freezing up in the Alps, and not due to its superior government.

Anyway, to the point, Japan. I know Japan. Very well. There's no fucking way in this universe or in any of the infinite universes out there that the 21st century is the Japanese century. Yes, Japan is a fairly pleasant place to live. No crime, by our standards. Very clean; awesome infrastructure. Amazing service by workers so polite they put Victorian butlers to shame.

But Japan is dying. Japan was the first country to stop breeding (and refuse to mask it with foreign workers), so right now it has a 25% old-age population. One in four Japanese are over 65 year old geezers. Who get pensions and consume untold amounts of free healthcare. Who pays for that? Well young people; who haven't seen their salaries raise, even nominally, for decades, mostly due to raising payroll taxes. The money-printing hasn't produced any inflation, but it has produced a bubble in the stock market and prime real estate.

Young people aren't stupid, they see the writing in the wall. If Western populations have been losing testosterone due to getting their balls busted by feminism since the 1970s; modern Japanese have lost the will to live[244], period. 40% of Japanese are virgins by age 30, men and women. You'd think it's all the lying Western press, fake news. Oh no, I know the place. It's true, people. National decline is a scary thing. Japan is in steep decline.

Oh, but the don't have immigrants! Bullshit they don't have[245]. Try to buy any groceries in central Tokyo and not see a Vietnamese or Bangladeshi kid in a 7/11 uniform. There's 2 million immigrants. There's foreigners everywhere. 2 million in total. Yes, of course, compared to what's going on in the West, that's nothing. Japan has a rational policy. It doesn't take "refugees". It takes workers, on their terms. Pretty harsh terms. Japan pays low salaries and makes people work really, really hard. Plenty of foreigners just won't take it. Japan is very far away, it's expensive, the language is crazy hard, there's little fun to do out there. And the sort of Japanese boss who takes foreign workers (agriculture, low-margin manufacturing and the like) are often nasty, nasty people. The conditions some workers are made to accept[246] would make many Dubai employers blush.

Of course, that's the only way to run an immigration policy that pays for the accepting country. Japan doesn't have an immigration industry. There are no foreign foundations paying for the colonization of the country by hostile foreigners. The government doesn't fund QUANGOs to bring them. It doesn't give welfare quotas to their cities to advantage foreigners over natives. The Japanese have their country, and want to keep it. Yes, they'll take any foreigner who is willing to work for them, without making any accommodation. Japan is their country and they like it as it is. Good for them.

But... Japan is not going anywhere. Don't believe the hype over the recent GDP growth figures. It's all bullshit. Japan is losing 1 million workers every year. The electronics industry is dead. Sharp was bought by the Chinese, Toshiba is bankrupt. The videogame industry is dying, completely outdone by America's. Japan tried to start an aeronautic industry, with the much hyped Mitsubishi MRJ, but the plane sucks and Mitsubishi Aircraft is bankrupt. Japan today can only afford to eat meat because Americans like to drive Toyotas and Hondas. Japan's future is closely tied to America's. As the USA declines, so will Japan. But the USA has the best real estate in the world. You can fill the USA with Mexicans and Africans and they'll still have plenty to eat, if

---

[244] https://www.steynonline.com/6320/alone-again-naturally

[245] https://www.bloomberg.com/news/articles/2016-10-25/a-wary-japan-quietly-opens-its-back-door-for-foreign-workers

[246] https://www.news.com.au/finance/business/travel/welcome-to-the-worlds-worst-internship/news-story/eeda395f79c84f4afde4744837724505

only. Japan though, is a bunch of volcanoes on the path of the Asian monsoon. They can barely feed 30 million people by themselves. Their economic boom only happened because they happened to be an American vassal in a strategic zone. But America will soon run out of money to feed their vassals.

What then? The Japanese century? Hah. In all likelihood they'll be China's bitch in 2 or 3 decades. And China will not be kind to them. The Chinese empire used to be kind to its vassals, giving them vast amounts of money in exchange for pathetic shows of allegiance. But China doesn't have an empire now. It has a micro-managed, internet-connected demotic regime, with hundreds of thousands of people engaging in government PR. Japan better practice their kowtows very well if they want the Chinese people to show them clemency.

So again, let us not lose sight of how the modern world works. Hell, how the world has always worked. Good government is nice. But nations don't live in a vacuum. Foreign policy is as important as internal policy. It doesn't matter how well governed a nation is, if the international situation isn't good. Venice was very nice, nicer than France; Napoleon crushed it. Same for all those nice bucolic principalities across Germany. If your neighbor is big he is going to crush you, sooner or later. This is a fundamental principle of history. To that, add globalized economies today. Hardly any country is self-sufficient today, even potentially. Every single developed country today is an American satrapy. How long will the US be able to afford them? What then? Certainly not the Japanese century. Nor the Swiss century. Gentlemen, there is no Patchwork, and there will never be. The logic of Empire always applies.

Have I mentioned there's a growing community of Japanese converts to Islam? Of course it's still tiny, but it's really funny. And given the sexual market in Japan these days (40% incels, remember), there's plenty of incentives for it to grow.

Capitalists and ropes

2017-08-29 // theory, capitalism, nrx

https://twitter.com/clairlemon/status/902498399634636800

How does this square with accelerationism? The forces of capitalism and the market feeding themselves into a self-catalytic process by which humans and their talents are consumed to form... Genderqueer Maoism?

A lot of people are completely focused in economics, like Marxists, libertarians or accelerationists. And yes, the economy is very important. Marx was an improvement over the religion-centered theories of history which preceded him. And the short-lived race-centered theories were worse. Yes, the economy is hugely important. It's one great pole of human society. How people organize to make stuff and exchange it can explain a great deal of what society is and does.

But there's another one pole. Violence. Or in other words, politics. How people organize to break stuff and kill people. That is also hugely important, and it explains a great deal of what society is and does. And it's always there. Violence is always there. You may not be interested in war, but Trotsky is, so you better be too.

Politics and the economy are obviously related. You need to make weapons before using them. And the other way around: what you are allowed to make and how to exchange it depends on those guys with guns. Yin-yang, folks.

Politics and Economics are bound together. They cannot live separately, as much as they'd like to. Politics can't do as it please, if people won't make stuff for it. The communists realized that the hard way. But economics can't do as it please either. The guys with guns won't let them. Capitalism won't consume everything for its own purposes. It has no purpose. It can only work in the small range that Politics allows it to. Right now, capitalism can consume everything, as long as it's for the benefit of advancing the holy cause of Marriage Equality, Transexual Toilet Rights *and* Protecting Muslim Feelings.

What's scary is that capitalism can work with that. And make money. Oh well. Skynet is going to be very queer.

Language is Culture

2017-08-30 // theory, language, singapore

https://www.nytimes.com/2017/08/26/world/asia/singapore-language-hokkien-mandarin.html?mcubz=0

Damn, New York Times link show up automatically like Tweets now. Talk about privilege.

Anyway; you know what Gell-Mann amnesia is. You read the news, and assume what you're reading is, well, worth reading. It's generally accurate. Then you read something on a topic you have some expertise about, and you find that it's worse than false. It's completely inaccurate and misleading. It just shows how the writer has absolutely no clue of what he's talking about. Then you realize: well, it's some journalist who has no expertise at all except in writing jargon, of course he has no clue.

Then you go on reading more news. As my mother says, you gotta talk about something.

So the New York Times ran a story on how dialects are back in Singapore. Because they're, you know, "vibrant". That's not how I would describe Hokkien, but then I did study some Hokkien, instead of taking journalism classes. The story itself is not very remarkable, besides how inept and ignorant it is. I'm tempted to just become a Chinese chauvinist and blame the anti-Chinese animus of the American establishment, now shaming Mandarin Chinese as something to be avoided. Then it would make some sort of sense. But as they say, never blame malice what is likely just stupidity.

I guess it's just me, but I feel there's few things more harmful than bad linguistics. Take a look at the crap the NYT is trying to pull here:

At the time of the founding of the Republic of Singapore in 1965, it was led by a charismatic and authoritarian prime minister, Lee Kuan Yew[247], who was a self-taught linguist. A product of the English-speaking elite who rarely spoke Chinese dialects, including Mandarin, Mr. Lee held the popular idea, discredited by linguists, that language was a zero-sum game: speaking more of one meant less mastery of another.

In short, he considered dialects a waste of the brain's finite storage capacity when it should be filled with, above all else, English.

---

[247] https://topics.nytimes.com/top/reference/timestopics/people/l/lee_kuan_yew/index.html?inline=nyt-per "More articles about Lee Kuan Yew."

"He felt that since he couldn't do it, the rest couldn't do it," said Prof. Lee Cher Leng, a language historian in the China studies department at the National University of Singapore, referring to Mr. Lee's inability to fluently speak multiple languages. "He felt it would be too confusing for kids to learn the dialects."

First of all, LKY, peace be with him, was not a "self-taught linguist". He's a guy who learned some languages as an adult. That doesn't make him a linguist. This makes him a language learner. There's billions of those across the world. Lee Kuan Yew certainly wasn't very good at it; the ability to learn foreign languages doesn't correlate very strongly with IQ.

Mr. Lee held the popular idea that language was a zero-sum game? No, Mr. Lee understood the commonsensical idea that your brain has limited storage capacity. Like anything else. Your brain is made of atoms. It is not made of magic. It is not made of godly dust. It is a material thing. It is, in a sense, a container of information, and information takes space. It obviously does in computers; pray tell, NYT, why the brain should have infinite capacity? It doesn't make sense.

Now I don't know if LKY thought of it in these terms. I think that, as a language learner, he went by experience. I guess the more time he spent practicing Mandarin, or Hokkien, or Malay, the worse his English prose got. And that's exactly how it works. Happens to me all the time, and happens to anyone who uses 2 or more languages regularly. The more different the languages, the less commons structures they share, the more acute the problem. Again, there is no reason why it should not be so. Information takes space. It isn't hard.

Alas, it is true that academic linguists will not tell you this, even though they probably did in the 1950s. That is not because common sense has been "refuted". It is because since the 1960s academia has morphed into a worldwide racket of fraud and deceit. If you read this blog you already know that; economics is bogus, climate science is bogus, psychology is bogus; even more than half of medical papers are bogus. Well, surprise surprise, linguistics is also bogus. The language learning industry is huge. There's a lot of money in telling people that the brain is made of magic dust, that they can learn whatever they want whenever they want, as long as they give you money. 3 languages at the same time? Go for it! Kids are like sponges, they can learn anything. No, they can't.

Now of course, all human traits are distributed in a Gaussian curve. Some kids are pretty good, can learn 3 or 4 languages given some exposure. Some can't even speak 1 language properly by the time they enter primary school. Lee Kuan Yew, who was in charge of spending Singapore's money, realized he didn't have money to waste, and he took what was the most rational decision: let's focus on having everyone learn English, then let's make some half-assed effort at teaching a "mother tongue"; mostly for political reasons, so tribalists didn't complain. Some kids will learn the mother tongue well; most won't. Not the government's problem. Lee Kuan Yew was CEO and what he wanted was an efficient workforce, so English it was. And English he got. Well, kind of.

Japanese researchers, fortunately isolated from their American comrades because of their ineptitude at learning English, have long found that Brazilian immigrants in Japan often end up not bilingual, but "halflingual". They end up speaking shitty Portuguese and even shittier Japanese. Because Japanese is hard, they don't speak it at home, and whatever they speak at home tends to have very low vocabulary levels. So they end up sounding retarded even if they really aren't.

You know who else sounds retarded? Singaporeans. OK, sorry, that's overly harsh. I apologize to my Singaporean readers, I love you all. But I had to say it. With all due respect, Singaporeans in general don't speak proper English. They speak Singlish[248], which is a pidgin English with a fair amount of Chinese grammar and vocabulary baked in, and a pretty weird (and what sounds to me a pretty big Indian influence) pronunciation. As you may remember[249], even Singapore's prime minister, Lee Hsien Loong, by every account a 150 IQ genius, speaks what can only be described as pretty goofy English. Again, it's not their fault, it's just the unintended consequence of public language policy.

How did this happen? By forcing diglossia (widespread bilingualism) on Singapore. After independence most people spoke some either Chinese dialect at home, Malay or Tamil. The schools taught English, what is a foreign language to everyone. So yes, they learned, the minimum required to pass the exams, and went on with their daily lives. Given that kids spent almost more time at school than at home, eventually the exposure of English was greater than their respective languages. Let's say a random Singaporean teen was exposed to 65% English and 35% Hokkien during their formative years. So, surprise surprise, he ended up speaking a language which is 65% English and 35% Hokkien, and so did most everyone else, with all languages and dialects getting some of their stuff in this hodgepodge lingua franca that evolved into Singlish. And once that got widespread it became almost impossible to change.

If Singaporeans speak bad English, their Mandarin is even worse. I've seen business owners who couldn't even write it. Again, I don't blame them. Chinese is hard, especially the writing system. I'm pretty sure Lee Kuan Yew was never very good at writing it. And most likely he never thought most Singaporeans would be able too. But he had two good reasons to teach Mandarin to every Chinese in Singapore. First; some talented people would learn it, and Singapore needed those people to go make business

---

[248] `https://en.wikipedia.org/wiki/Singlish`

[249] `https://spandrell.com/2017/06/20/the-fall-of-singapores-monarchy/`

in China. And second, dialects had to be stamped out. Chinese people were extremely clannish back in the day. They still are in some parts of China. Liberals think dialects are like race, this colorful thing that adds vibrancy points to a culture. But no. Race is in your genes, you are born with that. You can't change it. But dialect is a choice. Even if your parents teach it to you, children will forget it very soon, just as they forget everything their parents try to teach them.

Dialects survive because of a political choice. Language is a badge of loyalty; speaking Hokkien or Cantonese instead of Mandarin means that, as a child, you've reached the conclusion that Hokkien is more useful than Mandarin. Singapore, as all societies of Southeastern Chinese ancestry. used to be run by small dialect and family based societies, who did their thing unbeknownst to the state. Imperial China was laissez-faire about this kind of clan-based society, but Lee Kuan Yew was a legalist[250]), and he had to crush them to impose his authority. So crush them they did. Once the clans were crushed, speaking dialect stopped working as a signal; and so the signal died. Whatever the NYT says, dialects aren't coming back. There's no money there, and Asia doesn't trade in those vibrancy points which make New York housewives happy.

Why did Irish die soon after Irish independence? The signal wasn't needed anymore. They had their own country, and God knows speaking Irish is a costly signal. Hokkien or Cantonese aren't that costly for a competent Mandarin speaker, but they aren't cheap either, so most likely this "dialect revival" is just 10 bored housewives who happen to eat in the same noodle joint as the NYT correspondent there. Fake news, as usual.

What the article gets right is the cultural desert that Singapore became after LKY enforced the power of the state and broke every intermediate society. There's a lesson there: high cultural output depends on the identity of a people. It's a political statement. It thrives on conflict. But Lee Kuan Yew would have none of that. He had a multiracial to run in a very delicate balance, and he couldn't risk people developing a cultural identity without things spiraling out of control. He couldn't tolerate cultural diversity; but he, cursed by the knowledge of HBD, wouldn't allow race mixing. So he was left with a multicultural society where conflict wasn't allowed. So the culture died. Romans stop producing good literature after the Empire. Nobody remembers the great books written by the Ottomans. And I wonder if in the future anybody will remember the Singaporeans at all.

---

[250] https://en.wikipedia.org/wiki/Legalism_(Chinese_philosophy

Choose your side

2017-09-05 // china, redpill, Cold War 2

https://twitter.com/JEPomfret/status/902584060156903424

And people ask me why I cheer for China being a great power who can stand against the US.

ETA: I see that the poster isn't translated in the fake news peace, so I'll do it here.

做一个好主妇，

To be a good wife

好母亲

A good mother

是女人最大的本事

Is a women's most important skill

为什么非得削尖了脑筋，

Why must you squeeze your brain

累吐了血

Work until you're so tired you cough up blood

跟男人争资源，

Why must you compete for resources with men,

抢地盘呀？

Take away their turf?

Well said. Why indeed? Who the hell enjoys working?

Not that China is putting all the weight of the state behind traditional marriage. Plenty of feminism out there, both in private and public areas. But it's getting better. And the more evil baizuo like John Pomfret signal their disapproval, the more China will want to stick it to whitey by going back to Confucian marriage.

Which remember, had *unlimited polygamy*. And women couldn't cut their hair. Way better than Islam, people. And they can drink and eat pork. If it only got some more traction.

Fighting the bad fight

2017-09-06 // china, Cold War 2, hbd, russia

The United States is the world empire since, at least, 1991. There's no question about that. This hegemony has started to crumble in recent years. First, China refused to surrender to the Western-supported students in Tiananmen square, in 1989. Then Russia fell, some thought for good, but since 1999 Putin rebuilt the Russian state and its sovereignty, leading to very tense relations with USG. China also waivered between accommodation to the USG led order, signing all those UN human rights treaties. But since Xi Jinping came to power in 2012, China has been in open confrontation to the American led world order.

It is no surprise that Vladimir Putin has a lot of fans in the West, as the internal enemies of USG, or its state church, the Cathedral as we call it, follow the ancient logic that your enemy's enemy is a pretty good guy. The specifics don't matter. There's plenty to dislike about Putin and his regime. But he's one of the few enemies of the world empire that USG wants to impose on Earth, and for that he deserves our respect. That he goes the extra length of opposing the very things we object about American rule, e.g. gender ideology, is the icing on the cake, changing mere respect into gratitude, even admiration. I agree with this idea, and I'm very glad Vladimir Putin exists.

Putin gets a lot of fans also because, well, he's white. He looks like us, and comes from a fairly similar cultural background. China doesn't get many fans. Most of the same people who hail Putin still deride the Chinese government as "Chicoms", who are sleazy and nasty and just witchy. I mean look at those small eyes, you can't even see what they're thinking. That's, well, racism, but in this blog we are understanding of racism. Racism is a natural feeling of human societies. And while racism towards, say, black Africans was subsumed by virtue signaling, racism towards Asians will never die.

For a very simple reason. As you may recall from the late Larry Auster's First Law of Minority Relations, niceness towards NAMs is a moral command because NAMs are on average dumb and violent, i.e. uncivilized. People are naturally ill disposed towards dumb and violent people, so being nice to NAMs is a costly signal. It makes the signaler feel so much holy on her sacrifice. That's Economics of Religion 101. East Asians though are smart and law-abiding. There's plenty to dislike about them, of course, the stereotype of the boring Asian drone who only cares about money and takes infinite amounts of shit is often true; although there's regional differences, and I gotta point out that Northern East Asians tend to be much cooler and less drone-like than Southeastern Chinese.

But I digress, the point is that there's no holiness points in liking Asians. They're ok people who do their thing, nobody has any reason to hate them. And in practice nobody hates them, East Asians get along quite well in White countries, and intermarriage rates with second-gen immigrants are very high, on both sexes. But precisely because Asians and Whites get along well, because they live together, they also compete. They get on each other's throats. And there being no incentive to suppress natural outgroup resentment ("racism"), well haters gonna hate. For many reasons. There's the obvious sexual tension. Even I got called a "sexpat English teacher in China" by some weirdo on reddit. Incidentally I'm married with children, I don't live in China, and I'm not even a native English speaker. But by my talking about Asia I'm even closer to them in mindspace, so some Asian is naturally going to resent my white presence. It happens to when some Asian goes on Unz.com, and some white guy tells him to go home to the Commies.

I of course think this is very unfortunate. The problem that humanity faces now is not any real conflict between Whites and East Asians. The problem humanity faces now is the probably death of advanced civilization due to South Asians, Arabs and Black Africans outbreeding Whites and East Asians. sub-90 IQ populations outbreeding 100-plus IQ populations. That's a real and serious problem. If our civilization dies, there will be no second one. There's no cheap coal left to jumpstart a second Industrial Revolution. If we lose our present technology, we are back to the Iron Age, forever. Probably not even that, the cheaply accessible iron ore deposits are probably gone forever too. Back to the Stone Age, folks. That's our predicament.

It follows that Whites and East Asians should stop hating each other, as natural and understandable as that is, and fight the brown hordes together. That's happening to some point. There's zillions of East Asians in the West, and more whites in East Asia than, in the Middle East or Africa (not counting the colonial settlers stranded there). But there are still obstacles for an Alliance of Civilization (in the singular). First is that of course political actors have their own incentives. USG is divided in two broad factions, left-Bluegov (the State Department, academia), right-Redgov (the Pentagon). Bluegov must hate China because they want to spread their NGO human rights racket over there. Redgov must hate China because they need an enemy to scare the country into giving them more money for bombs.

Second is that, well, Asian PR is inept. Whites and East Asians have common interests, but we are still quite different, both biologically and culturally. I said that from the most deep admiration for Chinese political culture, about which I've written extensively and will continue to do so. But some stuff is still hard to swallow. Take a look at this.

https://twitter.com/XHNews/status/904380782638022656

That's... embarrassing. I'm the sort of guy who changes channels and even stops watching a movie when something embarrassing happens. And this was tough to watch. I'm a fan of Xi Jinping, I think he's a great guy and he's doing a fairly good job. But hell, if he had this made he needs some PR classes. Cults of personality are bad enough, but there's nothing lamer than a lame cult of personality.

Incidentally, Putin also has his cult of personality, which I criticized some time ago[251], although for different reasons.

https://www.youtube.com/watch?v=klcyPNIA698

That's pretty embarrassing too, but the music is better and the chicks are hot, so who cares. Hail Putin.

Now, I understand why the Xinhua video is so lame. It's basically why Asian PR is all lame. Japan's isn't any better, so it's not about Communism. Well, the cult of personality has all to do with Communism. By many accounts Xi Jinping has good reason to be drumming up his own cult of personality: the remnants of the Jiang Zemin era kleptocrats are being purged, and the more they resist (they got money) the stronger the need to check for bureaucratic loyalty by forcing them to be shameless sycophants.

But the lame culture itself is a result of the reclusive nature of Asian sociability. Asians just really like small, reclusive groups. They work very well inside them, they can focus, do their thing, and calculate their status very easily. Open, universalist societies are just exhausting in comparison. That's not exclusively Asian, of course, all biological bell curves overlap. Plenty of whites enjoy joining cults and developing wacky and cheesy culture of their own. But East Asians are patently more driven to small clique formation. Maybe it has something to do with cousin-marriage (no plagiarism here, hbdchick). Or something about pastoralism or a lack thereof, as agnostic had it.

It's a pity that Asia can't produce better PR. To the extent that Japan does produce any decent content (Anime, Kurosawa movies), it found plenty of friends in the West. China also has much to sell. Neoconfucian patriarchy was a pretty awesome deal for men. But alas, they don't care about us, and they have no good reason to do so. The West also has no good reason to give a shit about Asia. But we could at least leave each other alone and focus on keeping our civilization alive. But nah, China is too big, and the closer it gets to US levels of power, the more exciting the fight becomes. And we all like a fight. Even it kills us in the process. Think of Persia and Constantinople.

---

[251] https://spandrell.com/2012/03/04/panem-putas-et-circenses/

State and Church

2017-09-08 // china, redpill

I say we need a new religion; the Western State doesn't agree with me. They have their own, thank you.

China has its own too, and doesn't want a new one. What it wants is to dismantle the old ones. Which is pretty much what the West has been doing. We have freedom of religion. All churches can do what they want as long as they're progressive. Like the model-T. China finally figured out how that works. And so...

https://twitter.com/globaltimesnews/status/905689026421702656

Context is China just passed new regulations about religion (in English here[252]). The new regulations call for all religions in China (the 5 legally recognized) must do more to adapt to society and obey the government. Take proactive measures against extremism. Extremism being of course a relative term.

I want something. You want something. Say you draw a line, at one end it's what I want, at the other end it's what you want. If you accommodate to what I want, well you stop being you. If you try to do what you want but not too hard, then you're a moderate. If you try very hard to do what you want and don't care about what I want, then you're an extremist. Quite literally so.

---

[252] https://www.chinalawtranslate.com/%E5%AE%97%E6%95%99%E4%BA
%8B%E5%8A%A1%E6%9D%A1%E4%BE%8B-2017/?lang=en

Chinese mosque

Again, that's no fallacy. If you try very hard to get what you want and don't care about what I want, well the logical end is to kill me, then get what you want. And that's what extremists do. That's not good, obviously, and China wants to eliminate extremism. They very wisely have chosen to do away with the charade that a country can be multicultural. It can be multiethnic, given that the ethnic groups live separately, and the government has as little popular input as possible. But multiculturalism, of which religious freedom is but a subset makes no sense. The point of having a distinct culture is to set borders to the ingroup and compete with other groups. The very point of culture is to prepare for conflict. You don't want internal conflict in a state. That's bad for everyone.

Which is why everyone in the West must be progressive, and everyone in China must be... "sinicized". Chinese. Not Han, mind you. The official ideology in China is that "China" is this multiethnic utopia, of which the Han are an important, but not unique part. It's all still quite blood and soil though, compared to the universalist blank slatism of baizuo religion. And of course Progressive infiltration of religion is a fact, but never stated overtly. De jure we have Freedom of Religion. China insists on being honest.

Power

2017-09-16 // anglos, religion, power

There's this stereotype that says that people who apply to join the police force are the kind of people that enjoys having power and using it over others. Power is nice but not everybody is equally driven to it. But some people just love the stuff. To lord over others. Give orders. The right to be nasty. Innate bullies, so to speak. I don't know how accurate that is, but there must be something to it.

Well, take a look at this, hat tip to Handle.

https://www.youtube.com/watch?v=clNDUoxzSIc&feature=youtu.be

Before somebody on frog twitter publishes a copy of this video with a rhythmic BGM signing "cuck" all the time (please do it). Take a serious look at that policeman. Look at those closeup shoots. Now that physiognomic analysis is kosher again thanks to AI, take a good look at that guy. That's the face of a man who 200 years ago would have been a priest, a clergyman. A man who gives sermons for a living. Which is a very similar job to a policeman, really. The job comes with legal privileges. It's kinda high status, at least inside a small milieu.

I guess in order to get promoted inside a modern police force you gotta be both. You gotta enjoy bullying people with force, *and* with insufferable sermons. Stronger than you *and* holier than you. Take that. That's like the ultimate powerlust. The prerequisite for real power in the modern bureaucracy.

Anyway, I hope this guy is enjoying is Policepriest job in Vancouver. For when Chinese immigrants take over the half of the city, they aren't going to give sermons on the fundamental goodness of humanity on Youtube. That's Stuff White People Do. Stuff Anglos do, to be precise.

But maybe not; maybe the Sinocanadians just keep the nice parts of the city, and let the remaining whites be happy by giving them positions of authority over the worst parts of the country. Like the concentration camps (*reducciones)* the Jesuits used to run in South America to enjoy domesticating native tribals. That way race replacement could go on all over the white world and our liberals and cucks would enjoy every day of it.

What's the deal with the Rohingyas

2017-09-20 // myanmar, islam, bluegov, redgov

Myanmar opened up to the West, agreed to "democratize", and release Aung San Suu Kyi, in 2011. I blogged about it back then[253]. The rationale between the military junta dissolving itself was that China was eating up the whole economy. 100,000 Chinese have basically colonized downtown Mandalay, so the idea was to play USG against China. Which is a pretty good idea. Kim Jong Un is playing the very same game right now. Duterte in the Philippines kinda is too. This will be basically geopolitics 101 in Asia from now on.

Westerners of course didn't see it like that. They thought this was a great victory for Human Rights and Progress. Soros set up shop, and every American businessmen with spare change was in Yangon the very next weekend. Myanmar, The Last Frontier[254] they called it. Plutocrats starved for yield were watering their mouths watching a new virgin country with actual possibilities of growth, i.e. with a native population with an 80+ IQ.

So what happened? Not much happened.[255] And not much[256] is happening right now. The generals didn't really go away. And the democratic government isn't quite sold on the idea of selling out the country to Cathedral-aligned plutocrats. Doing business in Myanmar is still a nightmare, and very few palefaces have managed to make a buck out of their country. So what did USG do?

The usual trick, run a divide-and-conquer worldwide media campaign. And this one was extra easy, because USG didn't even have to pay for it. Myanmar has a problem with Muslims in Rakhine state. Why? Well there's plenty of theories about it. Foreign jihadis infiltrating the community and attacking the Burmese army and stuff. But even if that isn't true, which I guess it likely is true; there's still plenty of reasons to dislike the Rohingya.

---

[253] `https://spandrell.com/2012/06/18/the-price-of-becoming-the-usgs-bitch/`

[254] `https://www.forbes.com/sites/connorconnect/2012/11/09/myanmar-the-last-frontier/#78f67ae55dce`

[255] `https://www.chinalawblog.com/2014/06/myanmar-open-for-business.html`

[256] `https://www.chinalawblog.com/2017/02/a-report-from-myanmar-from-an-old-china-hand.html`

https://twitter.com/taslimanasreen/status/910052174192709632

The thing is these guys are Muslims, and Muslims abroad got money. Gulf money has pretty much bought half of London, a big chunk of Paris, half the American congress, and I believe a very big chunk of worldwide media. You don't need to watch Al Jazeera anymore, it's the same stuff in our own Westerns tations. There's a reason why they won't shut up about Syria. There's a reason why "Islamophobia" is a word. It started as marketing copy by CAIR. Surely somebody is greasing CNN and the wider fake news media. Some little example.

https://www.youtube.com/watch?v=p54hHhlLjRk

Muslims have money, and they like their signaling too. Muslim governments all across the world are rushing on, climbing on top of each other in order to be the one who is more vocal in defending ~~gaymarriage~~ the Rohingya and denouncing those evil ~~white supremacists~~ Buddhist supremacists in Rakhine. Erdogan is putting big money[257] on the proejct. Politicians, even local mayors in Malaysia and Indonesia are wasting their time talking about the plight of the Rohingya.

So USG is playing along, letting the latest Muslim signaling spiral work for their own objectives. It seems to me this is a long term plan of them. They certainly make good use of Chinas crackdown of militant Islam in Xinjiang in order to make China look bad. Fortunately Myanmar seems to understand what's going on, and it's not apologizing. Even the yesteryear London socialite Suu Kyi, in exquisite RP of course, masterfully dodged the question and announced to the whole International Community (i.e. Bluegov and its vassals) that the Burmese government has done nothing wrong. Well done.

https://www.youtube.com/watch?v=Qmp0FlONC88

The 400,000 or whatever Rohingya who have fled will be able to return to their homes (what's left of them) after a "verification process". And you know, that stuff takes time. Wow, tons of paperwork. And Burmese bureaucrats don't work long hours. Buddha no like that. So there you go. They can remain in Bangladesh to keep churning their 10 babies per woman.

Meanwhile Koreans and Japanese do get to make money in Myanmar. Why? Maybe because they're Redgov vassals. A different empire for all that matters.

---

[257] https://asiancorrespondent.com/2017/09/rohingya-crisis-turkeys-erdogan-appointed-voice-opressed/

Primitivism

2017-09-24 // myanmar, demographics, wat do

A while ago I argued that[258] if modern civilization collapses, which is a possibility given the relentless action of the worldwide IQ Shredder that we call "modernity", then humanity will never get a second chance to start industrial civilization ever again. By lack of cheap fuel mostly. We'd be stuck, at best, with a Chinese style "high-level equilibrium trap[259]", basically the middle ages going on forever.

To which many commenters surprised me by saying: good-riddance then. What's so bad about the Iron Age? Men were men, women were women, children were children. Yes, no air conditioning and no antibiotics is pretty bad. But you get used to that. What you never get used to is the never ending ratchet of contemporary madness. We call ourselves reactionaries for a reason; maybe we should celebrate the forcible return to Ancien Regime technology.

I honestly don't know what to say to that. I've a natural instinct to defend my current standard of living, but I can't really argue against the fact that preindustrial societies are just much healthier. It's not really comparable. As a datum, let me put forward this video. It comes from a channel that our resident Hindu nationalist, the good Lalit, put on my last post, on a white guy living in Burma, defending the Burmese against the attacks by the global islamoprogressive alliance. It's a nice channel, check it out.[260] And now look at this video of some rakhine state kids. As he says, just being kids.

https://www.youtube.com/watch?v=2ruy2s7ismA

Burma is not Africa. The TFR is a modest, but healthy 2.3. And interestingly enough they publish of the Marital TFR, which is extremely reasonable at 4 kids per married couple. I guess the Buddhist establishment takes care of the bachelors and spinsters.

---

[258] https://spandrell.com/2017/09/06/fighting-the-bad-fight/

[259] https://en.wikipedia.org/wiki/High-level_equilibrium_trap

[260] https://www.youtube.com/user/burmafriend88

Region	Crude Birth Rate (CBR)	Total Fertility Rate (TFR)	Total Marital Fertility Rate (TMFR)
Total (Myanmar)	18.8	2.3	4.0
Urban	15.8	1.8	3.6
Rural	20.1	2.5	4.2
Kachin	22.0	2.8	5.1
Kayah	26.1	3.3	5.7
Kayin	23.8	3.4	5.4
Chin	29.9	4.4	6.9
Sagaing	19.4	2.3	4.4
Tanintharyi	21.9	3.0	5.0
Bago	17.6	2.2	3.6
Magway	17.6	2.1	3.8
Mandalay	16.9	1.9	3.7
Mon	18.1	2.4	4.2
Rakhine	18.0	2.2	3.5
Yangon	15.5	1.7	3.3
Shan	21.2	2.7	4.3
Ayeyawady	20.2	2.6	4.1
Naypyitaw	18.7	2.1	3.4

But anyone, it's just a joy to watch children in a rural setting, where they can play around amongst themselves, unwatched by adults, unbothered by cars and buses, playing and laughing and just being there, learning to live in society. Instead of being thrown into cages ("classes") from age 2 where they are lectured 10 hours a day on inane stuff made up by evil fat women from the government. Like we do.

Everyone would be more than glad to have 4 children in this kind of environment. They're just much less work, children raise each other and they're just a joy to look at. Again, I'm not eulogizing poverty, life in rural Burma isn't easy, and the people aren't all happy and good-natured. Poverty is harsh. But the one thing the rural poor in traditional societies do better is raising children. Which is the very thing which we, the richest societies in human history, are utterly incapable of doing. And is this inability which will bury is, likely forever.

Show this video to your mother and just watch her giggle for 18 minutes.

The Money is in Religion

2017-10-23 // Jordan Peterson, religion, cucks, psychology

Haven't posted in a while, but everything's ok. Just been busy. Worry not, my dear readers, this blog isn't going anywhere. I might be lazy but I'm quite resilient. And I like my blog very much, so you can expect this blog to last for as long as I have fingers to type. If I go offline I'm either dead or in some hidden CIA prison for thought criminals. I expect to have good company if either of that happens.

Speaking of crimethinkers, Anatoly Karlin had a good review of the alt-internet at his blog.[261] The conclusion is quite clear: the old far-right is quite healthy. The alt-right, defined as Kek-worship and assorted Spencerites is very small. And NrX* is just tiny. Like really tiny.

**I'll just stop fighting the, in my opinion, lame branding and just surrender to the fact that everybody categorizes me as NrX so I might as well own it.*

I've said it before, and others have said it before and better than I have. But that's how it is: there is no great media revolution. Most people still get their news from TV. To the extent people get their news from the Internet, they like their mainstream stuff first, and to the extent they like edgy stuff, they like the edgy stuff that has always been around. Stormfront is still big, fellas. Or it was until a few months ago. Think about that.

This shouldn't be something to worry about, and it should surprise anyone. For one thing, the population is getting old. Old people don't like to change, they have their old ideas, and they're hanging on to them. The paleo-right was a thing, a very fine thing, and these good ol' rednecks aren't going to jump into Richard Spencer's wagon. Trump didn't change anybody's mind. He just said what his voters had been thinking for decades.

I have a blog, so I should be sad about this. I'm supposed to want to change peoples minds through my awesome writing. And to some extent I've achieved that; but the amount of people who are open to persuasion by strangers over the internet is, well, tiny. As tiny as the total audience of NrX. This is fine, many of these people are the smart people who might end up having some influence in the world. Neoreaction has been cited in the press, not always negatively, way more often than its numbers would warrant.

---

[261] https://www.unz.com/akarlin/state-of-the-altsphere-2017/

But if we look at the facts, and if I'm coherent with my writing, well the fact is most people just aren't open to persuasion. Because there's no reason they should be. Ideas aren't about logic. Ideas are badges of group membership. They are Schelling points. Ideas aren't things we hold in our "minds"; ideas are things we say. To others. For a reason. A social reason. A Dunbar reason. If saying the same things that NrX says isn't going to make you more friends, well you aren't going to say it. If saying what the Alt-right says isn't going to make you more friends, well you aren't going to say it. Ask Pax Dickinson about that.

So if the purpose of ideas is to, broadly defined, "make more (or better) friends", it should be obvious that old ideas have an advantage there over new ideas. The easiest way to make friends with someone is to adopt his ideas. New ideas by definition have no adopters, so it's hard to make friends with them. Of course just adopting someone else's ideas out of the blue is also not a very smart move. It's quite boring, and they must suspect you wanting something out of them. The way to make friends is not to make something out of people, but to offer people to make something out of you.

So the good move here is to adopt people's ideas, but give them a little bit of spin. By doing so, you signal yourself as something which is potentially useful; but you also give people something to fall back on. If your spin ends up not working for them; they can always fall back to their old ideas, with nobody noticing. No embarrassment, no loss of status. Nothing happened here.

Let me be more concrete here. I'm actually thinking of somebody very concrete. Who? Jordan Peterson. He has mastered the "old ideas with a bit of spin" trick. I've been writing of Jordan Peterson's ideas for quite some time[262]. Back then what I did was to take them at face value; but what I want to do here is to make a functional analysis. Or as Steve Sailer says of modern journalists, to make marketing criticism. I've been mildly critical of Jordan Peterson's ideas before: there's some logical errors and unclear philosophy in his speeches. But say what you will, he is a Genius marketer. With a capital G. The guy is good. How good? His Patreon[263] is making 67k a month. That's how good he is. He's making more money than the whole alt-right and paleo-right put together. And then some.

Why is he so popular? This article gives you a hint:

Bread Pilled: Jordan Peterson turning young, Western men into Christians Again[264]

---

[262] https://spandrell.com/2016/12/22/jordan-peterson-on-truth/

[263] https://www.patreon.com/jordanbpeterson

[264] https://tipolitics.com/bread-pilled-jordan-peterson-turning-young-western-men-into-christians-again-58864fa39385

Jordan Peterson is making a fortune (in internet politics terms) because... he's preaching. He's preaching the Christian gospel. And that's a very good business, especially in North America, which has a long tradition of innovative preachers. Now I'm not dissing Dr. Peterson. He's an insanely talented preacher. He's the best preacher I've heard in my whole life, and he's better than any of the preachers I've read about from the past. He is really good. He preaches Christianity with bits of HBD, of the manosphere, of evolutionary psychology and pragmatic philosophy. All great stuff. But this red-pill spin is not what is making him money. There's plenty of people preaching the red-pill, and they're not making a dime. It's Christianity what's making him the money.

And why would that be? Why would preaching be so profitable? Because Christians are a thing. There's hundreds of millions of Christians out there. Many of them aren't happy, they suffer from the diseases of modernity we all internet dissenters write about. The war on men. Diseases of modernity which affect organized Christianity itself. Many, I'd guess most of us here also come from Christian families; but we dropped out. However not everybody is willing to take that step, for many reasons. It's not so easy to accept that everything your family, your schools, your friends has been telling you about is a lie. Some people may have functional Christian social circles which they can't abandon. These people will never give money to Heartiste, even if they secretly agree with them. These people, these millions upon millions of unhappy Christians need something that gives them the red-pill but lets them keep being good Christians. Jordan Peterson sells exactly that. And he's brilliant at it.

They money, thus, is not in good ideas per se. The money is in religion. Good religion, and bad religion, they all make good money. Why? Because religions are, sticky, heavy social matter. Religions are designed to encompass one's social circle so that one can never leave. That keeps people civilized when the religion is good, and that makes society sick when the religion is bad, as in modern progressivism. But at any rate, the way to reach the bulk of the population is not just to sell good ideas, it's to sell a fallback. There's a hilarious amount of ways of saying this in Chinese, who understand the point very well. "To help them keep face". "To give them a step so that they can come down". "To find a slope to get down from the donkey". Nobody wants to lose status.

Any change is welcome, as long as it doesn't make people lose status. No change is welcome, no matter how good, if people feel the process involves them losing status, even a little, even just a tiny little slight embarrassment in the short term. These of course means there's a limit to what one can sell; you can only deviate so much from the status quo if you want people to buy in. But the power of compound interest is vast, if the will is there to keep on pushing.

Biological Leninism

2017-11-13 // Top Post, theory, status, leftism, power, democracy, history, bioleninism, hbd, loyalty

This is the first of three essays on the topic of Biological Leninism, the organizational principle of the contemporary left. You can find the second part here[265], and the third part here[266]. I also gave an interview with some more thoughts on the topic which you can read here[267].

It's 100 years now since the Russian Revolution. The Soviet Union. Lenin and the Bolsheviks. Leninism. It's been 100 years already, but you realize how present the whole thing remains when you look at the press these days. People are still praising or damning the revolution. As if it mattered anymore. As if it were something more than history. As if the left and right of today had remotely anything in common with the left and right of Lenin's day.

I won't praise Lenin, an evil man. But great men are often quite evil. I'm not very interested in Lenin, the man; but I'm very interested in Leninism. Lenin is very dead (if not yet buried, I wonder what Putin is waiting for); but Leninism is quite alive. And the Western press has just realized that China, the second power in the world, in place to become the first in a few years, is a Leninist state. It's taken 5 years of Xi Jinping shouting every day about the Leninist orthodoxy of the Communist Party of China for people to realize. Now the West is scared.[268]

The West is scared because Leninism is effective. Yes, sure, the Soviet Union collapsed in 1991; but lasting 74 years is no mean feat. And at any rate, the very establishment of the Soviet Union was a superhuman feat. It was something amazing, and amazed was the whole intelligentsia of the Western world for many decades. The kind of people who read my blog might not realize this, but Marxism was huge. Still is, really. Marxism completely captured the intellectual classes of the whole world for over a century. In China it's still the official orthodoxy, taught in schools. In the West it's still with us, if in the morphed form of Cultural Marxism.

---

[265]   https://spandrell.com/2017/12/13/bioleninism-the-first-step/

[266] 2018/01/21/leninism-and-bioleninism/

[267] 2018/12/27/interview-on-bioleninism/

[268] https://archive.fo/EGVjV

It's a staple of the right to speculate about why intellectuals hate capitalism. Reagan had a lot of quips about it. As usual, the right was good at cracking jokes, but it just never understood the problem. Which is why it lost, and keeps losing, and now we have gaymarriage and black transexuals running for office.

To understand Marxism you have to understand the world Marx lived in. 1848. The Liberal Revolutions. Europe had gone a long way since feudalism, through the absolutist wars of the 17th century, the rise of the modern state, and then the series of liberal revolutions starting in France in 1789 all up to 1848. A common thread on all this history is the rise of the bureaucratic state. Feudalism is a very natural form of government. It's basically transposing the hierarchy of a conquering army into peacetime. China started like that, 1046 BC. The German tribes that conquered Western Rome also run like that. The king at war becomes the king at peace. The generals become counts. The colonels become earls. Everyone gets a peace of land, a set of rules of behavior, a set of duties of fealty.

It works pretty well at keeping loyalty. It's not perfect, of course, after generations pass, the original ties of loyalty between army buddies aren't quite the same. But it worked reasonably well. Feudalism in both China and Europe lasted about 1,000 years. The problem with feudalism is that it's really hard to get anything done. It's hard to raise taxes, it's hard to get anything built. Everybody is very zealous about their inherited status and they won't tolerate the smallest change. Then the most centralized and obedient Ottomans come in and the most free and decentralized Kingdom of Hungary is slaughtered at Mohacs.

A state, like any organization, but even more so, wants to get things done. It wants to grow, expand its power and influence. And so feudalism led to absolutism. And absolutism led to liberalism. Liberal states were strong, had armies of bureaucrats and tax revenues that feudal states could only dream of. But while they were effective, they were a mess. Feudalism is good at generating loyalty. Liberalism is awful at that. And loyalty is very important. The fundamental problem of politics is the distinction between friend and foe, said Schmitt. A friend is someone who is loyal.

The 19th century, which destroyed the Ancien Regime in Europe, was an economic and scientific golden era, but politically it was a mess. A revolution every decade[269], governments which lasted months, huge scandals every week. Elections were a violent and chaotic affair.[270] If anything got done at all it was because the political chaos gave way to economic freedom, and the private sector got things done. A lot of things done.

---

[269] https://www.revolutionspodcast.com/archives.html

[270] https://carlsbad1819.wordpress.com/2017/10/25/electoral-violence-in-america-or-why-your-country-had-to-be-pozzed/

But the intellectuals weren't cool with that. Intellectuals are always the reserve army of the bureaucracy. They want the government to get things done.

With all the scientific advances of the last centuries, the 18th and 19th century intellectuals were just brimming with excitement with all the things they could get done. All those plans of social engineering. Utopia on earth! It just seemed so feasible. And yet they could never pull it off through the political process. They just couldn't pull it off. The politicians and bureaucrats just weren't loyal enough. Constant factionalism and infighting made any real reform impossible.

Until Leninism, that is. Now Leninism is most likely mislabeled. Lenin did indeed found the Communist Party of the Soviet Union. But Lenin died in 1924. And the Soviet Union was still a huge mess in 1924. It was Stalin, general secretary of the CPSU since 1922 who, through the means we all know, really built the Communist Party and stabilized the Soviet government. Stalinism is used to refer to his brutal purges and his approach to criminal justice, but it would be more accurate to use Stalinism to refer to what we today call Leninism; the structure of rule of single-party Communist regimes.

Say what you will about the Soviet Union: the Communist Party was loyal. They got things done. Every crazy and stupid thing that the Politburo approved got done. Yes, it took a while to achieve that result. Stalin had to kill a lot of people. But it wasn't through sheer terror and cruelty that the Communist Party worked. The Communist Party had a system. Which worked. It still works today in China. You might have noticed how people in the West today talk about China in these same terms. China gets things done, it does them fast and cheap. China got the world's biggest high-speed rail system in the time that it takes to dig a tunnel in Boston. And for not that much more money. That's not a coincidence. That's Leninism at work.

Any country has a ruling class. What I call "loyalty" you could also call asabiya; the coherence of the ruling class as such. Their ability to stick with each other and gang up, keeping the structure of rule stable. Feudalism got that; the nobility was the ruling class, they formed a society very much separate from that of the peasants, and they took much care that their rule was never contested. The destruction of that world by enlightened liberals resulted in a ruling class which was orders of magnitude less cohesive and orderly. You might be a libertarian and think that is a good thing, and you may have a point. But any organization wants to fight entropy and ensure its stability and reproduction. Liberalism historically has shown itself incapable of that. Leninism was the first solution to that problem.

Leninism is, of course, applied socialism. Socialism was huge before Leninism was even a thing, and that Marxism was and is still popular is not due only to Soviet patronage. Socialism works by hacking the Social Calculus Module[271] that humans have in our

---

[271] https://spandrell.com/2015/10/09/the-social-module/

brains. Remember, humans care deeply about status. Status is what drives human behavior. Everybody works to achieve more status, and to avoid losing status. Socialism of course sells egalitarianism. It tells people with low status that they can get some more. The Industrial Revolution had forced millions of peasants into the cities, and they all felt they had lost status in the process. Economists will tell you that the standard of living of industrial workers (according to some measures) had actually improved. And that may be so, but the workers didn't think so, and they were pissed.

So these socialists come by and tell them they have this plan to make them gain status, big time. That was huge. Yes, sure, Christianity had also started promising the meek that they were morally higher than rich people; they'd all go to heaven unlike those perfid rich guys. But that didn't translate into actual, real-world status. Socialism was promising actual goods. And so it became huge. It's still huge. It's pretty much catnip for humans. It's instant check-mate.

Socialism works not only because it promises higher status to a lot of people. Socialism is catnip because it promises status to people who, deep down, know they shouldn't have it. There is such a thing as natural law, the natural state of any normally functioning human society. Basic biology tells us people are different. Some are more intelligent, more attractive, more crafty and popular. Everybody knows, deep in their lizard brains, how human mating works: women are attracted to the top dogs. Being generous, all human societies default to a Pareto distribution where 20% of people are high-status, and everyone else just has to put up with their inferiority for life. That's just how it works.

Socialism though promised to change that, and Marx showed they had a good plan. Lenin then put that plan to work in practice. What did Lenin do? Exterminate the natural aristocracy of Russia, and build a ruling class with a bunch of low-status people. Workers, peasants, Jews, Latvians, Ukrainians. Lenin went out of his way to recruit everyone who had a grudge against Imperial Russian society. And it worked, brilliantly. The Bolsheviks, a small party with little popular support, won the civil war, and became the awesome Soviet Union. The early Soviet Union promoted minorities, women, sexual deviants, atheists, cultists and every kind of weirdo.[272] Everybody but intelligent, conservative Russians of good families. The same happened in China, where e.g. the 5 provinces which formed the southern Mongolian steppe were joined up into "Inner Mongolia autonomous region", what Sailer calls "consolidate and surrender".

In Communist countries pedigree was very important. You couldn't get far in the party if you had any little kulak, noble or landowner ancestry. Only peasants and workers were trusted. Why? Because only peasants and workers could be trusted to be loyal. Rich people, or people with the inborn traits which lead to being rich, will always have

---

[272]   https://abandonedfootnotes.blogspot.com/2017/10/utopia-and-revolution.html

status in any natural society. They will always do alright. That's why they can't be trusted; the stakes are never high for them. If anything they'd rather have more freedom to realize their talents. People of peasant stock though, they came from the dregs of society. They know very well that all they have was given to them by the party. And so they will be loyal to the death, because they know it, if the Communist regime falls, their status will fall as fast as a hammer in a well. And the same goes for everyone else, especially those ethnic minorities.

Ethnics were tricky though, because they always had a gambit which could increase their status even further: independence. Which is why both Russia and China soon after consolidating the regime started to crack down on ethnics. Stalin famously purged Jews from the Politburo, used WW2 to restore most of the Tsar's territory, and run such a Russia-centered state that to this day people in Kyrgyzstan speak Russian. The same in China, a little known fact of the Cultural Revolution was the huge, bloody purge in Mongolia and the destruction of many temples in Tibet. After that was done with, the Communist party became this strong, stable and smooth machine. The Soviet economy of course worked like shit, and that eventually resulted in the collapse of the system. But as China has shown, central planning is orthogonal to Leninist politics. China, of course, had to know. It had been running a centralized bureaucracy for thousands of years. Leninism was just completing the system.

So again, the genius of Leninism was in building a ruling class from scratch and making it cohesive by explicitly choosing people from low-status groups, ensuring they would be loyal to the party given they had much to lose. It worked so well it was the marvel of the intellectual classes of the whole world for a hundred years.

Meanwhile, what was the West doing? The West, that diehard enemy of worldwide Communism, led by the United States. What has been the American response to Leninism? Look around you. Read Vox. Put on TV. Ok, that's enough. Who is high status in the West today? Women. Homosexuals. Transexuals. Muslims. Blacks. There's even movements propping up disabled and fat people. What Progressivism is running is hyper Leninism. Biological Leninism.

When Communism took over Russia and China, those were still very poor, semi-traditional societies. Plenty of semi-starved peasants around. So you could run a Leninist party just on class resentments. "Never forget class-struggle", Mao liked to say. "Never forget you used to be a serf and you're not one now thanks to me", he meant.

In the West, though, by 1945, when peace and order was enforced by the United States, the economy had improved to the point where class-struggle just didn't work as a generator of loyalty. Life was good, the proletariat could all afford a car and even vacations. Traditional society was dead, the old status-ladders based on family pedigree and land-based wealth were also dead. The West in 1960 was a wealthy, industrial meritocratic society, where status was based on one's talent, productivity and natural ability to schmooze oneself into the ruling class.

Of course liberal politics kept being a mess. No cohesion in a ruling class which has no good incentive to stick to each other. But of course the incentive is still out there. A cohesive ruling class can monopolize power and extract rents from the whole society forever. The ghost of Lenin is always there. And so the arrow of history kept bending in Lenin's direction. The West started to build up a Leninist power structure. Not overtly, not as a conscious plan. It just worked that way because the incentives were out there for everyone to see, and so slowly we got it. Biological Leninism. That's the nature of the Cathedral.

If you live in a free society, and your status is determined by your natural performance; then it follows that to build a cohesive Leninist ruling class you need to recruit those who have natural low-status. In any society, men have higher performance than women. They are stronger, they work harder, they have a higher variance, which means a fatter right tail in all traits (more geniuses); and they have the incentive to perform what the natural mating market provides. That's the patriarchy for you. Now I don't want to overstress the biology part here. It's not the fact that all men are better workers than women. In a patriarchy there's plenty of unearned status for men. But that's how it works: the core of society is the natural performance of men; those men will naturally build a society which benefits them as men; some men free-ride on that, some women get a bad deal. Lots of structural inertia there. But the core is real.

To get to the point: in 1960 we had a white men patriarchy. That was perfectly natural. Every society with a substantial proportion of white men will end up being ruled by a cabal of white men. Much of its biology; part of it is also social capital, good cultural practices accumulated since the 15th century. White men just run stuff better. They are natural high-status. But again, nature makes for messy politics. There is no social value on acknowledging truth: everybody can see that. The signaling value is in lies. In the unnatural. As Moldbug put it:[273]

in many ways nonsense is a more effective organizing tool than the truth. Anyone can believe in the truth. To believe in nonsense is an unforgeable demonstration of loyalty. It serves as a political uniform. And if you have a uniform, you have an army.

Or as the Chinese put it, point deer, make horse.[274]

The point again is, that you can't run a tight, cohesive ruling class with white men. They don't need to be loyal. They'll do ok anyway. A much easier way to run an

---

[273] https://unqualified-reservations.blogspot.com/2008/05/ol4-dr-johnsons-hypothesis.html

[274] https://spandrell.com/2015/06/03/the-purpose-of-absurdity/

obedient, loyal party is to recruit everyone else. Women. Blacks. Gays. Muslims. Transexuals. Pedophiles. Those people may be very high performers individually, but in a natural society ruled by its core of high performers, i.e. a white patriarchy, they wouldn't have very high status. So if you promise them high status for being loyal to you; you bet they're gonna join your team. They have much to gain, little to lose. The Coalition of the Fringes, Sailer calls it. It's worse than that really. It's the coalition of everyone who would lose status the better society were run. It's the coalition of the bad. Literal Kakistocracy.

There's a reason why there's so many evil fat women in government. Where else would they be if government didn't want them? They have nothing going on for them, except their membership in the Democratic party machine. The party gives them all they have, the same way the Communist party had given everything to that average peasant kid who became a middling bureaucrat in Moscow. And don't even get me started with hostile Muslims or Transexuals. Those people used to be expelled or taken into asylums, pre-1960. Which is why American Progressivism likes them so much. The little these people have depends completely on the Left's patronage. There's a devil's bargain there: the more naturally repulsive someone else, the more valuable it is as a party member, as its loyalty will be all the stronger. This is of course what's behind Larry Auster's First Law[275] of minority relations: the worse a group behaves, the more the Left likes it.

This is also why the Left today is the same Left that was into Soviet Communism back in the day. What they approve of today would scandalize any 1920s Leftist. Even 1950s Leftist. But it's all the same thing, following the same incentives: how to build a cohesive ruling class to monopolize state power. It used to be class struggle. Now it's gender-struggle and ethnic struggle. Ethnic struggle works in America because immigrants have no territorial power base, unlike in Russia or China. So the old game of giving status to low-status minorities works better than ever. It works even better, unlike Lenin's Russia, America has now access to every single minority on earth. Which is why the American left is busy importing as many Somalis as they can. The lowest performing minority on earth. Just perfect.

If you think it can't get worse than transexuals or pedophiles, you're really not understanding how this works. Look at this NYT article[276]: a black woman, ex-con, convicted of murdering her own 4 year old son. She served 20 years in prison, which she spent studying sociology or something. After leaving prison, she applied to study a PhD at Harvard, which rejected her. Progressives were up in arms. How could you!

---

[275] https://www.amnation.com/vfr/archives/009226.html

[276] https://www.nytimes.com/2017/09/13/us/harvard-nyu-prison-michelle-jones.html

Go to the link, and look at that woman. Look at that face. She never expressed any remorse over killing her children. She lied about it in the PhD application. She disposed of the body and never told the cops where her son's corpse is! This is utter and complete psycho. Nobody in their right mind would want anything to do with this woman. But that's precisely the point. In most human societies before 1900 she would have been killed, legally or extralegally. But precisely this kind of person, someone who should in all justice be the lowest status person on earth; that's exactly the people that the Left wants on its team. You can count on her extreme loyalty to any progressive idea that the party transmits to her. And so, yes, of course, she finally got her PhD, at New York University. And unlike 97% of PhD students out there, you can bet on her getting a full tenured professorship very soon.

Yes, it's all madness, but it works. It really works like a charm. The richest parts of America, California and New York, are now a one-party state. America has legislation which forces every private enterprise of size to have a proportion of women, of black people and sexual deviants; who of course know they don't belong there, and thus are extremely faithful political commissars. More faithful than the actual official political commissars that Communist China has also in their private companies.

And Biological Leninism is extremely powerful overseas too. The same way that Soviet Communism all had natural fifth-columns across the world, with industrial workers forming parties and all doing Moscow's bidding across the West; American Biological Leninism is also an extremely strong means of agitation all over the world.

The United States has been the only superpower on earth since 1991. But that's changing of late, with China's growth into almost economic parity with the US, and Russia growing a pair, plenty of countries are now not following USG's line. Southeast Asia is now pretty much China's backyard. So now the United States is running an agitation campaign all over the world trying to undermine Chinese and Russian influence. As I'm most familiar with China, it's very obvious what the USG line is. Appealing to women and homosexuals to become their fifth column. And it's working. Every single article you see out there by a Chinese writing about how China should be more progressive (i.e. more American) is written by either a woman or a homosexual.

I read this article a while ago[277], which is infuriating. It's about a particle accelerator that China is building. A Chinese-American writer interviews the head scientist there: and all she does is undermine his project, saying how Communist censorship means the whole project is tainted. The guy doesn't get it. Why are you doing this to me, aren't you a fellow Chinese?

---

[277] https://foreignpolicy.com/2017/11/02/the-future-of-particle-physics-will-live-and-die-in-china/?utm_content=buffer824cb&utm_medium=social&utm_source=twitter.com&utm_campaign=buffer

No, she's not. You know what she is? An ugly woman on her thirties. I know China well and ugly women on their thirties are very much not high-status in China today. Unlike in the West, where they're the voluntary thought police, and you can't even look at them. So of course any Chinese, or Russian, or Saudi, or Indonesian ugly woman in her thirties is, to the extent that she's given access to US propaganda, going to become a fifth column against her country's independence. And of course the same goes for ethnic minorities, the dumber the better. You want to get funding as a China expert in Western academia? You better be researching about Uyghurs or Tibetans. Those dumb and hostile minorities. So much more important than the oldest civilization on earth.

The question of course is how Biological Leninism is going to evolve. Both Soviet and Chinese Leninism changed a lot during their tenure. Stalin purged the party very hard, and after some decades, when all the memories of the pre-Soviet era were gone, and their power was secure, the CPSU started promoting high-performing (by the requirements of a political party, not a rocket science department, that is) Russian males. Which didn't care much when the whole Soviet state collapsed. I guess they're doing quite ok right now. Same in China: today the CPC is by no means a peasants and workers party. It's a best-guy-of-the-class party. Loyalty is not ensured by the threat of landowners coming back to enserf them and their children; it's ensured with a next-gen surveillance and propaganda apparatus. Note that both Russia and China kept class-struggle as the official ideology which everybody was (and is) forced to parrot incessantly to keep their jobs.

But exactly that is what makes it vulnerable to progressive attacks. I just blogged[278] about how women and minorities have even less power than before in China. Let alone sexual deviants. No gay politicians in China. That alone makes a huge constituency, hundreds of million strong, of people in China that would prefer a Progressive government. That's the people who America is now addressing, unlike the previous strategy of selling democracy and its free economy to the Chinese middle class. Those don't look so good right now that the Chinese middle class arguably has a better standard of living that America's. Certainly less stressful.

Let's assume (hope) that America's Coalition of the Fringes doesn't succeed in destabilizing foreign countries. How is it going to evolve though? Again as I said, Russia and China both stopped their peasant kakistocracies after a few decades. But they already had a nominal single party dictatorship, and centuries of tradition of autocracy to feed upon. America is still 20 years away (if not 10) from a single party regime; and it has a tradition of adversarial democracy which makes it very hard to stop the ratchet. Even if it stopped, the ideology is already there. In the best-case scenario where a Democratic single-party regime gets its Stalin to purge the country of agitators

---

278 https://spandrell.com/2017/10/27/choose-your-side-2/

and stabilize the regime, you still get 2020 rhetoric frozen as the state religion: women are sacred, can't even joke about them, Islam is peace, transexuals get to retroactively change their birth certificates. It's not okay to be white. White men get to run the country but they must parrot all this stuff 5 times a day, facing at the Great Zimbabwe.

Or Brazilification collapses the economy and everything goes to hell. Yeah, that's more likely.

Bioleninism, the first step

2017-12-13 // Top Post, theory, status, leftism, power, democracy, history, bioleninism, hbd, loyalty

This is the second of three essays on the topic of Biological Leninism, the organizational principle of the contemporary left. You can find the first part here[279], and the third part here[280]. I also gave an interview with some more thoughts on the topic which you can read here[281].

Some things I said in Twitter yesterday. Man, 280 characters feel *way* better.

https://twitter.com/thespandrell/status/940723305265610752

Bronze Age warfare used to be about great lords going around in their chariots, shooting arrows here and there, then getting on foot and engaging in Single Combat. Early Samurais also did that. They'd go around on their horses, shouting who they were, their house, their pedigree.

But eventually somebody figured out that winning a war is really profitable. So they'd just raise a big army of common people, give them cheap weapons, a cheap shield, drill them into having rock-tight discipline. And they'd win. A disciplined team always wins against the most talented man.

The theory of democracy was that rich people, with the leisure to educate themselves about public policy, and a financial interest in the government of the nation, would run for individual office, represent their constituency, be reelected if they did their job well, replaced if they didn't. But laws are passed by majority vote. Soon somebody realized that getting a majority vote was very profitable; so the money was in finding a way to reliably organize half the parliament. So we got political parties.

A political party is a very different beast from an individual politician. A political party has no use for rich people. Well their money is welcome: but rich people tend to not be very loyal. They can afford to have a personality. As a political leader, politicians are your employees. You don't need staff who's very skilled or competent. They just need to be loyal, obedient, and have some ability to get elected. It helps if they can talk. Look good on TV. But that's about it.

---

[279] https://spandrell.com/2017/11/14/biological-leninism

[280] https://spandrell.com/2018/01/21/leninism-and-bioleninism/

[281] https://spandrell.com/2018/12/27/interview-on-bioleninism/

You want people who are loyal, who will vote what you want them to vote. As Roissy would tell you, a man, or a woman, is only as loyal as his options. So the ideal politician is the man who doesn't have anything else going on for him. Someone for whom being a politician is the best thing that ever happened to him. Somebody who positively known that if he ever leaves the party his status would drop. Marco Rubio, say. He'll play ball. He better.

Any system ruled by political parties will always move to the left. Their business model is based on getting low status people to work for them. Obviously they must give them something in exchange. And they must motivate voters to vote for them. Their promise is simple: You, low status people, help us out, vote for us, obey our commands, and we will give you high status. Don't vote for us, disobey us, let the right win, and you will remain low status.

Once the left wins, which it always does, because they are better organized, better able to form majorities in comparison to rich pricks who have no good reason to coordinate. High status people have been in the losing side in politics for 300 years. So what? They're still rich. Life is good. Yeah taxes are higher. And women are incomparably more annoying. But they put out better now, so there's that. Anyway, who cares. The Son also Rises.[282]

The left always wins. But once they win they become higher status. Come on, they got power. They try, very hard, to convince everyone that they're not really in power. No, the forces of reaction are lurking everywhere! We must keep on the struggle! 80% of the Left's energy is in producing propaganda about how the Right really runs everything. When the Left had 90% tax rates, they still talked as if they were in Charles Dickens world. After 60 years of feminism, affirmative action, and Jews in all resorts of power the Left of 2017 is obsessed with "systemic racism", "toxic masculinity" and "anti-semitism". Right.

But of course the Left has been in power for 200 years now. Once they got power, they got enjoyed their hardly fought high status. Naturally they lost discipline, until a party further Left appeared, and then won. And so on and so forth. Cthulhu always swims left. That's where power is.

First they captured the electoral system. Arguably it's the easie. But power is not only in parliament. Separation of powers is, or at least was, real. A Parliament can pass a law. The Executive could delay or outright ignore its execution. A judge could find or make up some flaw in the law and block it. It is of no use to have a legislative majority, having the ability to pass laws at will, if you can't effectively put them into practice. Power is absolute power or it is no power at all.

---

[282] https://www.amazon.com/Son-Also-Rises-Surnames-Princeton/dp/0691168377

But where there's a will, there's a way. And there is always someone with a will to power. Eventually the Left found a way. Well, two ways. Stay tuned.

Leninism and Bioleninism

2018-01-21 // Top Post, theory, status, leftism, power, democracy, history, bioleninism, hbd, loyalty

This is the third of three essays on the topic of Biological Leninism, the organizational principle of the contemporary left. You can find the first part here[283], and the second part here[284]. I also gave an interview with some more thoughts on the topic which you can read here[285].

Happy New Year everyone. I left a bit of a cliffhanger on my last post, which I intended to resolve in a few days, but I've been pretty busy, not really in the mood to write long form.

I am sorry about that, but do note, this blog is a free service, so I hope you understand it doesn't quite take the priority of my time. Again, there's a Bitcoin address at the sidebar, so if you want me to write more, I'm sure we can arrange something.

2017 has been a quite eventful year. I guess the overall mood was disappointment. Trump didn't get anything done. Doesn't seem like he'll ever get anything done. Europe slowed down the refugee invasion but not by much. And China has realized that AI makes state control so much easier. It's showing the way in censorship and crowd control. All China is doing will be done on the West in a few years, with the aggravating factor that Western states will use Orwellian tools to jack up Bioleninism.

Speaking of which, I gotta continue my last post.[286] So we left with the early evolution of Western liberal parliamentary system. In economics there's this great concept called the "invisible hand". In a free environment, if there is money to be made, someone will find a way to make it. Works the same in politics: in a free political environment, if there is power to be grabbed, someone will find a way to grab it. Economics and politics are really quite similar.

---

[283] https://spandrell.com/2017/11/14/biological-leninism

[284] https://spandrell.com/2017/12/13/bioleninism-the-first-step

[285] https://spandrell.com/2018/12/27/interview-on-bioleninism/

[286] https://spandrell.com/2017/12/13/bioleninism-the-first-step/

There's this aspect of economic theory called "the theory of the firm". Why do corporations exist? Why can't be all be self-employed? That's kinda how it worked during medieval guild days. Why are we all slaves of huge corporations now?

There's many ideas thrown around, but the standard theory is that firms are built because of "transaction costs". Basically in a free market, individual economic actors don't quite trust each other, for good reason. Too many people around, can't really know who's good and who isn't. A hierarchical firm fixes social relations and sets up a structure of trust and responsibility that makes economic action more predictable and safe.

The standard liberal theory of politics had it so that all political actors were self-employed. But, surprise surprise, political firms, i.e. political parties, turned out to be way more effective at political action than isolated individuals. And the same way that corporations tend to look for a certain kind of man, not quite the same as the old individual craftsman; political parties too select for a certain kind of person. One who obeys, who can be trusted. That was the seed of Leninism; and oh boy did that seed grow.

The thing about firms, or any organization really, is that there are no fixed limits in how large they can grow, and how many things they can make. A state is but a gang of dudes who then grows into an army, then conquers a territory. As a gang the dudes did little more than drink beer and the odd assault on trading caravans. But eventually the grew into a state which does pretty much everything. Plenty of examples of that in Chinese history. For something closer to home: the East India Company. Started trading spices. Then ended up ruling over 400 million people. Why? There was marginally more money to be made in every step of the process.

So happened when political parties started to form in the 19th century. Parties formed in order to secure power in parliament. But once you have a machine to grab power, why stop there? There's a lot of power out there outside of parliament too, whatever the constitution says. There's the executive and the judiciary too, for starters. There's the press, the power to shape opinion. There's education, the power to shape the minds of children and their social relations as they grow. There are lots and lots of social groups around, and they all have power dynamics in them. Why don't eat them up too? If there is power to be grabbed, someone will grab it. And the liberal revolutions were all about putting power out there in the open, up to grabs.

Well, surprise surprise, people started moving to grab it. And as in the magical invisible hand, which builds up an efficient economy if you only let it do its job; the invisible hand of politics also did its job. Economic firms are built around the pursuit of profit, and they grew through the joint-stock corporation. Political parties are built around the recruitment of low-status, or compromised (i.e. potentially low-status) people, and the promise of delivering high-status to followers and voters after power is grabbed.

We all know how efficient and sophisticated profit-pursuing mechanisms have evolved. Liberal politics were also this primordial soup where power-grabbing mechanisms were to evolve. And it didn't take too long for a strong, stable and hugely contagious mechanism to evolve. Socialism. It was always around, but Marx published the Communist Manifesto in 1848, just the year that the liberal revolutions were killing off all the monarchies across Europe.

Socialism refined liberal politics, the same way that double-entry bookkeeping refined business accounting. The base of electoral politics was to promise high status to low status people. Marx, starting this tradition where semi-assimilated Jews don't get the latent hypocrisy of the host society, didn't quite get the joke of liberal egalitarianism, and just took it to its logical conclusion. You're not supposed to do that, kids. You're supposed to get the joke. But he didn't. Liberty and Equality? Ok, let's abolish private property then. Hey wait a little there. Are you serious? Abolish private property?

He couldn't have been serious. I mean, come on. Private property. It's not only the basis of civilization. Even pre-farming tribes have private property. Even monkeys like to own stuff. How insane have you to be to say that private property has to be abolished? Who the hell is going to join that movement? Well, a lot of people. You see, capitalism was a big deal. It changed how the whole society worked. In more concrete terms, it changed what kind of person was high status and who wasn't. Under capitalism, the merchants ruled. And that made a lot of people unhappy.

https://twitter.com/jordanbpeterson/status/950253535417036800

Hey, some people just aren't capable of being successful at capitalism. It ain't that easy. And, you know, people are different. It's not their fault if suddenly some shtetl Jew who can't even speak properly is pretty good at making money and so is suddenly now 1000x more high status than he is; when just 100 years ago he would have been some decent member of feudal society and the shtetl Jew would have been widely scorned and hated. Not being good at something sucks. So yeah, people were resentful. And socialism catered exactly to that resentment.

Of course socialism didn't have to outright call for the abolition of private property. Feudal society had private property. They could have just called for progressive taxes, widespread welfare, usury laws, that stuff. But why be reasonable when it doesn't really matter? A political party doesn't have to deliver on its promises. Least of all a leftist one! A Leftist party is by definition fighting against the establishment; if they can't deliver on their promises they can always blame the powers that be. And people will believe them, because, well the powers that be have power. Or used to. And inertia is a real thing. People's memories can be inaccurate, especially if they have a good incentive to not update.

A political party can get away with lying; a political movement, i.e. a vague and embryonic version of a political party, can get away with murder. They don't need to deliver on anything. They don't have to be reasonable. They don't even have to make sense. They just need to be able to recruit committed people. And guess what, being unreasonable gets you more loyal followers than being reasonable. Why? Again, because reasonable, well-adjusted, normal people just have a wider range of options available for them. They don't need to commit to some crazy plan. They can just get a job and live a normal life. For an unreasonable, maladjusted, weird person, your options in life are much more limited. Joining a crazy political party which proposes the abolition of the very thing that makes society possible is, very likely, the best shot they'll ever get at achieving high status in their lives. So yeah, why not. Communism!

Again, there's many versions of unreasonable and maladjusted. Some people are genuinely just not very good at dealing with capitalist society. Born like that, to no fault of their own. Writers, journalists, middling lawyers. Rivers of ink have been spilled writing about how intellectuals are always overwhelmingly leftist. Which is odd given that communism didn't turn out to be very nice to intellectuals. But capitalism gives high status to precisely the opposite kind of person, the merchant, and intellectuals hate that. They are natural socialists. Very eager socialists.

An easy heuristic would to see the natural constituency of any political movement as the people who, in the grand zero-sum game of human social status, would rise in status if that political movement were to gain power. But it's not quite like that, if anything because you just can't know what's going to happen. Early socialists had no idea what was going to happen if socialism take power. They said they knew, but nobody knows the future. Uncertainty is the constant in human life. Any claims to the contrary are bullshit, or in scientific speech, signaling.

What is real is the present. And so the natural constituency of any dissenting political movement are the people who actually, very actually, in this very present, are losing out in the grand zero-sum game of human social status. These people are pissed and resentful, and they will do what they can to mess with society as it presently works. For good reason. Life is quite short, and you only get one. Nobody wants to lose out in status. The consequences of that are pretty bad. Losing out in the pecking order means, in general zoological terms, access to worst-quality mates, or no mates at all. So you bet all those intellectuals were pissed, and wanting to jump in to whatever movement promised them they would crush capitalism and those evil fat cats. Even if it took away everything that's good in life in the process. Who cares, that only made the process more engaging.

Again, the perception of losing out is subjective. Some people just are unreasonable and maladjusted and are not content unless they have absolute power and a harem with two thousand women. Political movements tend to house a disproportionate amount of those, alongside people who are really losing out to no fault of their own. A lot of people are losing out due to bad choices they did earlier in life, say, studied puppetry instead of something useful. So they are losing out, and it's their own fault, but they can't do anything about it either, and so they join up the ranks of the opposition.

The point here is not who forms the ranks of the opposition. The point here is that in a democracy the opposition has an actual shot at grabbing power. They have the freedom to do so. They are encouraged to do so. And so any smart political agent is going to find a way to organize these people. The same way any smart commercial agent is going to find a way to make money. There is always someone. An evolutionary process will produce it.

And the resentful will win, because upward mobility is a very strong motivator. Hope really does trump fear. People with a shot at gaining status are always going to outcompete people who are just trying to keep what they have. They are plenty of pathways, but the writing is in the wall. In a "free society", the politics will always move to the left. Always.

Of course the degree to which they move to the left depends on the degree of freedom on the political process. The first part to move left is the legislature, which is the part which is most open. Again as I was saying there are other parts to a power structure. The bureaucrats, the lawyers. The press, which provides conversation topics to all of them. The education system, which raises them and their children. It's fairly obvious that if any political agent is to take absolute power, he has to grab not only the parliament; he has to grab all these too. And those are trickier than just MPs. Again we saw the process by which politicians move to the left: a political party needs loyal people who follow orders; the lowest status people are more likely to be loyal, given their lack of options. But bureaucrats or judges are harder to control. For one they tend to be smarter. They have to be smarter, they need to do an actual job. States tend to try to hire smart people to work as bureaucrats or judges. China hired them (China had governors double as judges, didn't and doesn't believe in separating the executive from the judiciary). through a famously hard exam system. In most places bureaucrats are still hired through exams. Let alone judges and lawyers. They have to pass the bar.

So how do you control these people? You can't do it overtly, like you do with politicians. You can't organize them through a formal political party. That's against the rules. This is a very important point. How do you make sure the unelected parts of the power structure are in harmony with the elected parts? Here's where the Leftist Power Machine divided into two paths. I call it the branching of leftism between Formal Leninism and Distributed Leninism, which then for historical reasons became classical

Leninism and Biological Leninism. Historically this maps very well into what Moldbug called the Anglo-Soviet split.

Leftism in Russia had been advancing, slowly but steadily, for a very long time. Russia was formally an absolutist autocracy ruled by the Tsar. But during the 19th century the country opened up quite a bit, and as capitalism advanced, leftism grew in the same proportion among the people who weren't doing so well under capitalism. The Dostoyesvki types. Of which Russia had no lack of. I'd say Russia had a disproportionate amount of leftists because instead of capitalism growing organically as in say, the Netherlands, it came out of the blue into a very traditional and pious society. So of course all those people who had been conditioned over centuries to be loyal subjects and good Christians weren't enjoying all that freedom to build factories and make money. And so they hated the whole thing. Russia produced lots of leftists of the craziest sort before it even had electoral politics.

So then comes Lenin and stages a coup and actually grabs power as a formal communist. And what did Lenin do? He wanted absolute power. Like everyone else, but he actually had the guts and the will to pull it off. Lenin's way of achieving power was to do what I just said you couldn't do. Integrate all the ruling class into his political party. The judges, the bureaucrats, the teachers, the press. Everything into the party. The Communist Party. Political parties, remember, appeared as a way of ensuring discipline and organization in electoral politics. Lenin just extended the idea to every single organ of power in Russia. And it worked. It worked like a charm. It wasn't easy, by no means. It took a long and bloody war. Then long and bloody purges. Then some more. Then the complete terrorizing of society. Then some more purges. But after 20 years or so Stalin had it more or less set up. He had achieved absolute power. He controlled the party. And the party controlled everything.

That's Classical Leninism. There's plenty of literature about it, if you want to know more. And there's China right now, where the same principle still applies. Moreso these days after Xi Jinping tightened screws back on some areas of power which the Chinese Communist Party had let loose some decades ago. The point about Leninism is that after absolute power is achieved, the leftist ratchet stops. The country stops moving left. No new ideas. No new catering to low-status people and using them to topple the government. No, none of that. The ever advancing leftist movement was just a means to an end. The end was power. Once power is achieved, leftism dissolves. It doesn't disappear; it leaves some residue, in that states always try to have ideological consistency with what they said during their founding. Chinese dynasties framed that as filial piety of emperors following the ideas of grandpa the founder; but it's mostly just inertia.

This is not how things turned out in Western Europe and North America. No leftist party as such ever achieved absolute power in the West. It just didn't happen. And not for lack of trying. But it didn't pan out. As for why, well there's my theory back then.

Countries which developed capitalism slowly tended to produce less resentful losers than agrarian empires who were thrown suddenly into modernity. That's not quite my original theory, I've read it somewhere else, maybe someone can remind me who first said it. At any rate the success of Leninism in Russia and China has plenty of chance in it. Lenin could very easily not have taken power, he could have lost the civil war, he could have not had that precious Wall Street Jewish money to keep him afloat. No Soviet Russia, no Communist China either. But anyway, it did happen, and socialism was very strong in those places with or without actual takeover.

So what happened in the West, anyway? There's one guy who thought about it very deeply. For a long, long time. Mostly because he was in jail so he had plenty of time to study the problem. I'm talking about Antonio Gramsci. He was a communist agitator in Italy who got caught by Mussolini, and was sentenced to rot in prison. During that time he thought a very reasonable problem. Why am I here? Why did I lose? Fucking Lenin did a coup d'etat and he won, now he has power. Now look at me, rotting in prison. What went wrong?

His idea, which was hugely influential, and for good reason, was that the power structure wanted to keep being the power structure and you couldn't just throw it away and replace it with your boys. You can try your chance in electoral politics, but there's only so many resentful fucks who are willing to vote for the abolition of the very foundation of social life (property), at least in moderately prosperous Western countries. In these kind of places, if you want to take absolute power, you have to colonize the power structure very slowly. You have to influence their minds. You have to change the culture. This sounds very esoteric and spiritual but it's not. Basically Gramsci argues that you gotta grab the press and the education system, and slowly but steadily do in every institution with some power what you do in a political party. Political parties work by hiring loyal people by preying on their low-status. Well, find a way into HR of every school, every newspaper, every government department, every judicial board. And to the very same thing. Run a distributed covert Leninist party. Until you run everything.

Sounds easy, huh? No, it sounds complicated like hell. And it was. But not so much; after all there's fairly obvious economies of scale to influence peddling. A guy knows a guy who knows a guy. The great discovery of the 20th century wasn't atomic power. It was the power of cliques. A few people in positions of power sticking with each other is the most powerful force in the universe. They can make lies become truth. They can make toilets be sold as art, they can make women be combat soldiers. They can do anything. It was quite easy for socialists to get their hand in the media; after all journalists are all natural socialists. Smart-ish guys good at writing with no talent for making money. And the same goes for teachers. Teaching doesn't pay very well. And it's exhausting. Why would anyone want to be a teacher? Well, for the greater glory of socialism, that is.

So once socialists colonized the education system, the Gramscian distributed Leninist party got most of the job done. After all the schools are exactly where all the different power centers intersect. Montesquieu must have thought himself very smart saying that Legislators, Bureaucrats and Judges should be independent and in constant conflict. Well yeah, but where do they send their kids to school? To the very same places. And pray tell, cher Marquis, how do you plan on having those judges and bureaucrats and legislators and teachers and journalists and bankers and industrialists, who have all grown up together, shared a secluded life as a unified ruling class; how the hell are you gonna make them check and balance each other? That can't work. And it isn't working. They marry each other and send their kids to the same schools. Yeah, they'll do some show and play politics theater, or Kabuki as the American like to say for some reason (as if only Kabuki was fake and other theaters were real), but in the end they are an endogamic ruling class and they know it.

Gramsci's program was also called the Long March into the Institutions. A slow but steady Cultural Revolution. It was complete in most Western countries by the 1960s. And then we know what happened. I guess Gramsci's original plan was to then grab power in a classical Leninist way, a dictatorship of the proletariat of a sort. But that ship had sailed in Western Europe. The workers were rich. They could afford cars and houses and vacations to Florida or Spain. You couldn't motivate them with calls for hanging the capitalists and redistributing their property among the masses.

So the party was up and running. By the 1960s socialists cliques, more or less loosely associated with formal socialist parties, were running most schools and most newspapers and most government agencies and most courthouses and most parliaments. But you had to keep them together, keep them loyal and obedient. The early, the classical way was to get the losers of capitalism, i.e. workers and bureaucrat-inclined people, and promise them high status come the revolution. That had worked pretty well from 1848 to 1948. Hell they conquered half the world and were really close to capturing power in much of the West too. But by 1960 in the West they needed a new ideology to get people motivated and loyal.

So again, what they did was stick to the structure: promise high status to low status people. But change the content, adapt to the times. Western 1960 society was very much not 1860 society. It was much richer, much more equal, and much more pleasant. People worked 8 hours a day, they had cars and TVs, girls put out pretty easily and there was always a party to go. Absolutely no point in running a communist revolution. Well there was the 1968 "revolution", with the anti-Vietnam stuff and all that. But that was just a big ass outdoor party, not a real revolution. It just sounded cool to call it that. The teens from 1968 are now all in positions of power and they haven't abolished private property.

But again, the leftist ratchet isn't a particular set of people. It's a memeplex with a life of its own. A virus evolved to concentrate power, adopting ideas that help in the project, and discarding those that not. Economic socialism, organizing the poor wasn't working out in the West anymore. But the principle is sound; they just needed to find whoever was low status then. And there is always someone, status is zero sum. There's always someone on top, someone on the bottom. Even in egalitarian societies. Socialism had really pressured Western society into becoming a quite egalitarian and pleasant society by 1960. But even in the best of worlds, there's always low status people. Even if you re-engineer society so that there's complete equality of opportunity, even if you run a revolution and you dissolve every existing hierarchy and start anew. There will always be low status people.

Because there's always biology. Some people are tall, some people are short. Some look good, some are pretty ugly. Some are thin and some are fat. Some are pleasant some are annoying. Some are cool and some are awkward. Some are smart and some are dumb. Some make good choices some make bad choices. Some are law-abiding and some are criminally inclined. The latter of each pair is going to be low status anywhere on earth. Even in Soviet Communism under commander Trotsky. Some people just suck. That's the way genes work.

And so thankfully for Leftism, even after achieving affluence, even after the working class disappeared as a thing, there was still plenty of material to work with to advance the cause of complete control. And so Leftist groups started agitating status for people of African descent. For Jews. For single women. For drug junkies. For sluts. For fat people. For homos. For lesbians. For aggressive Muslims. For the disabled. For the retarded. For the mentally insane. For the trannies. All people who are were low status in Western society. And who would be low status in any society. Because they suck. They just aren't very productive. For no fault of their own. Some people are born tall, some short. Some smart, some dumb. Some empathic, some psychopathic. Some content with their lot, some greedy with powerlust. That's how it is.

And so the Long March through the Institutions that Gramsci first envisioned as a way of having the Italian Communist Party do what Lenin had done, ended up producing a different kind of Leninist system, one distributed and informal, instead of Lenin's unified and formal, and one which morphed into promotion of the dregs of society qua dregs of society, instead of promotion of Marx's idea of the wrongly oppressed proletariat. Marx was not a good man, but at least he tried to dress his ideas in a way that made sense. Das Kapital took some real work to write. But that was just some contingent accident of his time. Leftism doesn't need to make sense. It just needs to get the job done.

Or at least marginally. Because the very fact that we have Biological Leninism as the organizing principle of all centers of power in the West, and that it keeps getting worse all the time, is because it's not quite getting the job done. The job is concentration of power. It's achieving absolute control. What Lenin did. What once Lenin did that, or more precisely Stalin did that, the ideological content of the Left stabilized. Cthulhu stopped swimming left. But here in the Atlantic Cthulhu has been swimming for centuries, getting crazier every day. Because there's no one to stop him. We have a Cathedral, yes, an informal distributed Leninist party, ensuring very efficiently that only their people get in positions of power and influence. But there is no Stalin. No Xi Jinping. Not even a lousy Putin even.

As for why, is a good question. The unwritten constitution of English politics is just very robust. English liberty. Only Oliver Cromwell ever tamed that beast, and not for very long, and that was quite a while ago. The West is the US vassal empire, and the US just doesn't do absolutism very well. But it'll get there, it's getting close; the returns are just too great. If there's a way to grab power somebody will grab it. All he, or more likely she at this rate, has to do is say: give me power, or else, all of you, all those evil fat women with a make-work office job, all those foreigners living off the public purse, all those just plain unpleasant people with unhealthy lifestyles; all of you, give me power, or if you don't, we'll go back to 1959, it'll be ok to be white, and all of you will have to make your bed, clean up your room[287], and do actual work. You'll be on your own.

How long will it take? Can't be that much longer.

---

[287] https://www.youtube.com/watch?v=BBR5v89L6gk

The Jordan Peterson movement

2018-01-31 // Jordan Peterson, religion

Jordan Peterson is an old friend of this blog, which I'm sure he reads, even though for obvious PR reasons he can't quite admit to the fact. Mr. Peterson is getting increasing amounts of mainstream attention after he utterly and completely destroyed some dumb journo British woman a couple of weeks ago.

https://www.youtube.com/watch?v=aMcjxSThD54

I won't pull the hipster move of saying I was into Peterson before he was cool. But I have written quite a lot about the man, his ideas, and why he's so popular. Do check it out.

In short, the reason why Peterson is so successful is that he's selling a single proposition. It's OK to be Christian. More precisely, he's selling It's OK to be a White, Christian Man. That is of course a revolutionary slogan, as White Christian men are the officially most low-status people in the West. They're not even just deprivated, they're the enemy of the state. Not just low, positively evil. Well, we know[288] that selling hope and validation to low-status people is very good business. And as it happens, the low status of White Christian Men is not the result of any natural law, but the highly unnatural result of a centuries old political endeavor. Peterson slightly hints at that. Just pull yourselves together, White Christian Men, and you'll be the ruling class again. Nature Says So.

Anyway, the mainstream media has started to notice our good Dr. Peterson. That is not good. It's good short term, in that some sympathetic people will find them and give him money. But mid term it's very bad. The hornet nest won't allow anyone to give hope to White Christian Men. Some trolls in the US printed some fliers across the country saying: It's OK to be White. It went to every single Cathedral outlet and the response was unanimous: Nazis! It's most positively NOT OK to be White in the Current Year. So it follows that someone is going to come down on Jordan Peterson like a ton of bricks. And eventually someone smarter or more resourceful than the Channel 4 broad will be put in charge of taking Peterson down.

I wonder what it will be. Some fabricated (or not) #metoo scandal? Surely plenty of nubile co-eds have thrown themselves at their handsome alpha professor over the years. Accusations of racism? They've already found an old Tweet of him making a (pretty accurate) race joke. Maybe that sticks.

---

[288] https://spandrell.com/2017/11/14/biological-leninism/

The question is what he will do later. Apologize? We all know where that leads to. Instant death. Mr. Peterson is walking a very thin rope here. Conquest's Second Law is very clear: Anything that isn't explicitly right wing turns left-win over time. Will Peterson cuck down and submit? Or will he stand on his feet and fight back as the leader of the deprived young Christian masses?

Tales from the patriarchy

2018-02-20 // china, history, men, women

The way of properly learning a language is to do what languages are made for: use it. Ideally, live your usual life, do whatever it is you like doing, and just try to find a way to insert that language you're learning into your daily routine. So if, say, you like movies, and you're learning Persian, well, stop watching Hollywood crap and go pick up some Persian movies.

I get asked about books on Chinese history, and I tend not to know what to say. I haven't read a lot of Chinese history books in English. Certainly not any general ones. I read China in World History by Adshead after Steve Sailer recommended it. It's a fascinating book, not very accurate, but a fun read for beginners, so I do recommend it too. Generally speaking most English books on China are pretty bad, and badly written. With the exception of Frederick Wakeman's, which are awesome.

What I often do to read up on Chinese history is watch a historical TV show, then stop anytime something bugs me and go check out the primary sources out there in Wikisource. If the thing is interesting I check out 知乎, China's much improved version of Quora, where they have detailed explanations and book recommendations. If the topic is interesting enough I get the (Chinese-language) book.

There's a recent TV show in China about 司馬懿 Sima Yi[289], one of the most important leaders of the Three Kingdoms[290] period. The whole period, which lasted about 100 years, 180 to 280 AD, is the most written about in the history of China, mostly because of the sheer force of personality of the men of the time. Dozens upon dozens of great warriors and statesmen. Sima Yi wasn't the most colorful of them, but arguably he was the guy who won the game. He was a quiet minister of the northern kingdom, Cao Wei, where he served and outlived three emperors. The guy was so good at anything he did, so influential that part of the imperial family decided to get rid of him, lest he took power for himself and made a puppet of the imperial court. He let the court take away all his power for 10 years. Then out of the blue he run a coup d'etat, where... he took power for himself and made a puppet of the imperial court. At 72 year old he executed thousands upon thousands of imperial kinsmen. Then he died. His

---

[289] https://en.wikipedia.org/wiki/Sima_Yi

[290] https://en.wikipedia.org/wiki/Three_Kingdoms

soon took over, then died. Then his grandson decided to do away with the charade and took the throne for himself. He then started the 晉 Jin Dynasty.[291])

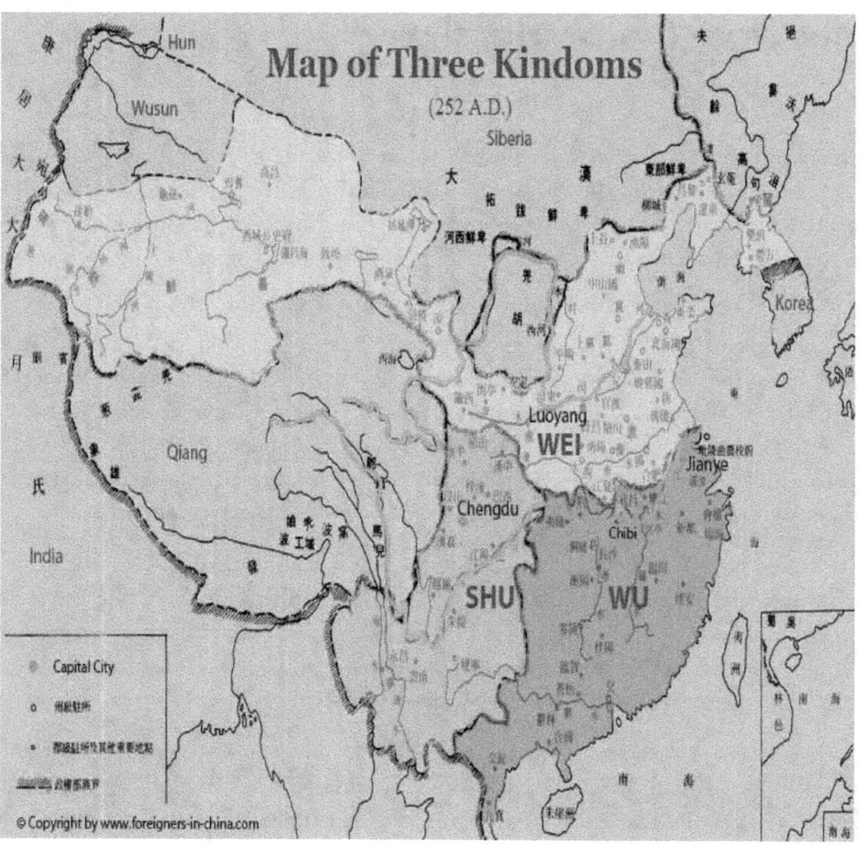

[291] https://en.wikipedia.org/wiki/Jin_Dynasty_(265%E2%80%93420

So anyway, the show is pretty good. But it's of course adapted to modern sensitivities. But not so much, I was very surprised to see a scene where he kills the whole family of his main rival in the coup, 曹爽 Cao Shuang. The usual penalty for treason in China was 夷三族, "leveling of the three families". There are conflicting records on which three families this referred to, but basically it meant killing the whole extended family, clients included. So all wives, brothers, children, parents, uncles and aunts. All beheaded, if possible together. The scene in the series shows Cao Shuang's 3 year old son, tied up in white clothes, in front of the beheading platform. They don't show his head being cut off, of course, but the mere sight of a 3 year old boy in front of a beheading platform would get most housewives in the West calling for their smelling salts and yelling at social media.

Anyway, kudos for China for their accuracy in that front. Shame on China for their lack of accuracy in what remains, in my view, the still biggest and most encroached area of progressive influence in modern China. Women. I write a lot about how Islam is a better deal for Men than Western culture, which is why Muslim immigrants refuse to integrate, and in fact radicalize further in their faith after moving to the West. But if Islam is a good deal, old Chinese culture was the freaking lottery. Polygamy among the gentry in China was not only legal: it was expected. And there was no limit to the number of wives you could acquire. Girls were sold as property at 13-15 years old, and no self-respecting men would not get a new wife every 5-10 years if he could afford to.

Of course having too many wives was frowned upon. It was a sign of lack of seriousness. Women are something men like, but men should like other things more, manly things. Warfare and government. Reading and the arts. Women were entertainment, who also happened to produce children, which are always nice to have, as they make heirs, and daughters which you can give to you friends' sons.

It is unconceivable that a man of the stature of Sima Yi would not have a handful of wives. And indeed he had, four of them in total. His first wife, Lady 張 Zhang, is said to have had a temper. That means that... she had a temper. In the TV show though, tailored to modern sensitivities, for commercial reasons if only, as most TV show viewers are women, Lady Zhang is a kung-fu master who accompanies her mild-mannered husband at war, does ninja work to help him in his conspiracies, and basically runs the household with an iron clit. Amazingly (progress!) the show has Sima Yi welcome a second wife. The show makes it look like the emperor forces upon him a second wife, Lady 柏 Bai to spy on him, and that makes his first wife, Lady Zhang, to flare up in outraged fury. How dare you get a second wife! A good 5 episodes are dedicated to this story. But she eventually accepts the fact and they get along together, the second wife being super smart or something.

Which I guess it's great fun for modern housewives, who like soap operas of women fighting for status. But as a historical show, the whole premise is ridiculous in the extreme. First of all, Lady Bai was his fourth wife. That's 4 women. Second, Lady Zhang was just some boring housewife with a temper, no super ninja. Third, while Chinese wives were indeed never happy about their husbands getting another wife, there was nothing they could do about it. Ancient China didn't recognize divorce, but wives nagging about concubines was one of the few cases where it was granted. Lady Zhang, first wife, may indeed have given shit to Sima Yi about it, but only so much of it, and the idea that Sima Yi would be apologetic about it, that he would feel sorry about getting a younger and hotter wife, is just preposterous.

Don't take my word about it though, the official history of the Jin Dynasty says it for me. The historian in charge was funny enough to add this piece of domestic life of Sima Yi.

其後柏夫人有寵，后罕得進見。帝嘗臥疾，后往省病。帝曰：「老物可憎，何煩出也！」后慚恚不食，將自殺，諸子亦不食。帝驚而致謝，后乃止。帝退而謂人曰：「老物不足惜，慮困我好兒耳！」

Sima Yi spent more time with Lady Bai; Lady Zhang hardly ever saw him anymore. One day, Sima Yi was sick, lying in bad, and Lady Zhang went to see him. Sima Yi saw her and said: "You annoying old thing, why did you bother coming out?". Lady Zhang was so angry and embarrassed that she stopped eating, and was going to kill herself. All her children [note: the elder, most legitimate heirs of him] stopped eating too. Sima Yi was startled and went to apologize, so she stopped (started to eat again). Sima Yi then left and told his men: "the old thing doesn't deserve pity, what bothered me was my poor good boys!".

This anecdote is not only funny today; it was funny even then, as it takes 3 lines of the 8 total lines that Lady Zhang, posthumous empress, got in the official history. I love how he called her, 老物, "old thing". Plenty to comment here: wives being annoying in any time and any social stratum, wives using their children as weapons in order to get what they want. Human nature.

Sima Yi was a huge prick, unlike the mild gentle man he is in this TV show. In previous renditions he's written more accurately. But hey, he founded a dynasty, he was the towering general and statesman of the most tumultuous and interesting era in 5000 years of China. Of course he was a prick.

China doesn't care about your opinion

2018-02-26 // china, redpill, Cold War 2

Well, the news is out: Xi Jinping has become dictator of China for life. He's the new Mao, a totalitarian ogre who will destroy human rights across the world.

Or so would the Western media have it. But that's why you're here reading my blog, of course, because you want a better take. Well this is mine.

https://www.youtube.com/watch?v=HWBw7mFTIGY

What just happened? Well, the Chinese Communist Party Central Committee, the de-jure highest power of the land, made by 205 members, has proposed a series of changes to China's constitution. Amongst them are the abolition of term limits[292] for the 主席 President and 副主席 Vicepresident. Previously, since 1982, there was a limit of two consecutive terms for both offices.

What do the president and vice president of China do? The offices have no power. The constitutions, and any other law, give them no power. None at all. They are completely ceremonial.

So what's the point? That's a good question. China has a weird double structure, where the party and state are distinct entities, but have completely mirror structures. For every province, city and county, there is a government, with its governors and mayors and vice governors and vice-mayors. And then there's a Communist Party committee for the same province city or county, with a secretary general. The secretary general calls the shots. The mayor isn't an entirely ceremonial office, but it is completely subservient to the secretary general of the local committee. There has been lots of calls for abolishing this nonsense and just unify the administration, but the system remains in place.

The central government, the 国务院, has a "prime minister", today Li Keqiang. That guy's not ceremonial either, he wields substantial power. But for some reason, Deng Xiaoping in 1982 decided to put a President on top of the prime minister. I guess for diplomatic reasons. Foreigners don't understand how Chinese politics work, not then and not now[293], so he wanted to make it easier to understand.

---

[292] https://www.globaltimes.cn/content/1090556.shtml

[293] https://www.chinafile.com/reporting-opinion/viewpoint/why-do-we-keep-writing-about-chinese-politics-if-we-know-more-we-do

https://www.youtube.com/watch?v=8Ft9YXJLPxI

There's this funny anecdote about the Second Opium War in 1860, when the British invaded Beijing and burnt the Qing Dynasty's Summer Palace, but didn't occupy the capital and left the Forbidden City alone. The Summer palace was the real place of government, had been for a century. The Forbidden City is narrow and urban and hot and hell, it was built by the previous dynasty. The Summer Palace was a country palace, away from the city, full of nice gardens and European buildings. But it was where the emperor lived, where all decisions were made. The British didn't get it; they thought it was this country garden, so they burnt it, but left the Forbidden City alone so the Chinese government could get to work. He was a gentlemen and wouldn't interfere with that.

So anyway, knowing how Westerners are, he having lived in Paris, Deng Xiaoping made the figure of the President, which has also coincided with the Secretary General of the Central Committee, i.e. the actual boss. So the actual boss and the fake boss have since 1982 always been the same. (ETA: Sorry, I got that wrong. During Hu Yaobang's reign the President was Li Xiannian, a figurehead).

Well, not quite since 1982. Interestingly enough, Deng Xiaoping has never been Secretary General. Nor president. He was "chief advisor" of an "advisory committee" he came up with. The secretary general during Deng's period of rule were Hu Yaobang and later Zhao Ziyang. Both renown liberals; Hu Yaobang is today hated by the nationalist right for ordering minority criminals to be treated lightly; Zhao Ziyang of course famously sided with the protesters at Tiananmen, for which he was sacked and detained. He died in house arrest.

https://www.youtube.com/watch?v=3ZxjV0s2CrA

Oh, there's this other piece of power which Deng did actually hold formally. The People's Liberation Army. He was chief of the Central Military Commission, which controls the military. He didn't leave that for Hu Yaobang or Zhao Ziyang. He kept that for himself, apparently forced by the army itself, who was not willing to obey those pesky liberal reformers he had put in charge of the civilian government. In 1989, after Tiananmen, Deng Xiaoping somehow decided to formally retire and give the whole package, the Secretary General of the party, the Presidency and the Secretary of the Military Commission to Jiang Zemin. Jiang took the three posts by stages, and soon controlled all formal levers of power. Deng was still calling most of the shots until his death in 1997, but Jiang had formal, and soon real power over the whole country.

Henceforth the idea that the same man must control the three offices has become an institution in China, which they now call the "trinity", 三位一体. Yes, that's actual Christian vocabulary. I really hate this part of CPC rhetoric, but anyway. In the 1990s Jiang Zemin controlled all levers of power, the real one, i.e. the Secretary General of the party; the fake one, the President, and the military one. The Secretary General has no term limits. It's not in the constitution, of course, that's about the state. The party has its party statutes. And no, no term limits. Same for the military commission. No term limits. So the only term limits are those for the Presidency, which is the fake office. Of course it's prestigious and all; but it has no real power.

This was some weird legal magic that Deng Xiaoping had done there. Jiang Zemin had the three offices now, again, party, state and army. True, fake, true. He kinda liked this idea of having it all. Jiang also spoke some English and loved, loved with a passion to hang out with foreigners and just brag with them on how cool he was. Go check it out[294], the guy's funny. So anyway, Jiang Zemin could have it all, but only for two terms, 10 years. After that he had to surrender one, but not necessarily all. He could keep the actual offices of power.

https://www.youtube.com/watch?v=UCA86xqa2o4

So what did he do? He was quite smart. He was Secretary General from right after Tiananmen, in 1989. But he delayed access to the Presidency until 1993. So he could hold onto the three offices until 2003, 14 years of actual power. And that's exactly what he did. He could have found some toady, some Medvedev, and give him the presidency. But he didn't do that; he chose Hu Jintao, a boring but competent guy, and put him as successor. In 1998 he was made Vice-president. Then in 2002 gave him first the office of Secretary General, then the presidency in 2003. And in 2005 (he was in no hurry), he gave him the military command.

Hu Jintao was no match for Jiang though, and it's widely acknowledged that Jiang Zemin till call the shots during Hu Jintao's time in power. But then another 10 years passed. Jiang Zemin was getting old, very old. He's 91 now. And people were getting fed up with his rule. The idea that Hu Jintao could play some game and hold onto power was just not in the cards. He wasn't that kind of guy. Hu Jintao followed Jiang Zemin's precedent, and in 2008 put his successor as Vice-president. That's Xi Jinping.

Now you'd read a lot about who Xi Jinping is, whose faction he belongs to, how he got the post, etc. Most of what you read is probably complete crap. He was often called a "princeling", a member of a faction made up of the children of old high-ranking politicians from the 60s and 70s. That's not important. What's important is what he's been doing since he took office. In 2012 he took the office of Secretary General, then immediately the military commission. Hu Jintao wasn't allowed to play there for a few years as Jiang Zemin had done. He surrendered it immediately. That gave signs that Xi Jinping was the real deal. Then in 2013 he took the presidency.

---

[294] `https://www.youtube.com/results?search_query=jiang+zemin+english`

https://www.youtube.com/watch?v=rDccUcm0ivU

Since then Xi Jinping has unleashed a massive crackdown on both Jiang Zemin's and Hu Jintao's protégés. And he's also jailed a big bunch of those princelings he was supposedly the leader of. Most famously Bo Xilai, who was this handsome, well-spoken guy who tried to outmanouver him out of sheer charisma and a very smart practice of making sure his friends were making a lot of money. Well, Mr. Bo is now in jail. Apparently writing daily (!) letters protesting about his outrageous treatment.

Besides cracking down on corruption, which he has undoubtedly done, Xi has also done a lot to tighten up the country. Most foreign journos would have you think that Xi is undoing the liberal legacy of his predecessors. But that's fake news. Xi Jinping didn't start internet censorship. He perfected it. Xi Jinping didn't start the crackdown against restless minorities (there's only two, Tibetans and Uyghurs). Hu Jintao started that as Governor of Tibet. Yes, that guy. Xi Jinping is only building on that legacy. China hasn't had a liberal in government since Zhao Ziyang in 1989. What China had were timid leaders of few words, who outwardly seemed to accept the superiority of Western democracy. They then cracked down on human rights and whatever, but without talking about it. Very subtly and with the lights off. Western politicians liked that; it meant that the Chinese Communist Party wasn't quite confident of its rule, and after a few time all the contradictions between rhetoric and reality would explode, giving USG and the Cathedral an opening into a market of 1.3 billion potential bioleninists.

That completely changed with Xi Jinping. He has completely changed the internal and external rhetoric of China. Now China has its own system of rule, which is different from Western democracy, and that's a good thing. China does not believe in separation of powers, in freedom of speech. And human rights, well yeah, but China interprets that as for example, having low crime rates, area in which China can claim wide superiority over the West. Xi Jinping is also making bold claims for (maritime) territory and influence. It is taking no shit, and giving plenty.

https://www.youtube.com/watch?v=t52tcNkFrbs

It should be no surprise that this drives Western politicians crazy. China is now fairly rich, it's buying property and high-tech companies across the world. China has made Southeast Asia it's diplomatic backyard, made a strong relationship with Russia against the US. It's practically vassalized South Korea, and eaten up so much of Taiwan economy that it's independence-minded government is limited to approving gaymarriage and bringing Muslim immigrants in order to beg for some Western sympathy.

All while internally the party's rule is tighter than ever. The standard narrative of Western democracy is that a developing economy creates a middle class, who then agitates for political rights. That may or may not be an accurate representation of the European experience, the revolutions of 1848 and all that. But it most certainly doesn't apply today. Today we have the internet. The internet creates monopolies by network effects. And governments just can't help themselves from merging with these monopolies. In the West, Google, Twitter, Facebook, are all arms of the cathedral. They censor, control and gather data for it. In China, Baidu, WeChat, Alibaba, are all arms of the Communist Party. The only difference is that in China, they are formally so.

And so Xi Jinping has now decided to do away with the term limits for President. Changing the constitution isn't unprecedented. The 1982 constitution has been ammended 4 times already. Some changes were quite big. Recognizing private property, for instance. The changes this time though have a very obvious theme: controlling the damn party. Enforcing discipline. They say Xi Jinping is obsessed with Gorbachov and the fall of the Soviet Union. On why the CPSU dissolved itself. It won't happen on his watch. He has created a new State Supervision Agency, a state-level agency, answering not to the government, but to the central committee, only to investigate illegal activity by public officials. That's a very, very old Chinese tradition, but let's leave it at that. The rationale is clear: all civil servants in the country must behave, obey orders, and stop trying to push for more power for themselves. It won't happen.

The Communist Party of China has close to 90 million members. That's bigger than the population of Germany. Coordinating and organizing 90 million people is no easy feat. Making sure they all obey order is borderline impossible. Civil servants in China have developed every way you can imagine to ignore the law and use their power to enrich themselves. The amount of money that civil servants in China have embezzled is in the trillions. And plenty have now families abroad, and many now kinda like liberal values. Everybody in China hates these people. Everybody in China has been scammed or cheated of victimized by some asshole politician. Well, if Xi Jinping wants to re-establish the legitimacy of the Communist party, and his personal rule, it is quite easy to see what his rhetoric is: People, I will protect you from evil politicians. I will jail them and get them out, and replace them with good people. That he has been doing, or he says he has been doing, and most people are quite content with it. The re-disciplining of the party has required cult-levels of ideological repression. The party media openly talks about the need for party members to have "faith". It's unseemly, but that's how large organizations work. Or isn't Facebook a cult? Have you seen Zuck talk?

Now, those local embezzlers are not happy. And those more or less honest business people who have fallen as collateral damage of the investigations are very much not happy about it. And everyone who just got used to liberal values, talking politics, and all that, are scared as fuck by internet controls and media censorship and talk of "faith in the party". All these people have endured 5 years of Xi Jinping, and probably were thinking they only have wait 5 more years until Xi's term limits come in. Then they could keep on embezzling money to buy Vancouver real-estate. Or go on gay-parties with drugs bought from Nigerians in Sanlitun. Well, tough luck. Xi Jinping is not going anywhere. That's the message of the constitutional change.

People should have figured that out when talk started to come of "Xi Jinping thought" going into the party statutes and the constitution. Xi Jinping thought doesn't mean anything. It's just a badge. A badge that says: as long as Xi Jinping is alive, his "thought" is one of the guiding ideologies of the country. So even if he's not Secretary General, any potential successor must follow his orders. His thought is in the constitution! Go ask the guy about what he thinks.

But it also happens that Xi Jinping is a formalist. He doesn't believe in tricks. He wants everybody to know that he's in charge, that he will be in charge as long as necessary, until he makes the Communist Party a disciplined organization without political machinations. No liberals will take power on his watch. China will not fall while he's there.

This may or may not be scary by itself; but it has nothing to do with being "a new Mao". Mao was not a dictator until 1966. And in order to become one he had to unleash the Cultural Revolution, where he physically killed every single enemy he had, and physically tortured about 90% of the party leadership. Mao did that precisely because he was not secure in his power. After 1959 he was removed from power due to, well, causing the starvation of tens of millions of people with the Great Leap Forward. He thought he would be purged and disgraced; and so he threw everything he had against the party. And he won. That's what Mao did. Xi Jinping is in a completely different situation. He has comfortable complete power over all the country, and in an orderly and formal way. He has nothing to fear.

As many of us now, it is not from secure power that bad government happens. It is due to insecure power, which leads the powerful to mess with society in order to secure it. That is what the Chinese historical tradition calls 乱, "disorder". Mao's time was a disorderly time. Xi Jinping's time, you may like, or not like, but it is most certainly orderly.

Now, a lot of people in China are kinda freaking out. Mostly liberal-ish college grads. If only because having a president for life does cut off some potential avenues for upward status mobility. And people hate that, of course, people want more status, more every day. If Xi is smart, he'll open up the economy a bit, so that status-maximizers can put their energies in making money and not in selling their country to USG's bioleninist outreach department. We'll see.

Mistakes happen for a reason

2018-03-09 // china, bluegov, capitalism, theory, philosophy

So the news from last week were how China changed the constitution and abolished term limits in the only thing that had term limits; the presidency. This was followed by the USG propaganda apparatus (AKA the press) going into fits of panic. "We got China wrong", they say. It took China changing its constitution without American permission for Americans to notice that they got China wrong.

What did they get wrong? China was dirt-poor in 1980. Really, really poor. It would have likely remained quite poor if USG hadn't decided to open trade relations with China, having them join WTO and all that. The theory, now stated openly, was that economic growth would eventually lead to the formation of a middle class, and that middle class would then agitate for democracy; a democratic China would naturally be a jolly good thing, aligned with USG's interests (also known as "Western values").

I don't quite see how that last line follows. Democratic politics doesn't correlate with "Western values" well at all. Look at Turkey or Iran. What does correlate with Western values is proximity of US military bases: that correlates pretty damn close. It also happens that proximity of US military bases correlates to some degree with democratic politics. But the causality starts with US tanks, not with democratic politics.

At any rate, Scientism on Twitter had a good elaboration of what it means that "we got China wrong". What did USG really think? Was it just the latest iteration of the Whig theory of Democratic Development, whereby democracy happened because of the rising incomes in the 19th century empowering the bourgeoisie into fighting against the royal houses of Europe for political rights? No, of course not. Nobody reads history anymore. Certainly not people in the American corridors of power. Whig history is stupid; but our ruling class today doesn't know Whig history anymore. What they know is a degraded version of Whig history as remembered by the guys on Wall Street, who have some faint recollection of reading about it in Harvard; but that was a long time and many many hangovers ago.

https://twitter.com/mr_scientism/status/971473572475621378

So the idea is that trade with China was a good idea because it was thought that China would always be poor, so the USA could always enjoy a sort of advantageous colonial relationship with Chinese factories. I can totally imagine some Goldman Sachs guy selling that to Clinton-Bush-Blair and those guys believing it hook, line and sinker. And the State Department QUANGO apparatchiks who had actually read the Whig theory of history could, on their end, support that thinking on all the opportunities for bioleninist missionary work. 1 billion souls to ~~save~~ organize!

That, of course, didn't work out. China grew richer than anybody thought it would, it didn't quite open up politically as fast as people thought it would, since 2012 it has instead closed up quite fast, and this closing up has not affected its economic might in the slightest. Yes, guys, you got it wrong.

The interesting thing about the recent media trends pressing for hostility to China is that it's a completely bipartisan point. The Left is extremely disappointed that China won't let them preach the supremacy of women, Africans and homosexuals in China; and the right is just pissed at the loss of American supremacy. See Pat Buchanan in this article[295].

The article is pretty lame; first in how it makes an analogy to WW2 in order to peddle more of Buchanan's book shitting on Churchill. We get it, Pat, you want us to buy your book. It is also lame in the whole tone of the article. It just states, in very strong terms, that We Got it Wrong. We Got it Wrong guys! Very wrong! Mistaken we were!

Well, ok, but why? How did this mistake happen? He of course does no attempt at explaining. Because his job, the job of Pat Buchanan is to be a conservative, and the job of conservatives is not to understand a thing. The job of conservatives is, and has been for decades, to state their confusion with a tone of strong indignation. I don't understand this! Hmm! I am angry, yes I am, this makes no sense, and that makes me angry. Join me in my indignation, oh and buy my book. Hmph!

Well as I often say, if you don't get something, that's a statement about the limits of your intellect rather than about the nature of the problem. If you don't get something, the problem is with you, not with the issue. Go try and understand it, and then come back. Your indignation solves exactly nothing.

That is of course my instinctive reaction, but I of course also do understand the meta quality of these kinds of statements. Speaking as a linguist, most instances of the string "I just don't get it" are not meant to state a lack of understanding; they are a way of signaling a political position. The underlying argument is "I just don't get it because I don't think that way, and I don't think that way because I am a proper person whose thinking only works inside certain limits, as is proper and just. I only think as people in the ingroup think". Understanding how the outgroup thinks is evil. You're not supposed to go and try to know what's going on. You're supposed to just not get it. And to loudly proclaim it.

---

[295]   https://www.vdare.com/articles/patrick-j-buchanan-fatal-delusions-of-western-man

This incidentally is a human universal. All languages I know have "I just don't get it!" as a short-hand for ingroup allegiance signaling.

Which leads me to this article by Scott Alexander[296]. He elaborates on an idea by one of his ingroup about their being two ways of looking at things, "mistake theory" and "conflict theory". Mistake theory claims that political opposition comes from a different understanding of issues: if people had the same amount of knowledge and proper theories to explain it, they would necessarily agree. Conflict theory states that people disagree because their interests conflict, the conflict is zero-sum so there's no reason to agree, the only question is how to resolve the conflict.

I was speechless. I am quite used to Mr. Alexander and his crowd missing the point on purpose, but this was just too much. Mistake theory and Conflict theory are not parallel things. "Mistake theory" is just the natural, tribalist way of thinking. It assumes an ingroup, it assumes the ingroup has a codified way of thinking about things, and it interprets all disagreement as a lack of understanding of the obviously objective and universal truths of the ingroup religion. There is a reason why liberals call "ignorant" all those who disagree with them. Christians used to be rather more charitable on this front and asked for "faith", which they also assumed was difficult to achieve.

Conflict theory is one of the great achievements of the human intellect; it is an objective, useful and predictively powerful way of analyzing human disagreement. There is a reason why Marxist historiography revolutionized the world and is still with us: Marx made a strong point that human history was based on conflict. Which is true. It is tautologically true. If you understand evolution it stands to reason that all social life is about conflict. The fight for genetical survival is ultimately zero-sum, and even in those short periods of abundance when it is not, the fight for mating supremacy is very much zero-sum, and we are all very much aware of that today. Marx focused on class struggle for political reasons, which is wrong, but his focus on conflict was a gust of fresh air for those who enjoy objective analysis.

Incidentally the early Chinese thinkers understood conflict theory very well, which is why Chinese civilization is still around, the oldest on earth. A proper understanding of conflict does not come without its drawbacks, though. Mistakes happen for a reason. Pat Buchanan actually does understand why USG open the doors to trade with China. Yes, Whig history was part of it, but that's just the rhetoric used to justify the idea. The actual motivation to trade with China was making money short term. Lots of money. Many in the Western elite have made huge amounts of money with the China trade. Money that conveniently was funneled to whichever political channels it had to do in order to keep the China trade going. Even without Whig history, even without the clueless idea that China would never become a political great power, the short-term

---

[296] https://slatestarcodex.com/2018/01/24/conflict-vs-mistake/

profits to be made were big enough to capture the political process in the West and push for it. Countries don't have interests: people do.

That is true, and should be obvious, but there are dangers to the realization. There's a reason why people dislike cynics. People don't want to know the truth. It's hard to coordinate around the truth, especially when the truth is that humans are selfish assholes constantly in conflict. Mistakes happen because people find it convenient to hide the truth; and "mistake theory" happens because policing the ingroup patterns of thought, limiting the capability of people of knowing too much, is politically useful. The early Chinese kingdoms developed a very sophisticated way of analyzing objective reality. The early kingdoms were also full of constant warfare, rebellions and elite betrayals; all of which went on until the introduction in the 13th century of a state ideology (neoconfucianism) based on complete humbug and a massively unrealistic theory on human nature. Roman literature is refreshingly objective and to the point. Romans were also murderous bastards who assassinated each other all the time. It took the massive pile of nonsense which we call the Christian canon to get Europeans to cooperate in a semi-stable basis.

But guess what? Conflict theory also exists for a reason. And the reason is to extricate oneself from the ingroup, to see things how they actually are, and to undermine the state religion from the outside. Marxists came up with conflict theory because they knew they had little to expect from fighting from within the system. Those low-status workers who still regarded their mainstream society as being the ingroup they very sharply called "alienated", and by using conflict theory they showed what the ingroup ideology was actually made of. Pat Buchanan and his cuck friends should take the message and stop assuming that the elite is playing for the same team as they are. The global elite, of America and its vassals, is not mistaken. They are playing for themselves: to raise their status above yours, to drop their potential rivals into eternal misery and to rule forever over them. China, Syria, and everything else, is about that.

Making Japan Great Again

2018-05-05 // japan, rightwingers, education, theory, history

The blog has been slow lately. Part of that is me being on Twitter, wrecking my long term IQ with short term dopamine hits. But man, those dopamine hits are good. If you're not following me yet, there's a link at the sidebar.

So anyway, one of the places I rely most recently for commentary is the online mag The Diplomat. It's some Cathedral foreign policy rag, apparently with some close relation to the Indian government. Lots of Indians shitting on China there, which is funny. But by and large it's a pretty standard Cathedral foreign policy rag, so if you want to know what USG, i.e. the compromise between the Redgov empire (the Pentagon and its foreign satellites) and Bluegov empire (the State Department and its foreign satellites) are up to, it's not a bad resource to follow.

Yesterday I took a look at their feed and they had this tweet, which I found hilarious.

https://twitter.com/Diplomat_APAC/status/988630863347945472

Seeing a picture of a woman academic I didn't bother to read the whole piece; I assumed it was a piece about the Abe's government long-discussed plans to nationalize college education. I thought some USG-supported feminist QUANGO had joined the plan and was salivating at the possibilities of extending Bioleninism in Japanese colleges. As it happens there's a #MeToo assault on Japanese politicians right now, and weaponized-vaginas agitating for leftist politics have been increasing a lot in the last year.

But I was mistaken. I got it backwards actually, the article is not about celebrating leftist agitation in Japan; it's panicking about that evil fascist Abe's early education policy. On hindsight it should have been obvious. "Make (country) great again" is Trump's phrase; as such it is tainted. Cursed even. Clueless provincials like Emmanuel Macron might have tried to appropriate it but that's not how the imperials in America do things. Puritans are about purity. You are not to talk about making things great again ever, as long as the English language exists.

So by all means read the article, which is interesting, as it does reflect a reality in Japanese schools. They have some low-profile Bioleninist academic in Japan, who says it quite bluntly: "Totalitarianism is a common feature of Japanese school education".

Of course throwing words like "totalitarianism" around means little, and it's not like this broad knows what totalitarianism is about, being a "sociologist" her job is not to read books. She's a political commissar, and as such her work does have value. Japanese education indeed has been moving right in the recent years. A couple decades, perhaps. And that is worrying if you work for the Left. It's her job to worry about losing power. Well, it's everyone's job. I can't think of any human trait more universal than worrying about losing power.

And yes, the left in Japan is losing power in Japanese early education. It used to be commies everywhere. And I mean real commies, actual card-carrying members of the Japanese Communist Party. They're still around, and still prominent in many school districts, but they don't own the school system as they should do. As I was saying, in the recent decades there's been a slow but steady pushback from the government, backed by some rightist organizations which have been lobbying for changes in the ideological orientation of early education.

On the face of it it's quite odd. Cthulhu always swims left, right? The history of the world, certainly the history of the modern world, is the history of the left waging war against the status quo and by their relentless vigor and sheer determination winning once and again. The Left always wins. The Left has been so victorious that you could make an argument that Left *is* what wins, it is change itself, the "Right" being just the hapless forces of reaction standing althwart at history and yelling "stop!". Not realizing that even if it stopped right there, the Cthulhu-truck had been driving left for centuries already. The position where it stopped would just happen to be wherever the Left was 5 minutes before. But that is the mainstream Right for you; those Leftists from yesterday who don't want to go further left.

It is of paramount importance to dispel the fiction that the Left and Right are both equal forces, armies fighting for their respective causes which are different in content but generally equivalent in size and culture. No, that's not how it works. There are no causes. There is only power. The Left is where the people who want (more) power flock to, and their ideas are contingent to that ultimate purpose. The Right are the people who do not want more power, either because they have some already or because they're just not into it. Risk-averse, perhaps. Whatever ideas people in the Right believe in are contingent to that ultimate purpose. To put it in military terms. Doctrines change. Strategies change. Weapons change. But the basic nature of war is universal.

That's the general theory, of course. I'm not a Platonist, but the above refers to some abstract, Platonic essence of Left and Right. Particular political groupings in the real world which get called "Left" or "Right" may differ somewhat from the definition; but that's just how language works. People put names to things, and somewhat the names stick through inertia for so long that the name doesn't refer to the same thing. But over time definitions tend to correct themselves. People learn words just once, then usage gets fixed and it changes much more slowly than its referent. As such people tend inevitably to associate the labels "Left" and "Right" which particular sets of ideas. And sure, there is some correlation. Some ideas do tend to universally to facilitate turnover of people in power. Say, universal rights to all humans. Other ideas tend to facilitate the Right's mission: stability of power. Say, the patriarchy. But that's all relative to the local language customs of a place. That's how words work; they are tools, who get made for a purpose, but then over time they are given other uses ("definitions") if the need arise. Problems happen when different people use them differently or when small groups develop their own idiosyncratic uses. That we call "jargon".

So to rephrase it again: In my theory, which you could call "neoreactionary theory" to give Moldbug his due credit, the Left is the forces of chaos, led by sociopathic status maximizers (SSM), while the Right is the forces of order. Outside the theory, the Left is whatever gets called the Left, and the Right is whatever gets called the Right in a particular place and time. There is of course correlation between the theoretical Left and Right and particular Lefts and Rights, but that correlation must be disentangled in every individual case.

So back to topic: does the Left always win? The theoretical always wins, at least since modernity, but in real world history, the left often loses. They lose the battle and go on to win the war. But battles they do lose. Particular real world Leftist movements do lose out every now and then. The death of economic communism in the West in the 1980s is a good example. Neoliberalism gets a lot of hate but there was a real danger of having state-planned economies and rationing in much of the West not that long ago. The Left did lose that battle. Or gun rights in the US: God knows the Left wants that gone. And yet it hasn't been able to.

The culture war in Japan is another example of Leftist failure. As I've mentioned before, many years ago when I first went to Japan I used to comment in the expat blogosphere there. There was this cool blog by American hipster types called Neomarxisme, written by a guy called David Marx. I wonder what became of him. I guess he's still in Japan; hipsters love Japan. Nobody else does. Anyway, as a hipster which loved the hipster side of Japan, Mr. Marx was quite worried about what he saw as a resurgence of Fascism in the Japanese internet. As it often happens Japan is the precursor of social trends that happen later in the rest of the world. A full 10 years before Trump, Japan had a full-fledged internet Alt-Right movement. And nobody understood why. David Marx and his friends surely didn't get it.

I did, though it did take me some years to understand it. Now of course I can fit my understanding in a wider framework, and relate it to general trends happening also elsewhere. The basic trend here was that the Japanese internet was full of people who were very nationalistic. In Japan a big divide between Left and Right is the question of patriotism, similar to Germany and for basically the same reasons. The Left thinks Japanese nationalism is this evil force which unleashed World War 2 which was this epitome of evil thing; thus modern Japanese must renounce their love for the fatherland and become all atomized universalist hedonists. Well not really hedonists, the Left would rather they all became lovers of communism and the Great North Korean Leader; but if hedonism keeps them busy enough consuming stuff to forget natural tribalism, then hedonism will do. The right in its most extreme form is for old-school chauvinism. Japan is the greatest nation on Earth, it's a Great Moral Power (yes they actually say so), and Japan dindu nuffin wrong in WW2.

While Japan didn't exterminate the Right like Germany did, the cultural consensus until the 2000s was quite firmly in the Leftist side of this divide. Your average Japanese in the 1970s, the prototypical Japanese boomer, didn't give a crap about the fatherland and didn't even know what this WW2 had been about. They were busy making money and listening to American music. Murakami Haruki is a fairly typical example of that milieu. If you have been unfortunate enough to read some of his novels you'll know his kind of braindead hedonist pervert. That's actually quite representative of his generation. If you have been fortunate enough to read some Mishima Yukio, you'll have noticed that he was desperate with how his beloved country of Samurais had become cucked to that extent. Mishima took a good look at the next generation (Murakami and his friends) and choose to stab himself with a samurai sword in front of TV cameras in a military base. That started to change in the 2000s. The mainstream media, TV and publishing industries and academia were 90% staffed by leftist boomers, so you didn't see any change over there. You only saw some of it in increased outspokenness of rightist politicians. And by far most importantly, in the internet.

The Japanese Internet is a really strange world, or it was in the 2000s. Japan never developed a blogosphere. The idea of writing for free just doesn't cross their mind; most people have neither the leisure nor the inclination of writing as a hobby. Why would anyone do anything for free? Those who can write and do not belong to a major media organization tend to issue mailing lists and charge $5-10 a month for them; which gets them some income if they're any good.

So where does one go to consume free content? 2chan. "Nichan" in Japanese. Absolutely everything interesting and funny to come out of Japan in the last 20 years has come from 2chan. So what is it? A website? Nope. 2chan is an obscure network which can only be accessed through a purpose-made Windows program. Think of it as a sort of reddit but much uglier and convoluted. There are many forums on a lot of topics; but you can't your start your own. It is completely anonymous, but the network generates temporary IDs; it also requires payment in order to post in some but not all the forums. It's really weird and I was never able to make sense of it myself. The Japanese relish in this sort of closed systems with weird rules to keep out outsiders. People think of Asians as bee-like collectivists, but they're not. Asian societies as a whole are by and large worse run than White societies. Asians don't work well in big groups. What they love is small groups; and to make sure the group stays small they come up with all sorts of bizarre and arbitrary rules, made up just on purpose to keep outsiders away and keep insiders loyal and invested. The Japanese are in my experience the worst in this. Even Japanese card games are abstruse. But hey, it works.

In a way it parallels the way that Thomas Kuhn said science works: first you establish a closed community of insiders. You make a lot of weird jargon that only insiders get. And once you have a coherent community of invested people, does progress happen. I don't know about that, but back to 2chan: it's the funniest place in Japan. It's jargon has been trickling down to wider society for years, a cottage of industry of blogs lives off exclusively of copying discussions from 2chan and putting them on the web; their traffic is huge. 2chan is, as everything in Japan, a closed network with bizarre rules, but it is free and anonymous. It is the only place where a Japanese can speak his mind. And what they say in 2chan is...

Fascism. Pure and simple fascism. 2chan is overwhelmingly a rightist place. Nationalistic, anti-immigrant, anti-feminist. In foreign policy the Left loves China and Korea and their domestic lobbies, while the Right hates them and wants to break relations, officially if need be.. They love anime and porn and prime minister Abe. They think that WW2 was awesome and that Japan should get a new Army right now. They get real mad whenever the Imperial army is slighted. Anyway, I could go on, but you get the point. It's not like they're all reactionaries who think democracy is a Western conspiracy agains the Son of Heaven. But there's enough red pills around in 2chan that saying women should marry at 15 year old and stay home like they've done since antiquity is not an uncommon opinion.

The funny thing is that only 2chan is like that. Japanese media is completely pozzed. Not to Western levels, of course, but they support leftist parties, argue against WW2 revisionism and for paying tribute to Chinese and Korean lobbies, have lots of homos around, and basically follow the slow attrition model of Cthulhu left-swimming that they always have. Japanese TV is like that: newspapers are mostly like that, with one exception (the rightist Sankei) and two typical cucks (Yomiuri and Nikkei). Academia is overwhelmingly leftist, often outright communist. And while there are many weird sects and associations in Japan forming a distributed conspiracy lobbying for rightist cultural points (the famous Nippon Kaigi et al.), they have close to non mainstream influence. They do have political influence and have managed to put some of their people in government, which is what the article linked at the beginning here was complaining about. Between 2chan and this weak conspiracy of housewives and retirees, the Japanese right has been slowly winning the culture war.

Now, don't think that these rightist masses populating the Japanese internet are nothing like the Western alt-right. They are not. I remember quite clearly when Satoshi Kanazawa, the evolutionary biologist in London became famous for writing in 2011 that by any objective measure black women are not attractive. I used to read 2chan back then and I expected the Japanese internet to come out in the defense of their countrymen who was so unfairly demonized for saying what should be an obvious truth.

But they did not. "You just don't say that. Why is this racist shaming the Japanese people abroad? Somebody get him shot or something, we don't need that". That was the almost universal tone of the responses, Some 10% or so did come out and say he was right. Japan does have its shitlords. But they are quite few of those who would expose any non-progressive ideas about race, individualism, or their Amaterasu-given right to not marry, not have a social life and spend all their money in anime-figures and Tenga masturbation-aids.

These are thus no trad masses defending the Japanese spirit. No. They are just as hedonistic and individualist as anyone else in Japan. But there are two things which they disagree on with the Left, and they will give no quarter about them. Women, and Immigration.

These are the only things in which Japan is at all different from any Western country. Japan has capitalism, brutalist architecture, alienated masses of hedonistic consumers with no religious affiliation whatsoever. What it doesn't have is feminist education, women doing slut-walks, fat women demanding to be complimented on their looks 24/7. And Japan doesn't have millions of dumb and hostile immigrants taking menial jobs from teenagers and filling up their prisons. And precisely because Japan doesn't have that, the Left has made its mission to introduce them in Japan. And that's where those internet masses, the 30-50 year old bored men in their bizarrely-structured internet forums have stood up, and said: No. Stop, right there.

Not that they will achieve anything. The National Review conservatives also stood up athwart history and yelled: "Stop!" It didn't. It just slowed down. Changed tactics. Turned down the fire burning the frog. Learned salami-slicing tactics. Japan doesn't have slut walks. But in just 10 years it has come from a country where a majority of married women were housewives to one where women work at Western levels, are increasingly present in high-level politics, and, who could've guessed it? are starting to agitate against sexual harassment. Big #metoo demonstration in Tokyo these days, I'm told.

As for immigration, Japan has more than 2 million foreigners working there, and it's steadily growing. They won't bring the yearly 200,000 brown men that the Japanese Business Association has repeatedly asked for; but they'll get there. To their credit, working conditions given to foreigners are so nasty that most of them end up leaving by their own accord way before their contract expires. US State Department reports, and those of their affiliated NGOs have been loudly haranguing Japan about this, so it could change with time, but I don't see Japan starting an immigrant welfare bureaucracy like Western countries have. They don't have the money.

Interestingly the most strongly held idea of the Japanese Internet is not opposition to feminism or immigration. Those are held-strongly but you can always feel a sort of defeatist mood, where they kinda understand they're fighting a losing battle. But the one thing they just love discussing is how Korea and China are evil and Japan should break relations with them. They are right about this.[297] South Korea and China have been extremely hostile to Japan in recent decades: and their lobbies in Japan, especially the Korea one, has been very influential. 10 years ago you couldn't watch Japanese TV without being lectured on how nice Korea is and how everybody should love them.

That has changed: the mood these days is extremely negative. Again, for good reason. But the thing is China's GDP is now more than double that of Japan. And Korean per-capita GDP is closing up with Japan's. Korean semiconductors have obliterated the Japanese electronics industry. Diplomatically Japan is without friends in its neighborhood, and its fading economic power means it is fast becoming a negligible actor internationally. Japan might hate China and Korea. They do hate them. But they won't, they can't stop 15 million combined tourists which come spend money in Japan. Oh, they complain a lot on the Internet about how nasty and smelly and rude they are. But they need their money. And that stings.

So you have a combination of revolt of the masculine masses against further encroaching by the International Left on the little pleasure left in their lives, and a generalized feeling of decline and powerlessness that leads many people to chauvinism if just to compensate. To this grassroots rightist mood, a small conspiracy of neotraditional cults has very effectively lobbied top politicians, bringing Abe and his ilk. Who have tried to deliver and bring up a Rightist movement. But their hands are tied. Japan is still a military occupied vassal of the United States. When the USA wanted Japan to sign TPP, they did, against the universal opposition of the Japanese economy. When USG asks for more feminism, Japan turns more feminist. Abe wants to restart his nuclear plants, but USG wants him to buy LNG from Qatar, so Japan spends all their trade surplus on that.

So what *can* Abe do? Change the school curriculum. That he can do. Tell babies left on kindergarten by their mothers who can't take care of them because they know have #metoo jobs that the Emperor is awesome and the nation is eternal. But can he do what he really wants to do? Reform the Constitution and establish a legally proper army? No. He's been trying for 5 long years, to no avail. He will likely step down this year, a defeated man.

---

[297] https://spandrell.com/2013/10/06/ghosts-and-diplomacy/

The imperial thing is a good analogy for the whole endeavor, as I wrote before.[298] The Japanese right wants to reform the Constitution and give some more meat to the Emperor's position. But the man didn't want it! He is stepping down next year, and his successor is world-famous as the cuck of all cucks, a crybaby liberal with a spendthrift and lazy wife who wouldn't even give him a son. And the Japanese government is cucked enough that they won't jump over him and give the crown to his brother, much more appreciated by the right. Oh, muh line of succession.

Abe has been trying to get his Rightist street-cred by being tough to China and Korea, but so what? Japan had 970k babies last year. China has 17 times that. North Korea has nukes; Japan doesn't. The only way Japan could recover even a little hope of being a rich and independent nation would be if Japanese women had more babies, but the trends are the exact opposite. Japanese feminism is growing partly as a result of USG pressure, and partly out of the increased bargaining power that women naturally get in times of decreasing fertility. I'll expand on that in some other post. But at any rate sex relations in Japan are getting worse, not better. Fascist education won't solve that. Because fascism is, at the end of the day, just the leftism of two weeks ago. Well, 90 years.

---

[298] https://spandrell.com/2016/08/16/the-will-to-not-power/

The Incel Question

2018-05-08 // women, incels, bioleninism, rationalists, cucks, theory, blackpill, Top Post

A couple of interesting things happened on Twitter last week. One was this:

https://twitter.com/robinhanson/status/990612769182507011

I'm a great fan of Hanson from years ago. Not of his weird sci-fi stuff, that I don't get. But his socio-psychology writing is top-notch. After an incel unleashed his Beta Rage killing several people on a van attack, the very word "incel" has reached the mainstream. And the normies are flabbergasted. What's an "incel"? Involuntary celibate? Like, some people aren't having sex? Well most male journalist aren't having sex either, at least by the soyboy-on-pajamas look of them. But they've been domesticated enough that they aren't unhappy about it. The thing about incels isn't that they can't get laid. It's that they dare to protest about it.

Mr. Hanson as usual didn't get the progressive joke. That's part of his charm, of course, it is his very cluelessness that pushes him to write, and to analyze well this kind of thing. But he's looking at things that the Left doesn't want him to look at; so he got burnt pretty badly. I won't link at Slate as a matter of principle, but Hanson is lucky that his patron is the dilettante, and secret Roissy/Heartiste fan, Tyler Cowen, and not some other normie academic.

Which brings us to this.

https://twitter.com/ekp/status/991817194987114496

As I was saying the problem that normies have with incels is not that they are losers for not getting laid. The problem is that they organize, that they gave themselves a name. That they have class-consciousness of a sort. Liberal states have "freedom of association" in their constitutions as a relic of the time they were fighting the old monarchies which wouldn't give it to them. And they wouldn't give it to them because "associations" are a hidden-in-sight form of political conspiracy, and any state which wants to survive doesn't admit political conspiracies. Try to gather 50 people in public in China and see how long it takes for police to ask what the hell you're doing.

Of course liberal states, i.e. Western states have freedom of association as a symbol of their revolution against the old order; but they aren't stupid. They don't really allow freedom of association. Ask Roosh what happened when he tried to organize a meetup of right-wingish PUAs. Ask any club or association of size that denies access to women;

or accepts only white men. The liberal state understands that only white men are potentially disloyal, and so any association of white men is illegal de facto.

Which brings us to incels: it's no coincidence that incels are now being discussed so widely. There's a huge question about incels. The current-year liberal state is based, as I've written at length, on the loyalty of biologically low-status groups of people. Bioleninism. White men, in white majority countries, are thought of as potentially disloyal given that their natural high-performance gives them other avenues of status-seeking.

What about incels though? Actually incels are a huge unsolved question in the Bioleninist framework. Many asked it in the comments of my Bioleninism essays: what about white leftists? What's their deal? I had actually meant to insert in the original essays a sizable analysis of the demographic represented by Scott Alexander. In the end I left them out because I didn't want to distract from the general theory; but now that incels are in the news, I've seen some people on Twitter discussing how to fit them in the Bioleninist framework. Which fills me with joy. Yes, that's exactly the thing that people should be doing. Bioleninism is out there, clearing people's minds, making sense of the world. Well, allow me to keep on helping.

Incels are, by and large, leftist. To the extent that some incels have organized qua incels, some of them have showed some mild disapproval over the progressive society which, well, prevents them from having sex. Something which 100% of their ancestors, every single one of them, was able to do repeatedly. But again, more broadly, the continuum that goes from 40 year old virgins to incels to married incels to literal cucks to average chumps, that is the Beta Masses of our societies are all loyal followers of the state religion. They are progressive.

And the smarter part of that demographic, the nerds, are enthusiastic progressives. It wouldn't be completely accurate to equate nerds with incels, but a vast majority of nerds are incels. Scott Alexander, which is a fairly representative member of that demographic, has been an incel for all his life, at least until his choice of medication rewired his brain to make a biological fact what was just a sad social circumstance.

Now this is an important point. Why are incels (or nerds at least) progressive? Where do incels fit in the Bioleninist structure? They are high-IQ white (I'll ignore the few Asians for simplicity) men after all. But... they are also nerds. Nerds are not high status. To they extent they existed in the past, they were never high status. The pre-modern world didn't have high schools, but extraverted early-maturing boys have been abusing the hell of introverted out-of-shape boys since social mammals first evolved. Probably since lobsters, someone ask Jordan Peterson about it. He won't answer my calls.

So anyway, a shortcut to understand Bioleninism is "a coalition of people who don't want high school jocks to rule the world". Which is the natural state of mankind, for better or worse. I wasn't a high school jock, but as a white man I'd rather they rule than the girls rule, so I am not Bioleninist. For the more awkward nerds in class though, they probably prefer the girls rule, out of some extremely misguided hope that the girls will be somewhat nicer to them. That's the vibe I get from Scott Alexander.

Or maybe it's just that nerds are awkward, know they are powerless, and so tend to obey whoever is in power, and since Bioleninism advanced after the 1960s nerds have just bent the knee and dropped to the floor and kissed the feet of Women and Africans and Muslims and whoever the fuck they're told to kiss. That's the vibe I get from Scott Aaronson. I think I'll regret defiling my blog with the following quote, but I guess it's better if you don't have to read the whole thing at his blog. I did write about him[299] before after all. Anyway, this is what Aaronson just published, in an hilariously misdirected defense of Robin Hanson.

Before going any further in this post, let me now say that any male who wants to call himself my ideological ally ought to agree to the following statement. I hold the bodily autonomy of women—the principle that women are freely-willed agents rather than the chattel they were treated as for too much of human history; that they, not their fathers or husbands or anyone else, are the sole rulers of their bodies; and that they must never under any circumstances be touched without their consent—to be my Zeroth Commandment, the foundation-stone of my moral worldview, the starting point of every action I take and every thought I think. This principle of female bodily autonomy, for me, deserves to be chiseled onto tablets of sapphire, placed in a golden ark adorned with winged cherubim sitting atop a pedestal inside the Holy of Holies in a temple on Mount Moriah.

Well, little chump, I don't think Robin Hanson is your ally.

At any rate, incels are leftist, either through mistaken affinity to the project of disempowering their chad tormentors, or out of sheer lack of spine. But none of this matters, and this brings us to Ellen Pao's tweet, who in case you are blocking embedded Tweets by some blocking extension said:

CEOs of big tech companies: You almost certainly have incels as employees. What are you going to do about it?

If you're not blocking tweets on your browser, here's one funny tweet of mine.

https://twitter.com/thespandrell/status/993045595286790145

The Bioleninist coalition is made of many parts, some of which are really hard to reconcile. Say, Muslims and homosexuals. But there's one combination which is way

---

[299] https://spandrell.com/2015/01/24/nerds-and-women/

worse than every other. Two groups which just can't coexist. Women and incels. Women hatred to incels is orders of magnitude greater than that of Muslims vs homosexuals. It is not just some vague disgust, or some religious commandment. No, women want incels dead, annihilated, out of the way, and they want it now. You see, the point of power is to get more of it. To get what you want. And what women want is hypergamy.

Hypergamy means that all women want the top men. The top 20%, the top 5%, definitions vary. Here's some data.[300] But even with the most generous definition, women see 80% of men as being completely out of consideration for sex. They just won't sleep with them. If they do (and they do every now and then for money or other motives), and other women find out, well that automatically means they're lower status, certainly lower status than women who sleep with better men. Not even sex really, the mere company of undeserving men is like a skin disease for women. It's like an old rag worn by a leper. The attention of mediocre men is low status itself, it defiles women in their own eyes. So it follows that if possible, mediocre men should disappear. Just die.

Incel men being the most mediocre among the mediocre, they are at the top of the list for things women want to eradicate. They just don't want them to exist. Wherever they meet them they try to make them disappear. You might have heard about "women in tech"; i.e. women trying to get nerds out of tech. Nerds protest. "We were here first! We built this from scratch!". Yeah whatever. There's money to be made, so women want in. Then they saw nerds there, and they can't help their instincts. Nerds must go. Women just won't live close to them; the same way humans don't like living close to snakes or rats. That getting rid of the nerds would destroy the whole ecosystem is secondary. When tech collapses after women chase the nerds away, women will just migrate to somewhere else, as if nothing had happened.

Robin Hanson got screeching calls to lock him up when he suggested that men with no access to women perhaps have good reason for being upset. Seems to me he doesn't understand how hypergamy works. He was accused of promoting rape and slavery. Which he denied of course, but feminists had a point. Women want hypergamy. For a woman to sleep with a man below the top 20% is by definition not consensual sex. It is thus rape. For a woman to work for or live with a man below the top 20% is by definition not consensual work. It is thus slavery. This is no joke.

When men get what they want; you get, well, Gengis Khan. What is best in life (for men)? Killing enemy men and taking their women. That is not a very stable situation but when men have all the power, which has happened now and then during history, the result is understandably not very agreeable for women. After all sperm is cheap and

---

[300] `https://web.archive.org/web/20180430011255/https://theblog`
`.okcupid.com/your-looks-and-your-inbox-8715c0f1561e`

eggs are expensive. The optimal strategies for males and females are adversarial. That's how it's supposed to be. That's how evolution works: conflict.

Well, what is best in life for women? What do women do when they have all the power? What is the female equivalent of Gengis Khan. We are finding out lately. It includes, obviously, complete privileges in every area of life for women. These two recent tweets were very illuminating. One complains that 19% of journalists killed were women. The other that 1 in 4 homeless are women.

https://twitter.com/framegames/status/993274599679954944

https://twitter.com/StefanMolyneux/status/993361737943482368

Well, say cucks, that means 81% of journalists killed were men! And 75% of homeless were men! What the hell are women complaining about? Well obviously they complain that there is even a single women being victimized, when it should be 0! When an Englishmen said that 10% of victims at something in colonial India were Englishmen, he was right to complain. We fucking rule this place, why should even a single of us have a rough time? That's what Indians are for. Well that's how women think. We are women; why should a single women have trouble? That's what men are for! There is no irony in this. It is only the cold logic of power.

And women have more power than they ever had. As I mentioned before; much of the power distribution between the sexes depends on the birth rate. The sexual targets of a man are, generally, women of his age or lower. The opposite for women; they are attracted to men their age or higher. Well, a declining birthrate means there's increasingly fewer amounts of women younger than any given man. Which raises the bargaining power of any given woman. Because every year there are fewer women being born to compete with her in the sexual marketplace.

When did men had a good time? In the 1950s to 1970s, when the birthrate was increasing and so every year more women were being born than before. Any woman had to shut the fuck up and be nice to men if she didn't want to be outcompete by the younger hordes being born every year. Now, though, it is the opposite. Women have the advantage. And they are using it. It won't be pretty.

The Past and Future of Korea

2018-06-14 // korea, history

So Trump just met Marshall or Chairman or whatever Kim Jong Un in Singapore.

I don't have any opinion on the meeting. Nothing substantial was agreed on. Seems to me nothing real happened at all. North Korea isn't going to give away its nukes. And USG isn't going to withdraw its troops from South Korea. Thus, nothing is going to happen.

The reasoning is quite simple. At the end of the day, North Korea is a small, poor, fairly inconsequential country 25 million people. It's birth rate appears to be close to 2, more than double that of South Korea, but still, it hardly matters at all.

Yes, it has nukes. But why would it give them away? Gaddafi gave them away. He was killed shortly after, as the evil fat women USG likes to employ laughed about it.[301] No way North Koreans with their 105 IQ are going to surrender their nukes. Not a good idea.

Unless USG packs and leaves South Korea, leaving the degenerate land of barren[302] K-pop whores and their long legs achieved through horrendous surgery open to domination by Kim Jong Uns soldiery. That would be a reasonable deal.

Which is not going to happen. The US military, or more precisely the military-industrial complex, as President Eisenhower put it, is today about half of the US power structure. It funds the larger part what Moldbug called Redgov, the Republican party and its appendixes. Redgov is the Pentagon and its friends. The US military being in South Korea means a lot of public money, a lot of budgets, a lot of salaries that US generals do not want to lose. These guys aren't going anywhere. The US military just doesn't leave unless forced to.

And certainly not today, when official doctrine is that China is America's Strategic Rival. We are in Cold War 2. Google it, it's already a thing. America is preparing for decades of juicy budgets to counter China and fight it in all fronts, so long as nukes aren't involved. Having troops in Seoul, 900 km from Beijing is just too good to just leave. It's an amazingly good strategic position. Not a single GI is going to leave, even if Trump really thinks he's getting a Noble Peace Prize, Which he isn't. Trump does not rule over the US military, and that is that.

---

[301] `https://www.youtube.com/watch?v=FmIRYvJQeHM`

[302] `https://twitter.com/Cicerone973/status/999210569247985664`

So again, my prediction is: nothingburger. China will lift economic sanctions over North Korea, the US won't, after Trump is gone USG will pressure China over North Korea's failure to denuclearize, and we'll be back to square 1. I really hope Temasek is getting some mining concession in Hamgyeong or the 20 million spent on this summit are going to look bad in Singapore's tightly held accounting books.

So all that said, I figured I might as well write a bit about how Koreans talk about themselves. We all talk about North Korea and South Korea. But surely you don't believe North and South Koreans talk of themselves like that? Of course not. North and South are just geographical adjectives we, ignorant foreigners use to make sure we know where each government is located. But the guys in the ground have access to millennia of history to come up with nice sounding words to justify their claim to power. After all, both Koreas claim to be the legal government of the whole territory. So of course they don't call themselves "North" or "South" anything. They call themselves the whole thing.

What thing, though? Surely they don't call themselves the same name? In English they do. The South is "Republic of Korea" while the North is the "Democratic People's... Republic of Korea". But that's not how it works in Korean.

Or may I say in Chinese, as Korean political words are almost exclusively Chinese words adopted in Korean, and that includes their own toponyms. All place names in Korean, North and South, with the very overt exception of Seoul, are Chinese derived words. That includes the name of the country, the names of all provinces and all cities. Most interesting of course is the name of the country, as that changes the most. Chinese-inspired polities tend to change the name of the state every time the dynasty changed. Modern Republics kinda count as dynasties, a fact which is often a matter of jokes, especially in China. The name of the country thus says a lot about the people who founded the government.

South Korea calls itself 大韓民國, 대한민국, Dae Han Min Guk. The first letter, 'dae' in korean, means big. The second, 'Han', is a proper name. Min-guk here is literally "common-people's country". It's an early Chinese rendering of the concept of "republic", and a rather elegant one. So South Korea is, literally "Republic of Great Han". On everyday speech it is shortened to 韓國, 한국 Han Guk, Han Guo in Chinese, Kan Koku in Japanese. "Han-land", sorta.

What is 'Han' though? Note that this Han has nothing to do with the Han of China's main ethnic group. That one is written 漢. South Korea is 韓. Zoom in, you'll see they're different. 漢韓. Tones are different in Chinese. No tones in Korean, so they do pronounce them the same, but such is life in China's area of linguistic influence.

So anyway, the Chinese letter which is now used by South Koreans to refer to themselves goes back to the Han state[303]) in warring-states era China, which was born of the dismembering of the Jin state in 403 BC. The Han state was somewhere between southern Shanxi and northern Henan in today's China, and while it wasn't one of the powerful warring states, it did give us the great philosopher Han Fei.[304]

Actually one can track the word back to an even earlier state, or rather a small fief given by the early Zhou Dynasty (1046 BC) to one of the many sons of the Zhou founder (the Warrior King, Wu Wang), which was located in... 韩城, the city of Han[305], which still exists to this very day, a small mountain town on the west bank of the Yellow River. Shaanxi province. Small towns having the same name for 3,000 years is one of the joys of the Chinese writing system.

So what does a Bronze Age walled town in the middle Yellow River have to do with post-WW2 South Korea? Their names are written exactly the same, 韓國. But that's about it. Obviously China's Bronze Age river town has precedence. 3,000 years worth of it. So why did South Korea took its name from it? That's a bit complicated, and fairly stupid if you ask me. Let me explain.

Korea is one of the countries with the least complicated history on earth. The country adopted Chinese statecraft early on, but Korean dynasties on average last longer than Chinese ones. Chinese states if lucky lasted at most 250 years. While the last two Korean dynasties lasted 500 years each (!). I think that's a record.

So anyway, as a unified kingdom Korea starts being a thing in 668. The first kingdom was called Silla[306] 新羅 (668-935), ruled by the Kim family, then came

Goryeo 高麗 (918-1392),obviously the origin of the Western name, ruled by the Wang family. And then came Joseon[307] 朝鮮 (1392-1897), ruled by the Li family.

As in China, a new dynasty changed the name of the country. So where did those names come from? Silla was the original name of a state in the South-west of the Korean peninsula. It then grew, and a smart alliance with Tang China got him the rest of the peninsula by 668. Nobody knows the origin of the name, nor much at all besides

---

[303] https://en.wikipedia.org/wiki/Han_(state

[304] https://en.wikipedia.org/wiki/Han_Fei

[305] https://www.google.com/maps/place/Hancheng,+Weinan,+Shaanxi,+China/@35.5856613,110.0873075,87302m/data=!3m2!1e3!4b1!4m5!3m4!1s0x36708106fd0aa7f7:0x846b27c0054461fb!8m2!3d35.476788!4d110.442846

[306] https://en.wikipedia.org/wiki/Later_Silla

[307] https://en.wikipedia.org/wiki/Joseon

that it was probably pronounced as "Sila" or "Sira" back then. Perhaps it meant something like "big city", which links to modern Korean "Seoul".

Silla was replaced by Goryeo, which got its name from the great kingdom of Goguryeo, a kingdom which was born in today's southern Manchuria in 37 BC, but eventually grew to conquer most of the northern Korean peninsula. They also founded Pyongyang, such as it was. As it happens the little evidence we have of Goguryeo's language suggests that it's more related to Japanese than to Korean, but it was a kickass warrior kingdom that everybody remembered fondly. And so when Silla was overthrown, new Wang family dynasty, who claimed descent from them, chose to recover the name for their new state.

So then after a good and eventful 500 years the Goryeo dynasty collapses, and it is replaced by a coup launched by this guy called Yi Seong-gye[308]. The background here is that as the Mongol Yuan dynasty, which ruled both China and Korea, collapsed, the recovered Goryeo dynasty tried to take advantage of the civil war chaos to win more territory from China. Yi Seong-gye was a Goryeo general, and he received the orders to attack Chinese armies. He thought it was a pretty stupid idea, so he came with a better one: he'd make peace with the Chinese armies and go invade the Korean capital instead. So he crossed the Korean Rubicon, and installed himself as new king in 1392.

Then he asked the newly founded Ming dynasty China if they'd recognize him, which of course they did gladly. He was the nice guy who had chosen to ally with them instead of attacking their armies. He then asked the Ming emperor to choose a name, out of a couple ideas, and the Ming First Emperor chose for him 朝鮮 조선 Joseon. Which is the name of a small kingdom, theoretically located around today's Pyongyang, which had payed fealty to the Zhou Dynasty way back in 1046 BC. So Bronze Age, again. The name was both ancient, Korean, and it symbolized the good relations with big bro China, and so Joseon it was.

So let's go forward again 500 years (how did Korean dynasties last so long I really have no idea). It's 1897, and the Joseon Dynasty is still around. Yi Heui is the 26th king in a straight line of Joseon kings. But it's 1897 already, it's the apogee of Western Imperialism, and it's also 2 years after the First Sino-Japanese war[309]. That war was launched by Japan explicitly with the aim of making Korea 'independent' from China. And Japan won, so it behooved Korea to take concrete steps to cut its traditional ties with China. Ties which had given it its name back in 1392. It took 2 years to convince the Korean king, who thought like many in Korea thought it was absurd to pretend to be diplomatically equal to China. Those 2 years included a series of coups, the murder

---

[308] https://en.wikipedia.org/wiki/Taejo_of_Joseon

[309] https://en.wikipedia.org/wiki/First_Sino-Japanese_War

of his queen, and an escape to the Russian embassy. But eventually in 1897 the Korean king made his mind. Same dynasty, of course, but new regime. And so new name.

What name to take, though? He couldn't ask China for one again. And he was still the king of the old dynasty, so he couldn't use his family heritage or something. He had to choose a new name out of the blue. And so after a while the Korean king, or I guess some of his ministers, came up with some old historical name which could fit the bill.

The original name, Joseon, had come from a Bronze Age Kingdom. Well, "kingdom", more like some chieftain and a couple hundred serfs. Way later in Korean history, around the first century AD, Chinese historians talk of a series of small chiefdoms in the southern half of the Korean peninsula. Specifically they talked of three: Mahan, Byeonhan and Jinhan[310]. The "han" part of the names was written phonetically, using different Chinese letters which sound like /han/, but eventually, and for no good reason, Chinese historians settled in using the letter 韓, which as I mentioned before refers originally to a fairly old Chinese fiefdom, and later a middle sized kingdom. It also happens to be a common surname. As for why those Korean kingdoms were called 'something-han', it's anyone's guess. The best scholarly theory seems to be that 'han' comes from the same root as Mongolian 'khan', i.e. boss.

So anyway, the reasoning here seems to be that the Korean king wanted a new name, he looked at the history books, couldn't find any name which hadn't been used before or that had any bad connotation, so eventually settled with this word which was kinda Korean so "anyway let's get done with this already gentlemen I didn't want to do this on the first place can I go home now?". The name chosen was 大韓帝國,대한제국 Dae Han Je Guk, "Great Han Empire". 'Empire' being also the formal titles of China and Japan and the time. So, equality, independence.

That was 1897. In 1910 Japan annexed Korea anyway and thought the whole thing was stupid. Under Japanese rule Korea was used by its previous name, Joseon (Chosen in Japanese). North Korea, being communist and down to earth, also calls itself Joseon. Well, the Democratic People's Republic of Joseon. China calls North Korea Chaoxian, which is the Mandarin pronunciation of Joseon.

South Korea though as a liberal democratic country had to do the virtue signaling thing, so they chose to signal that South Korea was a return to how things were just before the Japanese invaded. Just without the king. So South Korea chose the exact same name chosen back in 1897. Just changed a letter, "emperor" for "people". So instead of 大韓帝國,대한제국 it's 大韓民國 대한민국.

And that's the name today. South Korea has this weird ahistorical name, born of lazy Chinese historiography two millennia ago, but with a rich narrative of independence

---

[310] https://en.wikipedia.org/wiki/Samhan

and victimization. North Korea just keeps the old name of the 1392-1897 dynasty. China and Japan call each country by their chosen names. But of course North and South Korea *themselves* don't recognize the other's right to exist, so they call it by their own chosen names + north or south. <u>South</u> Korea calls North Korea, 北韓 북한 Buk Han "North Han", while North Korea calls the South 南朝鮮 남조선 Nam Joseon "South Joseon". China used to follow North Korean usage, not anymore.

Amusingly Taiwan and Hong Kong mostly follow South Korean usage, as good fellow USG vassals.

And yes, the Korean script, "Hangul" is Han-gul, Han letters. In the North is, you guessed it, Joseon-gul.

Long story short: history is fun, languages are different, and the difference allows for different ways of doing what everybody wants to do anyway: fight.

Black Swans of Common Knowledge

2018-07-11 // theory, china, power, psychology

As I write this, the news are coming out that the 12 boys trapped in 4km inside a cave in northern Thailand have been rescued, after having trapped in a cold, damp and pitch black cave for 10 long days until they were discovered, and another tense week when nobody really knew how to get them out. The rescue operation has been smooth, amazingly so.

The whole thing has been like a perfect movie. The setting is completely absurd. What were the boys doing there? Apparently the coach (apparently it's a soccer team) had a habit of taking the early teen boys hiking and exploring and doing boy-scouts kind of stuff. Which is fine; but why on earth did he get into 4 damn kilometres into an unexplored cave in the beginning of the raining season? What was he thinking? In some other place or time the coach would have been left to rot inside, and his whole family beat to death. In Japan today he would probably have to kill himself after he and his whole family are completely ostracized. The Japanese are quite amazed at how nice the Thais have been in general.

But again, like in a movie, the setting is not important. The drama afterward is, and this cave-rescue story has had all the necessary elements. The long search, eventually finding the kids. The kids being in good health, because their mysterious coach has taught them meditation (to 13 year old boys? come on). The international teams coming in, all rushing to find a solution. Discussing for several days what to do, with many giving up and saying the rescue could have to wait 4 months. Then the rains coming up, forcing everyone to find a solution right now. And the pressure worked; they found a solution: getting the kids full-face oxygen masks and bringing them out with two divers per kid, one pulling and one pushing them out. While looking for a solution one heroic diver tragically died, providing the necessary tragic scene to the movie.

There's even Elon Musk using the event to, of course, shamelessly promote himself, doing more harm than good[311], but of course any publicity is good publicity.

And now the kids are out. Happy ending. Which is good. Not because of the kids, mind you. Yeah sure, good for them. It wasn't easy to endure all that, and they came out safe. Good for them. But let's see the great picture. But 12 dumb boys and their dumber coach in Thailand are not something important. But the cave rescue story was so big, it attracted so much national and international attention, that everybody was

---

[311]   `https://www.abc.net.au/news/2018-07-10/thai-cave-rescue-elon-musk-submarine-wont-be-needed/9965698`

talking about it. And when everybody is talking about the same thing, that tends to have political consequences. That's how politics work, especially in our unfortunate era of mass communication.

"Thai authorities are trying to use [the rescue] for political gain," said Rangsiman Rome, a pro-democracy activist and leader of the Democracy Restoration Group. "Whoever saves the kids is going to be seen as a hero."

Thailand right now is in a tough spot politically. For over a decade the country has been torn between the traditional elite, based in the monarchy and the rich families from the capital, and a new movement led by some weird provincial guy called Thaksin who run a very smart political movement in which he pays rural peasants to vote for him, and he sticks it to the traditional elite in exchange. Every time the elite gets fed up with Thaksin and his party they stage a coup, rule for a few years, then run elections. Which Thaksin always wins. He will always win them. Why doesn't the Bangkok elite just pay the peasants 5 dollars more than Thaksin, I don't know. I guess they are cheap like that. Think they shouldn't have to. Schools are so expensive these days, you know.

Since 2014, a military junta rules the country, and it has wisely chosen not to hold elections just yet. As China becomes the largest trade partner of all countries in the region, USG has been losing control of Southeast Asia, so Thailand figured they could get away with that. In the Philippines they elected Duterte which has been telling America to fuck off since he got the job. Cambodia is an outright Chinese satellite. Myanmar has gone back to China since USG tried to force them to let themselves get killed by a local Muslim army.

But China hasn't been playing its hand too well. Its tourists are now everywhere, and well, nobody likes having too many foreigners around. Especially the Chinese, which are rude, crass, loud, and think they are hot stuff because they have money. They spend well, they don't screw the local women, they don't piss on the king's portrait... but they're kinda annoying. Most importantly, they move themselves and run the travel agencies, the bars, the hotels, the boats; basically every money that there is to make from the business, the Chinese will try to monopolize, and not let a single dime fall into hands of the locals. They do that in every business. The Japanese and Koreans do it too. It's good business, of course, but it's bound to anger your business partners. Especially if they are low-IQ, easy-going kind of people you find in Southeast Asia.

That was easily seen in the recent Malaysian election, when the party which had been ruling since independence lost the election, mostly because of anger against Chinese investment in the country, and the corruption it had enabled. The election upset of course galvanized all Westernized opinion. Democracy at work! Democracy is back! All that momentum is looking for a new target. Who is it? Not Vietnam, that's a communist regime. Not the Philippines, the guy just won, and he was the upset candidate in his time. Cambodia is now also using Chinese money to build a competent dictatorship. The obvious target is Thailand, which is formally a democracy, and a pretty lively one. The military junta has committed to holding elections next year, and opposition forces are mobilizing. The most promising candidate is a young 30-something billionaire. Which also looks totally gay[312]. Of course, the business of the Cathedral in 2018 is exporting Bioleninism.

Which brings us back to the 13 boys trapped in the cave. Who cares? Yeah, it's a good story. But let's say that Gnon rightly punished their stupidity and the boys had died the third day, and so been found dead after the long search. What would have happened? Absolutely nothing. Sad story, sure. The government would have made a statement, lamenting the news, calling for people to be more careful and not going to deep into caves. And that would have been the end of it. In a country where everybody drives fast motorbikes without helmets, 12 boys dying in a single day is not something uncommon.

40 people died on a boat accident in Phuket last week too. The news was huge in China, because most of the dead were Chinese, and yes, the operator of the boat was also Chinese. The Thais weren't interested in Chinese deaths, besides laughing at them, and the Western press isn't interested in Chinese deaths either, so that news is not consequential. It's not interesting, and so its not common knowledge. The 13 boys in a cave, though, that's a good story, and so it spread. It spread so much that it became common knowledge. And when something is common knowledge, people must have an opinion on them. You gotta talk about something, right? Conversation is a way to convey information, but there's only a real need for so much information most of the time. 90% of conversation is just a way of testing your peers and see if you can pick up some status from them. And that's the most basic form of politics.

The most important invention of the 20th century wasn't antibiotics, or the airplane. It was TV. The dumb box made everybody sit down and watch the same stuff, all day, every day. Why? Precisely because it gets everyone to watch the same thing, to have the same common knowledge. Suddenly everybody had something in common to talk about and play politics, big and small. Of course it's better if the TV has good, thrilling stories, like the Thai cave kids. But even if it hasn't. Or if the stories are fake, like all those soaps we love to watch. The thing is to have something in common to talk about, to coordinate around. Fuel for our social instincts.

And so as everyone in Thailand was worrying about the kids in the caves, opposition political parties such as the one quoted above starting salivating. If, just if, the Thai government botches the rescue attempt. Either through incompetence, or just because it's impossible to do; doesn't matter, only results do. If the government can't deliver

---

[312] https://www.dailymail.co.uk/wires/ap/article-5503965/Thai-billionaire-registers-new-progressive-political-party.html

and rescue those 12 dumb kids in the cave; a massive blame campaign could be launched, painting those 12 kids as innocent boys who were left to die by an evil dictatorial government. Many people would have agreed with that; after all they had been glued to their TVs and chatting non-stop about the cave kids for 2 weeks straight. Surely if the kids had died they would've felt compelled to reach some conclusion about it. Even if it had absolutely nothing to do with their lives, or with the quality of their government.

If the Thai government hand't delivered in rescuing the kids, it may very well have fallen. Which is crazy. Think about it. How many things are the responsibility of a government? Governments employ millions of people. They manage huge heaps of affairs, many of them extremely important. Food supply, the military, industrial policy, education, trade; you name it. A government should be judged by how it does the things it's designed to do. Not by how it manages to save 12 dumb kids and their dumb coach who in some fateful day as an election campaign was getting started, decided to go 4 km into a damn flooded cave.

Not that they can say anything like that, of course. Oh no, the government had to keep up good spirits. Thais, as one of the few peoples of the world which avoided colonization by Western powers, have kept much of their traditional culture, based on Theravada Buddhism in their case, so they are no strangers to public displays of nonsense. Everybody was praying for the kids, trying to be positive, lest one bad thought summon demons and cause harm to the poor boys. The government just announced that the kids, which were remember a soccer team, will get lifelong free tickets for their local soccers stadium, and a cash stipend to be paid immediately. Rewarding reckless behavior, you say? Shut up, you eeyore. Gotta be positive. The government's reputation depends on it.

You can see what happens when the government reputation is not on the line, even if the incident is arguably more serious. The Phuket boat which sunk killing 40 tourists; well that's pretty damn serious for a country where tourism is a big chunk of GDP. But the incident was Chinese people running a substandard operation, and the country's vicepremier said it openly. This is Chinese people killing Chinese people; it does not concern us Thais. He was pretty angry at the whole incident, and he showed it. He could do so, as there was little domestic attention on this incident. He later apologized[313], however, as I guess the Chinese embassy wasn't keen on the Thai government shitting on the source of half his tourists. Who do spend some money in the country after all, even if their countrymen try their best to capture all they can and ship it back home.

---

[313]   https://www.khaosodenglish.com/politics/2018/07/10/junta-no-2-sorry-for-chinese-ferry-deaths-remarks/

How does a government prepare against sudden black swans, random compelling stories which can draw the attention of a whole nation? You can't, really. You can do like China, and have a few million people controlling the whole media, and seeing that no story goes on TV or gets retweeted too many times before they've found a spin that makes the government look good. But that's a huge effort, and even China has chosen to co-opt stories instead of shutting them down as the irrelevant trivia that they really are.

But this instinct, the idea of using random events to test the mettle of a government is really quite ancient. Hell, the ancients actively sought random events, run them themselves, in order to test if a government was doing a good job. We call that divination. And of course there were always omens; particularly in China, any random weather or celestial event was thought to be a signal of Heaven's displeasure with the emperor. That's the psychology of common knowledge: if we have to take decisions in common, we must use things we all know about, such as the weather, or some ritual in which we all participated, as data for that decision.

People also want status, which makes any government inherently unstable. Everybody, or at least many people, want the king's place. Even if there's libraries upon libraries of law and custom saying that you can't take the king's place, the temptation is always there of trying to find some good reason to bring him down. Like, say, some big random event. Rulers after all, in our ancestral environment, when we spent time hunting and moving around, were not stable positions. Leaders in primordial human society exist because of a completely utilitarian calculus: rulers are there because they deliver the goods. They bring more meat, they defeat our enemies. Or they have awesome spells that make rain fall. Which don't always work if you think about it, but everybody believes them. That's what charisma is all about: the commonly acknowledged ability to deliver the goods, either proven, suspected or induced by propaganda. Biological variation and the nature of social animals make it so that having a leader to help the group coordinate and engage in collective action is incredibly useful, and some people will be more naturally suited to that leading role than others. But people will accept losing status to some guy only under very strict conditions. They must feel affiliated with him in some way, so that they can consider the ruler to be their guy. And he must deliver the goods.

Thankfully in this case Prayut and his guys delivered the goods, and Thailand will be spared of further turmoil at least until next year. The opposition of course cries "they're using the kids for political purposes". Of course! They were forced to, else that very opposition would use the kids in order to bring down the government. I'm sure neither Prayut not anybody in his government was happy about the huge problem the dumb kids had given them. In any pre-mass media society, the kids would have been left to die, and nobody would have cared, besides some locals who would have come with legends of cave demons one shouldn't disturb.

The BAP Trap

2018-08-26 // sexual deviancy, rightwingers

There's a lot of odd, deeply odd, profoundly strange things about modern society. Things that would make any hypothetical man traveling through time to our day from the past to have their heads explode in bewilderment. Perhaps one of the most salient characteristics of modernity, if not the most, is the presence of sexual identity groups. Sexual orientation, as they call it.

(This essay will be sprinkled with some completely random pictures and quotes I found on the internet to support my argument)

Traditional societies, according to the information they have, believe there are men, and there are women. Man and women marry and have sex (sometimes in reverse order) and have children and so on.

There are obvious differences in average behavior between men and women, which we can call masculinity and feminity. But there's also quite a lot of variation there, as in every single human trait, from size, to eye shape, to smell, to metabolism speed, you name it.

Now on sale at the #frogtwitter store.
A #HandsomeThursday mug --a great
conversation "set piece" and "opener"
for when thots come over

Some men are quite extreme in their masculinity. Some are rather closer to the middle of the spectrum. There's even some (a very little) overlap there. A woman in a million has a thicker beard than one man in a million. But still. Men are men, even effeminate men, and women are women, and that's it.

Now and then there are freaks who are *way* out of the spectrum. Again it happens in many other traits. Some men are taller than others, on a Gaussian distribution. Then a tiny few are midgets. Some people have more powerful legs than others. Some are born with a limp. Some men are manlier than others. Some are really girly. Some even pretend their are women or try to have sex with men. We call those homosexuals.

Bronze Age Pervert:

Heartiste has some good tendencies but someone eventually will have to address the cuckold/wimp-centered view of history you see in so many HBD (human biodiversity) writers like Peter Frost, Steve Sailer, and probably Greg Cochran. These are IT guys who have strong resentments of physicality and a weird relationship toward manliness (they all lack it, but where Frost seems to resent it, Sailer has some strangely erotic appreciation...still foreign though). They want to make the case that the white race or Western civilization is great because white men have evolved to be less masculine, more docile/tame, altruistic, cooperative, and possessing the sort of intelligence to do IT work or sit through an IQ test or do book-keeping.

Now that's quite of a problem. Sex is very important. Sex is the basis of society, the prime motivator, especially for men. Sex must be channeled and controlled if a society is to stick together.

Human societies reacted differently to the existence of homosexuals. Some ignored the issue, taking care of individually troublesome cases but generally ignoring the phenomenon as a whole. That's the case of East Asia. They're good at that. "If it stinks, cover it", as they say in Japan. 臭いものに蓋. It worked for them.

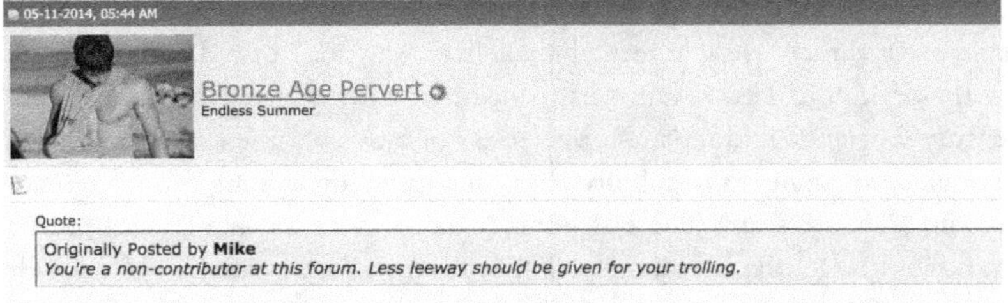

You were intimidated by superior power of the Brazilian stud. You wanted to submit to him...to be penetrated...used.

In others, perhaps a majority of human societies, behavior was given priority. So if a man insisted in having sex with men; well that's what women do. So you're a woman. Yeah, you might look completely like a man. Have male genetics, we'd say today. But if you behave like a woman, the looks aren't what matters the most. We'll take care of your appearance. And so in Iran, for example, homosexual men are forced by the state to undergo "gender reassignment surgery". That is, they try to shape them as much as possible into women, then given legal female status. And out they go. They aren't very good looking women, but there's plenty of unfortunate men around who will be happy to tap them now and then. They can't have babies of course, so marriage is not likely, but they'll have to accept their lot. The same way midgets do.

I do wonder what they do with obstinate lesbians, if there's some creative Islamic solution to have them to have penises. I suspect that given the legal environment, women who are into women find a way of not being too obnoxious about it. But I digress. Muslims, Indians, Southeast Asians, to my knowledge all take this sort of strategy. And it works for them.

In the modern West, for some reason, we chose to give appearance priority. So if you look like a man, you are a man. You may be very girly. You may like to wear female clothes. You may like dolls and make-up. You may talk like a fag. You may have sex with men. But if you look like a man, you are a man. A different sort of man. A gay man. Certainly not a woman!

The same applies to women who happen to behave like men. They aren't men. They are women. Just odd women. Lesbians, we call them. This way of categorizing outliers on sexual behavior slowly crystalized in the West around the liberal revolutions. So in a way it grow exactly with modernity, and as I argue here is indeed perhaps the most characteristic aspect of modernity.

I always loved the statues of the kouroi. I can safely say that upon viewing such statue by myself for three hours (someone let me in to look alone in museum), I was able to ejaculate without touching myself.

The operating principle here seems to be that choice of sexual partner is this one part of one's character, some kind of taste, not dissimilar from taste on food or drink. That men who have sex with men (MSM, as the medical bureaucracy puts it) happen to be effeminate in pretty much every aspect of their lives was not noticed very strongly, especially at the beginning. I guess it just happened that when gay men became a thing in 19th century England, middle and upper class homosexual men were socialized strongly enough into English masculinity that they just didn't come out as women trapped in male bodies. Oscar Wilde was homosexual, and he was kinda odd, but he didn't come out as being girly. For all the people of his time, he was just this bloke with weird sexual taste.

So perhaps because of this empiric lack of correlation among the elite (i.e. the people who shape the culture), or because Christianity doesn't contemplate sexual change, or because of Benthamite liberalism determining that all human behavior is about taste and pleasure and the most evil thing is to notice strange things about people's behavior (Bentham had good reasons to dislike people noticing his behavior); or perhaps because 19th century elites had low fertility and didn't want to lose the few boys they had even if they happened to behave like girls; at any rate, we in the West alone decided that homosexuality is about sexual taste, and not fundamental gender dysphoria.

Nor do I believe in the "miracle" that modern science has invented, hiding under the word "random mutation" and the hand-waving of "incremental change." There is not enough time, nor enough number of specimens, nor the kinds of "mutations" observed to support either natural selection or Lamarckianism as explanations for evolution. Many of the mathematical models for how a trait will spread in a population have failed — they don't tell you this." but then: " A healthy animal not under distress, not maimed, not trapped by man, seeks first when young: space. Animal seeks space in physical sense, territory. But this meaning isn't crudely physical, I give this as vivid image which is true for many animals that seek ownership of concrete territory. But more generally you must take it to mean something else, space to develop inborn powers.

Now this was a momentous decision. Never before in the history of the world, homosexuals, men and women, were given each a name, an identity. Names are no laughing matter. Names are socially approved categories. They are a social license to exist. Gay men now exist. Lesbians now exist. They never did before, but now they do. And since we gave them a name, Western society created categories of people where none existed before. And that has had very notorious consequences. Perhaps fatal consequences.

I should add that interpreting homosexuality as a sexual choice and not inborn gender dysphoria doesn't fit the scientific evidence we have, nor the historical evidence of what most of humanity has thought of the issue. For a very informative, and extremely readable book on the issue, look to Michael Bailey here[314]. Here's my take on the book[315].

I've always been attracted to filth and dirt, because something in me knew intuitively that it is only in the underseam of life as it exists today that you find the real "lacunae," the "holes" where its reach is limited or weak. I always sensed there was some real freedom in the blackest of red light districts among whores and junkies, perverts, and worse, with whom I've always chosen to take my dinners when I had the chance. I like the stories they told me, some showed letters from delusional Spanish engineer who wanted to marry her, another told me story of miscarriage her friend had in old pervert's bathroom, and how they flushed it down a toilet and then its name written on a piece of toilet paper.

Whatever your take on what homosexuals are and how they came to be, one thing is clear, by their own admission. Gay men generally want to have sex with heterosexual

---

[314]   https://www.amazon.com/Man-Would-Queen-Gender-Bending-Transsexualism/dp/0309084180

[315]   https://spandrell.com/2014/08/14/the-science-of-sexual-deviancy/

men. But heterosexual men by definition won't have sex with men. So homosexuals have two choices here. They can undergo a sex change, either surgically complete (as they enforce in Iran), or some half-way (as its easy to see in Thailand), and try to convince heterosexual men to take them as women. Or they can give up on heterosexual men and have sex with fellow gay men.

Neither choice is very satisfactory. Most homosexual man can't pass as an attractive woman, even after extensive extensive surgery. And sex with fellow effeminate gay men requires industrial amounts of LARPing, having to make oneself look like a tough man when they really want to wear dresses, and empirically not a small amount of drugs. It is a tough life either way. No good solutions. It must be irritating, which is why gays tend to look irritated and often driven into extreme self-harming behavior.

> They were true artistes: take, for example, Periander of Corinth. This man's name means literally "superman." At no point in his life as king of Corinth did he restrain his lust for the darkest paths: it is said he copulated with his mother, that he violated his wife's corpse, and much worse. He had all the boys on the island Corcyra castrated. And, having done all this, he was memorialized as one of the Sages, or Geniuses of the ancient world. A philosopher and a poet, he wrote an epic on the mysteries of nature… that showed themselves to him alone on afternoons when the long shadows make the blue-green shores of those seas whisper to ears ready to hear. He supported also the art and philosophy of others in the state, but only out of a careless generosity: I was there at his court, I played the harp and he once threw a well-used courtesan in my lap with a gesture of disdain.

Lesbians have it easier, if only by women having a much lower sex drive. Pretty women are out of reach, which sucks, but heterosexual women are much more open to persuasion in general, so it's orders of magnitude easier to get an average girl to date a lesbian than it is for a normal man to have homo sex. Women are just more into LARPing as a general rule, and as real manly lesbians tend to be much fewer than homosexual men, lesbianism seems to be an out of control mass-LARP game of women trying to play a game that nobody remembers who started and has actually very few real players in it.

Again, the key point here is that homosexuals don't want to have sex with each other. They want to have sex with heterosexuals. Which won't, by definition. The logical solution here would be for homosexuals to change their sex, which is again a very old and empirically attested solution practiced in many societies.

Nevertheless in spirit I would say even now the European has much more in common with the African than with the "Asian," meaning the inhabitant of the broad swathe of land stretching from Han China to the Near East, that includes the long-settled farming serf regions of the planet. I know many dorks who fetishize IQ above all else will disagree with this. The Orient and Asia has always been the enemy…Africa is mostly irrelevant. The "African" may even be an ally and only became a problem under conditions of modern mass democracy, when he has been manipulated and stirred up by others. 3

But mandatory sex-change has its drawbacks. You look like a freak, for one. And letting homosexuals keep their bodies unchanged also has many advantages. Not in the sexual realm, sure. But gay men in modern society get to choose whether to share their sexual choices. They may not come out of the closet, as we say, and just pass as a normal heterosexual man. That has many advantages. They get thus to dwell among heterosexual men; which they supposedly enjoy. And they also get to function as an effective secret society, helping each other covertly, promoting each other in jobs, giving each other businesses, covering each other's backs. Blackmailing each other. The Gay Mafia. It's a real thing.

They also get to influence men, persuading them into behaving in ways advantageous to homosexuals, while ostensibly offering advice as just one more man, one who happens to have a peculiar perspective on things.

> Some things make my blood boil far more than a direct physical challenge might. I once left the gym and some Chad came up to me and started to feel me up. Then I discovered he was feeling up my pockets, was trying to see if someone stole his missing stuff. I found this very amusing. Maybe was postworkout and I was very calm, but was not offended by this, partly his manner was not obtrusive despite what he was doing. It was possibly a form of muscle worship.

It is by no coincidence that gay men are extremely overrepresented in political parties or in the mass media, or as public intellectuals. Perhaps the enjoy the rather effeminate nature of the jobs' activities (talking a lot, sounding pompous, frequent parties and public gatherings, gossip and conspiracies, etc.). At any rate they are everywhere, in a way which would not be possible if they were forced or strongly induced to change sex. Although ladyboys are everywhere in Thailand too, so who knows. But still, stealth obviously has some advantages, enough advantages to make the rather unnatural and contradictory gay-man lifestyle be bearable for them.

Note that the same applies for lesbian women, perhaps even more so. Lesbian women have been extremely active in influence operations since more than a century ago. The case can be made that every single feminist movement was started by lesbians, for two purposes. One, to push society to allow them to behave as men, which is what they crave by their own nature as women born with masculine brains. The second, perhaps unintended consequence, is to push women, by persuading them to advocate feminist causes and raising their standards of acceptable male behavior, to become so unfeminine, annoying and obnoxious to men that no men can bear their companionship, and thus drive what were perfectly fine and fertile women into the arms of lesbians.

The populations of Europe and Japan, under the strain of life in high population density in the late 20th Century, chose to limit their fertility, and there's nothing wrong with this: it is the governments, corrupt and under the lash of financiers dependent on population increase, that forbad a natural retrenchment of population.

Note that women weren't just fooled by a small bunch of tiny lesbians. Well, they kinda were, but they were fooled for a reason. It's like the old argument about the Jews hijacking Western society with their socialism and other destructive theories. Well, yeah, but you need two to dance. Jews sold a product because there was a market to it. Lesbians too sold their feminism because there was a market of eager buyers. The arguments were quite compelling, and they came with perfect timing, just as the modern industrial economy was giving women more economic opportunities, and thus more bargaining power versus men. And the lesbian feminist arguments were very useful for women at a moment they wanted to increase their bargaining power. And you can't blame them for it. Everyone wants to get a better deal.

On hindsight, the war has been extremely destructive to both sides, but that's the nature of war. Humanity has been waging war forever, knowing perfectly well that it is destructive to both sides, but we keep fighting, because one side at the beginning often think it has much to win.

The frogs are to reclaim the great expanse of the land through scouting groups, in awe of pristine nature and their own bodies and daring! Form scouting groups use Wandervogel as model! #HandsomeThursday

5:41 AM - 10 Mar 2018

Now of course this this doesn't absolve lesbians (or Jews) from blame from selling toxic ideas. Every society has conflicts and contradictions of some sort. But the infighting tends to be limited by traditional norms of conduct which go by the personal ties between people. A highly motivated, hostile outside group can break that traditional balance, selling ideological drugs in a market which might be open to it, but also traditionally expected some restrain from the suppliers. When the suppliers, not being an integral part of it, are motivated to destroy society in their benefit, that breaks the traditional balance of debate, and chaos ensues.

You might be asking yourself now: sure, there is a stealthy Gay Mafia, notoriously in politics or the Catholic Church. But while lesbians have been indeed obviously (if not quite openly) agitating for feminism in academia and literature, what have gay men been advocating for? Sure plenty of them have been openly advocating for gay rights, "pride", sometimes even for legal changes to allow pederasty and other abhorrent behavior. But where have gay men been stealthily nudging heterosexual men into their camp, using cleverly packaged rhetoric that seems to increase the bargaining power of men, the way lesbians have been trolling heterosexual women into feminism as a pathway to lesbianism?

I will elaborate on the next post. On the meantime there are some hints hidden here, somewhere.

The Wars of the Sexes

2018-10-22 // women, theory, history, Top Post, demographics

What do Bronze Age Pervert and Brett Kavanaugh have in common?

https://twitter.com/bronzeagemantis/status/1044336637801615360

Not a lot. One is a nudist bodybuilder, a tropical Nietzsche who wants to burn the cities and reduce women to breeding stock. The other is a pasty Irish Catholic Yale graduate who was pretty much a virgin until his marriage at age 40, and to this day can't help crying like a girl when referring to the women "friends" during his life who gave him the slightest amount of attention.

Imagine these two guys in the same room. Would they get along? I don't think so. And yet here we are, in this strange world where not only BAP, but millions of people in and outside the internet defending this Irish cuck and his all-female team of legal clerks. So what's going on?

Let's talk about the Women Question (WQ). The WQ is the realization among a few select men of intelligence that female emancipation has been a complete and utter disaster for civilization. What started rather innocently with giving limited economic rights to women (having a bank account, inheriting property) has spiraled in less than two centuries into a full fledged war of the sexes, making life miserable for hundreds of millions. And most importantly, depressing the birth rate of the most valuable people on earth.

It used to be that genes for better strength and health, for higher intelligence, for physical beauty, made you leave more offspring, while the unfortunate carriers of genes that made you unhealthy, ugly or stupid were unable to reproduce themselves. Well not anymore. The best people on earth today are all, thanks to the open sexual market of all against all (the *extension du domain de la lutte* of Houellebecq's first novel) brought by female emancipation, squeezing themselves into big global cities, competing for status in a non-stop rat race which makes family formation impossible. They thus fail to have babies to inherit their precious genes, wasting them into these massive IQ shredders which dominate the modern world. I called them IQ shredders[316] as IQ is the most pressing concern (no IQ no electricity, folks), but it's really shredding all the genes of excellence that mother nature has spent millennia making for us.

---

[316] https://spandrell.com/2013/03/26/lee-kuan-yew-drains-your-brains-for-short-term-gain/

This is not exactly a race thing, as it's genes for excellence themselves which are being wasted in the global status rat race. It's not just Indians or Africans outbreeding Whites. It's the worst blacks and the worst Indians outbreeding the best of their kind. The first ethnic group to literally go extinct due to feminism won't be any European people: it would be the Parsis, long the highest-performing ethnic group in the whole of India. They are actually going extinct because their women would rather take PhDs than make babies. And they do that because women don't actually like most men. Women are wired to like the top 10-20% of men, "top" meaning bigger, stronger and more violent. It's how it works in most mammals, you can't argue with 500 million years of evolution. Hate the game, not the player.

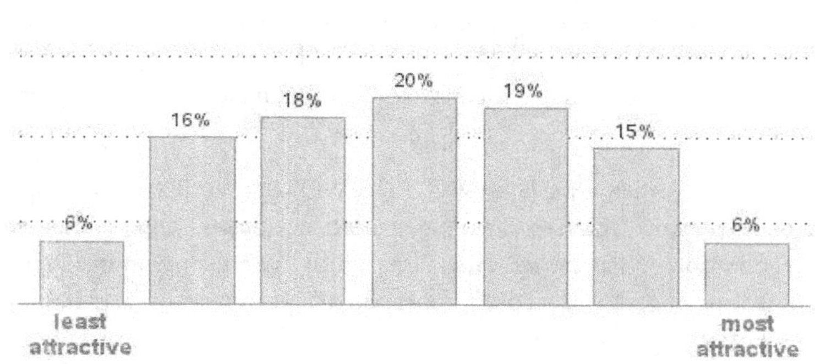

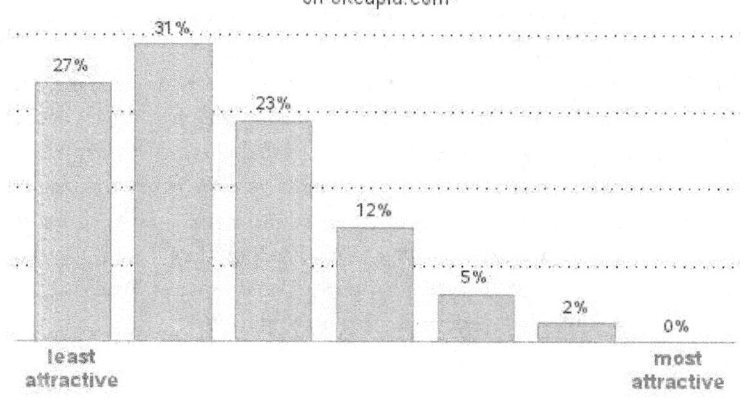

If you think this doesn't concern you, you're wrong. The whole Western world is slowly morphing into having the demographics of Brazil, roughly half white, half black. But Brazil itself is shedding its best people. The next step there is South Africa, 10% white. But again we know what's going on with South Africa and their planned dispossession of its white population. You know what comes after South Africa? The endgame is Haiti. If feminism isn't stopped and reversed, the whole world will be Worldwide Haiti (WWH). Now think of that.

So what do we do? Opposition to feminism has a long history, but as feminism advanced from demanding equal rights to achieving effective supremacy, more and more men are noticing what's going on, and are growing apprehensive at the dispossession of the male sex and the likely coming of Worldwide Haiti. I see four kinds of reaction to late-stage feminism.

1. Surrender. Marry, have children, live a life of enforced domesticity, take the risk of your wife destroying your life unilaterally on a whim, taking your assets and your children. Maybe you're lucky and you get a good woman. Or maybe you actually enjoy domesticity.It's not an ideal solution for most men, it doesn't solve the evil of feminism; but it does produce children, so credit where it's due, we should thank the sacrifice that these men do for the future of our peoples.

2. Quit. Men going their own way (MGTOW). The Japanese innovated here, as usual. In 2-chan they call live as a beta man today (80%+ of men) "playing in hard mode". What do you do if you just can't beat the game in hard mode? You quit and run a different game, of course. You buy a pillow with your favorite anime character of a 14 year old nymphomaniac with H-cup tits and a 10-inch waist and proclaim her your wife on your favorite internet forum. Not a solution, and really fucking disgusting on times. Withdrawal from the sexual market tends to make people into ambiguous freaks. At any rate it doesn't help at all. This is a "you can't fire me, I quit" kind of move. If you couldn't get laid anyway, you aren't quitting the sexual market, you have been fired. Withdrawing into a fantasy world, while an understandable instinct in some cases, doesn't affect the sexual market equilibrium in the slightest. Betas are just invisible to women anyway, getting out of sight just makes it easier for them.

3. Play the game. When playing a game in hard mode, some people quit. Some people take the challenge and master it. In the sexual game, they learn Game. Seduction techniques. Become an alpha, what women want. You read Heartiste[317], go on learning how to pick up women. Pump and dump. It's a risky game to play, but rewards are high. If the man is so inclined it might lead to a successful taming of a woman and the production of good children. In other cases it leans to decadence

---

[317] https://heartiste.wordpress.com/

and long-term misery. It's not an ideal solution, in that it doesn't quite solve feminism, and in fact provokes women into further escalating their demands for supremacy in order to rein down on men. Remember, women don't want "good men". They went the statistical "best men". They just want the top 20% alphas. Faking an alpha is a short terms solution that only leads women to recalibrate their algorithms to come up with a new 20%. But hey, as pointless as it often is, as a man I can only respect the man who takes up the challenge and beats the game in hard mode.

4.   Now I don't know how to call this strategy. I could just call it the BAP strategy. Or the Mishima strategy. Maybe call it Retreat, Regroup and Entice. Strategic Withdrawal. Or Sexual Cannae. Perhaps the best name would be the Mannerbund Strategy. Ever since the Industrial Revolution broke the equilibrium of the sexes in the civilized world, and brought men into the cities and into wage labor, plenty of people have deplored the effect this had on men, becoming effeminate and weak. Amusingly many of those who complained have been homosexual, as the leaders of the German Wandervogel in 19th century, or Mishima in 1960s Japan, or Jack Donovan in present America. This makes sense; homosexuals like real, strong men, even more so than women do, give their higher sex drive. While Bioleninism has been taking care of homosexuals of late, in a purely sexual way, homosexuals are the biggest victims of the dispossession of men and state-mandated effeminacy since the 1800s.

Of course not all of the strategic withdrawalists have been homosexuals; Nietzsche obviously comes to mind. At any rate, their idea is that men should recover their masculinity, go back not to pre-industrial times, but to the heyday of manhood, the culture where were not only in charge, their were heroic, and even beautiful. Ancient Greece. The Greeks just didn't saw much of a point in women, for them men were just perfect, got things done, were fun to be with, and were beautiful to see even. Women were annoying and not even that good looking. So what Greek fans argued is that, if women are gaining power and annoying men, men should withdraw, live together, form *mannerbunds* and do their own manly things. Have fun and stop caring about women   at   all.

That's fine and all. And in the 1920s and 30s, these male aesthetes were in some way responsible for the uber-manly fascist movements in Europe. The Nazis, and especially their armed forces, the SA, were full of crypto-homos such as Ernst Röhm. And they carried the day; Europe was this close to fall into communist horror, and it was only the handsome paramilitary armies of the post-Wandervogel boys that saved Western Europe from communism. So cheers to them. Homos saved Europe from communism once because they found mass rallies of armed muscular men arousing. And... then they were   purged,   with   long   knives.   Cheers   to   that   too.

While mannerbunds sound like real fun, they're not quite clear on how that solves the feminism problem. Well yes, Mannerbunds are different from omega MGTOWs in that the latter are invisible to women anyway, but the former, by the sheer size and hardness of their abdominal muscles, have a way of making women crazy[318].

But still, getting women horny doesn't solve the issue of producing quality babies if you don't actually go through the trouble of impregnating them. Which you can't in any civilized country, not if you want to stay in the mannerbund, given women's legal power to enforce serfdom to the genetic father of any of her babies.

While I sympathize with the idea, and hope history remembers me as the man who provided the theoretical justification for destroying IQ shredders and salting the land, for better or worse, we don't live in the Bronze Age anymore, and omegas married to their pillows are likely to be more useful at Razing the Cities through their knowledge of programming or nuclear engineering than Mannerbund Aesthetes with expertise in ancient art history.

The question remains, though: what can we do? How do we prevent Worldwide Haiti? Bring back the patriarchy? A subset of strategy 1, marriage, is trying to recreate a patriarchy inside an isolated society. A well known example is the Benedict Option, by religious-shopper Rod Dreher. The idea is that people should isolate from mainstream progressive society and try to pull a medieval Benedictine hill monastery kind of trick, and do their own thing in blessed isolation. A long but insightful review of the book by veteran blogger Handle can be found here[319].

The Benedict Option is a really misleading naming for what should have been plainly called "The Amish strategy". Because that's what you need to keep your women in control. The Amish have a patriarchy alright. They even get progressive journos sent to document how evil and patriarchal they are. But they are left alone, for some reason. Doesn't mean any neo-Amish movement starting from scratch would be. And that's assuming any woman born in our feminist supremacist society would actually join in. The Amish are already there, after all, and nobody's joining them.

The patriarchy only evolved in places where the local ecology made necessary the hard labor of men for survival. Places where women couldn't feed themselves. Places with

---

[318] https://www.vox.com/2018/6/1/17396182/jordan-peterson-alt-right-religion-catholicism

[319] https://handleshaus.wordpress.com/2018/09/10/excerpts-and-discussion-of-rod-drehers-the-benedict-option/

cold winters. Places where you needed granaries to store food for the winter, and men to guard those granaries from enemy peoples. In those places men got to rule, because what were women going to do anyway? They would starve and freeze without a man.

And so a system was set where every single women was subject to a man, either her husband or her father. Sexual access to women (and her labor, which was often quite useful at home) required a lifelong contract, or else. Now some patriarchies allowed polygamy. Europe didn't. But the general point that women were subject to men was respected; and that was what kept most men with skin in the game, willing to contribute their productive labor to society at large.

That was just a function of the economy. There's plenty of places where women can feed themselves without men. Warm, tropical places. You don't have patriarchies in those places, unless a northern tribe conquered them and kept it by cultural inertia. You never get a matriarchy, women are never physically strong enough nor organized enough to rule over men. But you do get matrilineal and matrilocal societies: places where women do their thing, feed themselves, fuck who they want, and interact with men mostly on the women's terms. The Chinese call one of these matrilineal hill tribes as having 走婚, walking marriage. Because the women live all with their womenfolk, sex happens when a man walk to the woman's house, screws her, and then leaves. The kid belongs to the mother's house, the couple can break at each other's whim (though there'll plenty of nagging and gossip in the village), and the guy may or may not feed the child depending on how much of an asshole he is. He usually is.

That's how society worked in much of Africa and Southeast Asia; women lived in their own villages, fed themselves. Men live with other men, have their cool mannerbund where they dress up and decorate themselves and work out and fight a lot, come and go to women's villages now and then to exchange food and sex. Of course it's not that easy going; it's heavily ritualized with festivals and ceremonies and so on, and sex pairings are supposed to be exclusive unless something goes wrong. The late Henry Harpending had a great writedown[320] of this sort of societies, and how men and women relate to each other in the absence of a pressing need for marriage, as in winter societies.

That's where we're moving now. That's the sort of society that arises when women can feed themselves. Of course our societies today are much worse than that. During the transition to a female-centered society, women want to have it both ways: they want the freedom of a tropical society, but they also want the amenities of a patriarchal civilized society. Every day they see their standard of living dropping as men refuse to marry them and pay for women's lifestyles, women nag and cry about how evil men are. Well, that's how it works. You can get to chase Chad to your heart's content. You

---

[320] ```https://the10000yearexplosion.com/human-cultural-diversity/">had a hilarious write down```

already do, and it's been a thing in tropical societies for tens of thousands of years. But what you don't get is to chase Chad and get Dad to pay for it.

https://twitter.com/Cicerone973/status/1045813263152422912

Matrilineal societies have reasonable fertility rates, even today, so the total collapse of sex relations in modern civilized societies is probably more a function of the slow motion breakdown of the patriarchy and women knowing they're screwed either way, than just a function of female choice. Women do like babies. They just want to have yours. And they want to travel too. And have a career. Aah! I can' even.

Can we go back to a patriarchy? We could. I guess the Mannerbund proponents envision a small army growing steadily, first a dozen kids, then one hundred, then one million, then revolting, razing the cities, conquering the world. That would work.

Absent that, though, capitalism is here to stay, female labor is 90% bullshit but still 10% useful. Most importantly, food is cheap. Women can feed themselves either way. They didn't like the patriarchy, they won't go back without force; force that men just don't have the organizational power to apply. The alphas are having a lot of fun, after all. A solution would be to flank the female army and come up with some technological innovation that made frontal engagement unnecesary. Embryo selection and CRISPR could again, in a few decades, produce quality babies without having to fix sex relations. Artificial wombs could make Brave New World a reality. Worldwide Haiti could be avoided, good babies produced and neither men nor women would have to cope with lifelong marriage, which let's be honest, 80% of men nor women don't really enjoy.

That's assuming that advanced civilization stays in a more or less stable way. In that case the breakdown is here to stay. If some big fat SHTF moment happens, if there's widespread collapse, then all bets are off. An old school patriarchy would have the upper hand there. But it would have to be solid, have a strong religion behind it. A new religion, perhaps.

Patriarchal Sexual Law

2018-10-29 // china, history, women, redpill

We live in a world of sexual license. Sexual freedom we could say. You can sleep with whoever you want and neither state authorities, nor most people, will interfere with your sexual life. You can even engage in the most unnatural, disgusting and disease-inducing activities; but criminal law just has nothing against you.

This alone is a sign that the patriarchy doesn't exist anymore. Patriarchies are systems in which all women belong to a man; the husband after marriage, the father before that, or the head of the household if she's a servant of some sort. Women have this uncanny ability to make men want to have sex with them, and at the same time prefer to have exclusivity in that matter. Not to mention the potential for disease or childbirth. So naturally their legal guardians had to take care that women, i.e. their property, was not captured by other men to have sex with them without proper compensation. As such, law regulating sex in the pre-modern period where every bit as complicated, and as harsh, as laws regulating finance and property in our day.

Imperial Chinese law on marriage is a lot of fun, but most interesting are their laws on fornication. Fornication belonged to criminal law, ever since the very first complete legal code on compiled during the early Tang Dynasty in 624, which has remained to us as the 唐律疏義 *tánglü shūyì*. More importantly, rape was understood as fornication + force, a more serious crime but nothing really different. The difference is stark between a legal code which lasted pretty much intact for 1300 years, and our present day of female supremacy, when rape has been reinterpreted every few years as the single most heinous crime that can be committed, while at the same time requiring no standards of proof.

What follows is a translation of the legal code of the Qing dynasty (1644-1911), the 大清律例 *dàqīng lülì*, tome 33. I have the book but you can find the text in Wikisource[321].

犯姦 Fornication

凡和姦杖八十 . Any fornicator gets 80 strokes of the big stick.

杖 *zhang* was a big wooden stick with a flat surface, the worst of two available corporal punishments. It was normally applied to the buttocks or the back. If done strongly it could kill a fit man after 50 strokes or so. The traditional maximum was 200, so it was

---

[321] https://zh.wikisource.org/wiki/%E5%A4%A7%E6%B8%85%E5%BE%8B%E4%BE%8B/%E5%88%91%E5%BE%8B#刑律·犯姦

usually never applied that strongly. Bribes to the executioner in advance helped make him feel weak that day.

At any rate, 80 strokes for peaceful, consensual fornication is a lot of strokes. 80%+ of the sex going on in any modern society is fornication. Think about that.

图四　对犯人执行杖刑

有夫者杖九十. If there's a husband, 90 strikes.

Obviously any consensual fornication with a woman with a husband is morally worse than if the woman is single, so you get 12% more strikes of the big fat wooden bat.

刁姦者[無夫有夫]杖一百. Seducers get 100 strokes, whether the woman has or does not have a husband.

> 刁姦 supposedly meant getting to fornicate on false pretences; the man (or woman, I guess) getting to seduce the other part by lying about its attractiveness or something. 100 strokes to you for lying.
> -

強姦者絞. Rapists [literally "forced fornicatiors"] get hanged. Not immediately, most death penalties were done after review on autumn. But rapists got hanged, period.

未成者杖一百流三千里. Attempted (but unfulfilled) rape gets exile to 3,000 li away.

> A li was a bit more than 500m during the Qing (set at 576m around 1900), so about 1,700km away. -

凡問強姦須有強暴之狀婦人不能掙脫之情亦須有人知聞及損傷膚體毀裂衣服之屬方坐絞罪 This is commentary to the law: "All cases of rape require proof of violence, and proof that the woman couldn't get away. Also they need someone in the know (i.e. a witness) and damage to the skin [of the victim] as well as her clothes, in order for the penalty of hanging to be valid."

若以強合以和成猶非強也. If intercourse starts as forced but ends as consensual then [it means] it wasn't forced".

> Important point here. Very important point. Again this is commentary later added to the law. I wonder what case(s) prompted this to be added.-

如一人強捉一人姦之行姦人問絞強捉問未成流罪 ""If one man forcibly captures [a woman] and another man rapes her, the rapist gets hanged. Attempted rape gets exile"

又如見婦人與人通姦見者因而用強姦之已係犯姦之婦難以強論依刁姦律 If a man sees a woman fornicating, and because of that rapes her, it's unfair to argue it's rape, and so it's sentenced as "seduction". So rape of a fornicator gets you 100 strokes of the rod, not the death penalty. Hey, she was in the market after all.

姦幼女十二歲以下者雖和同強論. Fornication with a girl below 12 years old gets treated as forcible (rape), i.e. hanged, period. Not unlike what Anglo countries call "statutory rape".

其和姦刁姦者男女同罪. In case of consented fornication and seduction, men and women get the same penalty.

姦生男女責付姦夫收養. If fornication results in a birth, the male fornicator must raise the child.

姦婦從夫嫁賣, 其夫願留者聽. If the female fornicator is married, her husband can sell her to someone else, or keep her if he so chooses.

若嫁賣與姦夫者姦夫本夫各杖八十婦人離異歸宗財物入官 If she is sold to the male fornicator, the fornicator *and* the cuck husband each get 80 strokes of the big stick. The woman is sent back to her father and her property is impounded by the government.

強姦者婦女不坐 Raped women have no punishment.

若媒合容止[人在家]通姦者各減犯人[和刁]罪一等. People who promote or provide lodgings for fornication get the same punishment as fornicators, with one degree less. So 70 strokes of the big stick instead of 80.

[如人犯姦已露而代]私和姦事者各減[和刁強]二等. People who, knowing fornication took place, do not denounce it to the authorities and instead helps the parties reach a private agreement, get the same punishment, with two degrees less. So 60 strokes of the big stick.

This part is important.

其非姦所捕獲及指姦者, 勿論. If someone claims there was fornication but didn't actual caught them in the act, there is no crime.

若姦婦有孕[姦婦雖有據而姦夫則無憑]罪, 坐本婦. If a female fornicator is pregnant, she alone is punished. After alone, there is proof of her deed, but not of the man's.

Again, you needed proof, which wasn't easy to come by. After the main articles come some further detailed regulations.

條例

一、凡職官及軍民姦職官妻者， 姦夫、姦婦女並紋監候. If a public official or military man fornicates with the wife of a public official, both male and female fornicator hang.

若職官姦軍民妻者， 革職， 杖一白的決. If a public official fornicates with the wife of a military man, he is fired and gets 100 strokes of the big stick, [maximum penalty]. In this case the sentence had to be executed, he couldn't evade it with money (as normal penalties could).

姦婦枷號一個月， 杖一百. Fornicating military wife must carry the cangue[322] for a month, and 100 strokes of the big stick.

---

[322] https://en.wikipedia.org/wiki/Cangue

The cangue was a square made of wood with a hole for the head, or sometimes the hands, which people couldn't get off. It's basically a very funny way of making everyone know you're a criminal. In this case a huge slut.

其軍民相姦者，姦夫、姦婦各枷號一個月，杖一百. If two military people fornicate, they get the cangue for one month, and 100 strokes of the big stick.

其奴婢相姦，不分一主，各主，及軍民與官員，軍民之妾婢相姦者，姦夫姦婦各杖一百. If two servants fornicate, whether they belong to the same master, or have different masters, as well as when military men fornicate with the concubine of a military men or a public official, both fornicators get 100 strokes of the big stick.

- Note that simple fornication between free people was 80 strokes. -

凡有輪姦之案，審實，俱照光棍例，分別首從定擬. For cases of gang rape, after investigating the truth, officials must follow the Thug Regulations, and sentence separately the leader of the gang and the followers.

> The Thug Act being apparently Qing Dynasty official jargon for a special law for hoodlums and petty gangsters that the dynasty set up pretty early on. A principle of that law was to punish gang leaders with immediate beheading, and followers with deferred hanging. I guess the idea was to get the followers to rat on each other with the hope of having their death sentence annulled before Hanging Season started in the fall. -

The following article was about 雞姦, literally "chicken fornication", which my dictionary tells me means "sex between men". That I think is matter of another post.

My classical Chinese isn't perfect and my legalese is even worse, so if there's any error please let me know. But I think my translations are decent. I hope you get the gist of the law. Sex happens within marriage; period. If you must fornicate, at least take care that nobody knows or cares.

China's CRISPR babies might have wasted our last chance

2018-11-27 // crispr, acceleration, china, eugenics

Yesterday I woke up to this piece of news:

https://www.technologyreview.com/s/612458/exclusive-chinese-scientists-are-creating-crispr-babies/

Chinese Scientists are Creating CRISPR Babies.

Hilarity ensued. This guy, Hè Jiànkuí 贺建奎 , professor at China's Southern University of Science and Technology, with good, manly posture, was bringing the future to our time.

I was feeling weird already. But then this other bombshell happens.

https://www.apnews.com/4997bb7aa36c45449b488e19ac83e86d

Babies are already born! Twin girls, Lulu and Nana. Which are quite standard names for Chinese girls today, even though that sort of name would've sound like prostitutes 50 years ago. But I digress.

The mad scientist who had created the first CRISPR babies out of the blue, in secret, just like that! Had set up a Youtube channel[323] where, in lousy English, he explained his whole project. Look at him here. His posture is not so good in the videos.

---

[323] https://www.youtube.com/channel/UCn_Elifynj3LrubPKHXecwQ

https://www.youtube.com/watch?v=MyNHpMoPkIg

His procedure involved knocking down the CCR5 gene, supposedly giving immunity to AIDS. The guy went out of his way to denounce the use of gene editing (he branded his procedure as "gene surgery". I'm just this doctor doing surgery, you see) for purposes of improving IQ. "That should be banned!" he said.

Oh man, we were just getting excited at the possibilities here. Immunity to AIDS? Getting AIDS is not a real concern for most people at all. Who cares about homosexuals really. Why is this guy using what might turn to be the most consequential technology in the history of mankind just to make life easier for homosexuals? And why is he bragging in English on Youtube? Which is banned in China. And why is his email in Gmail? Which is banned in China? Isn't this some kind of secret Chinese government project to produce SuperHan?

Short answer is, no. Long answer is: we were all getting excited as state media (People's Daily, The Paper, etc.) reported on the news on a fairly neutral tone. Those pieces were deleted a few hours later, as it surfaced that He Jiankui didn't make the CRISPR babies through his university research. Oh no, he had gone rogue, cooperating with a hospital called Harmonicare,[324] 深圳和美妇儿科医院. A maternity hospital, owned by the infamous, and I mean infamous, Putian hospital conglomerate. 莆田系.

If you search for the news in China, you don't get "ethics" or "horror" or "brave new world". No, all you get is "Those fucking Putian guys have gone crazy!!", again and again, and again. If this had been a state-run project, nobody would be saying anything. Yes, some western educated scientists would protest. But the mood would have been "oh, wow. Cool.". That was the general reaction of 90% of people when they first read the news, before the details started to trickle down. But once the Putian meme was out, most people in China wanted to grab Mr. He and tear him down to pieces.

He Jiankui must have known what he was getting into. He took a 3 year leave from his university post in February, supposedly to focus on this CRISPR baby project. The university has promptly disowned him, and 122 biologists come out asking[325] for his imprisonment. China has started an investigation. It's not looking good.

Putian is a small town in coastal Fujian province. There's nothing special about it, besides them being Fujianese, and thus a bunch of cutthroat money-grabbers with no sense of ethics and morals. Yes, nobody likes the Fujianese, especially in China. For some reason the Putianese have a virtual monopoly of private hospitals in China; or at

---

[324] https://www.hm91.com/

[325] https://www.sixthtone.com/news/1003265/first-gene-edited-babies-prompt-official-investigation-in-china

least that's what people in the street will tell you. Supposedly they created a good political patronage network under Jiang Zemin in the 1990s, and since then, no private hospital can get an operating license in China if they're not part of the Putian mafia.

Having a monopoly, and being (again, that's the stereotype) genetically evil, the Putianese run hospitals are famous in China for outrageous prices and making up diseases so they can do expensive surgery to cure them. Allegations of baby theft and organ trafficking are also common. Again, I don't know how true. I assume that the prices are high, and yes, unnecessary surgery happens, so the anger they have caused through those two things have escalated into Putianese doctors eating babies for breakfast and selling the organs to the Jews or something. Again, true or not, the street believes it, and that is newsworthy indeed.

It surprised no one that He Jiankui did his research through a Putian-owned hospital. Those guys will do anything for money. The question, however, remains: is this for real? Did he really pull it off? People on Twitter are saying they were classmates with the guy, and he was a physics major who only got into biology recently, no way he has the skill to pull this off. This could be just some marketing ploy to get fame for the Putianese IVF clinic he is now working for. Again, everything is fake in China. The Chinese will tell you so themselves.

I don't know what to believe. If CRISPR babies are real, this guy is in trouble. If the babies are fake, then this guy got into real trouble for no reason at all. Yes, he got his Youtube views, and some fancy videos where he speaks in English. But what he did is kinda illegal in China; and while China enforces its own laws when it wants to, making an international scandal of THE MOST IMPORTANT TECHNOLOGY EVER is pretty much the one thing that will trigger government attention in China. I hope for his own good that he's just some mad scientist who went rogue.

If he is a fake, he's gonna spend a long, long, long time in jail. All in exchange of 3 lame Youtube videos. If so, shame on you, He Jiankui. You are the dumbest guy ever, and you'd have brought shame on a great technology which could delay its application to humanity for decades. Decades which we don't have, at this rate of IQ shredding.

China was kinda ok with gene editing, but by associating the technology with the most hated institution in China, he could very much have forced the hand of the Chinese government and have it effectively banned for good. The future of humanity may have just died by the intersection of a greedy hospital, a vain scientist and social media.

Say it ain't so, He Jiankui. Better be true.

Interview on Bioleninism

2018-12-27 // Top Post, theory, status, leftism, power, democracy, history, bioleninism, hbd, loyalty

A few weeks ago, a great artist who runs the blog Parallax Optics[326] was kind enough to ask me for an interview on Bioleninism[327], to follow up on a great piece[328] he published recently where he interviewed the man responsible for the Twitter account Woke Capital.[329] That interview was great, and I had never done an interview before, so I thought it could be a good idea to try this new format. As it happened, the interview went great[330], and I very much enjoyed the process.

What follows is the whole text of the interview for those who missed it up at Parallax's. Let me use this chance to wish everyone a Merry Christmas and happy year end holidays. 2018 has been a quite eventful year. Hopefully it has been good for you personally as well (unlikely if you're invested in the stock market, but nobody's perfect). A lot has been going on in the reactionary sphere, much of it good. Bioleninism has become a widely known concept. Here's for a great 2019.

Bioleninism has widely been acknowledged as perhaps the most important contribution to reactionary discourse in recent years. It represents a coming together of several strands of your political analysis / theory. How did you first arrive at the concept of Bioleninism, and what specific influences / texts helped shape the theory?

Well, it's been a year now, and my episodic memory is pretty bad, so I can't really trace my thought process that clearly. I remember I had been discussing with some fellow reactionaries about the "Crazy Glue" concept, the question of what on earth it is that sticks the many different parts of the modern left together. The coinage comes from Steve Sailer, and his idea was that the different factions of the left, the "Coalition of the fringes" he calls them, are united by hatred/envy of white people, especially white men.

---

[326] https://parallaxoptics.wordpress.com

[327] https://spandrell.com/2017/11/14/biological-leninism/

[328] https://parallaxoptics.wordpress.com/2018/11/12/on-woke-capital/

[329] https://twitter.com/wokecapital?lang=en

[330] https://parallaxoptics.wordpress.com/2018/12/11/on-bioleninism/

I tended to agree with that formulation, but it's very rare that I disagree with Steve Sailer at all.

This fellow reactionary, though, pointed out that hatred only takes you so far, you can't really run a political coalition on just hatred. You must deliver some goods, even if abstract. The way he put it is that the coalition of the fringes is united by their very reasonable assumption that whatever social status they enjoy today in Western society is due to political power of Progressivism; and that if Progressivism were to fall, they'd all be back picking cotton, or barefoot in the kitchen, or freezing in the shtetl. It is this rational fear that keeps strange people like gays and Muslims together on the same side of the political divide.

It made a lot of sense, and it got me thinking. Not all leftists hate white people per se; even if they do today, I remember a time when they didn't. They could feel some envy and resentment, but hatred? After all, what is hatred? Hatred like any emotion is motivated by something. Hate is useful when directed towards targets which you can fight and plausibly win. There's no point in hating someone who can crush you and make your life miserable. So, hatred towards white people today seems to have been orchestrated from above, it's the result of a political campaign. That got me thinking about what kind of power or mechanism got this coalition together; the history behind the Left. That has long been one of my core interests.

I also remembered 10 years ago when I used to read Lawrence Auster's (RIP) blog. He used to have a commenter, a Canadian anarchist Jew, who would write to Auster and tell him how he got Muslim associations to sign up for gay marriage and other leftist causes, which had to be completely abhorrent to any Muslim. But he did, in a very business-like way.

At the time I was listening to the Revolutions Podcast, which is somewhat pozzed, of course, but explains in a very realistic way the complete and utter mess that liberal politics was in the early 19th century in Europe; how every little splinter group was out there fighting for himself, with no organization or loyalty whatsoever. I also had in mind some stuff I'd been reading on old Chinese imperial politics, how the court used eunuchs and minorities to keep the very fragile imperial governance working. The collapse of imperial politics in 1911 led to another complete mess as the Chinese gentry failed to build a cohesive movement, and China remained divided until the half-assed Leninism of the Kuomintang, and later the proper Leninism of the Communist Party, built a cohesive state by privileging the unprivileged.

So, comparing in my head the experience of building a workable polity in China from scratch, with how the left evolved in the West since 1950, two words just came to me. Biological Leninism. I put that as a title and started writing my post. I write like Houellebecq writes: no plot, no plan, just start writing semi-unconsciously and see what comes out of it. Sometimes it works great; other times I just start to ramble and have to rewrite again and again. It took me months to finish that one, and I was not too satisfied with how it came out. But it was very well received, which was great.

Central to Bioleninism, is the insight that humans are hardwired to seek status more than they seek happiness / comfort. Therefore, as a powerholder, your best strategy to ensure ongoing loyalty is to promise individuals / groups an uplift in status, tied to the success of the Party, which exceeds what they would have 'naturally' achieved within a merit based social order. Can you expand on the role of status as a currency within the Bioleninist system?

Status is well understood, we all know how it works, as it's the basic input of social life. But it's not a very well defined term, there's still work to do there. Status basically means whatever motivates people in any society once they have ensured the basics of survival. You could define it as "that which makes people want to become your associate and give you preferential treatment". The particulars depend on the culture you live in. If you live in a commercial society, status is mostly about money. If you live in a hunting band, it's mostly about hunting ability. If you live in a magical cult, it's mostly about ability to summon the spirits. If you live in a communist society, it's mostly about political favor. And so on.

If you're King, who do you want as minister? The Duke of Orleans, who has more money than you do and a plausible claim to the throne if (God forbid) something was to happen to you? Hell no, you want a guy who is going to follow your orders, someone reliably loyal. And who is going to follow your orders? Somebody who has no better options than following your orders. It's quite simple.

If you're in a free capitalist society, with freedom to acquire and dispose of wealth, status is going to be linked with the ability to earn wealth in the market. That is not a good situation to be in if you're the King; you basically have no power over people's behavior if the status assigning mechanism goes through the economy and not the state. Over time, the states of the world figured this out, and either went Leninist, thus abolishing the market altogether and controlling access to status from above; or they went hybrid, like in the West. The West allows a private economy, through which a lot of status is assigned; but the economy is heavily regulated, so the state gets a say in who gets what amount of money. And of course, there's also a wide propaganda system which includes the press, mass media and education. What we call the Cathedral (or the Polygon or whatever), in short. We can also just call it The Left.

The Left isn't formally the state, it's its own network which overlaps heavily with the permanent arms of the state proper (i.e. the bureaucracy) but is also larger than the state. It also spills over to other entities which aren't formally part of the state, but which are under its influence. Say education. Some of it is part of the state, i.e. public, but a big chunk is private. It doesn't matter, the social networks of public education workers are connected to private education workers, and so they all have the same opinions, marry each other, promote each other, etc. The same applies to the media, and increasingly to sheer capitalism companies, as we are seeing with Woke Capital[331]. Managers of big companies have been integrated in the same social networks as the bureaucracy and so they are basically the same social class. Again, they marry each other, have the same opinions, etc.

A lot of critics have said that Bioleninism is not real, the most wealthy and highest status people are still white men, black people are still poorer on average, etc. And of course, to the extent that in the West we still allow market forces, we still have a merit-based allocation of status. But everywhere else, wherever the Cathedral has any decision power: in public propaganda, in entertainment, in government hiring, in education: all of those are completely committed in giving status to *everyone but white straight healthy men*, in direct proportion to how different they are from white straight men. They give status in the form of hyping up in propaganda and cultural broadcasts they control (black surgeons on TV, female pilots, women with hijab in fashion ads, black history month, gay pride, whatever), and in preferential hiring for highly-paid sinecures and positions of influence. Again, that used to be mostly getting hired for some make-work job in the bureaucracy, or some professorship of Grievance Studies, but now they're increasingly moving into the corporate world, HR being a well-known reservoir for politically connected people.

Does Bioleninism function primarily by raising the status of low-status groups as a whole, or only the members of these groups who 'officially' join / pledge loyalty to the Party? Do you perceive a two-tier effect, whereby it raises the status of those who join the Party, but those that possess the inherent qualities of the group also get raised up / receive the benefits of protected characteristics, as part of a halo effect?

It does both, indeed. Black history month isn't about any individual black person; gay pride isn't about any prominent gay Party member. But the Left doesn't have infinite resources. It can't give a job to every black person in America, let alone on Earth. It can barely scrap enough to give each woman an Obamaphone to get her to vote on election day. But that's the good part of the trick: you don't need to actually pay cash to every single voter, in a Bueno de Mesquita sort of system. You can pay them with propaganda, telling them white people owe them because of slavery or colonialism or implicit bias, praising them 24/7, teaching in college about some Timbuktu pile of mud being the world's first University, or women having invented whatever. You as a person of a low-performance group may not have a fancy job and make 6 figures, but

---

[331]   https://parallaxoptics.wordpress.com/2018/11/12/on-woke-capital/

the people with the megaphones are shitting on your enemies on TV, and that sort of effort merits loyalty. You're certainly gonna vote for that guy and not for the guy who says you should be picking cotton or eating sand in Arabia. It's a modern twist on the idea that the meek will inherit the kingdom of God. And who knows, maybe some day you do get that fancy job, or if you're eloquent you can leverage your oppressed status© into YouTube fame or something. Maybe a seat in Congress!

You have described Bioleninism as a top down phenomenon, just like Leninism. Can you expand on the mechanics / incentive dynamics of the High and Low against the Middle, and why the Cathedral selects for loyalty over competence / ingenuity?

In any hierarchy, your enemy is the guy immediately below you. Because he wants your place, and he's close enough to come get it. A good example of this is dynastic politics. Who's the king most afraid of? His brothers, as they could take his place. The Ottomans famously had a period during which they enforced fratricide before any succession. The very existence of brothers was too big a risk. Chinese dynasties alternated between sending brothers far away to the provinces and keeping them under a form of house arrest in the capital.

To the extent that keeping your own position (your social status) depends on the loyalty of your underlings, everyone, everywhere, selects for loyalty over competence. No manager is going to hire a guy who's going to take his place and make him lose salary or status in the company hierarchy. No company owner is going to hire a guy who is likely to end up starting a competing company and put him out of business. No way. He can be a genius who'll make all the money in the world; but as a manager a subordinate's loyalty is the foremost concern. Only once loyalty is secure you can start to select for competence. So again, the ideal subject is not a genius. It's a genius who has nowhere else to go. There's a curve between loyalty and competence but it bends to the side of loyalty. It's better to have a mediocre 50% guy (provided he gets the job done) who's gonna stick with you, than a smart 70% guy who's gonna run to your competition. I'm sure many readers have seen versions of this phenomenon happening in their workplaces.

Same reason why every housewife wants a 40-year-old Honduran nanny instead of a 20-year-old Ukrainian, too. Given how human sociability works it's a miracle that competence gets rewarded at all. Once I understood this I stopped wondering why it took so long for humanity to develop science and industry.

How does the problem of *Imperium In Imperio* animate Bioleninism? To elaborate further, Moldbug discusses at length the problem of divided sovereignty – divided Power does not want to stay divided, it has a centrifugal attraction, pulling it back together, like the shattered pieces in Terminator 2. I wondered what your thoughts were on the problem of divided Power / *Imperium In Imperio* specifically in relation to the structure of Bioleninism: how the problem / fact of the divided, mendacious, un-formalized nature of Power in the West gave rise to something that looks like / is structured as Bioleninism?

It animates Leninism per se. In a way, it's the fundamental problem of politics. The way I described it in the original post was as the vengeance of Absolutism in an era of demotic politics. Power doesn't want to be divided. Power wants to be absolute. That's not only because there exist sociopaths among us; there's a perfectly innocent yet powerful motivation for power to want to be absolute. See, in my view the fundamental law of the universe is status-conservation. People don't want to lose status. Hence the guy in power doesn't want to lose power. Ever. And his children don't want to lose status either. In order to achieve status conservation for himself and his family, he pretty much needs to have power forever. In order to do that you have to stop other people from taking you out; which is hard to do, as they also want power themselves, again, sometimes out of sheer greed, but sometimes because they need to hold a more defensible position in order to achieve status conservation for their families. So, given enough time, power always tends towards concentration.

Given the restrictive mess that was feudalism, Absolutism was a way of doing away with all restrictions to monarchical power. When lesser nobles, merchants and country lawyers beat absolutism in Europe, they came up with liberal constitutions which made the division of powers into the basic principle of government. The result was completely unworkable, any decision by one power got blocked or stalled by the others. But given that all the powers of the state were occupied by the same sort of people (i.e. country lawyers), things got done by informal networking. I'm quite sure that this informal bypassing of legal limitations on power was what motivated Marxists to focus so much on "class consciousness". It's a really powerful thing, and Marxism-Leninism learned the lesson and engineered their own ruling class by giving poor people a class consciousness of their own. The Soviet Union and China then formalized the whole thing with a Communist Party, which controlled every single state organism *and* also gave privileged access to power for people of working class and peasant pedigree. Every single part of the government was controlled overtly or covertly by a party cell, and you just couldn't get to high places in the Communist Party if your family was high status in 1910. Communists had a double layer system to make sure that central commands always went through. Power wasn't divided.

Going back to the last question; Bioleninism is a top-down phenomenon insofar as it's basically a personnel policy. Leninism in general is, fundamentally, a particular way of hiring people for your organization, and Bioleninism a variant of that. But Leninism didn't come to exist in a top-down way; it was the result of a viral, memetic evolutionary process where power-hungry people tried to come up with effective ways of capturing more and more power. After a lot of trial and error, Leninism came up with class-struggle, and that not being a workable strategy in the wealthy West, slowly people started scraping the bottom of the barrel, hiring and promoting spinsters and gays and blacks and Muslims and whoever was unhappy with their status in the wealthiest and happiest society in human history.

Now every organ of state power, private corporations, religious denominations and every branch of the military, has a bunch of blacks and lesbians and transsexuals as political commissars to ensure that any order from the movement gets implemented faithfully. How is that different from Communist Party cells?

It's less formalized than classical Leninism because it didn't arise out of a complete break up of the old society, like in 1917 Russia. Bioleninism just slowly creeped little by little and colonized existing institutions without destroying them outright. And yes, they've had plenty of elite help, and increasingly so, but the elite didn't come up with the process itself as a sort of Elders of Zion conspiracy. These kinds of processes can't be accurately described as either top-down or bottom-up. It's a combination of both: people on the bottom are trying out ways to agitate, the organizations which are able to command loyalty survive, while others don't, in a classical bottom-up evolutionary process. People on top are watching for good organizations to invest in, so to speak, and they will integrate those which have survived the bottom-up competition into their top-down machines. So, there's a bilateral flow of interaction concerning what kind of political organization is going to work better.

The Coalition of the Fringes, mobilized by the Elites, self-conceptualizes / propagandizes as a Coalition of the Oppressed. How does Bioleninism relate to SJW activism, victimhood culture (sensitivity to slight combined with appeal to authority) and slave morality, as historically conceived?

There's a great article by this blogger called Devin Helton where he talks about "offense-bullying"[332]. In the old days, peasants were meek people whotrash talked each other constantly; they had thick skins. It was the aristocrats who were extremely thin skinned and challenged you to a death-match (a duel) if you went so far as to diss their choice of shoes, or whatever. They were full of righteous anger at any slight to their honor. Interestingly, there's an old quip of Chinese imperial bureaucrats, you may kill a bureaucrat, but you cannot humiliate him. They meant it. 士可殺不可辱.

Why were they like that? Because they could be. Being thin skinned is a signal of high-status, basically. An aristocrat must signal that he's high-status, and thus untouchable, by making a fuss over anything, lest the peasants forget whom they're talking to, the

---

[332] https://devinhelton.com/2015/03/23/standing-up-to-offense-bullying/

anger signaling confidence that you could make good on your threats by having access to higher authorities, or just more armed men. We all know that person who goes around saying "Do you know who I am?" in a menacing tone.

It's no wonder that it's now Bioleninist troopers who go around wailing in righteous anger at cross-dressers being refused to go to the female toilet, or packs of young, or tall, fit black men complaining that white women look at them in fear when they're alone with them in an elevator. What they're doing is signaling access to power, e.g. the ability to get physically violent without police intervention. Why are Antifa so in-your-face evil, shouting menacing slogans with a grin on their faces, and moving around the streets like they own the place? Because they effectively do, to the extent that law enforcement has double standards and they basically go unpunished.

They play this double game where they appeal for Christian charity (slave morality, if you will) from biologically high-functioning people, but at the same time use the support of state violence to engage in open extortion and random violence. Christian charity of course was its own power-play against the Classical-era pagans, who weren't into charity at all; Greco-Romans worshipped strength and heroism. Being nice to children or slaves or lepers was, besides a reasonable way of seeking recruits, also a way of shitting on everything that the Romans thought holy. Now the (modern equivalent of) slaves and the lepers are asking for more than charity, they want power itself, and who's going to come out and argue against that?

"Point deer, make horse" is the near epiphanic, central pivot in the first Bioleninism essay. How does your reading of Eastern thought, politics and history influence your understanding of Western thought, politics and history, and vice versa?

I would say my experience with Eastern peoples helped me in two ways. First, it gave me the detachment to look at my own history and culture in a more objective way. A great way of getting to really understand a concept is to try to explain it to a random Chinese person. You need to translate it into their language and explain the context in a way that makes sense to someone who shares absolutely no part of your cultural background. It's hard, but it's also very liberating. It forces you to come up with a narrative which is both simple enough to keep someone's attention, and makes actual logical sense, but it has to be almost pure logic. The only words you can use are those that are very down to earth, common-sensical, limited to universal human nature. Short words any random guy who hasn't read the same books you have can understand. A random Oriental doesn't know anything about Abrahamic religion or liberalism, so throwing words like "reason" and "liberty" around makes little sense to him. At most, if he's college educated he's learnt a few sentences to pass the college entrance exam, but he's long forgotten it.

The other way, and one trait of Asians I really like, is just how cynical and goal-oriented they are. To a large extent, discussing politics is just not done at all in Asia, unless you happen to work in politics or the media. That was boring, but also refreshing, coming from a European environment where everybody feels they must have a strong opinion on everything, from the price of bread to the Israeli-Palestinian conflict. Any abstract discussion of politics or philosophy in Asia is usually derided as a sophomoric attempt at showing off. Try to talk about anything not involving immediate money or gossip and you'll soon get interrupted. "So what?", "Your point?", "What's it to you?". A common Japanese quip when you use some uncommon word is, 言いたいだけでしょ "you just want to say that word", implying your vanity makes you feel good at using weird words that make you feel superior or high-status, but they've got you all figured out.

And they're right. It got me thinking. What's the point of all those conversations which don't concern personal, immediate interests? It didn't take long from that realization to finding signalling theory, and suddenly it all made sense.

Note that most of what we call Asian "philosophy" is also very down-to-earth, preoccupied with how to run a government, or how to live a good and content life. That's just how the people are, and I still believe that they are genetically incapable of caring about metaphysics and the pointless abstraction it so often encourages. I like that trait in them, but I also think it's deleterious to their building strong, cohesive polities. It's not that they don't ever peddle in bullshit or that they can't be brainwashed; the suicidal Imperial Japanese Army and Maoism obviously happened, but Asians are always only so far from caring about their own personal interest that they need really tight, often cruel, discipline to keep them going. The old guilt/shame dichotomy doesn't quite encompass it, but it's not wrong.

How is Bioleninism to be distinguished from Tokenism – how do Bioleninists reify / exercise their claim on Power in a way which is qualitatively / structurally distinct from political mascotism?

I get this objection a lot. "Blacks or transsexuals or whatever don't actually have high status. They're just given powerless sinecures and it's still white men calling the shots." Well I wouldn't mind one of those powerless sinecures with six-figure salaries for myself and my buddies. And one wonders how the demographics of the ruling class look in places where Bioleninism has advanced the most, like the USA, if you accounted for Jewish people. How many non-Jewish, non-gay white men are in positions of power in the USA? Not a lot, and its decreasing fast.

Mascotism does happen but it's not a stable strategy. At some point, younger generations are going to ask for and get actual positions of influence; and we are seeing this right now. No lack of female CEOs, of black congresswomen. The USA just got its first Somali. To some extent Bioleninist commissars are all likely to become tokens or puppets of some sort; but that's only because they are dumb and lazy by nature. At some point we'll get a high-energy black Muslim woman and it's gonna be bad.

What confluence of political factors / dynamics served to give Bioleninists the "whip-hand" in contemporary Western societies?

Well, basically it was the defeat of Communism in the West. The "invisible hand of power-grabbing" (invisible hand of politics I called it in the third essay) came up with Socialism early on in the West, during the Industrial Revolution, using the (quite reasonable) resentment of the working class of the time. When that didn't quite work out, after the working classes lost their resentment once mild-socialism became prevalent in the 1930s, and the boom times of WW2 made everyone rich, any aspiring agitator had to come up with some other resentful group. The first one was women; that had already arisen in the 19th century, and they got the vote mostly before WW2, but feminism was only developed thoroughly after WW2, when socialism wasn't selling well, and the sexual revolution was throwing women into the open sexual market and the workforce, creating industrial amounts of usable resentment.

Gays and other sexual deviants also came out the sexual revolution, and they're resentful by the mere fact of existing. I've written extensively about that: it must be hard when all the people you're really attracted to find you disgusting.

And then obviously the foreigners. Third worlders came to the West to supply the cheap labor that the mild-socialist policies of Western governments were supposed to abolish. They soon became very useful to leftist political machines. Foreigners by definition are a low-status group in any society; unless the king protects them personally. That happened often in history; it's basically the reason Jews still exist at all. Foreigners are weak, awkward, and so are loyal to whoever has the power to protect them.

Once all these groups were in place and had been agitated properly by the press and the academic establishment, basing a political coalition on giving official status to these people against the majority of, well, normal people, wasn't a hard decision to make.

Do you regard the intersectional tensions at the heart of the Coalition of the Fringes as ideologically / politically stable in the long-term; or do you perceive the hotbed of contradictions as too inherently unstable to endure / govern as Power becomes further consolidated in Bioleninist hands?

I get that a lot. "Muslims and gays can't get along, come on". Well, they seem to be getting along quite happily in Leftist parties all over the West. I do imagine they'll end up in conflict, but only after they've seized complete power. When all leftist parties in the West have become basically leaders of one-party states, then sure, the factions will start fighting each other. But in a one-party state you can unleash violence very easily. The early Soviets fought each other a lot too. Then they were all purged. And then purged again. And then Stalin came and unleashed the mother of all purges. I don't know if Biolenin or Biostalin will be brown gay men or black lesbian disabled women; but I imagine violence will happen in due course. But they have to win first. While they're still following the rules of liberal democracy they will stay put. They have to.

The concept of Bioleninism is simultaneously Essentialist, it draws on the explanatorily power of aggregate HBD forces; and Constructivist, it explains how political coalitions are socially constructed according to group-incentive dynamics. How do you conceive the inter-relationship of Essentialism and Constructivism in relation to Bioleninism, and which is the more dominant tendency in your thought?

I'm not an academic person but I think this is not a helpful way to put it. If there are two different academic cliques, one the "essentialist" and the other the "constructivist", and I have to choose which one Bioleninism belongs to; then we're doing something wrong. This is not a useful game to play; unless I'm gonna get tenure and a six-figure salary for choosing the right team? Am I?

I'm both Essentialist and Constructivist. I think reality is a thing, it's out there, and it's the same for everyone. That may map to "essentialism". There's real stuff out there and it has properties. IQ is real. Race is real.

But again, I'm a linguist. And language is constructed; it's the result of social agreement. The only reason the sound string /dog/ forms the word "dog", and that the word "dog" is used to refer to a certain animal is perfectly arbitrary and can be perfectly called a social construction. Every single word, every single part of grammar, every single linguistic pattern is like that. Every single "concept" is like that. It's not *completely* arbitrary, and world languages have much in common, because there's only so many ways to use language to form a society which is conducive to human existence. So, there's an evolutionary process limiting how arbitrary social constructions can be. That applies to language (most languages – but not all! – have categories such as noun and verb), and to any other social institution. No human society that we know of (before modern Anglosphere) has had 20 "genders".

To a large extent you could say that reality is non-constructed, but human perception, or at least public signals of perception (which is all we know. No matter how many MRIs you take, you can't really know what's going on inside somebody's head, you only know reliably observed behavior), is all "constructed". If only because going against social consensus is likely to get you killed or ostracized at some point, so you better follow the flow.

Then again, all political systems based their rhetoric on being objectively aligned with reality, following natural law of some sort. Constructivism as a theory arose as a way for the left to undermine Western society. It worked because constructivism points at a very real phenomenon: the fact that human knowledge is mostly mediated by other humans and not the result of any direct contact with nature. The right wing to a large extent is still trying to fight that fight, so they're still pushing objectivism.

But that fight was lost many, many years ago. I'm one of the few, or at least one of the first, rightist writers who have been using constructivist arguments. Not only because they're true; but also because they're useful. Useful to undermine the present power structure. Let's face it: we are not in power anymore. We've lost. Decades ago. Leftists are in power, they have a solid (if extremely flawed) theory behind them, and constructivist arguments can help destroy that.

You have been amongst the most insistent and articulate advocates of the need for a New Religion as a central / system of Schelling Point/s around which reaction could begin to build a parallel status system / coherent opposition to Bioleninism / progressivism. Which religions do you see as primary candidates to reboot, or would you prefer to work from a *tabula rasa*?

My idea was to start from scratch. Hence "a new religion". I do understand now that it's much easier to just co-opt or make a fork of an existing religion: that way you can attract a lot of people without implying they were completely wrong all their lives. But I honestly don't know what's going to work. At the beginning I thought the success of a religion depended on the ideas, it was a problem of 'design'. I now tend to think that a sufficiently charismatic (and evil) prophet can get literally anything running, by sheer force of personality and tight discipline, however absurd the ideas may be.

That said, I'm just not a very religious person, and neither a very social person, so I probably won't be involved with any of that. But at some point, I'm quite sure it will happen. It may be Zensunni, or the actual rebirth of a Deus Vult Crusader Catholic Church. Or something completely new.

If Bioleninism continues to proceed unabated, what do you see as its failure mode? Will it die of inherent contradictions, as Marxists fantasized capitalism would; or collapse of internal entropy and get overrun by external enemies; or ease up on adverse counter-selection dynamics, let competent people run things again, and transition to a neo-feudal oligarchy; or do you have faith in narratives of decentralization, fragmentation, Patchwork or neocolonialism; or do we face the eternal current year, on repeat, forever... or perhaps you envisage an End Game even more hideous than the possibilities I've highlighted above?

The scary thing about Bioleninism is that it has no alternative. Leninism existed for decades in Russia and China; but the obvious material success of the capitalist West provided a clear alternative. And at the point where internal contradictions went too far, Leninist countries could always say: fuck this, let's just go Western. And that's exactly what Soviet Union elites did. China took a middle way, but it basically dismantled much of its own system. Xi Jinping has been working hard to rebuild it, but he doesn't have the old proletariat to man his system, so he's basically running it on enforced sycophancy and internet surveillance. It doesn't look very sustainable and cohesive to me, at the very least after the man dies.

Bioleninism has no alternative. Nobody in the West can get fed up with Bioleninist dysfunction point at one country and say: let's do that! Well, there's Japan and other wealthy places, which have not inflicted third world mass-immigration on themselves. But Japan still has big problems with feminism and sexual deviants. The fertility rate tells you it's not a healthy society. And it just passed a law to finally bring mass migration of third worlders. At any rate, neither Japan nor anyone else has a solid, working non-liberal political theory to base their politics on.

On the right we may have many ideas of what to do, but we don't have a clear, existing, successful example to point out to normies as a thing to emulate. Leninism died because Russians did have that. Let's do America. We don't have that. At some point Soviet Leninism became lower status than American capitalism. Right now, Bioleninism is the most high-status system in the world.

Taken to its logical conclusion, it will die of internal contradictions. As I said previously, at some point a Biostalin is going to come up and start purging people. Once he has complete and uncontested power he may change the Bioleninist theory by fiat to let competent people back into positions of power. At least the minimum number of competent people necessary to keep things running for another day. That's a likely scenario. Slow, very slow decline. Collapse is also possible: Stalin was, after all, a very gifted man, and odds are the Bioleninists won't be able to come up with one.

Then again, we might also see an ersatz Bioleninist rise to power. One of those Scott Alexander guys, who are perfectly smart and healthy straight white men but completely exaggerate any teenage trauma into a full-fledged mental illness, if not outright cause themselves a mental illness through excessive psychiatric medication, in order to fit in with the wider Bioleninist coalition of actually innately dysfunctional people. It's no coincidence that reports of gender dysphoria and myriad mental illness are growing fast among young white people. Especially women: they know what our society demands, where status is, so they adapt themselves to it. Blacks and Muslims will protest that these guys are fake, that white people are all evil no matter how fucked up in the head, but odds are they'd lose in a frontal confrontation. So, look forward to the Dictatorship of depressed incel programmers. I'm only half-joking.

As for Patchwork and total fragmentation, the idea is cool and all, but I don't see how the military equilibrium works for that. Ethnogenesis is in the end mostly a function of military technology. Fragmentation would be bloody, very bloody. And at the end of that war, I don't think we'd get all that many polities after all. But I could be wrong.

Nassim Taleb is Retarded

2019-01-02 // eugenics, hbd, cucks

Happy New Year folks, welcome to the 8th (!) year of Bloody Shovel. Let me start this sure to be eventful year with one of these posts which just need writing. A quick internet search didn't come out with any article with this title; so if I'm lucky this post will at some point become viral on Google. You think Taleb is retarded? You heard this exact phrasing here first.

What am I talking about? Most of you should know who Nassim Taleb is; a finance man turned maverick public intellectual by virtue of a book, called the Black Swan, which basically saved all the western financial establishment from blame about the great financial crisis of 2008. If you read Steve Sailer you very much knew that all those Mexicans buying real estate with no down payments were going to unleash a subprime mortage crisis at some point. Not so! Said Taleb: that was a Black Swan.

A what? Some completely unpredictable scenario, a massive statistical outlier, he meant. He then colored the theory with a lot of fancy math. All those financial traders in Wall Street then could finally look themselves at the mirror again and not feel like evil failures. "It wasn't our fault! It was unpredictable! Look at all that fancy math in the book. Only a genius like Taleb could understand that stuff". It helped that Taleb is a Brown Man; hence a genius by default in our modern culture.

I know nothing of Taleb's theories; although people who I respect intellectually, such as Eric Falkenstein, have written at length[333] that they aren't buying them. On the other side I see thousands upon thousands of bugmen and cucks who have nothing but praise for the swarthy bearded brown dude who likes to talk like an Italian mafioso because he's convinced himself that being born close to the Mediterranean makes one white.

I could be wrong and the guy is actually a genius. But the geniuses I respect have a habit of not saying retarded things; at least not in public and when sober. That is not something that applies to Taleb anymore. One could read with some interest his stuff about finance math or "antifragility", but now Taleb has come out as a full-fledged retard by saying what amounts (in my book) to the most retarded claim anyone can claim.

Taleb went on a Twitter rant (then about how IQ is a "pseudoscientific swindle"). His observation was based on his experience with "quants", high-IQ math people who

---

333   https://falkenblog.blogspot.com/2012/11/taleb-mishandles-fragility.html

work for financial firms. He found them to be good at numbers but lacking at other skills, e.g. LARPing like a New York downtown mafioso or taking instagram pics doing low-weight deadlifts.

Now, to be fair to the guy; he's right there. IQ explains some things. But it doesn't explain personality, drive, extraversion, focus, dominance; a lot of stuff. But it doesn't have to. Quants are quants. If he found them to be bad at making money in Wall Street; well maybe making money in Wall Street is not just about IQ. Big deal.

But IQ is real all the same. All else equal, a higher IQ is a desirable trait in any living thing. A high IQ may not guarantee success at any particular endeavor, but a low IQ absolutely guarantees failure at pretty much any advanced skill.

But of course everybody knows that. Which is why nobody really finds IQ to be controversial in normal life. Yes, it's better to be smart than to be not smart. But to be smart, but a pussy, or a coward, or annoying, or just weird in personality is a bad thing. Nobody contests that.

IQ and psychometrics in general are only controversial, only a topic of discussion when applied to groups. Most importantly, to racial groups. That's the only one reason why anybody objected to IQ research. To be put it even more clearly, the only reason IQ is controversial is that black people test low in IQ tests. And that's why Taleb *had* to come out and say, oh, saying black people have low IQ on average is *insensitive*. After all, northern Europeans weren't rich until after 1600.

Letting alone the point that the Chartres Cathedral was up by 1220; the very simple point that Taleb here is ignoring is this thing called genetics. Surely those "Meds" he feels so proud of (after all, the concept allows him to claim the glory of the Roman Empire, instead of accepting that the Levant has been a complete backwater for 2500 years) are genetically quite close to those Northern Europeans who, besides beating Roman legions pretty much all the time, were indeed not living in societies as complex as those of Southern Europe or the Middle East. Germanic and Celtic tribes even spoke closely related languages to Greece and Rome.

Not something that Africans can say; they're the most distant race to Caucasians (and Asians) that lives on earth. And late last year we found very very interesting data[334] on their genetic make up.

We estimate that individuals in two African populations have 6 – 8% ancestry through admixture from an unidentified archaic population that diverged from the ancestors of modern humans 500 thousand year ago.

---

[334] https://www.biorxiv.org/content/biorxiv/early/2018/12/07/4
89401.full.pdf

Does Taleb know about this? Does he know about anything? Of course not. He makes a living by selling books to the soul-less bugmen in the finance industry; and he won't be able to be able to keep being called to TV if he can't claim to be part of the Bioleninism racket by hating on white people at regular intervals. He may not like being brown (half his waking hours are spent in loud reminders that he's not an Arab), but he surely enjoys the privilege of not looking white.

The Intelligence Question

2019-01-06 // theory, hbd, eugenics, cucks

So my last post on Nassim Taleb's mental retardation has triggered quite a lot of laughs and chuckles, and also some criticism. Some people say I was not rigorous enough when writing about Nassim Taleb's books.

To those people I say: hold my beer. Seriously, people, this is a blog. A free blog, which I write under a pseudonym. I seek nothing from my writing, besides it being an avenue to make interesting friends. Which I have, dozens of them, and God bless them. But surely in this little place of mine which I offer free of charge, I'm entitled to shit on people for fun once in a while, especially if they've given good reason, as Taleb did by saying the most retarded thing that anyone can say: that black overpopulation is not a problem because they'll turn out just as smart as the Germanic tribes did in post-Roman Europe.

That's not just retarded, that's the most harmful and dangerous thing that you can say, period. The most dire danger to Western Civilization, to our lands, to our families, to our friends, to everything we hold dear, is the demographic replacement of Western populations by immigrants from Africa and the Middle East. Taleb is saying that's not a problem! Well, fuck Taleb, fuck his books, his goatee, his accent. Fuck his deadlift, his insecurity about his racial background, and everything about him. And fuck you.

And besides, this kind of pedantic arguments about "oh you didn't spend weeks reading his book to understand the math", or concern trolling about the effects on group morale of criticizing a man who (to his credit, which I had always given before this week) at least makes a point of looking and sounding like a real man and not a soy-infused mangina, reveal you are the kind of person that Taleb hates. Taleb is a middle-eastern man who, by sheer biology, just can't stand North-Western European nerds. And to be honest I can relate to that. So at any rate, don't be a nerd and defend Taleb with nerdy, over-rigorous arguments. I don't care, and he hates your guts.

Going back to the gist of Taleb's argument, all he said was a bunch of wrong and disingenuous arguments about the importance of IQ (you can read a good summary here[335]), all done for the sole purpose of signaling his long dislike of nerds. And again, I can relate. There's much to dislike about nerds. They are often annoying, and their lack of skill at enjoying the many pleasures of life is *very* harmful for many of us who just want to have a pleasant life and not live a life of drudgery at work. Let alone the harm

---

[335] https://www.unz.com/jthompson/swanning-about-fooled-by-algebra/

that nerds do at showering thots and assorted single women with heaps of attention and money. Yes, nerds are bad. If Taleb had just said if he were King he'd randomly kill 5 nerds every fortnight just to make a point, I'd probably have retweeted that with implied approval.

But that's not what he said. He went on a long obfuscating tirade about IQ being pseudoscience. And yes, IQ fetishism, the idea that IQ is all that ever matters, is weird and wrong, and mostly a vehicle for nerds who have nothing besides IQ going on for them, to feel good about themselves. But so what? Are nerds and their small attempts at mutually licking their wounds and achieving some tiny amount of self-esteem a serious problem for our world?

No, not even close. The real problem in our world is that high-IQ people, not just nerds, but just basically everybody half-functional, is failing to produce children, leaving a huge demographic vacuum which greedy business-owners and evil politicians are using to import dumb and hostile foreigners into our lands. *That* is the problem. And in our modern world, where the rights of ethnic peoples to their own homelands on purely ethnic and historical grounds is not accepted (because Nazis), in our modern scientistic modern world where the only acceptable public arguments must be written in the form of formal science, the only effective, true, empirically provable, and most importantly, legal argument to oppose the influx of millions of dumb and hostile immigrants into our lands, is the biological basis of IQ, and the different distribution of IQ between racial groups.

I wish it weren't so. I wish the French could just say that France belongs to them and their posterity because they freaking say so, and everyone else will be expelled or killed. I wish White Americans could say they colonized and developed the continent, so it belongs to them, period. Talking about IQ is just a roundabout way of saying that dumb and hostile foreigners don't belong to our countries. It has the obvious pitfall that East Asians are even higher-IQ than Whites, and yet nobody wants 100 million Chinese to immigrate to their countries.

Yes, it would be much better if we had solid measures of not only intelligence, but creativity, integrity, decisiveness, leadership abilities, and whatnot. If we had, we'd surely find out that different ethnic groups have different distributions of every trait. We could even use them to define the national character of many countries, and perhaps plausibly use that definition to set a psychological legal standard for the demographics a country wants to maintain. Perhaps we'll get there some day. But we're not there yet.

All we have is IQ, which individually tells you indeed very little about how useful a man is going to be for a particular task, but when averaged over populations tells you if a place is a shithole full of dumb people, or it's a civilized and mildly pleasant place. IQ does an *exceptional* job at predicting that. Japan is nice. Denmark is nice. Morocco is not nice. Black Africa is awful. You may not like China, but it's orders of magnitude more pleasant to live in than India.

So again, I understand all the criticisms about IQ itself, or about IQ-fetishism, or about nerds in general. I get it. I really do. My IQ is nothing special, I'm no nerd, I do my deadlifts myself. But that's completely besides the point. The fight right now is for every civilized country to defend itself and its people. It's a tough fight, and right now we're losing it. Nerds are part of my people. Taleb, and the Africans he is so "sensitive" abut are not. A time will come to de-emphasize the importance of IQ and all that. But now it's not that time.

Tucker Carlson's war against Woke Capital and the future of the Right

2019-01-21 // theory, rightwingers, trump, capitalism, leftism, demographics

Well, well. Everybody predicted that 2019 would be an eventful year, with Trump realizing he must start to build the wall if he wants to be reelected; Cold War 2 against China heating up, and the trade war doing some serious damage to the Chinese economy, and China's slowdown dragging down the world economy in exchange. It's gonna be bad, but it's not gonna be boring.

And just after we welcomed the new year, this video by Fox News' Tucker Carlson[336] came out and has owned the attention of political media for more than a week now. And for good reason: it's good. Well, he's usually good, but this time he was something more than good. He stated very clearly what the right half of his country wants, what got Trump elected. And he made it very clear to the media, think tanks and the wider propaganda apparatus of the Republican party what they must do to survive. They must go to war with libertarianism. To war with Woke Capital.

The cuckservative media went immediately in panic. Ross Douthat on the NYT, who, besides being the physical incarnation of being a cuck, is a pretty good writer, made a good summary here[337].

As we all know, the political left, born out of the chaos of the French Revolution, came of age when Karl Marx produced a working formula: class struggle. You go find the low status people in your country, tell them the world is divided in two sorts of people: them, and the guys on top of them. The guys on top are oppressors, the guys on the bottom are oppressed: if you, the oppressed follow me, we'll turn the table, "liberate you" i.e. grab their stuff and their status and give it to you.

Then after WW2 the Western left realized that the oppressor/oppressed template worked much better with groups disadvantaged biologically than with mere social class. Hence we got Bioleninism. The industrial worker who was so much into socialism could after all become a manager, or start his own company and not be so interested in socialism anymore. Happened all the time. That's not a good deal if you're a leftist politician. You want your underlings to stick around and be loyal, and the underclass

---

[336] https://video.foxnews.com/v/5985464569001

[337] https://www.nytimes.com/2019/01/12/opinion/sunday/tucker-carlson-fox-news-republicans.html

doesn't feel so oppressed if there's not an underclass anymore. Of course, you can change class (in modern Western societies), but you can't change biology. The average racial minority, the sexual deviant, the mentally ill, the fat cat lady, those will always be low status, always feel oppressed. That's firm, absolute loyalty right there.

Ever since the Left found out this trick, the ball has been on the Right's camp. How do you deal with Bioleninism? The only workable strategy was formulated by Steve Sailer decades ago: if the Left is the Coalition of the Fringes, the Right must be the Party of the Normal. In the US, where demographics mean that the minority-supported Democratic party will by 2025 or so have a rock-solid electoral majority, that meant the Republican Party becoming the party of White people. It's taken a while, but as the critical date when Texas flips blue approaches, the Republicans have slowly, if somewhat unawares, moved in that direction. Hence, Donald Trump.

Of course the Right has to do a lot of work before that change of direction is complete. The Left is more flexible and responsible to change, because its basic formula is simple. They're the party of the oppressed. If things change they just need to change the identity of the oppressed, and they're set. Easy. The Right though, can hardly be the party of the oppressors. At its core, sociologically, the Right is the party of the people who wanna be left alone. That's not a very exciting way of running a political movement, though, so they must always come up with random reasons to justify their attachment to the status quo. The usual are traditional religion, which is useful as it doesn't need to be justified, and has centuries of history fighting the Left, long a force for atheism. There's also nationalism, to the extent it is allowed to exist post-WW2, which tends to be the refuge of secular, masculine people who dislike the Left's push for egalitarianism.

And of course, capitalism. When the Left was primarily about economic socialism, about state-control of the economy, the Right had a very strong Schelling Point in free-market ideology. Opposing socialism made for good politics for non-leftist people, it has a ready source of funding from business owners. And it just makes a lot of sense. Socialism is a very stupid economic policy, which produces poverty. And nobody likes poverty, least of all the poor. So the political Right in much of the Western world, and even out of it, became mostly a coalition of religious people, nationalists, and business owners. God, Country and Capital.

This kinda worked for a while; but it was never very stable. And most importantly, it was never very strong. Of those three parts of the coalition, the religious have the actual numbers. In America, by far, in Europe it's a closer contest with the nationalists, but I'd say the religious still have a small edge. At any rate, the ones with the money, funding the whole thing was the business owners. Capital. And money talks. Capital was funding and basically running the political right for a long time; and completely so since the Thatcher-Reagan revolution where they took over the whole movement with force, and took over the governments of much of the Western world for quite some time.

What came out of the increasing influence of Capital in the political right was this weird intellectual movement called "libertarianism". Libertarianism is a completely American phenomenon; in Europe it has appeared somewhat in the last 10 years, but it's still completely marginal, and for a long time it was completely non-existent. In the US, though, libertarianism is quite big. Not in numbers, of course, but it is very influential in the economics departments of American academia and, as an extension of that, as economic advisors for the political Right. The DC think tanks and all that crowd. It would be an exaggeration to say that all Republican politicians in the US are libertarians, but they are very influential in those circles, and their academic prestige is quite high.

Libertarianism strikes me as an escapist strategy. Democracy was founded in the idea of frequent changes in government. We have a team of guys running the state; if they stop doing a good job, you change them. Most places developed a two-party system, around a left-right axis, which disagreed more or less on how to do things; but the point is change is built into the system. So everybody has an incentive to play the game, and try to be there when the next change happens.

But at some point, somebody discovered that this theory was crap. Power doesn't work that way. Governments don't work that way, fundamentally. You can't change everything all the time, the incentives are just too big for people in power to find a way of keeping power amongst themselves. Like most important discoveries, different people across the world realized, independently, that alternation in power was absolutely not what happens in democracies at all; that most resorts of power are occupied by permanent bureaucrats, and that the different parties which prima facie compete for power, eventually find ways of helping each other achieve a stable sharing of power and money. The first to make a solid theory on how this works were the Italian elite theorists, Pareto, Mosca and Michels.

Libertarianism is what you do when you realize that the government is socialist by definition. Socialism being the control of the economy by the government, well, yes, odds are the government is going to want to control the economy. So if you don't trust the government to respect your interests, then you go libertarian. You do that because you are a business person and have an actual reason to want the government to get away from your business. Or you do that if you are opposed to the government for other reasons, say cultural reasons, and just want to signal your distrust of the government. Libertarianism came from both sides of that. Not by coincidence, much of libertarianism came of the American South after the Civil Rights movement. US Southerners realized the US Federal Government wanted to destroy their culture; and many of them became free market fundamentalists as a way to oppose that. That again connects with the 3-way coalition of religious, nationalists and capitalists that has formed the Political Right for decades.

Well, Tucker's speech basically said this alliance was over. The alliance of God, Country and Capital has achieved some electoral victories over the decades, but it has failed miserably at the only important task: the Culture War, influencing the behavior of the people so that they form stable and moral families. The Left has destroyed traditional culture bit by bit, and neither Nixon, nor Reagan, nor Bush, nor anyone, has been able to do stop it even by an inch. And why is that? Has God failed us? Do the people not love their Country? No, it's the other guys. Capital has betrayed us. The libertarians have been playing a double game, and they are now pretty much the enemy. They haven't just surrendered, or been neutralized. Capital today is perhaps the biggest force of the Left. They're the biggest enemy.

Tucker Carlson makes his argument much better in this video where he is interviewed by Charlie Kirk, one of those classical cuckservatism propaganda guys, doing both the evangelical and the libertarian thing. It goes without saying that Tucker completely destroys him, and he has fun doing it. Understandably given what a complete tool this Kirk guy is. Do watch the whole video.

https://www.youtube.com/watch?v=ybYvAZqo0KA

Of course not all the video is good. The first 10 minutes are actually a very disappointing collection of cuckservative platitudes, where he talks how the increased insanity of Leftist activists is a sign of "fear" on their side. That they're "losing control". What is Tucker smoking? The Left is losing control? Of what? They can put transexuals on kindergartens. They have 10 year old boys in drag on national TV. They have successfully derailed pretty much everything that the elected president of the USA Donald Trump has tried to do for 2 years: a point which he makes himself all the time. Yes, sure, Donald Trump is actually president, and he confirmed two justices for the Supreme Court. But the Left is in complete control in pretty much everything they care for. Most importantly, the Left has the demographic advantage. They control the votes of every single Bioleninist constituency, and they are all growing. Single women? Growing. Gays and assorted sexual deviants? (can we call them GASD?) growing. Ethnic minorities? Growing. White Americans just posted the lowest fertility rate in history. It won't be long until the Hispanic population of Texas grows to the point where the state votes Democrat, and then the Democratic Party will have a permanent electoral majority.

So no, they aren't losing control. They aren't "terrified". Well, maybe they are, but that's besides the point. When Stalin launched his purges in the 1930 Soviet Union, he was quite terrified of losing control. That's indeed why he launched the purges. Which were wildly successful, killed a million people, displaced tens of millions, and made him a dictator for life. So yes, besides the point. The cuckservative idea seems to be that the utter defeat of the Right in the Culture War is a sign of some sort of demon-induced "insanity", and that through a few exhortations to calm down given by DC aristocrats (like, say, Tucker Carlson) everybody will calm down and we'll be back to the 1950s like nothing ever happened.

"When you are standing on principle, and when you truly believe you're right (...) that you'll be proving right at some point; you don't need to get mad (...) you can softly chuckle, and you can persist in the face of all the threats, in saying what you think is true, if you really believe it is. If everybody did that, this crap will end tomorrow."

No, Tucker, no. I'm sorry, that's not how it works. The current-year Leftist insanity is not a sign of anything, it's just the logical progression of the Culture War, which the Left has won, utterly, and is now engaging in mop-up operations, gearing up the insanity just to gloat, to show off the power they have. Which they have, and we don't. You can't just tell people to "believe", i.e. to have "faith", and everything bad will go away. It won't. When people oppose the left, they lose their jobs, they lose their friends, they lose everything. Sure, if everybody made a stand, and you had 100 million people in the streets, that would be something. But you don't have 100 million people. You have at most 80. You have 200 million white Americans, of which taking out gays and single women and weirdos and nerds and snobs and cowards, you have at most 80 million people who oppose the left Out of a country of 330 million. So no, let's not play the numbers game.

And the Right isn't even right. The Right doesn't have a coherent theory of how things work, "consistent with thousands of years of human experience" as he puts it. The Left does: it has Marxism-Leninism, the old template of oppressors and the oppressed, now applied to biological groups. That may be wrong, quite bogus really, but it's simple, and it works at the job it has to do: building a political coalition. Meanwhile the Right, which prides itself in caring about reality more than politics, can't even agree on the reality of Human Biodiversity! No, Tucker, no. What we need is not just faith and courage. We need something more. We need smart politics.

But he knows that, and he elaborates that very well in the next part of the talk, where he puts forward his political platform. Tucker Carlson's political platform is not about Freedom. Or God. Or Improving the world. He makes a much narrow commitment, which sounds strange for the absolute obviousness of its desirability.

—-The goal [of government] is to have an economy which makes it possible for normal, average young people to marry and have kids.

"Period, that's it". Yes. That's exactly it. That's the one thing that all human societies since the beginning of time. Hell, that's the one thing that all apes, all social animals are able to achieve. But modern liberal society is incapable of doing. You could rephrase this in more scientific terms to make it even more obvious.

The goal of human society is to have a normal biological cycle of reproduction.

The genius of this is that in order to achieve this utterly obvious, minimal goal of existence, you'd have to completely dismantle liberal society from its foundation. And you could do that without hard feelings, without hate, without outright enmity towards liberalism. Nothing personal here, we're just optimizing the government in order to achieve a normal biological cycle of reproduction.

Tucker then goes on explaining why he places the focus on government in the economy, not in cultural values per se. He says that the reason why young people can't get married and have kids early is because of economic reasons, not cultural values, as the Right has been saying for decades. This is an important point. This is the most important point. This is everything.

Everyone, from rat-voice Ben Shapiro to Cuckold General David French has come out against Tucker and his suggestion that economic policy may have something to do family formation being unaffordable in the only cities in the world where good jobs are available. It's all about culture, they say. If people just pulled themselves up by their bootstraps and read Shapiro's or Jordan Peterson's latest book, they'd be able to be productive enough to get a high-flying job in a big city and afford their their USD 5k a month rent.

Now, it is certainly true that many of our ancestors used to have lots of children, up to 5 or 6 children per woman, while being much poorer than we are. It is also true that other people, say Africans, have way more children than we do while being much poorer than we are. So sure, cultural values are more of a factor than economic factors are.

But it's also true that economic policy is orders of magnitude easier to change than cultural values. It may be that people today are spoiled consumerist drones who think they are entitled to living the Sex in the City lifestyle, and even then won't have much children anyway. That may be right. But it is also the case that economic activity is increasingly concentrated in a few global centers all across the world, and that people who don't get access to those are increasingly depressed, with an epidemic of suicide by opioid abuse killing thousands of people a year.

The way that cuckservative pundits with their double libertarian-religious shtick (see Kirk and his "Proud Capitalist, Saved by Jesus" line) think of present economic trends reminds me of my friends back home who argue for the legalization of drugs. "People should have freedom", they say. "Drugs are no worse than alcohol", they say.

Alcohol is actually a great example. Obviously alcoholism is a big problem in some parts of the worlds, but oddly not everywhere. In many parts of Southern Europe, alcoholism barely exists at all, while in Northern Europe is quite serious. And with peoples like US Amerindians ("Native Americans") or Australian Aborigenes, alcohol causes severe physical and mental problems to pretty much every single one of them. "Liquid fire" some call it, for how it wastes them.

The only explanation for this fact is that humans in societies with a long history of agriculture have developed genetic adaptations to digest alcohol, while people with shorter histories of agriculture have not. This doesn't mean that people slowly developed an adaptation while merrily drinking their wine. No, that means that every single alcoholic in France or Italy who couldn't hold their liquor died, while the few (at the beginning *very* few) who didn't become addicted were able to survive and leave descendants. I have no idea what percentage of the population of early farmers in Southern Europe had to die in order for widespread adaptation to wine to spread, but given how Amerindians hold their liquor, it may have been in the order of 80%.

Legalizing drugs would start the process all over again. Sure, some people can get high on coke or meth and still be productive. The vast majority can't. If we legalized coke and meth, we would be basically killing off the 80% of the population who would get addicted and waste away. Is that a reasonable price to pay for "liberty"?

The same applies to our present economic system. At this moment, every single human population with an IQ over 95 has a fertility rate below replacement; and the places where the most intelligent and productive people tend to live, big cities, have generally fertility rates below 1. Not below 2, replacement, but below 1, half of replacement. As I've said again and again, big cities today are IQ shredders, where the genes that code for high intelligence go to get shredded in the corporate and bureaucratic rat-race, depriving humanity of the biological building blocks for a better future.

Why? Because some people are making money out of it. Who? The same people who fund the likes of Kirk, Shapiro, and the vast libertarian and associated free-market pundit ecosystem. Why are these guys on the Right at all? Says Tucker Carlson. And he's right. It's time they left. The cucks, cry, though "you can't do this! Capitalists are our allies against Socialism and the Left".

No. They aren't. Not anymore. Capitalists were indeed mostly in the Right side of the Culture wars for many decades. But not anymore. Libertarianism was a rational strategy to signal one's complete rejection of the state and the Cathedral and its associated cultural ideology; because the state wanted Socialism. It still wants it, of course. But not so hard, the Left has long reached an agreement with Capital, through which Neoliberalism lets Capital make some money in exchange of Capital going Woke. Woke Capital is a real thing now. It took decades of brainwashing and back-rubbing and cross marriage and outright coercion, but in 2019, the vast majority of capitalists, of investors, of bankers, of corporate executives, even down to the average middle manager, are now culturally leftist. They are Woke. If you don't believe me, go read this guy for a couple hours[338].

And as Tucker mentions, in an age of technological revolution, in an age where Facebook, Amazon and Google (FAG) have more capability than any state bureaucracy, these guys are dangerous. And these guys aren't in our side. They are completely sincerely Leftist. On average the tech population may be even more leftist than your average bureaucratic agency. Google is particularly crazy.[339]

If Capital is now Woke, if the Left has successfully captured the capitalists, why should the Right be nice to them? Because muh-free markets? That was a means, not an end. The goal of the Right is, again…

The goal [of government] is to have an economy which makes it possible for normal, average young people to marry and have kids.

Or in other words, to ensure a future for our children. There's another version out there in 14 words.

If it takes import tariffs to achieve this? Let's have them. If it takes higher taxes for some industries or people, let's have it. If it takes strict anti-monopoly laws, or even the outright nationalization of some companies, Let's have that. If it takes strict controls on the media, let's have those too. Whatever it takes. Liberty is a means, not an end.

The problem of means and ends, of process and goals, is of course an old one and a very hard one when you need to coordinate millions of people and keep them focused and loyal. An important point there is the careful use of language. When people speak of Capitalism it can mean a million things. You can have completely unrestricted markets or 90% tax rates, and they'll both be Capitalism, because the only thing that the word Capitalism means is "not Socialism", and the actual referents of those two words depend a lot on whether the Soviet Union still exists. National Socialism was less socialist than most capitalist countries today.

See that Tucker is careful to say he's still a proud Capitalist, even though he'd probably crush most capitalists that live today. At least he sounds like he would. At any rate, using the same words as the Right has for decades is good rhetoric: you do want to signal continuity to the people you want to support you. And besides, Socialism *is* bad for you. Everything else equal, economic freedom does create economic growth.

---

[338] https://twitter.com/wokecapital

[339]   https://dailycaller.com/2019/01/16/google-family-triggered-meltdown/

Which is why any good plan to crackdown on Woke Capital must be phrased in a way that blames big Capital of socialist policies, and promises to bring economic freedom to the middle classes and small business owners. That was also Trump's rhetoric, Salvini's rhetoric, and the rhetoric of every single successful right winger in a long time.

What the Right needs to do now is to reflect on how the Left was able to capture Capital and turn it into its most lucrative constituency. Any successful country needs a business community, and the capture of the West's by the Bioleninist left has been so unexpected that still many people refuse to believe it. But happened it has, whether by political coercion, infiltration, or just mere cultural prestige. We better think carefully on what happened, how to reverse it, and use the same tools for our own cause.

Acceleration by Yang

2019-03-22 // yang, acceleration, hbd, trump, economics, capitalism

Tl;dr. It really is that simple.

Long version:

I've never voted. Well, I lie, I voted once. I was 18, and my mother sorta forced me. It also felt like some rite of passage, you know, you grow to 18 and you get to do grown-up stuff like voting, having a voice in the political process. I've never been into rituals though, and I felt stupid immediately after putting my vote in the box. I didn't even like the guy! I thought he was retarded. All of them, really. I still do.

Of course ever time there's an election people would ask me now and then who I'm gonna vote to. I evolved a series of bunch of canned answers. First one was "Nah they all suck". Then I read Bryan Caplan's Myth of the Rational Voter and started saying "one vote doesn't count anyway". This triggered huge discussions if there was even a single Boomer at home. "But if everyone thought like you nobody would vote!!".

-"Well sure but my not voting doesn't influence other people's behavior".

"But you have to vote, if nobody voted..."

-"It doesn't follow that if I don't vote then other people don't vote".

"But you have to vote, if everyone did like you"

-"Where on earth are you taking that 'if' from?

"But you have to vote......"

You should try this, it's hilarious. They just go in an endless loop bug. Talk about NPCs.

Later I started reading Moldbug and got into this little sphere, so when in good company I'd just say "nah, not voting. Democracy sucks". I was exquisitely detached about most elections during my adult life. I honestly didn't give a crap. The Deep State, the Uniparty, the Swamp, call it what you will, it's all the same. I was beyond all that.

And then... Trump happened 3 years ago. It took me a while to get into Trump. I didn't care about elections, you see? Elections don't matter. It's all the same. And not being American I knew little about the guy. I'd seen him on TV now and then but besides him being this kinda sleazy showbiz guy I couldn't care much about him.

But I was on Twitter, and I was watching all the outrage, and man, Trump was good. He wasn't good, good. He wasn't Moldbug. Not even Pat Buchanan. Trump is really inarticulate, I don't know his verbal IQ but he has the vocabulary of a dumb 10 year old. And yet he got his points across. Good points. Drain the Swamp. NATO is pointless. Make America Great Again. China is ripping us off. You'd be in jail. No more senseless wars. BUILD THE WALL. All great, and most importantly, hilarious ideas. Trump was trolling everyone that I hated, the press, the bureaucrats, the whole Cathedral was up in arms against him, and *he was fighting back*. Successfully! He was talking shit to AIPAC! I just couldn't help myself. Trump was my guy. I couldn't vote for him, I'm not American, but I would have. Honest to god, I'd wake up early and vote for Donald Trump.

The Trump campaign triggered in me a feeling of community, of adhesion that I'd never felt before. And I'd never felt it before because Trump was the first candidate ever who wasn't representing the conservatives. Which I'm not. Or the Christians. Which I'm not. Or the fiscal conservatives or whatever. Which I care about but not very strongly. Trump arose in 2016 as the candidate of the fast-dying white majority of the United States. And again, I'm not American, but my homeland has a similar predicament, and American politics eventually trickle down to Europe in a few years, so it was easy to identify with. I hadn't written that essay yet, but I had it in mind, and Trump was the first guy ever to appear to be fighting Bioleninism, then incarnated in the odious, horrible body of Hillary Clinton. And so I really supported the guy. When against all odds he won the election in November 2016, I got drunk and had a blast. I'll always remember fondly that night.

Fast forward 2 and a half years later. No wall. No jail for Hillary. Narrowly avoided jail himself! The swamp is a big as always. Forever war still going on. Spending more time tweeting about Israel than his own country. Shits on Ann Coulter and says he wants more legal immigration. Did I mention no wall? What a disaster. Trump has been a huge and complete disappointment. Again, I don't dislike the guy personally. I mean I never *liked* him. He's weird, talks like a retarded 10 year old. I'd say I'd probably wouldn't enjoy having a few beers with him but he doesn't even drink. But I don't hate the guy, I think odds are his heart is in the right place. He just can't get stuff done. He's incompetent. I mean, it's hard. It was always hard. One just doesn't come in as a complete outsider and reform the whole government from scratch. Then again, people who work in the heart of the beast, in Washington DC, tell me he's just incompetent. He could get stuff done. Some stuff at least. But he's messing everything up. He's just bad at the job. Incompetent. A boomer after all, who gave his most talented child to a dumb Jew son of a criminal who doesn't let her or his grandchildren eat proper food because muh Jewry.

So now what? Back to Moldbuggian detachment? Nothing ever changes, huh. The Cathedral really is all powerful. Ever since Trump made some protests about the intelligence agencies being disloyal or outright attacking him, the Establishment feels so powerful they just blatantly say in the press that the CIA are the good guys. Does nobody remember that the CIA being evil was pretty much proven by the 1960s, and that evil CIA ops have been a staple of books and films for decades? Not anymore; they're not content with being powerful in the shade. They want outright public submission.

Democracy really is a sham; but it's hard to go back to detachment now that Bioleninism is out in the open. Elections now are openly not about economic policy or social conservatism. Elections now are about the speed of the dispossession of white straight males. It's for or against Bioleninism. The majority of candidates of the Democratic party are openly talking of "reparations" for black people, i.e. outright Danegeld. And don't get me started with open hunt to mess with the sexual hormones of white children in schools. It's going on right there in the open.

The US has an election next year, the campaign is starting now. Given the present demographic trends, it is very likely that Florida, if not Texas, will flip blue very shortly; that means a rock-solid majority for the Democratic party, forever. Donald Trump is likely to be the last white male president in American history. The 2020 election is probably going to be the last election which is more or less contested. Trump does still have a chance.

But Trump is incompetent. He's not helping. He's just treading water while another million Third-world immigrants sneak in, another middle-school boy gets injected estrogen because he doesn't like football, and another hundred-thousand white men just overdose on opioids because you can't even play a videogame today without being forced to play a black woman avatar. Can you support this guy? I sure can't. Again, not my nation, but I wouldn't. I won't call him a traitor, although many have. But he didn't build the wall. He's letting Amazon, Facebook and Twitter campaign openly against him and censor everything to the right, and he hasn't lifted a finger. He doesn't deserve support.

It doesn't seem anyone to his right is going to run third party, and even if he was removed as candidate, the most likely replacement would be the despicable bugman Mitt Romney. So what are the Democrats running? Beto, a tall white guy with a small face (as they say in Japan) which chicks dig, but sounds pretty much clinically retarded. There's Elizabeth Warren which is the stereotype of the annoying high school teacher who thinks she's an intellectual because she's memorized Jane Austen novels. I'm being unfair to her, she did write the Two Income Trap which is a great book on the complete scam which is the modern economy. But still, come on. Pocahontas.

Then there's Kamala Harris, which is like when you've beaten the final boss after an arduous fight, with only 10% HP left, but then the actual final boss comes in and he's 5 times as powerful and more aggressive. Kamala Harris is a black woman who's pretty much openly calling for the disenfranchisement of the white male population. She's

Bioleninism incarnated. Hillary in black. Not good. And precisely because of that the most anticipated to win the primaries.

There's Bernie of course, the last hope of the residual white left. Not the modern Baizuo. The old White left. The Classical Leninists. Who haven't still realized why they lost that battle. Why socialism is dead in the West. Bernie didn't work last time, won't work this time. A bunch of black girls will twerk to his face in his rallies and then spew some poison gas to his crowd. The press won't even report it.

Seriously though, to the extent Bernie represents a constituency that's not for instant Brazilification, I wish him well, but he's old and frail, and his program isn't very interesting. And most importantly, his own constituency is being taken over by a guy who's 10 times smarter, is young, has actual good ideas, is not white and will give the Bernie crowd everything they want, and more. Much more.

To be precise, $1,000 a month more.

Come Andrew Yang.

He became famous after an interview with Joe Rogan, which I strongly recommend. He's good.

https://www.youtube.com/watch?v=cTsEzmFamZ8

He was also good on Tucker Carlson's (!). Note how he mentions that GDP and unemployment rates are completely bogus figures which hide more than they reveal. He deserves a 10 year dictatorship just for that. But I get ahead of myself.

https://www.youtube.com/watch?v=GzksqTu9UY4

He's just very good. I mean look at him.

https://www.youtube.com/watch?v=LUolzAltwKI

He's the only candidate in this whole race that doesn't talk like a bugman. You know what a bugman is. All those politicians and corporate guys who talk in that odd and disingenuous jargon designed to obfuscate. High-grade NPCs, that's what bugmen are. Well, he isn't. He goes straight to the issues, analyzes them intelligently, and then has a plan. It may be or may not be a good plan. But I dare you to show me a presidential candidate with a higher IQ than Andrew Yang in the last 30 years. That's even more of a feat because the guy is East Asian, and God knows East Asians tend to be bugmen too.

The guy even wrote a book called The War On Normal People, which is the perfect definition of the Left. I should use it as a subtitle for a Bioleninism book.

I've been comparing him with Lee Kuan Yew, another famous non-bugman Asian. Well, LKY he's not. I don't think he'll ever go public saying this:

https://www.youtube.com/watch?vWblg2EM758

But Yang is perhaps the second Asian politician ever to be widely liked by the White right. The 4chan and related crowd which heavily supported Trump in 2016 has now gone wholesale[340] to the *Yang Gang*. Part of it is justified disappointed about Trump not delivering on his promises. Most of it is Yang's promise of Universal Basic Income (UBI), $1,000 dollars a month for every adult US citizen.

But a big part of it is just pure appreciation for the guy. Look at his interview with Tucker. You might remember my last post on Tucker, and how he's revolutionized conservative commentary in the US by arguing that the focus of government should be taking care of working families. Well, Tucker himself liked Yang, and it's no wonder he did. Yang is the candidate who's using the closest arguments to Tucker. By far. He's lamenting the plight of the working man. He's calling to help the rural white middle class who's being ravaged by the opioid suicide crisis. Note that Trump has said some stuff about that, and has tried to get China to stop exports of fentanyl, but he didn't mention white people by name. Yang did, just like that. He's the only guy who's not only overtly or covertly calling for your extinction; he's the only guy on the record for trying to stop it.

And, he's promising to stop it by taxing the hell of the Enemy. Which again, as Tucker mentioned, isn't a huge abstract thing The Jews or the Left. No. The enemy is Big Tech. It's Amazon, it's Google, It's Apple. It's Facebook. It's Twitter. It's Woke Capital. It's those guys who aren't only taking your jobs, they're using their monopoly in the management of information to censore us, hide us, slander us and ostracize us. You might remember that Trump also hinted at doing something about that. Regulate Facebook and Twitter as utilities to make sure the Right could actually fight the Culture War, and perhaps show that there's a majority of people against injecting synthetic hormones into 12 year old children. That he'd make big tech build in America and stop avoiding taxes with blatant laundering tricks. Well, Trump did nothing, and he's avoiding the topic. Yang isn't. I have nothing against Amazon's business, but Bezos chose sides by buying the Washington Post and recently going on a censorship spree, banning right wing books from Amazon. He must pay. Yang says he will.

I don't know if UBI would work. Americans are crying bloody murder about a proposed 10% VAT. I say cry me a river. Europeans have a 20% VAT. It's annoying, but it's not a big deal. Smart people say that automation is overhyped, it's not growing

---

340   https://www.occidentaldissent.com/2019/03/15/yang-gangs-interrogation/

that fast, self-driving cars, one of the biggest talking points of Yang, are likely to not even happen after all. That may be true. But I'd like to say that the beauty of UBI is not that it's actually necessary in the way Yang says it is, to give people something to fall back on while they find a new job.

Tucker is also worried about the middle class trucker. But Tucker's answer is to ban automation. Go full Luddite. Yang is talking about automation a lot. But he doesn't want to stop it. By implementing UBI he wouldn't stop automation, he'd accelerate it. Businesses would start automating like crazy once people left unsatisfying jobs to go play Fortnite on UBI or try an instagram e-thot career. A big majority of white collar jobs are complete and utter bullshit make-work made by government regulation to keep people busy and have some income to tax. If Yang succeeded in his proposed plan to completely change the regulatory paradigm to adapt to the computer economy at last, companies could actually get rid of all the inefficiencies, and automate everything. Starting with the bureaucracy.

You know who else is doing this? China. In 2017 when Xi Jinping basically named himself president for life, I was asked to look into his alleged eminence grise, Wang Huning. This guy wrote a book after a trip to America in the 1980s, when China was trying to find a way to square the circle of their adoption of free-market enterprise in the country. Wang realized he could justify free enterprise by saying that the United States "manages the people through their businesses, by regulating employment and taking taxes from labor". Basically arguing that Communism and Capitalism weren't so different, the latter as just outsourcing the "people management" to the business corporations.

Well China is pushing hard for developing AI and automation. Which is weird in a country which could have a serious unemployment problem if automation goes on. But China doesn't care. Why not? Because China has realized that with Internet and modern computing, they don't need the corporations to manage the people anymore. They can do it directly. Everybody has a mobile phone with a camera and a microphone 24/7 with them. The government knows your every move. You don't need to shame people into buying your ideology by threatening with firing them from their jobs, like America does. That's so 20th century. Now you can control behavior directly with internet surveillance. Social credit is an extension of this trend. It boggles the mind that accelerationists aren't talking more about this. Not saying it's a good thing. But the tech is here and it's happening anywhere. The only place where it isn't happening is Europe because we've outsourced it to American companies.

If you think UBI might work at giving people hope and readjusting the economy in a more just and fair way, sticking it to the oligarchs, vote for Yang. If you just want $1,000 a month, vote for Yang. If you think UBI would crash everything, vote for Yang, as this gay earth deserves crashing. If you just want UBI to show people that democracy inevitable ends with the people voting themselves money and thus proving democracy is a sham and discredit it as a political system, vote for Yang.

And if you want the final death of 20th century politics, and a new paradigm which breaks with the thievery of Boomers inflating the currency so that asset prices are rising through new records every year, while young people have to go through unpaid internships and 'gig economy' servitude until their 40s, while the Bioleninist government is busy with the soft genocide of every productive person with natural biological instincts.

Then Vote for Yang. I rest my case.

Debt

2019-04-22 // history, economics, capitalism, theory

A few weeks ago I had a short exchange with Nick Land on Twitter on the issue of debt.

https://twitter.com/Outsideness/status/1115053094654451712

Debt is a huge issue, a big part of what's wrong with the fabric of modernity, a big factor of what's driving modern civilization into collapse. And yet it has remained largely underdiscussed in these circles. Moldbug, who to the end still remained something of a libertarian, did have a keen interest in finance, and after the great crisis of 2008 made a series of long posts[341] on financial crises and how to design a properly sound banking system. His "favorite topic[342]" he even called it. Well it's certainly not my favorite topic, nor I'm sure it's Mr. Land's, but it's nonetheless a fascinating issue, and more importantly, a critical one.

Again, my approach to all intellectual issues is to think about its history, and the one thing that strikes one when thinking about debt is how easy-going the ancients were about them. Sovereign bankruptcies were routine, and nothing really happened. But most importantly, debt jubilees were *very* common. Mr. Land here seems to think it's a horrible idea, and he may be right, but I can't be faulted for liking something that Chinese emperors did every few years as part of general amnesties. New emperor? Cancel the people's debt. Emperor has a change of mood and sets a new regnal era? Cancel the debt. Cute imperial baby is born? Out with the debt. Some Emperors had general amnesties almost every year. It's interesting to note that the Song Dynasty, famous for its fabulous wealth, commercial mindset and urban culture, and thus a polity which you would expect to have more care about enforcing contracts, had over 200 debt jubilees over its 318 year history. That's one every eighteen months.

Again, you could say that the one thing that ensured the Great Divergence, the Rise of the West, the Industrial Revolutions and basically everything that's nice and productive about the modern world (and there's plenty of that, I do like fast transport, air conditioning and modern hygiene, thank you very much), was the establishment of the Sanctity of Contracts as an important part of Western culture. There's certainly

---

[341] https://www.unqualified-reservations.org/2008/10/misesian-explanation-of-bank-crisis/

[342] https://www.unqualified-reservations.org/2011/10/professor-krugman-on-maturity/

something to that. A non-negligible part of reactionary authors will spit on Libertarianism a dozen times a day, but they will stay give you a 2 hour speech in praise of the Joint Stock Corporation as the fundamental basis of the modern economy and Western Civilization as we know it. By that line of reasoning, the only reason we ever got away of the Malthusian trap was when we stopped forgiving damn debtors and we used state authority to enforce commercial contracts.

And yet, reactionaries since Moldbug have also been very concerned with the problem of sovereignty. Most precisely, the lack of it. We bemoan the lack of ability of the holders of political power in the West to take hard measures that could fix many of the social problems which afflict us. But, you know, that's not surprising given that we don't allow our political authorities to mess with "the sanctity of contracts". If routine commercial transactions are held to be above the supreme power of the land, how the hell do we expect them to get anything done at all?

Why did the kings and emperors of yore issue decree debt jubilees so often? Why at all? Not just to get debt out of their own shoulders, obviously, they had the power to do that and just that, and do not relieve the commoners from their own debt obligations. And yet they did that, all the time: have commoners be free of paying back their debts. Again this sounds outrageous to our modern sensibilities, and yet it was routinely done for millennia, and everybody thought it perfectly natural. Part of that is because anything the Sovereign did was perfectly natural. The whole point of being king is that you get to do things like issue debt jubilees and screw the merchants royally. Pun intended. There's such a thing as different sorts of power, and economic power, the power that arises from having massive amounts of wealth, is very real. And yet, all that power is good for nothing in front of the King's authority, who on a whim can wipe out all your claims of debt collection. The merchants cry, and the indebted peasants rejoice. That's just good politics for the king: gains him popular favor, and signals his power.

But was that all? Just the King, sticking it to the merchants because he can? The whole frequency of the measure seems to hint there's something more going on. Maybe debt jubilees were an actual tool of governance. A good tool, a necessary tool, in order to achieve some positive outcome. Surely in terms of political stability, the most immediate concern of kings. And maybe something more. Maybe debt relief just actually fixes something in society, corrects some imbalances which lead to not just more safety for the king, but actually a better society, in terms of economics, natality and just general happiness and prosperity.

If you have read Peter Turchin's book War and Peace and War, and if you haven't you should stop right here and just go read it right now (if you have time for my blog you really should be going and read that book), you might recall Chapter 10, which Turchin titled "The Matthew Principle". That's a rather forced coinage from a quote of the evangelist. The idea is basically that the rich always get richer and the poor always get poorer. That's a historical reality and there's plenty of evidence for it in premodern times, those very times I'm referring to as having frequent amnesties and debt jubilees, canceling everybody's debt and starting over, screwing with creditors every few years.

Now, when talking at this level of abstraction it's always important to take a pause and think carefully of the definitions we are using. Think of the proposition "the rich always get richer". Who exactly is "the rich" here? Are we talking of individuals? Do rich men, on average, grow their fortune over time until their death? I'm not sure that's true, but even if it were, analysis of a single lifetime are hardly interesting. What about families? Are rich families, again on average, richer over generations? That seems intuitively to be true, and Gregory Clark has written an interesting book arguing that case, The Son also Rises. The difference between families and individuals is that families to some extent get to choose their members, so rich family names persist by accepting rich heiresses and the like, and gently expelling underperforming sons, helping maintain or grow the family "honor".

What about the rich as a class? That was the focus of Turchin's argument. What he meant is that absent political action to counter it (i.e. violence), economic inequality always grows. And grows. And grows. It happens that it always ends, or at least has ended to this point in history, with some eruption of violence, either a popular revolt, a civil war, or some kind of crackdown by the government against the wealthy. But if you were somehow able to avoid violence from ever happening, inequality just would continue to grow, slowly but steadily, by its implacable mathematical logic, until we got a Gini coefficient of 1. That's just a law of nature. Pure, abstract math, in practical terms. Just the way humans work. The rich just keep getting richer, and the poor keep getting poorer, and there's nothing you can do about it except using organized violence (i.e. politics) to stop the process. Those processes of growing inequality and eventual freak-out tend to last about a 100 years, so Turchin calls them "secular cycles".

Turchin, who may be right or wrong but is nonetheless a great writer, describes his argument with a very easy example. In any competition, he notes, the poor are at a disadvantage against the rich, having fewer resources, and so overtime tend to lose ground. Think of land, the almost only source of wealth in civilized societies until very recently. Assume an initially completely equal distribution of land. And that's, by the way, not an absurdity. There's actually a very good example in China's Tang Dynasty, which adopted an "equal-field" system. All land was owned by the state, which allotted equal sized fields to individual peasant families.

What happened afterwards? Concentration. Little by little, some peasants were thriftier, others more prone to spend. Some were luckier, some more unfortunate with weather, or disease, or family issues. Some peasants started mortgaging away their fields to other peasants who again, due to thrift or luck had money available to spend. Those latter peasants then ended up with more land. Rince and repeat the process for several decades, and you get some very rich guys and a lot of landless vagrants. Keep the process going for even longer and you'd get even more inequality.

As Turchin himself says it:

"The mathematical model I developed, however, tells us that this mechanism by itself will not produce a vast gulf between the rich and the poor. When land becomes a scarce commodity, however, another process begins to operate. Human beings need to consume a certain amount of goods to survive. Most basically, they have to get enough food. Those who do not have enough land to feed themselves will have to start selling what they have to make up the difference. As a result, they become poorer. By contrast, those who have more land than they need to feed themselves will have a surplus income that they can use to acquire even more land. Thus, the rich get richer. The positive feedback of the Matthew principle arises as a result of threshold of the minimum consumption level. The Matthew principle ensures that all people whose land holdings are below the threshold—the poor—gradually lose their remaining property, which ends up in the hands of the rich. Finally, the population is divided into a tiny minority of wealthy landowners and a huge majority of landless proletarians."

But that seldom happened, as eventually some ambitious man always found a way of organizing those landless vagrants into a rebel army and started a big fat war. Chinese dynasties tended to all last exactly 250 years, with a big rebellion in the middle. Two secular cycles. And the Chinese historians always agree in the culprit. 土地兼并, land concentration. Every single time. Europe had less obvious closure but also plenty of wars to stir things up. And eventually, of course, the Age of Revolutions.

Things are of course different now in our incredibly diversified economies; even landless peasants or the equivalent today can work their way up some corporate ladder or find some new economic niche and start a successful business. But the fact that poor people, on average, are at a disadvantage in resource competition against the rich. The rich just have less to lose. As Half Sigma, unsuccessful candid Jew always says, talk of "risk-taking entrepreneurs" is just bullshit. Rich people have enough money stashed away to live comfortably all their lives. They are investing their spare wealth, and yes, there's always a risk there. But big deal. They're covered.

Again, I'm following Turchin and talking like evolution ends at the neck. Which it doesn't. People are genetically different, not only in intelligence but appearance (a very important part of individual capital), and a myriad personality traits which affect one's ability to gain wealth. Those successful genes, "moxie" as Greg Cochran[343] calls them, also get sent up to wealthier families as successful people choose to marry into them,

---

[343] https://westhunt.wordpress.com/2014/03/23/the-son-also-rises/

depleting the lower classes of the most fundamental resource, the very physical basis of economic success, especially in a culture like ours, without marriage taboos or formally separate social classes.

Modern debt has perhaps little to do with the debt of a peasant mortgaging his small plot of land to pay for his father's funeral. While commoners today have plenty of student or consumer debt, most debt is hold by corporations or public entities, in a complete madness of intertwined obligations going on for trillions and trillions. But it's not unreasonable to see corporations as the perhaps foremost subjects of the modern state, and not humans, who are but appendixes to corporations in the eyes of many bureaucratic agencies. Debt in the modern economy might not be as obvious as the poor medieval peasant of Turchin's tale, but the deleterious social effects, and the existence of a class of advantaged people using their position to increase their wealth against the debt of the masses is still very similar, and fits Turchin's equations.

Back to the beginning of the post, you can now see what debt jubilees were meant to achieve. Interestingly, Turchin's book doesn't mention the word "jubilee" even once. He probably didn't think them important, as economic inequality historically did grow anyway. But surely periodic legal debt relief made the process slower. Eased societal contradictions to a more manageable level for the court. But it was never enough, it was barely a stopgap to the inexorable trend. But at least it served to lower the gas boiling the frog.

I just realized that I started this post with the intention of arguing in favor of debt relief, of learning from the ancients how to pacify society. But given the limited power it historically had, and given the trends we are seeing now, the complete obliteration of Western Civilization down the road to becoming Brazil, then South Africa and ultimately Haiti, maybe the proper accelerationist position is to make the fire stronger and make the damned frog jump from the pot once and for all. No jubilee. No peace. Let's just observe the coming of the age of the oligarchs, and hope it breaks down fast.

If it does, though.

The reactionary tax code

2019-05-12 // economics, theory, nrx

What are we all doing here? By 'here', I mean the internet, by 'we', I mean the sort of person who very kindly reads this blog of mine regularly and/or writes similar stuff in blogs or Twitter or whatever.

My original goal was to understand what is leftism, why leftist people exist and why our societies are decaying by enabling leftism to dominate all the levers of power. After years of writing, years of reading, and years of talking with like-minded gentlemen over the internet, I think I've succeeded at that task. You can read some examples of it in the sidebar as "best posts".

I've also been meeting some readers in person over the last few years, and they all agree that the "analysis phase" of this little movement we've come to call neoreaction is done. Moldbug started the whole thing, asked the right questions, showed how everything we thought we knew was wrong, then he left to build interesting stuff. Nick Land asked another set of right questions, found out nobody dared answer them, and then he left to write horror fiction. I here have done my little part on finishing what I considered was most important: an analysis of the history and the psychology of leftism.

Well, that's done, we know leftists are sociopathic status maximizers who seek groups of people who, for contingent or increasingly genetic reasons, have low status, and thus a great incentive to disturb the political process and create chaos in society. They have much to gain, little to lose, and thus are ideal employees with an incentive to keep loyal. Ok we know that one. Now what? What do we do? We should do something.

Well, I'm not the first one to be asked that. Moldbug was asked that. What did he say? Become worthy. Funnily it seems he took that from the Chinese concept of the "Mandate of Heaven", i.e. the post-hoc rationalization of successful rebels after they took the throne by force. The idea is that if I was able to take over the throne by force, by definition the previous monarch didn't have the favor of Heaven (i.e. we'd say God), and the fact that I took it means Heaven likes me somehow, so it's alright if I rule now. QED.

So was Moldbug advocating for armed rebellion à la Zhū Yuánzhāng? Not quite. Well, nobody knows. I don't think he himself knew (he's welcome to comment here to clarify now that he's retired. We miss you M). And let's face it, nobody knows what to do. The Bioleninist left rules the United States, which rules the Western world, and they're hellbent in destroying any slight hint of opposition. They're winning, and all we can do is root, anonymously, for enemy countries such as Syria, Russia or China in the vague hope that at least some balance in international affairs will stop, or even just stall the Cathedral from destroying the native cultures of Europe and North America for good.

Now even crypto-homo influencers like Paul Joseph Watson or thousand-cock-stare wacko Jewish broads like Laura Loomer are blacklisted from all social media. Other, more consistent right-wingers who were vain enough to go public with their real names are being physically banned from many countries or being denied the ability to open bank accounts (!). Meanwhile President of the United States, Donald J. Trump, does nothing but screech on Twitter about how Surprised he is, and that he's Monitoring the Situation. Thanks Don.

So yeah, Moldbug had a point. Do nothing, until you're ready to go all in. We're not ready to go all-in, not even close to that point. So just do your thing, take care of your family, have a bunch of kids, and make sure they're not groomed into the Bioleninist sewers. And make money. A lot of money.

That said, there's one thing I wanna do, which is to continue blogging. One thing that I miss reading around is policy ideas. Yes, the Left is still moving further Left, we have less power than we ever have, it is absolutely impossible that any idea that we may have would ever be implemented in our present political structure. Our ideas tend to be, as an elder of neoreaction put it, coup-complete problems, problems which are completely untractable in our modern political structures and would require Fnargl to materialize in this world to be implemented. Be that as it may, it is still important to put some ideas out there, if just in order to exercise our brains and refresh our eyes seeing how a more intelligent way of governing would work. And who knows, maybe Xi Jinping or Putin senpai actually notices me some day.

So I was thinking of taxes. That modern Western tax codes are a big, a huge pile of ultra-condensed evil is beyond question. They're outrageously long, convoluted, designed so that normal people are scammed routinely every year, and rich people get undue advantages thanks to the aid of an army of tax accountants and their nefarious tactics. The very existence of an occupation such as "tax accountants" is of course an artificial result of how complicated the tax code is, and that very complexity is very likely done on purpose in order to ensure that evil guild of tax accountants still have a job. I, with Andrew Yang, am an ardent supporter of automation, and thus I can't wait to the day where the tax code is simplified, automated, and all those tax lawyer bugmen are out of a job, and have to do something actually useful for a living. Or they can also just live off UBI, because UBI is Great and Merciful, and protects even poor boring bugmen such as them.

Speaking of Andrew Yang, peace be on his name, I should have elaborated a bit more on my enthusiasm for UBI and other ideas of his when I wrote about him[344] a few weeks ago. It is a fact that in pure economic terms, human labor is just not worth as much as it used to be up to the 1970s. Real wages have dropped all over the developed world, and the income share of labor has plummeted. Whether that is due to automation, or to competition from China, or due to women entering the labor force, that can be debated, but it doesn't really matter. Labor is losing out, that is a fact. A sad fact. But whatever Tucker Carlson and his fellow nostalgics say, you can't just go full Luddite. You might do that, but Napoleon won't, and eventually Napoleon always conquers beautiful Venice. So I say we try to think how one could use the current economic circumstances to promote a better way of governing the economy.

Well, if labor is losing value across the economy, the least modern governments could do, is to stop taxing labor. Not only are income taxes the main source of tax revenue in all of the developed world, payroll taxes are also a crushing burden, and an increasing one due to low birthrates. Well, stop that crap. No payroll taxes. Stop all that crap of deducting social security and healthcare from wages, with some part masked as "employer burden", which only makes the paperwork of hiring people all the more burdensome. Make all old-age pensions and healthcare costs go to the general budget, and streamline the hiring and firing process to make it transparent how much money every employee actually makes and how much he costs his employer.

Speaking of income tax, punishing people for making money really isn't the best way of incentivizing work, is it. And don't get me started with tax filing and all that paperwork. It's medieval. Now, you may say that the government has to take money from somewhere, and today people earn their income in form of cash, so that's what you tax. And sure, that was the case when the whole thing started about 100 years ago. But look at today. Most countries haven't balanced their budgets in decades. Japan is a famous example, with about half of public expenditures being financed with public debt. The US federal debt issuance is also out of the charts. And yet there is no inflation.

Why not? Because governments today are more advanced than they were in the 1930s. They can now not only print money, but target it into where they want it to go. Governments today print money, and make sure that the excess money supply goes to the stock market or real estate to prop up asset prices and make rich people richer, and thus happier. Modern Monetary Theory is on the news lately, and that reflects the growing consensus among economists that governments don't need to collect taxes to finance themselves. They can just print money and use their coercive powers to make sure it flows where they want it to.

---

[344] https://spandrell.com/2019/03/23/acceleration-by-yang/

Why collect taxes then? Not to collect money. But just as yet another mechanism to control the economy and the population. Tax collection is a way of removing money from the particular places or people where you want it removed. You could, today, theoretically just not collect taxes at all and just run the government by printing money. But why would you relinquish the power to tax people at will? Besides, tax revenue is a useful economic indicator.

If we're lucky, the likes of Alexandria Ocasio-Cortés and her brown dancing milkers will serve to bring to the public the idea that taxing is about power, and not about the economy. And if it is so, taxing becomes a matter of government discretion. After decades of somewhat disingenuous "technocratic" government, modern politicians are increasingly moralizing their agendas and running government in order to advance their ideas of morality. I approve of that mindset. Confucius would be proud. It indeed follows the same principles; Confucianism and its reboot as Neoconfucianism represented the victory of the bureaucrat civilians (one might call them the priestly class) over the military establishment. That's a process that we are seeing in the West only recently, but powered further by women joining in the process, and women of course can only be priests, never warriors. So moralizing it is. I say we join in, at least tentatively.

So what would a reactionary tax policy look like? Let me propose a few ideas. First, as I mentioned above, don't tax labor. You want people to work. Use tax policy to discourage the worst parts of human nature, not the best ones. What I called before "social failures"[345] in lieu of the "market failures" the economists talk about. Could just as well call them "psychological failures". Just the parts of human behavior that evolution hasn't had the time to fix after the Neolithic Revolution, and especially the problems which have arisen in modernity due to motorized transport and electronic communications.

You shouldn't tax labor but you could very well tax corporate power. A lot of people seek promotions and positions in corporate management not because of the money, but because they're sadists who get a kick out of lording people around. Others stumble upon positions of management against their actual disposition due to common problems such as the Peter Principle.[346] You could modulate that with a Management Tax. You want to brag about being an executive? Then pay. I'm sure most people would pay gladly. At the very least a tax on corporate board seats could change the presently pervasive revolving door of "retired" politicians given discrete payment for previously rendered services. Might as well call it the Committee Tax. Only the owner doesn't pay.

---

[345] https://spandrell.com/2017/05/14/the-role-of-government-2/

[346] https://en.wikipedia.org/wiki/Peter_principle

Given that our future government (and all future governments) is going to be a Moral Government, it is imperative that we bring our modern knowledge of the failures of human nature into our new governance structure. Since the dawn of humanity, people have known that humans have such a thing as vices. Christians frame it as the seven "cardinal sins", pride, greed, lust, envy, gluttony, wrath and sloth. That's not bad, but individual differences are quite huge here, and it's hard to set a standard definition of where the line is between a glutton and some guy who likes to eat. And things like pride or envy are a mental state, not a behavior, so it can hardly be dealt with.

A more scientific way of putting this is to address the problem of addiction. I said before that neoreaction is reaction with better knowledge of history and some modern cognitive science. We know now that there are some substances or behaviors which for some reason or another hack our brain chemistry and make them hard to stop. A good example is the classic male vices: gambling, whoring and drinking (i.e. drugs more generally). Men do these things, some more, some less, I guess over a Gaussian distribution. But we do it, and will always do. It feels good. Some puritanical cultures (mostly Abrahamic) have banned some or all of these behaviors, driving them underground, but hardly extinguishing them. Other more enterprising cultures (e.g. the Chinese) historically decided to run them as public enterprises and tax them heavily. Men are gonna whore and gamble anyway, might as well regulate it and make them fill the public coffers with it. Alcohol and tobacco are taxed heavily today for exactly the same reason, and everybody understands it's a good thing. Do the same for cannabis now that it's being legalized. Although I'm a fan of Andrew Yang and others' idea of granting a monopoly of pot trading to black people; might as well fund their welfare that way. Fellow fans of Brave New World may also get the hint.

To that we might also add videogames today. Videogames are a huge deal, millions upon millions of people spend untold thousands of hours on them. Videogames are by now the most important entertainment industry. It's time the state give it the status it deserves. How? By taxing the hell out of them. You wanna waste your youth on Fortnite? Your call. But it can't be free. It stands to reason that online subscription services like Xbox Live are taxed at a 100-200% rate. Note also that internet gaming in China requires logging in with one's real ID card so that minors are legally restricted from playing up to a certain age, and have time limits for teenagers. I think it's a great idea. No SWATing in China either.

History has given plenty of attention to male vices, but it is only fair that we also put some spotlight to female vices, of which there is also no shortage. Women's vices perhaps have never been addressed because women didn't have financial independence until 60 years ago, but now they do, so let us make them pay. Women have their own vices of superstition (e.g. astrology and divination), attention-whoring (e.g. constant revealing selfies on social media), and celebrity-chasing (we've all seen teenage girls going literally insane over some midget singer with makeup). I saw we tax the shit out of all those industries; and preferably nationalize them and run them effectively as a government department. Again China is innovating here, with their tight censorship of social media and recently enforced ideological control over celebrities.

To this, add a universal consumption tax, which is easy to enforce, especially now with the coming cashless society, and which you can tweak to charge higher for pointless luxury goods. Tax the stuff the rich like at, say, 50%. Tax cooked food, but not raw ingredients. But do charge salads. Fuck those. Americans really need to get over their hatred of value-added taxes. Surely they beat being taxed for making money? Don't you want all those unproductive net tax-receivers to pay something?

I'm also a big fan of wealth caps. Roosh, who's getting interesting as he transforms into a Sufi monk after his T levels started crashing down at age 40, recently put it very well[347], while proposing a wealth cap of $100 million:

"Jeff Bezos, Bill Gates, George Soros, and many other billionaires will all go back to being one-hundred millionaires as long as the bulk of their business and social activity takes place in the United States. That leaves them plenty enough money for penthouses, yachts, and high-class whores, but not enough to subvert society with a globohomo agenda."

Of course a wealth cap would be tricky to enforce; none of these men have all their billions in cash; they just happen to own trillion dollar companies, and it wouldn't make sense to punish a person as his company gains in value. Now of course we can all argue about how modern states have engaged in artificial asset inflation in the stock market, about how valuable these companies really are. But surely some companies out there really are valuable and efficient, and taking stock from their founders because they've reached a wealth cap doesn't sound like a good idea. Any commenters with good ideas are welcome to share them here.

On a different note; for all the panic about global warming, which we all know is an evil plot by government and associated entities to have an eternal excuse to control more of the economy and have an excuse to request bigger budgets; isn't the modern logistics industry to blame for some of that? We talk of globalization as this amazing human feat. Which it is; but isn't it wasteful that every little piece of machinery requires world-length supply chains, moving a myriad little components from a dozen countries until its final assembly? Actually there's a good way of fixing that problem. Tariffs. The WTO was set up with the ultimate goal of having zero tariffs across the world. Make that a 10% universal tariff. Try to encourage supply chains to be country-sized, or at least trade-block sized. That would get some much needed revenue for UBI too.

---

[347] https://www.rooshv.com/6-policies-i-would-enact-as-president-of-the-united-states

In my last post on Debt[348], I argued that the world's financial system is obviously in the verge of collapse due to the egregious amount of debt being issued in all countries in the past 10 years. Something's gotta give, and it's increasingly obvious that the financial system we have is absurd, with its automated algorithmic trading depending on milisecond speed advantages by bribing NYT officials to put their servers 10 feet closer to the NYSE, cultish scams like Herbalife[349], or the constant IPOs by unprofitable Silicon Valley gypsy-economy e-gig companies[350], which are basically just doing regulatory arbitrage by virtue of being Woke. Of course stock exchanges are a big part of the great story of the success of capitalism, but a few well placed taxes and restrictions should be put to rein in that huge, evil mess.

A big problem, well, the biggest problem of modern societies is the IQ-shredding problem. Intelligent people have the fewer children, and the decline in human capital we've been having for the past 150 years is bad enough. There's been lots of talk all over the world about how to encourage birth rates through tax policy. While many argue for sheer cash payments per child (a Japanese TV show was just advocating for $100k per child, no questions asked), it shows that governments are actually HBD-aware at some level and do not want the sheer increase in trashy population that immediate cash payments would ensure. The people who you want having the children are those who *don't* need the money. I still think a child-less tax is a good idea. No kids after 25, you get taxed. Less than 2 kids after 30, you get taxed. Less than 3 kids after 35, you-get-taxed. I'd say a TFR of 2.5-3 should be the aim of public policy, no more, no less. Child-less taxes shouldn't be crushing, just annoying. You want to nudge people, but the freaks who just hate family life should be allowed to weed themselves out of the gene pool.

We know what we don't like about modern society. We (now, finally) know why we got here and how it happened. But what do we stand for? What do we want? Let's think about that. We have nothing better to do anyway.

---

[348] https://spandrell.com/2019/04/23/debt/

[349] 2013/08/18/clausewitz-lenin-robin-dunbar/

[350] https://www.unz.com/isteve/hot-high-tech-startup-ideas-of-2014/?highlight=startup+startup

Class Struggle is underrated

2019-05-30 // status, hbd, theory

So our good Russian friend Anatoly Karlin had this take on his blog

https://www.unz.com/akarlin/climate-bioleninism/

I paste the complete link because the URL is quite ominous, "climate bioleninism". Imagine that. Karlin there makes a point that ideas that flatter the upper-class, like global warming, become entrenched, while ideas that they find inconvenient, like the genetic load of IQ or HBD more generally get killed or ostracized, no matter how solid the science behind them.

https://twitter.com/akarlin88/status/1133547242588168195

Seems Karlin thought I wouldn't like talk of Class Struggle, but he's wrong. I'm a great fan of the idea. The perhaps most basic part of my thinking is that whatever exists, exists for a reason. It follows that whatever is popular must have something going on for it. I'm certainly no Marxist, but there is much wisdom in Marxist theory, and I personally think that Class Struggle was a conceptual bomb which was so good and so powerful at the time that it basically destroyed and replaced Christianity all by itself. Well, I exaggerate, but not by much.

Incidentally, and I only learned of this recently, apparently in China, the idea that "everything exists for a reason", 存在即合理, is taught in high-schools and universities across the country, and is part of the official Communist Orthodoxy there. Apparently they took it from Hegel, I guess through Marx being a Hegelian and all that. The original being *was vernünftig ist, das ist wirklich; und was wirklich ist, das ist vernünftig*. It more accurately translates to "if it exists, it is reasonable". Pretty much half of Chinese websites frequented by college students are a debate on this one clause, mostly because college students there as everywhere else are all obsessed with morality and they interpret the word "reasonable" as meaning "good". Yes, it's all so tiresome.

Anyway, I wrote many, many years ago, that Class Struggle is the reason that things like HBD will never in a million years become widely accepted. Check this 2012 post.[351] The idea is: the most powerful force in the world is the drive for upward status mobility. People crave more status. The second most powerful force in the world is the need for status conservation. If you can't raise in status, you want at least to keep what you have, and you want to keep the status of your whole family; ideally your whole

---

[351] https://spandrell.com/2012/11/22/the-brain-drain-trap/

Dunbar circle. That's what Social Class is, a big fat fence to make sure your family never ever drops in status. Given that actual performance is mostly genetic, social class tends to persist over centuries, (as Karlin mentions quoting Gregory Clark's *The Son Also Rises*), but there's some randomness to genetics too, and upper classes tend to do strange things to their mating practices in order to aid their status-conservation plans, like having too few children or marrying late, so some degree of social class movement does still happen.

Unless you take the Status Conservation Drive to its final logical conclusion, and go full-Hindu on it. Indians went full-retard on social class, and divided their society in 30,000 jatis, ranked more or less in castes, and never ever shall they mix or change their rank. They made social classes into full-fledged ethnic groups. That's what happens when the upper-class gets what they want. Complete and Eternal Status Conservation. Of course that's in the end just a psychological thing, if inter-subjective. Brahmins are high-status but they're not necessarily rich or handsome, and those are sources of real-world status too, at least today in capitalist society. But Indians seem over all to be quite happy with their system, and everybody knows their place.

All other societies failed to codify social class, and Abrahamic religions went out of their way to demonize the idea and preach universalism. Everybody is valuable, it's all about the individual. That has its advantages, as it allows high-performers to rise in status no matter their pedigree. It is not by chance that Muslims have lorded over India for 1,000 years and not the other way around. But no amount of preaching by Christians or Muslims is able to cancel that fundamental mental drive of humans: we all want our children to inherit our social standing, or improve it if possible.

That's what I mentioned in that old post of mine, and I still stand by it. I think a big part of the motivation for foreign immigration into Western countries is that white people like that their social inferiors are visibly so. Canada has (had?) this funny way of talking about non-white people, Visible Minorities. White proles are just as white as White Aristocrats. But a Guatemalan or Pakistani maid is just obviously made of a different stock than her master. And she likes that. Her son won't fool around with the maid. She can talk differently with her, be ruder or more annoying than a native prole, who knows more of local manners, would tolerate. The way I put it back then is: Prole co-ethnics are the personification of downward mobility. And everybody hates downward mobility, so the physical replacement of proles who look like you is actually a very good proposition for most people. Call this the Housewife Theory of the Great Replacement. Somebody put it in French please.

The same applies for the male business owner. If I had a dollar for everytime a white business owner has praised their brown employees over the native kids, I'd be a billionaire. "They work harder, they're hungrier, they're just better and more honest people". Nah, they just take more shit, mostly because they can't really understand what you're saying. And you love giving it to them, because half the reason you started a business is because you just enjoy giving people shit.

And indeed, the reason why IQ-realism, which is the most obvious of all obvious aspects of human nature, will never get anywhere, is because we have a "meritocracy". Access to the ruling class today is mediated by "education", i.e. by schools and universities, in which supposedly some magical things are said, and students there listen to a lot of those magical things, read some others, then re-write them into "papers", and suddenly they become smarter, so that's why they deserve the highest status that our society allots. It's all designed so that every piece of status gained can be traced to some piece of "work", i.e. "merit", so if you don't have high status, well, you should have worked harder! This moral logic only works if the output per unit of work (i.e. intelligence, or 'performance' if you will) is assumed to be equal among all humans,.

If intelligence is not equally distributed, then social status is not about work (merit), but about whatever it is that intelligence comes from. If it's genes, bad, because then everyone and their dog (remember, *everyone*'s paramount interest in life is social status) will try to interfere in genetics and mating, most likely through the power of the state. If it's random, that's somewhat better in that the likely government intervention wouldn't be as jarring (no interfering in who mates with whom), but still not good enough, as it deprives high-status people of the satisfaction of their status being "earned". Aristocrats didn't think their status was earned, and they were perfectly happy, but our modern liberal ruling class, as good Puritans has taken their Christian universalism to heart, and must believe that they not only get to rule over you, but that they earned the right to rule over you. This relates with the much greater willingness of liberal elites to interfere in the lives of their subjects.

Note the hysterical reaction against genetic determinism is in no small part motivated by fear of public interference in mating. Or to put it plainly, in sex. It is rather odd that liberals, not really leftists but pretty much 90% of modern white people go batshit crazy at hearing the word "eugenics". Why? Eugenics is the science of improving the population's genes. What is wrong with that? "Aggh!! Evil!!" Evil? How so?

Because it would entail breaking up couples and having a cold, rational appraisal of who should be fucking whom. And people hate that idea. For good reason, to be fair. You like who you like. Attraction is not a choice. Men often like their sluts, or grow fond of the plain Janes that the so painstakingly were able to attract, but they don't want to talk about it. And women all too often get carried away by their hybristophilia and decide to mate with dumb, evil, violent men. All of which would not just be disapproved of, but actively impeded by a society and a state with eugenics in its mind. So in order that people can keep having sex with the bad partners of their choice, the word "eugenics" must be made a taboo, and the mere concept must be erased from the minds of all the good-thinking.

That won't change until either liberal society dies, replaced by whichever traditional society outbreeds it (Islam if we're lucky, Black Africa if we're not, some brand of Christianity if there's a miracle). Or until somebody develops a viable means of ectogenesis, i.e. artificial wombs. That would mean procreation is completely divorced from sex. An optimistic take on that possibility is Aldous Huxley's masterpiece, *Brave New World*. In these days of feminism and Globohomo, I fear it wouldn't be as pleasant. That said, it could be here soon.[352]

---

[352] https://metro.co.uk/2019/05/14/human-babies-born-using-an-artificial-womb-possible-in-a-decade-8156458/

Tiananmen

2019-06-06 // china, history, redpill

It's been 30 years this week since the famous riots in Beijing. I refuse to give any attention to an incident which was of little consequence, which nobody in China knows about, and to the extent they know about it nobody but a small number of dieharders (i.e. the people rioting back then and their families) gives a shit about.

If the Western press won't shut up about something, odds are is all a pig pile of fake news, of official propaganda which has been concocted up at some upper level and been issued hierarchically to the Cathedral press so everybody toes the official message. That applies to things like #Metoo, to the idea of "Russian interference" in the 2016 American election, the goddamn Rohingya, and yes, the stories of the "Tiananmen massacre".

So I won't add my blog to that message volume. Which is what they want, of course. Attention. To occupy mental space and crowd out other ideas, so the fake news gets around. Don't give it to them.

That said, some people do ask me what Tiananmen was about. Short answer: nobody knows, they won't tell, everybody is lying. Long answer: probably an internal coup attempt by a pro-Western faction of the CPC (led by premier Zhao Ziyang) with some Western intelligence support; a coup attempt which perhaps was aided by other factions inside China which disliked Deng Xiaoping and just wanted to take advantage of the disorder to drag him down.

Didn't work. Suck it up. Zhao Ziyang died in captivity, and all his team and their families went to exile to the US where, to this day, they still LARP as a sort of liberal government in exile. As CIA largesse has dried up, many of them have converted to Evangelical Christianity in a desperate attempt to get some Americans to give them money. Just take a look at dorks like this guy[353] to see what sort of people we're talking about.

Here's a short Twitter thread with some useful links on the topic.

https://twitter.com/thespandrell/status/1136535187431538688

---

[353] https://en.wikipedia.org/wiki/Wu%27erkaixi

How far is far enough

2019-06-18 // theory, Top Post, nrx, power, nationalism

A while ago I wrote a post on tax law[354], proposing some ideas that I thought could plausibly make for a better existence if implemented by a sane government.

Reactions to that were mixed. It was, admittedly, an uncharacteristic post. I am not a "policy wonk", I'm usually more interested in deeper questions of history and human psychology as it applies to our political environment. As such, some people said that that sort of piece, proposing some tweaks to tax policy or this or that law is not just beside the point, it's actively harmful. The problems of modern society are, they would have it, not something that can be fixed through the legal political process. And talking as if the state could just tweak this or that law to make our existence better is to be guilty of cuckservatism, if not something worse.

On the same topic, Chris Nahr posted a translation[355] of an article by some right-wing Austrian writing about this problem. "Full Speed into the Void", it's titled. Reminds one of the "Flight 93 election[356]" essay in 2016. Austria has, by modern White standards, a fairly large and successful far right political party, who has managed to get into the government now and then. That article says that vanity of vanities, all is vanity. Politics is completely pointless, even if we manage to get one of our guys in the government. Even if we managed to get all of our guys in the government, it wouldn't work. Why? Many reasons.

1. The sort of people who man a political party are just dumb and not deep thinkers

2. Even if you manage to conquer the executive, the judiciary is against you, the bureaucracy is against you, the media wants you dead, foreign countries will sabotage you, and you'll never get big enough majorities in parliament to do anything

3. You gotta follow existing law, so people become incrementalists, never daring to do any radical changes.

---

[354] https://spandrell.com/2019/05/12/the-reactionary-tax-code/

[355] https://news.kynosarges.org/full-speed-into-the-void/

[356] https://www.claremont.org/crb/basicpage/the-flight-93-election/

4. Eventually the Iron Law of Bureaucracy prevails and the very far right parties become led by bugmen cucks of one kind or another.

What do we need? A Profound Social Transformation, he says. We might as well call it PST. And how do we achieve PST? Not through politics, but out in the streets. We need a grassroots movement which builds a new world, "a spiritual preparation for a new European myth that binds us to our oldest past and reconciles us with our future."

He could have just said We Need a New Religion. Which I've been saying for 8 years now myself[357]. Unfortunately the guy is also hyping the Nouvelle Droite, famous for French uber-dork Alain de Benoist who used to sell Nazi Crystals by mail and has a following of about a dozen people and his dog. Hardly encouraging.

The question this guy is posing is not a new question. It's a very basic question, and even in our circles it was debated very early on. Are politics useless? Should we be in politics? Moldbug's answer was a definite No. We can't win there, for exactly the same reasons the Austrian guy is saying. The Cathedral is too strong, it is everywhere. The paths for formal power open to the democratic process are but a small fraction of the whole. Donald Trump has more power than any European government, and yet all he has been able to do is whatever neocons would have done anyway.

That said, there are things that seem to be possible. Trump has slowed things like H1B, seems to be getting somewhere with Mexico in the southern border, and is royally fucking with China. In Europe, Hungary's Orban is a thing, a right-wing guy who has managed to capture all levers of power. In Italy, Matteo Salvini stopped all illegal immigration and is now steadily moving to fuck with the EU financial policy. All of these are good things, some of them very good things, and all were achieved through the legal political process.

Will they last? I don't know. Salvini had a 15% support when he was elected; now he has 35%. Orban isn't going anywhere. Things aren't looking too good in places like France or Germany, but not even Macron is talking about bringing more Africans to Europe. So it seems some degree of engagement with the mainstream can achieve marginal gains.

The real problem here is not whether doing politics works or not. Effectiveness is not a binary concept. Almost everything has some effect on the margin. That effect can be big or small, and the size of the effect might make the time and effort put to it worthwhile, or not. That is the real question: is time spent in setting up a political party, making election campaigns and legislative work worthwhile for our cause?

---

[357] https://spandrell.com/2011/11/09/we-need-a-new-religion/

Well that depends on what your cause is, of course. You might be a cuck and just want a 4 year respite from leftism, to Stand Athwart History and Yell: Stop! But Stay There. If so, you can very much achieve your goals by going into politics. Happens all the time.

You might also be a white nationalist, and just want Liberalism Without Foreigners, as the Austrian guy put it. Then it gets rather trickier, as a big part of the modern political structure all across the West is hellbent on preventing white countries from preserving the demographics of 1970. But on the face of it, it shouldn't be impossible to kick out all foreigners while keeping everything else in place. The videogames, the drugs, the promiscuity, Instagram, gaymarriage, bullshit jobs. Just get the foreigners out. You could even do that more or less legally if you put yourself to it.

It wouldn't be easy, though. Some political problems are coup-complete problems, things that you can't possibly achieve unless you run an outright coup d'etat and suspend the legal system for a time. The more you want to cut out into the Cathedral's network of patronage and spread of degeneracy, the more you're going to need more than just electoral support.

To be honest, most of the ideas of my tax policy post are coup-complete problems. There's no freaking way we could get any of that passed through a parliament without some judge somewhere shutting it down as unconstitutional, or no way to deal with it against a hostile bureaucracy dragging its feet in "resistance".

Some other causes, though, aren't achievable even with a coup d'eat. That's what I think people complaining about my very talking about taxes were talking about. And what this Austrian guy is talking about with his Profound Social Transformation. An important neoreactionary tenet is that Culture is downstream from Power. You can and do get Profound Social Transformations by seizing a government. Happened all the time in history. The French Revolution. The Meiji Restoration. Communist China. But we shouldn't oversell this. Power is also downstream from Culture. This thing is not a river, it's a Yin-Yang sort of thing. The people in Power are humans too, and they inherited a culture themselves. So to the extent that people in Power set their minds to achieve a Profound Social Transformation, they tend to do it only in one direction. On rails. Mostly accelerating trends which are already ongoing (the French Revolution), or adopting mores from foreign countries which are readily available (Meiji Japan).

What is much harder is to achieve a Profound Social Transformation which goes against the flow. Fighting Globohomo, fighting feminism, fighting technology-addiction, fighting atomization, fighting dysgenics. That's not a coup-complete problem. That's a jihad-complete problem. You don't need a well run coup d'etat to achieve all those goals, you need a full-fledged religious war of all against all. And I'm not talking Muhammad scale here, I'm talking Dune's Butlerian Jihad scale. We Need a New Religion, and one armed to the teeth.

So if your cause is a jihad-complete cause, then sure, tax policy isn't going to solve it. A far-right political party with an Executive Committee and Local Assemblies full of normies isn't going to solve the problem. If the very existence of a state apparatus manned by bureaucratic managers is incompatible with your goals for society, then you better have an army of camel archers or Fremen worm riders up to the gills on spice.

Is the state going to go anywhere though? Are we going to do away with large-scale organizations with middle management bugmen? The only way I see that happening is after a massive collapse of civilization and a new (a third) Dark Ages. So it seems to me what PST-advocates are betting on is on start to build a new civilizational package to be deployed once the Third Dark Ages get started.

Which is not a too unreasonable bet. But I'm not sure it's a winning bet. At any rate, some people choose a a cause, an end, and then take whatever method, whatever means, are appropriate to that end. Other people choose means, and accept the end which those means are likely to bring about. We should all make clear what it is that we are doing.

Hong Kong and the Perils of Nativism

2019-08-25 // china, Cold War 2, nationalism, ethnicity, status

There's an old saying, that Paris would be lovely without the Parisians. I don't actually agree with that. They can be a bit arrogant, sure, but on the whole I find Parisian men quite civil and Parisian women classy and sexy. So I hope they stay.

There is one place though where that saying absolutely fits. Hong Kong. HK is a very cool city. It is a first world city built on a landscape of high tropical mountains, and you can see how the force of modern industry has made humans conquer the environment, fitting skyscrapers into the mountain bedrock and open-air escalators to reach them with ease.

https://twitter.com/CarlZha/status/1165490546883715074

Hong Kong also produced Hong Kong cinema, one of the few non Anglo film industries with a distinctive style and which aims to entertain and not preach to the viewers. There's also Hong Kong music, which...well, no, that's pretty bad. On the other hand Hong Kong has, in my view, one the best food industries in the world, or at least had until 5 years ago when mainland China started to up its game. All in all, Hong Kong is a great place. I used to go often and enjoy every visit. But that doesn't mean it has a great people. Oh no. Hong Kong is indeed a cool city, but it would be much cooler if you just replaced its population wholesale. Hong Kongers are, generally speaking, a bunch of rude, uncultured, materialistic, annoying, semi-glossic, entitled twats with a chip on their shoulder, who think they're hot shit because they were lucky enough to be licking British ass while their fellow Chinese fell under the boot of Communism for 3 decades. Their average looks, famously the ugliest in China, don't add to their appeal.

https://twitter.com/_cyphe/status/1165291966202044417

So what's going on in Hong Kong? A massive riot sponsored and organized by the United States Government, that's what's happening. What we call a "color revolution". Funds by USG's National Endowment for Democracy have been revealed, US diplomatic staff have been found organizing the rioters, and the whole mass of Western journalists (i.e. half the Cathedral) have been pushing the most egregious propaganda for weeks. There's nothing special, nothing unique about this. Color revolutions aren't new. This isn't the first one, and won't be the last one. The day Germany grows a pair and starts to push back against US meddling in European politics, rest assured that Berlin will burn for weeks under a massive Antifa riot lionized by the US press.

That said, the US isn't that powerful. Not that generous; the money USG is sending around isn't enough to motivate every single rioter to get out of home. USG isn't stupid and it only pulls the trigger in places where the powder is already plentiful and ready to burn. It needs a fifth column of people willing to burn it all, a place where people hate the status quo so much they'd rather sell their country to USG. Hong Kong is indeed such a place.

https://twitter.com/Gerrrty/status/1163136288792481793 How did that happen? To put it briefly, Hong Kongers think they are a superior people to the rest of China, and to the bottom of their hearts hate being ruled by Beijing. This isn't about Communism or muh Freedom or muh Human Rights. This is a basic, deep problem of self-perceived social status. As I've said again and again, 90% of human concerns are about social status. Hong Kongers think China is low-status and hate every association with it. On the flip side, Hong Kongers think that Japan is high status. Also England. Well, the Anglosphere as a whole. So they revel in associating with it. Hong Kongers will spend 2,000 dollars to get on a plane on a Friday evening to fly 5 hours to Japan and spend the weekend there eating lame high-carb food and buying cosmetics that don't really work just to be able to go back and say they've been to Japan again. That's on Hong Kong where work hours are long and leisure time very precious. But that's just part of the culture.

Why do HK people think China is so low status? Well because for a long time, and for a critical time period in Hong Kong history, the time period where Hong Kong's population stabilised and its culture took form, China was indeed a poor shithole of peasants who shat in the street and were ruled by a bunch of retarded communists. Societies are just an aggregation of people, and people are dumb and stubborn. Memories taken as a child get fixed as culture, and are almost impossible to update after adulthood. Hong Kong collectively grew up being somewhat understandably disgusted by China's backwardness. That all that is 40 years in the past and Chinese living standards in most cities are by now higher than in Hong Kong just doesn't register to them. They just won't admit it, the same way old men never admit their experiences just aren't relevant anymore. Things never change if that change results in lower status to oneself. That's how human brains operate. Scale that to a whole society and it can be brutal.

https://twitter.com/spt1171/status/1161595680193839107 When shown that salaries in Shanghai are higher, the food is better, apartments are incomparably bigger and better designed, internet services are an order of magnitude better; Hong Kongers just double down and talk about Human Rights and Internet Freedom not because they actually care; but because that's all they have left to justify their culturally engrained sense of superiority. Even if you get a HKer to admit that Human Rights is all bullshit he'll just come and say that Cantonese is a superior language and Mandarin just isn't as expressive. Which is rich, as Cantonese, which has for decades had a workable writing system, is almost never written in practice, because the local intellectuals never bothered to learn and spread it. All literature in Hong Kong is written in 1920 style Mandarin prose, read out loud in Cantonese but with Mandarin grammar. It's as if all books in Italy were written in 19th century-style French but read out in Italian pronunciation, and all Italian kids learned to write in French at school, with Italian writing being an extremely low-class affair left for tabloids and shady internet forums.

Most Hong Kongers can't even type Chinese characters phonetically, resulting in typing speeds several times slower than in China, or people just typing in English because it's easier on the hands. These aren't people who really care about their linguistic culture. They're just arrogant chauvinists. It's ethnocentrism at its most retarded.

https://twitter.com/qin_duke/status/1161995495625113602

Hong Kong exists because the Hong Kong economy exists, and that exists because as China went communist, Hong Kong was the only sizeable place with a decent commercially-minded government and a land border with China. Hong Kong was the middleman for making business in China, and as China opened up and developed, the economic rationale for Hong Kong slowly eroded. Again, starting salaries for college grads in Hong Kong are already lower than in the richest cities in China. Hong Kongers aren't superior anymore, by any metric. The city is decaying, little by little, and there's nothing unnatural about that. Urban economies rise and fall, that's just a normal result of economic cycles. Happens all the time in every country. In normal circumstances when a city's economy starts to falter, young people just pack up and leave for growing cities. But HKers won't do that. They may leave the country, move to the Anglosphere if they have a chance (not to Japan, that's only suitable for LARPing in the weekends, the language is too hard), but the vast majority of HKers would hang themselves in the nearest lamp post before considering the logical option of just packing up and moving to Dongguan. Why? Because China is low status, and they are high status. Why? Because it has always been like that, Mommy and Granny told them so. So they will stay, and complain endlessly about why HK isn't as rich as they believe they're entitled to be. A life is not worth living if you can't live in a 50sqm apartment and hire a Filipina to clean it because you're too busy commuting to your corporate lawyer secretary job.

https://www.youtube.com/watch?v=rUXowE-Futo It doesn't help that there's much fucked in Hong Kong for it being a tax haven where all of China is parking their money in real estate, and the government is captured by Lee Ka-shing and fellow oligarchs. But hey, that's the whole point of Hong Kong. The day it stops being a tax haven run by oligarchs is the day the economy actually collapses completely. There's just no other point to the place. People should stop whining and just move where their productivity can actually afford them human living standards.

But again, they won't move. Why? Because they think they're hot shit, they're superior to those people living in places with lower rents. And why are they so fucking stubborn? Because Hong Kong is (or used to be) a city state, and it has its own culture. And culture is extremely hard to change. Basically impossible without organized, constant state intervention (i.e. violence) applied for decades.

https://twitter.com/thespandrell/status/1161398330079043585 This is the clusterfuck that is Hong Kong today, where basically a majority of higher educated young people have collectively become Antifa in a desperate attempt to retain a distinctive culture which is just destined to die. But culture dies hard, and cultures which give you a sense of status superiority are basically permanent. They won't die, you have to kill them. The culture, I mean.

I could go on on how annoying and duplicitous and violent-yet effeminate and just outright evil the Hong Kong protesters are being, beating people to a pulp, throwing bricks and fire bombs into people's houses, vandalizing the whole city while jumping in the air crying bloody murder like soccer players every time a policeman just but looks at them. Violently preventing foreign families with small children from going reaching airplanes to go home, justifying openly the targeting of policemen's families. See at how HK rioters operate and (if you still had any) you will lose all hope in the power of rationality and debate. If the motivation is strong enough, people will lie, steal, hit and steal like there's no tomorrow. Sociopathy can be induced. Very easily.

https://twitter.com/mibuxiaode/status/1160436543204425729 It's quite the sight to see to what insane lengths Hong Kongers go to slander China and make it public that they just won't be associated with it. This in a city where the majority of population moved from China barely 50 years ago! See this Hong Kong "scholar" arguing that China is a cannibalistic culture, where eating human meat was just part of the usual savagery of life. Nothing to do with Hong Kong themselves, of course; the light of British enlightenment and bastardized Christianity (you really gotta check out local Christians for yourself, it's hilarious) has purified them of all that yellow savagery.

But the Hong Kong riots have a deeper lesson than just how evil people can become when they want to, how a basic sense of honesty and decency go down the drain when a movement is allowed to be captured by its left-wing of sociopathic status maximizers. The deeper lesson here is about the Patchwork, this old libertarian concept about competitive governance inherited by neoreaction. The idea that bad government is the result of a lack of competition, that countries today are overall too large, and an ideal world would have city-state sized countries experimenting with different types of government and culture, and having them compete to develop the most effective ways of managing human affairs.

https://twitter.com/thespandrell/status/1161396428310241280 The problem with that is provincialism, the nativism of small places. Political units tend to develop particular cultures among the population. Humans all want to be high status. Absent obvious signs to the contrary, given enough time humans will convince themselves they are indeed high status. Smaller political units will do it just the same as bigger political units. Poor places will do it just the same as rich places. Hong Kong, historically a malarial rock with at most a few dozen fishing huts, think they are hot shit, a paradise of civility and hard work with the most moral people and the wittiest language in human history. North Korea, a miserable half of what already was a destitute slave nation of Chinese emperors for 2,000 years, a country which still struggles to feed its own population, thinks they're hot shit too, heroes of anti-imperialism and the birthplace of everything worthwhile in Asian history.

A patchwork city who is underperforming economically compared to some neighbouring city isn't just going to copy whatever government structures or cultural practices of a richer neighbour. Most likely it will just come up with some lame rationalization about how their backwardness is actually just a sign of their superior status, and before changing a iota of its own habits, will rather go to war with the richer city for having the audacity of not accepting the poor city's cultural superiority. That's just what humans do. That's exactly what all the Greek polis did until they were invaded and thrown to the dustbin of history by Macedon and Rome.

https://twitter.com/XinqiSu/status/1161233443809714176 Larger countries indeed can become complacent; but the mechanisms that produce that aren't just about size, it's just humans being humans and culture being stubborn. What a bigger size gives you is more time to decay until the whole thing collapses; while city states have less ability to be unproductive until they collapse or get invaded. But that's the thing: Science advances one funeral at a time. The Invisible Hand of Capitalism works its magic through bankruptcies, redistributing idle capital into productive purposes. Underperforming city states in a patchwork must also be annihilated if the competitive principle is to work: but unlike libertarians who assume that underperforming city states would just lose their assets (its capital and population) and see it redistributed elsewhere, humans don't work like that. People will stay and deny the decline until the bitter end. It will always end in violence, either through invasion and takeover by a foreign power, or if that is not an option, through the violent rebellion of the deracinate locals going full retard on nativism so they can assign status on their own without looking out of their own borders into the real world.

This is Hong Kong we're talking about, the textbook example of rampant free market capitalism, a monument to the power of impersonal Capital, the unlikeliest of global cities, with its skinny skyscrapers built on top of a typhoon-prone tropical rocky island. And yet this very monument to rootless capitalism has evolved one of the nastiest and dumbest forms of chauvinist culture you can encounter on earth, and that provincialism, ignited by USG's agitation machine, is menacing to bring down the economy now too, undergoing now the closest thing to a Cultural Revolution the world has seen since Mao's days. And that one was a top-down conspiracy orchestrated by Mao and his cronies! Hong Kong youngsters are destroying their own city this on their own.

https://twitter.com/Birdyword/status/1161299001414578177 After the successful rebellion of the United States against Britain, there was this debate about the powers of the Federal government. One of the best arguments of the federalists, who won in the end, was the dangers of the dangers of local tyranny. The fact that a state is small doesn't necessarily mean it will be better controlled by its citizens, it could very well be captured by a strong man or a few families and run as an effectively feudal state forever. They should have added the stultifying effects of local cultures without ease of movement of its citizens. That's not so much of a problem in the Anglosphere, with a common language for 500 million people across 20 million square kilometres, but places with a more distinctive culture, especially if they have their own small language, can go full retard very easily. Even Scotland, which merely has a (admittedly strange) dialect of English, is going full retard in their cultural distinctiveness, again rationalizing its economic failure by reassigning status locally to be whatever it is that can make them feel superior to their neighbors.

Ever since I started this blog I've felt ambivalent about nation-states. I will readily agree that globalism is a plague and that different forms of government are suitable for different peoples, diversity in government being generally a good thing. And yet the pursuit of diversity and distinctiveness for its own sake has also always striked me as a conspiracy of academic collectionists. One thousand languages are dying every year! Big fucking deal. As a linguist I do feel sorry I'll lose some potential objects of study, but my entertainment isn't a good enough reason to keep alive things that are meant to die. Should I care if some yellow frog in the Amazon is going extinct? Hell no. Unless it tastes good, but if it did we'd be farming it already. Is it a world priority the conservation of the Latvian national identity? Would it be a big deal if Denmark were to disappear as a distinct unit? What about Ireland? Doesn't seem that they care themselves that much about their own culture.

https://twitter.com/SFkUSLyimKiCvnG/status/1163665657403023361 Do the nations of the earth have a right to preserve their own culture? Many antiglobalists would instinctually answer "yes". But the proper answer to that question is that there's no such thing as "rights". Some cultures are good, some cultures are bad; some nations make sense, some nations just don't have the means to subsist, and so won't, and should be allowed to dissolve, instead of insisting on keeping everything alive artificially, making the world a ethnic group zoo where every single distinct culture which existed at the end of World War 2 must be preserved as part of the American project to freeze everything at the moment where its power was at its peak.

What is a "nation" anyway? What is a "people"? The usual attributes are easy to spot: common language and folklore, self-perceived status as a unit distinct to its neighbors. But all those attributes didn't come out of thin air. They evolved over time, and they evolved because they worked in their particular historical environment. If perceiving yourself as a distinct nation implied your annihilation after a few weeks, like, say, in the case of a Mongol subtribe under the rule of the Khans, or a small fief close to the Kingdom of France, well odds are you aren't going to perceive yourself as a distinct nation, because the moment you do you get invaded and destroyed. If national status gets you money, women, and lionized in the international press as a Champion of Liberty, well odds are that the among the most impressionable people on earth, i.e. young men and women, who the West has the retarded habit of assembling daily in these places we call Universities, are going to feel like a nation very very fast.

https://twitter.com/CarlZha/status/1165416559122141185 In other words, ethnocentrism only exists when it pays. While many in the far right talk about pathological altruism and a lack of ethnocentrism dooming many white nations, it is important to understand under which conditions does ethnocentrism actually work to produce a powerful nation. Not always. Not at all.

Is China going to destroy Hong Kong the way France destroyed all its regional cultures? Not outright, that's not how the Communist Party of China does things. The CPC are real believers in materialism. They really think that Uyghurs for example go into Islamism because they're poor, and the day they're lifted out of poverty (through education, of course. The blind belief in Education is the one thing that the West learned from Confucians and then re-exported as one of the main tenets of Progressivism) they'll just become deracinated hedonists like everyone else. The propaganda line about Hong Kong right now is that a lack of economic opportunity for young Hong Kongese, in addition to outright mobilization by the United States of the worst thugs and lowlifes in the city, is behind the riots. Which is completely missing the point. No amount of money is going to change the deeply engrained feeling of status superiority of the HKese towards China. It would only make it worse. The same way that more money would make Muslims even more arrogant and violent towards outsiders. The comparison with Muslims really is apt. Two million Hong Kong citizens demonstrated against the extradition bill. It doesn't mean that two million people participated in the violent riots, the beatings of police and dissenting citizens, the physical wrecking of roads, the blockage of the airport. But they won't condemn it either. "These kids are just too hot headed but their heart is in the right place". The sort of thing that your average Muslim says about Al Qaeda.

The only effective answer to make Hong Kong a loyal city for China is one that nobody wants to hear: cultural genocide. It would basically take that to make a majority of Hong Kong residents stand up and sing the Chinese anthem with enthusiasm. But that takes decades of very unpleasant effort, especially in a time, as ours, where the prevalent ideology of the Anglo-Jewish elite ruling the American empire and its vassals is committed to the preservation of ethnic identity across the world as a supreme moral mission. A very crafty version of classical divide and conquer, but based on the Holocaust story. Discouraging Cantonese in schools would be tantamount to Auschwitz, HKers will tell you with a straight face.

https://twitter.com/OedoSoldier/status/1165202605640835072 Right now China's propaganda department is putting videos of HK protesters with American flags shitting on China and beating up Chinese citizens 24/7, proving to mainlanders what a bunch of despicable traitors the HKese are. The victimist narrative is working wonders and a pretty massive boycott on everything Hong Kong has already started. China is gearing up to play the long game, as it can't afford to get sanctioned by USG and its allies on trumped charges of "massacring students" as happened after June 1989 in Tian'anmen. Hong Kong isn't that important.

It's funny that Progressivism holds racism as the supreme evil, and yet spares no effort in supporting provincialism and ethnic chauvinism, which are basically the same primal xenophobic instinct, but applied in a narrower and much more irrational way. Races after all do differ in behavior in much larger ways than neighboring ethnic groups. But that's how Bioleninism works: you're allowed, even encouraged to hate your family, especially your smarter and more productive relations. What you're not allowed is to hate complete strangers, especially the nastiest and most hostile ones.

https://mobile.twitter.com/EconGeopolTech/status/1165419636763938817

Those who show up

2019-10-28 // Top Post, theory, demographics, blackpill, eugenics

Hi everyone, sorry for neglecting the blog. I blame glycine: I'm the descendant of a long line of night-owls, but I'm able to sleep early now for the first time ever. Alas I've always been a late-night writer, and my healthy lifestyle was getting in the way of my blogging. Trade-offs. I should think of something.

Also apologies to my commenters: the comment notification system was broken so I had a backlog of unapproved comments: they're all online now.

Years ago, back in the times before Bioleninism and all that, I made a name for myself in the intellectual parts of the right-wing blogosphere (≈neoreaction) in a large part because I was the best at categorizing the different strands of dissident thought. Back then I said[358] there was by and large three different factions, the religious, the nationalist and the technological, what then Nick Land rebranded[359] as the trichotomy of theonomist, ethno-nationalist and techno-commercialist.

That was 2013 though, and a lot has happened since. Most of it bad. Some good things too: Russia grew a spine, annexed Crimea and kicked USG out of Syria. China grew two spines, destroyed their liberal fifth-column, is forcibly assimilating their native muslims and is fast approaching military parity with USG.

And yes, Trump happened. That was fun. It unleashed a renaissance of right-wing memery. But Trump also failed to get anything done, he's likely to lose the next election, and now not even the memes are safe, as the CIA has co-opted 4chan talent for export, as seen in Pepe frogs in Hong Kong and Joker thots in Lebanon. Not cool.

https://twitter.com/thespandrell/status/1188656046220267520

I won't say that Trump killed neoreaction. It wasn't him. It was just time. 12 years have passed since Moldbug started blogging. Hell, 8 years have passed since I started this blog. Have things got any better? No, they're getting steadily worse. Politics is getting more toxic, with the NYT feeling so cocky they outright admitted[360] the Deep State rules and there's nothing mere electoral politics can do about it. The culture is getting

---

[358] https://spandrell.com/2013/04/10/conflict/

[359] https://www.xenosystems.net/trichotomy/

[360] https://www.nytimes.com/2019/10/20/opinion/trump-impeachment-testimony.html

ever more toxic, with now even (ostensibly) straight males declaring their pronouns before talking. And most importantly, Demographics are getting worse, both in macro-HBD (race replacement) and micro-HBD (dysgenics within each race) terms.

https://twitter.com/Cicerone973/status/1144622840584572929

Follow this guy, by the way. If you ever have a good mood and feel optimistic he'll solve that for you fast. All he does is show birth rate data across the world. And it's not looking good. Not good at all.

Yes, I'm a demographic pessimist. I see the above figures and see how the Western world is slowly becoming Brazil, half white, half black. But Brazil itself is not stable; white people are having less babies than black people there. Brazil is slowly becoming something like South Africa, 10% white, 90% black. But again, South Africa is not stable itself, is it? Birth rates are different, and if that didn't suffice, blacks there are outright murdering white people and chasing them off the land. The actual endgame is actually worse than South Africa, which still has (people tell me) some very fine spots, such as Cape Town.

The end game is Haiti. 100% black, and arguably the nastiest, poorest, worst shithole on the face of earth. That's what we're facing if demographic trends keep worsening as they are.

"Oh come on", you may say. It's never going to get that bad. At some point demographic trends self-correct, right? Evolution will run its course. Leftists aren't having children, eventually the differential fertility of conservative people will make sure everyone is based and redpilled.

If I had a dollar for every time I've heard that, I'd be the pope. Yes, Catholics love this argument. Christians, more widely. They have sacrificed a lot to have children and stable families in this society which does everything it can to promote unhappiness and dysfunctional lifestyles. If there is a God, surely at least their sacrifices will win them the future of the species? History will talk about them as ancestors of the next stage of humanity. Right??

Wrong. I'm sorry guys, but evolution doesn't work like that. Yes, sure, evolution is about differential reproduction. Whatever genes make you have more babies in a given environment, spread in the genepool. And whatever genes do the opposite, make it marginally harder for you to reproduce, disappear from the genepool. So yes, on the face of it, "genes that make you want children" are by definition being promoted by natural selection. The argument, as explained by promoters such as Anatoly Karlin[361], is that humans until now have been fruitful and multiplied perfectly well through a basic motivation: seeking sexual pleasure. But that motivation doesn't work anymore in an

---

[361] https://unz.com/akarlin

environment with easy contraception, so the future belongs to people with psychological traits that make them enjoy family life.

Does it work like that, though? Are there any genes that "make you want children"? Does the brain work like that? The human brain is complicated, you see, but it is also an evolution of the more basic mammal brain, and its circuitry must follow roughly the same pathways. And last time I checked all mammals reproduce exactly the same way. The male produce quadrillions of sperm every minute, and are at the hunt of every ovulating female. The moment they find one they jump onto her, copulate semi-forcibly, and babies ensue. Yeah, this pretty much includes humans.

The idea that humans are going to single-handedly evolve, over single-digit generations, a completely different pattern of reproduction to replace one which has been functional for 60 million years strikes me as pretty wild wishful thinking. Not that it's not an interesting thought. Karlin himself recently linked[362] to a post by a guy called Alexander Turok. The post is titled "The Age of Malthusian Industrialism[363]", and man, that was interesting. I'm a fan of this sort of down-to-earth sci-fi. And while Turok's Malthdustrial world isn't very exciting, it surely is a productive line of speculation.

So Turok's idea is that if this idea of natural selection fixing the demographic problem by itself ends up working, eventually birth rates will rise above replacement, and so we will hit the carrying capacity of the planet at some point. So, Malthusianism. Too many people, the same amount of land, so people keep getting poorer and poorer. Go read Turok's post, he makes some interesting claims about how the economy and society would evolve. He puts very well how this future society will be made of dumber people than today.

If the primary reason fertility is low despite an abundance of resources is because people are trying to climb the latter of social status, trying to get more money and live in a better neighborhood, trying to attract the highest quality of mate, (or quantity of mates) then natural selection will act against those who play this game, promoting the genes of those who do not care about it or those too incompetent to play it well. Though the particularities of "the game" differ by culture, it can be recognizably found in many different cultures, and accounts for the fact that the correlation between fertility and intelligence is negative everywhere[364].

---

[362] https://www.unz.com/akarlin/alexander-turok-on-the-age-of-malthusian-industrialism/

[363] https://alexanderturok.wordpress.com/2019/08/27/the-age-of-malthusian-industrialism/

[364] https://www.unz.com/akarlin/nor-breeding-their-best/

Supposedly though, at some point of impoverishment, the downward drift of average IQ would stop, as intelligence would begin to pay again. Without welfare and Bioleninist political machines with an incentive to bring ever stupider people into a country in order to lower the cost of clientelism, at some point the drift into Global Haiti ceases to function, and you get some sort of stable equilibrium of, say, 90-95 IQ people. Living in more or less permanent starvation wages and some sort of low-level medieval warfare.

Quite depressing, huh? Well remember, that's a best-case scenario. That's what happens if that Conservatives-inherit-the-earth mantra actually succeeds. Remember the trichotomy I mentioned at the beginning? Well the above scenario is what theonomists are for. They won't say it, they probably never thought it through that much. But that's undoubtedly what a Theonomist Revolution against progressivism would entail.

But again, this is a somewhat depressing but still acceptable scenario. This assumes most populations in the First World remain a less intelligent but still recognizable version of what they are today. History will go on, and perhaps with a downward IQ correction men will be men, women will be women, children will be children, and if you're into that, people will be more religious than today. Global Mexico, in a way. Well, what Mexico was before the Narcos took over. Theonomists would enjoy that world. Eth-nats... hey, they can secure a future for white children.

But again, I just don't see it. The Kuwaitis aren't very smart; their birth rate is in 1.6. The Arabs across Europe aren't replacing themselves. The Mexicans in the US are also below replacement! Even if, and this is a big if, there was some easily assemblable collection of genes by which people would love having children far above their love for playing status games in a modern society with Tinder and cheap contraception, odds are by the time those genes have starting to spread, in a few generations time, 90% of humanity is already African. And so, again, Global Haiti.

"But wait", you may also say. "Africans in the US aren't having that many babies either. Maybe the high-speed train of African fertility is stopped during this century, and after that evolution does have enough time, even if it takes thousands of years, for Malthdustrianism to happen". Well sure, that's a possibility. But why are so sure that those Malthdustrian genes will evolve at the same speed among all human populations? What if it's Africans the first to evolve the pattern of "reproducing by liking babies"? Which by the way sounds perfectly likely, if the arrow of natural selection is towards promoting "people too incompetent to play status games".

So that's it? Either Global Haiti or Global Mexico?

Well not quite. Tech-comms have something to say too. Humans aren't all dumb, not yet. What if there's a technological way out of the demographic crisis? Well, there kinda is. And it's a year old actually. Has everyone forgot about He Jiankui?

He's still missing, by the way. Not arrested. Not detained. Not on trail. Just... disappeared. Somehow I don't think he's sitting idle in a room. China is not known for wasting scientific talent.

Genetic sequencing is advancing fast these years. Perhaps the only thing which is still progressing fast after computing's Moore's Law stopped working 10 years ago. We already know dozens of genes involved in increasing IQ, and we'll sure know of hundreds, maybe thousands. It seems likely that within our lifetimes we'll have the capability of safely increasing the IQ of IVF embryos by 10-20 points. Would you take that? Perhaps not. Would that Chinese Tiger Mom-in-becoming living across the street take the chance? Of course she will. Do you want your own kids to be the dumbest at class? I thought so.

The bottleneck here would be IVF, which is still a rather slow and ineffective process, although perhaps with some room for improvement. That bottleneck could be solved, though, with a technology which is still quite far away. Strangely so, given the obvious incentives to develop it in what is effectively a feminist world. Ectogenesis, i.e. artificial wombs. Don't women complain about how unfair it is they get pregnant and lose all that time to build their careers, while men only bust a nut and keep climbing that dear corporate ladder? Fear no more, ladies. Just put your eggs in this machine, and 9 months later you'll get your baby delivered to your home. Free delivery if you sign up for Amazon Prime.

If this is sounds like Brave New World, well yes, that's pretty much what that was about. Aldous Huxley came from a long line of distinguished biologists and couldn't see things like TV and computers coming. Eventually he got into drugs, but I'm sure he died still puzzled by why ectogenesis didn't become a thing during his lifetime. It stands to reason that eventually it will. And once artificial wombs are reliable and affordable, in a world with CRISPR, you don't really need families anymore. Anybody can 'produce' children, raise them in 'villages' (because it takes a village!) and just be done with the whole problem. Progressivism taken to its logical conclusion. It's better conclusion, the way that progressives of the 1900s saw it, the production of a race of ever more rational and free humans. Yes, it's kinda messed up, but it has its logic. The twisted mechanics that led to our present Biological Leninist politics were, in the end, just the result of a lack of state authority. That may resolve itself quite soon. Again, with modern technology.

So yep, let me offer you a new Trichotomy. Global Haiti. Global Mexico. Or Brave New World. Pick your poison. I know mine.

Coronachan

2020-04-18 // eugenics, china, blackpill, leftism

People have been asking for a blog post on the coronavirus crisis, and I've demurred. Mostly because I have little facts to add. I'm no virologist, no epidemiologist, I basically know nothing useful about the virus, and I'm not in the business of making up shit or speculating for clicks. I try to offer insight in this blog and I really have no insight about viruses.

Is the virus man-made? I don't know. Is it just the flu? I don't know. Did China release it on purpose? I don't know. Was it made by Americans to fuck with China? I don't know. Is bat soup that good? I don't know! I'd say I'm sorry that I'll never get to try it at this point but nah, I've had the chance but never tried it. I'm high-openness but not that high. I've never even tried cat meat. Or bugs. Or pangolin! Oh pangolin. That I wouldn't have minded trying. Friend tells me it's pretty good.

What I can write about is the all sorts of realizations I've had over this already 3 months of global crisis. And I'd say by far the most salient thing that's struck me is the sheer amount of bullshit going around. People literally making up shit all the time and peddling on Twitter, on Reddit, on WhatsApp, everywhere there's an audience.

And sure, some of that is Hasbara, i.e. covert state propaganda by China to shit on America, by America to shit on China, etc. But you can mostly tell the state-sponsored fake news: it's yelling CUI BONO!! to anyone with a room temperature IQ. "US intelligence sources have concluded that the virus was made by China". Oh, really? You don't fucking say.

But by far the largest portion of fake news is random people doing it I guess for lulz or to get attention. And oh man are they fucking annoying. Back when the very term "fake news" was coined in early 2017 by the US mainstream media to blame it for Donald Trump's election, I remember thinking what a pathetic cope the whole thing was. Then some countries started making government "Fake News Suppression Taskforces" and I thought the whole world had gone insane. Surely people making up shit on Twitter isn't a big deal?

I retract that. Shoot them all. Every single one. Put them against a wall, shoot them in the head, and then feed them to the dogs that China isn't eating anymore. The whole heaps of disinformation going around getting everybody and their mother confused, it's infuriating. Shut the fuck up already. 10 million cases in China! Cover up in Italy! Vietnam is not testing! Animals spreading it in Australia the government isn't acting! Shut up. Now. Sheesh.

Then again there's a reason why so many disinformation gets an audience at all. Where are the experts? People who supposedly know what they're talking about respect to virology and epidemics have been saying pretty much every single possible take on the pandemic. I thought Economics was the dismal science which is not really a science and you can find an economist taking 2 completely opposite takes on every conceivable topic. Well, they're not alone anymore. Is the virus man made? Got two experts saying yes and no. Is the virus more or less deadly than we think? Experts disagree. Do we actually need ventilators? Well, it depends. Will the virus become endemic and come back every winter? Who knows.

It's been more than 3 months since we got the complete DNA sequence of coronachan and we still don't know the real death rate! Just yesterday a new paper came in[365] saying that a lot more people are infected than we think so the death rate isn't that much higher than the flu. Just the flu! Is it though? The death rate in some Italian towns[366] shot 6x compared to last year, that's not the fucking flu is it? Oh well, nobody knows shit.

Nobody Knows Shit. That's the real moral of the coronachan story. We don't have a fucking clue about anything. It's 2020 guys, and a lot of people just realized that. This is gonna be a fun decade.

On my personal opinion about coronachan, again not about the actual science of the virus, just its societal repercussions. As my followers on Twitter know, I'm a big fan. One thing we *do* know, even though the media and all the hysterical virtue signalers out there deny it, is that the virus pretty much only kills the old and weak and the fat. This blog has always been a supporter of eugenics, and also a deplorer of the modern life cycle where people just marry too late, have kids too late, and die too fucking late. I firmly believe that people should have children in their early 20s, be grandparents in their 40s and have intense and enjoyable lives so that their bodies are exhausted by their 60s and die in their mid 70s at the latest. Aldous Huxley started doing hard drugs in his late life and died while tripping on LSD age 69. If everybody did that we wouldn't have had to murder the world economy for corona.

---

365   https://www.unz.com/isteve/infection-rate-in-silicon-valley-was-under-5-in-early-april/

366   https://westhunt.wordpress.com/2020/03/25/just-another-flu-in-bergamo/

That said, that's not the world we live in, and yes many of us have parents or grandparents who we don't want dead just yet, so I get it when people get emotional about it. But one (at least men) should be able to abstract oneself from personal circumstances and see the whole picture. Have you guys been to rural Japan? Or rural Italy by that token. It's miserable. You have no idea how dark and sad a country's culture becomes when you have more old geezers than toddlers. Not to mention public finances. Japan is basically murdering itself, having fallen into a vicious trap where there's too many old people taking pensions and using the national healthcare system, and the government raising the taxes of the young generation making it even harder for them to have babies to solve the problem. Sure, to this date the country has been rather conservative in taking immigrants, but it's still literally dying off, and the effects on the culture at large and the national psychology are there for everyone to see. Despair, detachment, sadness and ennui.

If it takes 10 million 80+ year olds dying of pneumonia to solve that, to get taxes low again so people can actually make money again and form families and have babies and have spare time to write books and scripts and songs, to revive the culture, well bring it on coronachan. BTW this is not just me being evil, every single Japanese under 50 will tell you that all the problems in Japan are caused by the 老害, "old vermin". And yet when coronachan comes to put the vermin out of their misery, people start panicking. Ah, the humanity.

On politics, what will happen next? Finance types sure have been enjoying the crisis. Moldbug, i.e. Curtis Yarvin, has been having a field day with the collapse of the financial markets worldwide, writing a few pieces[367] on how financial policy could be fixed to deal with the pandemic. I've always liked the Unfulfilled Financial Engineer part of Moldbug's career so by all means go take a look. It's been funny seeing how every country but especially the US is printing money like crazy, all restraint thrown to the window. 6 trillion? Sure. And more coming! Talk right now is for USD 2,000 *monthly* for every American resident until the crisis is over. Nobody will remember Andrew Yang (serves him right for letting his wife dominate him in public during the campaign) in 3 months but hey, I was into UBI before it was cool.

Alas I also have no financial advise to give. Bitcoin fell a lot but has recovered a bit; stocks collapsed until the Fed started artificially propping it up, real estate seems to be taking a big hit on the collapse of the global tourism industry. Oil is so dead it's quite funny really. We're at (or almost at) pre 1973 oil crisis levels! Who see this happening 2 years ago? Hell, 1 year ago? Again, nobody knows shit.

---

[367] https://medium.com/@curtis.yarvin

But I guess what most people want me to talk about is international politics. Will China came ahead after the crisis? Well whatever the volunteer (and paid) Trump propagandists tell you, China surely is looking, and most importantly, feeling good after corona. China may have produced the virus, but it got it under control in record time given the circumstances. And it got it done precisely because it had the administrative apparatus that Xi Jinping has been introducing for years, the very weapons of totalitarianism that China has been criticized for the last 5 years. Massive surveillance, complete control of the internet, party cells in every neighborhood and residential compound. China got hit bad, but it recovered, now restaurants are open and people are back to work. 4k dead officially, 80k infected. Say it's double that, it's still nothing.

Meanwhile 1 million infected in Europe, another 1 million in the US. The EU completely collapsing as a political actor, with European countries not only not helping each other but actively sabotaging them, e.g. France confiscating medical supplies bought by Italy from Sweden as it passed through French territory. Trump denying the whole thing, then getting shamed by Tucker Carlson to do something, then getting AMOG'ed by state governors into taking a harder line than he wanted, then pushing for hydroxychloroquine as a cure all, then having the whole Cathedral campaigning against the treatment, preferring people die than proving Trump right.

The Chinese are watching Tiktok all day, which in China feeds them government news videos randomly among the first 10 or so videos, and last month it was all about "see these dumb white people not wearing a mask! Partying as the virus spread! Saying it's like the flu! What are they thinking?!". So yeah, the Chinese are feeling very damn smart right now. Which I think it's great. As you all may know, my stance is that the world needs political diversity. China is the only world power not under the control or influence of USG, the Cathedral and progressive ideology. No Globohomo down there. China was way more admiring of the West 10 years ago, when they felt poor and inadequate compared to the wealth and sophistication of the West. Now they think they're rich and smart and we're stupid and incapable of manufacturing even fucking paper masks. China is making a point of selling medical equipment as a diplomatic endeavor, "winning hearts and minds". But the fact remains that the West is physically incapable of providing basic goods for the healthcare of its citizens. Which is something you'd expect of the Third World.

So yes, the prestige of the West in Asia is pretty much dead. I hear in Vietnam (a very poor country with a long land border with China who has nonetheless masterfully managed to control the outbreak) people cross the street when they see white people because they think they might be infected. We laughed when people stopped eating Chinese food in February because of corona. Casual racism against Asians is cool because they're kinda small and well behaved. Hell, Brad Pitt could beat the shit out of Bruce Lee! These Asians they just suck. And now they got the virus hahaha. Oops, shit, it's us who got it. 10x prevalence! Oh fuck fuck.

So by April the Chinese don't look dumb, they actually look too smart. Devious! Hence the Redgov (i.e. the Republican Party and the Military Industrial Complex that funds it) propaganda machine (which is smaller than Bluegov by an order of magnitude but getting quite big now under Trump and Bannon) are openly demonizing China and basically begging for war. China covered the virus up for months! (looks notes) ... 2 weeks (looks newer notes) 6 days![368] That the West had 2 months (that's 6 x 10 days by the way) advance notice and still pretty much did nothing to prevent contagion doesn't really matter. I get it, I get it. Nobody likes feeling incompetent. And there's good reasons for China-Western hostility. Trump from the beginning has an agenda of reducing commercial ties with China so that manufacturing goes back to the US. Which is a great idea. And the Pentagon just wants more money and Cold War 2 is the perfect excuse for it.

---

[368] https://apnews.com/68a9e1b91de4ffc166acd6012d82c2f9

The Pentagon is very greedy and very [369] wasteful but for better or worse they are the only political actor with enough money to be able to resist the Leftist political machine in America so, sure, good for them. China is also enjoying the hostility, it has made its population so much more loyal to the government. Arms races are a great thing. We owe much of our technology to them. But again, Cold War 2 has been gearing up for years. Corona is just yet another excuse to drive it up.

The whole thing is just sad, though. Sad and dumb. Lockdown is boring. I'm not that much of an introvert to enjoy it. And the whole official response is just retarded. Why can't we get antibody tests for free and a certificate of immunity to be able to do a normal life? Why can't old and vulnerable people ~~be left to die~~ be isolated and the rest of us be allowed out? The world economy is gonna contract something like 30% in a year. The whole thing is crazy. Where are the greedy Scrooge Capitalists furious with the shrinkage of their bank accounts, using their billions to force governments to open the economy? Trillions left there on the table! The Corona crisis has proven that the driving force of world government isn't greed or evil. It's just bureaucratic cover-your-ass. Do No Harm. Or more exactly, Do No Harm That You Can Be Blamed For. If everything goes to hell *but* bureaucrats had been following their manuals to the T and can't be blamed for it, everything's cool. But don't innovate! Oh no, you might be blamed for the results. Or take credit for the success! And we can't have that either. Nobody is better than anyone else. Just shut everything up and if people die it's their fault.

---

[369] very

Oh yes, people have asked me if the corona crisis is going to end Bioleninism[370] as we know it. Well it sure seems that people have less interest in transexual men trying to force normal people to have sex with them or the plight of Somali taxi drivers struggling to organize a competent jihad with their meager Uber earnings. Gotta say it' s been quite hilarious to see the grunts of the Cathedral trying to shoehorn their causes into the corona crisis. Black people more affected! Men are dying more but the nurses in the hospitals are mostly women! Can't get an abortion while on lockdown!

But let's all remember: the progressive memeplex is a means to an end. The end is absolute power, a tight single-party regime. Feminism and Globohomo and all that are things that in recent decades have helped organize leftist movements to that end, getting people motivated and loyal. That indeed has changed. Right now the easiest way to achieve absolute control is go absolutely hysterical about Corona, and that's exactly what we see in the left, many of whom are pushing for outright economic communism.

But corona will pass. Worst case scenario it will infect everyone and after herd immunity it will go away in less than a year, so corona-hysteria isn't a viable long-term strategy. Nobody is talking about climate change these days, of course, the whole thing was bullshit and we have better things to think about now; but I'd imagine we'll go back to the good old progressive days of Climate-histerical-globohomo very quickly after corona disappears. I guess someone could run a single-party regime on pandemic grounds, "just to prepare for the next virus". But that's not gonna work in any large-ish country; very hard to get enough people motivated to staff it on those grounds.

---

[370] https://spandrell.com/2018/01/21/leninism-and-bioleninism/

Bioleninism works because it motivates large amounts of people. That's not gonna change.

So yes, the whole crisis has been rather underwhelming. Just lame and gay, as pretty much everything. No massive financial collapse. No political collapse (although California declaring itself a nation-state has been interesting). No war, no riots, no nothing. We'll see though. The loss of prestige of the Western ruling class will have some consequences. The EU is looking particularly bad. I'd be surprised if it survives this long term. At any rate it has absolutely lost the ability to expand its power any further. Lost the legitimacy to do that, I'd say forever. America is in a different plane, I don't see secession happening and partisanship isn't that much worse than it's always been. At any rate the crisis isn't quite yet over. Some countries (Germany most importantly) are now opening up, but Russia and Japan are only getting started, so restrictions on international travel are going to stay well into summer if not beyond. The world economy may take some unforeseen hit in a few months. These are interesting times, just not amazingly entertaining ones. Yet again that's what degeneration looks like. A process, not an event. The Romans also thought that everything was lame and gay. Then the Goths sacked Rome. But it took a while.

Cold War 2 Propaganda

2020-05-05 // china, redgov, Cold War 2

So it seems that hostility to China is now official American policy. Redgov, i.e. the Military Industrial Complex has been pushing it for quite a while, and for good reason: they want war, or at least a plausible threat of war so they can get bigger budgets and waste more money so they can embezzle their cut and invest it in things like Theranos. That's their job. And it happens that the narrow pecuniary interests of the Military Industrial Complex now fit very well with the electoral interests of the Republican Party. Trump wanted to run on the economy and the stock market, but Corona-chan has completely wrecked it. The strategy now is "It's all China's fault, let's make them pay". Again, lame, but understandable.

All in all it's been a while since these two sides of Redgov, the Military and the Republican party have interests so tightly aligned. As a result we've been having a massive onslaught of Pentagon-led propaganda this last year, and man, is it lame and stupid. The left really is better at this stuff. The left is not only smarter (on average, it attracts social strivers and smart people want status), it's also more motivated, and the internal competition is way higher. I've blogged before about how retarded Chinese propaganda tends to be due to a lack of market incentives: you could say the same about official right wing propaganda in the West. It's all for the boys, to fill up the resume. Not that promotion depends on anything but pedigree and connections, but it's always nice to have some stuff in there for when the Democrats come making questions.

So this guy called Matthew Pottinger yesterday published a speech to commemorate the May 4th movement in China[371]. More on May 4th in a minute. What's remarkable of the speech is that he did it completely in Mandarin. And pretty good Mandarin at that. Very impressive for an Anglo I must say, pronunciation was tight. I don't give such compliments lightly. The guy is pretty good. If... very odd. His pronunciation is so textbook-ish it sounds like a text to speech generator. Tonal languages have tones, sure, and the guy nails the Mandarin tone contours. His first are high his seconds rise up and his fourth fall all the way. But you're not supposed to! Not like that. In actual speech tones vary according to syllable length and stress and just basic rhythm. The guy sounds like an A+ student who has never actually been to China. Biggest tell is that he doesn't do the 5th tone, the "light tone" of many common words like 父亲, "father". Imagine not pronouncing the word "father" properly.

---

[371] https://www.youtube.com/watch?v=MyBSDYkDUso

It's really weird how accurate but mechanic he sounds. Either he's just some new category of cyber-bugman, or perhaps he wasn't reading actual Chinese writing, but a pinyin transliteration, i.e. an automatic romanization of Chinese letters. Transliteration engines usually translate letter per letter instead of words as a unit, so they lose light tones and other semantic influences on pronunciation. That would explain it.

Which makes it even funnier how some chattering heads (mostly co-workers of him in the USG foreign agitation apparatus) have come out saying his Mandarin is *perfect*. "Better than Deng Xiaoping's" said some banana retard. For fuck's sake. Sure, he's pretty good, easily top 1% of white guys in China. But please, apples to oranges. Deng Xiaoping was from Sichuan, he barely went to school, Mandarin was barely standardized at his time, and he didn't have access to teachers who spoke standard Mandarin. He also didn't need to learn a good accent, Sichuanese accent is quite strong but still intelligible to 90% of Mandarin speakers if not spoken too fast. Incidentally the first Chinese leader to speak unaccented Mandarin is Xi Jinping. Not because he's any kind of genius, but because he just happened to grow up in Beijing.

A bit of context on the timing: the May 4th movement (called 五四 in China, "five four". months in Chinese don't have names, just numbers) happened in 1919. China was in a rough spot in 1919. The Qing Dynasty fell in late 1911 and the Republic of China was declared; old general Yuan Shikai kept things more or less together until 1916 when he suddenly declared himself emperor and not even his own generals obeyed him. He died of sheer embarrassment weeks later, and China officially entered the "warlord era".

That was in the midst of WW1, where European powers were murdering each other in sight of the whole world. In theory China was lucky that Europeans were killing each other instead of carving out pieces of China as they used to. And the Chinese government (to the extent there was one) did the fairly rational thing of joining the allies at the last minute in the hope of getting something out of the peace treaty. That didn't quite work out though. China did send laborers to France to man the factories, but it didn't have the ability to send troops. And without troops, no leverage.

You know who had troops? Japan. Plenty of them. Japan did a smart bet and joined the allies from the beginning, and very early on took over Germany's colonies in Asia. Conquered them, by force. Among them Qingdao, where the Chinese beer comes from. The question at Versailles was then whether German possessions go back to China, the rightful owner, or to Japan, who actually made the effort of conquering them and already had troops in the ground. Well, Britain and France and America weren't going to send troops to China and make Japan surrender Qingdao. And so China got shafted, Japan got all it want, and it proceeded to use its position of strength to keep bullying China little by little, in what eventually became what we know as the Pacific theatre of WW2.

The Chinese were furious, of course. The government (to the extent they had one) could do little, but the intellectuals really felt the nation was at crisis. China was in disarray, starving, ruled by a bunch of tragicomic iliterate warlords[372] who fought each other all the time, and bullied and ridiculed by foreign powers. 8 years after the foundation of the "republic", and all the hopes for a national renaissance, that obviously hadn't worked out. China was fucked, more than ever. Что делать?

Chinese academia, i.e. the university faculty and their students concluded that what was needed was... demonstrations. So a few thousand people in Beijing went out in the streets with banners demanding the government do not sign the Versailles treaty, and that they got their shit together and reunified the fatherland. The first they could do and did, the second wasn't possible obviously. Not like the students were forming an army and offering themselves to do the job of retaking Qingdao from the Japanese military. No, they just were there shouting and nagging what they knew was impossible. The warlord government just suppressed the demonstrations, and that was that.

The actual outcome of the May 4th movement wasn't political. Again, it was a fairly tame student demonstration at most. The importance comes from its link to the New Culture Movement, which was a burgeoning intellectual movement in China which argued that traditional, confucian culture was dead and harmful, and China should westernize utterly, and fast. This had several branches: one argued for Western style democratic politics, another argued for writing using vernacular language instead of classical Chinese (akin to the transition between Latin and local languages that European countries did from the 15th century), another for gender equality, etc. You get the picture.

All that was a small minority view at the beginning, but after China kept decaying more and more, the May 4th movement did get a lot of people to stop for a minute and think that maybe these guys were right. Maybe we should change the way we write and improve literacy among the masses. Hey, have you guys heard about Russia? They got this communism thing going on. Didn't take long for China to get its own Communist Party in 1921.

So in short, May 4th 1919 was one of the peaks of Western cultural and intellectual influence in China. It was a time where everyone in China agreed that China was inferior to the West and that China should adopt Western culture and politics. You see why the United States Government is making a point of celebrating this date? The gist of Pottinger's speech is, not surprisingly, "Hey, you guys used to worship us and do everything we said. Go back to that".

---

[372] https://en.wikipedia.org/wiki/Tang_Yulin

Who is this Matthew Pottinger[373] guy though. His resume is... weird. His father was a high ranking bureaucrat in the 1970s[374], Harvard grad who ended up in Wall Street making millions. I'm sure those two parts of his career are a mere coincidence. He also was Gloria Steinem's boyfriend for 9 years.

Matthew himself studied at Amherst, majoring, of all things, in Chinese. He learned it well apparently, and after that went to Beijing as a Reuters, and later Wall Street Journal reporter. Spent seven years there, seems he got in trouble and police roughed him up a couple times. After his good career in American journalism, in 2005 he quits reporting and... joins the Marine Corps. Age 32. What?! "He spent several months in Beijing getting in good physical shape" so he could pass the requirements. Huh?

The whole thing is just... bizarre. He spent 5 years in the military, did some tours in Iraq and Afghanistan where he met many people of influence, and after leaving the military he goes to... a hedge fund in Wall Street. LOL. I mean, come on. I'm just gonna come out and say that the whole thing is fishy, this guy was an intelligence operative from the minute he left college, and his whole career is a CIA op. So following the example of Peter Buttigieg, who has a rather similar profile, I'm gonna come out and call Matthew Pottinger - CIA Matt.

CIA Matt I guess was lucky to leave China when he did, before the Chinese government got a list of names of CIA operatives in China and shot every single one of them. Seems he had a much safer life in Iraq and Afghanistan writing reports and drinking tea.

So much about the guy, let me fisk his little speech. It really is quite something. It's hard to ignore how... demeaning the whole thing looks. A guy who looks like him, the Uber Anglo, with his blue eyes, pasty skin and preachy tone, exhorting the Chinese to learn from all those white academics and their research on the real meaning of Chinese history. Listen to us, we know better! The aesthetics are just awful. But again, the US really is the hegemon, so arrogance of this sort is to be expected.

Again, as you know, the United States is an empire, but it's not one empire. By and large, following Moldbug's parlance, we can divide USG in Bluegov and Redgov. Bluegov is what we call "the Cathedral", i.e. the US government bureaucracy, the State Department, journalists, international institutions, NGOs, academia, etc. They all look and talk the same way. That's "the Left". Bluegov's imperial outreach works through international bureaucracies, the media and NGOs, and they talk the language of Bioleninism. Privileging feminism, LGBT, ethnic minorities. They do that very well, have a *very* polished rhetoric on the subject, and have been very successful in

---

[373] https://en.wikipedia.org/wiki/Matthew_Pottinger

[374] https://en.wikipedia.org/wiki/John_Stanley_Pottinger

spreading their ideology in foreign countries. Xi Jinping has had to work overtime for 10 years to push away this stuff in China's media and academia. Bioleninism is dangerous stuff. It works.

Redgov though is much smaller. It's basically the Military Industrial Complex. It's well funded, and quite competent, but propaganda it's just not its forte. It can more or less sell old school patriotism inside its own country, but there's some basic conflict between a patronage network centered in the armed forces of a certain country and their ability to persuade foreigners. Armies are just not in the business of persuading. Their business is in threatening, that's what they do. The Melian Dialogue is the beginning and the end of military rhetoric. That and Gengis Khan's admonitions to Nishapur. There's really little else you can say.

Alas, we live in clown world, where everything is fake and gay, so the US military is now in the business of trying to trigger an uprising of the Chinese people against their government by appealing to that time 101 years ago where China was weak and poor and felt inadequate.

First of all it was obviously written in English and then translated to Chinese. Here's a transcript[375]. The tone, the pacing, the rhetoric is just full 100% American political speechwriting. I mean… don't do that. Ostensibly this was a speech to the Miller Center of the University of Virginia. But why do it in Chinese? So that Chinese people can see it, right? This is an attempt to agitate Chinese people, give them some first hand American official speech. That's quite valuable, if done right. This wasn't.

If you're writing a speech for a specific audience (to the Chinese people, supposedly) then you should write it from the beginning in the language of those people. This will force your mind to use their idioms, their pacing, their rhetoric. You'd put yourself in a position to persuade a Chinese person, and if you've ever done that before, you know the language you're supposed to use. It doesn't seem like CIA Matt does. He doesn't even get the basic difference between writing for readers and writing for a speech; you're supposed to use more colloquial language for the latter, avoiding words which come down well in Chinese logographic writing but are hard to pronounce and parse by ear when uttered aloud. This may sound very hard but it really isn't rocket science.

I mean, he even doesn't get basic vocabulary right. Pandemic as 传染病大流行 when in China everybody says 疫情. Whoever translated his speech hasn't been reading *any* news from China for the last 5 months. Internet as 因特网？ That's Taiwanese Mandarin, in China it's 互联网. Why would you write a speech where even basic words aren't translated properly? Isn't this supposedly about reaching the Chinese

---

[375]   https://www.whitehouse.gov/briefings-statements/remarks-deputy-national-security-advisor-matt-pottinger-miller-center-university-virginia/

public in their own language? Seems not. They must have outsourced the translation to the Taiwanese government, because who cares. This isn't supposed to work. This is just a LARP, a piece of theatre for domestic (and vassal) consumption, where Americans can pat themselves in the back about what a great job they're done. "That'll show them", they must be saying.

Note how much time he spends thanking his teachers and think-tank pals in the beginning. Who in China gives a shit about Governor Jerry Baliles? Why on earth thank that guy in public in Mandarin? This is typical bugman speech, the point is to show one's good standing at the ruling class, scratch the right backs. Quoting John Pomfret! Who the fuck cares? Again, bugman speech, the same thing that makes academic papers and books be 70% about quoting the right people with appropriately groveling adjectives and 30% to making the actual argument (in arcane prose lest the commoners read it).

It's just incompetent. You're not gonna reach any potentially friendly Chinese citizen like this. Not if you fail to do the basic job of using proper language. That's hard, though, most translated stuff is like that. There's a basic problem with translations which is that the consumers don't have enough information to judge the quality of the product. By definition, really. So translations tend to be atrocious. The only cases are in literature where you need a polished product to sell and make any money, and the original author takes an interest in seeing that his work hasn't been adulterated. Which he often doesn't, or if he does only about languages he more or less understands (not many).

It's hard for me to ignore the form and focus on the content, but this horrible, lame, kitsch, fake and gay speech needs a takedown. Let's focus on the first point he makes after speding 5 minutes licking the asses of all those western academics. Hu Shi's "gift of language" to the Chinese masses.

Again, what a gay way of putting it. "Hu Shi's gave the Chinese people the gift of language". Huh? Were they all speechless before? Pre-human savages who couldn't talk? No, of course, China has the longest uninterrupted literary tradition of all humanity. What he means is that Chinese writing was mostly done in classical Chinese, and Hu Shi argued that people should write in vernacular.

What CIA Matt seems to ignore is that Hu Shi didn't invent vernacular writing. Have you ever heard of the Romance of the Three Kingdoms? The Journey to the West? The Water Margin? The Dream of the Red Chamber? Those are known as the Four Great Novels in Chinese literature and... they're all written in vernacular. Yes, Chinese have been writing in vernacular since at least the Tang Dynasty, and vernacular fiction has been a major literary genre since the early Ming Dynasty (the 14th century). The Qing

Dynasty had a flourishing literary industry of pulp-fiction (sort of) written in very colloquial language. The Qing Dynasty emperors wrote official letters in vernacular!

Sure, vernacular wasn't prestigious among the literary establishment. It was considered kinda trashy by any self-respecting intellectual in China. A properly educated man was supposed to read his history and his poetry in classical, vernacular novels were for kids and women. What the May 4th movement, and Hu Shi did, was argue that smart people should stop being so conservative and go populist, try to write newspapers, essays and political philosophy in vernacular too. Make it prestigious. Which they did; nobody writes classical anymore, the 1920s and 1930s saw a boom in very good literature written in vernacular. The Communists made a point of vulgarizing the language even more; CPC documents sound positively peasant-ish. That has been changing a bit recently though as China has developed a new chattering classes. Literacy in classical has also been strengthened in the school curriculum of late.

So again, it's quite a show of academic autism to make a change in the prestige of a type of prose into some sort of religious awakening ."The gift of language". Give me a fucking break. He makes fun of Gu Hongming as this conservative boogeyman who opposed the abolition of classical Chinese prose. What he fails to mention is where Gu Hongming[376] came from. He was a British subject! Born in British Malaya, educated in Scotland; he was the first Chinese kid who became an anti-Western reactionary after experience with Western education. I'm sure he's crying of joy from the other side as he sees how millions of Chinese students abroad these days are sharing his experience these days. Gu was so much of a shitlord, he made a point of wearing the Manchu queue even after the Qing Dynasty fell.

As a counterpart then he chooses P.C. Chang. If Gu Hongming was a Chinese born in the West who grew to dislike it and ended up living in China growing a queue and wearing traditional clothing, P.C. Chang was the opposite: born in China but moved and died in America. Supposedly he helped draft the UN's Universal Declaration of Human Rights. Helping balance Western individualism with his input of Chinese collectivism. Wait, the Declaration of Human Rights has "confucian collectivism" in it?? Chinese Socialism?!! Sacrilege! Has Tucker Carlson heard of this. Might have to leave the UN now too.

Then he says the fact that P.C. Chang put some confucian perspective on the UN charter means the Chinese people can have democracy, and Taiwan is "the living example". Mmm quite the leap of logic here buddy. Guess somebody read the first draft and asked for Taiwan to be put there, somewhere, fast.

And then, he mentions Li Wenliang. Oh, Li Wenliang. Li Wenliang. It's all so tiresome. Would anyone remember the guy if he hadn't died? The guy wasn't arrested or

---

[376] https://en.wikipedia.org/wiki/Gu_Hongming

incarcerated, let alone tortured like Steve Bannon's propaganda kids were claiming months ago. He was telling his fellow doctors on chat groups that SARS was back, and *his fellow doctors* called police because they thought he was annoying. Local police then followed the book and told him to shut up and sign a statement by which he promised to shut up. China is a big country, nobody up there in Beijing knows about any random doctor in a random hospital in a random city. No conspiracy to silence a hero. He turned out to be mostly right, and oddly for a man his age he died. Given his own coworkers ratted him to police it wouldn't surprise me some fellow doctor poisoned him at the hospital. He surely didn't have many friends around. Again, shitty thing that happened to him, but if he hadn't taken two selfies nobody would remember the guy.

He also didn't tell a reporter "in his death bed" that China needs "more than one voice". He wasn't even positive at that point! He told that to Caixin[377], whose reporting has been openly critical of the Chinese government early response (and somehow their reporters don't get sent to Gulags). Plenty of people in China are against censorship, even China's Troll in Chief Hu Xijin[378], who argued China has enough shitlords by now to deal with American propaganda online. Xi disagrees.

CIA Matt goes on. "China has expelled more foreign journalists in a year than the Soviet Union in decades". Hah. That says more about the Soviet Union that it says about China. Ever heard of Anthony Sutton[379]? Read him.

Then he goes on to mention all those local Christians and Hong Kong protestors. Again, this is not a speech meant to reach common Chinese. This is meant for domestic consumption, a speech to all the clients of USG, a message to all his corporate employees, to thank for them for their service, sure, payments haven't been very regular, but we love you guys! Great job! The big boss is aware of you! Keep working for free just a little longer, any day now the Communist Party will collapse and we'll make you ministers or something.

Then he raps up by again mentioning Hu Shi, making a yet another weird link between Hu Shi's promotion of vernacular writing and democracy and whatever. Dude, wtf. Why make a hero of Hu Shi? Nobody in China likes the guy. Not even in Taiwan. It's real funny. I mean, *I* like the guy. He was a pretty good writer, a decent historian and a brilliant columnist. But he lived in an era of great encompassing ideologies and the guy refused to fit, refused to put his prestige to a cause. He was his own man. And that

---

[377] https://www.caixinglobal.com/2020-02-06/after-being-punished-by-local-police-coronavirus-whistleblower-vindicated-by-top-court-101509986.html

[378] https://twitter.com/huxijin_gt?lang=en

[379] https://en.wikipedia.org/wiki/Antony_C._Sutton

exasperated everyone. Mao Zedong and Chiang Kaishek both hated him, not a mean feat. He was also known as a whoremonger and general bon vivant. Famously argued that China should not waste energy fighting the Japanese given that at some point they'd overreach and get fucked by the Soviets and America and China could easily finish them off at that point. Cool guy in my book, if somewhat of a weasel, and a really really bad fit for the 30s.

Best story about him is how he chose his own name, Shi 適 (used to be common in China to change names to rebrand oneself). You know what that name means? "Fit", in the Darwinian sense. He loved the Origin of Species and changed his name to make a point of his Social Darwinist ideology! So again, great guy, but a very unlikely saint for the cause of American hegemony. The guy spent some years in exile in the US after the Communist takeover but he eventually left and died in dictatorial Taiwan. Obviously didn't like freedom. I don't know if there's some academic thing in America where some Chinese Studies prof who CIA Matt likes has made a point of promoting Hu Shi, but he really is not a guy you want to canonize.

And then the guys end a speech with an apology of "populism". "It fueled Brexit and Trump's election" he says. China could use more of that. Really, Matt? That's your argument? That China needs more populism? I mean, lol. If China had *more* populism they'd have nuked Washington and Tokyo just for lulz. Be very careful what you wish for.

I mean, I'm not in the business of helping USG subvert China, you couldn't pay me enough to do it, but hell, it just bugs me at an aesthetic level. There's so much more effective ways of doing it than this sanctimonious crap. Trump needs better advisors, he's a genius at trolling domestically, he could do so much better. If you made a speech in Chinese saying "actually it was the Democrats and covert commies in the US government that helped the Communist Party win the Chinese civil war. If it wasn't for American leftist help, the Kuomintang would have never lost and you wouldn't have had massacres of landlords and the 1960 famine killing 40 million people. Sorry 'bout that". Xinhua would get so angry the whole building would explode. Hu Xijin would get a stroke and go on a coma. But nah, all USG can do is get CIA Matt to exhort the Chinese populace to read John Pomfret. Pfff.

The Father of Taiwan

2020-8-2 // china, taiwan, history

Lee Tenghui is dead. 97 years old. I won't wish he rest in peace, as his life was dedicated to making peace harder on earth. He was the man who single handedly prevented Taiwan from reuniting with China, thus prolonging the life of the American Empire in Asia for a good 3 decades. Of course I exaggerate, but only a little. The man really was a force of nature. Readers of historiography might now that there's a factional battle among historians, between the proponents of the "Great Man theory" which says historical change is driven by extraordinary men and their raw energy and ambition; and it's opposite, what you could call the "naturalist theory", that history is driven by larger forces such as modes of production or religion or whatnot, and individuals don't really matter that much.

Large ideological battles are of course always bullshit; they are driven by factionalism, status infighting inside the guild in order to capture monopoly rents and vanquish your factional enemies. I'm not an academic historian, hence not a member of the guild, so I won't give fuel to any faux dichotomy. Obviously history is both influenced by overarching forces *and* the actions of extraordinary man. The same way wars are generally determined by fundamental factors such as production and manpower, yet some decisive battles are very close and pretty much decided by random chance.

Well Lee Tenghui was a most extraordinary man, a man who for decades did what very few humans are capable of, and achieved what nobody thought possible. But also a very ordinary man, with hilariously petty motivations. Let me explain.

Let me first disclaim my attitude towards the guy. I wish no ill to the people of Taiwan; I've been there, it's a fine place. Not a huge fan myself, though, I have no special amity towards them either. If anything I feel a slight dislike towards a very weird, schizophrenic culture who doesn't really know what it is and what it wants. A place where people dress like Americans, talk like Americans, all entertainment is either copied from American or Japanese templates, etc. You know a culture is dead when a big portion of the population follows foreign religions, and there's loads of Christians in Taiwan. Again, not very good Christians, the whole thing is a sad LARP, focus on sad. It's just not a healthy culture. Japan is weird in many ways but at least they know who they are.

Another good example of that is how Taiwan has the most profoundly disorganised linguistic culture on earth. Taiwan is the only place where people will juggle two languages (Taiwanese Mandarin and South Fujianese) constantly, code-switching a dozen times per utterance. It's maddening. Taiwanese Mandarin is ugly enough (a very, *very* gay sounding mutilation of northern Chinese speech by Fujianese phonetics), but a big chunk of local Taiwanese won't even stick to it, switching back and forth to their native dialect (yeah technically a language but whatever) every few seconds. I like clean, well designed structures, both in the physical and the mental world. And the Taiwanese mental world as messy and tortuous as the room of a depressed teenage rebel chick. By comparison Hong Kong's retarded diglossia is a white marble ancient Greek temple.

But putting my aesthetic sensibilities aside, I am against Taiwan independence because I want China to be strong, because I believe the decline of civilization that this biog has been discussing for 9 years now is caused by American power. I want the American empire to be weak, so I want competitors to be strong, and China needs, absolutely needs Taiwan to be secure in its sovereignty. As of now China is militarily surrounded by hostile powers. Securing Taiwan would break the island-chain blockading China, giving its navy a free pass to the wider world. And it would also destroy two ideological problems: having a Western-aligned, democratic ethnic Chinese polity as some sort of political alternative, and also having an sub-ethnicity of the Han people as a sovereign country, serving as a precedent for potential separatism among other Chinese dialect groups. Han provincialism in China has never been much of an issue; separatism even among the Cantonese has always been an extremely minority taste, and to the credit of Xi Jinping's regime, the allure of western-style democracy in China has plummeted in recent years.

Still, getting back Taiwan would obliterate both issues for a very long time. So again, China may be more or less based (I'd say it's quite based), and more or less in a path to uphold technological civilization (demographics are concerning but I'd say they're doing OK), but what counts is that China is orders of magnitude more based and more orderly than any country in the West today, so I'm on their side on this one. And if you know anything about China you might guess that my aesthetic issues with Taiwan and HK go away in northern China. The Chinese know who they are. And Beijing Mandarin is *clean*. I like it there.

Anyway, back to Lee Tenghui. The man was born in Taihoku in 1923. Taihoku? That's what the Japanese called what is today Taipei, as Lee was born a Japanese subject. Taiwan belonged to Japan from 1895 to 1945. The Japanese run a rather efficient colonial administration in the island; developed its infrastructure, educated the natives, both Chinese and aboriginal (Taiwan has a bunch of native hill tribes, who happen to be ancestral to all Malay-Polynesian peoples), and run things pretty well. Of course Japanese were privileged above the natives, but as it happens in colonial regimes, a small minority of natives who are particularly friendly to the overlord can also attain very high status. We often call those 'compradors'. Compradors in fact have a better time than colonial overlords. Colonials have to move to a foreign, hot, musty, barbaric place, surrounded by (to their mind) dumb and dirty natives. Yeah you get called sahib and have lots of servants, but eventually you go home anyway, and while you're away you lose access to your social networks back home, which is usually bad for your career There's still much to hate about the whole deal. Native collaborators though have the best of both worlds. They get to live at home, comfortably among their own people, *and* get to lord over their own Dunbar neighbors. Status is relative, the point is not being rich or poor, the point is being richer than the people you know, your cousins, your school classmates. Seeing people worse off than yourself releases shitloads of dopamine, it's science. Colonial lords often don't get laid much as there's taboos about bedding the natives, but compradors are basically gigachad. It's a great deal.

Lee Tenghui was getting that deal. His own father was a police officer in Taiwan, and he and his brothers got access to the Japanese *cursus honorum*. As the wiki[380] says:

Lee—one of only four Taiwanese students in Taipei College-preparatory School class —graduated with honors and was given a scholarship to Japan's Kyoto Imperial University. (...) In 1944 he too volunteered for service in the Imperial Japanese Army and became a second lieutenant, in command of an anti-aircraft gun in Taiwan. He was ordered back to Japan in 1945 and participated in the clean-up after the great Tokyo firebombing of March 1945. Lee stayed in Japan after the surrender and graduated from Kyoto Imperial University in 1946.

---

[380] https://en.wikipedia.org/wiki/Lee_Teng-hui

We wuz samurais

Lee Tenghui went to college in Japan! A massive honour for a dirty colonial. He naturally spoke fluent Japanese. He even got a Japanese name (and surname), Iwasato Masao. He had a bright, bright future ahead of him, had not Japan lost WW2. Oh, feels bad man. Really bad. This top comprador in the whole damn island, this guy who was projected to get probably *the* best gig in Taiwan, lost it everything in 1945, when Taiwan was given back to China, to Chiang Kai Shek's Kuomintang. The guy didn't even go back! He wasn't a Japanese subject anymore yet he stayed in firebombed, double-nuked, literally-starving 1945 Japan for a whole year until he went home. The guy didn't want to admit reality; his comprador career was over, for good. Fuck.

But he had to go home, and so he did. And what did he do in now Kuomintang, nationalist China dominated Taiwan? He enrols in the Chinese Communist Party! Lol. You can't make this stuff up. He resented the death of his sweet comprador gig career at the hand of the KMT so much that he joined whatever he thought would piss them off. The enemy of your enemy thing. But God was no kind to poor Tenghui. He didn't like being a commie too much. Compared to LARPing as a Samurai doing Kendo in Kyoto University, being a Chinese Communist was surely a joyless gig. But what's most fucked up is that even though the Communists did beat the Kuomintang in China, the KMT not just kept ruling Taiwan, the whole thing moved there, making it its headquarters. If he hated the KMT, now he had the whole fucking thing at home, there in Taipei.

Oh man. Why can't a guy get a break? Well Lee Tenghui needed a break, so he got the fuck out. He moved to America, where he got a masters. Then he moved back to Taiwan where he taught agronomy at a middling university. In the 60s he move back to America and gets a PhD. Tenghui wasn't the most handsome guy (his brother got all the good genes there), but he had a tall, imposing physique, and he was very smart. Off the charts. And he was also disciplined, and driven. Good genes all around, although I guess he credited his Japanese education for that. The man was bright and in America he became a rather popular figure among the American political establishment regarding Taiwan. He became... if I may say so, a comprador for the Americans. Because of course. People don't change. And he was good at that. In America he converted to Protestant Christianity, because again. He was that kinda guy.

After getting his PhD he moves back to Taiwan, 1968. It's been a long time, but Chiang Kai Shek is still running things. Lee Tenghui is appointed professor of agronomy at the top university there, and in 1971 he... joins the KMT. Hey wait. No way? Didn't he hate them? He actually did, he confessed to that many times later in his life. But a guy's gotta eat, and this guy was ambitious. He wanted a political career, and to get a political career in Taiwan while the Chiangs lived you needed to join the Kuomintang. Single party regime and all that.

It wasn't easy to join the KMT, they did background checks and all. This guy had been a Japanese collaborator, a *hanjian*. The KMT used to shoot those in China. Not in

Taiwan, there were (understandably) far too many of those. But they sure didn't get to join the KMT. Hell, it was hard enough for any native Taiwanese to join the KMT, let alone an ex-comprador. And this guy had even been a communist!! There's a few theories about why that could happen at all. Apparently Chiang Chingkuo, crown prince and de-facto ruler at the time, had made a point of getting native Taiwanese into the party in order to win hearts and minds, and Lee Tenghui indeed a brilliant and distinguished native Taiwanese scholar. He had also American backing which I'm sure helped. So either the KMT internal spies by 1971 had gone old, soft, senile, fucked up and couldn't do their jobs properly; or Chiang Jr. just liked the guy and got him in, ignoring all standard procedure. Or the CIA called Taiwan and said this is our guy you get him in, pronto. Who knows.

As it happens 1971 was also when Nixon betrayed Chiang Kaishek and basically canceled his country, expelled his Republic of China from the United Nations, and let the commies, with Mao Zedong still kicking, to replace him. Bad, bad year for the Kuomintang.

Anyway, Lee Tenghui after joining the Kuomintang showed himself to be a very capable politician, and a very loyal one at that. At every chance he got he would crackdown on any Taiwan localism, any democratic activism, anyone who would even slightly show any displeasure against Chiang Kaishek and his dynasty. In 1978 he was appointed mayor of Taipei. That's the capital of the realm! A guy with a very dubious history and who had just joined the party a mere 7 years ago! Madness, madness. But again, smart guy, did a great job as mayor. Chiang Chingkuo, by then ruler of Taiwan after the old Chiang Kaishek died in 75, was very happy about his controversial choice. He had had his doubts himself. At some point he made a habit of going to Lee Tenghui's house every day to check up on the guy. He (the ruler of the country!) would show up at Lee's house in the early afternoon, knowing he wasn't home yet, and just sit there or look around his house. Checking up the house furniture, how expensive it was, if he had some jewelry stashed somewhere. Looking if he was corrupt or not.

Chiang Chingkuo and family

And he was apparently satisfied, as in 1981 Lee Tenghui was appointed governor of Taiwan province. The Kuomintang since the very beginning in the 1910s in China had been riddled with wild factionalism, it was very hard to rein on all those. Chiang Chingkuo had dynastic legitimacy but he must have lacked his own team of loyalists, people he could trust to implement his policies and not use state resources to benefit their own clan on the side. Lee Tenghui was a great choice there. He had no faction in the KMT, he was an outsider, a native with no political clout, a guy with absolutely no leverage against the king. The equivalent of a commoner bureaucrat, much easier to use than some landed aristocrat. Lee Tenghui didn't even have a family! No sons. This is underappreciated, but many a great leader was chosen because he had no sons, and so was trusted to not have ambitions of building his own political dynasty. Putin is another good example.

In 1981 Lee Tenghui is appointed governor of Taiwan province. "Taiwan province" is a funny one, as the Republic of China since 1949 has only had (besides the few offshore islands) control over one province, Taiwan. But of course abolishing the provincial system meant recognising they'd never get China back, so the Kuomintang could never do that, and kept the Taiwan province administration as a thing. It was a pretty big deal, having an outsider as governor of Taiwan province; but not a huge deal. Plenty of powerful people above him. But then in 1984 Chiang Chingkuo choose Lee Tenghui has his vicepresident! Now that's a big deal. People in the party were livid Just how good is this guy at licking ass?. He's his eunuch! But worry not. He won't get any further than that. Once the old man is dead, Lee Tenghui goes away with him. Most importantly, Chiang Chingkuo had sons of his own (hapa sons, children of his Soviet wife as it happened), so Lee Tenghui had reached the pinnacle of his political career. He couldn't possibly get any further while Chiang Hsiaowu and the old clique was around.

Oh boy. They didn't see it coming. In 1984 soon after Lee Tenghui became vice-president, a Taiwanese journalist in the US who had been critical of the KMT, Henry Liu, was murdered. As it happens he was an FBI informant, so the American government took that case seriously, and they found that all pointed towards Chiang Hsiaowu, second son of the president, had ordered the hit. USG was not pleased and they mobilised everything they got against the guy. Chiang Chingkuo had no choice but to throw him under the bus. He started talking about democracy, how he had never thought of continuing the dynasty, oh no. Poor guy. Yet another Redgov ally destroyed by Bluegov.

Utterly destroyed by the way. Chiang Chingkuo died unexpectedly in January 1988, and his *three sons*, every single one of them, died within a few years. Funny how that worked.

Anyway, Chiang Chingkuo died quite suddenly, leaving no will and no successor. His son was out of the picture, so the fight was between all the big shots in the party and government. The vice-president, the chairman of the KMT, the president of parliament, you get the picture. Lots of good claimants. Everybody raising troops and trying to make a run for the throne. Lee Tenghui wasn't a leading candidate, given his lack of pedigree and factional affiliation. And yet... as if often happens, it's those outsiders who end up coming on top. Lee was skillful, played the field well, leaked stuff (he had legendary dossiers about everyone) against his top competitors, bribed some key factional leaders, and against what had been almost universal opposition by the Kuomintang elite... came out on top.

▲ Photo by Academia Historica

Chad pose

Picture this, Chiang Kai Shek ruled the whole of China from 1928, then moved to Taiwan after losing the civil war in 1949. He ruled Taiwan until his death in 1975, after which his son Chiang Chingkuo took over. This was still the Republic of China and the Kuomintang, a single-party dictatorial polity which officially still claimed the whole of China (and Mongolia!) and had actual plans of reunification. Then upon the death of Chiang Kaishek's son, the helm passes to... Lee Tenghui? A Christian, childless native Taiwanese wannabe samurai with an American PhD? What the hell? And not through a popular election, no, he actually went through the internal standard procedures of the Kuomintang. What the fuck happened?

So thought a lot of people, but what can you do. The guy was smooth. Very smooth. On assuming power he, slowly but steadily, started the controlled demolition of the Kuomintang and the Republic of China edifice. He started harbouring Taiwanese separatists, speaking in the local dialect, changing the school textbooks, praising Japan, basically making Taiwan what it's today: a country which feels little connection to China. People think the Taiwanese have always opposed reunification but in 1990 a big majority of the locals still thought unification would happen, and on their terms. Yeah, kinda funny, I know. Lee Tenghui slowly disabused them of the notion.

That's a guy who for 20 long years had worked inside the regime, made speeches on how proud he was of being Chinese, on how reunification is his dream, on how he loves and respected the Chiang dynasty, etc. I've talked before on how East Asians like to grind, have a patience and dedication which is hard to fathom for most Whites. But this guy, he's beyond the charts. 20 years he took all amount of shit until he rose to the top and he could take his vengeance. Again, I disagree with everything he stood for. But I can't help admiring the guy. He was a fine, genius-tier politician.

Lee Tenghui dismantled the single-party regime, allowed other political parties and instituted free elections. Changed the constitution, all that. The first elections were in 1996, and he won, fair and square, but he of course had good reasons to be popular. Then he went on pissing off China, building the grounds for Taiwanese independence. And by the 2000 elections, which he couldn't compete because of term limits, he pretty much openly helped the opposition! The president of the KMT, campaigning against his own team! His, again, genius-tier machinations, surgical strike of leaks and other manoeuvres made it so Chen Shuibian, the leader of Taiwanese separatists, won the election with 39% of the vote.

Lee Tenghui was still the head of the Kuomintang, the party of the Chinese army that flew to Taiwan only after losing the civil war in 1949. He might have manoeuvred his way into the committee by skillfully playing elite politics but the vast majority of the party supporters were people who had actually been fought in the Chinese Civil War, and their families. On losing the 2000 election the KMT masses surrounded the party HQs and were pretty close to grabbing the guy and quartering him on the street. Things didn't get that violent but he was forced to resign the party leadership and soon after he was outright expelled. After that he founded his own, openly separatist party, and I don't believe he has ever been seen speaking Mandarin again.

He has been seen speaking Japanese quite a few times though. He raised quite the ruckus when he visited Yasukuni shrine in Tokyo, which he felt so strongly he visibly cried while praying there. Of course the guy is a rockstar among right-wingers in Japan; the man openly defended Japanese imperialism. A guy who used to run the Kuomintang, the party which bitterly fought Japan for 15 long years. You can't make this stuff up.

We wuz samurai

Why would he do that? The guy owned the place, he was by far the most powerful man in Taiwan. Why did he throw everything away, why did he go out of his way to destroy his own party? Because he hated them, he hated the Chinese transplants of the Kuomintang and everything they represented. The guy had been a privileged comprador elite, doing Kendo with his imperial master in Kyoto. He felt so damn good there, knowing he had access to stuff that 99.9% of people in Taiwan would never get. Then Japan lost the war and his family lost everything they had. The other way around, as former collaborators they were very likely the target of all manner of harassment.

The guy then eventually became even more elite, even more privileged, but the feelings of youth don't go away so easily. He gave it all away to hang out with his old Kendo buddies in Japan, and spite the old Kuomintang clique who he had suffered for 20 long years in Taiwan. Lee gave dozens of interviews and wrote a bunch of books basically shitting on the Kuomintang. That must have felt good. But that also shows what ideology is most often about. Feeling good.

I'm not just deducing this, you should have seen the guy, before and after he achieved power and started pushing for Taiwanese independence. The guy was happy, funny, talkative, a joy to watch. Nothing like the stiff, old-school politicians out there, or his former self in the old Chiang days. You could really tell he was enjoying every minute of his destruction of the party that made him president.

Now the man is dead, but his legacy lives on. Taiwan is not only de-facto independent, it now has, very much due to him alone, an independent, if somewhat confused, identity. A large majority of Taiwanese don't call themselves Chinese anymore, and shiver at the thought of reunification. Separatists have run the country for 12 out of 20 years since Lee left power, and will likely do so indefinitely until China actually sends troops. China hasn't been idle either, it has bought off a big chunk of the local media, is by far the biggest factor in the economy, and has infiltrated so much of the Taiwanese military the the joke is China might have enough ships to transport its troops to invade Taiwan but it doesn't have enough to exfiltrate all the spies it has in the island.

Xi Jinping has hinted that reunification will happen in his watch, and that he'll invade he has to. So I'd predict Taiwan will fall during this decade. Unless America intervenes, after first sight of PLA fighter jets I expect the Taiwanese to surrender before you can say "bubble tea". But America may very well intervene, and if so there will be much blood and destruction. Also more closure, and a more meaningful geopolitical outcome. Lee Tenghui won't be there to see it, but the bunch of childless, gaymarried anime cosplayed cat ladies he left leading the country will be there.

What's gonna happen with social media

2021-1-11 // trump, politics, china, tech

Hi, it's been a while.

I don't know if anyone was expecting my take on the 2020 US Presidential election. I mean, I called it. I won a few hundred bucks betting that Trump would lose. But of course I'm not happy about it.

I mean, I'm personally cool. Quite cool really. US global power is coming down, and fast. Pressure on China will soften up (not disappear), Europe is starting to show some balls in asserting some independent foreign policy. See the EU-China Investment Treaty, and Germany actually going on with Nord Stream 2.

Most importantly Trump's loss has been a massive, hilarious steal, a farcical fraud where they blatantly took two weeks to slowly cook up the election results and scam 75 million Americans. The whole thing was the epitome of "not even funny". To think that most of the world today is ruled by such a dumb, ham-fisted third world country is infuriating.

I mean, people, please. Elections in civilized countries take 24 hours, tops. Japan is a big country with 125 million people. It's also fairly low tech, and American political influence means that their government is handicapped in many ways. There are no ID cards, for example. That's part of why Japan has been by far the country worst affected by Corona in East Asia. Well, election results in Japan come down the same day or at most the next morning. In Europe they usually confirm in 4 hours after poll closing. The closest thing I can think of is the Thailand elections in 2019 where the junta took a whole 2 months to cook their elections resulting in ... the junta staying in power. Of course.

From the perspective of accelerating the demise of the American empire, the election results were almost ideal. Trump lost, so America will be weaker, and Trump lost in such a disagraceful way that America will be weaker still, as infighting diverts much of its strength, and the few people with both a 3-digit IQ and some sense of decency suddenly realize that the state that governs them is but a third world kleptocracy.

So yeah, that's cool, but Trump's defeat also signals that decay has already set in, and it's quite bad already. And even though a Gaul or Dacian patriot might have enjoyed the sight of the Roman Empire falling into constant civil war in the 3rd century, odds were the Gothic invasions that followed ended up with his daughters being raped and his head severed and put on some German's lance. So yeah, not funny.

Not that I expect actual barbarian invasions or anything: even Islam in 2021 is fake and gay. But I do have many American friends: about half the readers of this blog are American. They are all good people and I feel for them. They lost their country in the most disgraceful way, and they're in for a world of pain in short notice.

See the January 6th incident at the Capitol and it's aftermath. Let's first not discuss why it was allowed to happen; whether it was a set up by the government, or just a random event allowed by an incompetent police force. To this day nobody knows why the Reichstag was set on fire in 1933. It doesn't matter, the aftermath was what it was: the Nazis suspended the constitution and installed themselves as a single-party regime.

And that's what's happening in America too: Massive purge on Twitter and Facebook, including the still legal president Donald Trump (!). Trump who is most likely kidnapped. Remember when people were outraged about people "disappearing" in China? Well in Woke America they disappear the fucking president. Why? Because they can.

Twitter is purging, well I'll go to Parler. No chance. Parler has been banned from both (!) Apple and Google's mobile app stores, and they can't even keep the web app online as Amazon Web Services has also kicked them out. And that's not about the Daily Stormer which can be argued is quite extreme. Parler's audience is mostly pretty lame boomer rightwingers. MAGA hats. Well those aren't allowed to gather online anymore.

Now everyone is running around thinking on what to do next. Obviously mainstream platforms aren't hospitable anymore. I've been telling people for a while now to get on Urbit. It's perfectly functional and future-proof. My group address on Urbit is ~docteg-mothep/bloody-shovel. Go to urbit.org for details on how to install the app. The thing with Urbit is that it's not a public forum. It's more of a fancy decentralized Telegram, an instant messaging application with some extra features, but there's only chat groups, more or less private; there's no central node. Well, some people just want Twitter. They want that public forum. They want the central node. They want to fight.

tl;dr: don't fight. You're not gonna win. This links with an older and more important debate. The debate on passivism, which Moldbug introduced long ago, most famously on his commentary on Anders Breivik's incident.[381]

Moldbug's idea is that the Left is the ruling class for a reason; that it reached power through insurrection, and is memetically invulnerable to subversion itself. In fact it's

---

[381] https://www.unqualified-reservations.org/2011/07/indisputable-humanity-of-anders-behring/

anti-fragile: it grows stronger the more you oppose it. The Left has this never-ending myth of being the underdog, the party of the downtrodden masses who fought against oppression by the evil old white man. So the more that you, old white man (doesn't matter if you're not old or that white, they'll make something up) oppose them, the more it validates their narrative, so the stronger they become, and the more resolute in their backlash.

Let's let aside the actual mechanics of this. How exactly "narrative validation" results in more effective crackdowns is indeed an interesting topic to explore. Let's just assume Moldbug is right, and I think he largely is. Right wing activism really isn't working, and our standing today is incomparably weaker than it was 10 years ago. Whether this was the result of mere Cthulhu swimming left as a law of physics, or the contingent result of Trumpism and other right-wing populism in the world is inmaterial. The shit is getting bad. We're in serious danger of being silenced, fired from our jobs if not outright arrested and jailed just for dissenting with leftist ideology. This is a fact.

So what about Twitter? A lot of people have been making the analogy that US Big Tech censorship is already tantamount to that of China. Well I know something about China so let me share a very relevant experience in Chinese social media during the past decade.

You see, China used to have something quite similar to Twitter. It started as an outright clone, later evolved on its own, quite interesting way. I'm talking of Weibo[382] 微博

Weibo started in 2009, and a year later already had 100 million users. Chinese people are very online, and they very much enjoy the sort of casual, easy dopamine release that comes from microblogging. The Japanese are also avid Twitter users, incidentally, while they never had much of a blogosphere. The language also helps: 150 Chinese characters amount to about triple that in English, so you can say quite a lot.

As usual in China, there's little regulations, and little enforcement of existing regulations, so once Weibo came in it was very free and open. It was the first national forum of public opinion that the Chinese had ever seen. It became huge almost instantly, and of course the most popular part of it was political debate. Everyone and their mother had become a political pundit on Weibo, rather amusingly forgetting they lived in a Communist single-party state. For a couple years people shat on their mayors, their governors, this or that politician, this or that policy, or even the Communist party itself. The American Embassy joined the party with their famous Air Quality reports (at the time air quality in China was really awful and the government refused to release figures), which were promptly retweeted by 300 million boomers with added comments on how much better America was at everything.

---

[382] `https://weibo.com`.

Well that situation couldn't last. China was at the moment undergoing a rather big leadership transition (Xi Jinping assumed power in late 2012), so the massive agitation going on at Weibo went on undeterred. But governments, certainly the Chinese government, might be slow, but once they get moving they're unrelenting. In 2013 China decided to crack down on free speech on Weibo, and crack down they did. Famous accounts which had been too edgy politically got visits by police, if not outright arrested. Some were jailed, others had to make public proclamations of loyalty to Socialist values. We're talking of people with tens of millions of followers; China is a big country.

Once the big guys were dealt with pour encourager les autres, the masses were targeted with the beginning stages of what has now become a very sophisticated apparatus of keyword censorship. In Weibo today you just can't search what you want. If there's a rumor that Xi Jinping has farted this morning, the word "fart", "frt", "f4rt" and all permutations that might come up are all promptly banned from searching at any sizable Chinese social media. That's step 1: stop the thing from going viral. Step 2 is deleting already existing mentions of the fart. The thing. That takes time but they have an army of censors (which Weibo was forced to hire at their expense) to take care of that. Step 3 is banning you from tweeting about the fart, but that's a last resort, as it's the most annoying and harder to implement.

Soon enough Weibo just became unusable. Most people up there were on the platform precisely to shitpost on politics, to be edgy, to shit on the government, to be a viral pundit, retweeted by 50 million people at least once in their lives. The new regulations were so oppressive that most people just left. Not to some other similar platform. There had been some at the beginning but they all lagged off and eventually were killed, and the government wouldn't allow a new microblogging site. When Weibo was censored people just left, period. They abandoned the public square. They mostly retreated to WeChat, the national instant messaging app. Some didn't get the message and started being edgy on their public statuses, but most just retreated to private chat groups, where they could be safe from the prying eyes of government. The public square was killed, on purpose, and it never recovered.

Well, not quite. After politics were banned from Weibo, only the most inane stuff was allowed to remain. Mostly celebrities and PR accounts, and the odd clueless boomer. But it's been years now, so plenty of people who need an easy internet exposure but have no intention to talk politics are still on Weibo, many producing quite decent content. A lot of aspiring intellectuals have also learned what is politically correct and what not and have managed to survive. Plenty still get banned mercilessly after some innocent mishap though, as Carl Zha (by all indications a paid propagandist for the government) who lost 10 million followers after dissing some Chinese fighter jet or something. But the platform is lively again, if in a more boring, sanitized way. Half a generation of youngsters have grown up without knowing what legal shitposting was like, and so just don't do it. You can't miss what you've never known.

Now, America isn't China, so there's no guarantee that the situation will evolve in the same way. Maybe Parler or Gab manage to survive the multi-pronged assault by every single part of the tech stack, and they thrive as a hotbed of right wing activism. I don't find it very likely though. I see Twitter becoming a sanitized platform where only government-approved speech is allowed, and most people will be fine with that. I'll stay on Twitter if only to follow a bunch of academic linguists who I find interesting. Also Japanese Twitter has its charm, as Twitter censorship is much, much weaker in exotic languages.

So to recap: I think we should do what the Chinese did, which is retreat to private groups. So go to Telegram, to Urbit if you're smart. I'd avoid Slack but you can run a private Mattermost server which is very similar and actually private. There's a million things you can do. You can also hang out here: this blog is safe and will stay up as long as I can afford it. I expect I'll have more time to write long form this year as Twitter shitposting gets outlawed.

On private groups: so yeah, all the agitation in China retreated to private groups, but note that China only allows one mobile IM application: WeChat. Well there's a few others but people are sheep and everyone is on WeChat. WeChat is not even encrypted or anything, the government can get access to your logs fairly easily. Of course it's not like your local police gets a transcript every night of what you're telling your mistress, there's a long process with a lot of layers to go through, but it can and does happen. So you can imagine that private groups engaging in actually subversive stuff will get in trouble sooner or later.

Well, they did. Since 2019 administrators of WeChat chat groups are legally liable for all speech uttered inside the group. Of course this was framed about drug dealing, cyber-bullying and other illegal behavior; but "spreading disinformation" is illegal behavior too, so you can imagine the chilling effect that had on chat groups in China.

Thankfully in the West we have more of a choice, and it's very unlikely that we ever get to a situation in which even our private chat groups are being surveilled for, say, climate change denial or transphobia. Gotta watch out though, the Left is most certainly going to try. They're preparing a "domestic terrorism" law in the US which promises to be quite Orwellian, and WhatsApp is integrating with Facebook soon. Do yourself a favor and get that shit out of your phone.

So to recap: stay safe. See you on urbit, and expect a big renewal of the blog soon.

There's always a way

2021-1-12 // china, history, military

There's a nifty book in China called the 三十六計. The "36 stratagems". Nobody knows when the book was written, though it must be old, the first mention of it goes back to the 5th century AD, when it was attributed to Tan Daoji 譚道濟, a general for the Liu Song Dynasty. The consensus is that he did indeed write it.

The 36 stratagems are organized as six different scenarios, with six stratagems each. Each stratagem is phrased as a catchy four letter idiom, the staple of Chinese vocabulary, and most of them have since become common idioms known even by small children. The book also quotes extensively the Yijing 易經, the Book of Changes, the famous book on divination. For no good reason really, but it does sound cool.

The six scenarios vary on the balance of power they apply to. Generally speaking half the stratagems apply to when you have an advantage in the war, when you are stronger than your enemy, while the other half are for when you are in a weaker position.

The last scenario is outright called 敗戰計 "tactics for when you're losing the war", and describe crafty attempts to gain an advantage or reverse the course of the fight. You may not be able to fight your enemy head on in the open, but that doesn't mean there's nothing you can do. There's plenty of tactics that a committed force can use even when fighting a vastly stronger enemy.

For no reason in particular, certainly nothing to do with current events[383], I am going to make a series of posts translating the last 6 stratagems in the book, those to be used when you're losing the war. Interestingly the 6 last stratagems are the only ones not phrased as with 4-letter idioms. They are instead titled with two letters each, with the last one being three. I guess the author wanted to make the point that when you're losing the war you have no time for florid language and witty metaphors: just get to the fucking point.

And that he did. I'll translate the very last stratagem, also the most famous during the ages, being quoted in many pieces of literature since the book was written 1600 years ago.

On the translation: First line is the name of the stratagem. Second line is the original text, purportedly going back to the 5th century. Then comes the " 按語 ", an

---

[383] /2021/1/11/what's-gonna-happen-with-social-media

elaboration written much later, probably in the mid Ming (15-16th century). I like my translations as literal as possible.

走為上

To run is best.

全師避敵 左次無咎 未失常也

Avoid the enemy with all your troops. There is no fault in retreat, no loss of normality in it.

敵勢全勝，我不能戰，則必降，必和，必走。降則全敗，和則半敗，走則未敗，未敗者，勝之轉機也。

如宋畢再遇與金人對壘，度金兵至者日眾,難與爭鋒。一夕拔營去，留旗幟與營，豫縛生羊懸之，置其前二足於鼓上，羊不堪倒懸，則足擊鼓有聲。金人不覺，相持數日，始覺之，欲追之，則已遠矣，可謂善走者矣。

If the enemy is achieving total victory, and we are unable to fight, one must surrender, make peace, or run. Surrender means complete defeat. Peace means half defeat. Running means no defeat. To be undefeated can be turned into victory.

Like the Song dynasty general Bi Zaiyu, who fighting the Jurchens, realized the Jurchen army was growing stronger every day and he couldn't compete. One evening he dismantled his camp, leaving his army banner in place, then got a sheep and hanged it from a rope, so that its front legs would be on top of an army drum. The sheep, distressed at hanging in the air, would hit the drums with its legs and make them sound [TN: as if the troops were still around]. The Jurchens didn't realize what was happening, waited in place for days until they finally noticed the retreat. They wanted to pursue the Song army but it had run too far by then. We can say he did well by running.

That's it for now, more stratagems to come later this week.

The Honeypot

2021-1-21 // china, history, women

Biden was inaugurated yesterday. Didn't watch the thing, it's kinda depressing, so I went back to my old disinterested, cynical self. I used to be very happy ignoring mainstream politics. Damn you, Trump, you pulled me out of my detached cool lifestyle. Well it was more the pepes and other 4chan memes created since 2016. Damn you guys. I used to not care. I didn't want to care. But you draw me in. It was great. I had a lot of fun. But it was wrong. We all knew it was wrong, that it wouldn't get anywhere. And yet... Oh well. What is done is done.

Now back to regular programming. As promised I'll go with my translation of the 三十六計[384], the 36 stratagems of ancient Chinese warfare. Well, I'm only translating six stratagems, the six stratagems to use when you're in the weak side, losing the war against a strong enemy. Last time I did the very last one, which can be summarized as gtfo. Today it's turn for Stratagem #31.

美人計

The Honeypot

(literally: The Beautiful Person Trick)

兵強者，攻其將。將智者，伐其情。將弱兵強，其勢自萎。利用禦寇，順相保也。

When the enemy army is strong, attack its commander. When the commander is smart, attack his emotions. When the troops are strong but their commander is weak, its momentum withers on its own. Use this to resist your enemy and you will protect yourself successfully.

兵強將智，不可以敵，勢必事之。事之以土地，以增其勢，如六國之事秦，策之最下者也。事之以幣帛，以增其富，如宋之事遼金，策之下者也。惟事之以美人，以佚其志，以弱其體，以增其下之怨，如勾踐以西施重寶取悅吳王夫差，乃可轉敗為勝。

When the enemy army is strong and its commanders are intelligent, you just can't compete, you have to surrender something.

If you give them land, it increases the enemy's power. That's what happened to the six states and Qin [which eventually destroyed them and founded the first Empire]. That's the worst possible tactic. If you give the money and silk, it increases the enemy's wealth.

---

[384] https://spandrell.com/2021/1/12/there's-always-a-way

That's what happened with the Song Dynasty vs. the Khitans and Jurchens. Also a bad tactic. The only good tactic is to give them hot chicks. That shaves away theirs resolve, weakens their bodies and increases the resentment of their subordinates. That's what happened with Gou Jian, King of Yue, who sent Xi Shi [legendary beauty in China to this day] to Fu Chai, King of Wu. That's the way to turn defeat into victory.

My book has some extra examples for illustration, let me introduce a funny one:

During the An Lushan rebellion, Tang Dynasty general Li Guangbi was sent to resist [An Lushan's second in command and later successor] the rebel armies of Shi Siming. The two armies soon found each other and dug trenches across a river and the situation stagnated.

At the time Shi Siming's army was slightly stronger than Li Guangbi's, having more than 1,000 high quality war horses. One day Shi Siming ordered a subordinate to take their thousand hourses to the river to drink and wash, but actually he just wanted to show them off to intimidate the governmenet forces. Li Guangbi heard of this and thought of a trick. He sent a subordinate to gather every single mare in his army, a total of around 500, and sent them close to the river where the rebel army's horses were drinking.

The mares started crying and moving excitedly as they approached the 1,000 war horses of the rebel army, and those horses on seeing the mares run straight away towards them, crossing the river and leaving their soldiers behind.

Thus, the government forces easily captured 1,000 strong war horses, and the rebel armies had to retreat several miles after losing much of its military advantage.

Commentary:

This might seem quite irrelevant for my readership and current affairs. Honeypots are indeed old as sin, and quite effective. And they don't require strong armies so they can be used by people in a weak position in order to gain some advantage.

But they're also not a trick which is exclusive to people in a weak position. Honeypots are just as powerful when used from a position of strength. Governments, police forces use honeypots all the time to capture criminals or dissidents. It's just a good and rather cheap trick no matter who initiates it.

If anything, I think you could say that using women against their enemies is a trick that the left has been using a lot. For centuries really. To a large extent the victory of leftism against traditional society, since the very beginning really, has been a long, centuries-long, sustained honeypot. Not just sending hot chicks to get some short term advantage or extract some incel. It's a rather more insidious sort: it's using all our women, our wives, our sisters, our daughters! in a life-long mission to sow discord and division among our ranks. The mother of all honeypots.

What to do? Write your suggestions in the comments.

By the way my call to people to join my Urbit group has been massively successful. ~docteg-mothep/bloody-shovel is right now the most active group on Urbit! You're missing out. This post will be published there too, do come and join the discussion.

The Empty Fortress

2021-1-25 // china, history, war

Today it's Stratagem 32:

The Empty Fortress

虛者虛之，疑中生疑，剛柔之際，奇而複奇。 Those who are empty, empty it. Create uncertainty inside uncertainty. Between hard and soft, be strange and strange again.

虛虛實實，兵無常勢。虛而示虛，諸葛而後，不乏其人。

如吐蕃陷瓜州，王君焕死，河西恟懼。以張守珪為瓜州刺史，領餘眾方複築州城。版乾裁立，敵又暴至。略無守禦之具，城中相顧失色，莫有鬥志。守珪曰：“徒眾我寡，又瘡痍之後，不可以矢石相持，須以權道制之。”乃於城上，置酒作樂，以會將士。敵疑城中有備，不敢攻而退。 又如齊祖珽為北徐州刺史。至州，會有陳寇，百姓多反。珽不關城門。守陴者皆令下城，靜座街巷，禁斷行人，雞犬不亂鳴吠。賊無所見聞，不測所以，或疑人走城空，不設警備。珽複令大叫，鼓譟聒天，賊大驚，登時走散。

Empty or full [weak or strong], there are no constants in warfare. Of weak armies who show openly their weakness, ever since Zhuge Liang, there have been many.

For example when the Tibetans conquered Guazhou [in 776], Wang Junhuan died, and the West edges of the Yellow River all fell into panic. Zhang Shougui, governor of Guazhou, took the remainer population and started to build a new fortress. With the scaffolding for the walls was just finished the enemy attached again.

They had no means of defense, and everyone immediately turned pale, with no will to fight. Wang then gave a speech: "The enemy are many, and we are few. We've just survived a defeat, we can't fight again with arrows and stones, we must use other means to defeat them". Saying this he went to the top of the fortress, served some wine, played some music, and held a banquet with his soldiers. The enemy on seeing this thought the fortress was well prepared, so they retreated.

Or like Zu Ting of the Northern Qi, governor of Xuzhou. On arriving to his post, he found enemy troops from the Chen Dynasty, and many peasant rebellions. Zu ordered to let the city gates unshut, and have all the defendors go downtown and sit quietly in the alleys, while forbidding people from walking around and making sure roosters and dogs made no noise. When the enemy arrived they saw the open gates but nobody in the streets, not knowing why, with some suspecting perhaps everyone had left and the city was empty and undefended. At that moment Zu loudly shouted commands, the war drums blasted their sound up to heaven. The enemies, frightened, scattered away immediately.

Commentary: This is a bit of a stretched metaphor, but in a sense we're already running an empty fortress trick, and we have for a long time. Just that it's not we running the trick, but us being forced to.

The Left is strong and has dominated most wings of government for centuries. Their rhetoric however makes them repeat the mantra that they are the underdog, the weak and vulnerable, while the right is this scary mass of violent power, eager to attack them at any time.

In ancient war, the most important thing was discipline. If an army kept formation and obeyed orders, 9 times out of 10 they were pretty much invincible. Most deaths were not during battles, but after one side had lost cohesion and scattered troops could be hunted down easily by the victors. In that circumstance numbers didn't really matter. Scattered troops running away are useless, whether there's one thousand of one million of them.

Hence the scariest thing for an army commander was being ambushed and caught by surprise. Showing yourself to the enemy to be too weak just doesn't make sense: you're basically begging them to attack and kill you. The only rational explanation is that it's a trap, and traps are dangerous. So it's a neat trick to use, assuming the enemy doesn't have good information of your strength, and you have the massive balls to pull it off.

Does the Left have good information on the Right's strength? They surely have, but can they use it? The truth is highly inconvenient for them. They're always pretending that any affront on the right will unleash a "violent backlash" by the fierce right wing masses. Which don't really exist anymore. But they need them to exist. So the Right is kept alive, barely, left to exist not because of mercy, but to be forced to play a part in the Left's running LARP.

Sow Distrust, and Profit

2021-2-13 // history, china, loyalty

Time for our next stratagem, the 反間計.

It's rather hard to translate the name itself. Literally it's "counter-between". A "between" is what foreign agents were called in ancient China. Half spies, half agents to sow discord in the enemy ranks.

Original text and translation follows:

疑中之疑比之自內不自失也

Doubts inside doubts. Befriend from the inside, you won't lose.

間者使敵自相疑忌也 反間者因敵之間而間之也

Secret agents [lit. "betweens"] spread doubt within your enemy. Counter-agents do that to your enemy's own agents.

如燕昭王薨，惠王自為太子時，不快於樂毅。 田單乃縱反間曰： 樂毅與燕王有隙，畏誅，欲連兵王齊。 齊人未附故且緩攻即墨，以待其事。 齊人唯恐他將來，即墨殘矣。 惠王聞之，即使騎劫代將，毅遂奔趙。

When King Zhao of Yan died, King Hui took the throne. He didn't like General Yue Yi ever since he was crown prince. Tian Dan [general of Qi during a massive war with Yan], unleashed a counter-op, saying: "Yue Yi doesn't have a good relation with his King, and fears he might be executed. He's thinking on bringing his trips and install himself as King at Qi. The people at Qi haven't committed to him yet which is why he's delaying his attack on Jimo [a city of Qi he was besieging]. The people of Qi are most afraid of Yue Yi being replaced by some other general, as then Jimo will certainly be sacked." King Hui of Yan heard of this story, immediately sent Qi Jie to replace Yue Yi, and Yue Yi fled to Zhao.

又如周瑜利用曹操間諜，以間其將。 陳平以金縱反間於楚軍，間范增，楚王疑而去之。 亦疑中之疑之局也。

Or like Zhou Yu [famous general of the state of Wu during the Three Kingdoms period] fooled an undercover agent sent by Cao Cao to mislead his general. Or Chen Ping, using money to spread doubts on the Chu Army, making it look as if Fan Zeng was disloyal. The King of Chu grew suspicious and removed him. All these were tricks to spread doubts inside doubts.

Commentary:

This is one of the classics, used very, very often in history, often with great success.

The strongest thing in the world is a cohesive army of men who trust each other and have a common purpose. They can literally achieve anything they work on. Make them distrust each other, though, and no matter how numerous, how strong, how wealthy or how technically advanced, they just lose the ability to project power effectively. You can't get anything done if you're afraid your underlings (or your superiors!) are going to stab in your sleep. Any human organization runs on trust. It follows that to win, you must undermine the trust among your enemies. Especially if you're in a position of weakness.

Of course that assumes a flat, meritocatic scenario with a lot of mobility, which was often the case in China, or in the Roman Empire, up onto the very end of Constantinople plagued with dissension and betrayals and all sorts of stratagems. European or Japanese warfare was less afflicted by that because feudalism is quite good at enforcing loyalty, and in Europe warfare often had ethnic or religious background to it.

Well, do we live today in a feudal, fragmented society, or a global meritocracy? You might see now why I write about Chinese history so much. It's not just that I like it, it's actually much more relevant than you'd think.

Now, the stratagem above and their examples give the general idea of the counter-op. But there is a variant of this strategy not detailed in this collection, a variant which I find of the utmost importance. It is much more insidious, but so much more effective. It's the counter-op on steroids. The mother of all counter-ops.

Let's talk about Ying Bu 英布. Also known as Qing Bu 黥布, i.e. Bu the Tattooed. More on that soon.

The time is 209 BC. The Qin Dynasty, the First Empire, has collapsed after only 12 years, as the death of the first emperor ignited a palace crisis and the whole country, nostalgic of their recently vanquished kingdoms, rose in rebellion against the heavy handed rule of the Qin. The Qin dynasty was known to history as following the ideology of Legalism, an idea of government through clear laws of rewards and punishment, strictly applied, with no loopholes or privileges. Confucians, who eventually became the mainstream ideology in China, always refer to Legalism as cruel and inhuman. What they don't say is that Legalism works, and is almost wholly responsible for the rise of the state of Qin from frontier backwater to the founder of the First Empire.

Sometimes Legalist do over do it, however, and the early Qin empire was famously harsh with their punishments. They might have felt that it was necessary in order to tame a recently conquered massive population, but they certainly overdid it. They had two basic problems: one was the overly wide use of the death penalty. The death penalty is important to remove shitty people from the population. But you must only use it to punish the worst crimes of all, basically murder and extreme cruelty; else you're pushing lighter criminals into murder. If you punish rape with death, rapists might as well kill their victims too.

Well, the early Qin famously punished arriving late to a military commission with death. And so Chen Sheng and Wu Guang got bogged down by torrential rains in Dazexiang, and knew they would be killed for it, they famously said: 等死，死國可乎 "If we're dying anyway, might as well die for our [old] country". And so they rose in rebellion and proclaimed the restoration of the State of Chu.

Second problem with the harsh criminal laws of the early Qin was that any man with a slightly above average level of testosterone was likely to see himself in the wrong side of the law; and the relentless, thorough Qin legal machinery would see him branded for life (an old Chinese punishment is tattooing the word "criminal" in the forehead) and sent to hard labor. Hard labor sucks, but if you have a bunch of big, strong guys, branded for life, expelled for good from polite society; well you better make sure that this relentless state machinery is kept well oiled and stable all times. Because if it's not, at the slightest show of unrest, these guys are not an embryonic army. They're an army alright.

So this takes us to Ying Bu. Ying Bu was a big, tall, strong guy, who for some probably violent crime got tattooed in the face and sent to build Qin Shihuang's mausoleum at Lishan. There he was, shoveling earth around with a bunch of several thousand big, tall, strong, violent tatted bros when news come that there's a bunch of big rebellions all over the place and the government is basically not functioning anymore.

Ying Bu naturally decides that he wants a piece of the action, so he raises a gang with his fellow prisoner bros and goes around robbing caravans, stealing women, claiming territory and raising more troops. Good times.

Soon Ying Bu was commanding a few thousand men, and as it happened, he was a masterful commander and brave warrior, winning a series of battles against government troops. As the civil war progressed, Ying Bu was persuaded to join the, at the moment, largest army of all, that of Xiang Yu, who controlled the heir of the house of Chu, the largest of the pre-unification kingdoms. Ying Bu again showed himself to be a brilliant commander and was made a nobleman of the kingdom of Chu. In 207 at the great battle of Julu, the Chu armies destroyed the main force of the Qin Dynasty, a battle in which Ying Bu had a decisive role to play, holding the flank of his army against superior government forces.

After the battle of Julu, Xiang Yu went around burying alive hundreds of thousands of Qin troops, mopping up any opposition he found, and triumphantly conquering the Qin capital at Xianyang, which he burnt to the ground, no fucks given. The amount of ancient treasure and literature that was lost at the time, I shudder to think. Oh well. The wages of war.

Soon after his triumphant tour, Xiang Yu, now basically lord of the realm, decided he just wanted to grill. He had Ying Bu kill the King of Chu he supposedly served, put himself as King of Western Chu, and divided the rest of the country among his underlings, 18 of them. Among them obviously was Ying Bu, his loyal general, always at his side leading the shock troops, doing the dirty and dangerous work while Xiang Yu stayed at the rear. Ying Bu was made King of Jiujiang, just south of Xiang's own territory. From mutilated prisoner to King, Ying Bu had gone a long way. Good times. Very good times.

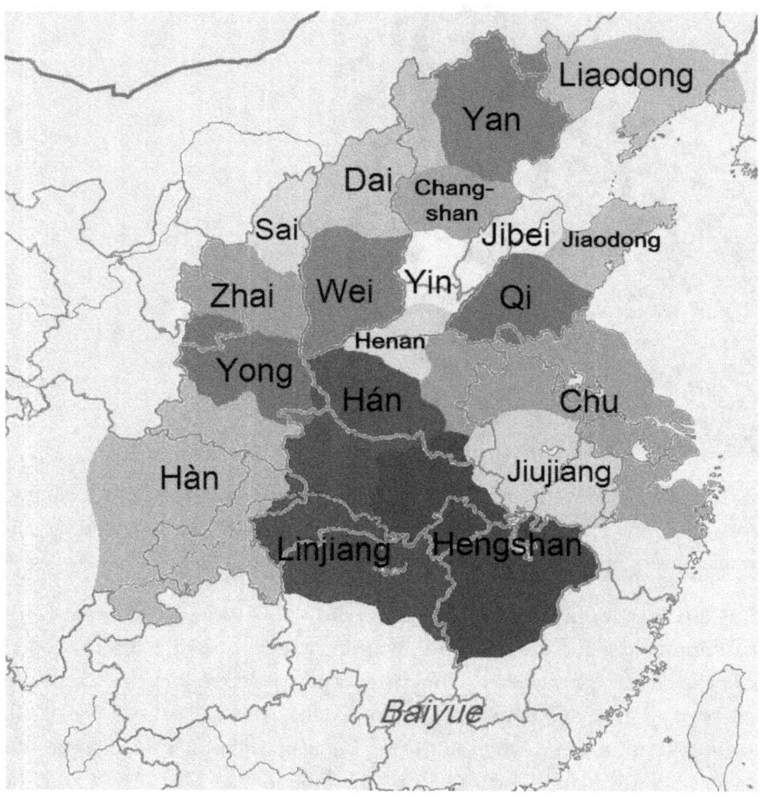

But of course it didn't end that way. Everybody in China knows about Xiang Yu, but what they know about Xiang Yu is how dumb he was. First, don't fucking burn the capital, there's good stuff there. Second, once you burn the capital don't fucking go home and retire. What the hell. How is dividing the country randomly in 19 pieces to random dudes who 10 years before were mutilated prisoners working hard labor sentences going to be a stable arrangement. It almost immediately broke down, as Liu Bang, just made King of Han, decided he wanted a bigger piece of the pie.

The rest is history, as Chinese people today are known as Han, so called because of the Han Dynasty, so called because Liu Bang conquered the country as King of Han, a title given to him by Xiang Yu during that weird 19-fold division of the country when he retired home to grill in 206 BC. So yes, that guy won, and Xiang Yu got wrecked, little by little, for a long 4 years. Poor guy didn't see it coming. But he should.

So Liu Bang eventually conquered the whole thing, the 19 statelets. So what happened to Ying Bu? Was he killed defending his little kingdom of Jiujiang? Oh no, this is where it gets interesting. So this is the thing, Liu Bang was no strong, 7 foot chad warrior. He was a rather short, scrawny, cowardly guy. But he was smart, and most importantly, he was both evil and nice, and had exquisite timing on when to be which. Liu Bang famously said that he didn't have any talents, but that he got so far in life (the guy was a village drunkard before he became Emperor of one of the largest empires known to man) because he had good friends. And that's indeed the most important talent in life: how to make useful friends.

Well Ying Bu was a useful friend to have, obviously. One of the best military minds (and bodies) in the world. But at this point (206 BC, Liu Bang attacks Xiang Yu), Ying Bu was not Liu Bang's friend. He was Xiang Yu's friend, the other guy's friend. What's to be done? Well Liu Bang had to turn the guy. Not easy though, Ying Bu had been one Xiang Yu's right hand man for years, accompanying him around in almost every campaign, and even killing the nominal emperor (the erstwhile King of Chu; long story) for him.

But he was now king for his realm, and after a couple years of kingship, Ying Bu had grown a bit lazy. Several times his erstwhile big brother Xiang Yu had asked him to raise troops and help him in his campaigns, but Ying Bu claimed he was sick and refused to go out. For all we know he was actually sick, but Xiang Yu wasn't happy about it, and people who angered Xiang Yu had a tendency to ended up stabbed and thrown in a ditch. At any rate there was a civil war going on and Ying Bu had perfectly good reasons to not commit on either side just yet. The smart play was obviously to let other people fight it out, conserve your strength, and then sweep them both, with a bit of luck maybe pull a Muhammad against Persia and Byzantium.

That was not to happen though, as Liu Bang was just too crafty. He sent an envoy to Ying Bu, telling him Xiang Yu is cringe, everybody hates him, Han is taking him down any day now, might as well join the party now while the going is early and we're feeling generous. We'll give you a bigger patch of land or something. Ying Bu remained uncommitted, reasonably taking his time to think about it. But the Han army was not going to give him that time. On seeing that a Xiang Yu envoy was meeting Ying Bu, Liu Bang's envoy rushed in uninvited, pushed away the guards and just yelled: "Ying Bu is with us now! Why the hell would he send troops to help Xiang Yu!".

Ying Bu was aghast. That fucking Han envoy had slandered him in public in front of the one guy who could and most certainly will kill him if he got suspicious of defection. Xiang Yu didn't joke around. He didn't need proof. He just got angry and killed people all the time.

You can imagine the Han envoy, giggling, wispering at his ear. "Well, if that's the case... you might as well, like, do it. Kill Xiang Yu's envoy, rally your troops, and come join the Han army. Come on, you'll like it there. We'll treat you well."

And so Ying Bu was very much forced to take sides in favor of Liu Bang. He killed Xiang Yu's envoy, left his fief, and run to the Han camp. He was soon made a great general of a big Han army and after the final victory he was made King again of a slightly bigger kingdom. So it all turned alright (well, not in the very end, but that's another story).

But the fact is Ying Bu didn't take sides himself. He was forced to. By an ally, a guy who needed him and treated him well. But he had to be forced to defect. And by forcing Ying Bu to defect, Liu Bang didn't only sow discord and perhaps deprive his enemy of one of his best generals, which is the basic idea of the stratagem. He deprived his enemy of a good general *and* obtained the general for himself. Genius.

If you still don't get it, I'll elaborate on lesson of this story on the next post.

The Based Draft

2021-2-18 // politics, bioleninism, wat do

I'm accused of timing my last post[385] just before the New York Times launched it's much awaited hit-piece on Scott Alexander.

It's all a funny coincidence. But funny it is. Indeed Scott Alexander was the subject of a post I wrote[386] exactly 5 years ago where I also mention the story of Ying Bu.

It's been interesting to see Scott's development since then. On one hand he hasn't changed much. He's got progressively more famous, and deservedly so. He's also got progressively more fat. Which is sad, but not unexpected. Neutered animals also get fat, and Scott talked about himself being basically chemically neutered.

I was pleasantly surprised though with the way he dealt with the New York Times doxing him. Closing the blog was a smart move (and now that I think of it, a great example of a 苦肉計 stratagem 34, the very next one!), and his recent move towards financial independence by moving to substack and starting a private practice is actually pretty ballsy. Good for him. Hopefully at some point he realizes that the best cure for depression is regular sessions of weight-lifting and parties with abundant MDMA and hot chicks.

As it happened we didn't have to pull a Ying Bu on Scott Alexander; the left banished him of their own accord. As such he didn't move to our side, he pulled a Stratagem 36 and just gtfo to his own turf. Which is fair. But you can only run for so long. The NYT will be back to haunt him and he obviously doesn't have the strength to fight them head on. The IDW crowd isn't sleeping soundly, that's for sure.

By the way TIL that Scott's ex poly-gf or whatever, the infamous camgirl[387] with a masectomy fetish got married (to some other weirdo) and has a kid! Oh boy. What a cursed image.

Any way, I'll spell it out. We need to pull a Ying Bu not just on Scott Alexander. We ned to run a massive, complete, society-wise Ying Bu on every single non-bioleninist person who is still working for the enemy. We can define the enemy as the wider Left,

---

[385] https://spandrell.com/2021/2/13/sow-distrustand-profit

[386] https://spandrell.com/2016/02/16/picking-sides/

[387] https://slatestarcodex.com/2014/09/15/ozy-a-response-to-spandrell/

which includes our governments and corporations known to have helped the left, either with money or with influence.

The point of the Ying Bu story (henceforward "stratagem 33b") is that we need to find a way to deny our enemy the use of their best human capital; and not only that, we must do it so that our enemy sends their best human capital *to our side*. And we do that by implying that they are disloyal to the government side. All of them.

This should be easy, really, the left itself is busy making the point for us, implying that white people are born evil and incapable of loyalty to the Woke cause. Especially in America, Europe is nowhere as bad in this department yet (yes, Europe doesn't include Britain), so what follows applies especially to Anglo countries.

I don't watch TV and haven't done for years, but I bought an Oculus Quest recently and there's this app where you can watch some American TV news channels. I was just browsing for a few minutes on CNN, ABC and a few others and it's outstanding how demonic talk about "whiteness" this and "privilege" that is now completely normal. The loyalty of white people is suspect already. Bioleninists at your company or department are already agitating to get your place and have you fired.

I say let them. Let's see how the federal government and Globohomo manages to even function without white men. I really want to see it. Now of course, most white men won't leave. They need the money. They have mortgages to pay and kids to provide for. I get that; but guys, they're after you anyway. So I'm sorry, I'm very sorry, but you gotta join our side. And sooner rather than later. You may not want to, you might be afraid, and we get that. But we're not gonna give you the choice. You're being drafted.

"But I'm not Nazi!!" you might say. "I'm not even based!". Well, you are now. Besides, nobody will believe your denials. Lateesha at HR saw with her own big black eyes that you have a Gab account where you like Hitler memes. "But I was hacked!!". Yes you were. But who cares? You are white. We are your only friends. *We were always your only friends.* Don't worry, it's all for your own good. We won't even make you lift. Yet.

Back when I wrote Biological Leninism one of the earliest criticisms was that I didn't explain white male leftists. The first response to that is that if you take out core Bioleninist constituencies like Jews, sexual deviants of any sort (homosexuals, troons, furries, whatever), there's very, very few actively loyal white men working for the Left. What there are though, in spades, is a lot of passively loyal NPC types who are risk averse and dont' want to rock the boat. Some people have very slavish personalities and they'll parrot the government line as second nature. I'm sure some men in Turkmenistan buy books of Turkmenbashi and eagerly watch TV to see their president kick a ball or something.

There's also lots, probably a plurality, of men who at some level know something is bad but again, they're risk averse and cant' just afford to make a stand and fight the system just yet, or at least think they can't. Those kinds of people are the exact target of a Ying Bu counter-op. We must deprive them of the choice of serving the enemy.

This is not going to be pleasant. As Mao said, a Revolution isn't going out to dinner. It's a violent affair. Stratagem 33b hurts. It's brutal. Ying Bu's wives and children were all murdered by Xiang Yu. But he won, and he got new ones.

Now, I don't expect the Left to go around murdering the wives and children of every competent engineer that we slander as being a Nazi with a Gab account. But there'll be some short-term financial damage. And probably a lot (a fucking lot) of divorces and personal trouble.

But it'll all be for the better. Scott Alexander was forced out of polite society, but after some short-term pain he'll be happier and (way) wealthier than he could ever expect to be as a wage-cuck in the government healthcare system. And once his polyamorous friends have all ostracized him and he has no choice but to make new based friends... then he'll have to hit the gym, get fit and healthy and even look good. The horror!

If you're a numbers guy but has read some history you might often be surprised on how often very few men were able to conquer vast populations. Mongols at their peak were probably no more than 100k warriors; yet they conquered literally 70% of the civilized world. They way they did that was by co-opting the locals. The Mongol armies conquering Baghdad were full of Muslims. The Mongol armies conqurering China were *led* by Han generals. They paid them well.

Thankfully the modern Left isn't quite as smart and competent as the Mongol armies, and they're already busy expelling every single man (and increasingly woman) of talent out of high-status positions. All I'm saying is we weaponize this very internal tendency for our own purposes. YouTube wouldn't be able to censor us if every single straight white and yellow man (which are also being victimized plenty) stopped working for them. They couldn't even function.

And don't even get me started with law enforcement. BLM and their buddies salivate about a police force without white men. Red-blooded white men are being purged off the US army just as we speak. Do you want secession but are worried that the US army would destroy you? Not once you pull a Ying Bu on them and every single soldier is a stunning and brave curvy black woman.

You might think I'm joking. This is no joke. But sure, things have to happen gradually then suddenly. You want to test the stratagem to see how it goes? The IRS. Every single white man (and married white woman with kids) working for the IRS must be outed as a White Supremacist 1488 acolyte who doesn't check their privilege twice every morning. Have the token blacks working there panic twice a day that the evil eye rays of white people are lowering their eye-queue.

Imagine purging the IRS the way Stalin purged the Soviet Army before the Winter War. Thank me later. Or better, send me part of your tax savings to the bitcoin wallet at the top.

Guys, this is not on me. I'm at a safe place; my homeland is not that bad either, I'm not at war. But you Anglos, you are being preyed on. You have to fight back. And you have to fight smart. This is, by far, the best and most actionable stratagem. It will be painful, for sure. Very. But it'll work.

Do you want to win?

The Self Harming Trick

2021-3-4 // china, history, war

Hi, welcome back to our series on Ancient Chinese War Stratagems.

Today we will translate stratagem 34. 苦肉計, the Self Harming Trick.

人不自害 受害必真 假真真假 間以得行 童蒙之吉 順以巽也

People don't hurt themselves. If they are hurt, it must be true. Fake the true, true the fake, between and you will succeed. It is auspicious that children are ignorant, as they can be thus molded.

間者，使敵人相疑也；反間者，因敵人之疑，而實其疑也；苦肉計者，蓋假作自間以間人也。凡遣與己有隙者以誘敵人，約為響應，或約為共力者，皆苦肉計之類也。如：鄭武公伐胡而先以女妻胡君，並戮關其思；韓信下齊而驪生遭烹。

Betweens[388] cause the enemy to suspect themselves, counter-betweens make those suspicions of the enemy become real. The Self-harming trick is sort of like running a fake op on yourself in order to run a real op on your enemy. Self-harming tricks make it look like there's a gap in your own line in order to lure the enemy in, promise him you will undermine your own side for him, or at least help him. As when Duke Wu of Zheng 鄭武公 who before attacking the state of Hu 胡, gave a daughter in marriage to the lord of Hu and killed a minister who argued for attacking them. Or when Han Xin 韓信 attacked the state of Qi 齊 and Li Shiqi 驪食其 got boiled alive.

Commentary:

Well this is an odd one, but the idea is clear. You need to fool the enemy, distract him, get his attention off you somehow. A way of doing that might be to harm yourself in order to feign weakness; feign so much weakness that the enemy stops bothering to attack you. Then you attack.

You might call this the Art of War version of being passive-aggressive.

As I said recently Scott Alexander shutting down his blog in reaction to the New York Times announcing they would dox him was a sort of Self Harming Trick. Sort of like a crazy girlfriend saying she'd kill herself if you flirt with the waitress. Signals earnestness. But again, people never harm themselves, if they do, it's always a trick. Now you know.

---

[388] https://spandrell.com/2021/2/13/sow-distrustand-profit

On other news, I've been banned from Twitter. It would be cool to say that this was a crafty ancient oriental stratagem on my side; but no. I just woke up in the morning, saw a dozen messages telling me "F" on telegram, keybase and email, next thing I know Twitter says I'm suspended. No reason given. Oh well.

I won't be back on Twitter. Fuck them. Banning me is one thing, after all I did go around posting pictures of mediocre women to assess their sexual value. I even called Roko a faggot for being a faggot. But banning @rtsukazaki? @real_xi_jinping? That's just disgusting. Twitter won't get my content again.

I'll spend more time here. And especially, I'll spend more time on Urbit. Urbit, which will soon be such a superior alternative to Twitter, Jack Dorsey will be soon sent to Guantanamo to atone for his misusing CIA funds in that fake and gay platform.

Next post will be about that. Stay tuned. And join my group (address at the header, click the urbit icon).

We don't have to tweet like this

2021-3-4 // tech, urbit

As I said yesterday, I was just banned from Twitter. They didn't give me a reason, nor a way to restore my account. I did file an appeal, and maybe I get lucky, but I doubt it. My ban was part of a massive purge of thousands of accounts, many of them much milder than myself.

I won't register a new account. I'm done. I've pumped Jack Dorsey's bags with my stellar content for long enough. Screw that faggot, his CIA handlers, his Saudi investors and his troon moderators. The Twitter link at the navbar is gone, and good riddance. I quit Google in 2011. I quit Facebook in 2012. It's taken a while but now I'm completely out of Globohomo social media. Feels good man.

I'm not angry at losing a platform to broadcast my thoughts. I've had a blog for far longer than I've been on Twitter. And this is *my* blog. My territory. It is mine. I moved off Wordpress years ago when I saw all this coming. This is my house now. I built it. I wrote the code it runs on, the post CMS, the comments system, everything. I host it myself, in a neutral jurisdiction, nobody can take it away from me. I write what I want, edit my content as I will, moderate the comments at my pleasure.

And that's how it should be. I'm a publisher, and a publisher should take care to not be subject to the will of anyone else. This much should be obvious. It's my fucking content. I'm not angry at all at my tweets going away. Most of what I did on Twitter was shitposting, WYBs; the equivalent of just shittalking with the boys at a red light district bar while laughing at the passing hookers. Often it was literally that. I deleted all my own tweets every few weeks or so; for me it was a place for ephemeral musings. I didn't keep backups. I find it quite odd that people are fine with every shit coming out of their brains after 3 beers remaining permanently (in public!) on the internet.

What I'm quite angry about is that I did follow about a thousand people myself, and now I can't access that content. I mean I'm not stupid, I did keep a backup of my follows (and my followers), I already have them set up RSS feed made with Nitter. That took some work, though. And I should've done it earlier, to be fair. Same with my followers: thousands of them; I have a list, I can contact them again. But it's a huge hassle. And some of them are gone, perhaps forever.

It shouldn't be like this. We don't have to live like this[389]. We can do better. And we will do better. As my readers know I saw all of this coming, and since Twitter banned Donald Trump I've been actively preparing for my eventual expulsion from Twitter. There's many options out there, plenty of Twitter clones. Gab, the Fediverse. Good people have offered to help me move to many platforms, and I thank them for that. But I won't; we don't need another Twitter. We need to change the whole damn system. We don't need vulnerable centralized platforms just to say "Based" and paste a URL and have people read it. We need to take back the Internet.

Most internet applications today are built as a client-server system. A computer somewhere serves code to other computers who consume it. The code-server computer is a, duh, server and the code receiver is a client. But that's completely incidental to how the internet works. The server and the client are pretty much the same sort of computer. Might be running the same operating system for all we know. The internet, TCP/IP, at its base, is a peer to peer system. Computers sent packets to other computers. That's it. All computers are the same as far as the network is concerned. The internet is just a pipe, it doesn't care who or what is funnelling stuff into it.

As a publisher, with a blog or a microblogging feed, you are literally serving content. You are writing stuff and broadcasting it on the internet. You, little shitlord on Twitter, You Are a Server. You should be serving your content yourself. That's what this blog does. I have a server and I serve you my writing in the form of HTML/CSS/JS code; your browsers are clients which receive the code I serve. But that's not how Twitter works. On Twitter you're just some pansy who has to register, give them your email (!) and cellphone number (!!!). Then you upload your content through a client (a Twitter mobile app or their web app) and then Twitter, at their leisure and discretion i.e. hiding your content if you like a Trump tweet, or outright banning you for undermining confidence in the stability NATO alliance[390], serves your content on the internet. Twitter also keeps your list of followers, your own reading feed and your DMs and they can dispose of them at their complete leisure.

Why are we doing this? Why can't we just serve our content directly on the internet? Well there's an obvious reason. It's hard. This blog took some effort to put online. It also costs me money (which my btc link in the navbar isn't covering, bitches). Twitter is easy to set up, and it's free. It's a fact that people are dumb, lazy, and cheap. And so Twitter gets to ban them for undermining confidence in the stability of the NATO alliance.

---

[389]　https://graymirror.substack.com/p/we-dont-have-to-live-like-this

[390]　https://www.rt.com/russia/516484-twitter-ban-accounts-undermine-nato/

A lot of problems with the internet today (censorship, platforms just shutting down, spam, tracking, etc) would be solved if we had more servers and fewer clients. People should possess their data and serve it themselves. Everyone should have a personal server under their control which served their blogs, their microblogs, their chats, their notebooks, their spreadsheets, their identification data, their monetary transactions: anything they want, at *their* discretion, and no one else's.

The problem with that is that it's hard to do so. There's a reason 99.99% of internet users are just dumb clients of Globohomotech servers; serving is hard. Thankfully I'm not the only person thinking about that problem. In fact I only started thinking about this last year when Twitter purges started to get more frequent and I saw the writing on the wall. Brighter people than me have been thinking about this for decades, and they have a solution. A solution I buy, a solution I joined some time ago, and which I've been promoting now for months. Urbit.

Urbit is a personal server. Plain and simple. It is designed from the ground up to be a completely programmable server which belongs to you, forever, with a permanent ID system that can't ever disappear, be destroyed or taken away from you. And you can do anything you want with it. It's a server, you go serve what you want with it. It's a brand new operating system which functions as an overlay applicaton on top of any Linux or Mac system. But the details aren't important here. If you need help setting it up you can ask these guys on Telegram[391] or check out https://subject.network/.

Yes, running Urbit as of today isn't exactly easy. But it's not that hard, provided you're the sort of person who can type without looking at the keyboard. And it's getting easier every day. Even if you're just not good with computers, by the end of this year at the latest you will be able to pay people to run a server for you for the cost of a couple drinks, or you can buy hardware to run it in the privacy of your home. Hell, pay me 10 bucks a month right now in the cryptocoin of your choice and I'll host you a comet (a free Urbit account) at this very moment. 20 bucks if you want email/telegram support.

I've been in Urbit for months now; I host a big group there, with hundreds of smart and based people being able to chat, write posts or share links in complete freedom. I serve that group, myself, from my computer. And it's glorious. By a mile the smartest group of people online in the whole world. "OK that's cool, but that's not Twitter" you might say. You're wrong: my Urbit group is *really cool*. But yeah, good point, it's not Twitter. You need to be inside Urbit to access my blog, it's not on the public internet as Twitter is.

But that's just incidental. As of now most applications run on Urbit use it as a closed network. You have to log in to Urbit's built-in web client and access Urbit groups from inside that sandboxed network. That's just the state of the network as of now. But it is

---

[391] `https://t.me/UrbitLiveGroup`

perfectly possible to use your Urbit server to publish a website and expose it to the public internet. And that's what we will do very soon.

It's infuriating that I have to keep manual backups of my Twitter followers, my own follows, or my own tweets. It's infuriating that some bluehair future evil-fat-woman-in-government can ban a guy I follow and I completely lose access to that guy, period. How much of Hakan's tweets were lost forever? How is that not outrageous? If he were on Urbit and for some reason his content went down, I'd just ping him and say "hey, ~master-basted, what's up?" and he'd be accessible. Forever. Unless he blocks me or quits or something, but that's up to him.

It's infuriating and it shouldn't happen. But it won't for long. We don't have to live like this. UrbiTweet is happening. It doesn't exist yet. But I'm confident it will by the end of the year. And it will annihilate Twitter, in time.

The idea of Twitter is that you can publish stuff, mostly short stuff. People can read that stuff. and interact rapidly with it. You can like a tweet, you can reply to it, you can quote it, and you can retweet it. That's all fine, and God knows it can be addictive. But you don't need some cash-burning Globohomo company in San Francisco to do that. Ideally we would have our own UrbiTweet app in our personal server, in which we would write stuff. And sure, let's give it a length limit too. 280 characters or whatever. Maybe even ban threads. Get a damn blog if you want to write long form.

The writing side of Twitter is fine (besides the threads). The problem is the reading side. You can only read Tweets on Twitter. But ideally I'd like a feed with all the content I subscribe to. I'd like a unified feed with Twitter stuff, with Gab stuff, with Mastodon stuff, with Weibo stuff, with anything I want. And I'd like to be able to get all that stuff in my unified feed and interact with it the same way I can interact with Tweets. I'd like this one Tweet. I'd quote this Gab retard saying JESUS IS KING while his centralized database gets dropped on a motherfucking SQL injection attack. I'd retweet this video of a chinathot on Weibo so that people answer "WB" without me even asking. I would interact as I please with my feed because it's my fucking feed and it's my fucking server.

Why can't we do this? Because Twitter, or Gab, or anyone else, has an incentive to keep us locked down in their own platform, and we don't have a server of our own to customize. Oh wait, now we do. We have Urbit. We could easily do this. We could feed our UrbiTweet with data from Twitter, Gab, Mastodon, Weibo, Facebook, VK, or whatever, and we could publish anything we want while seemlessly interacting with all that stuff. We'd have the microblogging equivalent of multi-protocol chat apps (you remember those?). And we would own the data. Brilliant.

There is only one problem with this approach. If you're on Twitter's sandbox and somebody quotes a Tweet of yours, or mentions you by name, you get a notification.

And that's useful. You get to react in real time, get a conversation going. The problem with interoperation is that a guy who's on Gab or Twitter wouldn't know he's being retweeted on UrbiTweet, so he wouldn't be able to respond. You can read stuff from Twitter even if you don't have a Twitter account, but you sure can't post anything to Twitter.

There's two answers to that problem. Short one: screw him. Maybe he shouldn't be on Twitter giving his content to Jack so he can hire more blue-haired troons to write reports for the Biden Administration on the perils of Domestic Terrorists Undermining Confidence on the Stability of the NATO Alliance.

Long answer is that the business of UrbiTweet is the users of UrbiTweet. UrbiTweet users would get notifications if their content has been interacted with by other UrbiTweet users. UrbiTweet users could even get notifications if they have been mentioned on other platforms. If you're on Facebook you won't know what Urbit users are saying about you; but maybe you should be on Urbit instead of selling your soul to Zuckerberg so he can buy yet another Hawaiian island. If you are on Urbit, publishing as publishing should be done, by yourself, on your own terms, then you'll have access to the same features and community reach that Twitter has; and then some. You'll have access to the whole internet.

This is not a trivial enterprise. There's work to be done. We need a way to feed data into the system. Twitter data is easy to scoop from Nitter, others will have to be hacked some way. But it's not hard; worst case scenario we can just scrape the shit out of Twitter and any other website. As long as the content is on the public internet, it can be read and fed into a machine. Content which is not public, as much of Facebook or private accounts on Twitter won't be accessible: but the sort of faggot that runs a private account on some Big Tech platform doesn't deserve his content being shared.

And of course a proper backend should be built on Urbit, but that shouldn't be too hard. Urbit servers already have a built-in social database called the Graph Store, which was explicitly inspired by Twitter.

So again, this is happening. Soon. We are going to eat Twitter's lunch, and we're gonna have a great time doing it. In the meantime, join the party (group address up in the navbar, click on the urbit icon), there's lots of other stuff going on. And all the cool kids are there already. See you in the future.

Better people

2022-2-17 // corona, urbit

Hey, it's been a while.

Apologies for not writing much these days, but you know, shit happens, people form families, move countries, change jobs, get busy with this and that. And they just get plain old and run out of things to say. Even if they won't admit to it. Looking at you, sir[392].

Or shit just gets so bad that there's little to say either way. I have plenty I could write about, but I hardly see the point. I certainly have better things to do, and even if I didn't... would it help? The utter and complete obliteration of even the pretense of liberal government after Corona. What does one write about it? Plenty of people are laying the facts on the table, better than I ever could, and all their effort does is prove that facts don't matter at all anymore. All this bullcrap is doing is eliciting despair, and for good reason.

Good thing is I didn't need covid to despair, I despaired long ago. In a way there's been plenty of silver linings coming from this wretched pandemic. The remote work revolution, for one, has been a godsend, personally. And having plenty of smart people come closer to my long-held positions has been also quite nice to watch.

https://twitter.com/phl43/status/1485409009377193984

Note that I reached that conclusion in the very first post in this blog. Time does nothing but prove me right. Increasingly so, as people are demonstrably getting more stupid, for the old fact of dysgenics that we all know.

If corona has proven something is that Nationalism as a Schelling point is dead, destroyed, completely unworkable. What do nations matter when they are all divided on basic matters of the freedom to show your face in public? I love my country, I still get emotional when groups of men sing army songs or people stand to the national anthem. But whenever I see a person with wearing a mask outdoors in 2022 I immediately lose any little sliver of collectivism in my soul. Those are not my countrymen. Even if it's family. Just fuck that. Fuck my homeland, fuck my heritage, fuck my language and culture. I just don't want anything to do with anyone who thinks getting a vaccine (a booster!) for corona is a good idea.

---

[392] https://graymirror.substack.com/

"Oh but normies are normies man, they just follow the script", you'll say. Sure, my point exactly. The problem is normies. I don't want to share a nation with normies. "Oh but we just have to recapture the media". Hah. Good luck with that. Why even try, though? For what purpose? To attract the loyalty of that mass of mask wearing retards? How can any red-blooded man even keep the motivation to engage in mass politics after these two years?

Seriously. Sure, nationalism, even the most retarded type, would be an improvement over Globohomo. No question about that. But it's just not good enough. Hungary got a lot of attention for Orban being based and redpilled. And yeah. not letting his country be swarmed by niggers was very nice of him. But he's still a disgraceful coronacuck. That's just not good enough. Nothing is. We can't go backwards. Or even rightwards. We gotta go up. We gotta solve the real problem, the root problem. People are fucking stupid. We need better people.

How to do that? Well, it's gonna take time for sure. Bit of a long shot. But it's the only worthy goal. As for intermediate goals... just make money, move to a nice place, and have a good life, surrounded by loyal friends, hot chicks and loving children. That's all there is to it.

Oh, people were complaining that the link to my Urbit group was wrong, and it was indeed, I had to change it a while ago. The easy solution to that problem was to DM me inside Urbit, and kudos to the people who were smart enough to realize that. Those who couldn't figure that out are probably better staying on Twatter. Anyway, the link is now updated, and Urbit planets are now (from this week really) very cheap, so by all means try it out.

This isn't a goodbye, this blog will stay up. The internet needs a place where people can say nigger. I'll still write now and then. So stay tuned.

By their fruits

2022-9-9 // europe, history, ngmi

England's Queen Elizabeth is dead. 96 years old.

She was obviously a very likeable lady. Discreet, polite. I dislike vacuous words which are hard to define, which people usually use because they sound old and educated. "Dignity" is one of those words; you can search this blog and you'll probably never see me use that word. But if someone could be described as "dignified" Queen Elizabeth II was one of those. May she rest in peace.

It was just very hard to dislike that lady, as a person. The people who did or today claim to have done are without exception very bad people. The usual suspects, really.

Good or bad she was just not a very interesting person, was she? Again everyone is today writing pieces qualifying her and her reign, which I find rather unfair. She was a woman! What did you expect? Yeah sure, she reigned over the complete destruction of the British Empire and unprecedented decay of the British nation. The death of it, really. The physical death of the nation; the stock of the British race is gone, probably forever. On that note, sure, she was the worst monarch ever. Ye shall know them by their fruits.

But was it her fruits? Look at that nice lady, how could she have any fruits at all? She's a woman, women have generally no agency, how can you blame her for all that? Her office had no power, by law, but even if it had, she was still an unremarkable woman. The only responsibility we could ask her is about her children. Her own children, which... lol. Well OK, those aren't too good either. But hey at least she had a bunch of them.

Tucker Carlson had a rather moving video[393] on the Queen's death; which turned into nostalgia about the British Empire. The most benign empire that human history has seen and will ever see, as he put it.

Well yes, hopefully it won't happen again. I mean, why would that be the case? Why would it be that no future empire will ever be as benign as the British Empire was? Surely the British Empire was very successful. We learn from past successes, there surely is much to learn from British imperialism. But I agree, future empires won't learn from it's benignness. Because that was it's undoing, the cause of it's ultimate failure, and the ultimate destruction of the British nation itself.

---

[393] https://www.youtube.com/watch?v_OzymdJ03c

Future historians, if humanity is to get much further, will qualify past events by their contribution to human advancement. That means ultimately, their contribution to eugenics, their contribution to the improvement of the human genetic stock, most importantly its cognitive ability. What the Benign British Empire ultimately left to the world was the multiplication of the human population of black Africa and the Indian subcontinent. Hundreds of millions of people there. People who are incapable of doing anything of remark. Barely able to feed themselves. All for what? So that Tucker Carlson could brag about it to his Boomer American audience. "See how benign our cousins were".

No, buddy. All the problems that your country has right now, which are exactly due to the proliferation of the wrong sort of people, can be quite directly tracked to the British Empire, or at least the mindset that they created and popularized, which became popular thanks to the very success of the empire. That's what you get when your rulers are "benign". Multiplication of bad people.

It's sad because of course some British did understand that; in point of fact they very much discovered the notion of eugenics. And some of them even understood what their Empire had to do in order to prosper. See things like this map:

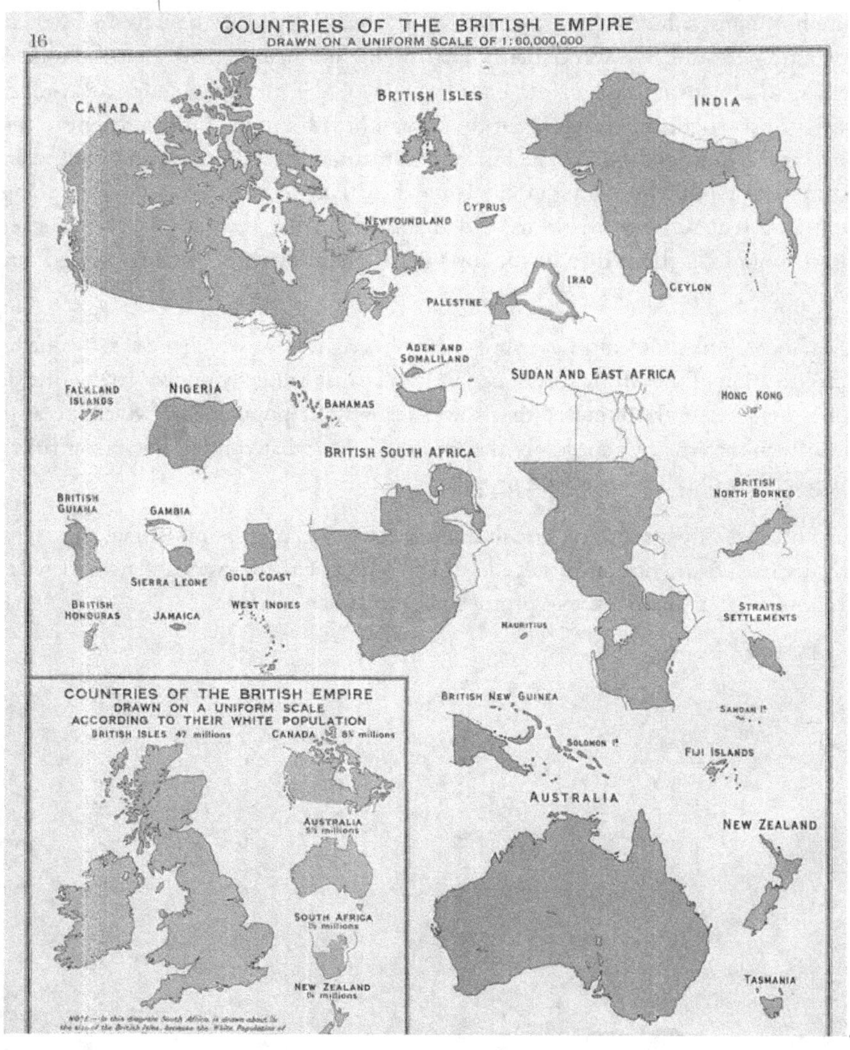

Some people quite obviously got it. And yet, they couldn't do what had to be done. And now their home government looks like this.

That said, the Bombay train station really is nice. One does hope that the empires of the future build more stuff like it. But not out of the goodness of their heart. But because they enjoy making their possessions more beautiful.